ARMS CONTROL, DISARMAMENT, AND NATIONAL SECURITY

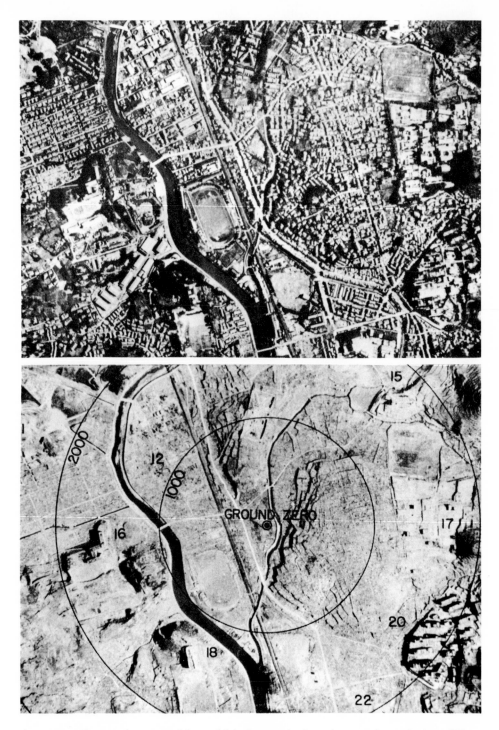

Area around ground zero at Nagasaki before and after the atomic explosion. (*These photographs are reproduced by courtesy of the United States Atomic Energy Commission.*)

ARMS CONTROL, DISARMAMENT, AND NATIONAL SECURITY

Edited by
DONALD G. BRENNAN

GEORGE BRAZILLER

NEW YORK   1961

The following essays or earlier versions thereof were originally published in *Dædalus,* the Journal of the American Academy of Arts and Sciences, under the general editorship of Gerald Holton, in the issue devoted to "Arms Control" (Vol. 89, No. 4). Donald G. Brennan served as guest-editor of this issue.

"Setting and Goals of Arms Control," by Donald G. Brennan.
"Basic Requirements of Arms Control," by Robert R. Bowie.
"Characteristics of Recent Arms-Control Proposals and Agreements," by William R. Frye.
"The Arms Race and Some of Its Hazards," by Herman Kahn.
"The Feasibility of Arms Control and the Principle of Openness," by Edward Teller.
"Limited War: Conventional or Nuclear? A Reappraisal," by Henry A. Kissinger.
"Economic Implications of Arms Control," by Kenneth E. Boulding.
"Reciprocal Measures for Arms Stabilization," by Thomas C. Schelling.
"The Case for Unilateral Disarmament," by Erich Fromm.
"Comprehensive Arms-Limitation Systems," by Jerome B. Wiesner.
"The Inclusion of Communist China in an Arms-Control Program," by A. Doak Barnett.
"The Role of the Smaller Powers," by Paul M. Doty.
"Inspection Techniques of Arms Control," by Bernard T. Feld.
"Public Opinion and the Control of Armaments," by Ithiel de Sola Pool.
"Adjudication and Enforcement in Arms Control," by Louis B. Sohn.
"Recent Policy Making in the United States Government," by Saville R. Davis.
"Government Organization for Arms Control," by Hubert H. Humphrey.
"Arms Control through World Law," by Arthur Larson.

The section titled "Foreign Comment" was originally published in the Winter, 1961, issue of *Dædalus* (Vol. 90, No. 1).

Contents

* Starred chapters comprise the "short-course" form of the book.

unacceptable solutions; and (3) The pursuit of solutions by purely military means has led to a dangerous technological arms race of continually increasing speed.

PART III. THE SUBSTANCE OF ARMS CONTROL

PART IV. THE OTHER PARTICIPANTS

PART V. TECHNIQUES OF ARMS CONTROL

PART VIII. FOREIGN COMMENT

Comments on some of the preceding chapters by four well-qualified foreign observers.

Editor's Preface

THIS BOOK SEEKS TO PROVIDE A FAIRLY COMPREHENSIVE EXPOSITION OF the subject of arms control as one of the means toward eliminating the risk of nuclear war and improving national security. Its several chapters explore some of the potentially feasible routes as well as obstacles to arms control. They also illustrate many of the major considerations bearing on decisions of national policy. The volume is primarily designed for the generally informed reader.

Although this book has been written by twenty-three authors, it is not a routine collection of essays that are largely unrelated. Every chapter has been written specifically for this volume, and written to fill a definite need in the book. At least in outline, therefore, we have been able to achieve a degree of unity not often found in symposia, while calling on a range of expert knowledge not accessible to any single author.

In one respect, however, the kind of unity achieved is rather unusual: it is a unity that embraces a highly diverse range of views concerning the subject. This is one of the basic strengths of the book. Much of the considerable complexity of arms control stems from the fact that it is highly subjective; no two specialists see the issues in quite the same way. Any book on the subject by a single author, or by a very few authors, is therefore almost certain to reflect much less than the full range of outlooks actually to be found on the subject—even in policy-making quarters. The rather wide range of views represented in the present volume is narrowed to some extent by the fact that our authors all represent points of view to be found in the United States. However, this orientation is partially offset and enriched by the comments on the body of the book by four foreign observers which appear at the end of the volume.

There are three points, however, on which I think every one of the authors would agree. The first point is that the present state and direction of the world is not at all satisfactory. The second is that it will not become ideal at any time within the foreseeable future, on even the most optimistic assumptions that are yet within the bounds of reason. And the third point of agreement is that the basic values of Western civilization are well worth preserving. There are differences over ways and means, and in sophistication; but *there are no basic differences in the morality of the authors.*

This fact bears on a false dichotomy that certain extremists have been trying to create—that of "disarmament *versus* arms control." The point of view of this book (as with most students of these affairs) is that "arms control" is a generic term that includes the possibility of literal "disarmament" among other possible cases. In the recent past, unfortunately, a few writers have been attempting to create a new meaning of their own for "arms control," a meaning that seems to embrace only limited and rather special forms of arms control. These writers hold that "arms control" (in their limited sense of the term) is a distinctly wicked doctrine, and those who advocate it (as opposed to "disarmament") are made to appear as immoral proponents of the continuation of the arms race. No careful reader of this volume can escape the conclusion that this view is absurd.

Although the book has been designed to display a full range of views, it would be less than honest to pretend that the over-all volume does not reflect *a* point of view, principally that of the Editor. It would be difficult even for me to say precisely what this view is, except to the extent it could be summarized by the word *experimental*. However, perceptive readers may find indications, such as the distribution of emphasis in the volume and the placement of certain chapters.

For those who wish a "short-course" form of the book, chapters 1, 2, 3, 5, 6, 7, 9, 11, 14, and 22 are recommended for this purpose. (These are indicated by asterisks in the Table of Contents.) Professional students of national-security policy will probably wish to include chapter 12 as well.

A word about the inclusion of chapter 7 (Henry A. Kissinger, "Limited War: Conventional or Nuclear?") in this list may be in order. Several readers have asked why this chapter should be in a book on arms control at all. In point of fact, the subject of this chapter is of vital importance to arms control. Decision-makers in the United States are most unlikely in the near future to accept significant constraints on nuclear capabilities unless the basic viability of a nonnuclear strategy is accepted. This problem is especially related to the question of significant Chinese cooperation in arms-control arrangements. If a nonnuclear strategy seems feasible, then some bilateral Soviet-American controls on nuclear weapons and forces may be feasible for the *near* future, even without Chinese participation; on the other hand, if it is held that nuclear forces are necessary to contain Chinese conventional forces, the scope of possible nuclear controls is heavily dependent on Chinese cooperation. The subject of chapter 7 is vital to the evaluation of such arms-control possibilities as a nuclear-test ban, a cut-off of production of nuclear materials, the prohibition of first use of nuclear weapons, and zonal denuclearization arrangements, among others. (The relevance of this topic to the question of a nuclear-test ban is explored in some detail in chapter 12; it is also relevant to several other chapters.)

Mention should be made of the limitations in coverage of this volume. Relatively little background material on the present politico-military environment is provided because of the enormous literature extant on this subject, though enough is included in chapter 1 and others to serve as an introduction. We have not included any material on the domestic legal implications of arms control because this topic has been thoroughly studied

by Louis Henkin.[1]* And there is relatively little detailed analysis of specific
arms-control measures, partly for reasons of space (compare chap. 12),
but partly because few such specific measures have been studied sufficiently
at the time of organizing this book.

Readers wishing additional guidance through the volume are advised to
consult the summaries in the Table of Contents.

ACKNOWLEDGMENTS

This book is based on a special issue (Fall 1960) of *Dædalus,* Journal
of the American Academy of Arts and Sciences, published jointly by the
Academy and Wesleyan University Press. Eleven of the chapters in the
present volume (2, 4, 6, 7, 8, 9, 10, 15, 16, 19, and 23) appeared in
Dædalus in what is substantially their present form; seven others (1, 5, 11,
14, 17, 20, and 21) are based on chapters in *Dædalus* with moderate to
extensive revisions; and five chapters (3, 12, 13, 18, and 22) are completely new. The foreign comments in Part VIII appeared in the Winter
1961 issue of *Dædalus* in substantially their present form.

The initiative in the inception of the special issue of *Dædalus* came from
Gerald Holton, Professor of Physics at Harvard University and Editor-in-
Chief of the American Academy of Arts and Sciences. A guest Editorial
Board was appointed for that issue, consisting of Jerome B. Wiesner,
Director of the Research Laboratory of Electronics at the Massachusetts
Institute of Technology and then a member (now Chairman) of the
President's Science Advisory Committee, as Chairman, and with the fol-
lowing as members: Robert R. Bowie, Director of the Center for Interna-
tional Affairs, Harvard; John T. Edsall, Professor of Biology at Harvard
and Chairman of the Committee on the Technical Problems of Arms
Limitation of the American Academy; Bernard T. Feld, Professor of
Physics, Massachusetts Institute of Technology, and Chairman of the
Operating Committee on the Technical Problems of Arms Limitation of
the Academy; William T. R. Fox, Director of the Institute of War and
Peace Studies, Columbia University; Stephen R. Graubard, Historian at
Harvard and Managing Editor of *Dædalus;* Dr. Holton; Henry A. Kissinger,
Director of the Harvard Defense Studies Program; Louis B. Sohn, Professor
of International Law, Harvard; and the present writer, who served as Guest
Editor (and principal architect) of the issue. All the members of this
board contributed substantially to the issue, some of them in many ways.
In particular, much of the success of the undertaking was due to Gerald
Holton, who not only took the initiative in getting the issue under way and
securing the necessary financial support, but also contributed heavily to
the substantive organization and editing of the issue and to the publication
arrangements for the present volume—as did Dr. Graubard. I am also
especially indebted to Jerome Wiesner for helpful guidance at many points
in the organization of the issue.

* Numbered notes are in the "References," pp. 457 ff.

In addition to members of the guest Editorial Board, three of our present authors contributed substantial assistance to the preparation of this volume. I should first of all like to thank Herman Kahn, partly for many constructive suggestions on several of the chapters, but even more for his willingness to devote much time in the midst of a busy schedule to the preparation of his own chapter. Bernhard Bechhoefer and Lewis Bohn also provided many helpful comments.

Many others have also aided in the preparation of this volume, either by helpful suggestions on one or more of the chapters or in other ways. These include Raymond Aron, Hans A. Bethe, Lawrence S. Finkelstein, Betty Goetz, Arthur T. Hadley, Louis Henkin, Spurgeon M. Keeny, Jr., L. Addison Lanier, Ralph Lapp, Charles L. Mack, Jr., Carl F. J. Overhage, Philip W. Quigg, Henry Rowen, Max Singer, Ronald I. Spiers, John W. Tukey, Harry Waters, Victor F. Weisskopf, and Christopher Wright. Some of the revised material in chapter 1 can probably be traced to discussions at the joint Harvard-MIT Faculty Seminar on Arms Control, and chapter 12 owes much to this body. Chapter 3 is based in part on a study done by Roger Fisher for the 1960 Summer Study on Arms Control of the American Academy of Arts and Sciences, which was supported by the Twentieth Century Fund.

A conference sponsored by the Johnson Foundation was held at the House of the Academy in May 1960 to discuss drafts of the papers for the special issue of *Dædalus,* at which most of the authors and many of the others named above were present. Other participants and observers at this conference, which aided materially in the final formulation of the *Dædalus* chapters, were Harold Brown, Herbert S. Dinerstein, David C. Elliot, W. A. Higinbotham, Fred C. Iklé, Harold Kuhn, Ernest W. Lefever, R. Duncan Luce, Kirtley F. Mather, J. Alden Nichols, Paul H. Nitze, Colonel Kent Parrot, John B. Phelps, Howard Raiffa, David Riesman, Matthew Sands, Herbert Scoville, Jr., J. David Singer, Harry Starr, Lester Van Atta, and Albert Wohlstetter.

Thanks are also due to Mrs. Katharine Strelsky, Assistant Editor of *Dædalus,* Miss Susan Levitt of the *Dædalus* office, and their editorial assistants, all of whom effected no inconsiderable improvement in the prose of many of our authors, and otherwise assisted in the undertaking.

A special word must be said of the great debt owed the Johnson Foundation of Racine, Wisconsin, whose financial support made possible the Conference, the special issue of *Dædalus,* and consequently the present volume. The quick and generous decision of the Foundation and its President, Leslie Paffrath, has enabled the timely production of what several experts have called "the 'bible' of arms control."

DONALD G. BRENNAN

Massachusetts Institute of Technology

February 1961

Foreword

JEROME B. WIESNER

THIS BOOK, DEVOTED TO THE PROBLEMS OF ARMS LIMITATION, ATTEMPTS TO provide some of the basic information and understanding needed for an intelligent public discussion of the disarmament problem. To a distressing degree American citizens, who normally insist on free and open discussion of important issues facing their country, have turned away from the problems of arms control as being of such complexity and requiring access to so much secret military and political information as (supposedly) to be beyond the comprehension of the ordinary citizen. But, without a widespread understanding of the options available to the nation and without some ability on the part of the general public to judge the relative security of various alternatives, it will not be possible for the United States to find acceptable arms-limitation agreements or to accept the constraints such agreements will impose on the military activities of the country.

During the past two years discussion groups and seminars on problems of arms limitation were held in the Boston area. These groups found themselves badly handicapped by the lack of published material relating to their studies. When the Editor of the American Academy of Arts and Sciences decided to devote a special issue of *Dædalus,* the Journal of the Academy, to the topic of Arms Control, they were quick to encourage it and collaborate on it. This book is largely based on that issue of *Dædalus* (Vol. 89, No. 4), but includes several additional chapters, as well as various additions and modifications to the original papers.

One cannot deny that the political, military, and technical issues involved are complex. Moreover, even in the classified literature there is little on the substantive problems of arms limitation. The lack of popular or technical literature in this field indicates that until now there has actually been little intellectual effort expended on it, a disturbing fact that is pointed out by several of our contributors.

Secrecy, it may be noted, has not greatly inhibited the appearance of *military* information. Technical and military journals, leaks to the syndicated daily columns, and even the *Congressional Record* provide a voluminous flow of technical and tactical information regarding military weapons and the official assessment of the politico-military situation. This flow of information, much of it officially regarded as secret, is in fact impossible to stem. It is the lack of anything to publish, not secrecy restrictions, that accounts for the absence of a body of literature on arms control.

The primary motive, therefore, in preparing this collection of essays was to stimulate public discussion of the arms-limitation issue by providing the views of a number of persons who have given some thought to the problem, and, if possible, to make a contribution to the serious literature in the field. Nearly all the contributors have had an intimate association with the military or political aspects of the United States government during the past decade and so can write with considerable understanding on the complicated issues involved.

One idea stands out very clearly in these chapters: the general consensus that civilization is faced with an unprecedented crisis. There is a growing realization among knowledgeable people that if the arms race is allowed to continue its accelerating pace, our country will have less security, not more, with each passing year. As a result, there is an ever-increasing likelihood of a war so disastrous that civilization, if not man himself, will be eradicated.

My own experience is not very different from that of many others who have worked hard during the past decade and a half in an effort to provide the country with a strong military defense. We have seen each of our advances matched by Soviet developments, so that, as time passed, the only discernible result has been that both our nations have produced more and more destructive weapons against which there is no defense.

One of the most ironic aspects of the situation in which the United States and the Soviet Union find themselves is that each is running an arms race with itself. Because of the technical capabilities of both countries, neither will for long lag behind the other in developing any new weapon. As a consequence, we are forced to work harder and harder in the effort to maintain a given degree of security. Thus we create twin spirals of invention and production, which, because of the nature of the weapons involved, appear to lessen, rather than enhance, the possibility of that security.

While the Doomsday Machines discussed in Herman Kahn's chapter may appear somewhat far-fetched, it is an unpleasant fact that almost any invention the weapons engineers can conceive of can now be built—and the logic of the arms race seems to require that any possible weapon *be* built, no matter how horrible. Furthermore, both the Soviet Union and the United States already own enough nuclear explosives, and are fast getting the delivery capability, to kill each other several times over. The prospect of the spread of large numbers of such weapons to other nations only adds to the nightmare.

Obviously, the most important task confronting us today is to find the means of halting the arms race and eliminating the danger of nuclear war. This does not appear to be something that can be safely done by unilateral actions on the part of the Western allies, and it is doubtful whether the Soviet leaders would regard unilateral disarmament as a course on which they could embark with safety. Like it or not, the nations of the world must make a superhuman effort, working together, to reach agreements leading to some form of rational system of world security.

Yet most people do not quite believe in disarmament. In fact, some people view with suspicion any attempt to impose restrictions on military activities, and many more are skeptical of the possibility of actually achieving a meaningful agreement on arms control. Such cynicism is strongly supported by historical precedents. On the other hand, history also indicates that until now wars have occurred with distressing regularity, and that in recent times each successive major war has been larger and more destructive than the previous one. There is every historical reason to conclude that, if we drift along as we are now doing, another major war will certainly occur. We can only avoid that disaster if the nations of the world regard war itself as a common enemy and make a truly consummate effort to work together in resolving the important issues that are involved.

Unfortunately, nations, like most individuals, become interested in adequate fire protection only after the house has burned down. At least in the past, there has been little official willingness anywhere to undertake the effort required to make a success of arms control. Shall we wait until after the next world war, in which hundreds of millions of people will undoubtedly be killed, uncountable future generations condemned to genetic death or malformation, and thousands of billions of dollars worth of property destroyed—before it becomes obvious to the survivors that war should be outlawed? In retrospect, it will be impossible to understand why the consequences of the arms race were not crystal clear beforehand, and why an otherwise rational people like the citizens of the United States did not insist that their leaders make a reasonable effort to find alternatives.

I feel a word of caution to the reader is needed. Partly owing to the small amount of sound research in this field in the past, there are many real gaps in our understanding of the military, technical, and political problems involved. Many of the authors, myself included, stress the need for intensive study. We are hopeful that such studies will provide knowledge which will make it possible to proceed with more confidence, but I should like to warn against the expectation that any amount of advanced planning and study, no matter how thorough, will see the problem completely solved. But a start must be made. First, and second, and continuing studies must be initiated. Research and development on a large scale are necessary. And the nations must be willing to try out the results of these carefully thought-out studies without insisting on a blueprint to completion. We must accept an understanding of the desirable objectives and of the multitude of technical details involved, so as to gain the confidence to set off on the road to peace.

I believe we already have a sufficient understanding of the problem of arms control to make an effective start, and I am confident that if the nations of the world were to devote one-quarter of the effort in terms of manpower and money now being expended in the arms race to the quest for a lasting peace and a better world, the goal, though a difficult one, could be achieved in our lifetime.

PART I

BACKGROUND

1. Setting and Goals of Arms Control

DONALD G. BRENNAN

INTRODUCTION

THIS CHAPTER HAS TWO MAIN OBJECTIVES. THE FIRST IS TO ESTABLISH THE military and strategic setting in which arms control must operate, at least initially. This section includes a brief review of contemporary military doctrine, principally (but not entirely) for the purpose of introducing the relevant concepts and terminology to readers who are not experts on these matters. The second major objective is to enumerate some of the major goals of arms controls. A third objective, subordinate to the first two, is to provide at least some coverage on topics of major pertinence to arms control that are not sufficiently treated elsewhere in this volume.

The emphasis on the present military environment indicated in the first major objective should not be taken to mean that the subject of arms control is purely military in character. Quite the contrary; although certain kinds of potentially valuable arms-control arrangements involve only relatively narrow military considerations, the bulk of the potential arms-control or disarmament measures that have come under consideration entail political factors of great importance. However, the political environment is quite well known to the general informed reader, while the character of the military environment and the jargon used to describe it are much less widely known. Topics such as the ideological conflict, the division of Germany, and the division of Korea are just as much a part of the initial "setting" of arms control as are military forces and strategic doctrine, but they are not treated in detail in the present chapter.

It should be mentioned that this chapter is not a survey of the topics treated elsewhere in the volume, nor is it intended as a synthesis of all the elements central to arms control. It is also not meant to provide a discussion and an emphasis representing a consensus among the other authors. Although most of the authors would probably agree with most of what I shall say, it has not been written with this objective in view, and the agreement would not in any event be complete.

The Goals of Armament Policy. It is desirable at the outset to review some fundamental facts. Most of us do not regard either war or the means of war as ends in themselves. We regard military force as means to other, nonmilitary goals. This simply means that there is a consensus among a large number of people that military action is not one of the ends of life.

What, then, are the goals that armament is intended to serve? The first answer to this question is seemingly easy: it is simply survival—national survival at the level of the nation, personal survival at the level of the individual. But it is possible to distinguish different kinds of survival—physical survival, political survival, survival of a standard of living.* The significance of such distinctions is that different armament policies would support some kinds of survival without necessarily supporting others. For example, some people believe that a policy of complete unilateral disarmament and nonresistance would possibly support sheer physical survival. Even if true, this policy would surely be unlikely to support political survival, and still less likely to support the survival of our standard of living. (I am here speaking of the possibility of another nation making large demands on our economic output or other resources, and not about the problem of internal adjustments to disarmament.) On the other hand, modern weapons are so impressive that a strong "Fortress America" armament policy would probably support national survival in all three senses, but might fail to support other national goals and purposes.

The simple problem of national survival, in its various senses, is sufficient to indicate the character of the enormously complex interaction among armament policy, armament-in-being, and national goals and purposes. Of course, the present and projected armament and national goals of other nations—or, rather, our beliefs concerning them—are components of this interaction. To affirm that armament should be only a servant of national purposes is not to say that there is a simple cause-and-effect relation between them; the interaction is much more complex. Radical technological developments sometimes influence armament policy more profoundly than do explicit decisions of national policy.

The visible complexity of this interaction increases in both degree and kind when national goals beyond mere survival are considered. The increase in degree is fairly obvious; it stems from the increased complexity of the added armament required—overseas bases, logistics, different weapons—and the broadened spectrum of goals. Most of the added goals are in the realm of foreign policy, and relate to such matters as the maintenance of independent nations in Western Europe and South America. The increase in the kind of complexity is less obvious; it stems from the fact that the fundamental ends the foreign policy itself is intended to support are less clearly defined than the simple ends of physical and political survival.

A reasonable view of the objectives of foreign policy is that it is intended to secure a world order with a structure that is compatible with the funda-

* Henry Kissinger has suggested adding "moral survival" to this list. This is a very important point, and I should do so but for the fact that it would complicate the following discussion.

mental purposes of the United States. This view has recently been set forth with considerable clarity and detail in a broad study [1] of the interaction under consideration here. But this view immediately raises the question: What are the fundamental purposes of the United States?

Several critics have maintained that we do not, in fact, *have* an adequate sense of national purpose, and that this problem infects the formulation of foreign policy and, consequently, the formulation of politico-military strategies to support such policy. On the other hand, there are many who have more or less explicit ideas about the fundamental ends of what has been called "the affluent society." But it is not my present purpose to enter this debate *per se*. It is sufficient here to point out that there *is* a debate—which, perhaps, may be intrinsic to a pluralistic society. While we have a consensus that military action is not among the ends of life, and that survival *is* among the ends of life, we have no similarly complete consensus concerning the basic national purposes (beyond survival) of the United States.

At bottom, therefore, armament policy is one of many aspects of the general problem of achieving a world to our liking; but we seem to lack a clear collective sense of just what that world should or could be like in the long term.

All this is not to say, however, that there are not eminently sensible intermediate goals that have constituted the immediate objectives of our foreign policy of the recent past—goals on which, moreover, there is general agreement. We do not think it desirable that the political future of the South Koreans should be determined by the armed forces of North Korea and the People's Republic of China, nor do we wish to encourage the idea that such aggression can pass unnoticed, possibly to be repeated elsewhere; we do not wish to see the farmers of Japan collectivized in communes; and we have made promises to the people of West Berlin that should be kept.

The most significant aspect of our foreign policy of the present and the recent past is perhaps best characterized as a holding operation. This is the main virtue of the doctrine of containment; whether or not we have good collective ideas of what we are ultimately holding *for,* we certainly have good ideas of what we are holding *against.* This agreement, while minimal, is important. The aggression in Korea is too fresh in our minds, and the possible loss of Western Europe to other Communist aggression seems too great a potential catastrophe to permit us to contemplate the philosophical basis of our foreign policy while the world around us burns. At least to the extent that it does not directly conflict with national survival, and possibly to the extent of considerable risk that it may eventually do so, most of us feel obliged to support and defend the non-Communist world in general and our allies in particular. This obligation has heavily dominated our armament policy of the last decade.

NATIONAL SECURITY

The Notion of Security. The phrase "national security" is one that receives much use but little analysis. Various views of security are possible, and a brief indication of the range of possibilities is useful.

To begin at the level of individuals, there are some people who on moral or religious grounds oppose violence so strongly that no ends whatever, not even the preservation of life itself, are sufficient to justify such violence. The avoidance of violence being a primary end, security for this goal would reside in complete unilateral disarmament and nonresistance.

The most basic view of national security commonly held is the protection of national survival, in all three senses discussed above. This is usually the minimal demand on "national security." Beyond this, the concept quite generally extends to the military and politico-military support of national goals in general and foreign-policy objectives in particular. Improvement of relative military capabilities to support such goals may be obtained at the expense, sooner or later, of impaired national security with respect to national survival. This can and does happen because of economic or political limitations on the armament that can be bought; because of the armament obtained in response by hostile powers; because of a basically defective strategy or armament policy; or because of any combination of these factors. In spite of this conflict, the common consensus of national security is that it relates to the protection of national survival and the support of foreign-policy goals, in some mixture of the two. The character of the mixture and the extent of the interaction and conflict between the two objectives is at best dimly understood, and sometimes not perceived at all.* However, it is probably the view that would be set forth by the majority of informed students of these matters, and it is certainly the concept underlying the remainder of this paper.

Current Views and Concepts. The evolution of ideas on the contemporary state of national security, including those on current military doctrine, strategic thinking, and armament policy, is a subject on which there is very extensive literature. To mention only a few of the more substantial studies in addition to the one already mentioned,[1] there are earlier books by Kaufmann[2] and Kissinger[3] and more recent volumes by Brodie,[4] Knorr,[5] Morgenstern,[6] and Schelling,[7] among others. An especially fine brief survey has recently been given by Rowen,[8] and books by Kahn[9] and Kissinger[10] have been published since this volume was initiated. Studies of Soviet strategic views have been published by Garthoff[11] and by Dinerstein.[12] It is not possible here to include a detailed study of this area, but I shall

---

* That is, it is sometimes held intuitively that support of foreign-policy goals is equivalent to support of national survival. As suggested above in the remark about a "Fortress America" policy, it takes very little thought about the potency of modern weapons to dispel this notion, whatever validity it had before 1945. This is not to say that there is not some interaction, but it is quite short of "equivalence."

attempt a very cursory survey and critique of contemporary Western ideas in this section.

The central concept in current strategic doctrine is that of deterrence. As a phenomenon, deterrence is as old as man—perhaps much older. As examples of deterrence, the protective equipment of a skunk serves to deter *some* enemies from troubling him. The existence of the Roman legions served to deter *some* attacks by invaders. A policeman walking a beat serves to deter *some* crime. The United Nations Emergency Force in Palestine is supposed to deter the resumption of active war between Israel and the Arab powers. The missiles, bombers, and nuclear weapons of the United States Strategic Air Command (SAC) are supposed to deter a nuclear attack on the United States.

The essence of a deterrent is a threat to carry out some punitive measure in the event that the action against which the threat is aimed does transpire. Deterrence is therefore a basically defensive phenomenon, and, as such, has always been present in military strategy to the extent that the strategy was defensively oriented. However, as the first three examples above illustrate, and as the fourth tends to suggest, deterrence can fail. The consequence of a failure of military deterrence is at least the increased likelihood of military action, and perhaps war itself, unless the deterrent threat involved proves to be an empty bluff. In the past, a failure of military deterrence has undoubtedly been painful for the participants involved, but not intolerably painful for Western society as a whole; in particular, it has not been catastrophic for the United States. The deterrent aspect of defense military forces was formerly taken for granted.

But, today, the doctrine of deterrence has assumed paramount and explicit importance in contemporary strategic thinking. The consequence of a failure of strategic nuclear deterrence could be a general nuclear war and a resultant catastrophe for Western society of a magnitude unparalleled in the whole of human history. This possibility has focused attention on the problem of keeping a nuclear war from happening—that is, of deterring it.

The idea of deterrence has become a central organizing concept for all types of strategic problems and for all manner of enforcement threats—for example, the use of conventional limited-war forces to deter aggression by other conventional forces, and the deterrence of evasion under an arms-control agreement. In the process, we have learned a good deal about deterrence. To quote a brief summary by Schelling:

> We have learned that a threat has to be credible, that credibility may depend [inversely] on the pains of fulfillment for the one who makes the threat, and that to make it credible one has to get "committed" to its fulfillment. We have recognized that a readiness to fight a limited war may detract from a threat of massive retaliation; that a threat may be more credible if the means of retaliation are in the hands of those whose resolution is strongest (as in recent suggestions for "nuclear sharing"); that the rationality of the adversary is pertinent, and that madmen, like small children, often cannot be controlled by

threats; that the success of the threat may depend (in the analogy of the trapped lion) on whether the threatened party is left some tolerable recourse; that a threat of all-out retaliation gives the enemy every incentive, in the event he should choose not to heed the threat, to initiate his transgression with an all-out strike at us; and that the threat of massive destruction may deter an enemy only if there is some assurance of nondestruction in the event he complies, so that too great a capacity to strike him by surprise may induce him to strike first.[13]

This passage is primarily oriented toward nuclear deterrence, but the basic principles are applicable to other types.*

Other than deterrence, the main strategic and military concepts requiring mention here are general war and limited war. The distinction presents semantic difficulties. General war is universally understood to mean a nuclear war involving the major nuclear powers, one in which the homelands of these major powers are subject to nuclear attack. The detailed conduct and the consequences of a general war are subject to an enormous range of possible variations,[9] which, however, will not be explored here. "All-out" war is the extreme case of a general war. Broadly speaking, limited war is usually taken to mean a war that involves major powers but one that is not a general war in the above sense. However, it is very important to distinguish between a limited nuclear war and a limited high-explosive (HE) war—a distinction not always as sharply maintained as it should be. A few writers occasionally insist that a limited war is impossible, but this assertion is untenable; the Korean War was limited in numerous ways, gas was not used in World War II, and pre-1939 history is filled with examples of conflicts that were limited in important ways—in objectives, in the resources employed, and in the manner of employment.* Mention should be made of the considerable illumination provided by Schelling[14, 15] on the kinds of qualitative and legalistic distinctions that may serve as "limits," and on the tacit methods of communicating such limits.

It is useful to analyze some of the strategic requirements a national security policy must meet in terms of the different kinds of deterrent functions that must be provided. Many different breakdowns are possible; a widely known classification introduced by Herman Kahn[9, 16] is as follows:

Type I: Deterrence of direct nuclear attack on the United States.

Type II: Deterrence of extreme provocations. These include major attacks on United States forces, on our NATO and SEATO allies, and on other important areas of the non-Communist world.

---

* Some writers use the term *deterrence* to mean only "nuclear deterrence," most often of the "massive retaliation" kind. This is an abuse of language and is to be regretted on several counts.

* As this suggests, the definitions of general war and limited war as given above are defective, principally by reason of their brevity. A really sharp distinction (other than a geographic one) between limited nuclear war and general war does not exist, given the possibility of any sort of "limits" or restraints in the conduct of a general war.

Type III: Deterrence of moderate provocations. These range from the shelling of Quemoy and cutting submarine cables, through shutting off access to Berlin, up to aggressions on the scale of Korea.

This classification is helpful because it serves to isolate the different functions that must be provided and to separate them from the various types of capabilities that might be employed to implement the functions. The functions must always be provided in some degree for the indefinite future; the capabilities employed depend enormously on complex estimates of the world situation in general, and on hostile intentions and forces in particular. (For example, there is a rather abstract Type I requirement to deter a direct attack by Canada, but no specific capabilities whatever are required to implement this function.) Even for a fixed situation, estimates of the capabilities required differ widely, as in the recent debate over the presumed "missile gap." A more extreme example of differing estimates resides in a comparison of current "official" views with the position advanced by the advocates of unilateral disarmament, most of whom would not question the desirability of providing the functions by some sort of means. In addition, the situation can change with the passage of time and with the changing intentions and capabilities of other nations. It might be appropriate to introduce here the idea (to be elaborated below) that arms-control measures are oriented toward improving the performance of the functions by adjusting mutual capabiilties.

In a general context such as the present discussion, however, the specific breakdown given above can be improved by distinguishing between extreme *nuclear* provocations and extreme *nonnuclear* provocations. The lack of this distinction (a lack probably traceable to people who place primary reliance on "massive retaliation") can be rectified by a breakdown of deterrent functions such as the following.

Type A: Deterrence of direct nuclear attack.
Type B: Deterrence of extreme nuclear provocations.
Type C: Deterrence of extreme nonnuclear provocations.
Type D: Deterrence of moderate provocations.

The distinctions between these four are worth brief comment. It has occasionally been held that each of Types A, B, and C deterrence could be adequately implemented with a single type of threat capability, namely, the capability of delivering a major nuclear strike on the homeland of the aggressor. The use of this threat to implement Type C deterrence could be, and was, questioned trenchantly on moral grounds alone (among others), even in the days when we had an essential monopoly of nuclear weapons. To any reasonable person, the growth of Soviet nuclear capabilities has since placed this policy nearly or entirely beyond the realm of credibility, on several counts. To name only three: first, a Soviet retaliatory strike on the United States could be extremely painful—with perhaps 10 to 70 million people dead, with grave hazards to the health, to political survival, and to the standard of living of the survivors. Second, there is only slight likelihood that our strategic nuclear response to a failure of Type C deterrence would in fact secure the protection of the original object of the provocation. Third, and perhaps most important, there could be an alternative response that could be at once much less painful and much more successful: the use of conventional (HE) forces. We could, if necessary, mobilize and equip a 15-million-man army that would probably be able to defeat the aggressive conventional forces of any nation in the world, not excepting China, which could mobilize the men, but could not adequately equip, train, or transport them. An army of this size need not be in existence on the first day of the provocation, and probably would never need to be that large.*

For such reasons, there should no longer be any serious intention of responding to a failure of Type C deterrence with a major nuclear strike. For example, former Secretary of State Christian Herter said in the United States Senate on the occasion of the hearings on his nomination: "I *cannot conceive* of any President involving us in an all-out nuclear war unless the facts showed clearly we are in danger of all-out devastation ourselves." (As quoted by Herman Kahn; [16] emphasis supplied by the present author.) Apart from a few people who would probably be quick to change their minds about the issue in a crisis, the policy of responding to a conventional-force attack with a strategic nuclear strike seems to be an essentially dead issue.

An issue that is much less dead, but seems to be rapidly dying, is the use of a response intermediate between conventional forces and a strategic nuclear strike, namely, tactical nuclear weapons and limited nuclear war. Close analysis of limited nuclear war appears to indicate that it would be militarily disadvantageous if used by both sides, at least, in most cases where it might be employed. In addition, it would be highly dangerous and would be likely to produce undesirable political effects, such as hastening the spread of nuclear weapons to other countries. Some of the difficulties of this response are indicated in the chapter by Kissinger.

It should be noted, however, that in the absence of a comprehensive arms-control program, an extremely good general-war capability might be required in the event of a failure of Type C deterrence, simply to persuade the enemy that it is unmistakably in his interest to refrain from transgressing the HE-nuclear boundary when the subsequent HE war begins to go badly for him.† This last might be called "escalation deterrence"—prevent-

---

* There is an important and unresolved question as to just how large the army should be on the first day of the conflict. It obviously depends somewhat on the HE forces-in-being of other nations, among other things. As noted in the essay below by Kissinger, the need for good conventional forces-in-being is greater than at any time in the past, but the potential role of mobilization and industrial capacity for Type C and Type D deterrence has been overly neglected in recent years.

† There may be, of course, a limit as to how badly it might go; "unconditional surrender" is a dangerous objective in an HE war between the major powers if one wishes to keep it an HE war.

ing the scale of initially limited conflicts from growing to disastrous proportions.

The kinds of capabilities currently being procured (or discussed for possible procurement) to implement the various types of deterrence are too well known in outline to require more than the briefest mention here. They include a wide variety of nuclear weapons (together with the requisite aircraft and missile delivery systems), active and passive defense systems, and conventional-war forces.

There is a very general consensus among military experts that our current conventional forces are unnecessarily inadequate. There is, however, a complicated trade-off (which is hardly ever recognized explicitly and is not at all well understood) between large HE forces-in-being and consequently limited initial gains achieved by an aggressor on the one hand, and limited HE forces-in-being and (possibly) the consequent necessity of large mobilization to retake lost ground, on the other. To some extent this is a trade-off between present national resolve and future national resolve. Some analysts seem to discount our future national resolve excessively, as did the Japanese in 1941.

There is much less of a consensus as to the adequacy of our present and projected nuclear deterrent forces. There is an increasing recognition of the fact that the simple form of the "balance-of-terror" theory to implement Type A deterrence is inadequate, and that the balance, as was aptly noted by Wohlstetter,[17] is "delicate." This stems from the fact that contemporary nuclear-weapon systems provide an enormous potential advantage to an aggressor, who, in launching a Pearl Harbor style of surprise attack on his victim's retaliatory forces, might reduce the possible level of retaliation below that which would deter the attack. In consequence, there is much current emphasis on protecting such deterrent forces (often referred to as "hardening," a term stemming from the protection of "soft" objects against blast overpressure) by mobility, by concealment (as in POLARIS submarines), and by sheer concrete, so that much of the deterrent force could survive a surprise initial strike.[17] This type is sometimes called a "second-strike" capability, to distinguish it from a "first-strike" force*—i.e., one which would be highly vulnerable to destruction if struck in a surprise attack. Another distinction often made is between "countercity" (or "counterpopulation") and "counterforce" capabilities.

It has sometimes been held that Type B deterrence can be implemented with a vulnerable "first-strike" force; as of 1961, however, so much of our own strategic nuclear capability (such as aircraft carriers with the Sixth and Seventh Fleets) is inextricably involved with NATO and SEATO forces that a failure of Type B deterrence without simultaneous failure of

---

* I am using "first-strike force" in a more restricted sense than that conveyed by the term "credible first-strike capability," which implies the ability to limit retaliatory damage to a level at which the initiation of a first strike would be credible, not merely possible. See Kahn.[9, 16]

Type A deterrence is most unlikely.* Partly for this reason, and partly because it does not seem likely that a general nuclear war would consist simply of an all-out attack salvo followed by an all-out retaliatory salvo, distinctions between "first-strike" and "second-strike" forces are becoming somewhat blurred. The detailed facts concerning the composition and functioning of strategic nuclear deterrent forces are highly technical, and for the most part are set forth in literature that is either classified or otherwise unavailable; however, unclassified illustrative computations and considerations have been given by Phelps and his colleagues at Ohio State, among others.[18, 19, 20, 21]

The major point of controversy concerning our present and future strategic nuclear forces is whether the United States should adopt a position of approximate equality with the Soviet strategic forces, or whether we should continue to maintain a considerable margin of superiority in such forces. While the effectiveness of our present forces in a general nuclear war would depend considerably on just how the war broke out, it is probably true that our present forces would yield a considerable margin of superiority in any of the more likely ways in which a general war might arise. This means that our present forces could probably assure a purely military victory in such a conflict, though the nonmilitary cost of the conflict might be enormous. Advocates of the continuation of a posture of this type, which is probably feasible as a purely technical and economic matter for at least the next decade, correctly point out that this type of capability increases deterrence. On the other hand, those who oppose the continuation of this type of policy point out that it is certainly incompatible with the establishment of agreed arms limitations of substance, and probably likely to lead to long-term political and military effects of an adverse character, such as increasing the pressures for the further spread of nuclear weapons.

As is often the case in such matters, the policy decision involved here is one of balancing short-term costs against long-term potential gains. To begin with, current Soviet long-range nuclear striking forces seem to be relatively modest, though of course the available information on this subject is far from complete. The Soviet forces may well be so modest that even the implementation of an arms-limitation program of the type discussed in the later chapters by Wiesner and by Leghorn might not result in any major reduction in these capabilities, though such programs would certainly affect our own long-range forces radically. To reduce our strategic forces to a level comparable to the Soviet forces might well impair our ability to reduce the destructiveness of Soviet attacks in the event a general war were to break out. Therefore, the net immediate effect of accepting a pos-

---

* The statement of Herter's quoted above is therefore not particularly relevant to our response to failure of Type B deterrence, except in so far as it explicitly indicates that we might pre-empt under such conditions. This again indicates why it is vital to distinguish between B and C deterrence; indeed, it is probably much less vital (but still vital) to distinguish between A and B deterrence.

ture of approximate equality in Soviet and United States strategic forces might be simply to increase the level of damage sustained by the United States in a general war if one were to arise. In turn, this effect might have secondary political effects, arising principally from a corresponding reduction in our ability to stand up to nuclear blackmail threats, though the extent to which these effects would be real or imaginary may well be open to question. To be balanced against these short-term costs of a posture of equality are potential long-term gains, such as the possibility of ultimately reducing net Soviet destructive capabilities through arms-limitation programs and the possible world that might evolve if a sufficient degree of East-West cooperation is achieved.

Although this policy problem is central to this subject, it has received astonishingly little intelligent discussion, either inside or outside the government, at least to the time of writing. The problem is worthy of a book in itself, but as of early 1961, no one known to me is prepared to write such a book. It would be fair to say that most of the advocates of arms-control programs have not even perceived this problem, much less discussed it explicitly; they usually assume simply that it *is* acceptable to adopt a position of approximate equality, or that we are in such a position already. (R. S. Leghorn and a few others are exceptions.) On the other hand, advocates of the continuation of a posture of considerable strategic superiority simply assume that a posture of equality is not acceptable, and do not usually analyze the potential long-term costs of their own policies. Personally, I am at least tentatively in favor of a posture of approximate equality, but I should feel more comfortable about this opinion if there had been more thought devoted to the problem.

The Role of Arms Control. As the foregoing survey might suggest, that part of our national security that is measured by our ability to guarantee national survival in all its various senses his undergone a precipitous decline in recent years. At the close of World War II, no nation had the capability of inflicting any damage worthy of the name on the United States. At the present time, the Soviet Union could mount an attack that would kill tens of millions of citizens and leave the standard of living of the survivors very seriously depressed. Every projection based on this trend points to an increasingly serious capability; by the late 1960's, the USSR might be able to launch a strike that would extinguish 90 per cent of our populace.

This is sometimes taken to mean that the national security of the Soviet Union, relative to ours, has been improving. Perhaps it has, perhaps not; it depends on what is understood by the term and on when the comparisons are made. In the mid-1950's, for example, we had a very nearly one-sided capability to obliterate the Soviet Union, so that their relative position has improved since then—*they* can now threaten "massive retaliation" to deter provocations. On the other hand, our capability of this type was all but negligible in 1946, so that their relative security has not improved from 1946 to 1960.

But talk of relative security is somewhat beside the point, in any event. The central fact is that the absolute national security (measured in the same sense of their ability to guarantee national survival) of the Soviet Union has also undergone a precipitous decline since 1946. The Soviets cannot be sure that our forces will never be used, whether because of accident, misunderstanding, or our response to a crisis. Neither can we be sure that the Soviet capability will never be used. It is possible to feel moderately relaxed about these facts at the present time, but anyone who feels completely relaxed about them either does not understand the situation or is not acting in a manner that is rational with respect to the goals of society.

For it would seem that each side is likely to be able to inflict far more damage on the other in a general war than either would find at all justified by the original objectives of the conflict, whichever side suffered the greater absolute damage. And the possibility of a general war occurring is a real one. The chance of a general war within the next year is not zero, and, assuming the present course of events continues, the likelihood of a general war within the next ten or fifteen years appears very disturbing. Again, assuming the present course of events continues, the possibility of a general war involving China as a participant in the era of 1975 and beyond must appear a very disturbing one indeed—both to the Soviet Union and to the United States.*

It appears, therefore, that the armament policy pursued by the two major nuclear powers for the past fifteen years has brought us both to a situation we should like to see modified. There is no need in the present context to attempt to assign the responsibility for this situation. The question at issue is whether we and the Soviets and others can find means of improving our security by modifying our armament policies, perhaps cooperatively. There seem to be large common interests.

This brings us to a definition of "arms control." It is neither necessary nor desirable to formulate a precise definition that would include everything thought of as "arms control," "arms limitation," or "disarmament," and would exclude everything else. However, it is useful to think generally of arms control as a cooperative or multilateral approach to armament policy —where "armament policy" includes not only the amount and kind of weapons and forces in being, but also the development, deployment, and utilization of such forces, whether in periods of relaxation, in periods of tension, or in periods of shooting wars. The approach should be thought of as oriented toward improving the national security of each of the nations involved by adjusting at least some armament capabilities and uses to those "actually" desirable in the light of the intentions, actions, and adjusted capabilities of the other nations.

It is necessary to put "actually" within quotation marks because a

* It may be worth pointing out that it has been estimated [8] that by 1975 China will have an industrial capacity equivalent to that of the Soviet Union in 1960.

sharply defined consensus of what is "actually" desirable is in no way to be expected in any circumstances in even the remotely foreseeable future. In the first place, we are dealing with a very nebulous concept labeled "national security," which has an inherent conflict between the support of national survival and the support of other national goals. In the second place, the "intentions" are also nebulous, not so much in concept as in fact; we ourselves do not know how we might respond to certain crises or provocations, and the Soviets do not know in detail just what actions they would take in support of their national goals. Last, even if precise statements about security and intentions were both possible to formulate and were also known, the interaction of such statements with specific armament policies is so enormously complex as to be utterly beyond a detailed and precise understanding. But these problems of understanding and analysis are with us already, even with a largely unilateral armament policy. They do not necessarily make the problem of improving the world by arms-control measures impossible of solution.

Some further clarification of the concept of arms control may be useful. To begin with, it includes the possibility of an actual reduction in arms, that is, disarmament, either in limited or extensive ways. It also includes the possibility of constraints on armament that may or may not entail a reduction of forces, of the sort sometimes described as "arms limitation"; for example, a weapon-test ban and deployment restrictions (e.g., disengagement) are "arms limitation" measures but not "disarmament" measures. And there is nothing in the concept of arms control to prevent the increase of certain types of armament, if it appears in the interest of national or world security to do so. Nor does the concept require the "cooperation" involved to be explicit or to be set forth in detail in a formal agreement; the cooperation may be tacit, partial, nebulous, or even grudging.* For example, the advocates of partial and graduated unilateral disarmament can make a strong case that this policy might, through economic and political pressures, induce others to follow suit—in other words, to "cooperate," without impairing national security in the process.

A few cases in point will illustrate the range of possibilities. The recently concluded agreement to abstain from developing or deploying weapons or forces in the Antarctic is an arms-control measure—notable at the moment of writing as being the only one to which both the United States and the Soviet Union have explicitly and formally subscribed, but one that otherwise seems rather insubstantial. We have a more substantial but completely tacit agreement with the Canadians not to arm the border between the United States and Canada. The nonuse of gas in World War II was a tacit

---

* Many students of arms control prefer to reserve the term for measures that are explicitly agreed upon, and they would not concur in this extension. However, I do not see how otherwise to include graduated unilateral measures (among other things) as a special case of arms control. (On the other hand, the cooperation should at least be recognizable as such, if the notion is not to be too broad to be useful.)

arms-control measure, at least in the sense used here. To cease the production of fissionable nuclear materials would be an arms-control measure, as would general and complete disarmament—if it can ever be achieved. The point these examples are intended to suggest is that there is an enormous range of measures for cooperative security that nations might take to reduce the danger of war, most especially the danger of nuclear war, or to mitigate the consequences of war if it comes. But there are problems in arriving at such measures.

The Problem of Evaluation. From the point of view of the United States (or any other country), any specific arms-control measure or program that has been proposed has two basic aspects: it may improve some component of our security, either in the short or the long term, and it may degrade some other—again, either in the short or the long term. Both the hazards it may protect us against or reduce and the hazards it may introduce are often subtle, complicated, and difficult to understand. Indeed, they may not be at all apparent when the measure is first considered, and may never be completely understood. The problem of deciding whether or not the proposed measure is "actually desirable" is one of deciding whether the hazards reduced do or do not outweigh the hazards introduced. Some brief indication of the nature of the problems involved will be useful.

The Central Hazard of the Present Environment. Most of us probably find it difficult to grasp what a nuclear war could be like. Numerical estimates of x million dead, y cities destroyed, and z per cent of our industry obliterated seem unreal. The frontispiece shows photographs before and after of Nagasaki [22] that convey an immediate sense of the scale of the problem. The energy release of the Nagasaki bomb was equivalent to about 20 thousand tons (20 kilotons) of TNT. This size of weapon is now often regarded as "tactical," that is, suited primarily to use against troops and other forces in a limited nuclear war, rather than strategic bombardment. However, the frontispiece illustrates why Europeans and others on whose territory a limited nuclear war might be fought may be disinclined to view such a war as sufficiently "limited."

In several senses, the frontispiece is obsolete. Seven years after the Hiroshima and Nagasaki bombs, the first thermonuclear device was tested. The Soviets tested their first the following year.* Today there exist thermonuclear weapons with an energy yield approximately one thousand times as great as the Nagasaki bomb, a yield measured in millions of tons, or "megatons," of equivalent TNT. It is often said that a single high-yield thermonuclear weapon can release more energy than all the high explosive used in the whole of World War II—perhaps more than was used in all past wars altogether. Most people have not yet really assimilated this development. To the present day, experienced newspaper reporters often confuse "kilotons" and "megatons." In their defense, it should be said that these units

---

* The Soviet weapon was actually the first operational bomb; our 1952 device was not transportable.

of measurement are indeed difficult to grasp. Even among professionals, I have observed an occasional tendency to think of "kilotons" as "tons." The frontispiece is a good antidote to this tendency and is worth occasional study as a reminder, whether "obsolete" or not.

There is another side to this problem. Nuclear weapons very much smaller than the Nagasaki bomb are possible. For example, weapons having a yield as low as 55 tons (0.055 kilotons) have been tested. Weapons having a yield of 10 tons or less could presumably be developed, and much of the motivation on the part of weapon scientists to continue the development of nuclear weapons stems from the possible development of weapons in this range. There is no question but that such weapons, which are sometimes overlooked by critics of limited nuclear war, would not produce anything like the damage indicated in the frontispiece. And they probably would be militarily advantageous for the United States, *provided that they did not lead to the use of much larger weapons.* The difficulty, of course, is that as soon as one side achieved an advantage by the use of 10-ton weapons, the other side could promptly neutralize it (and possibly much more besides) by introducing 10-kiloton weapons.

Megaton-class weapons have not yet been used in war, and there is no analogue to the frontispiece to provide a graphic sense of their effects, for which numerical estimates must suffice. To begin with, a high-yield thermonuclear weapon can reduce a standard frame house to absolute rubble as far as 12 *miles* from the point of explosion, and leave one very seriously damaged as much as 20 miles away. This implies an area of blast destruction of several hundred square miles. The radioactive fallout from a single such weapon can kill unprotected people throughout an area of several thousand square miles.

The cumulative effects of a large attack involving many such weapons are much more difficult to estimate. As of 1959, a hypothetical attack on the United States analyzed for the Holifield hearings[23] involved 263 bombs with a total yield of 1,446 megatons. It was estimated that this attack would produce 50 million deaths, 20 million serious casualties, would destroy or damage 50 per cent of all homes, and leave the remainder radioactive from two weeks to a year.* Herman Kahn and his colleagues[24] have analyzed a hypothetical attack of the late 1960's that assumes a total fission yield† of 20,000 megatons delivered on 150 major cities in the United States, about half of which would necessarily have a population of less than 100,000. It was concluded that this attack would kill about 160 million people out of an assumed population of 180 million, in the absence of a substantial civil defense program.

It is instructive to compare thermonuclear-weapon yields to large natural forces. In the series of earthquakes in Chile in the spring of 1960, the

---

* The real force of Secretary Herter's "cannot conceive" remark should be apparent at this point.

† A technical distinction; the total yield would be larger, perhaps 30,000 megatons.

largest shock was estimated to have an energy release equivalent to 200 megatons. This not only created great physical damage in Chile but also generated tidal waves that produced destruction and casualties as far away as Japan. The total yield delivered in a large-scale thermonuclear attack might be from 10 to 100 (or more) times larger than 200 megatons.

Such grim figures are only part of the story, however, as they only relate to what could happen—in other words, to the capabilities that now exist or that may exist. Yet we should not be very concerned over the capabilities if only we and, say, the British had them. The other part of the story is that it *might* happen. We do not expect Type A deterrence to fail, but it would be rash to assume that it cannot. There are a number of ways in which it might fail. Many such possibilities are set forth in the chapter by Kahn.

The Hazards of Arms Controls. It should not be thought that any and all arms-control measures can be guaranteed as resulting in a net improvement. The major problem, and one that rightly troubles most critics of a casual approach to arms control, is the fact that in the present state of the world our need for armament is just as pressing as the need to take seriously the possibility and the consequences of nuclear war. In particular, as long as the Soviet Union (and perhaps somewhat later, China) has the capability of launching a surprise attack, armament to deter such an attack is necessary.

It is worth an effort to put the contemporary problem in perspective, for reasons explained below.* Let us first consider the *likelihood* of a Soviet surprise blow. An extreme view sometimes encountered is that the Soviets will strike us at the first moment they see a reasonable chance of escaping overwhelming retaliation. Does this "preventive war" outlook really represent the Soviet doctrine that guides their actions?

The evidence seems overwhelming that it does not. To begin with, the Soviets for many years have been conducting among their own people an intensive propaganda for peace by means of films, radio and television broadcasts, and newspapers. It is conceivable that this campaign is merely a smoke screen (it can obviously be turned off at a moment's notice) but it would surely affect young men moving up into positions of power and responsibility, some of whom would be startled, to say the least, to discover that it was merely a smoke screen. In addition to their overt campaign, the Soviets are surrounded by many reminders of World War II, which hurt them very badly; to the present day, many of their cities still show scars.

Official Marxist-Leninist doctrine has never suggested a preventive war. To be sure, it has affirmed the inevitability of war, but one always envisaged as an attack on the Soviet Union by declining capitalist powers. Even Stalin apparently held that the capitalist powers would exhaust one another in war before they attacked the Soviet Union. More recently, however, Khrushchev,

* The ensuing discussion has been improved by the helpful comments of Harold Brown and H. S. Dinerstein at the Johnson Foundation Conference of May 20-21, 1960.

in an address to the Supreme Soviet that enunciated major policy, asserted that there is "no fatal inevitability of war." [12] Coexistence seems to be the order of the day, at least as far as major military action is concerned.

It is sometimes reported in contemporary stategic literature in the United States that the Soviet Union has been taking steps for civil defense that might be considered suggestive. However, the extent of this activity is rather limited; it is more extensive than our present program, but much less than many proposed United States programs. The Russians do not appear to have a substantial program for shelter from fallout. It is certain that the Soviets have not been conducting drills for evacuating their largest cities, drills which would be spectacularly visible to consular officials and tourists, and which would seem imperative for a nation seriously considering an attack.

The weight of such evidence (of which this is only a fraction) therefore suggests overwhelmingly that preventive war is no more the guiding Soviet doctrine than it is the guiding United States doctrine. It is true that we cannot prove it is not; but neither can we prove many other assumpions of equal importance on which our policies are based.

To accept this fact does not by any means dispose of the problem. The central truth is that many of the goals of the Soviet Union conflict with those of the United States. It does not presently appear that any of these conflicting goals are such as both of us would be prepared to support by going to war. If this situation should ever develop, however, war of some kind is certain to result, and this is what imparts substance to the following problem.

The Soviet rulers are quite well aware that large-scale military power casts a certain shadow. They undoubtedly expect to achieve certain goals, *perhaps* only defensive ones, simply from the implied threat of military power. Indeed, all the gains the Soviets have achieved since World War II have been initially obtained without the use of any Soviet military force. We surely cannot treat the threat these forces represent simply as an empty bluff. We must therefore consider the possibility that they might some day feel that a goal for which they would indeed go to war was being thwarted, and that thereby they would be motivated to strike us. Even those Soviet citizens who count themselves our sincere friends could not give a guarantee against this eventuality.

It is necessary to establish some perspective on this problem, for our own strategy must be based, at least to some extent, on a reasonable appraisal of the opponent. Not everyone would agree. One able student of these matters has questioned the wisdom of guessing Soviet intentions, as I have been doing in asserting that preventive war was not guiding Soviet doctrine; and another has suggested that there would be some scope for successful arms-control agreements even if preventive war were the guiding Soviet doctrine. I do not believe that either of these views will stand a close scrutiny. If the Soviets were firmly and unequivocally committeed to preventive war, they would surely enter an arms-control agreement with the sole objective of using it to enhance their relative advantage and diminish their losses in conducting that war—if only by postponing the war to a time of their own choosing. And if we were convinced this was their strategy, we should not wish to enter an arms-control agreement, but might rather double or triple our defense budget—which we have the capability of doing, though the Soviets do not—and spend a large fraction of the increase on measures to protect our population. This would make the world much more dangerous for the Soviets and much less dangerous for ourselves, and it would be likely to persuade them that the doctrine of a preventive war should be abandoned. This would not necessarily be the only, or even the best, course of action, but it illustrates a strategy that we have not so far pursued because in fact we do not think it necessary.

We do not know Soviet plans or intentions in detail, and in any event they are most certainly subject to modification in the light of our own policies. We are therefore faced with the necessity of designing our strategies and our armament policy for *some* range of possible Soviet strategies. We must take into account not only the pleasant possible Soviet strategies but also the unpleasant ones; and one of the unpleasant, if perhaps the least likely, is the real possibility of a Soviet strategy of preventive war, if not now, then at some time in the future. It must be recognized, however, that our own strategy will not be optimum for that particular Soviet strategy, any more than it would be optimum for the Soviet strategy that would be implied by a completely friendly outlook toward the United States. The problem cannot be solved simply by our being excessively conservative in designing our armament policies, as this would lead us straight to the problems discussed in Kahn's chapter. Both our unilateral armament policy and also the possible range of arms-control agreements must be conditioned by our having a reasonable perspective of the world situation. We cannot escape the hard necessity of appraising our prospective opponents.

In particular, it is irrational to treat every Soviet arms-control proposal as if their sole motive in advancing it was to help them achieve world domination. On the other hand, it is worth emphasizing that both we and the Soviets do have conflicting national goals, and that the Soviets are intensely and skillfully opportunistic. It would be entirely possible for a carelessly drawn or carelessly inspected arms-control measure to present them with opportunities they might be tempted to exploit—whether they had originally intended to at the time of signing the agreement or not. Possibilities of this kind include the clandestine development, production, and deployment of prohibited weapons, the misuse of certain types of inspection systems to enhance the surprise of a surprise attack, and the subversion of group-decision procedures for applying force or sanctions. Some of the problems of this type are explored in various chapters in this volume.

There are genuine hazards of a different type, associated with certain kinds of arms-control measures, that are less often discussed. These might be called "irritation" hazards, and they arise as follows. The basic origins of world tensions (and therefore of armament, with the consequent possibility of war) are hostilities between nations, and conflicting national goals. No one would seriously maintain that arms control *per se* could solve these problems, or that arms-control measures are certain to survive in the long run if these problems are not solved. But it is of course an important possibility that arms-control measures may contribute to the easing of these problems, and that in any event they should not be so designed as to aggravate these problems by introducing avoidable irritations.

Such irritations may be introduced by arms-control measures in any of several ways. Differences may arise in the interpretation of the agreement, in the methods of enforcing it, or over the question as to who is going to pay how much of the bill. Irritations that affect a substantial segment of the population more directly may stem from the operation of inspection systems. Inspection has sometimes been called "institutionalized distrust," and in fact that is what it is. A certain minimum of irritation is probably bound to arise out of inspection. But it is important to avoid aggravating such irritation. Most important, the operation of an inspection system should not in itself become the object of distrust on the part of the host nation. It would be tragic if the implementation of an arms-control measure or program produced temporary alleviation of some immediate problem at the expense of aggravating the basic problems to the point of the ultimate breakdown of the program, thus perhaps leading to war. This hazard is also a real one, but it can be minimized or even avoided altogether by paying it careful attention when formulating a control agreement and when designing an inspection system. To do so, however, it is necessary to keep clearly in mind the character of the long-term underlying problems, and it is not always easy to do this while simultaneously devising measures to deal with more immediate ones.

VARIOUS GOALS AND MEASURES

The basic goal of arms control, as has already been indicated, is to reduce the hazards of present armament policies by a factor greater than the amount of risk introduced by the control measures themselves. In other words, arms control aims at improving our national security in all its various short- and long-term aspects. This definition, unfortunately, is rather like a general statement against sin: no one would disagree until the specific "sins" were defined. Let us consider some of the specific examples currently being discussed or likely to be discussed.

Broadly speaking, approaches to arms control are of two kinds. The first is to examine current and projected armament policies, to isolate their major unnecessary hazards, and to attempt to reduce or eliminate these, one at a time, leaving the basic armament policies largely unchanged. This is the realm of *limited* arms-control measures. The second approach is to attempt a survey of the basic requirements for armament to implement the various types of deterrence that must be provided for the participating nations, and to adjust all types of armament to fit these basic needs in such a way as to give maximum net security. This is the realm of *comprehensive* arms-control systems. In both cases, of course, the analysis should consider both unilateral and reciprocal points of view and should take into account the performance obtained under both calm and stressed conditions, the possible consequences of clandestine or overt evasion or other failures in cooperation, the possible failure of various types of deterrence, and the irritations introduced.

Comprehensive arms-control programs seem much more attractive on several counts than do limited measures. The goals of such programs may be better matched to basic needs, they seem generally safer, they may provide economic savings through substantial disarmament, and they may actually require less inspection than a small collection of independent limited measures. Comprehensive controls are studied in some detail in the essay by Wiesner.

Comprehensive controls, however, have not proved to be at all easy to negotiate, and are not likely to be so in the future. Some of the reasons for this difficulty operate with little or no force in certain limited measures of arms control which may prove to be more negotiable. (This "may" is very weak; they well may not.)

Although the goals of such measures are limited in scope, they are not necessarily trivial. The major hazards stem, not from the armament *per se* in the possession of the major powers, but from the fact that it might be used. Several measures are aimed at inhibiting such use. For example, two of the hazards to our security are the "catalytic war" (i.e., the initiation of a major nuclear war by one of the smaller powers) and the "escalation" problems; the major goals of a nuclear-weapon test ban are to eliminate the problem of catalytic war altogether (by preventing the spread of weapons to other nations) and to eliminate those escalation problems that might result from a limited nuclear war initiated by one or more of the smaller powers. Most of the various types of accidental war depend for their initiation on misinformation about what the other party is doing in a crisis; Schelling[25, 26] has proposed the use of special surveillance forces whose primary goal would be to minimize such misinformation. Many other potential limited measures may have considerable merit, as is shown in Schelling's chapter.

It is possible, and sometimes useful, to view arms-control measures of practically any type as intended to provide warning. In some cases, this objective is explicit, as with measures designed to monitor strategic forces and provide immediate warning when an attack is launched. Many of the measures proposed by the Western delegation to the Surprise Attack Conference were of this type.[27] However, even a very comprehensive arms-control program that provides a substantial reduction of military forces can be regarded as a measure to provide warning, but in this case the warning given would be a long-term strategic warning of hostile intentions. As long as such an agreement was functioning satisfactorily, it would provide some evidence that the participants did not intend to launch an overwhelming attack—they would not have the capability. Any observed failure of cooperation in the carrying out of the provisions of the agreement, such as the repudiation of the treaty, would then provide a warning of aggressive intentions. The amount of time this warning would provide might range from a few months to a few years, depending on the extent to which disarmament had gone and on the scale of the aggression contemplated by the violator. Intermediate types of measures would provide intermediate degrees of warning; for example, certain deployment restrictions, such as a disengagement of Soviet and United States forces in Europe, would provide a warning of from several hours to a few days. In general, the more severe the restrictions in force levels or deployment, the longer the warning time provided by the corresponding arms-control measures.

To pass to goals less military in character, it is entirely possible to employ arms-control policies for achieving political as well as military objectives. For example, it might well prove possible to achieve the political reunification of Germany (on terms acceptable to the West) in connection with an arms-control program that provided for the disengagement of Soviet and United States forces in Europe and for the disarmament of Germany. The evaluation of such measures is especially complex because the pros and cons to be balanced are so subtle. Indeed, such an arrangement might seem to be something of a horse trade; however, bargaining arrangements in which both sides emerge with net gains are not only possible but common.

A different type of political goal is found in the realm of propaganda. Some of the connotations of this word are unfortunate, for it is certainly a legitimate objective of our policy to achieve the allegiance of the other nations of the non-Communist world. The difficulty with this goal (at least for the West) arises when measures are proposed purely for this purpose; the objective is then likely to be self-defeating.

One goal often stated by major political leaders is that of freeing the economic resources now devoted to arms for other purposes. This might happen in a significant degree only with rather comprehensive arms controls, as far as the near future is concerned. Among contemporary students of arms control, it is fashionable (and probably correct) to point out that arms control is very likely to cost more, not less than present armament policies. This is because adequate inspection systems are likely to be sufficiently expensive to more than offset the relatively slight reductions (if any) in arms that may be achieved. (This would not, of course, nullify the value of arms control. We should be prepared to spend a good deal to achieve a less dangerous world.) In spite of such reservations, the goal of economic savings is nevertheless reasonable *qua* goal, and is worth stating explicitly.

One way in which arms control could lead to a safer world is rather indirect but deserves mention. This would be to educate the Soviets in mutually desirable strategies and armament policies. For this purpose, we would first have to educate ourselves in some detail as to what these were —which hardly prevails at the present time. But if we did understand these matters in depth, and if we did have specific arms-control objectives fixed clearly in our own minds, it is highly likely that we could persuade the Soviets (and others) of the desirability of such objectives. Also, if we were better prepared ourselves, we should then be in a better position to understand and evaluate Soviet proposals.

One goal of either limited or comprehensive arms control is to contribute to the solution of the basic problems of international hostilities and conflicting national goals. Besides taking care to avoid the hazards of unnecessary irritations, various constructive contributions are possible. For example, the careful design and use of mechanisms for adjudication and enforcement in arms-control programs may lead to an increased dependence on peaceful and orderly means of resolving conflicting national objectives. The very fact of implementing arms-control measures might therefore improve the world climate. This presumably accounts for the ardor of those arms-control advocates who think the military problems can safely be ignored. But it is quite possible that such an improvement would not result. This problem is one of the major imponderables of arms control.

Although the possibility of achieving such beneficial political effects in consequence of arms-control measures is highly uncertain, many students of these matters—including the present writer—consider the possibility of such effects to be one of the major motivations for the pursuit of arms-control arrangements. The hope that such effects might be achieved is not without rationale; the basic considerations are as follows. At the present time, East-West political cooperation is inhibited by a number of unresolved political problems, such as the division of Germany, the division of Korea, the status of Formosa, and the division of Vietnam. Problems of a slightly different type are illustrated by the difficulties relating to the Congo, and by potential sources of difficulty in Iran. Beyond these lie the basic ideological conflict and the problem of conflicting national goals. Progress on these problems by direct frontal attack seems incapable of achievement; there is simply no political agreement on acceptable methods of solving these problems. There is also very little political motivation even to search for possible solutions. On the other hand, there is a great deal of political pressure, and some apparent political willingness, to achieve at least some degree of cooperation in the field of arms regulation and control. And if the habit of cooperation can be established in the field of armament policy, it may well prove "catching" in other, nonmilitary areas. The establishment of arms-control programs might therefore have a catalytic effect on the political problems and tensions. An optimistic view of the situation would be that the achievement of modest arms-reduction programs would facilitate the achievement of some political solutions, which in turn would facilitate further measures of armament cooperation; and so on. It is even possible to imagine that this process might go sufficiently far as to alleviate to some degree the basic ideological conflict, and that we might ultimately learn to live in at least relative peace, much as Mohammedans and Christians ultimately learned to live in relative peace and as Catholics and Protestants ultimately learned to live in relative peace.

I repeat, the achievement of such far-reaching objectives through the device of arms control can hardly be regarded as certain. One of the basic problems is that neither the United States nor the Soviet Union seems to have clearly defined collective views on the role large-scale military force *should* play in implementing their national objectives, apart from national survival itself. The Chinese, on the other hand, do seem to have clearly defined views, but their views do not appear to be such as to encourage enthusiasm for the prospects for early achievement of general and complete disarmament. These considerations suggest that the entire subject of arms control should be approached in something of an experimental, "try-it-and-see" spirit. But, bearing all these reservations in mind, the achievement of an improved political climate should definitely be counted as one of the major goals of arms control.

CONCLUSIONS

The foregoing enumeration of goals will surely leave many readers unsatisfied. It will seem much too optimistic to many and much too moderate to others. In particular, some readers will doubtedly have noticed that I did not define the predominant goal of arms control as the total elimination of all war. Several students of arms control would do so, including one as eminent as Philip Noel-Baker. It is undoubtedly a desirable goal, and one well worth pursuing with vigor. But the obvious difficulty is that it may not be susceptible of achievement. It seems to me that attaining this goal is likely to require either a radical alteration in national outlook—which no one seems to have the faintest idea of how to accomplish—or the general acceptance of peaceful international machinery for adjusting conflicting national objectives. The latter may or may not be possible, but it should be noted that the machinery in question must be capable of dealing not only with the United States, the Soviet Union, and China, but also with Israel and the Arab powers, North and South Korea, France and the Algerian Nationalists, and so on. At the very least, this is likely to take a considerable time.

Yet we can use this time to good advantage. If in the meanwhile we can avoid major nuclear war, without necessarily resolving such problems as that of Berlin or the Algerian conflict, we shall have done something profoundly useful—useful to ourselves, to the several nations involved, and to Eastern and Western civilization.

2. Basic Requirements of Arms Control

ROBERT R. BOWIE

THE CONCEPT OF "ARMS CONTROL" INCLUDES ANY AGREEMENT AMONG several powers to regulate some aspect of their military capability or potential. The arrangement may apply to the location, amount, readiness, or types of military forces, weapons, or facilities. Whatever their scope or terms, however, all plans for arms control have one common feature: they presuppose some form of cooperation or joint action among the several participants regarding their military programs. Is such cooperation feasible between major powers whose national purposes are in basic conflict? Concretely, is there any basis for such arrangements between the USSR and the United States? If so, what are the conditions and limits of reliable arms control?

DEFINITION OF THE PROBLEM

Many are convinced that agreements for arms control with the Soviet Union are not possible or in the national interest of the United States. In general their view derives from some or all of the following propositions:

1. Military forces are only the reflection of political hostility. They are not the source or origin of tensions and conflicts among nations. Consequently, it is futile to try to regulate or reduce military forces separately from their underlying political causes. When basic hostility is resolved, reduction in arms will follow automatically as the nations feel themselves more secure and less threatened. To attempt control of military forces before removing the political sources of friction or threat is to put the cart before the horse.

2. The purposes of the Sino-Soviet bloc are fundamentally hostile to the non-Communist nations. In the Communist view the conflict between their "system" and any other is irreconcilable and will be resolved only by the ultimate victory of the Communist order. Its leaders believe that Communism is destined to triumph throughout the world, and they intend to advance their cause by the vigorous use of all feasible means. Apparently, the Communist ideology no longer considers a global military showdown inevitable

43

under present conditions. But the Communist leaders still define "wars of liberation" as "progressive," and have not abandoned the use of force (as in Hungary) or threats (as in Berlin) when either serves their interests.

3. The Communists would not make or carry out any arms agreement in good faith. Any means are legitimate in seeking to promote Communist advance. Treaties are only instruments for pursuing their basic aims and will be violated or evaded as suits their interests. In 1939-1940, the Soviet Union overran and divided Poland and absorbed Esthonia, Lithuania, and Latvia, in flagrant violation of nonaggression treaties with each of these nations. Soviet disregard for commitments regarding Eastern Europe, and of its Potsdam obligations regarding Germany, is too well-known to need laboring.

It would be rash indeed to disregard these lessons in devising and analyzing any arms-control proposals. The grounds for distrusting the Soviet Union and its purposes should make even the optimistic cautious. The record of broken agreements should warn us not to rely on Soviet promises or good faith as the basis for arms-control measures. And the only safe course is to accept at face value the constant Communist assertions of their basic hostility to our social order.

But, this does not dispose of the problem. One could also cite many agreements which the Soviets have carried out. The crucial point is to understand what kinds of arrangements they can be expected to comply with and why. The safest premise is this: in breaking or keeping agreements, the Soviets *can be trusted* to pursue their own interests as they see them. Hence, measures for arms control should be reliable if they can be so devised that compliance will be more in the Soviet interest than evasion or violation.

Distrust is not, of course, limited to one side. The Soviets, reflecting Communist ideology, are deeply suspicious of the "capitalist" nations and of their "ruling circles," which are seen as ruthless and unscrupulous in maintaining and improving their power and position. Within this conception, however, they are expected to pursue their interests.

The remaining discussion will be mainly concerned with how to make compliance conform to self-interest, given the fact of basic antagonism and distrust. It will examine, *inter alia,* how far the first proposition above—the relation of politics and arms control—remains valid under modern conditions.

BASIS OF COMMON INTERESTS

At the threshold is the question: How can the Soviet Union and the United States have parallel or common interests in measures to control armaments if their basic purposes are antagonistic?

The answer lies essentially in the changing nature of war, especially general war. Until recently, large-scale military force could be used as an effective instrument for the pursuit of political aims. An aggressor might hope to win and to benefit from his victim's defeat. Conversely, potential victims could normally assure their own security by confronting the possible aggressor with sufficient opposing strength, either alone or with allies, to deter attack or defend themselves if it occurred. The resulting balance might preserve peace for extended periods under favorable conditions.

The development of modern weapons has changed the situation radically. As always, threat has produced deterrent which has largely succeeded thus far in preventing large-scale war. But the military balance remains unstable, entailing substantial risks and burdens. More important, these conditions jeopardize both sides. The loss of one need not be the gain of the other. If large-scale war meant mutual destruction, it would not advance the political interests of either side; both would be better served, *despite basic political hostility,* by preventing its occurrence. Thus, military instruments, while still related to political conflict, have taken on a life of their own and have become a separate source of tension and danger. These matters are analyzed elsewhere in detail in other chapters in this book, such as Herman Kahn's. Here it is sufficient to explore them briefly in order to indicate the limits on unilateral action to cope with them.

One serious factor of instability arises from the disparity between offense and defense. The state of military technology puts a heavy premium on striking the first blow. Surprise attack not only could grievously injure the victim; it might also knock out much of his capacity to retaliate, so long as delivery systems remain relatively vulnerable. Even so, an aggressor would run a serious risk of severe damage from even a limited surviving retaliatory capability. While that situation prevails, an aggressor is not likely to be tempted to initiate an attack unless he believes himself in peril of an attack. The sense of exposure and vulnerability, however, creates strong pressures for rapid reaction to strike in case of threatened or apparent attack, before the means of striking are jeopardized. The necessity for quick decision creates serious dangers of war by accident or premature response, due, perhaps, to the misreading or misjudging of warnings. Progress in reducing vulnerability by hardened, concealed, and mobile weapons may lessen these risks, but may also introduce new instabilities; it may, for instance, complicate communication and central control.

The dynamic character of military technology forces each side to strain constantly to develop new or improved weapons systems in order to better its position or at least maintain the balance. Whenever one or the other achieves an earlier success, it creates tension and uncertainty and the necessity for adjusting on both sides. The rapidity of change entails the risk of rash action prompted either by a fear of imminent inferiority or by a belief, whether correct or mistaken, of overwhelming superiority. The latter could lead to efforts at blackmail which could precipitate unintended large-scale war.

The spread of nuclear weapons into the control of more and more nations seems likely to enhance seriously these risks of instability and to introduce additional ones.

The effort to maintain an effective deterrent and to keep up in the arms race will probably become more burdensome. In any case, the greater part or all of the effort will only serve to neutralize the capability on the other side. Neither alone can safely stop its frantic activity, but the question is certain to arise as to whether mutual deterrence could not be achieved at lower levels of forces and expenditure.

As even so brief a summary indicates, both sides have possible common or parallel interests * in preventing an unintended all-out war and in minimizing the burden of the deterrent. Each side can continue its unilateral efforts to make its deterrent more effective. If these efforts merely produce enhanced or more secure capacity to damage the opponent, the result will still be a system of mutual deterrence, subject to risks of the sort outlined. Conceivably, one side might achieve a technical breakthrough, reducing its own vulnerability to an opposing strike so radically as to destroy the "stalemate." But, the chances and value of that possibility must be weighed against the opposite danger and the other risks inherent in an unrestricted arms race. In making that appraisal, both sides could readily conclude that their interests would be better served by measures to stabilize the system or reduce its burden. There are limits, however, to how far this can be achieved by unilateral action. Certain kinds of measures useful for these purposes require joint action or cooperation. This objective fact must be the basis for any progress toward arms control under present conditions.

CRITERIA OF ACCEPTABILITY

The thesis of this chapter is that the validity and stability of any arms-control system will depend ultimately on the same kinds of motives and factors as those which underlie the existing "system"—namely the self-interest of the parties. Arms-control measures broaden the arsenal of instruments available for constructing and reinforcing a viable deterrent system by means of agreed standards, limitations, or safeguards. They may serve to reduce the likelihood of war, or (possibly) the burden of effective

* Since these parallel interests result mainly from hazards inherent in major nuclear-weapons systems, they extend to any activities or violence entailing risks of the ultimate use of such weapons. Hence, the desire to mitigate that danger can be the basis for measures to control conventional weapons. If the use of such nuclear-weapons systems were, however, fully neutralized by technology (as might happen) or eliminated by arms-control measures (as seems remote), would this common interest persist for controlling conventional weapons? It might not if a potential aggressor considered that nuclear-weapons systems had been finally removed from the equation; but that condition is hardly likely to be fufilled, at least by arms-control measures. Moreover, even in that case, there could be a common interest in reducing the burden of conventional forces if both sides concluded that a standoff existed in such forces and could be maintained at lower levels.

deterrence. But any proposed system of arms control must be judged by whether it makes it more attractive to the parties (in terms of their own interests) to maintain the system and its safeguards than to disrupt it by resorting to violence or evasion.

Constructing an arms-control plan that meets such a test is far from easy and must overcome serious technical and political obstacles. The existence of common interests does not assure that practical methods for working together are attainable. To establish arms control, the parties will have to be in accord on: applicable limitations; methods of verifying compliance; and the consequences of violation. These three aspects, which interact as will be discussed later, may affect the several parties differently. In appraising any plan, each party will compare its benefits and risks under the plan with its prospects without it. Before accepting any plan, each nation will have to be satisfied on two issues:

First, if carried out according to its terms, how will the plan serve its security or other interests compared to the situation without it? Will it lessen the risks of war, whether deliberate or unintended? Will it allow reductions in military expenses without loss of security? These two aims are not necessarily complementary. Some joint actions to stabilize deterrence might even require increasing expenditure. For example, if the all-out nuclear deterrent were virtually neutralized, stability would depend on the balance in other weapons and forces. Unless attained by major reductions in Soviet and Chinese forces, this would probably require increases in those of the West.

And, second, would possible violations of the arrangements entail undue risks to its security compared to the situation in the absence of the arrangements?

In essence, this question breaks down into several parts. What are the chances that another party could evade some or all of the agreed limitations without prompt detection? How seriously might any such violation upset the military balance? Could the victims redress the balance or compensate for the violation if detected, and, if so, how rapidly? What detriment might the violator suffer from detection? Taking all these questions into account, how likely is it that evasion would be attempted? And, how do these risks compare with those without an agreement?

To be acceptable, any arms-control plan must combine its limitations, safeguards, and remedies so as to satisfy both criteria for all parties. In seeking to do so, it is essential to understand how these several elements may reinforce each other or conflict, and what limits they impose on the feasible scope of such a system.

The remainder of this chapter attempts to analyze some of these limits and interactions and their implications. Its purpose is not to develop a specific proposal but to examine certain conditions and relations inherent in the situation, which apply to any arms-control measures in existing circumstances.

BALANCING OF RESTRICTIONS

One serious obstacle to arms control arises from the difficulty of equating the impact of specific restrictions or other terms on the several parties. The task of assessing the effect of any acceptable change in military forces or armaments on the absolute and relative capability of the parties is extremely complex.

Since the armed forces of each nation rely on their own special "mix" of armaments and men, any restriction of a particular weapon has different impacts on each of them. In the 1930's enormous amounts of energy and time were devoted without success to efforts to equate different kinds and numbers of conventional weapons. Nuclear weapons and missiles have, if anything, made this task even harder because of the wide range of uncertainty regarding their effects on offense and defense and the relations between nuclear and conventional capabilities. Moreover, with dynamic-weapons technology, each side is likely to be ahead in developing specific fields, and therefore will appraise the prospects and significance of newer weapons in quite different terms. Especially under these conditions, military experts on each side almost inevitably tend to overestimate the harm to their capability from any proposed restriction and to discount its effects on the potential enemy. Hence, the greater the uncertainty regarding the value and equivalence of weapons and forces, the more likely is the conservative bias on both sides to block agreement on any material change.

A second obstacle arises from differing appraisals by the United States and USSR of the value and costs of inspection inherent in the divergence between a "closed" and an "open" society. Effective inspection is more vital for the United States than for the USSR. The vast range of published data on the United States military programs available to the USSR through the press, Congressional reports and hearings, etc., would greatly reduce its dependence on the inspectorate, and provide cross-checks and leads for its operations. Moreover, the very nature of an open, democratic society would make it far more difficult, if not impossible, for the government to carry on any large-scale secret evasion or violation, even if it desired to do so. Conversely, the closed character of the USSR necessitates more intensive inspection to provide data and greater dependence on the data so obtained with fewer chances for cross-checks, etc. Hence, the United States is forced to insist on a degree and reliability of inspection for which the USSR is likely not to feel a corresponding requirement.

In terms of costs or burdens of inspection, the appraisals will also differ. The Soviets undoubtedly look on their secrecy as a military asset. In allowing it to be pierced by inspection, they consider they are making a separate, or additional, sacrifice of their military potential. Hence, they will assess the cost of reciprocal inspection (particularly, if intensive) as high, especially as compared to its value for them. The United States will certainly not estimate the burden as nearly so great, though it might appear more onerous (at least for private activities) if negotiations ever got down to practical details.

The consequence is that, in striking a balance between costs and value of inspection, the United States will inevitably favor more intensive and thorough systems and methods than the USSR. In this respect their interests tend to diverge materially and to obstruct agreement on a common system.

Their interests may diverge in another respect. A system which succeeded in neutralizing the all-out deterrent could have ancillary consequences differing according to the purposes of the two sides. For the Soviets, widespread confidence in the system might make it more difficult to utilize the fear of war for attaining political advantages. For the United States, one result might be to narrow the value of the all-out deterrent in inhibiting aggression in peripheral areas. Today, lack of certainty about its use may deter rash Soviet action, especially where the stakes are small compared to the price of a mistaken judgment. Some forms of arms control, by more effectively neutralizing the strategic capabilities, could erode this effect in the less vital areas. Finally, the prospect of rapid technological change complicates the creation of an acceptable system. Where radical innovation has become usual, a nation may hesitate to tie its hands too tightly when the future is so uncertain.

LIMITS OF INSPECTION

Inspection (used here to mean any method of obtaining or verifying evidence) has come to be the cornerstone of arms control. Indeed, it is often said that inspection must be "foolproof." If, in fact, 100 percent certainty were required in the inspection system, virtually no arms control would be feasible. In practice, no technique depending on human skills and judgment can be infallible. This truism is especially applicable in a field where actual experience is so lacking. Moreover, the Soviet Union (certainly) and the United States (probably) would not agree to inspection of the scope and intensity which would be necessary to attain the highest feasible reliability.

But infallibility is not the proper criterion. Inspection should be viewed as a technique for reinforcing and maintaining the self-interest of the parties in the continued effective operation of the system. The restrictions and the related inspection should be considered as a system of deterrence. Their combined aim should be to create *risks* of detection which a rational participant would not consider worth running. He need not believe that the inspection techniques are certain to discover the violation: he need only be convinced that the odds of discovery are too high to make the attempt worthwhile in the light of the possible benefits and costs. Of course, the reliability of the inspection process is still a vital factor in determining the extent of feasible arms control. But it cannot be judged in isolation. It is intimately related to the nature of the restriction and remedies included in the system, and to the interest of the parties in its continued operation.

This interplay is apparent even when the primary purpose is to provide reciprocal information for reassurance or the avoidance of mistakes, as in some schemes for preventing accidental war or for inhibiting surprise attack. Inspection to prevent mistake or surprise may be greatly facilitated by agreed-upon restrictions concerning readiness or disposition (of strategic air forces or missiles, for example) which would almost surely have to be violated to mount such an attack. Inspection could not prevent such restrictions from being disregarded, but their existence would enable inspectors promptly to interpret as hostile an action which might otherwise be ambiguous.

For any specific restriction, the potential violator will weigh the value of the evasion against the risks and consequences of detection. He will hardly assume the risks of discovery (whatever they may be) unless he can foresee some commensurate advantages. Thus, the crucial question is not whether the inspection system could discover every *technical* evasion, but what prospects it offers for detecting any *significant* one. In assessing this, several factors become relevant.

One is the scope and duration of activity required for a significant violation. If evasion had to be carried out on a large scale or over a long period before yielding benefits, there would appear more chance of its detection by cross-checks or random sampling or other means. Thus, if conventional military equipment had been reduced to a certain level, its replacement in substantial amounts should be reasonably risky with even moderate inspection in operation.

Also, the amount of clandestine production required to be "significant" would also depend on the levels to which agreed reduction had dropped. If other powers had reduced virtually to zero, relatively small violations might give the offender a great advantage. But if they retain major capabilities, much larger evasions would be necessary.

In assessing advantages of evasion, the violator must think in terms of usable weapons systems—fragmentary evasions may not give any real superiority. Thus, if restrictions were applied to existing nuclear material, the fact that it could be secreted in little space without continuing activity would make the prospects of detection very small indeed. The significance of a violation, however, would depend partly on the level to which others had reduced and partly on how much else the violator would have to do to make his secret stockpile usable. Added safeguards might arise from other reinforcing restrictions which could be inspected more readily—such as limits on delivery vehicles which might involve a much wider range of activities for evasion.

Inspection seems likely to present some of the hardest problems at the start of an arms-control system. Time will be required for it to be organized and installed, to gain experience, and to earn the confidence of the participants. Moreover, at that stage, the degree of intensity of inspection is most likely to seem out of proportion to the modest initial restrictions or reductions: checking on certain kinds of isolated limitations could require nearly as much probing as that for more extensive reductions. For this reason, under a comprehensive system put into effect by successive stages, the inspectorate would hardly need to expand in step with the restrictions. In selecting initial limitations, therefore, one major factor should be to find those which minimize the scope and burden of inspection.

One method for facilitating inspection at all stages is to require the participants to prove their compliance with specific obligations. They may be in a position to produce convincing evidence of their action much more easily than inspectors could establish the facts without assistance. The making of reports of various kinds by the parties can serve a similar purpose of facilitating inspection. The early stages of a system should capitalize on such techniques by beginning with limitations for which they are especially helpful.

The nature of the inspection system and its value are also related to how the data it produces will be used. The deterrent effect will be affected by how violations are established and redressed.

MEASURES RELATING TO VIOLATION

Since the purpose of the inspection system is to assure compliance, a central issue involves the treatment of violations. Actually, two factors are involved: the method for determining that a violation has occurred; and the remedies available for redressing it.

Determining Violations. In considering procedures for determining violations, two alternatives can be conceived: the inspectorate could be required to produce and submit evidence of any violation to an impartial tribunal which would judge the issue like a court; or the evidence could be furnished to the parties for their information and decision as to how to act on it. Some have taken for granted that the first method is inevitable or desirable.

This is by no means self-evident. In some cases, the state of the evidence may require a court to find that the violation is not proved despite suspicious circumstances. The other parties may still suspect evasion, and be tempted themselves to evade in "self-defense," if the decision of the court leaves no alternative. If the parties have the privilege of deciding how to interpret and act on the suspicious data the deterrent to violation may be enhanced. The practical effect might be that they could then take overt counter-measures. Indeed, they could announce the protective counter-measures, and offer to withdraw or terminate them upon satisfactory proof that the suspicions were unfounded. The suspected party would then have a real interest in establishing innocence. And it will frequently be far simpler for him to offer persuasive proof that he is not in violation than for the inspectorate to prove the real state of facts. Consequently, if the system is designed to serve the continuing interests of both sides, the right of the parties to interpret suspicious evidence may be better calculated to maintain the viability and stability of the system than final authority in a tribunal for this purpose.

There are, however, considerations favoring a tribunal. Any agreement will entail some ambiguous provisions on which there is room for legitimate dispute. Both sides might well be willing to allow a tribunal to resolve the issue. Similarly, it may be useful to have a forum for presenting evidence of violations, especially where clear, in order to exert pressure on the violator or to have the support of a judgment of the tribunal to justify any counter-action the victim might decide to take.

Hence, the best solution may be to seek to combine both methods. To obtain the benefits mentioned, a tribunal could be available for resolving disputes about the terms of the agreement or the evidence of violations; but the parties might still have the right to suspend or cancel the agreement if the result seemed to require it for the protection of their security.

Remedies for Violation. What remedies are available in case of violation of the arms agreement? The answer to that question sets a basic limit on the kind and extent of restrictions which are feasible.

In their comprehensive plan for world disarmament, Clark and Sohn provide for an international agency with authority to require compliance and adequate power for enforcement. No such agency now exists. Even if the International Court had compulsory jurisdiction to determine a violation, it would lack effective means to enforce its decree or to provide remedies to the other parties. Under existing political conditions, the Soviet Union and the United States could not agree to create an international agency with sufficient power to coerce their compliance with its decrees. The existing distrust and cleavage make joint action for that purpose wholly impracticable.

If that solution is now unfeasible, it is essential to realize that dependence in case of violation must be placed on self-help. Consequently, in making any agreement, the parties must seek to appraise the following: If they fulfill their obligations under the agreement, how will their relative capability compare with that of a violator who has whatever advantage he could reasonably be expected to obtain by evasion before detection? The crucial question is whether or not the honest parties would still be able to assure their security under these conditions. Would the violation be likely to upset or jeopardize the deterrent balance?

The answer to the question depends on a variety of factors involved in any specific plan. Of course, if the plan affects the capabilities of either side only in ways readily rectified or reversed, its cancellation could leave the parties substantially where they had been before its adoption. Some forms of limitation might operate in much this way. For example, the plans for depositing weapons in international stockpiles on the territory of the several members are designed to have this effect. If one party should re-claim his weapons, others might quickly follow suit.

Moreover, the effect of a violation depends on the general level and character of forces retained. Smaller evasions might not be really significant to upset the balance if major deterrent forces were kept in being by all parties; but, as the general levels were reduced more and more, the sig-nificance of the same violation could grow.

Violations which do not threaten to upset the military balance might be more difficult to handle. For example, one party may impede the work of the inspectorate in various ways which infringe on their rights under the agreement. The experience under the North Korean Armistice offers many examples of such methods. The other parties might be loath to terminate the agreement with all that would entail, just as was the case in the Korean Armistice. They might, however, be able to resort to lesser pres-sures to coerce compliance, such as imposing similar restraints on inspec-tion (which might not be adequate) or suspending other provisions or restrictions until the noncompliance was corrected. Of course, this could lead to an ultimate breakdown of the agreement—but it would confront the offender with the necessity of choosing whether to comply or to run that risk.

In deciding whether or not to attempt a major evasion and risk detec-tion, however, a potential violator would have to weigh a wider range of considerations.

An evasion might so shock and solidify world opinion against the violator as to create a stronger coalition against him than would have existed before-hand. It could produce crash programs of rearming such as resulted from Korea. Moreover, the violator might run a serious risk of provoking pre-ventative action based on the conviction that the other parties have no choice in view of his demonstrated perfidy. The uncertainty and unpredicta-bility of these consequences would be likely to exercise very great restraints against major violators.

CONCLUSION

The basic point should be stressed again: no arms-control plan will remain effective and dependable unless it continues to serve the national interests of each of the parties, as its leaders conceive those interests. In reaching their judgment, however, they will appraise the alternatives. The main function of inspection and of the remedies available to the other parties is to make evasion unattractive as an alternative course. To achieve that result, the inspection system should confront the potential violator with risks of detection and counter-measures outweighing the significance of the violation for the relative capabilities of the participants. The system as a whole must be designed to offer benefits to all participants which they are likely to prefer not to jeopardize.

The analysis leads to one tentative conclusion. It may be wise for the agreement to allow any participant to withdraw at any time (or after relatively brief notice) without cause. Such a privilege has several merits.

First, it emphasizes the fact that the validity and continuance of any plan depends on its *continuing* appeal to the self-interest of the participants. It underscores the fact that their *promise* to comply should not be the basis for reliance.

Second, it resolves the problem of the determination of compliance or violation. If one party becomes suspicious of another's compliance, he can protect himself at once by suspending some or all of his own obligations. The threat to do so, or conditional suspension, could be one means to require the suspected party to provide positive evidence of compliance.

Third, such a provision would underscore the necessity for each party, either alone or with allies, to be able to protect his security at all times if the agreement breaks down. This again is calculated to forestall any false reliance on the agreement which it cannot provide, and to confront each participant constantly with the need for realistic appraisal of the operation of the plan.

Fourth, it would meet the problem of revision of the agreement. An arrangement in this field may not operate exactly as anticipated, either with respect to restrictions or safeguards. As a result, they might bear unfairly on one or more parties. Moreover, technological progress could easily skew the initial effects of a plan in favor of one side or the other. It would be extremely difficult, if not impossible, to prescribe detailed procedures for modifying or revising the plan by arbitration or other usual methods for breaking deadlocks. The privilege of withdrawal may be the simplest way to force renegotiation where justified.

It must be recognized, however, that such a privilege has some drawbacks. The fact that ending the agreement would not entail the breaking of a commitment might reduce the pressure to preserve the system under some cases. In practice, however, that pressure could hardly prevail if the continuance were considered to imperil the security of a party for whatever reason. In the case of the democracies, it might delay the decision somewhat more than in the dictatorial regimes.

Even with the privilege, however, there would still be substantial forces inhibiting a participant from withdrawing from or upsetting a working system for light causes. The dangers of reviving an urgent arms race with less likelihood of renewing arms control later would normally give serious pause. Such action, if taken for arbitrary or narrow reasons, would also involve major political costs all over the world, and, at least in the democracies, at home as well. Consequently, if the system were operating fairly and effectively, it seems reasonable to assume that the privilege of ending it would not be used casually by any major party. So long as they felt the system served their security interests, they should also be able to assure that its continuance would not be jeopardized by the withdrawal of others.

The privilege of canceling or suspending could be used as a very flexible device. The choice need not be all or nothing. A party could suspend specified portions of the restrictions or other provisions commensurate with the violation or evasion, or adequate to adjust to changed conditions. Moreover, any such suspension could be made conditional, or to be effective after a certain interval, in order to induce a negotiation for agreed modifications in the agreement. The experience with the Korean Armistice indicates that changes can be made in this manner without destroying the agreement, even when it contains no such privilege. In that case, the Communists introduced planes into North Korea contrary to the armistice; thereafter, the United States, in compensation, suspended certain restrictions on bringing new weapons into South Korea. Despite these changes, the armistice itself has remained in effect.

Some may feel that the foregoing analysis is unduly pessimistic or that it virtually forecloses any prospect of an extensive arms control. That, in my opinion, is not a proper conclusion. Within the limits discussed, there is room for substantial measures to stabilize the deterrent and to make initial modest reductions. Moreover, experience with inspection, and the application of imagination and invention to developing its techniques, could broaden the area for further measures. In particular, by cooperation through such means, the major opponents might be able to work out ways of maintaining the strategic deterrent at lower levels of resources and expenditures, especially if newer generations of missiles create the possibility of relatively invulnerable defensive capability. If their role comes to be recognized as one of essentially mutual neutralization, more modest levels might be adequate within an operating arms-control system. Moreover, in such a context, a reduction in the levels of conventional forces is within the realm of feasibility and could serve to lower the general level of defense expenditures below what otherwise might prevail.

These prospects fall well short of total disarmament. But realism seems to require recognition of the fact that such a state can be approached, if at all, only under conditions which permit international enforcement to operate effectively. In particular, it appears to call for an international agency with adequate authority and coercive means to punish and constrain a violator of the system. And that presupposes such fundamental changes in the political sphere as would pose a different range of problems within a new context. Such changes, if they occur, will depend on a wide range of policies and actions, involving many fields besides arms control. Limited progress in arms control to stabilize the situation will help in providing the time for such other actions to produce results.

3. Constructing Rules That Affect Governments

ROGER FISHER

AN EXPLICIT PREMISE OF THIS CHAPTER IS THAT ARMS CONTROL REQUIRES rules—that the task at hand is to design, create, and maintain rules that effectively restrain governmental conduct. In the light of rapidly changing technology and political conditions one might suggest that nations should not be tied up by rules but should be left as free as possible to alter their conduct quickly to meet new circumstances as they arise. That suggestion must be rejected. The problem is to create order out of chaos, and the essence of order is rules. Just as collisions on the highways are reduced by such rules as driving on the right, so the chaotic conditions of the arms race are reduced by rules restraining governments.

Much discussion of arms control rests on the assumption that the only way of creating rules to limit the arms race is to negotiate a treaty. It is suggested here that in fact there is a variety of ways in which restraints upon governmental conduct may be created. To appreciate the spectrum of rule-creating procedures, one must understand what it is that causes a government to respect a rule.

WHY GOVERNMENTS COMPLY WITH RULES

Before turning to international rules that may guide governmental behavior, it should first be recognized that within a country the laws that restrict governments are quite different from the laws that restrict individuals. If one makes a contract with an individual and he breaks it, there is a third party, the government, which will use the superior force of the state to make that individual either comply with his contract or pay damages. If the individual does not pay, his property may be seized by the sheriff and sold. But if one makes a contract with the government, and the government does not pay, there is no third party to make the government do so. All that a court can do is to say that the government ought to pay. If the government does in fact comply with court decisions and with the Constitution, it is not because of the physical power of any marshal or sheriff.

The same is true of rules in the international field. Short of world government, there will be no superior force to compel compliance by the major powers with such rules as may be applicable to them.* Governments comply with treaties and other international rules as they do with constitutions and other domestic rules by a process of composite self-restraint.

If, having signed an arms-limitation treaty, State A decides that it now wants to abandon that approach and go full steam ahead in the arms race, there is no way to "enforce" the treaty. The most that State B can do is also to go full steam ahead in the arms race or take actions that are even more warlike. Short of world government, there is no physical control in arms control. If an arms-control rule is broken, the most that the community can do is to destroy the rule; it cannot, as it can in the case of a violation of a municipal ordinance against carrying guns, re-establish the rule. Any country, certainly a major power, acting as a unit, is physically free at any time to terminate a rule restricting its conduct, no matter how clearly it was written or how many times it was signed. In some ways a treaty is just a scrap of paper. A treaty cannot be iron-clad. It is egg-shell thin, within the power of a state to smash it, and all the king's horses and all the king's men cannot put it back together again. And a treaty, like an egg, is kept from getting smashed by the enlightened self-interest of those who deal with it, not by anything inside it.

Among the limitless considerations which affect a governmental decision there appear to be four basic factors which tend to cause a government to respect rules—rules which it, as a unit, always has the physical, factual ability to violate.

1. Apprehension of Action by "the Other Side." One factor causing governments to respect rules is the apprehension of the action which would be taken by those directly benefited by the rule—those on the other side of the rule. The decision of the United States government to respect the constitutional limitations on its power is influenced by an apprehension of what the people of the United States might do if the Constitution should be ignored. Similarly, the United States respects a treaty by a process of self-restraint which is influenced by a fear of what the other party to the treaty might do.

In the case of nontreaty rules, and even in the case of treaties such as those governing the Panama Canal, to divide governments into those on one side of the rule, those on the other side, and third states appears to ignore the China problem and is obviously a simplified model. But for any given act by the United States, even such diverse countries as Egypt, China, India, Brazil, France, and the USSR can probably be divided

---

* Although the discussion is directed at the problem of controlling the major powers, most of the discussion is equally applicable to the small powers. A big power cannot automatically compel a small power to respect a rule. E.g., the United States may not be free to compel Cuba to respect the international law protecting foreign investments.

among those "on our side," those who might take prompt action hostile to us, and those where our primary concern would be with the long-range effects.

The deterrent effect of the fear of retaliatory action by those "on the other side" is well known. It supports not only rules against the use of gas, but rules establishing diplomatic immunity, rules keeping arms out of the Antarctic, and most other rules limiting the behavior of one government with respect to another.

2. *Apprehension of the Effect on Third Parties.* A government is concerned not only with what the party most directly affected by the breach of a rule might do, it is also concerned with the effect of the breach on others. In the international sphere, this concern is usually with what is called "world public opinion." Should the United States resume U-2 flights over the Soviet Union, one category of consequences that we would fear would be the steps that the Soviet Union might take, such as to hit with rockets the bases or carriers from which the planes had taken off. A whole additional range of feared consequences would be, for example, political action in the United Nations and the loss of confidence in us by other countries.

If a government were convinced that it would have to violate an undertaking in order to maintain a military position necessary for survival, it would no doubt do so, and hope that it could justify its action to the world. But in some circumstances the views of third states may be more feared than retaliatory action. Presumably the Soviet decision to respect the rule of nonintervention in the Congo was brought about in significant part by concern for the views of third states. In a world in which actions speak louder than words, governments which engage in propaganda weigh the effect of their actions on third states.

3. *Individual Morality.* In addition to the two types of external consequences that may cause a government to respect a rule, there are two internal factors which tend to work in the same direction. The first of these is that by and large man is a moral creature who must convince himself of the "rightness" of a proposed action. However evil we may think particular governments or individuals to be, we cannot ignore the extent to which people's behavior is influenced by their own notions of what they "ought" to do, independent of their judgment as to what the rewards or punishments might be for the particular act.

The fact that a government cannot afford to trust a potential enemy does not make the morality of individuals an unimportant consideration in arms control. Rules will have greater practical strength when they are reinforced by the moral principles of the individuals in the governments affected. We could expect rules against the assassination of officials of a foreign government to be respected for reasons going beyond a cold calculation of the consequences. On the other hand, rules requiring officials of one country to inform upon their colleagues might be violated because of moral scruples, despite a recognized theoretical advantage in compliance. Moral strength may depend not only on the substance of rules but also on the process by which they were established. When solemn promises are given or rules of recognized authority established, many government officials will tend to respect them because of their belief that they "ought" to, without basing each day's continued compliance upon a Machiavellian weighing of the pros and cons.

4. Institutional Resistance to Breaking Rules. The second internal factor affecting a governmental decision to comply with rules is the restraint that results from the fact that a government is not a single unit but an elaborate political structure involving a great many people. Once a rule is established and a government is complying with it, any breach requires a change in governmental direction. Sheer inertia will tend to keep the government doing what it was doing before. Any change of policy requires recommendations, conferences, memoranda, and some kind of collective decision.

In particular, a decision to break a rule will have to overcome the individual moral notions of those who might think the rule should be respected. It will also involve attempts to reconcile differing appraisals of what the external consequences of the breach would be.

Finally, a government is a structure that is held together and operates on the basis of rules. The entire power of a government depends upon the officers and employees within it continuing to function in accordance with an elaborate scheme of rules. The government's ability to break a rule depends upon whether that particular rule can be sorted out and ignored, leaving respect for the other rules intact. Within the United States the government is not free to ignore decisions of the Supreme Court or to ignore the Constitution without jeopardizing the whole governmental structure. For many government officials direct respect for the Constitution would outweigh respect for a Presidential request to ignore the Constitution. Currently, treaties and other international rules are not so interwoven into the governmental fabric. But in the future, government officers may acquire a higher loyalty to an international rule, particularly to a rule that seems to them essential for world survival, than the loyalty which they have to the request of a superior. The critical point comes when the government officer considers the international rule as applying directly to him, rather than as applying to him only through the governmental chain of command. Once an individual official recognizes a direct duty to the rule, that government's freedom to break the rule is seriously reduced. Such a rule has become an element in the structure of a government which depends for its strength on respect for rules.

If the above analysis is correct, rules governing governments can be created by any process which defines a norm of governmental behavior and which marshals in support of that norm one or more of the forces which tend to bring about governmental compliance: fear of retaliatory action, fear of the effect on public opinion, the moral views of government officers, and institutional resistance to breaking rules.

The durability of a rule will depend upon the strength of the forces behind it. This strength will depend to some extent upon the rule-creating process. An act of acceptance by a state will create a moral commitment of some of its officers, will set up institutional resistances to change, and will require a state to consider the effect of a breach upon public opinion. The same forces will support any rule that is created by a process which makes it "law." The more solemn and formal the procedure is, the greater the commitment. Also, because of the force of public opinion, a rule accepted as binding by most of the countries of the world is by that fact alone a rule with which every other state must reckon. Public opinion and moral scruples will be less upset if the rule is in a form which can be "terminated" without "breaking" it, although the consequent action to be expected from the other side would often be the same.

The retaliatory action to be expected depends in part upon whether the rule was being respected by the other side and, if not, what an appropriate response to a breach would be. (There are rules about breaking rules: concern for public opinion, moral scruples, and the fear of further retaliation tend to deter one government from retaliating more than in an amount justified by the original breach.)

Because democratic institutional arrangements require clearing a decision with so many people, the less autocratic a government, the greater the strength of a rule accepted by it. Even in a democracy, however, the possibility of a secret breach reduces substantially all the forces which tend to support compliance. Fears of consequential action by the opposing party and an adverse public opinion are discounted to the degree that it is thought that the secret can be kept. Moral and internal resistances to breaking the rule exist only among the reduced number who are privy to the secret.

The strength of public opinion will further depend upon such factors as how clear it is that there is a rule, how clear it is that the rule applies to this case, and the extent to which the rule is easily understandable and appeals to common sense. An arbitrary rule will not have the strength of one that has a rational, historical, or geographic basis.

From such considerations it is apparent that the forces that produce governmental compliance with legal rules, including treaties, are also available in support of nonlegal rules of governmental behavior. Although the breach of a rule recognized as legally binding will usually involve more moral and institutional resistance and more of an adverse effect on world public opinion than in the case of a rule not considered to be one of law, this need not always be so. And the retaliatory considerations may be just as great in the absence of a treaty as with a treaty. Arms control need not be limited to rules that are thought of as legal.

METHODS OF CREATING ARMS-CONTROL RULES

The science of game theory has shown that an understanding of international relations may be acquired by comparing the rules of governmental conduct to those of a game. In such terms, what we are concerned with here is the kind of a game in which one makes up the rules as one goes along. Take, for example, a situation in which several boys are starting to throw snowballs at each other. How does it become understood that the activity is to be limited to a snowball fight, and that neither side is to grab boys on the other side, or to wrestle with them, or to punch them in the nose? If one player thinks there ought to be a rule against putting stones in the snowballs, what is the best means of getting the rule established? Should he build up a reserve of snowballs with stones in them and agree to give them up in exchange for an agreed adoption of the rule, or should he promptly declare: "No stones in snowballs!"?

What we need to become is experts in the art of creating new rules to the game while the game is being played. There is scope for ingenuity. The other players do not have a veto over all the ways of creating rules. The following are suggested, in roughly ascending order in terms of the clarity and strength of the resulting rule, as illustrative types of processes for the creation of arms restraints.

Engaging in a Course of Conduct. A single nation may create a norm by a uniform course of conduct which conforms to that norm, even though the implied rule which it is respecting is never made explicit. A series of precedents creates a rule. The more years that go by without maneuvering near the Soviet border, the more unusual and hence provocative such an act would be. A pattern of conduct may tie a country's own hands.

If many nations follow a similar course of conduct, the rule that is established may affect not only themselves but all nations. If most nations conduct their military affairs consistently with certain restraints, those restraints tend to turn into custom. And the violation of custom involves, to a lesser degree, the same considerations of external consequences and internal restraints that are involved in breaking a rule recognized as binding.

Articulating a Rule. Making explicit a particular norm may create a rule as to whether or not that norm reflects a contemporaneous course of conduct. If the articulation does define a course of conduct, it adds strength to any rule established by the conduct itself. Consider, for example, rules about testing long-range missiles. If the United States were to test a missile by firing it directly toward the Soviet Union but so arrange the missile that it would alter course and drop into the sea thirteen miles off the Soviet coast, would this violate any existing rule? So far as I know, neither country tests its missiles by firing them toward the other, but no rule against it has been mentioned. When the first person, looking at the specific facts upon missile testing, articulates the concept of not shooting missiles toward the other country, the rule begins to take life. A significant fact about a rule is the frequency and extent to which the underlying concept is articulated, repeated, and accepted as a valid concept, whether or not it is accepted as a rule to be followed.

To some extent, the process of creating restraints through effective articulation is in the field of propaganda. The public hue and cry against the atmospheric testing of nuclear weapons created a norm against such conduct, a norm that induced considerable self-restraint on all countries of the world even without the corroborating effect of declarations and promises. But drawing lines is not simply a matter of words. The line articulated should reflect a concept that has internal validity, has a physical, practical, or historical basis, is readily understandable, and distinguishes a pattern of restrained conduct from a pattern of conduct that is meaningfully different and less restrained. Before countries can respect lines, the lines must be created, and some lines will work better than others. Through study and effort, valid concepts of arms restraint can be articulated.

A country is not only able to tie its own hands by making articulate the restraints it is respecting, it can also tie the hands of the other side. If there is conduct in which we are not engaging and in which we would like the Soviet Union not to engage, defining the line we have not crossed in terms that appeal to common sense and public understanding would, by that fact alone, cause the Soviet Union at least to pause at that line and appraise the consequences of crossing it. Such articulation by one side makes it increasingly easy for the other side to recognize the line as a convenient place to maintain a modus vivendi if it wishes to do so. Equally possible, though more difficult, is the articulation of rules which the other side is currently not respecting but which thereafter it will be persuaded to respect by the feared external consequences of not respecting it, the moral views of its officers, or both. Articulation can most effectively be done, perhaps, by governments, but it can also be done by organs of the United Nations, by private citizens, and by public and private groups.

Making a Unilateral Promise. A course of conduct, or the articulation of a course of conduct, contains at most an implied promise. Unilateral restraints can also be created by express promises. A country may undertake on its own to behave in a certain way. The United States might, for example, promise never to place a nuclear warhead in a satellite or might promise not to fly any of its military aircraft within fifty miles of the Soviet Union. Either of these promises would create a rule which would have a significant restraining influence on the future conduct of the United States. Breach of the rule would require overcoming appreciable internal resistances to going back on a promise—and some concern over the external consequences of the breach.

Unilaterally Limiting Capability. A promise of future conduct can be made absolutely binding for a while by a country's limiting its physical capability to act contrary to its promise. Switzerland may promise never to use nuclear weapons and may so conduct its affairs, by not training person-nel and by not producing any nuclear weapons, that at any given time the world is sure of what Switzerland's conduct will be for some time in the future.

Another illustrative restraint in this category would be the unilateral disarmament of weapons that do not presently seem decisive. The total elimination of existing nuclear stockpiles seems extremely difficult, inas-much as it is not subject to verification. On the other hand, the military risk of unilaterally disarming types of middle-grade weapons, like poison gas, would be comparatively slight. It need not be conditioned on reciprocal action by the other side; to the extent that it was not, the deterrent for the other side's using the "prohibited" weapon would depend upon a credible fear of a retaliatory use of bigger or worse weapons among those which were retained.

If two men, A and B, each armed with their fists, a knife, and a gun, are hostile and become involved in a fight, it might make sense for A to throw away his knife. Such a move would create a rule against using knives and would have a tendency to keep any fighting at the fisticuff level. A new pressure would have been created against B's using his knife. If B should pull his knife, A might have no reasonable choice except to draw his gun, and, if B is going to get into a gun fight, he would not want to start it with a knife but would want to be the first on the draw. (Of course, there is always the danger that A may end up being shot by quick-drawing B, or having to fight B's knife with his fists, having in turn been deterred by other factors from using his gun. But the example does suggest how a uni-lateral limitation on capability can create rules for the other side.*)

It should be noted that in the rule-creating processes considered so far, the restraint is created unilaterally † without any aspect of agreement. The rule, which a state may be caused by the factors previously discussed to respect, is established without a treaty or even a tacit understanding. To be sure, the restraint is effective only if the restrained state "voluntarily" complies, but the forces, such as world public opinion, tending to cause such compliance are basically the same as those which would tend to cause compliance with rules that had been agreed upon.

Unilateral Action Plus United Nations Articulation. Still without any acceptance by the other side, either the Soviet Union or the United States might be able to tie the other's hands quite effectively by a resolution of the General Assembly recommending a particular restraint for all coun-

---

* It also illustrates how such gaps in capabilities may create strong pressures on the other side to exploit the gap or to pre-empt the use of more potent forces. Such limitations must be selected with great care.—ED.

† Some discussions of "unilateral" measures fail to recognize that the number of states restrained by a rule may not be the number involved in creating the rule. A rule which binds only one country may have been established by treaty, and a rule that creates a restraining influence on two or more states may have been created by the unilateral act of a single state.

tries. The United Nations, to a very real degree, has legislative powers. The rules it "enacts" can have the same types of compulsion behind them as do treaties and general rules of international law. They may be stronger or weaker, but this will depend upon many factors, including the inherent merit of the rule. It may sometimes be easier for a country to explain to the world why it had to break a bilateral promise than to explain why it had to act contrary to the expressed consensus of the world. Working through the United Nations has its risks. The United Nations might recommend a rule we would be unwilling to abide by, for reasons, for example, such as the difficulty of verifying compliance. But a country's day-to-day concern that particular rules might not be to its liking should not obscure its fundamental and long-range interest that there be rules.

Unilateral but Reciprocal Self-Restraints. One process for limiting the arms race is for each side to demonstrate self-restraint. The more self-control one side undertakes, the more self-control the other side can afford to undertake, and vice versa. This is the process by which limited wars are limited. The process would seem equally applicable to limiting preparations for war. Although no clear line can be drawn between the case in which the restraining influence is established by the act of one side (but respected by the other) and the case in which the rule is established by the reciprocal acts of the two sides, the core concepts should be distinguished. In the first, the restrained government finds itself trapped by world public opinion and other forces in support of a rule announced and respected by the other side. In the second, rules are established by a deal—by a tacit agreement under which, as under an express agreement, performance is exchanged for performance. The essential difference between unilateral but reciprocal self-restraints and bilateral agreements would appear to lie in the fact that one side takes the first step without having the promise of the other side that it will take any step whatever.

There are infinite variations on the process. The continuance of the action taken by the first state may be made, expressly or impliedly, contingent upon the over-all restraint exercised by the second state, or upon the second state's demonstrating that it is subjecting itself to the identical restraint. The United States, for example, may conclude that it will not engage in an all-out nuclear shelter program so long as the Soviet Union does not launch such a program. Another form of reciprocal self-restraint is the case in which the second state adopts a quite different restraint which may be considered an appropriate quid pro quo. Examples of such reciprocal restraints may be taken from the limited-warfare area. In Korea, United Nations troops did not fight across the Yalu, and North Korean forces did not bomb Pusan harbor or Japan.

The process of unilateral self-restraint, contingent upon reciprocal self-restraint, lends itself more readily to some kinds of rules than to others. It would seem easiest when the action being restrained is action in which neither side has yet engaged, and when compliance with the rule is subject to ready verification at any time by the other side.* The process seems least useful when the first step taken by one side would require a major shift in conduct from that in which it is currently engaged and when the risks are such that if the other side did not follow suit, the first state would feel obliged to shift back to its original course of conduct. The United States could hardly scrap all its long-range missiles and promise not to have any in the future, conditioned on the Soviet Union's doing likewise. Should the Soviet Union fail to follow suit, the United States would promptly have to recreate its whole missile program.

A major difficulty with the unilateral approach lies in the very fact that the determination of what step shall be taken and what reciprocal action will be deemed satisfactory is made by only one country. If we assume that the first state is seeking a fair and equivalent restraint on both sides rather than seeking to gain a military advantage, it still may not have appraised the risks and benefits in the same manner as does the other side. Unless there is a good deal of negotiation and communication between the two sides, the one will not know what is bothering the other, what steps each side thinks it can undertake, and what steps it considers equivalent.

The measurement of the respective military positions of the Soviet Union and the United States is not so fine that any single step of a modest sort could be said to alter the balance. The gamble that one side takes in not attempting a few unilateral steps toward military restraint is probably greater than the military risk those steps would involve. But a basic issue that must be faced in suggesting that a particular step be undertaken unilaterally is whether the first state would do better to hold out and get a promise of something in exchange for the restraint that it is adopting. In resolving this issue, it must be recognized that to rely wholly on bilateral agreements gives the other side a veto power over the creation of rules in support of which one may rally world public opinion.

Forces similar to those that would persuade the other side to honor an agreement once signed can be brought to bear through unilateral action. A series of unilateral steps by the Soviet Union—disarmament through deeds, not words—would bring some pressure on the United States. Also, the United States could be expected to take steps simply in order to encourage the Soviet Union on. We would far rather see their defense budget go down than up. And any encouragement, to be effective, would have to be demonstrated. If this analysis is correct, it is equally valid with the roles of the countries reversed.

One side can tailor a unilateral restraint on its own conduct to get the maximum effect toward military stability with the minimum interference with strength it considers essential. It can recognize that the other side, in whatever reciprocal action it may take, may have to tailor its restraints

* A particularly good example would be the renunciation of the *first* use of nuclear weapons.—ED.

similarly. The process is thus well suited to situations in which the identical rule would affect the two sides quite differently.

Where one side judges the action it can afford to take on the basis of the actions which the other side has demonstrated it is taking, there is no necessity of negotiating first the promised performance, and then the promised inspection. Of course, neither side will rely on what the other says it is doing. But neither could it rely on what they promised to do if there were a treaty. In either case, it must judge from day to day what military preparations it must make and what restraints it can afford to exercise in the light of what the other side has demonstrated its performance to be.

The Bilateral or Multilateral Negotiation of Mutual Obligations. The process of negotiating an international agreement is well understood. It has the great advantage of disclosing, at least in part, the relative interests and positions of the two or more sides. In the negotiating process, the full pressure of the bargain can be brought to bear: "I won't unless you will." If a treaty is concluded, obligations are defined that are acceptable to both sides. A government that concludes an arms-limitation treaty will be more firmly committed to that policy than if comparable actions were taken unilaterally. Therefore, it is easier to take bigger first steps, since it is quite likely that the other side will take the first step it has agreed to take.

The negotiation of a reasonably detailed, general, over-all disarmament agreement is an extremely complicated task. Any comprehensive treaty would require the participation not only of the United States and the Soviet Union but also of Communist China and many other countries of the world. Once a treaty was negotiated, there would be ratification problems, of which obtaining the advice and consent of two-thirds of the United States Senate would not be insignificant.

After a treaty has been negotiated, signed, and ratified, each side has the bare promise of a potential enemy which it is physically free to ignore at any time. Each side will be under pressure to construe the agreement favorably to itself and to take all military action which it can legally take up to the edge of the agreement. We, in the United States particularly, tend to believe that if a proposed action is legal it is all right to take it. However comprehensive a disarmament agreement might be, it could not preclude the possibility of the opposing side's conducting an arms race around its edges. If the two sides did not conduct such a limited arms race, it would be because of self-restraint—restraint which, perhaps, they could have exercised without the treaty.

A quite different kind of treaty might be one which simply tried to set the tone for a joint policy of arms limitation. A joint declaration by the heads of state that each side would adopt a policy of limiting its weapons and of demonstrating to the other side that it was not preparing a surprise attack might be quite useful, if it was not taken as a substitute for action.

Assuming that a comprehensive arms-control treaty is sufficiently valuable so that great effort should be made to obtain one, regardless of the difficulties and regardless of the substantial chance that it could never be obtained, the question still remains, Should each country put all its arms-control efforts in the treaty framework? Should it accept the policy of all-out defense while trying to negotiate an arms-control treaty? Should each side assume that it is safer to exercise no self-control, except along lines agreed to by the other?

CONCLUSION

Within a country, the line between legal rules and other rules is fairly sharp. In general, a rule which is legally binding upon an individual has not only such moral force as it may carry with it, but also the superior physical force of the state behind it. In the international sphere, and more broadly in the sphere of rules that regulate governmental conduct, the line between legal rules and nonlegal rules still exists, but the consequences of that line are quite different. Legal rules carry with them a greater sense of "ought" than do other rules. But the same forces which persuade a government to comply with a legal rule can be marshaled in support of other rules.

Those who are concerned with reducing the risk of catastrophic war by developing rules of governmental conduct should not confine their activities to the attempt to create legal rules, whether through an international treaty or otherwise. The technical possibilities of desirable rules should be explored in the widest way. We should work out potential rules of governmental conduct, having in mind not only the military aspects but also factors such as ease of comprehension and appeal to common sense, which add strength to a rule. And for each potential rule all possible avenues for establishing that rule as one to be accorded respect should be explored.

4. Characteristics of Recent Arms-Control Proposals and Agreements

WILLIAM R. FRYE

THROUGHOUT RECORDED HISTORY, DEDICATED MEN AND WOMEN HAVE sought to limit the destructive effect of human quarrels and reduce their incidence by controlling or eliminating the instruments with which men fight. The effort has been very largely futile. It has been likened to the legendary medieval quest for the Holy Grail, that "cup hanging in the sky like a burning jewel" for which so many knights of the Round Table searched in vain. Invariably those setting out on the quest for arms limitation and control have sought to restrict or eliminate primarily the instruments with which their enemies were best supplied, or in the use of which the enemy was most proficient. (One's own weapons never threaten the peace; they are defensive in character.) An element of society which was superior to its adversaries in power would refuse to sacrifice that superiority, and one which was inferior would resist curbs on its efforts to close the gap. Except for theologians, few have probed at the root causes of the quarreling—the fear, greed, hatred, and lust for power in men's minds. The causes being untouched, the derivative instruments were virtually impossible to control.

The advent of the nuclear age in 1945 gave new impetus to the quest for disarmament, but did not make it any easier. On the contrary, it immensely complicated the task. Whereas previously the advantages to be gained or lost from a badly negotiated or imperfectly executed disarmament treaty were important, now they were quite literally matters of life and death for whole nations and alliances. "A quantity of plutonium—probably less than would fill this box on the table," said the then British Prime Minister, Winston Churchill, patting the dispatch box in the House of Commons, "and quite a safe thing to store—would suffice to produce weapons which would give indisputable world domination to any great power which was the only one to have it." The risks of *not* negotiating an agreement on arms control were also multiplied by the atomic age; but these risks seemed less immediate in many eyes.

Perhaps the first recorded effort to limit manpower and armaments was the agreement reached in 600 B.C. by the Chinese states of the Yangtze Valley. Tired of recurrent wars, they entered a disarmament league and were able to achieve 100 years of peace. In modern times, in the Rush-Bagot agreement of 1817, the United States and Great Britain, recently enemies in the war of 1812, agreed to limit their naval power on the Great Lakes to three vessels each, of equal tonnage and armament. The arrangement worked well and helped lay the basis for nearly 150 years of peace on the Canadian-American frontier.

EFFORTS TOWARD DISARMAMENT BEFORE 1945

Instances of successful arms limitation, however, are few. In 1899 and 1907, there were efforts at The Hague to curb the arms race which preceded World War I; but they failed. Between wars, the effort for disarmament was redoubled, but it had no lasting results. The 5-5-3 ratio among the navies of the United States, Britain, and Japan, established at the Washington Naval Conference in 1921–1922, remained binding for only a few years. By the end of the 1920's, Japan was openly demanding, and covertly achieving, the power necessary for her outward thrusts of the '30's and '40's.

The Covenant of the League of Nations had committed its members to the proposition (Article VIII) that "the maintenance of peace requires the reduction of national armaments to the lowest point consistent with national safety and the enforcement by common action of international obligations." Efforts to carry out this principle, however, broke down over the question of which came first, the chicken of national safety or the egg of arms reduction. The same basic dispute had preceded, and would follow, the League of Nations debates. Britain, the Scandinavian countries, and the United States (the latter, of course, not a League member) argued that disarmament would produce security and peace; France, Belgium, and Eastern Europe wanted to give priority to national security.

Efforts were made to satisfy both schools of thought. A preparatory commission was set up in 1925 to explore the ground of disarmament.. It did much useful technical work and studied a number of plans, including a spectacular plan for total disarmament offered in 1927 by Maxim Litvinov, then the foreign minister of the Soviet Union. (A generation later, Moscow was to return to this theme with similar fanfare.) Meanwhile, there were also explorations in the realm of security. The Geneva Protocol of 1924 was the first of several attempts to ease France's fear (well justified, as subsequent history proved) of a German military revival. Other such efforts to buttress European security included the Locarno Pact of 1925 and the Kellogg-Briand Pact of 1928. But none provided genuine security—in considerable part, no doubt, because the United States, gripped in postwar isolationism, held aloof. Denied the essential precondition, France refused to disarm. The world disarmament conference of 1932, one of the best prepared conferences in history, broke down on what was essentially the same basic issue, though many other cross currents of politics and diplomacy played their part.

In retrospect, France's proposals for security first, through an international police force, and for strict control over all disarmament appear sound and far-sighted. Indeed, they could be projected with little change into the year 1960. But they were minority aberrations at the time. They became majority views only after the United Nations came into being in the 1940's.

Chapter VII of the United Nations Charter provided for security through a world army. All UN members were obliged to contribute "armed forces, assistance, and facilities" to it (Article 43). The eleven-nation Security Council was placed in charge; and on the assumption that the five great powers would cooperate, they were given full control over the army's establishment and use. That provision was, of course, a fatal weakness; negotiations in the Military Staff Committee broke down on questions of organization and composition, and could not be resolved in the Security Council because of the rule that on all matters of substance the great powers must be unanimous. The Soviet Union of 1945–1948, engaged in spreading its power and influence through eastern and southeastern Europe, was not interested in establishing a world-wide system of collective security which would curb those ambitions. The West eventually set up a substitute security system for Europe in the form of NATO.

Lacking global security, the members of the UN, like the members of the League of Nations before them, set out to attempt disarmament first. They were no more successful. Under cold-war conditions, the goal was remotely feasible only if two conditions were strictly met: that no step be undertaken which would compromise the relative military power of any participant; and that all participants be certain their adversaries were faithfully carrying out their obligations. Disarmament without security, in short, would have to be balanced on a knife edge and subject to the most stringent international controls. In the nearly fifteen years of negotiations which have been conducted in the atomic age, everything from limited "first steps" to comprehensive total disarmament has been discussed, but only one measure—a ban on the testing of nuclear weapons —has been found which both East and West considered would hurt the other's power posture as much as its own and in which adequate control seemed politically feasible. Critics of the test ban, moreover, have constantly challenged both assumptions.

THE ADVENT OF THE NUCLEAR AGE

The Western powers first attacked the problem of the nuclear age on a broad front, seeking the elimination of nuclear weapons for all time.

When this did not prove feasible, they accepted the inevitability of such weapons, at least in a few hands, and set out to make the world as safe as possible under that Damoclean sword.

On November 15, 1945, the United States, Britain, and Canada, which had combined their wartime efforts in making atomic bombs and thus had let loose the genie, proposed that it be returned to the bottle. They asked that a United Nations Atomic Energy Commission be established for the purpose of "entirely eliminating the use of atomic energy for destructive purposes." The awesome fate of Hiroshima and Nagasaki had stirred world demands for such elimination, and the three-power proposal was in large part a response to those demands. It also served a further purpose: the proposal and the steps which followed it firmly fixed in the public consciousness the fact that under certain circumstances the United States would give up its new weapon, despite the temporary damage such a sacrifice would do to its strategic posture. This, in turn, gave the United States the moral freedom to use that weapon if, as the result of Soviet obstructionism, the bomb remained in the American arsenal and the Red Army then went on the march. In short, one of the principal effects of proposals to eliminate the atomic bomb was to strengthen the national security of the United States and its allies by helping to make credible the threat of atomic retaliation. Such proposals strengthened the bomb's value as a deterrent. All during the period of American atomic monopoly and for years thereafter the Soviet Union for its part did everything possible to neutralize the A-bomb by portraying its possession and use as immoral. Moscow attempted to reimpose the moral restraints which the Baruch Plan had cast off. This was the strategic meaning of its "ban the bomb" propaganda.

From the beginning, as we now can see in retrospect, there was no likelihood that the Soviet Union would agree to the Baruch Plan. This fact may have been its principal virtue in the eyes of some cynics, though there was also a great deal of idealism and dedication in the minds of many of the authors of the plan. The United States proposed to destroy all its bombs and share its peaceful atomic know-how—indeed, to turn over all its atomic energy establishments to international ownership and management—if the Soviet Union and all other countries would agree to similar treatment of their future atomic industries. The UN was to have a complete monopoly of atomic energy for peace. There was to be no atomic energy for war.

Taken at face value, history has seen few such magnanimous gestures. In Soviet eyes, however, this was an effort to perpetuate indefinitely the American monopoly. Stalin saw little difference between United States control of atomic energy and control by the proposed International Atomic Development Authority, a majority of whose members would presumably be friendly to the United States. The capitalist West, as he saw it, would own, manage, or license a substantial segment of the Communist economy, that segment which would be related to or dependent upon atomic power. Moreover, the Soviet Union would never be able to obtain legitimately the know-how to build atomic weapons (since all legal research would be under UN auspices), whereas United States personnel would retain that know-how and could fall back upon it in an extremity. Indeed, existing American bombs would not be dismantled until after the control system had been established and was adjudged to be in "effective operation"—a judgment which the Russians professed to believe would be indefinitely postponed.

Whether for these reasons or simply because the Kremlin was determined to possess nuclear-weapons capacity, it utterly rejected the Baruch Plan. In an effort to combat its propaganda appeal, Soviet delegate Andrei Gromyko proposed on June 19, 1946—four days after the presentation of the Baruch Plan—what was to become the Soviet leitmotif: that atomic weapons be prohibited by decree. Gromyko offered to join in formulating a control plan, but did not then offer one. An unenforced obligation of this kind might have been persuasive in the atmosphere of the 1920's, which had given birth to plans "outlawing war," but it was wholly inadequate, even as propaganda, in the 1940's. Rarely before or since have the United States and its allies held such unchallenged mastery of the propaganda field.

In June 1947 the Soviet Union made its first serious move to pull abreast. The lines along which disarmament debate was to be waged for the next ten years thereupon became visible. Gromyko now offered a control plan. Whereas Baruch had proposed the international ownership and management of atomic materials and processing plants, the Soviet Union suggested that they be left in national hands but made subject to inspection. The inspection was to be fairly extensive but periodic, with special inspections on suspicions of violation. Control would begin after the United States had destroyed its bombs.

EAST AND WEST: CHIEF POINTS OF CONFLICT

Two fundamental differences between East and West thus emerged. Whereas the United States thought of control in terms of ownership, management, and veto-free authority to punish violators, the Soviet Union thought of it as inspection only, with punishment left in the hands of the veto-bound Security Council. The very word "control" in Russian and French means to check, to inspect, to verify; one "controls" a bank statement at the end of the month. By contrast, the United States believed, as the Baruch Plan said, that "there is no prospect of security against atomic warfare in a system of international agreements . . . which relies [only] on inspection and similar police-like methods." Not until well after the Soviet Union had broken the American atomic monopoly (making the idea of "condign punishment" academic), and after the accumulated production of fissionable material had slipped beyond the point of fool-proof audit (making a complete ownership transfer unverifiable) did the United States alter its view. Today, "control" and "inspection" are virtually synonymous for both East and West.

The other major difference between the United States and the Soviet Union in 1947 was on the timing of disarmament and control. The United States wanted control first and the scrapping of bombs second; the Soviet Union sought to reverse that order. This difference seemed to have been overcome in the early and mid-1950's, when the concept of simultaneity gained wide acceptance; but in 1960, at the ten-nation disarmament conference in Geneva, the two sides found themselves back at the point from which they had started in 1947, arguing which should come first, disarmament or control. It was a more sophisticated argument in 1960, since both sides professed to want disarmament and control simultaneously; but, with considerable justice, each accused the other of deviating in practice from the agreed norm.

The 1948 UN General Assembly gave overwhelming endorsement to the Baruch Plan, as the UN Atomic Energy Commission had done before it; but this fact had no appreciable effect on the negotiating process, however greatly it benefited the Western moral position. "We are willing to disarm, but the Russians won't agree to control" became the virtually universal popular impression of the situation, an impression which of course contained a large element of truth and which persists to this day, even in fields where Western willingness to disarm could legitimately be questioned. The popular appeal of the Baruch Plan placed Western policy makers under great temptation to avoid public pressures for distasteful steps by linking them to more inspection than the Soviet Union would be prepared to accept, thus effectively shifting to Moscow the blame for lack of progress and perpetuating the popular impression of the East-West postures.

The Soviet Union set off its first atomic explosion in 1949. This achievement, breaking the American monopoly, basically changed the terms of reference of the negotiations, but governments were slow to acknowledge the change and make the necessary adjustments. The United States began hinting in 1950 that it knew the Baruch Plan was out of date; in 1951 it reconfirmed the plan only "unless and until a better or no less effective system can be devised." But it was not until May 1954, after the Soviets had exploded a hydrogen bomb, that the key features of the Baruch Plan—ownership and management—began to disappear from American proposals.

Meanwhile in the early 1950's Jules Moch of France, virtually alone, was warning that the point of no return had been passed, that such a large quantity of fissionable material had been produced on both sides of the Iron Curtain that no inspectorate, however great its theoretical powers, could ever be sure of tracing it all down and ascertaining that it was all being used for peaceful purposes. The margin of inevitable error might be moderate; but expressed as a percentage of a sizable stockpile it would represent an amount of fissionable material too large to be ruled out of consideration. A formidable amount of firepower— enough, as Churchill had said, to "give indisputable world domination to any great power which was the only one to have it"—could be hidden where no inspectorate could hope to find it.

This fact was of the utmost importance. It negated one of the two basic preconditions for disarmament in the midst of a cold war: the possibility of verifying the adversary's compliance. No rational govern- mental leader on either side of the Iron Curtain could now contemplate signing in good faith a treaty for the elimination of his country's nuclear weapons, intending to carry it out, whatever theoretical provisions for control might be written into the treaty. Even the possession of equally destructive (or, more destructive) bacterial and radiological weapons would not justify the sacrifice of an atomic stockpile, since such "Buck Rogers" weapons might not be adaptable to the same tactical purposes. Since there was no serious intention of eliminating nuclear weapons, it was dishonest, in point of fact, to go on proposing that a treaty for their elimination be drafted. But for a long time neither side had the courage to say so. Moch remained a voice crying in the wilderness.

A new approach clearly was called for. In December 1953 President Eisenhower suggested one such approach. Appearing before the UN General Assembly, he proposed a cooperative international effort in the field of atoms for peace, revolving around a pool or bank of nuclear fuel to be contributed by the "haves" and used primarily by the "have- nots." By-passed by the industrial revolution, the latter thus would benefit from its atomic counterpart in the twentieth century. In return, they would forswear atomic energy for war and accept UN inspection. Thus the spread of nuclear weapons would be discouraged.

The Communists' first reaction to the Eisenhower Plan was that the proposed International Atomic Energy Agency was just the Baruch Plan brought in by the back door; but they were forced by the enthusiasm for the plan among underdeveloped countries to reconsider this view and ultimately, within distinct limits, to cooperate. One by-product was a world-wide atoms-for-peace conference in 1955 at which much classified material was discovered to be in the possession of the enemy after all, and where as a result the wraps were taken off a great deal more, thus transforming the atmosphere in the peaceful atomic field. The Inter- national Atomic Energy Agency, established in 1956, has made a dis- appointingly slow start, its activities consisting primarily of atomic technical assistance. In part this has been because the pool or bank of fissionable material has not come into existence as such; the United States, Britain, and the Soviet Union have earmarked modest amounts of fuel which the agency may purchase and then sell, as a broker would do, but no attempt has been made to build an agency stockpile. The United States has preferred to conduct many of its atoms-for-peace programs on a bilateral basis outside the Agency, and this, too, has severely restricted the latter's scope of activity.

THE SOVIET ATTITUDE AFTER STALIN'S DEATH

Simultaneously with the presentation and development of the Eisenhower Plan, a change took place in the face the Soviet Union turned to the Western world. The death of Stalin in 1953, combined with a number of other factors, produced a major Soviet "peace offensive" which began to sprout in the fall of 1954 and took tangible form on May 10, 1955, in the first Soviet disarmament plan considered by Western experts to be a serious effort at negotiation. It contained many objectionable features; but for the first time in any official disarmament proposal from either side of the curtain, it acknowledged the fact that nuclear stockpiles were now uncontrollable. "There are possibilities," it said, "beyond the reach of international control for circumventing this control and organizing the secret manufacture of atomic and hydrogen weapons, even if there is a formal agreement of international control."

Moscow did not draw the logical conclusion as a consequence and stop proposing the elimination of nuclear weapons; this step came, temporarily, the following year. What it did do was to downgrade the prohibition of *possession* (as distinct from the prohibition of *use*) to the later stages of the plan (where the West had previously put it). The Soviet Union also had what were, for it, some startlingly new things to say about inspection "on a permanent basis" with an inspectorate which, "within the bounds of the control functions they [the inspectors] exercise," would have "unhindered access at any time to all objects of control." This phraseology left important questions unanswered, but it was in striking contrast to anything the Soviet government under Stalin had been prepared to say.

Possibly the most interesting aspect of the May 10th plan, from the Western point of view, was what it proposed with respect to surprise attack. Because of the possibility that nuclear weapons could be made in secret, the world stood in danger of an atomic Pearl Harbor, Moscow said (though it did not use that precise metaphor). Logic, therefore, required measures to prevent surprise, the Russians said, proposing that inspectors be stationed at fixed ground posts where they could detect the large-scale preparations necessary for "sudden attack."

This approach to the disarmament problem—acknowledgment that atomic weapons could be secretly produced, and so were here to stay; and that consequently the most practical course was inspection so as to minimize the danger that they would be used—appealed to many in the West. The most likely, indeed, the most rational use of such weapons against a major nuclear power would be a massive effort to knock out the enemy's capacity for retaliation—an effort requiring preparation which could be detected. Inspection, therefore, could make major nuclear aggression impractical. Preliminary thinking along not dissimilar lines had been going on in the office of Presidential Disarmament Assistant Harold E. Stassen, who had been appointed in March 1955. It led the United States to say frankly and publicly, later that year, that it no longer favored the elimination of atomic weapons; that it wanted to focus on ways to make the balance of power more stable, with fewer temptations to rational war and much greater protection against disastrous accident. The "open skies plan" offered by President Eisenhower at the 1955 summit conference was one such plan. Later the President offered to combine it with the Soviet scheme for fixed ground observation posts, the whole to make up an early-warning system so effective that massive attack by surprise would be improbable and hence an unprofitable venture.

THE NUCLEAR STALEMATE

It is one of the anomalies of arms negotiation that with so much apparent agreement in principle, East and West have not yet, as of March 1961, gotten down to a serious negotiation on ways and means. There was an attempt in 1958, but it broke down on what in retrospect seem ridiculous grounds: the United States insisted that the talks be purely technical, the Soviet Union wanted them purely political. No doubt a sounder reason was that comprehensive aerial inspection, as distinct from limited ground observation, would deprive the Soviets of the advantage in the field of military intelligence which they derive from the Iron Curtain. But this advantage is being greatly whittled down as the era of the reconnaissance satellite dawns; soon all skies will be open, within the technical capabilities of cameras in space vehicles. Moreover, the strategic damage the Soviet Union would sustain from the loss of its freedom to strike the first blow is being reduced to the vanishing point as atomic deterrents become harder and harder to knock out. Khrushchev is reported to have acknowledged in 1960 that a knockout blow against the enemy is now impossible.

Less ambitious plans have been offered from time to time to minimize the danger of surprise attack on a smaller scale or in a different form. Schemes for disengagement and/or denuclearization in Central Europe would serve this purpose, among others. But they have all foundered on political rocks. Some plans, for example, would freeze the partition of Germany, or place severe restrictions on the military potential of the Federal Republic, and hence would have been unacceptable to Bonn.

Much else could be done in many directions to help make the nuclear stalemate less precarious. Proposals to this end have been put forward by all the great powers. In March 1956 the United States offered one such plan, a scheme to keep additional countries from obtaining nuclear weapons (there were then only three members of the "nuclear club"). Reasoning that a proliferation of atomic weapons would sooner or later bring them into irresponsible hands and thus make the world a much more dangerous place in which to live, President Eisenhower proposed in a letter to Marshal Bulganin, then the Soviet Premier, that the production of weapons-grade fuel for atomic and hydrogen bombs be halted and that all future production be used for peaceful purposes. Strict international inspection would verify compliance—a task which probably could be performed with an acceptable margin of error.

In 1956 the United States could afford to stop bomb-fuel production far better than the Soviet Union could; its stockpiles, accumulated by then over a period of at least eleven years, presumably were larger by a considerable factor than those of the Soviet Union. And a "cut-off" would freeze the advantage. Realizing that this fact made the plan not only unacceptable to Moscow but unpersuasive to much of world opinion, the United States subsequently added a provision for the progressive reconversion of existing stockpiles to peaceful uses in amounts which could be larger for the United States than for the Soviet Union. Apparently Washington felt that the margin of error involved in determining the size of accumulated stockpiles would not be so great as to make invalid a ratio of transfers to peaceful uses based on the relationship between the size of the stockpiles. (If, for example, the United States had ten times as much fuel—so far as could be determined—its transfers would be ten times as large at each step.)

The real difficulty with the cut-off was that the permanent inspection necessary to verify compliance would make formidable inroads on national sovereignty and freedom of action. If it was to have maximum effectiveness, as the United States of course would want it to have, it would be comparable to inspection envisaged under the Baruch Plan (though of course the ownership, management, and enforcement provisions of the Baruch Plan, as distinct from its *inspection* provisions, would be irrelevant). This much inspection could have a major impact on the Soviet society and economy. Few Westerners genuinely expected the Soviet Union to accept the cut-off, despite benefits to Soviet as well as Western security in keeping nuclear weapons out of irresponsible hands. Indeed, the tactic of linking the cut-off to other disarmament measures came to be used as a protection against premature agreement on the other measures. During the period 1955–1959, for example, when Moscow was pressing for a test ban, the West contrived to avoid frontal opposition by linking the test ban, first to a package including the cut-off, and then to the cut-off alone. Only when the United States had completed its highest-priority testing and Britain had become a member of the "nuclear club" with full access to United States technology did Washington and London trade away the link to the cut-off for corresponding Soviet concessions at the three-power test-ban conference in Geneva. France, which wants to go on testing, continues to insist on the liaison; indeed, she has expanded the package to include steps which the West, as well as Moscow, can be counted on to resist.

THE TEST BAN

Prohibition of the testing of nuclear weapons is a measure designed tangentially to ease the "fifth" (or nth) country problem, that is, to help prevent the spread of nuclear-weapons technology. Few countries will invest the formidable amount of money and man-hours necessary to build a nuclear weapon if they may not legally test that weapon, once produced, and thus become thoroughly familiar with its performance. To bar testing, therefore, is to discourage the manufacture of the weapon. The prevention of radioactive contamination of the atmosphere is a second motive for the test ban, a more important one in some eyes. A formidable head of public steam has been built up on the subject in many parts of the world, despite official efforts to shunt it off—efforts which have included the establishment of a special United Nations Scientific Committee on the Effects of Atomic Radiation, which some of its sponsors mistakenly thought would deflate the dangers.

The test ban is unique in one respect: it is the one measure which at this writing has seemed genuinely negotiable between East and West. Soviet motives for seeking a test ban are generally supposed to include these: (1) desire for the propaganda advantage of successful advocacy (in point of fact, it was India which first proposed the test ban, but the Soviet Union quickly became its godparent); (2) concern over the spread of nuclear weapons to "fifth" countries, including notably Germany and quite possibly Red China—a China which, ten or twenty years hence, industrialized, with a population nearing 1,000,000,000 persons, might become less of an ally to the Soviet Union than a menace; (3) belief that the Soviet Union would be at an advantage in a weapons-technology race conducted wholly in the laboratory; and (4) desire for an East-West *détente* at minimum cost in terms of inspection behind the Iron Curtain.

The West too believes a test ban to be, on balance, in its interest. At least, dominant majorities in the American and British governments so believe, though there are powerful and influential dissenters. (The Russians have said privately at Geneva, "We have a lot of trouble with our military men, too.") The immense pressures of world opinion, reflected for example in repeated, overwhelming United Nations resolutions, have made the ban unacceptably costly for the West to resist, whether frontally or by more devious methods. There is concern over the fifth-country problem, including the problem of Red China. There is a desire to get the first olive out of the disarmament bottle. There is the possibility that even the limited amount of inspection involved in a test ban would have beneficial effects on the Soviet system, impelling or hastening what George F. Kennan has called an "erosion from despotism." Whatever the governing motives, East and

West have from time to time appeared to be coming together on the test ban. At this writing, its fate is in doubt, but despite setbacks to East-West rapprochement, hopes remain high.

SPACE CONTROL AND MISSILE CONTROL

At the outset of this chapter, it was pointed out that the Western powers, against varying degrees of Soviet resistance, at first set out to eliminate atomic weapons, and then, when that step could no longer be adequately verified, have sought to limit the danger of their use—that is, to render the nuclear stalemate less unstable. Two methods of doing so have been mentioned: inspection to make surprise attack unprofitable, and curbs on the proliferation of nuclear weapons—the latter to be accomplished via a production "cut-off" or via a test ban. These approaches have by no means exhausted the list of possibilities.

The control of outer space, if effective, would put a kind of ceiling on the area in which warfare could be conducted. It would help minimize the danger of a push-button Pearl Harbor, deliberately planned and executed; it also would reduce the peril of accidental war. Such super-Damoclean threats as H-bombs in earth satellites, ready to be propelled downward on seconds' notice, would return to the realm of science fiction. Many persons, in and out of government, have therefore urged space controls. But they have run up against a virtually insuperable obstacle: effective space disarmament would upset the existing balance of East-West power. It would remove the "missile gap," the presumed Soviet advantage in the numbers, motive power, and sophistication of long-range missiles.

The West, in proposing such peripheral measures of space disarmament as the banning of bomb-carrying satellites, has reminded the Soviet Union that when the West had an advantage in nuclear weapons it offered via the Baruch Plan to subordinate that advantage to the larger good of humanity. Moscow, however, has shown no inclination at all to take the hint. It has linked missile control to the prohibition of all means of delivering nuclear weapons to an enemy target, and has said that one part of the package must be the dismantling of "alien" bases on foreign soil. Moscow thus has proposed in effect that its temporary lead in space-weapon delivery systems be traded for permanent abandonment by the West of its globe-encircling base system. This deal has had no appeal for the West—even though, in the era of intercontinental and submarine-launched missiles, air bases are losing some of their strategic importance. Alliances are much less cohesive when not backed by a physical "presence"—and the United States will continue to want alliances in some parts of the world even when it can strike at the Soviet Union from its own soil. On the other hand, the desirability of clinging to Asian bases is being questioned by some in the wake of President Eisenhower's frustrated trip to Japan and his mixed welcome in Okinawa in June 1960; some commentators are coming to regard the bases as counterproductive in the over-all cold-war struggle. Pentagon planners are reliably reported to be seeking out alternatives to peripheral military containment. However, the Soviet plan—destroying all means of weapon delivery—is regarded as too ambitious to be taken seriously, and present United States policy is still very much keyed to preserving the base system.

Neither the United States nor the Soviet Union appears to be genuinely eager for space control—the United States, because it wishes a free hand to close the missile gap, believing, perhaps too confidently, that time is on its side; the Soviet Union, because effective space control would deprive it of the advantage it now possesses.

If agreement is long delayed, the day may soon arrive when 100 percent effective missile control may become—like the verification of nuclear stockpiles—a technical impossibility. Indeed, there are some who contend that the point of no return has already been passed. It is by no means 100 percent certain that clandestine launching platforms in the Soviet Union, even those of fixed location, could all be found and hence outlawed or subjected to surveillance. The much greater problem of finding mobile platforms—which could be on submarines, railroad freight cars, even trailer trucks—is staggering. The practical effect of an attempt at prohibiting such platforms might be to make cheating immensely profitable. No one in the West has any doubt about who would be most likely to succumb to the temptation. Moreover, there is the added fact that such military uses of outer space as the reconnaissance satellite would benefit the West far more than the Soviet Union, since the West has much more to learn about the adversary's territory. For this reason, too, the West has been less than eager for early space disarmament. It has repeatedly proposed cooperation on space-for-peace, but not until March 1960 did it come up with anything more than first, tentative feelers toward the control of space-for-war. And that proposal—in the early stages, covering primarily the prohibition of bomb-carrying satellites—was such a fragmentary approach as to be widely classified as a headline-catching device.

An exception to this Western reluctance for space control has been France, which, beginning with the fall of 1959, has proposed extensive controls over space-weapon carriers; but there is more than a suspicion that General de Gaulle has been doing this in retaliation for American and British willingness to halt atomic tests. The Anglo-American stand on testing brings pressure on France to curb her nuclear-weapons technology at a time when the United States is unwilling to share the knowledge and equipment which would make French testing unnecessary.

THE CONTROL OF CONVENTIONAL ARMAMENTS

Finally, among the principal measures which could be taken to stabilize the nuclear stalemate, there is the limitation and control of manpower and conventional armaments. This has been a particularly controversial field, though overshadowed in urgency by the nuclear problem. A UN Commission for Conventional Armaments was set up in February 1947, parallel to the UN's Atomic Energy Commission. It had scarcely begun to work (after delays over procedure and a lengthy debate on which should come first, disarmament or security—the same issue on which the League of Nations became impaled) when in 1950 the Soviet Union staged a walk-out over the issue of Chinese representation. The Korean war followed.

In February 1952, the General Assembly united the two arms commissions into a single UN Disarmament Commission competent to handle both atomic and conventional arms. On May 28, 1952, at one of the first meetings of the commission, the United States, Britain, and France laid before it for "illustrative purposes" manpower ceilings of 1,000,000 to 1,500,000 men for the Soviet Union, China, and the United States, and 700,000 to 800,000 for Britain and France. Other countries were to have armed forces numbering roughly 1 percent of the population. In June 1954, Britain and France (though not the United States) again proposed similar ceilings, reducing their own maximum to 650,000 men each. The proposal was one part of a carefully integrated, stage-by-stage plan for comprehensive disarmament.

The Soviet Union, for its part, repeatedly called in the years 1948–1955 for a one-third cut across the board in armed forces and armaments—a measure which, as the West pointed out time after time, would have kept intact the numerical superiority of the Red Army. Confidence that the Soviet Union would cling to that formula, and hence would go on rejecting numerical ceilings, may have tempted the West to offer lower force levels than it really wished to "live with." At any rate, it was a surprise to many when in May 1955 the Soviet Union adopted as its own proposal the force levels contained in the British-French memorandum of June 1954, with a minor variant applying to countries other than the Big Five. In this case, too, the proposal was part of a larger stage-by-stage plan.

In the summer of 1955 Harold E. Stassen "placed a reservation" on all United States disarmament proposals to date, in effect withdrawing them— a step which his aides said he later regretted, since it took such a long time to get new policy through the government machinery. One result was to pull back from the force-level ceilings. In March 1956, Mr. Stassen offered a "first-stage" plan which included new figures of 2,500,000 men for the United States and the Soviet Union and 750,000 for Britain and France. In the meantime, the Pentagon had privately pointed out that a cut below that level would require the abandonment of some (or, if a severe cut, all) of the United States' overseas bases, including those which were the backbone of NATO. The Soviet Union had apparently perceived this fact earlier, and like a jiu-jitsu fighter had used the adversary's thrust to help throw him off balance.

When Moscow felt it had gained as much propaganda advantage as it could by deriding the American shift, it accepted the 2,500,000 figure also. But there was a difference of view as to whether other steps should be taken in conjunction with force-level cuts, and if so, what they should be. Soon both sides began a unilateral reduction of their armed forces, which, if Soviet statements are to be accepted at face value, will bring both sides down roughly to the "first-stage" level they were (and still are, as of 1961) seeking to negotiate. Had the West been willing to isolate force levels from other aspects of disarmament, it might have been able to extract a useful price from the Soviet Union, in terms of inspection, for the reduction which was in fact made. But instead the cut was made voluntarily, in large part, apparently, to balance the American budget. If this reduction was regarded by the Soviet Union as a contribution to its security and budgetary stability, as Soviet diplomacy implied, Moscow got it for nothing. Moreover, the Soviet Union, benefiting from less intense American competition and therefore feeling more free to cut its forces, trumpeted to the world those cuts, claiming to have initiated the idea, and reaping a propaganda harvest; whereas the United States, perhaps for domestic political reasons, sought to minimize the significance of what it had done.

In any event, many have felt there was a large element of unrealism in talk of force-level cuts, whether supervised by an inspectorate or not. Manpower, once trained, is of military use, whether in uniform or civilian clothes; a man in the reserves is obviously subject to quick call while he remains in good physical condition. Moreover, how would an inspectorate go about verifying, with 100 percent certainty, the number of men under arms? Would it not be possible temporarily to "demobilize" a certain number of men while a census was being taken? One of the best methods of checking, it is said, is to take inventory of supplies, including perishable food stuffs. But this suggestion evokes the image of international inspectors going through quartermaster warehouses counting every orange, banana, and potato—a formidable task, to say the least. Other methods, including cost accounting and budget checks, are not infallible. The latest United States proposals with respect to manpower, put forward in 1960, rely upon spot checks at unexpected places and times.

Similar difficulties are encountered when one sets out to reduce conventional armaments, under adequate inspection. It is obviously not feasible to inventory every grenade, mortar shell, and bullet in a country the size of the Soviet Union or the United States. Unless every factory—literally every factory in the country, of whatever size—were to be put under surveillance to make certain it did not convert to war, there could be no certainty that weapons, once destroyed, would not be replaced. In 1955 Stassen proposed an approach to conventional weapons which circumvented some of the problems involved: internationally controlled supply dumps, within national territory, where a government would put some of its weapons into cold storage, as it were. The proposal figured again in the Western disarmament plan offered in March 1960. If the number of weapons stored were substantial, their replacement would be so costly as to defeat one of the presumed purposes of entering into the disarmament treaty. Meanwhile they would be available for use if a crisis made it necessary to denounce the treaty.

In one respect, force-level cuts and arms reductions have become more difficult since 1954 because France has been embroiled in Algeria and hence has needed its military strength. No mention was made of force levels for Britain and France in the West's 1960 plan, though it reaffirmed 2,500,000 men as the initial level for the United States and the Soviet Union. When and if the time comes that the problem is no longer academic, the West will also have to decide how to approach Red China to seek its acquiescence in a disarmament agreement. Would the United States be prepared to recognize the Peiping regime—the minimum price that Peiping could be expected to demand for participation? Already this problem is becoming pressing in the area of a test ban.

THE GENEVA CONFERENCE OF 1960

Disarmament is an almost unending series of difficult, seemingly unanswerable questions. There is great temptation for the skeptic to throw up his hands. Soviet Premier Khrushchev gave the skeptics considerable grist when he appeared before the UN General Assembly in September 1959 and (reviving the Litvinov thesis of 1927) proposed "general and complete disarmament." The West regarded this as an outrageously hypocritical travesty on sense and logic, but Western diplomats felt obliged to pretend to take it seriously lest they be maneuvered into an unenviable position before world opinion.

Anticipating Khrushchev's move, Britain had offered its own comprehensive disarmament plan twenty-four hours earlier; and at the Geneva disarmament conference of 1960, the five Western powers (the United States, Britain, France, Canada, and Italy) joined in sponsoring a similar proposal. They then tried to persuade the Soviets to discuss some one concrete aspect of the plan, offering first one approach, then another. But Soviet delegate Valerian Zorin continued to ride his premier's white horse of general and complete disarmament. Each time the West thought he might have finished the exercise, he would dig in the spurs once again and go galloping down Geneva's Avenue de la Paix, heraldic flags flying. Only if the West would take full responsibility for abandoning total disarmament would he join in discussing partial measures, he said; and this the West would not do. On June 2nd, Zorin mapped in greater detail the road to the goal, making route changes which some, at least, in the West considered improvements. He offered to begin, for example, by dealing with the means of delivering nuclear weapons; and he mentioned the nuclear-production cut-off as one subject that might profitably be given early "joint study." The plan also contained somewhat more realistic-sounding passages about control. But the objective remained the same: total disarmament, beginning with total destruction of delivery systems (including overseas bases); and this atrophied the negotiations from the beginning. The West felt obliged to profess the same desire; it even stole the copyright on the Khrushchevian phrase "general and complete disarmament" and made it a part of the West's "ultimate goal." But few believed privately that this was, in fact, the objective of either party, and so the negotiations wandered in a maze of unrealism until, on June 27th, they broke up in a Soviet-bloc walkout.

Perhaps if the West had offered a more tempting alternative to general and complete disarmament, Zorin might more quickly have given up his three-ring horsemanship. But the Western plan—both in its original form on March 16th and in a slightly revised version presented June 27th—was a conglomeration of fragments, representing the lowest common denominator on which the Western capitals could agree. Among the very first steps would be the establishment of a control organ—a time sequence which, whatever its logical justification, is to the Soviet Union like waving a red flag in front of a bull. "Control without disarmament" has always meant espionage to the Kremlin because of the Soviet mania for secrecy. In the wake of the U-2 incident, which Khrushchev used to torpedo the May 1960 summit conference, anything resembling information-gathering provoked even more frenetic outbursts in Moscow.

One striking element in the Western plan, as presented March 16th, was the linkage of ultimate total disarmament to the "establishment" of an "international organization to preserve world peace." The implication that the UN is not now such an organization, or at least is one only in embryo, and that therefore one must be "established" *de novo,* irritated supporters of the UN and evoked a protest from Secretary-General Dag Hammarskjöld. Chapter VII of the Charter, Hammarskjöld pointed out, blueprinted a peace-keeping world police force; if the great powers could agree on building one outside the UN, they could at least equally easily agree on reactivating Chapter VII. If they wish to bypass the veto and are agreed on so doing, let them amend the Charter, he said; if they are not agreed, the veto reflects the facts of international life and cannot be bypassed. In the revised version presented June 27th, the West corrected this defect; the new plan specified that the "peace force" would be "within the United Nations." On June 2nd, the Soviet Union had envisaged reactivation of the Chapter VII police force, though at a later stage in the disarmament conference. On paper, therefore, there was considerable agreement on this point.

Advocates of world government have been pleased that the idea of organized force to keep a disarmed peace should be a part of official Soviet and Western policy. However, just how an international police force could today deal with a world in which hidden stockpiles of nuclear weapons in formidable quantities might be in the hands of a peacebreaker is not clear. Nor is it clear, despite lip service from the West to "general and complete disarmament," and despite a phrase in the plan about the "final elimination" of weapons for mass destruction, what the West is in fact proposing with respect to such weapons. The Western plan is careful to predicate that "all measures of disarmament must be observed and verified by an appropriate international organization." This leaves in a shadowy zone the measures of disarmament which are listed as objectives but which could not be observed and verified.

Perhaps it is not surprising, therefore, if we consider the positions taken on both sides, that disarmament negotiations in the spring of 1960 bogged down in empty propaganda haggling. The Soviet historian, E. V. Tarlé, has written,

> The idea of disarmament has been one of the most favored forms of diplomatic dissimulation of the true motives and plans of those governments which have been seized by a sudden "love of peace." This phenomenon is very understandable. Any proposal for the reduction of armaments could invariably count upon broad popularity and support from public opinion.

The public has become somewhat more sophisticated since Tarlé's time (the period between the two world wars), but large sections of it are still prepared to swallow outrageous propositions.

Diplomats, therefore, go on seeking needles of serious intent amongst haystacks of propaganda. The very process of confrontation and maneuver sometimes is considered beneficial. And the alternative, as President Eisenhower has put it, is that the "two atomic colossi" should be "doomed malevolently to eye each other indefinitely across a trembling world."

PART II

MAJOR POLICY ISSUES AND PROBLEMS

5. The Arms Race and Some of Its Hazards

HERMAN KAHN

PREFACE

IT IS EASY TO WRITE GRAPHICALLY AND PERSUASIVELY OF THE DANGERS of the arms race, nuclear and otherwise. Such documents are often well received: the author's heart seems to be in the right place; he is for people and against the abominations science and technology have produced. Yet, this question remains unanswered: Why do nations in general, our own in particular, continue to play such a dangerous and pointless game?

Here we hit on the nub of the matter: the game is indeed dangerous, but not pointless, since not to play it (even to reduce forces or submit to arms control) can also be dangerous: a Pearl Harbor or a Munich is all too possible. If we examine the whole range of possibilities, beginning with unilateral disarmament, surrender, appeasement, or accommodation, and ending with an accelerated arms race, preventive war, Mutual Homicide Pacts, and Doomsday Machines, we discover that there are no pleasant, safe, or even unambiguously moral positions for the individual, for a nation, or for civilization. Unfortunately, the discussions that concentrate on one facet of our dangerous future tend to create a psychological atmosphere conducive to the neglect of the remaining problems of security. This is no reason for not discussing the dangers of the arms race (or any other dangers), but only for emphasizing the ultimate need for a balanced comparison of all the dangers.

I have written elsewhere * on why adequate arms control may be essential if we are to reach 1975 and later years without a major thermonuclear war, while emphasizing that we may also need military establishments of a much higher quality than is usually conceded, even by people who think of themselves as "militarists," and the many difficulties and dangers of arms control. I will not summarize the arguments here. I would only be doing myself a disservice if I did so. This is a difficult, unpleasant, and emotional

---

* This chapter is based in part on my book, *On Thermonuclear War* (Princeton, N.J.: Princeton University Press, December 1960).

subject; the points raised are often irritating or dismaying, and many readers transfer their irritation and dismay to the author. For example, if one presents a balanced account of the risks an attacker might face from a retaliatory blow, it is easy to show that, subject to some chilling uncertainties, there are many circumstances in which the risks the attacker faces are considerably less than is generally believed. As a result, there are plausible situations in which a perfectly sane (but calculating, decisive, or ruthless) attacker might decide that "it is less risky to go to war than to live with the current situation or crisis." At this point, many readers conclude that the analyst is advocating preventive war; in other words, instead of examining the arithmetic, they conclude that anyone who calculates this way wants to act this way.

While the most important problems of the 1960's and 1970's may result from the arms race itself, rather than from the political and military dangers against which the arms race is supposed to protect us, those dangers exist. Today they are manageable only because the arms protect us from them; *ill-advised* measures to control the arms race can still reduce our security.* We are trying to negotiate some very rough and dangerous terrain. While it is by no means clear that there are any "reasonable" routes to wherever we want to go, it is clear that there are precipitous and unscalable heights in all directions. Let us now examine some of this terrain.

VARIOUS WAYS IN WHICH WAR CAN START

The major danger of the arms race lies precisely in the fact that the arms may be used; thermonuclear war may be unthinkable, but it is not impossible. Arms control can reduce the risks that ensue from the everpresent possibility of war by reducing:

1. The number of events, both international (tensions and crises) and technical (false alarms and misunderstandings), that could give rise to war.

2. The probability that an event of the kind that could cause war will actually result in war.

3. The damage of an actual war, not only by abolishing the use of certain weapons and controlling the use of others, but also by facilitating ahead of time the machinery by which wars are ended before they become overwhelmingly destructive.

There is no space here to expand on these possibilities; they are all discussed elsewhere in this book. However, it may be well now to discuss systematically how a war could arise and indicate some of the problems to be considered. I will begin by listing a number of possibilities, in a semi-technical jargon intended to categorize and describe them.

1. *Unpremeditated war* (human or mechanical error, false alarm, self-fulfilling prophecy, unauthorized behavior).

* The possibility implied by the author's use of the word *still* in this sentence is to be noted.—ED.

2. *Miscalculation* (game of "Chicken," rationality of irrationality strategies, escalation, overconfidence).

3. *Calculation* (Type II Deterrence situation; preventive war; pre-emptive war; world domination; solution to a desperate crisis).

4. *Catalytic war* (ambitious third nation; desperate third nation).

The items in these four categories are neither exhaustive nor distinct from one another. They are not exhaustive because our weapon systems are so new, and their impact, both on one another and on international relations, is so little known that it would not be surprising if a war started in some manner not heretofore thought of. However, I have made the list as exhaustive as possible; in doing so it has been convenient to list categories that occasionally overlap. This is probably better than to strain too much to prevent duplication or leave out some important possibility.

Unpremeditated War. The four categories are ordered by the writer's personal estimate of their likelihood of actually being a cause of war in the next decade or two. I have put unpremeditated war at the top of the list, the fearful possibility that a war may occur almost unintentionally. There is a widespread fear that this could occur; that a button may be pressed accidentally, an electrical circuit short, a relay stick, a telephone call or other message be misunderstood, an aurora borealis or meteor or flock of geese be mistaken for an attack, a switch fail, some ICBM's launched through some mechanical or human error, some stockpile weapons accidentally exploded, and so on. Such things have happened in the past and may happen again. However, unless one side or the other is careless enough to install a quick-reacting, nonrecallable strategic system, it is most unlikely that any single one of the above events would trigger off a retaliatory attack. It is just because radars do indeed occasionally give false alarms and accidents do happen that it is essential for both sides to install weapon systems that either have so-called "fail safe" or "positive control" features built into them, or that are large enough and well enough protected that they do not need to be "trigger happy" to survive. If a system can accept the enemy's attack and still strike back effectively, the decision maker has time to evaluate and decide—time to be careful. Such systems may use an ambiguous warning so as to take some temporizing measure that will reduce vulnerability to enemy attack or provide a better posture from which to retaliate. But the commander can then wait for further confirmation before making any irrevocable commitments.

There is a danger that the temporizing measures that are instituted on an ambiguous warning will remove some of the psychological, legal, and physical safeties that normally govern the strategic force, so that there is a greater load thrown on the remaining safeguards. For this reason several accidents in a row or even a simple accident during a period of considerable tension could be dangerous. Actually, the greatest danger is the possibility that a chain of "self-fulfilling prophecies" is set into motion. It is perfectly conceivable for one side's temporizing action to be observed by the other side and to be misinterpreted as being aggressive rather than defensive, thus causing the other side also to make some temporizing defensive move. This second defensive move can in turn be misread by the side originally alerted as confirming his suspicions, so he may make some further moves. It is then possible for reactions and signals to be set into motion which trigger off further reactions and signals by both sides until a point of no return is reached. This is one reason that it is necessary for each side not only to be cautious and responsible, but also to make sure that the other side also understands what is happening. In so far as any temporizing measures depend on doing things which raise apprehensions on the other side, it is important to be prepared to allay those apprehensions. This is possibly a very fruitful area for arms control.

The Soviets are completely aware of the problem. For example, in a Security Council debate of April 21, 1958, Arkady S. Sobolev made the following statement:

American generals refer to the fact that up to the present time the American planes have taken off on their flights and returned to their bases as soon as it became clear that it was a case of false alarm. But what would happen if American military personnel observing their radar screens are not able in time to determine that a flying meteor is not a guided missile and that a flight of geese is not a flight of bombers? Then the American planes will continue their flight and will approach the borders of the Soviet Union.

But in such a case the need to insure the security of the Soviet people would require the USSR to make immediate retaliatory measures to eliminate the on-coming threat. The Soviet Government would like to hope that matters will not go so far.

In order to get a clearer idea of the extremely dangerous character of acts of the United States [that are] dangerous to peace, it is enough to ask the question what would happen if the military Air Force of the Soviet Union began to act in the same way as the American Air Force is now acting? After all, Soviet radar screens also show from time to time blips which are caused by the flight of meteors or electronic interference. If in such cases Soviet aircraft also flew out carrying atom and hydrogen bombs in the direction of the United States and its bases in other states, what situation would arise?

The air fleets of both sides, having observed each other, having discerned each other somewhere over the Arctic wastes or in some other place, apparently would draw the conclusion natural under those circumstances, that a real enemy attack was taking place. Then the world would inevitably be plunged into the hurricane of atomic war.[1]

In spite of their awareness of the problem, the Soviets have tended to emphasize disarmament almost, but not quite, to the exclusion of other aspects of arms control. For example, at the 1958 Surprise Attack Conference, they stressed larger issues and refused to discuss narrow technical issues although our own position may have been excessively narrow. To this writer it seems dangerous to wait for a settlement of the political issues before considering this problem, but in this kind of a problem it takes two to make an agreement. However, even informal implicit agreements or, on some aspects, unilateral concessions can be helpful.

It is also conceivable that some pathological or irresponsible person will deliberately try to start a war or crisis. The Soviets have made much of the possibility that a deranged or irresponsible American pilot on airborne alert would take it into his head to attack Russia alone. Not only are there many safeguards against this, but it is most unlikely that a single-plane attack would touch off a war. A much more ominous possibility is given in the book *Red Alert*,[2] in which a determined SAC general, who, unknown to his superiors, is sick with an incurable ailment (and whose judgment and sense of discipline are thus affected), decides personally to end the Soviet problem once and for all. The most interesting part is the clever way he gets around the rather elaborate system set up to prevent exactly this kind of behavior.

I should make clear that I believe that, currently at least, the probability of unpremeditated war is low. The reason I put it on the top of the list is because I believe (assuming, perhaps optimistically, that both sides are careful, competent, and responsible) the other ways in which a war could occur should have an even lower probability. It is also clear that many of the methods recommended to reduce the probability of war by accident might very well result in increasing the likelihood of war from one of the other causes. After both these points are made, it must also be mentioned that nobody can estimate realistically what the probability of accidental war is. (There seems to be some tendency to underestimate the probability of war. For example, Wheeler-Bennett reports in his book, *Munich: Prologue to Tragedy,* that on January 1, 1939, Lloyds was giving 32 to 1 odds against war in 1939. This was three months after Munich and eight months before the war actually started. While it would be hard to convince me that it is as high as, say, 1 in 10 a year, still, if it were this high, the situation would be entirely unsatisfactory. Even if it were 1 in 100 a year, it would still be unsatisfactory, because the current state of affairs could not be allowed to continue indefinitely. One must eventually introduce a major change in the situation, or expect to get into a war anyway.

The really dangerous intensification in the probability of unpremeditated war is likely to come in the future, partly as a result of increased alertness or dispersal of weapons carriers in the missile age, partly as a result of the increase in the number of buttons that can be pressed accidentally, but mostly as a result of the proliferation of independent nuclear capabilities to other countries, each with its own standards of training, reliability of personnel, and safety practices.

War by Miscalculation. Nearly as worrisome as the possibility of unpremeditated war is the war which is more or less premeditated (perhaps as in the *usually uncalculated* "calculated risk")—but the decision maker doing the premeditating has miscalculated or misunderstood the risks or consequences of his actions. Many believe that the most likely way for this to occur is as a result of the use of a committal strategy. For example, one side may make it clear that it is going to stand firm in some crisis in the belief that "since neither side wants war," the other side will back down. If the other side does not back down, then war can result. A graphic if somewhat oversimplified example of such a situation is given by Bertrand Russell:

This sport is called "Chicken!" It is played by choosing a long straight road with a white line down the middle and starting two very fast cars towards each other from opposite ends. Each car is expected to keep the wheels of one side on the white line. As they approach each other mutual destruction becomes more and more imminent. If one of them swerves from the white line before the other, the other, as he passes, shouts "Chicken!" and the one who has swerved becomes an object of contempt.[3]

It is clear that if one side really wishes to win this game its best (rational) strategy is to commit itself irrevocably to going ahead. If one can convince the other side that one has done this, then the other side must back down. However, if the other side still refuses to back down after the irrevocable commitment has been made, it would be irrational to carry out the rationally made commitment. Since both sides will be attempting to use this strategy, it is also quite clear that the game may end in a disaster.

According to Bertrand Russell, the game is played by degenerates in America, and by nations everywhere. It is a caricature, because Russell ignores the fact that it is a major purpose of diplomacy to prevent a crisis from arising which can only be settled by the total and humiliating defeat of one side or the other. Most bargaining situations involve gains for both sides, and the major question is on the division of these gains and not the humiliation of the other side. However, the game of Chicken may occur. Barring enforceable adjudication, the less one is willing to play the game, the more likely it may be that one may end up having to play it. Life, liberty, and security may depend on being willing to play this dangerous game. As Russell states:

Practical politicians may admit all this, but they argue that there is no alternative. If one side is unwilling to risk global war, while the other side is willing to risk it, the side which is willing to run the risk will be victorious in all negotiations and will ultimately reduce the other side to complete impotence. "Perhaps"—so the practical politician will argue—"it might be ideally wise for the sane party to yield to the insane party in view of the dreadful nature of the alternative, but, whether wise or not, no proud nation will long acquiesce in such an ignominious role. We are, therefore, faced, quite inevitably, with the choice between brinkmanship and surrender."

The game of Chicken is an extreme example of the use of "rationality of irrationality" strategies. Because these are so important it may be worthwhile to dwell on them briefly. In any bargaining situation, even the most innocuous, it can make sense to commit oneself irrevocably to do something in a certain eventuality, and at the same time it may not make sense to carry out the commitment if the eventuality occurs; if one could, one would revoke the "irrevocable" commitment. The analogy with the game of Chicken should be clear. It should also be clear that if both sides commit themselves to incompatible positions, there will be no bargain. But if the bargaining is carried on with skill, and if both sides are cautious, then the bargaining will take on the aspects of a normal commercial transaction in which both sides gain, the exact division of the gains depending on their relative skill, but in which neither is driven to the wall.

Unfortunately, in any long period of peace, there is some tendency for governments to become more and more intransigent. The thought of war may become unreal. Even more important, every government is likely to build up a background of experiences in which it did very well by standing firm and very badly when it displayed a flexible, reasonable, or conciliatory attitude. It is only when peace fails that the governments are likely to learn that standing firm on incompatible positions is not a feasible symmetrical strategy. One can almost confidently predict that unless arrangements are made for adjudication or arbitration, somebody is going to play the international analogue of Chicken once too often.

The rationality-of-irrationality war should be distinguished from one caused by the two sides having incompatible objectives which they are determined to achieve, no matter what the risks: in this case war must result. The rationality-of-irrationality war corresponds to a situation in which neither side really believes the issue is big enough to go to war over, but both sides are willing to use some partial or total strategy of commitment to force the other side to back down. As a result, they may end up in a war they would not have gone into, if either side had realized ahead of time that the other side would not back down, even under pressure.

A typical circumstance in which such a situation could arise results from the use of Type II Deterrence.* Imagine, for example, that the Soviets had done some very provocative thing, such as invading Western Europe with conventional armies, on such a large scale that we felt that we could not stop the invasion by any limited actions, and that we would not be able to rescue Europe at a later date. We might still not be willing to strike the Soviets with our SAC, in view of the terrible price we would have to pay to their retaliatory blow, even if we struck them first. However, we could evacuate our cities and place our forces on a super-alert status, and thus

---

* As in my book, I would like to distinguish three kinds of deterrence. Type I is the deterrence of an "all-out" direct attack. Type II is the deterrence of extremely provocative acts, other than an all-out attack on the nation using the deterrence. Type III might be called a graduated or controlled deterrence: it is the deterrence of provocations by making the potential aggressor afraid that the defender or others will then take limited actions, military or nonmilitary, which will make the aggression unprofitable.

put ourselves in a much better position to strike first and accept the retaliatory blow. We might then present the Soviets with an ultimatum. We would in effect be presenting the Russians with the following three alternatives: to initiate some kind of strike; to prolong the crisis, even though it would then be very credible that we would strike if they continued to provoke us; or to back down or compromise the crisis satisfactorily. We would hope that the Soviets would prefer the third alternative, because our Type I Deterrence would make the first choice sufficiently unattractive, and our Type II Deterrence would do the same for the second; but we might be wrong, and they might take the first alternative. Or they might take the second alternative in the assumption that we would back down, and we might not.

Another method of getting into a war by miscalculation would be as a result of a limited move that appeared safe, but which set into motion a disastrous sequence that ended in all-out warfare. This increase is called escalation. One can imagine some sort of crisis which gradually increased in violence or scope until it triggered one of the reactions already discussed. This could occur either because the limits of a limited war are not being observed, or because more parties are being drawn into it, or because the isues themselves become fraught with significances that did not initially exist, or because of some unauthorized or accidental behavior by subordinates. It is difficult to supply a plausible reason for escalation (except, of course, as a move in the game of Chicken), when it is to everybody's interest to control things, yet almost everyone considers that it can and perhaps will happen.

Escalation is possible particularly if one of the two contending sides does not think through the consequences of its actions. To return to the Type II Deterrence situation discussed above: it is perfectly conceivable that the Russians, looking at the 60 million hostages we have in our fifty largest cities, might decide that it was safe to attack Europe, and that we would not attack them in retaliation. They might also vaguely realize that if they attacked Europe, we would probably evacuate the 60 million hostages; but they might not understand the full consequences of that evacuation, in terms of the psychological stiffening of the backbone and the enormous decrease in the risks this country would be running if it went to war.

The possibility of escalation may actually play a useful role in deterring certain kinds of crises or limited wars. For example, it is quite clear that the nuclear-weapon systems we and the British have in Europe are on the whole fairly vulnerable to Soviet attack, so that they have little second-strike capability. Yet the Soviets might be afraid to destroy them in a limited European attack, for fear that the level of by-product destruction would automatically cause escalation into an all-out World War III. On the other hand, if the Soviets did not destroy them, the Europeans might use them, and this in turn would not only be damaging to the Soviets, but might also cause escalation into World War III. This means that lower than all-out attacks may be deterred for fear they will escalate. The same mechanism holds, for example, if we decide to open a route to Berlin by force if the Soviets or East Germans try to close it. As of 1961, the Soviets have the capacity to apply all the counterforce they need to stop any such action. The purpose of the action is not to overwhelm Soviet countermeasures, but to make it clear to them that the stakes are large. It is clear that we might be willing to take a small but appreciable risk of an all-out war, even if we were not willing to go immediately into an all-out war. The action might be effective precisely because it was so dangerous. To the extent that various types of arms-control measures reduce the possibility of escalation, then to that extent the deterring effect of escalation on limited actions is decreased. The author finds this no reason for not carrying through such control measures, but he knows many Europeans who are antagonistic to any reliable limits on the use of violence, for the very reason that such limitations may increase the probability of a provocation at that limited level.

Another possibility of a war by miscalculation occurs when one side goes to war in the mistaken belief that it has a sufficient preponderance of force or a clever enough war plan to be able to win satisfactorily. The mistake can occur through some uncertainty being underestimated, some imponderable ignored, or sheer ignorance or recklessness. Given current beliefs in the West, it is almost impossible to imagine this happening to a Western government unless the decision makers have their judgment clouded by desperation or madness. The situation is less certain in the Communist bloc. The Chinese clearly underestimate the effects of nuclear war. Hopefully, it will be some time before they have the power to use nuclear weapons, and time may bring them greater wisdom. The Soviet estimates, as gleaned from their public statements, seem plausible, though whether this comes as a result of more or less sophistication than is prevalent in the West is hard to tell. They talk of the possibility of great destruction and suffering together with the likelihood of the "victor" surviving and recovering. The Soviets do not seem to be trigger-happy or reckless, one judges at this writing, so that it does not seem to be necessary to put much effort into attempts to educate them on the danger of being overconfident about the use of modern weapons. The Soviets may underestimate the need for collaboration in controlling the technological development and dissemination of new weapons and thus be unwilling to make the necessary compromises entailed in getting feasible arms-control programs accepted by both sides. If they go to war, however, it is as likely to be as a result of calculation as of miscalculation. This thought brings us to our next topic.

War by Calculation. War could result from calculation. After due study, a nation might decide that going to war would be the least undesirable of its choices. Common belief, of course, holds just the opposite: that war could arise only as a result of miscalculation—but this is based on the unsophisticated view that all wars result in automatic mutual annihilation.

This could happen, but in all likelihood it would not. One type of war by calculation could occur in the Type II Deterrence situation referred to above. If at that point we attacked the Soviet Union, the damage we received in return would be considerably reduced. We might well decide that our nation was better off to accept this retaliatory blow rather than let Europe be occupied, and also to accept the costs of living in the hostile and dangerous world that would result.

Or, to give another example, the Soviets suffered from 20 to 30 million casualties in World War II, and in addition they lost about one-third of their wealth. It is sometimes pointed out that this did not happen from calculation but was inflicted on a day-by-day basis: no alternatives were ever really put up to them. However, given the nature of the Nazis and their program, I would believe that even the average Soviet citizen (not to mention the government) would have been willing to accept the cost of World War II in order to achieve the position they have since won, as an alternative to Nazi domination.

Another war by calculation would be the so-called preventive war. This does not necessarily mean that one side believes the other is planning eventually to attack the first, which is therefore merely getting in the first blow. One side has only to feel that a war is inevitable—or so likely that it might as well get the disaster over with as soon as it gets a sufficient lead, so that it is safer to seize the opportunity than to wait. Such an edge is most likely to result from a technological change to which the other side has not reacted. The so-called missile gap illustrates how this problem could arise.

The United States SAC (Strategic Air Command) is supposed to be based upon about fifty home bases. If the Soviets happened to acquire, unknown to us, about three hundred missiles, then they could assign about six missiles to the destruction of each base. If the Soviet missiles had, let us say, one chance in two of completing their countdown and otherwise performing reliably, then there would only be 1 chance in 64 that any particular SAC base would survive a Soviet attack. There would be better than an even chance that all the bases would be destroyed, about one chance in three that one base would survive, and a small chance that two or more bases would survive.

A missile gap of the sort described is especially dangerous because missile attacks are so much more calculable than any other kind of attack. They are so calculable that many people feel that even a cautious Soviet planner might be willing to rely on the correctness of his estimates; that Soviet decision makers might find it the path of caution to attack while the opportunity was still available.

Actually the results of missile attacks are not mathematically predictable. There are imponderables and uncertainties with regard to such things as reliability of basic data, field degradation, intelligence leaks, and firing discipline so that the probability of something going wrong cannot be predicted. But so many laymen and professionals persist in regarding the reliable prediction of the results of missile attacks as simple problems in engineering and physics that it would be irresponsible to rely on Soviet caution and sophistication alone as a protection. And if such an attack were successfully carried out, it would truly be a war by calculation.

The need for a quick reaction to even "hypothetical" changes in the enemy's posture is likely to persist indefinitely, in spite of the popular theory that once we get over our current difficulties we will have a so-called minimum nuclear deterrent force that will solve the Type I Deterrence problem. (Some even maintain that it will solve all strategic problems.)

It should be noted that if a serious deterrent gap ever occurred, then, even if the Soviets were not willing, either out of caution or morality, to use their superiority, the situation would still be dangerous. They might well be tempted to a strong (even reckless) foreign policy, if they believed that their military technology entitled them to some gains, or that if they got into trouble they could use their missiles to rescue themselves. This kind of situation could be especially dangerous if the Soviets considered that they could not disclose their superiority, since if they did so, we could take remedial action (e.g., an airborne alert). Still, they might be willing to hint at their superiority, in the belief that this would be just enough to make us weak or uncertain in our response in a crisis, but not move us prior to a crisis to institute the airborne alert in time.

Another possibility for preventive war could occur if an arms-control agreement broke down and one side had a considerable lead, either because of its previous success in evading detection, or its greater ability to rearm. This side might well feel that, rather than see the world subjected again to all the dangers of an arms race, it would be doing a public service to stop the race, once and for all. And this could best be done by stopping the cause of the race—its opponent. It might be especially willing to start the war soon after the arms-control agreement terminated, because the risks, even if things went awry, would not be so great at the existing low level of arms than before the arms-control agreement had lowered the absolute level of the balance of terror. The rather high probability of war breaking out after the arms race had begun again (but before both states were fully armed) is often ignored. Most writers focus attention on the situation existing at the time of the breakdown, when the posture is still determined by the agreement and on the feasible violations of the agreement, rather than on the situation some months or a year or two later.

Then there is the idea of "pre-emption," or as Einstein called it, "anticipatory retaliation." Almost all authorities agree that at present the advantages of striking first are so great that if there seems a high probability that the other side is actually attacking, it may be better to take the certain risk of a relatively small retaliatory strike rather than the high probability of a much more destructive first strike. This calculated pressure for pre-emption is especially likely in one situation very similar to that of "self-fulfillment," previously discussed. Even if only one side suspects that the other may attack, each can easily become convinced that it should attack—not because it wants to, or even because it believes the other side wants to, but only because it believes the other side may attack simply to pre-empt a supposed attack by the first (which is itself being launched as a pre-emptive attack). Schelling has labeled this situation, "the reciprocal fear of surprise attack."[4] As described, it is not a case of miscalculation, but a case of calculating correctly. This is clearly a situation in which each side has nothing to fear but fear, yet the knowledge that the other side is afraid fully justifies that fear.

Many things could touch off a "reciprocal fear of surprise attack" situation. The only reason I have put this possibility low on the list of possible causes of war is because of the belief that as long as decision makers are consciously in control of events, they are very much more likely to draw back from pressing buttons and accept any resulting risks, than to do something which would make war inevitable—particularly, if this war were to occur at a time and under circumstances not of their choosing. However, complicated and dangerous situations can occur. For example, suppose that one of our own Polaris submarines accidentally launched some missiles at our own country. Even if the submarine commander succeeded in informing us of what happened before the missiles landed, the accident could still cause a war. The Soviets might observe these missiles exploding and if they did know where the missiles came from, they might decide that it would be too dangerous to wait. Even if the Soviets knew that the missiles had not accidentally come from a Soviet submarine, they might not believe that we would wait to find out.

We might ourselves be under pressure to attack even if we thought the Soviets knew nothing about the incident because we could not be sure they did not know. It might appear safer to pre-empt than to let precious minutes slip away while we tried to persuade the Soviets that we knew they were innocent. The possibilities for trouble are almost infinite, and it would be wise to reinforce the natural caution of decision makers with explicit measures, both unilateral and multilateral, to facilitate communication and persuasion and to make waiting safe.

The line between preventive and pre-emptive war is sometimes very fine, and it is on this line that some of the most plausible war-making situations can occur. For example, let us imagine the Type II Deterrence situation discussed earlier, in which the Soviets were hypothesized as invading Europe, and we as evacuating our cities as a preliminary to delivering an ultimatum or otherwise exerting pressure. If the Soviets struck us at that time, it would not be a pre-emptive war, because very likely we would not have made up our own minds as to whether we would strike or not; in particular, we would intend to give them the option of backing down or compromising. However, we are so close to making up our minds that this cannot be labeled as a preventive war, either—a war to head off some generalized future threat. Similarly, if after evacuating our cities, we gave the Soviets an ultimatum, and the Soviets chose the alternatives of prolonging the crisis, we might decide to strike, even though we thought there was a big chance that they were going to back down eventually. We would not be sure, and if we had already evacuated our cities, the risks of going to war would have been sharply diminished.

There is also a possibility of going to war simply to achieve world domination. Most people (the author included) believe the risks involved in going to war are so great today that no matter how promising an attack might look on paper, the "imponderables" and other "uncertainties" are large enough so that not even a moderately irresponsible decision maker would go to war for positive gains—though one like Hitler might. However, if we ever disarm, either unilaterally or bilaterally, to the point where the available weapon systems do not present the awful potentialities present today, then, of course, this possibility reappears.

Even if decision makers are unwilling to go to war for positive gains, they may still be willing to go to war, if, in their opinion, "going to war" is less risky than not doing so. There are many situations in which this could occur. One could imagine an internal or external crisis getting out of hand, and one which was being aggravated by the opponent, perhaps merely by his very existence. One may then be tempted to go to war, not because it looks so tempting, but because it looks like the least undesirable alternative.

Catalytic War.[5] The last possibility is the catalytic war. This is the notion that some third party (or country) may deliberately start a war between the two major powers for reasons of its own. As it is usually discussed, the concept holds that some power which is third, fourth, or fifth in the international hierarchy wishes to improve its position by arranging for the top two nations to destroy each other, thus moving itself up two notches. This is one of the major reasons why some people fear the dissemination of nuclear weapons to "ambitious" powers. However, there are several reasons why this particular concept is not considered plausible: (1) risks are so great for the triggering power that it is difficult to believe that one power could make and carry out such a decision, (2) more important, the United States and the Soviets will probably put into effect slow-reacting systems with a lot of stops in them before the decision for all-out war is reached. This means that it will be much harder for a third party to start a war than is often imagined, though if it tries hard enough and has a large enough capability, it is not impossible.

There is another type of catalytic war which I think much more likely and important: a desperate third nation thinks it has a problem that can be solved only by war. Let us imagine a war between India and China which the Indians were losing. The Indians might feel that if they induced the United States to strike at China and Russia, this would solve their problem, and any method they used to achieve this end was as good as any other. Conversely, let us imagine a situation in which the Chinese felt hard pressed (possibly over Formosa) and told the Russians, "We are going to strike the United States tomorrow, and you might as well come along with us, for they will undoubtedly strike you, even if you do not do so."

As stated, the situation may seem somewhat implausible, but one can devise hypothetical situations which make it seem more plausible than I have done here. One may wish to broaden the definition of catalytic war. Any method by which a nation uses military or diplomatic power to embroil larger nations or increase the scope of the conflict could be called catalytic. By this definition, World War I was a catalytic war, set off by Serbia and Austria, which also had some overtones of "reciprocal fear of surprise attack" and "self-fulfilling prophecy," because the side which mobilized first was likely to win. It meant that even a defensive mobilization (by the Russians) touched off a defensive-offensive mobilization (by the Germans), in much the same way some believe that a badly designed, quick-reacting force can be touched off by defensive moves by the other side.

SOME HYPOTHETICAL ULTIMATES

Stability Is Not Enough. Many experts and laymen believe that the best method of preventing any of the four potential causes of war from actually causing a war is to procure what are called "stable deterrent systems." This term implies a military posture which will deter a surprise attack and also not be accident prone or "trigger happy." Even this limited goal is not enough for those strategists who also want stability against provocation (i.e., they also wish to have adequate Type II and Type III Deterrence). However, many strategists, and even some arms controllers, overlook the important requirement that a failure of stability should result in limited and "acceptable" consequences.

In order to illustrate this remark, I would like to discuss the strategic theory of three conceptualized devices, which I shall call respectively the Doomsday Machine, the Doomsday-in-a-Hurry Machine, and the Homicide Pact Machine. To discuss these hypothetical (almost allegorical) devices will not only focus attention on the most spectacular and ominous possibilities of the arms race, but it will also clarify a good deal of our current strategic thinking. In particular the discussion should make clear that:

1. The sole objective of maximizing deterrence is an unacceptable criterion for a weapon system;

2. There is a very difficult fundamental problem in deciding the permissible stakes at risk in the event of failure of deterrence;

3. Although current weapon systems are already quite disturbing, their potentialities could be dwarfed by some of the devices that may be practical in the near future.

The Doomsday Machine. A Doomsday weapon system might hypothetically be described as follows: let us assume that for 10 billion dollars one could build a device whose function is to destroy the world.[6] This device is protected from enemy action (perhaps by being situated thousands of feet underground) and then connected to a computer, in turn connected to thousands of sensory devices all over the United States. The computer would be programmed so that if, say, five nuclear bombs exploded over the United States, the device would be triggered and the world destroyed. Barring such problems as coding errors (an important technical consideration), this machine would seem to be the "ideal" Type I Deterrent. If Khrushchev ordered an attack, both Khrushchev *and* the Soviet population would be automatically and efficiently annihilated. (The emphasis is deliberate: most deterrents are more likely to destroy populations than decision makers.)

Even if this is the ultimate in Type I Deterrence, the Doomsday Machine is an unsatisfactory basis for a weapon system. It is most improbable that either the Soviet Union or the United States would ever authorize procuring such a machine. The project is expensive enough so that it would be subjected to a searching budgetary and operational scrutiny, one which would raise questions the project could never survive.

The Doomsday-in-a-Hurry Machine. Before considering these questions, let us consider how one might adapt the Doomsday Machine to purposes of Type II and Type III Deterrence. For reasons that will become clear, let us call this model the Doomsday-in-a-Hurry Machine. The computer would be given all the facilities it needed to be "well informed" about world affairs. We could then publish a "Soviet Criminal Code." This would list in great detail all the acts which the Soviets were not allowed to commit. The Soviets would then be informed that if the computer detects them in any violations it will blow up the world. The logicians (and some so-called practical men) might then believe that we had solved all our deterrence problems. After all, we would then have drawn a line the Soviets would not dare to cross. We could relax forever our interest in defense and turn our attention to other matters.

Unfortunately, the world is not that simple. First, the Soviets would rush to build their own machine. There would be a race to publish first. This race to publish first involves more than prestige. There is almost a certainty of an incompatibility between the two sets of rules, since Paragraph I of each probably states that the opponent shall not build a Doomsday Machine! To many people, to build a Doomsday Machine would be the greatest provocation short of an attack that the opponent could commit. In fact, because it may destroy so many people, some find it more provocative than an attack. Even if we succeed in publishing first, and even if the Soviets believe our machine will work as advertised, and are deterred from publishing, trouble is still almost certain. It will simply prove impossible to draw a useful, unambiguous line that covers most Type III Deterrence situations—it may even be difficult to cover unambiguously all possible Type I and Type II situations. The first time there is a difference in interpretation the world would be blown up.

The Unacceptability of Doomsday Machines. Let us examine the use of both the Doomsday and Doomsday-in-a-Hurry Machines as deterrents. It is desirable that a deterrent should be: frightening; inexorable; persuasive; cheap; and nonaccident-prone.

As measured by these characteristics, both Doomsday Machines are likely to be better than any current or proposed competitor for deterrence. They are as *frightening* as anything that can be devised. They are more *inexorable,* since they can be made almost invulnerable to direct physical destruction (electromagnetic waves which would set them off go faster than shock waves which might destroy the device); the operation is in principle so simple and reliable that one can really believe it would work (as opposed to a complex weapon system which requires the split-second coordination and almost perfect operation of many complex parts in a strange post-attack environment); and the automatic operation eliminates the human element—including any possible loss of resolve as a result of either humanitarian consideration or threats by the enemy.

The machines are certainly *persuasive.* Even the most simple minded should be able to understand their capabilities. Most likely such machines would be *cheap,* compared to present weapons expenditures.

Finally, they are relatively *foolproof,* in the sense that the probability of an accidental or unauthorized triggering should be low. This means, while the possibility of an unauthorized or accidental use of the machine, in spite of all precautions, would be too high to be acceptable, it would still be lower than the probability of such an action in complicated and dispersed systems such as Polaris, Minuteman, and airborne alert. Not only is the number of buttons very low, but the Doomsday weapon system is so simple that one should be able to see clearly the places where trouble could occur, and then take all possible precautions.

The difficulties lie in the fact that the Doomsday Machine is not sufficiently *controllable.* Even though it maximizes the probability that deterrence will work (including minimizing the probability of accidents or miscalculations), it is totally unsatisfactory, for one must still examine the consequences of a failure. A failure will kill too many people, and kill them too automatically. There is no chance of human intervention, control, and final decision. Even if we give up the computer and make the Doomsday Machine reliably controllable by the decision makers, it is still not controllable enough. Neither NATO nor the United States, possibly not even the Soviet Union, would be willing to spend billions of dollars to give a few individuals this particular kind of life-and-death power over the entire world.

If one were presenting a military briefing advocating some special weapon system as a deterrent and examined only the five qualities on the list, the Doomsday Machine might seem better than any alternative system; nevertheless, it is unacceptable. We thus see that our list of properties should have included a sixth: It is desirable that a deterrent should be *controllable*. The fact that most public discussion ignores this last requirement could imply that either some of the weapon systems currently being proposed are unacceptable, or that the way we talk about these weapon systems is wrong—very likely both.[7] Most decision makers seem to feel very strongly about the unacceptability of Doomsday Machines. If forced to choose among accommodation to the point of surrender, a large risk of surprise attack, or buying a Doomsday Machine, they would choose one of the first two as against the last one.

This last statement may surprise many who feel that irresponsible governments on both sides have already bought the equivalent of Doomsday Machines, almost without a second thought. I used to be wary myself of discussing the concept for fear that some overenthusiastic colonel would issue a General Operating Requirement or Development Planning Objective for the device. For whatever it is worth, my experience in two years of briefings has been exactly the opposite. Except for some intellectuals, especially certain scientists and engineers who have overemphasized the single objective of maximizing the effectiveness of deterrence, the device is universally rejected. Doomsday Machines do not look professional to senior military officers (in a way it threatens them with a fourth service), and they look even worse to senior civilians. The fact that more than a few scientists and engineers do seem attracted to such devices is disquieting, but as long as the development project is expensive, even these dedicated experts are unlikely to get one under way.

A Fundamental Problem. The concept of the Doomsday Machine raises certain awkward questions which must be considered by both policy maker and technician. If it is not acceptable to risk the lives of the *three billion* inhabitants of the earth in order to protect ourselves from surprise attack, *then how many people would we be willing to risk?* It is clear that both the United States and NATO would reluctantly envisage the possibility of one or two hundred million fatalities (i.e., about five times more than those in World War II) from the immediate effects, even if one does not include long-term effects due to radiation, if an all-out thermonuclear war results from a failure of Type I Deterrence. Under somewhat more controversy, similar numbers would apply to Type II Deterrence.* We are willing to live with the possibility partly because we think of it only as a remote possibility. We do not expect either kind of deterrence to fail, and we do not expect the results to be that cataclysmic if deterrence does fail. However, even those who expect deterrence to work might hesitate at introducing a new weapon system that increased the reliability of deterrence, but at the

---

* For example, Brennan would concede the statement for his B Deterrence, but not his C Deterrence. [Primarily because I believe we have the capacity to deal with failures of Type C Deterrence by drastically less expensive methods.—ED.]

cost of increasing the possible casualties by a factor of ten, so that there would then be one or two billion hostages at risk if their expectations fail.

Neither the 180 million Americans nor the half billion people in the NATO alliance would be willing to procure a security system in which a malfunction could cause the death of one or two billion people. If the choice were made explicit, then the United States or NATO would seriously consider "lower quality" systems, i.e., systems which were less deterring, but whose consequences would be less catastrophic if deterrence failed. They would even consider such possibilities as a dangerous degree of unilateral disarmament, if there were no other acceptable postures. The West might be willing to procure a military system which could cause such damage if used in a totally irrational and unrealistic way, but only if all of the plausible ways of operating the system would not inflict anything like the hypothesized damage. Nor would we knowingly build a strategic system which forced the Soviets to build a Doomsday Machine in self-defense. On the other hand, we would probably be willing ourselves to go to desperate measures rather than give in to a cynical attempt by the Soviets to blackmail us by building or threatening to build a Doomsday Machine.

Possible Future Problems. Aside from moral and political reasons, and aside from the repugnance policy makers and practical men feel for a device that is poised to strike at their own population, the main reason the Soviet Union and the United States would not build a Doomsday Machine is that they are both *status quo* powers; the United States is one because it has so much, and the Soviet Union is one partly because it also has much and partly because it expects to get so much more without running any excessive risks. However, even if we believe that neither the Soviets, nor the Americans, nor other technically competent and wealthy but "satisfied" powers (such as England) would at present deliberately build a Doomsday weapon system, at least three important problems arise. Would a nation build one inadvertently? If not now, will it change its mind in the future? Would a determined non-*status quo* nation build one?

I do not believe that any nation will build a Doomsday Machine inadvertently, partly because it is so hard to build one, but mostly because current discussion is focusing attention on this problem, and decision makers are becoming conscious of its implications. As for a technically advanced *status quo* country's changing its mind, I could easily imagine a crisis in which a nation might desperately wish it had procured such a machine. Fortunately, it seems less likely that a nation would procure a standby capability that could be connected up at the last moment than that it would procure a continuous capability in being. The lead time for designing and constructing such a machine would be so long that the crisis would be settled before the project could get under way. In the long run (one to three decades), the third question, "Would a determined non-*status quo* nation build one?" may turn out to be the most important.

Many scientists believe that Doomsday Machines will inevitably become both clearly feasible and much cheaper than I have suggested, so that the developmental gamble will be much less risky than it is today. In addition, a number of powers which, unlike the United States and the Soviet Union, may not be cautious in outlook, will be getting both richer and more competent technically, yet may retain their non-*status quo* outlook. For example, there may be a nation (like the Germany of 1933) which is wealthy enough and technically competent enough to have an advanced military technology, yet desperate or ambitious enough to gamble all.[8] Or some of the underdeveloped nations may become rich in terms of gross national product, but have such a low per capita income or other social anomaly that they retain attitudes more appropriate to a desperate claimant on the world's resources than a responsible "bourgeois" member of international society.

China presents the outstanding possibility of this last type in the next decade or two. Such a third nation might well decide that an investment in a very high-quality Type I Deterrent would pay dividends. It is unlikely (though not impossible) that the leaders of that nation would plan on threatening the world with annihilation or extreme damage unless given their way. If they can do the damage gradually, they can make the threat clear and demonstrate their resolve, without actually committing suicide. As an example, suppose that the blackmailing nation started a process which it could reverse, but which could not be reversed or negated by others, in which the temperature of the earth was artificially dropped five degrees a year. If they also had a Doomsday Machine to protect themselves from attack (one which might depend on the same mechanism), one could easily imagine that they could demonstrate enough resolve to bring most of the other major nations to terms. A much more likely possibility for the possessor of a Doomsday Machine would be to exploit the sanctuary afforded by his "excellent" Type I Deterrent to be as aggressive as he pleased against his neighbors and to threaten any who interfered with all kinds of punishment—for example, some form of controlled nuclear retaliation, in which he destroyed two or three of the major cities of his interfering opponent. Even if it were feasible to retaliate in kind without setting off the Doomsday Machine, the social and political impact of accepting such losses would raise much more serious internal and external problems in the United States than in China. It seems most likely, for example, that having to accept and explain the rationale of an exchange of two or three major United States cities for an equal number of Chinese cities would result in political suicide for the party in power in the United States, as well as in some instabilities in our alliances, but only in some serious inconvenience to the Chinese government. It should therefore be a major objective of arms control to prevent such hypothetical, but not unimaginable, problems from occurring. (Here is one clear case of joint Soviet–United States interest.)

The Homicide Pact Machine. There is another hypothetical deterrent which, while not a Doomsday Machine, is still an "ultimate" of a sort. This could be called the Homicide Pact Machine, an attempt to make the failure of Type I Deterrence mean automatic *mutual* homicide. The adherents to this somewhat more practical device hope to divide the work of deterrence in a natural way—we poised to destroy the enemy and the enemy poised to destroy us, and neither of us buying any effective active or passive defenses for our respective societies.[9] The Homicide Pact Machine is clearly more satisfactory to both humanitarians and neutrals than the Doomsday Machine, and both should note the distinction. As far as patriots and nationalists are concerned, I believe that the Homicide Pact systems have many of the same drawbacks as the Doomsday Machine, though not in so extreme a form. The major advantage of the Homicide Pact is that one is not in the bizarre situation of being killed with one's own equipment; while intellectuals may not so distinguish, the policy makers and practical men prefer being killed by the other side rather than their own.

It is just because this view no longer strikes some people as bizarre that it is so dangerous. The Homicide Pact used to be, albeit only half-intentionally so, NATO policy and recently has come extremely close to being consciously adopted as official United States policy. It is not known to what extent the Soviets are planning to live up to "their part of the bargain" and move in the same direction. While Khrushchev's speech of January 14, 1960, indicated that Soviet decision makers have begun to accept some of the concepts of deterrence which have so persuasively swept the West since the mid-fifties, there is no indication that this acceptance will lead to a relaxation of current Soviet attempts to attain a capability of fighting and surviving wars as well as of deterring them. The opposite may be true. The main point of the speech was not that the Soviets were disarming, but rather that, by cutting back on conventional capabilities, they would gain in their capability to fight a modern thermonuclear war. Whether this is the somewhat misleading "more bang for the buck" program we once followed or a serious attempt to be prepared for any eventuality, only time or Khrushchev can tell.

THE ARMS RACE ITSELF

In discussing the Doomsday Machine as a weapons system, including computer and sensors, I have ben dealing with a somewhat romanticized and (one hopes) very remote possibility. I have spent so much time on it partly to highlight and satirize some current strategic notions (e.g., some extreme forms of Finite Deterrence). For this reason, much of the section on "hypothetical ultimates" has been cast in a "reassuring" tone; but the mere fact that one feels it necessary to discuss soberly the use and construction of Doomsday Machines indicates in the most dramatic manner that the current arms race has changed in character from previous arms races. The issues are bigger and may eventually come to the stage of Doomsday Machines or close approximations of these devices. While this possibility now seems rather remote, if the event should ever transpire, it would of course constitute *the problem* of the twentieth century. However, one does not have to allude to the Doomsday Machine to be concerned about the arms race and current capabilities. Our normal military forces are frightening enough, and they are improving rapidly (though in some ways the newer systems—Polaris and Minuteman—are less destructive than the old ones).* The most spectacular thing about the arms race is that it *is* a race, and one that is being run with some celerity.

This is also a new thing. There has been some tendency in the past for the military to exploit the products of civilian research and development, but this attempt has been remarkably lackadaisical. There has been even less research and development done specifically for war. (The common belief that the search for improved weapons has been a major source of technological progress seems to be grossly exaggerated, at least for periods of peace, though long wars such as the American Civil War and World Wars I and II did see technological advances spurred on by the requirements of the war.) Previously, really big wars have tended to occur twenty and thirty or more years apart, and there has been a tendency for each war to start where the last one left off or even with more ancient techniques.

Even so, each war has brought startling and unexpected surprises. (For example, the development of the most characteristic feature of World War I, the long line of trenches stretching from the Alps to the English Channel, seems to have been considered by only one writer, Jean de Bloch, and though widely read, he had no impact on military planning.) Now, for the first time in history, we are having a complete technological revolution in the art of war approximately every five years. As a result, we are now three technological revolutions away from World War II. Any attempts to apply the concepts and rules of common sense derived from that experience run the grave risk of being as outmoded as some American Civil War concepts would have been in World War II. In so far as we are trying to plan for the late 'sixties and early 'seventies, we are projecting into an environment which is two or three revolutions ahead of where we are today. An examination of the development of military doctrine in the postwar years, in both the official agencies and the *avant garde,* indicates that the possibility of great success in such planning is not high. While doctrine has evolved with meteoric speed as contrasted with the rates before World War II, it has been hopelessly behind events rather than successful in anticipating the future. I will not try to describe this process in any detail, though I would like to describe the technological revolutions, so as to emphasize the difficulties both we and the Soviets have in understanding and coping with just the military environment in our search for security.

* This is because of weight restrictions on the warheads for these missiles, not because of humanitarian considerations.—ED.

The Technology of 1951. Let us start with the situation in 1951, a convenient date to mark the first peacetime revolution. What follows is a very partial list of the new possibilities (with particular reference to the United States and air warfare) that the military planner (or arms controller) of 1945 would have had to anticipate by 1951: third- or fourth-generation fission bombs; the B-50 and B-36, forming the backbone of the United States SAC; the initial production of the B-47; the first flight of the XB-52; a manual air defense system started; air defense having F-80, F-84, F-86, F-94; production order for Nike A; experimental aerial refueling; a nuclear-powered airplane under development; many organizations, in and out of government, formed to institutionalize innovations in air warfare and to rationalize research, development, procurement, and operation; the Russians possessing TU-4 and MIG-15, and having tested three nuclear weapons.

I will discuss only a few items on the above list and on other lists to be given later, but the whole list will remind us of the complexity and speed of the arms race.

The most pressing questions involve the impact of fission bombs. These devices had had a very vigorous development program, and in 1951 we had third- or fourth-generation models available. Would their use have been decisive or not? The Soviets did not think so: they talked smugly of the "permanently operating factors" and the impracticability of blitz-krieg tactics. Many Americans, particularly the advocates of air power, tended to think that nuclear weapons would be decisive, but we had not bothered to get as many bombs as we could or (from the strictly military point of view) should have. Of course, the Soviets had gone into a vigorous development and procurement program for nuclear weapons. But they did not seem to have made any preparations specifically designed to meet the threats that nuclear weapons pose, though they had done a great deal to meet conventional threats typical of World War II.

In 1951 there was still much talk of the scarcity of uranium, a view which was reinforced by most of the technical people. Few people in or out of government thought of the atom bomb as soon being plentiful; nobody realized that practical and convenient thermonuclear bombs would be available before long. But a few people with high security clearances knew that some work on a rather impractical thermonuclear device was going forward. Though there was some discussion in 1951 about "baby atom bombs" with about the same power as the Hiroshima and Nagasaki bombs but much smaller in both weight and size, not even the experts had any idea of the flexibility, efficiency, and economy soon to be available in the atomic weapons arsenal.

Almost all 1951 discussions of defense against nuclear weapons assumed that the bombs were too precious to be used on anything but important cities or the most valuable production targets, such as Oak Ridge and Hanford. Similarly, NATO planned on the assumption that nuclear weapons would not be generally available for the European theatre except for very special and very high priority targets. However, a few economists were already pointing out that since there was a large disparity between the value of uranium and the marginal cost of production, there was every reason to imagine that much more uranium could and would be produced. There was even some reason to suppose that this large increase in production would be roughly at current prices. Most of the military, the scientists, and the engineers did not think that way.

This overvaluation of bombs as being too precious to use on military targets affected defense planning in our Zone of the Interior. Because of the threat of Soviet attacks, the Air Defense Command and the associated Army Anti-Aircraft Command was set up in Colorado Springs in 1951, but they thought of their highest priority job as the defense of large cities and nuclear facilities; the initial deployment of their facilities (radars and fighters) almost ignored warning and defense for SAC in the event of a surprise attack directed at SAC and not at the cities.

In spite of the emphasis on short wars it was not until 1948 that we seriously started to mold SAC into an ever-ready instrument of war. (The accession of General Curtis LeMay to the command of SAC and the Berlin Blockade apparently played the main roles.) We had not quite finished the process by 1951. Neither had we accepted the implications of the Soviets' testing of an atom bomb. For example, the official point of view (to be reflected soon in the investment of some 11 billion dollars in war reserve tools and raw materials), as opposed to that of the air-power enthusiasts, held that an all-out war of the mid-1950's would be long—from three to five years—even though initiated with atomic weapons.

While it is easy to show that most of these planners had not thought about the problem and were just reacting in a World War II fashion, given the official asumptions as to the scarcity of bombs, they may well have been right about the length of the war. Nobody could show just by physics and engineering that a small number of fission bombs dropped on Russia would in fact have caused them to sue for peace. In fact, one could almost have shown the opposite: that the Russians accepted much more damage in World War II and continued to fight, so that unless such imponderables as the psychological and disorganizing impact of using even a small number of bombs were great, a long war would have been possible.

One thing was almost always completely overlooked in 1951: the possibility that war could have broken out under such circumstances that the United States might not have succeeded in using very many bombs. We had only a small number of SAC bases (18 in 1950,[10] including some strategic fighter bases that did not pose a serious threat to the Soviets) and no organized warning system worthy of the name. (There was not even a Ground Observer Corps, for this organization dates only from July 14, 1952.) Furthermore, under normal conditions, SAC operated unalerted and would have taken some hours before it could get its planes into the air just to evacuate—even longer before the airplanes could have been prepared to go on a mission. Under these circumstances, just a handful of Russian planes carrying a very small number of atom bombs might well have been able to wipe out a large segment, possibly approaching 100 percent, of our strategic military power in a few hours. (I use the term "few hours" deliberately. The Russians needed no superb coordination or piloting to do this task. They simply had to be able to fly from one point to another point, more or less on a Great Circle route.)

In some ways the lack of concern in 1951 for the ground vulnerability of bombers was surprising. Many people had written or lectured about the importance of our having a secure and invulnerable SAC. Furthermore, it was part of both Douhet * and Air Force doctrine that war in the air is decided by the destruction of the enemy air force on the ground. Last, less than a decade had passed since the "bolt out of the blue" at Pearl Harbor. Nevertheless, there was a real doctrinal lag, which by the mid-fifties was just being made up. It is rather interesting that it was the advent of the ICBM, rather than the fact that the Soviets had acquired a strategic bombing force, that persuaded most people to think the vulnerability problem through and learn to distinguish between First Strike (attack) and Second Strike (retaliatory) forces. As long as the problem had any subtlety at all, most people managed to ignore it. One wonders what subtle doctrinal lags exist today.

It was quite true in 1951 that even though the Russians had the basic equipment they needed—the bomb, and a plane which when refueled could reach its target—they probably had neither the tactical knowledge, the operational capability, nor the strategic doctrine which would have enabled them to launch such an attack out of the blue. In fact, given their strange lack of emphasis on aerial refueling (an absolute must for any Soviet war planner devising an attack on the United States), one could have argued that the Soviets were basically planning to refight World War II, and, for example, had built hundreds of submarines to stop convoys of the type of World War II.

In addition, Stalin and his military advisers seem to have been reasonably, if not excessively, cautious. They were willing to fill power vacuums and press relentlessly, but not too aggressively. They were willing to take small but not large risks. There is even evidence that they tried to restrain the Yugoslav, Greek, Indochinese, and Chinese Communists from being too provocative.

However, it also seems likely that Stalin's caution did not stem from fear of the atomic bomb as a decisive weapon. What alarmed him about the United States was Detroit—not SAC. He appears to have been convinced that no sensible government should tangle with a nation that had a gross national product of 350 billion dollars a year. We had both assets, the

---

* Douhet was an Italian strategist who developed in the 1920's much of the air-power strategy later used in World War II. See Bernard Brodie, *Strategy in the Missile Age,* Princeton University Press, 1959.—ED.

bomb and the GNP, so that any difference between the point of view of the United States and the Soviet Union was not crucial.

It should be quite clear, even from the superficial discussion above, that any arms-control system set up in 1951 might easily have been based on some serious misunderstandings of the implications of the technology then current, and on even more serious misunderstandings of the future. In particular, some kinds of inspection schemes might have resulted in making our vulnerabilities both crystal clear and very tempting to Stalin or some of his military advisers. Even to force the Soviets to go through the intellectual exercise of thinking these problems through might have been dangerous. Before we could have safely started discussion of "the control of surprise attack," we would have had to fill in the gaps in our defense posture—that is, engage in a limited rearmament program.

The Technology of 1956. Let us now look at the technology of 1956. It included such factors as: third-generation thermonuclear bombs; three nuclear powers; the last B-47E produced; B-52 and KC-135 being phased into SAC; B-36 being phased out (the last B-36J was produced in August 1954); B-52D in production; B-58, Snark, and XP6M-1 (Martin Seamaster) flying; Regulus I, Nike-Hercules, and Falcon missiles in service; Atlas, Titan, and Thor in crash programs; many other missile programs in progress; Century Series of fighters (F-100 to F-104) being phased into the Air Defense Command; the DEW line being built; MB-1 (nuclear warhead for air-to-air rockets) being tested; production order for Missile Master and SAGE; classified intelligence projects such as the U-2, Turkish Radar, etc.; an atomic-powered plane and rocket under development; an atomic-powered submarine launched; research and development becoming the major business of the aircraft industry, and procurement becoming secondary; the Russians having the Badgers, Bears, Bisons, IRBM's, and their own models of H-bombs.

The most startling change was the development and perfection of thermonuclear bombs. Probably this introduced a more radical change into the technology of war than the introduction of the atom bomb did. The difference between megaton and kiloton is very large, in some ways relatively larger than the difference between kiloton and ton.

The effect of the innovation shows up in the nature of the questions one tends to ask. For kiloton bombs, one asks how much is destroyed—but, barring an extreme course of military events, no one doubts the the nation will continue in some form. With multimegaton weapons, the question of the continuation of the nation (to some, of civilization) is raised even in the shortest of wars. Megaton weapons are comparable to gross forces of nature such as earthquakes, hurricanes, etc. The prospective effects of the use of such weapons are not only extremely widespread, they are also occasionally very subtle and hard to predict. As a result, for the first time in the history of war we have what might be called *the problem of the post-attack environment.* Partly because of one of these environmental effects (fall-out), and partly because we had not thought about or prepared for nonmilitary defense including recuperation, it is most unlikely that the United States really possessed in 1956 and later years much objective Type II Deterrence. But nobody knew it, so we did not suffer any disastrous losses in 1956. However, the instability of such psychological capabilities began to show up even before the next technological revolution in 1961.

Let us look at this notion of post-attack environment in more detail. Multimegaton bombs are so powerful that even if they do not destroy a system, they may damage it by some subtle effects or so change the environment that the system will be temporarily inoperable. The various effects of nuclear weapons include blast, thermal and electromagnetic radiation, ground shock, debris, dust, and ionization—any of which may affect people, equipment, the propagation of electromagnetic signals, etc.

It is quite possible that some of our current systems may have important hidden defects that will only be disclosed by an attack. In the last few years I have worked on several weapon systems in which new weapon effects or new interpretations of old weapon effects were found that had not been thoroughly allowed for and which could have been disastrous. I therefore find it hard to believe that we have uncovered all of the problems from which our systems may suffer. An extreme dependence on such theoretical investigations as a substitute for (unobtainable) experience can be dangerous. For example, imagine that our total posture has ten serious weaknesses in it, but by dint of hard work and much investigation we discover nine out of ten of the weaknesses and correct them. Imagine also that the enemy is trying to find these same weaknesses and succeeds in finding nine of them. Unless the overlap is complete and we have found exactly the same weaknesses, then the enemy has discovered a weakness which he can exploit. If the processes involved were purely random, there would be a 90 percent probability that the enemy had found the one weakness we failed to correct. In practice, the situation should not be that bad: the weakness that was hard for us to find is probably just as hard for the enemy to find. But even if the enemy does not find some weakness that he deliberately exploits, it is not at all clear that we will be able to predict the post-attack environment in enough detail to be able to take into account adequately all of the phenomena that will occur.

Technological Advances by 1961. Let us now glance at some of the technology we shall be facing in 1961: arms control (techniques and capabilities); satellites, such as Tiros, Transit, Notus, Discoverer, Pioneer, Mercury; soft Atlas and soft IRBM's deployed; 25-psi Atlas, 100-psi Titan, and Polaris being phased in; several guidance "breakthroughs"; a crash program on Minuteman and other second-generation missiles; B-47E, B-52H, B-58 forming the bulk of SAC; BMEWS being phased in; Goose, Navajo, Regulus II, Seamaster, etc., canceled; SAC operating alert and dispersed; inexpensive, efficient, and versatile bombs; four nuclear countries; SAGE and Missile Master partially deployed; Bomarc A and Hawk being phased in; Nike-Hercules, F-100, 101, 102, and 104 in service; limited Civil Defense (?); X-15 test vehicle; a nuclear-powered plane and rocket still under development; experimental nuclear explosives; the Russians having . . . ?

The year 1961 will find arms control having some influence on our military posture. On October 31, 1958, the United States suspended the testing of nuclear weapons, and 1961 is likely to be the third year of no weapon-development testing on the part of the United States. Thus, 1961 should be the third year of an uninspected moratorium, and, in addition to all the other uncertainties of a United States military planner, there will be such questions as, "Are the Soviets cheating? If so, to what extent? And what is the military significance?" Even if a treaty were to be signed by the time this book is published it will take a period of from two to five years to install and proof-test whatever inspection network is agreed upon.

The test-suspension negotiations at Geneva illustrate the importance of doing our homework. In July and August of 1958, the Western and Eastern experts at Geneva agreed, after a short hectic conference (at which most of the technical facts were worked out in late evening sessions) that about 180 stations around the world (about 21 in the Soviet Union) would suffice to pick up illegal explosions greater than 5 kilotons in yield. Within months, on the basis of new data and experiments, the Western experts decided they had been off by at least a factor of four. A few months later, several ingenious schemes (testing in big holes or outer space) were worked out to evade the proposed inspection system almost completely, as far as tests of the kiloton type were concerned.

From the viewpoint of arms control, one of the most dangerous innovations of 1961 is the possibility of the experimental use of nuclear explosives in one or more peacetime applications. In May 1959 the Atomic Energy Commission sponsored the Second Plowshare Symposium on the Industrial and Scientific Uses of Nuclear Explosions. At an earlier symposium there had been much interest in the subject, but nobody expected anything to happen very soon. By the second one, many of the ideas had had time to mature. There were about fifty papers presented at the symposium on various aspects of nuclear explosives. The suggestions for peaceful uses of nuclear explosives included: artificial harbors, sea-level ship canals, underground oil storage, power, isotope production, geothermal steam plants, salt water distillation, improvement of underground water supplies, mining, shale oil production, meteorological experiments, and other scientific experiments.

The length of the above list should not surprise the reader. Nuclear explosives are a uniquely concentrated but very simple and relatively cheap source of power, heat, and pressure, as well as of neutrons and other radiation. Once they become even slightly available, many people will look for and find applications for these new devices, which in turn will make them even more available. In fact, the terms on which they are available at this writing were spelled out by the AEC at the Second Plow-share Symposium as follows: roughly a half million dollars will buy explosives in the low kiloton region, and perhaps a million dollars will buy them in the low megaton region. The AEC is careful to note that the above charges are for small quantities.

Very few people at the 1959 symposium would have accepted even odds that a number of the ideas discussed would not be in programs by 1961. In particular, a project to dig an artificial harbor in Alaska is definitely programed at this writing. Since some of the individual projects promised to use hundreds or even thousands of bombs, it is not impossible that even a private international market of buyers and sellers of nuclear explosives could eventually spring up. This last is particularly likely if there is technological progress in the design of very simple bombs made of readily available materials. Once there develops a legitimate market for nuclear explosives, then in the absence of controls many nations will manufacture them for sale or peaceful use, if not by 1970, then by 1980. However, unless one of these nations is very irresponsible, there should be a fair degree of voluntary control over the distribution of these devices.

I will discuss later some of the problems that might arise as a result of the possible dissemination of nuclear weapons. I should point out that at the present writing, however, it is rather unlikely that nuclear explosives will be as successful as I have indicated they might be. As Lewis Bohn has pointed out to me, the above discussion mirrors almost exactly the early (incorrect) postwar expectations on the speed of development of nuclear reactors and the consequent strategic and control problems. Much of the Baruch Plan for the control of nuclear weapons was preoccupied with this much overestimated problem.

I believe that a much better economic and technical case can be made for the use of nuclear explosives than could be made for the early postwar reactors. In addition, there is a much smaller distance between a nuclear explosive and a bomb than between a reactor and a bomb. In the first case, the distinction is often a semantic one; in the second case, one may need a major chemical industry. I therefore believe that if nuclear explosives do not present a problem, it is likely to be because of legal, social, and political obstacles to this development rather than technical and economic ones. This is one place where the pursuit of a higher standard of living for all may result in a drastic reduction.

The Mid-1960's. We have just been looking somewhat superficially at the early 'sixties. I would like to give only a bare listing of the possibilities of the mid-sixties, labeled 1965 for the sake of definiteness. (The reason there are only four years between this technological revolution and the last—I had been using five years between these revolutions—is that technological innovation seems to be even faster today. We are spending more money on research and development, and getting more skillful in its management.) By 1965, then, we would expect to have some of the following:

independent nuclear deterrents; Minuteman B and Polaris C; second-generation Atlas and Titan; Dynasoar; BMEWS-B, Midas, and SAMOS; protected B-52G and H, B-47E, B-58A and B; the limits of bomb technology (if testing is continued); commercial nuclear explosives; an airborne ballistic missile; super-guidance; SAGE B, Bomarc B and C, Nike-Zeus A and B, Hawk B, F-108, B-70 technologically possible, but perhaps canceled; antiradiation drugs; protected command and control; exotic fuels and propellants; an inexpensive reliable research missile; inexpensive satellites; a nuclear-powered airplane(?) or rocket (?); experimental climate control; bacteriological and chemical warfare; and astronauts.

The 1970's. Rather than comment on any of the above, I would like to deal with some of the possibilities for the late 'sixties and early 'seventies, which I will label 1969. We now have to take into account more than just the extrapolation of current technology. We have to consider the possibility of "breakthroughs" and other surprises. Although it is not possible to limit or describe in advance what breakthroughs might occur, it is possible to discuss some projects currently being studied which might be called breakthroughs, if successful. This method of trying to estimate the total impact of technological progress is likely to involve some large underestimates of the total change, since one can almost guarantee that many startling and unexpected developments will occur. I will try to make up for this by some judicious exaggeration in the areas to be discussed, for such an exaggeration will give a better "feel" for the over-all possibilities for the late 'sixties or early 'seventies than a more sober discussion of the few items I will consider: cheap, simple bombs; cheap, simple missiles; cheap satellites; controlled thermonuclear reaction; other sources of cheap neutrons; other sources of nuclear fuels; californium bullets; ground-effect machines; reliable sensors; super-calculators; cheap calories; medical progress; advanced materials; cheap, fast transportation (for limited wars); reliable command and control; Doomsday Machines; and disguised warfare.

When we enter the 1970's, the most advanced nations at least will know in theory how to make simple bombs and missiles, and in the absence of explicit or implicit controls will be making them in practice. For this reason, I have put cheap simple bombs and cheap simple missiles at the top of the list because, even with arms control, and certainly without it, these are likely to be the most characteristic features of the late 1960 or the early 1970 period. They may or may not present the most important (and dramatic) problem. This will depend on which nations actually have weapons in their stockpiles, on the explicit and implicit controls, and on the state of international relations.

Under the current programs, 1969 may be a little early for the diffusion of these devices to other than "advanced" nations. It is very difficult to predict the rate at which the technology, materials, and information will be disseminated. Even without explicit controls, it might be the mid-1970's or even a later period before they become cheap and simple for the majority of "developed" nations. But there are many things that could accelerate this dissemination process: the use of nuclear weapons in a limited war; successful programs for the peaceful uses of nuclear explosives in the mid-1960's might at least make nuclear "devices" widely available; the deliberate diffusion of nuclear technology, by either the United States or the Soviet Union, to enough allies so that there will be no more secrets; a breakthrough in technology or materials, etc.

As an example of this last possibility, consider the fusion reactor. It is improbable that this device will be practical by 1969; most experts in this field are somewhat doubtful about any real success before the year 2000. Let us, however, go ahead and outrage the experts by assuming not a qualified, but an outstanding success—such a success that even relatively primitive nations will find it possible either to build or buy a fusion reactor and thereby to acquire a virtually unlimited source of cheap power. This spectacular gift of technology has a significant side effect: it gives off neutrons very copiously, so copiously that it may not be exaggerating to state that the neutrons are for all practical purposes free.

Free neutrons would mean that many kinds of nuclear fuels would be very cheap. With these nuclear fuels and with the kind of technology that is likely to be available in 1969, it may literally turn out that a trained and technically minded person, even one who is a member of a relatively primitive society, would be able to make or obtain bombs. This would raise forcefully the question of the illegal or uncontrolled dissemination of bombs. (One can today buy machine guns, artillery, tanks, and fighter aircraft on the gray market.) Thus the 1969 equivalent of the Malayan guerrillas or the Algerian rebels or the Puerto Rican nationalists, or even less official groups such as gangsters and wealthy dilettantes, might be able to obtain such bombs.

Even if the controlled thermonuclear reaction does not prove to be a success by 1969, there are other possibilities for the cheap production of neutrons. For example, many of the commercial uses of nuclear devices would release neutrons as a by-product. This might lead to either the clandestine or open production of weapon-grade nuclear fuels. There are also possibilities that simple and inexpensive methods for producing weapon-grade nuclear fuels will be developed. It is also possible that we and others will learn how to make bombs using only or mostly materials already widely available, such as deuterium and lithium. (The widely discussed small "clean" bomb would probably use such materials.) In a word, 1969 (though more likely 1979) may see the introduction of the era of the conventional nuclear bomb in which (in the absence of adequate controls) any "legitimate" nation can get some models, and some illegitimate groups or governments may also get access to nuclear weapons, but presumably under more onerous conditions than those to which legitimate purchasers are subject.

Consequences of the Spread of Weapons. We may be too frightened of the possible consequences of the widespread diffusion of weapons. It is quite clear that if one gave the Egyptians and Israelis atomic weapons, one is likely to find both nations acting much more cautiously than they do today, simply because the consequences of "irresponsibility" would be much more disastrous. On the other hand, even a greatly increased sense of responsibility may only mean that, instead of falling upon each other the week after they come into possession of these weapons, the attack may be deferred for a year or two.

In fact, almost any sober analysis indicates that it is somewhat harder for "Nth" countries to cause a cataclysm than is often believed.[11] It is difficult to imagine that China or France, for example, could in the next decade obtain a large enough strategic force to strain United States Type I Deterrence seriously, although the situation in the 1970's and 1980's could become much more difficult. It is even difficult to imagine one of these nations being able to start an accidental war, if the Soviets and the United States have made sensible plans to prevent this eventuality, and it is a little difficult to understand why they would want to start one, unless they were in some kind of a crisis which would be helped by such an action. In this last case, the Soviets and the United States would be likely to be on their guard.

All of the above may be true. Even though it is going to be difficult to get nations to make the necessary concessions until the dangers are both more apparent and more pressing than they are today, nevertheless, I believe that we should still try to make international arrangements *before* the weapons have been distributed, rather than *afterward*. While it is quite possible that many laymen overestimate the immediate impact that the widespread dispersion of weapons will have, I strongly suspect that the "sober" analysts underestimate both the immediate and long-term problems. I will list ten such problems here. It would not be difficult to list many more.

In a nuclear world, the "small" powers, vis-à-vis one another, would have: greater opportunities for blackmail and mischief-making; greater likelihood of an accidental triggering of weapons; an increased possibility of a "local" Munich, a Pearl Harbor, and blitzkriegs; pressures to pre-emption because of the preceding three items; a tendency to neglect conventional capabilities because of an overreliance on nuclear capabilities; internal (civil war, a *coup d'état*, irresponsibility, etc.) and external (the arms race, fear of fear, etc.) political problems.

Nuclear diffusion to small powers would also: create a situation in which the diffusion of nuclear weapons to irresponsible or criminal organizations and individuals is facilitated; complicate future problems of control by making such control involve the small powers' having to accept an obvious reduction in their sovereignty (that is, they would give up something, rather than abstain); give the Soviet Union or another large power many opportunities to act as agent-provocateur; and create the capability, and therefore the pressure, for many nations to make a crisis serious or to exploit an ongoing crisis (such as by catalytic war or escalation).

In short, the diffusion of nuclear weapons may or may not increase the number of crises, but it will almost undoubtedly tend to increase the seriousness and the grim potentialities of any crisis or even the misunderstandings that do occur, besides increasing enormously the importance of having responsible and competent governments everywhere.

The widespread possession of nuclear weapons and delivery systems strikes many observers as similar to situations in physics that may be described as semi-stable equilibrium. For example, imagine a ball balanced on top of a small cup so that small movements of the ball can be tolerated, but not large ones. If this ball on the cup is isolated, it might sit there on top of its cup forever, but if it is submitted to the vagaries and chances of a sufficiently uncontrolled environment, one can guarantee that sooner or later it will fall. This may be true even though every "reasonable" analysis of the situation that looks at probable or plausible disturbances showed that the forces were in close enough balance so the ball should stay where it is. It takes an improbable or implausible force to topple the ball. But some improbable and implausible events will occur and, barring a major change in the situation, almost certainly the ball will eventually fall. While the analogy may simultaneously be apt and yet misleading, many who have thought about this problem have come to the conclusion that reliable stability can only come through an international agency with an effective monopoly of force.

For many reasons, I do not believe that the twentieth century will see a disarmed world, but it may see a world government or the equivalent.[12] Until that day arrives, it will be of great value to try to keep, indeed *make,* the problem of national security intellectually and diplomatically simple, and the diffusion of nuclear weapons would seem to go exactly the wrong way. The "two-power" case seems both intellectually and practically more controllable than the "N-power" case. The diffusion of nuclear weapons not only complicates the over-all "analytic" problem, but the stakes at risk if events go badly would seem to be less in the "two-power" than in the "N-power" case.

CONCLUSION

In this chapter I have scarcely been able to touch upon the complexities of the technological arms race and the stability of the United States–Soviet balance of terror. I have tried to point out that technological progress is so rapid that there are almost bound to be doctrinal lags. These doctrinal lags will in themselves be dangerous, leading to important gaps in our preparations, the waste of badly needed resources on obsolete concepts, the neglect of possible strengths, the excessive use of especially glamorous tools, and, possibly most important of all, heightened possibilities of serious miscalculations or accidents because we have not had time to understand and make provisions for the requirements of the newly installed systems. To the extent that arms-control measures are supposed to alleviate dangers or costs by allowing the current "balance of power" status and military competition to be conducted, by agreement, at cheaper or safer levels, or to the extent that one hopes to increase each state's objective capability of preventing surprise attack or other disaster, this inability to understand "the military problems" introduces almost intolerable complications. (The reason for the adverb "almost" is that we have these complications, whether or not we have arms control.) I have almost ignored the even more complex problem of the conduct of international relations in a world in which force is becoming both increasingly more available and increasingly less usable, a problem that is complicated by the spectacular increase in the number of sovereign nations, by increased nationalism, militarism, and "ambitions" in these new nations and governments, and by the revolution of rising expectations.

Any attempts to control the arms race must be able to live with all the stresses and strains that the above problems will create. It is most unlikely that all of these problems will be solved in an atmosphere of good will and common fellowship, or by the use of *ad hoc* committees and intuitive judgments derived from experience in almost irrelevant situations. And we may not have much time in which to work.

6. The Feasibility of Arms Control and the Principle of Openness

EDWARD TELLER

THE ISSUE OF PEACE IS RIGHTLY UPPERMOST IN THE MINDS OF OUR generation. Those of us who have participated in the invention of modern means of destruction feel a special desire to contribute toward peace as best we can. In the popular mind peace and arms control are closely linked. It is clear, however, that disarmament is desirable only to the extent to which it will promote peace.

THE RELATION BETWEEN ARMS CONTROL AND PEACE

Historically it would appear that the relation between arms control and peace is dubious. Most people believe that World War I was brought about by an arms race. There is good evidence to support this view. On the other hand, there can be little doubt that World War II was caused by an uncontrolled race for disarmament. The peace-loving nations disarmed; thereby they gave one lawless government a chance to bid for world domination. Historical analogies are not conclusive, but it seems to me that it is more valid to compare the present situation with the history of the 1930's rather than with the history of the early years of our century.

There are many well-known arguments both for and against arms control. Perhaps the strongest driving force toward arms control is the conviction that without it a world catastrophe of unimaginable magnitude cannot be prevented. It is hoped that an arms-control agreement can prevent the further spread of the knowledge of nuclear explosives. It is argued that arms control is in the interest of both the Russians and ourselves, and therefore we can come to an agreement. It is hoped that arms control will be a first step toward increasingly friendly relations and genuine cooperation between all people in the world.

On the other hand, arms control may well lead to a change in the balance of power with the result that the Russians could gain overwhelming superiority. This can happen by reducing those categories of arms in which we enjoy an advantage. Or else it may happen that the arms-control agreement cannot be enforced; it may then be observed only by our side but not by the Communists.

Finally, it may be urged that the regulations and the policing which will have to accompany arms control will give rise to suspicions and to friction. Thus arms control would become a source of irritation rather than a first step toward peace.

There is no doubt in my mind that human contacts between all people will promote the cause of peace. This is particularly true if these human contacts lead to positive and valuable accomplishments. Joint work on medical problems or on the exploration of our globe and the oceans of air and water are cases in point.

On the other hand, it is undeniable that disarmament may lead to frustration, friction, and failure. Therefore, there is at least some doubt whether or not arms control is the proper first step in creating a peaceful atmosphere.

A THIRD WORLD WAR

That a third world war would be catastrophic cannot be questioned. Some people have argued that it is better to surrender than to risk the dangers of such a war. This point of view cannot be attacked on the basis of logic. But, in viewing it, it is relevant to reflect how catastrophic a third world war may in fact be.

Extremely little thinking has gone into the question of passive defense against an atomic attack. I believe that an extensive shelter program would save the great majority of the people in the United States even in case of a most ferocious attack. It is certain that such an attack would wipe out our industries, but past experience as well as some research on the question of possible reconstruction have shown that the United States could recover from an all-out attack in a small number of years. This, of course, could be done only if we prepare properly. It is estimated that forty billion dollars, which is equal to one year's military expenditure, could go a long way toward insuring the survival of our nation. Twice that amount would make our passive defense satisfactory. Unfortunately, we are now spending for passive defense an amount which is approximately one-thousandth of our military expenditure.

It is, of course, of paramount importance to avoid the great suffering that a third world war would cause. But it does not seem proper to state that there are no alternatives to surrender. Arms control is justified only in so far as it decreases the probability of war without creating a situation in which surrender will become inevitable.

THE SPREAD OF NUCLEAR WEAPONS

A short time ago we were worried about the fourth-nation problem. We are now faced with the fifth-nation problem. How long or how short a time will it be before this turns into the sixth- or seventh-nation problem? It has been claimed that the cessation of nuclear testing is the only hope we have for limiting the number of nuclear powers. I wonder whether this hope is realistic.

We like to believe that to produce nuclear weapons requires great skill. We imagine that there is a secret of nuclear weapons which we can continue to guard. The fact is that every nation which obtained a sufficient amount of nuclear explosive found out within a very short time how to make nuclear bombs. The really difficult step is the production of plutonium or some equivalent substance. After one has this substance, the rest is relatively easy.

Unfortunately, the production of nuclear explosives is closely connected with the peaceful use of nuclear reactors. We have powerfully assisted in the spread of the knowledge of nuclear reactors throughout the world. We were right in doing so. Otherwise, the world would have bypassed us. But in accepting the unavoidable we have handed to the nations of the world more than peaceful nuclear power. We have also handed them the key to the atomic bomb. This is unpleasant, but it is a fact.

A moratorium on testing is likely to delay the development of nuclear weapons by some nations. These are the nations which are law-abiding, in which the individual citizen has most rights, and in which the government is both unwilling and powerless to pursue secretly a development which the family of nations has outlawed. On the other hand, dictatorships may find it relatively easy to produce nuclear explosives. They may find it unnecessary to perform a test prior to usage or else they may be able to carry out their tests in secrecy. The results will place more power in the hands of dictators throughout the world. Establishing laws which cannot or will not be enforced favors the lawless element. A test ban may demonstrate the truth of this statement on a world-wide scale.

There is one circumstance which mitigates the danger from the spread of nuclear weapons. The next nations in good position to develop these weapons are our friends and allies. We could prevent the uncontrolled spread of nuclear arms by replacing it with a controlled sharing of our own knowledge and nuclear resources. If we did this, the incentive for independent development would disappear. At the same time we could coordinate to a much more complete extent research on defense problems within the free world. Soviet progress on rockets has shown how necessary it is for the free world to utilize its research and development facilities in the best possible manner.

Of course, the sharing of nuclear weapons with our allies will create difficult political problems. But perhaps it is not correct to say that new problems will be created. It might come closer to truth if we state that the sharing of nuclear weapons will make such problems which already exist more apparent. The interests of the free democracies are quite similar. In fact, the very survival of each of them is gravely endangered if any one of them is conquered. In a shrinking world it is increasingly urgent to link the democracies by a single supranational government. NATO is a first attempt in this direction. The sharing of nuclear explosives may well be the catalyst which will make the establishment of common institutions and common loyalties both necessary and possible.

In the long run it is impractical to limit the knowledge of nuclear weapons to the advanced democracies. The significant fact, however, is that we have some time in which to solve the urgent problem of atomic control among the democracies. Once this has been done, an example and a nucleus will have been created. On the basis of such a new experience in international cooperation we might then be in better position to find the proper way to share full knowledge of nuclear technology with additional nations.

The spread of knowledge is unavoidable. The only practical hope we can have is to find ways of directing and influencing a process which, in the long run, we shall be unable to prevent. If we fully realize that the difficulty is unavoidable, the difficulty itself may become a stimulus. The secret of the atomic bomb is vanishing. If we face this problem, we might make a great and necessary contribution toward constructing a better world.

THE QUESTION OF CONTROL

The crux of the test ban is the question of control. It is a long-standing and well-founded position of our government that disarmament must not be unilateral and that disarmament must be subject to reliable verification. To proceed otherwise would be to return to the disastrous mistakes of the 1930's.

At first it appeared that nuclear tests could be observed and policed with reasonable ease. The test ban can indeed serve as a good example of the potentialities of policing. Big nuclear shots can be heard around the world, if not by human ears, then at any rate by the big ears of appropriately constructed apparatus. Nuclear reactions also produce radioactivity. It is widely and incorrectly believed that this activity constitutes a serious danger. It is, however, quite true that the activity can be observed at great distances. Furthermore, a detailed investigation of the radioactivity will disclose the time at which the event took place.

In the summer of 1958 experts from the Soviet bloc and from several Western countries, including the United States and the United Kingdom, recommended a system of controls for atmospheric testing. With the help of a moderate number of stations distributed throughout the world and within each of the bigger countries and with the further help of appropriately planned airplane flights, nuclear tests can be policed down to a strength of one kiloton. Even smaller explosions might be noticed, and violators would have to count seriously on the possibility that their acts will be detected.

A similarly favorable technical situation was reported for testing in the oceans. The acoustic signals from underwater tests can be picked up with ease and it seems possible to pick up the radioactivity deposited in the water and thereby to verify that a nuclear explosion has been detonated.

Unfortunately, the observation of underground tests encounters much more serious difficulties. One is that the crust of the earth is a noisy medium. It is hard to distinguish nuclear explosions from the normal noise caused by major or minor earthquakes.

The second is that radioactivity from an underground test is confined to a distance of about one hundred feet or at best a few hundred feet from the explosion point. On the other hand, the uncertainty in locating the event amounts to several miles. To verify by inspection becomes difficult. In the end it boils down to an intelligence operation which must be aimed at tracing the preparations for the nuclear explosion and at finding the actual shafts through which the nuclear explosive had been put into position.

The final difficulty is that nuclear explosions can be muffled. If this is done, they will emit a greatly reduced seismic signal which is exceedingly hard to distinguish from quite minor disturbances in the earth's crust. With the simplest procedures it is possible to reduce the seismic signal by a factor of 300.

The present situation is best characterized by the fact that surveillance of muffled nuclear explosions above twenty kilotons will necessitate 600 seismic stations in the Soviet Union alone. (It is quite possible that many of these stations could be unmanned.) This would have to be accompanied by an extremely high number of on-the-spot inspections. Probably many inspections per day would be required.* The only way that has been proposed to re-establish effective control is to discover by intelligence operations the activities of preparing a site for muffled nuclear explosions. It happens that these preparations are not necessarily conspicuous. Therefore we are led back all along the line to a reliance on intelligence.

The hope that purely technical means will allow us to establish easy control of nuclear tests has not proved well-founded. Big nuclear explosions —above hundreds of thousands of tons of TNT equivalent—can be noticed and identified. Below one hundred kilotons detection of underground shots is dubious, and below twenty kilotons, the detection seems at present practically impossible.

The situation is no better for testing in interplanetary space. One can send out a rocket containing a nuclear warhead and also equipment for detection and communication. The rocket should be fired in such a way as to leave the gravitational field of the earth. After waiting until the rocket reaches a distance comparable to that between the earth and the sun, it

---

* The argument assumes that cavities in limestone can be constructed in a reasonably expeditious manner and that muffling is not limited by the occurrence of salt formations.

should be separated into a portion containing the explosive and another portion containing the rest of the equipment. These two portions should be allowed to drift apart to a distance of approximately ten miles. Then the bomb would explode and the package containing the apparatus would perform its function of observation and coded reporting.

It has been established through careful discussions that this type of operation is feasible. It has also been established that by using this method and by establishing appropriate procedures of concealment nuclear explosions up to the size of five hundred kilotons or half a megaton can be carried out without chance of detection. These discussions were based on optimistic assumptions concerning the background of radiation in space and therefore concerning the possibility of detection. It is entirely possible that even bigger explosions in space can be concealed. Therefore, nuclear explosions underground and in interplanetary space could be carried out up to a considerable size even if we assume that the best possible controls known today have been established.

There is one way in which nuclear explosions in interplanetary space could be policed in an adequate manner. One could establish a limited number of stations throughout the world which will reliably detect the firing of any outgoing space vehicle. It could then be agreed that every outgoing rocket would be inspected before it is fired. In this way we could be certain that no nuclear devices will leave the earth. Unfortunately, the Russians have rejected suggestions of this type. Therefore, the only plan of policing interplanetary tests which is feasible from a technical point of view is at present excluded because of the attitude of the Soviet government.

It is not obvious to me why this point has not been emphasized more strongly both in the Geneva discussions and in the American press. The on-site inspection of underground shots has developed into a crucial issue. Yet these inspections, even if they were granted in sufficient numbers, would turn out to be difficult and possibly futile. On the other hand, another big area of possible evasion could be adequately policed by a simple and straightforward method. It is this area in which Soviet technology is known to be ahead. Why do we focus our attention almost exclusively on the prevention of underground testing and neglect the parallel issue of testing in interplanetary space?

At the present time no world-wide system of control exists, and it will be several years before such a system could be put into effect. We could start constructing seismic stations in the United States, England, and Russia as soon as an agreement is signed. To establish the right kind of stations will be a lengthy job even in these three countries. However, it is clear that the inspection system will have to be extended to China, and this will take further time. Finally, if outgoing rockets are not inspected, the policing of interplanetary shots makes it necessary to establish an expensive and intricate system of well-equipped observational satellites. At present these satellites are not even designed.

Thus it is clear that several years must pass before any world-wide inspection system can be put into effect. In the meantime there is no objective evidence that the Russians have actually stopped nuclear tests. Underground tests up to one hundred kilotons and interplanetary tests of arbitrary size could have gone on and could continue to go on for several years without any possibility that such tests be detected by any of the physical methods of observation.

There always remains the possibility of Soviet nuclear tests' being discovered by our intelligence. We should remember, however, that the first Soviet atomic bomb test and the Soviet hydrogen bomb test were not predicted by our intelligence. It will not be easy for our intelligence observation to pit its strength against the secret police of the Soviet Union. Furthermore, it is most doubtful whether it will be possible to use intelligence data which are not clearly confirmed by physical organization in conjunction with the international inspection system. Even if we should find out by methods of espionage that the Russians are testing, it will be hard to convince other nations of our findings.

If we have to fall back on intelligence methods, one has to question why arms control should start with a nuclear test ban. Preparation for conventional war involves more people and could be more easily detected by intelligence operations. The proposal to begin with a test ban was based precisely on the argument that a test ban could be controlled by objective methods which do not require conventional intteligence. It seems that this particular argument did not stand up well under detailed scrutiny.

METHODS OF DETECTION

We have seen that detection of underground and interplanetary shots is difficult. The obvious answer is: Let us find better methods of detection. The total effort that has so far been expended on such detection systems has not been impressive. It is fair to estimate that in the United States approximately twenty million dollars had been spent on this subject through mid-1960. This is a small sum, particularly when one remembers how deeply the results of such investigations could affect our security.

At the same time any such investigation would yield interesting scientific results. Better detection and analysis of the natural movements of the earth's crust would be a most welcome addition to the knowledge of our planet. Satellites sent out to gather information about possible interplanetary explosions would necessarily have to investigate in detail all the various types of radiation which exist in interplanetary space. Quite recently a great and hitherto unknown zone of radiation was discovered: the Van Allen belt. The finer observations which nuclear detection requires will possibly lead to the discovery of other more or less similar phenomena and we shall learn about particles and electromagnetic waves which are present in space but from which our atmosphere is shielding us. If we set out to detect tests, we shall certainly gather scientific facts which in themselves will amply repay the efforts made.

At the same time it may turn out that continued investigation will not lead to an improvement of the detectability of tests. The main difficulty with test detection is not that our equipment is insensitive. The main difficulty is that the effects produced by the tests are small enough to disappear in the natural noise level. One can attack the troublesome question of discrimination but one cannot promise to succeed.

This is particularly true because it is not proper to consider the improvement of detection as an isolated issue. Together with such improvement we must consider methods of concealment. To do otherwise would be tantamount to the efforts of a person who practices playing chess while introducing the rule that Black must not move his pieces.

During the past two years methods of concealment have developed much faster than methods of seismic detection. Yet the amount of money spent on the methods of concealment was relatively small—three million dollars. The reason is that detection is closely related to seismology, which is relatively speaking an old art. Whatever progress could be obtained easily has already been achieved and is now available. On the other hand, the manipulation of nuclear explosions is a new experience. It is relatively easy to invent methods to reduce the effects of nuclear explosions or else to modify the characteristics of such explosions in a way which will make it more probable that man-made events will become confused with natural ones.

The most effective concealment to date was obtained by the simple expedient of placing an explosive in an underground cavity.

This method could be further perfected by placing in the cavity substances which can absorb the energy of the nuclear explosion without producing a corresponding pressure. Since it is the pressure that transforms the nuclear energy into earth motion, a reduction of this pressure will decrease the signal. It is entirely possible that the muffling factor can be increased from its present value of three hundred to a value of several thousand. This might be done without an increase of the size of the cavity needed. In fact, one might use this additional expedient to reduce the cavity's size. In this case one probably would not increase the decoupling but would instead make the execution of decoupling easier.

Another approach would be to wipe out the marks which distinguish an explosion from an earthquake. Generally speaking, an earthquake is a complicated and irregular event, whereas a nuclear explosion gives a simpler signal. Two or more explosions could be cleverly arranged in such a way as to produce a type of signal or signature which is not characteristic of a single nuclear explosion and appears more like a disturbance of the earthquake type. At the same time, simultaneous detonations could falsify the apparent position of the disturbance. Explosions set off twenty miles around a center would give signals which would indicate an event at the center. Thus inspection teams would go to the wrong place and could never find the radioactivity.

Recently we have discussed the possibility of a gentleman's agreement which will give us time to develop better methods of detection. We have argued that this gentleman's agreement should be of relatively short duration, such as one or two years. This was done because of the proper apprehension that a longer period would give the Russians a longer time for clandestine experimentation. This indeed would put us at a great disadvantage.

On the other hand, if we limit the gentleman's agreement to one or two years, we run into a different difficulty. Such a proposal will be accompanied in the public mind with the implicit promise that at the end of this period reasonably satisfactory methods of detection will be available. Such methods are not in sight. It is possible that eventually reliable methods of detection will be developed, but it is most likely that if this is at all possible it will take a period of the order of ten years. A gentleman's agreement of one or two years carries along with it a promise and a hope which is completely unrealistic.

All this does not mean that we should not try to improve methods of detection. We should indeed do so. We should spend a considerable sum —for instance, one hundred million dollars per year—on this enterprise. We should execute these experiments publicly and invite the cooperation of everyone who wishes to cooperate. But we should carry out this work on a broad basis including methods of both detection and concealment, and we should not permit that the detection program be hamstrung by the conditions and restrictions which the Russians are attempting to impose. There is so far no shred of evidence that the Russians are genuinely attempting to contribute to the art of detection.

FUTURE DEVELOPMENT OF NUCLEAR WEAPONS

An agreement to discontinue nuclear tests will not hamper work in the Soviet Union. The Russians can violate a treaty in secrecy and with certainty that the violation will not be discovered. This holds even if they perform extended series of nuclear tests. The only question is whether they choose to do so.

Our own situation is rather different. If there is an agreement to stop testing, we shall abide by that agreement. For reasons both moral and practical it is impossible for us to engage in organized cheating.

It would appear most relevant to state in what way the Russians might gain by additional tests. Unfortunately, such a statement requires a detailed knowledge of Soviet military planning. This we do not possess. It is also interesting and relevant to discuss in what manner the United States could benefit from a resumption of the testing operations. We can answer this very much more fully. Apart from the inherent interest of this question, it may also throw some light—by the way of analogy—on the possible advantage which the Russians may derive from further test operations. Progress on their side might be directed toward different goals. These goals could be as significant, however, as are those connected with American developments. Therefore, the following discussion has a double purpose. It demonstrates concretely the advantage we can derive from continued testing. It also demonstrates by way of analogy that the Russians could make decisive one-sided progress if we agreed to an unenforceable test ban.

It will help in a minor way to clarify our ideas if we recognize that the expression "nuclear testing" is a misnomer. The idea of a test is to check a device whose functioning you already know rather accurately. You may test a car and find out whether it gives 23 or 25 miles per gallon.

In the program of developing nuclear explosives, we are not concerned with tests of this type. Each nuclear explosion is, in fact, an experiment whose outcome is very much in doubt. Sometimes the explosive performs much better than we expect. On other occasions the performance is disappointing; sometimes it is a fizzle. We have learned at least as much from the failures as from the successes. The experiment would not be worthwhile if we knew the outcome in advance.

The aim of this experimentation with nuclear explosives is a continued and rapid advance. This advance actually has been both impressive and continuous. It has produced its important results not by unexpected jumps but by steady and rapid improvement based on ever increasing understanding. Each of the experiments has been in fact accompanied by complex and intricate measurements which have allowed us to find out not only the energy released in the explosion but the particular way in which each portion of the apparatus functioned.

The picture which has been created in the popular mind is quite different from this. It is believed that in 1945 we found the secret of the atom bomb; in the early 1950's we developed the hydrogen bomb; and this ends the story. It is important to emphasize that this picture is false. In fact, each year has added its discoveries, and it is the cumulative results which have produced the present situation. It is accurate to state that, in comparison with the nuclear weapons of 1960, those of 1950 appear completely obsolete. If the development should continue, there is no doubt that in 1970 nuclear explosives can be produced compared to which our present weapons will appear similarly outdated.

Most people believe that any such further development in nuclear weapons is of no importance. It is the general opinion that we have reached a state of saturation. We have enough weapons to destroy the world. Why should we want more? Indeed, we do have enough weapons to destroy the world if we strike the first blow. But this we do not intend to do. In fact, we should make very sure that we shall never do this nor be tempted to do it. If, on the other hand, our nuclear weapons are to survive a Soviet attack and be available for retaliation, then it is questionable whether we have the right kind of weapons to perform this task. Similarly, if nuclear weapons are to be developed into discriminating instruments of tactical warfare, much remains to be done.

The idea of massive retaliation is impractical and immoral. It has caused considerable damage to our position in the world. We have announced that an infraction of the peace, even if were not a major infraction, might give us cause to strike back at Russia with devastating weapons. Such an action, which responds to evil with much greater evil, is contrary to our sense of justice. We did not put this policy into execution. I doubt whether we ever seriously intended to do so. Today we know that an all-out attack by us will be followed by an all-out attack from the Russians, and this will devastate our own country. It is a certainty that we shall never engage in such folly. The only result of the doctrine of massive retaliation was this: it created a militaristic picture of the United States. This picture is false. It has never had any validity. Unfortunately, it has appeared credible to many people abroad.

It is my opinion that we must not use our all-out striking power except to deter a massive blow upon the United States itself. This, however, requires that we establish what is called a second-strike force—a force which can inflict upon an aggressor intolerable destruction even after we have been attacked ourselves. If we are in the possession of such a second-strike force, we need not have a nervous trigger finger. We need not unleash our retaliation prematurely because we know that our ability to retaliate will not be destroyed.

Such a second-strike force can be created with the help of our present nuclear stockpile. However, this will be exceedingly expensive. It will cost many billions of dollars. By further nuclear testing we can reduce the weight of our nuclear explosives. This will result in smaller and more mobile missiles. The final effect will be that a second-strike force will cost a fraction of what we would have to spend for it today. Thus, a test ban will not reduce the cost of armaments. It will do the opposite: it will force us into a much more expensive program.

LIMITED NUCLEAR WARFARE

Massive retaliation has appeared to have one justification. It provides a shield over our allies. If we drop the idea of massive retaliation, it is necessary to find another counter-move to deter Russian nibbling. Today the Communists enjoy great military advantage: central location, superiority in massive conventional weapons and in manpower, and, finally, a political orientation which permits them to assume the initiative without any moral scruples. If we do not want the free world to succumb to piecemeal aggression, we must find a way in which these advantages can be counterbalanced.

Tactical nuclear weapons could enable us to build up a counterforce which would neutralize these Soviet advantages. Nuclear warfare makes it both necessary and possible to employ widely dispersed forces. In fact, concentration of forces in a nuclear war becomes quite impractical. At the same time light tactical nuclear weapons can be carried by small commando-type forces. These small forces are therefore in possession of very great firepower and they can accomplish the same purpose for which in previous wars we had to employ numerous troops.

It is by no means claimed that the use of tactical nuclear weapons will insure victory for our side. There can be little doubt that the Russians possess such weapons also. But, it is claimed that these small nuclear weapons will neutralize the Russian advantages of central location, massive conventional manpower, and surprise. The great power and mobility of the new weapons can be used to regain an equal chance in a limited conflict.

One can go a step beyond this point. With the help of nuclear weapons we can impose the need for extreme dispersion on the armies of an aggressor. In this way the invader will become vulnerable to guerilla tactics. Thus, we give a chance to any determined people to defend themselves if they want to do so.

But, can any nuclear war remain limited? The opposite has been asserted so often that by mere repetition it has almost assumed the status of a self-evident doctrine. Once small tactical nuclear weapons are employed—so the argument goes—the way is open for the employment of progressively bigger explosions. Eventually all-out nuclear war will follow.

The natural limitation of a nuclear war does not consist in limiting the size of nuclear explosions. The main point should be to limit the aims of the conflict and also its areas. This is the classical method by which wars have been limited in the past. In a limited conflict one should use nuclear weapons of such a size as best serves the military purpose of that conflict. In most cases the targets in a limited war will not warrant the use of big nuclear explosions. It is also most doubtful that the bombing of cities will help to win a limited war. I certainly do not consider such an employment of nuclear weapons to be helpful to our side, and I doubt that it will be considered advantageous by the Russians.

I can see no clear-cut reason why a limited nuclear war should necessarily grow into an all-out war. The assertion of this necessity is merely the Russians' way of advancing the threat of a massive retaliation. They know very well that the employment of tactical nuclear weapons would be to our great advantage. They try to use every possible means of dissuading us from using them. They are doing it more subtly by stating that all-out war is a necessary result of any use of nuclear weapons rather than by stating that all-out war will be started by their side as a measure of retaliation.

All-out war will never be in our interest, and we should never start it. If the Russians should want to embark on such a desperate enterprise, they will probably pick a time when our guard is down. While a limited nuclear war is in progress, we shall be much better prepared than in times of peace. The time of a limited nuclear conflict, therefore, would be the worst time for the Russians to launch an all-out-attack.

It is my belief that limited nuclear warfare can very well stay limited. In fact, during the course of such a war danger of an all-out war will be at a minimum. Preparation for limited nuclear war is desperately needed if we are to maintain the power to defend our allies.

For all of these reasons it is necessary to continue the development of light, cheap, and flexible tactical weapons. We are at the early stages of such a development. The most important nuclear experimentations which have to accompany this development are explosions below one kiloton. During our last nuclear test series such small explosions gained a rapidly increasing importance. It is precisely these small explosions which are hardest to detect. In fact, there does not exist any realistic prospect of working out reliable detection methods, no matter how far into the future we may look.

THE PRINCIPLE OF OPENNESS

Toward the end of World War II and in the years following Hiroshima and Nagasaki, Niels Bohr suggested a method of dealing with the problem of nuclear arms. The suggestion was clear-cut and radical. Its central part was to abandon secrecy. He strongly advocated that we return to the free discussion of discoveries and ideas which were characteristic of scientific work before World War II.

It is obvious that if freedom of information were fully established throughout the world all arms-control problems would at once become much more manageable. It would be necessary to bring about the situation where the freedom to exchange information would be guaranteed by enforceable international law. Under such conditions it would become extremely difficult to keep the development of new weapons secret, whether the development were to be pursued by testing or by other procedures. The production and deployment of weapons might become known at the same time.

Of course, this proposal could not become a reality except by a very thorough change of the world as we know it today. It would effectively mean that Russia would have to cease to be a police state. Police states cannot flourish in the full light of world publicity. Thereby a reason and perhaps the major reason of world tension would have disappeared. The possibility of arms control would become only one facet of a situation that appears to us now too wonderful to be realistic.

Nevertheless, I believe that Niels Bohr's suggestion deserves serious consideration. It strikes at the root of our difficulties. It stresses that kind of openness which is natural in free countries and which has been the lifeblood of science. In this connection, Bernhard G. Bechhoefer has pointed out to me the provision contained in Article VIII B of the Statute of the International Atomic Energy Agency. Article VIII, Sections A and B read as follows:

Each member should make available such information as would, in the judgment of the member, be helpful to the Agency.

Each member shall make available to the Agency all scientific information developed as a result of assistance extended by the Agency pursuant to article XI.

Mr. Bechhoefer adds that these provisions should be interpreted in conjunction with Article VII, paragraph F, which requires that the members of the Secretariat "shall not disclose any industrial secret or other confidential information coming to their knowledge by reason of their official duties for the Agency." What this means is that any States securing assistance—material or otherwise—from the Agency have a fairly extensive obligation to disclose their entire Atomic Energy programs; States not calling for Agency assistance—which would include the United States and the Soviet Union—have a far less extensive obligation.

The background and interpretation of these provisions are set forth in the recently published volume, entitled *Atoms and the Law* (University of Michigan, 1959), pages 1375–1376. This particular section, entitled "Atoms for Peace—The New International Atomic Energy Agency," was written by Eric Stein and Bernhard G. Bechhoefer.

At the same time there is no doubt that serious problems will be raised. Can we abandon secrecy in the present state of affairs? Will such a plan not endanger our military safety? It is not true that openness will accelerate the spread of nuclear weapons among other nations? These questions merit thought. In my opinion they point to the fact that a sudden and sweeping abandonment of secrecy on the part of the United States should not be proposed. But in order to obtain a sense of balance we should investigate the possible answers to the questions mentioned above.

Secrecy has not prevented our most powerful enemy from developing the most powerful weapons we possess. It is not even obvious that our secrecy measures have slowed down Soviet progress. It is quite obvious, however, that secrecy has impeded our own work. Because of secrecy we have had to limit the number of people who could contribute to the development of our own weapons. Due to secrecy it has become difficult to exchange information with our allies. This led to duplication. It has also led to a less than complete realism in the planning of our common defense. Secrecy has also prevented full public discussion of the possibilities of the future development of our weapons. The fact that most of our fellow citizens consider nuclear explosives as weapons of terror rather than of defense may be due to a considerable extent to secrecy. This is only one face of the more general truth that the democratic process does not function well in an atmosphere of secrecy.

It cannot be denied that the full publication of all nuclear facts will aid further nations in developing nuclear explosives. However, the gradual spread of this knowledge is unavoidable. It has been stated above that the main limitation is the absence of nuclear materials rather than the absence of knowledge. If we can guarantee a completely open flow of information, it will become much easier to check the production of nuclear materials. In the long run this will more than offset the dangers introduced by publishing the facts about nuclear explosions.

It seems to me, therefore, that we should give most serious thought to a gradual and well-planned abandonment of all secrecy concerning technical and scientific facts. We should at the same time exert as much pressure as we possibly can on every nation in the world that they likewise permit complete freedom for the flow of information. At the present time some technical facts are subject to secrecy in many nations. We should try by every means to reverse this trend toward secrecy. Every additional secret is an obstacle to the free collaboration and the eventual union of nations. A strong and widespread condemnation of all practices of secrecy may in the long run have a strong effect even on those countries which value this form of security most. Direct influence upon the Soviet government is not likely to produce quick results. Individual Russians and particularly Russian scientists are likely to be susceptible to an approach which stresses openness together with collaboration and increasing mutual confidence. In this way we shall put ourselves in the position in which the obvious advantages of a free democracy will have the greatest effect. Instead of more restrictions and more suspicions, we shall create more freedom and more trust.

If we make progress along these lines, we may well find that arms control will become feasible. It will then become an academic question whether arms control has brought about more stability or whether greater stability has made arms control possible. The two will go hand in hand and will reinforce each other.

INSURING PEACE

One can look at the problem of peace from an even more general point of view. Science and technology have made the world small. Our interrelated problems can no longer be solved on a narrow national basis. The administration has stressed this fact and has tried to proceed along the road of creating a lawful family of nations.

The need for supranational organizations is most obvious when we try to find ways by which to avoid war. But it is not only through common dangers that we are closely tied to our neighbors. Big-scale enterprises like the exploitation of atomic energy, the prediction and the eventual modification of weather, the study and cultivation of the oceans are all undertakings which are best carried forward on an international scale. It is hardly possible to do otherwise.

These positive undertakings can most easily furnish the first steps toward peace. Work toward a mutually desirable aim brings about the type of collaboration whereby no secrecy or suspicion can arise. Work along such lines can lay the foundation of friendships, and success will give the feeling of a common accomplishment on which future extended cooperation can be based.

One feeble attempt in this direction was the international geophysical year. It was a wonderful undertaking. It is a pity that it was limited to a "year" which lasted for only eighteen short months.

To state that international cooperation is difficult is to state the obvious. But we should use all possible ingenuity and determination to overcome this difficulty. We may start by close and meaningful cooperation with the NATO countries. At the same time we should work together with as many further nations as possible on projects which at first may have to be limited. Would not a yearly amount of a billion dollars be well spent on such international enterprises? Every common undertaking will help in the difficult long-range task of establishing a stable world organization which commands the loyalty of all people.

Our problem is how to insure peace and how to create a lawful world. It has been argued that only arms control can bring about a rapid solution. It is true that the more ambitious developments which I am advocating here will take a longer time. It is necessary, however, to consider this question: Is the proposed quick solution a solution at all? Is it even a step in the right direction? I believe that the road through a comprehensive and responsible world organization is longer and harder; but it is the only one that is realistic and that promises eventual success.

7. Limited War: Conventional or Nuclear? A Reappraisal

HENRY A. KISSINGER

THE NATURE OF THE DEBATE

FEW ISSUES HAVE AROUSED MORE CONTROVERSY THAN THE RELATIVE ROLE of conventional and nuclear weapons in Western strategy. Its resolution is of vital significance for our strategy, our policy in alliances, and the future of arms-control negotiations.

Two facts need to be understood at the outset: no war in the nuclear age can ever be completely free of the specter of nuclear weapons—at least, not until arms-control measures are much further advanced and much more reliable. In a war between nuclear powers, even if no nuclear weapons are used, both sides would have to take account of the possibility that they *might* be. The tactics would necessarily differ from those of World War II; deployment would have to guard against the sudden introduction of nuclear weapons. Diplomats would have to negotiate with the knowledge that any prolonged conventional war may turn into a nuclear conflict, if not a final show-down. Every war henceforth will be nuclear to a greater or lesser extent, whether or not nuclear weapons are used.

A second fact is equally important: the choice between using conventional or nuclear weapons is no longer entirely up to us. The Soviet nuclear arsenal is growing. Soviet military journals report tactical exercises with nuclear weapons. We cannot gear our strategy or stake our survival on the assumption that nuclear weapons will *not* be used against us. Even if we prefer to resist with conventional weapons, we have to be prepared for nuclear war as well. Only our being ready for limited (in addition to general) nuclear war will give us the option of a conventional strategy.

ARGUMENTS FOR A NUCLEAR STRATEGY

With this background, we can summarize the arguments for both sides. The advocates of a nuclear strategy—a strategy of initiating the use of

This chapter appears in another version in the writer's *The Necessity for Choice: Prospects of American Foreign Policy* (New York: Harper and Brothers, 1961).

nuclear weapons in limited war—emphasize the disparity in mobilizable manpower between the Communist bloc and the free world, a disparity made even more acute by the Communist ability to concentrate their whole weight against states much smaller and much less well-equipped. Nuclear weapons, it is claimed, can serve as a substitute for manpower. At the very least, they will force an aggressor to disperse his forces and prevent break-throughs of established defensive positions and the consolidation of oc-cupied territory.

The proponents of a nuclear strategy admit that if nuclear weapons were simply added to the tactics of World War II the result would probably be the complete devastation of the combat zone. They point out that such a course would be senseless. The cost of a nuclear strategy must be judged in terms of the tactics appropriate to nuclear weapons. Since nuclear weap-ons are so destructive and at the same time so easy to transport, large mili-tary formations cannot be maintained in the field. And they are unnecessary because fire power is no longer dependent on massed armies. To concen-trate is to court disaster. Safety resides in mobility. Logistics must be simple. The traditional supply system is too cumbersome and too vulnera-ble. Accordingly, a great premium will be placed on small, self-contained units of high mobility. In such circumstances, it is argued, damage would not be excessive; indeed it might be less than that of a conventional war of the World War II variety with a flankless front line rolling over the country-side.

A nuclear strategy according to its proponents would have these advan-tages: (1) The dispersal of troops would separate the requirements of victory from those of controlling territory. To prevail in a nuclear war, it is necessary to have small, highly mobile units. To control territory, larger concentrations are required, particularly in the key centers of administra-tion. For example, the Soviet army required some twenty divisions to crush the Hungarian rebellion. Crushing the rebellion, it is argued, would have been clearly impossible if the Soviets had had to face nuclear weapons. (2) Nuclear war would complicate the aggressor's calculations—if only because it is an unfamiliar mode of warfare. The Soviet Union and Com-munist China possess many "experts" in conventional warfare; but with respect to nuclear war, the calculations are theoretical. There would always remain the inevitable uncertainty of embarking on a course in which no experience is available. (3) Nuclear war would be an effective device to weaken the Communist control of Soviet dominated areas. The small de-tachments that are appropriate for nuclear war will be extremely vulnerable to guerila activity and can be handicapped severely by a hostile population. Since the population on the Western side of the Iron Curtain is more loyal to its governments than are those under Communist rule, a nuclear war is thought to be the best means of exploiting Soviet political difficulties—at least, in Europe—and therefore the most effective means of deterring Soviet aggression. (4) Nuclear weapons are our "best weapons," the result of our most advanced technology. To forego using them is to deprive ourselves of the advantages of a superior industrial potential. (5) Any other course would impose impossible force requirements. It is admittedly impossible to fight a conventional war against a nuclear enemy without having a nuclear establishment in the field—otherwise, the temptation for the aggressor to use nuclear weapons and sweep all before him might become overwhelming. This means that we would need a well-protected retaliatory force, a capable limited war force, and increasing conventional strength. Since the expense of maintaining each category even at present levels is multiplying, and since the military budget is shrinking, any attempt to build up conventional forces must result in a fundamental, perhaps fatal, weakness in each category.[1]

ARGUMENTS FOR A CONVENTIONAL STRATEGY

The advocates of a conventional strategy reply that the decision to use nuclear weapons is inconsistent with the very concept of limitation. Pointing to such military exercises with nuclear weapons as "Carte Blanche" in Europe and "Sagebrush" in the United States, they stress that the inevitable consequence of nuclear war will be the desolation of the combat zone and the decimation of the population. No country would wish to be defended at that price. Even a "successful" nuclear war would provide a conclusive argument for future Soviet blackmail.

Moreover, once nuclear weapons are used, so this school of thought reasons, all restraints may disappear. It will be difficult enough to establish the limits of a conventional war. Because of their very unfamiliarity, nuclear weapons would make the task nearly impossible. The very fact that there exists a continuous spectrum of destructiveness in nuclear weapons, so often invoked by advocates of a nuclear strategy in defense of their thesis, is used by their critics against them. If the distinction between the low-yield and high-yield weapons is so difficult, if so much depends on the manner of employing them, any effort to set limits based on explosive equivalent will be meaningless. The temptation to resort to even more destructive weapons will be overwhelming.

Proponents of a conventional strategy question not only the possibility of limitation but also the efficacy of the tactics thought to be appropriate for nuclear war. Small detachments, they contend, whatever their nuclear fire power, would be extremely vulnerable to harassment and defeat by conventional forces. When confronted by an opponent possessing both a nuclear and a conventional capability, they are almost certain to lose, for they would be largely defenseless against small conventional raiding parties. Nuclear weapons, it is contended, are not a substitute for manpower. On the contrary, because of its high rate of attrition, nuclear war would probably require more manpower, not less.

Finally, our industrial potential will be less significant in a nuclear war.

Since nuclear weapons provide greater destructiveness per unit cost than do conventional explosives, reliance on them enables economically weaker nations to redress the strategic balance much more easily than they could with conventional forces. A point is likely to be reached for any given objective or area at which additional increments of explosive power are no longer strategically significant. When this "saturation point" is reached, superiority in nuclear weapons may be meaningless. And nuclear weapons place a premium on surprise attack and sudden thrusts to which the defender is much more vulnerable than the attacker. To rely on a nuclear strategy, it is urged, would thus be adopting a course of conduct which rewards the qualities in which potential aggressors excel.

A conventional strategy according to its advocates would have these advantages: (1) It would provide the best chance to limit any conflict that might break out. (2) It would use our industrial potential to best advantage. Since the destructive power of individual conventional weapons is relatively low, victory can be achieved only through a substantial production effort which puts a premium on our special skills. At the same time, the relatively slow pace of military operations—at least, as compared to nuclear war—and the need to build up supplies before such a new advance give the maximum opportunity for attempting a political settlement. (3) Conventional defense provides the best means of preventing the occupation of threatened countries. The concept of a flankless line which advocates of a nuclear strategy wish to abandon is likely to be considered by threatened countries as the best guarantee of their safety. Liberation will always be a less attractive prospect than protection. (4) If, after all, nuclear weapons were used, the onus of initiating such a war would be shifted to the Communist states.

DETERRENCE VS. CONDUCT OF THE WAR

One of the difficulties in resolving these arguments is that the moral fervor of the debaters sometimes obscures the nature of the issues and often causes them to claim too much: those who think that to forego nuclear weapons is an offense against progress have as their counterpart those who are passionately convinced that even to consider modalities of nuclear warfare is to insult morality. As a result, arguments that closer examination would reveal at least as imprecise and sometimes as erroneous have been elevated into dogma.

For example, it is often said that a nuclear war cannot be limited because neither side would accept defeat without resorting to even larger weapons. Now there are many good reasons for concern about the possibility of limiting nuclear war. But the argument that neither side will be prepared to accept a setback implies that it is somehow worse to be defeated in nuclear than in conventional war. In reality, it seems much more likely that the decision as to whether a war is to be expanded depends more on the value attached to the objective than to the weapons used to attain it. It is not clear why a country should be more willing to acquiesce in a conventional than in a nuclear defeat. Whatever the technical difficulties of limiting nuclear war, the political argument that it makes defeat unacceptable does not bear scrutiny.

On the other side of the debate a nuclear strategy is often justified by the spectrum of available weapons. The smallest nuclear weapons, it is said, are less destructive than the most powerful conventional devices. There is therefore no technical reason to recoil before nuclear warfare, and every reason to use our most "advanced" technology. However, the effort to base a nuclear strategy on the discrimination of nuclear weapons surely goes too far. The chief motive for using them is, after all, their greater destructive power and their lower weight per explosive equivalent. Nuclear weapons no more destructive than conventional ones would probably not be worth the increased risk of "escalation" inherent in an unfamiliar mode of warfare.

The frustration in the debate is all too often caused by the fact that both the proponents and the opponents of a nuclear strategy are right: their disagreements arise from the perspective from which they consider the issue. Looking at the problem from the point of view of deterrence, the advocates of a nuclear strategy argue that nuclear weapons are the most effective sanction against the outbreak of a war. Considering the actual conduct of a war, the opponents of a nuclear strategy are above all concerned with reducing the impact of military operations and increasing their predictability. The destructiveness of individual weapons and the uncertainties of an unfamiliar mode of warfare which are correctly adduced as contributing to deterrence can, with equal justification, be cited as working against effective limitation.

Much of the debate therefore turns on the question of what should be stressed: deterrence or the strategy for fighting the war. Obviously, an overemphasis on destructiveness may paralyze the will. But an overconcern with developing a tolerable strategy for the conduct of war may also reduce the risks of aggression to such a degree that it will be encouraged. While the deterrent threat must be credible, the quest for credibility must not lower the penalties to a point at which they are no longer unacceptable. The frequency of warfare since the Middle Ages demonstrates the difficulty of achieving deterrence with conventional weapons alone. On the other hand, a course of action that increases the opponent's uncertainties about the nature of the conflict will generally discourage aggression. If war should break out, however, through accident or miscalculation, it may make limitation extremely difficult.

DIRECTION FOR UNITED STATES STRATEGY

Some years ago this author advocated a nuclear strategy.[2] It seemed then that the most effective deterrent to any substantial Sino-Soviet aggression was the knowledge that the United States would employ nuclear weapons from the very outset. A nuclear strategy appeared to offer the best prospect of offsetting Sino-Soviet manpower and of using our superior industrial capacity to best advantage.

The need for forces capable of fighting limited nuclear war still exists. However, several developments have caused a shift in my view about the relative emphasis to be given conventional forces as against nuclear forces. These are: (1) the disagreement within our military establishment and within the alliance about the nature of limited nuclear war; (2) the growth of the Soviet nuclear stockpile and the increased significance of long-range missiles; (3) the impact of arms-control negotiations. The first of these considerations raises doubts as to whether we would know how to limit nuclear war. The second alters the strategic significance of nuclear war. The third influences the framework in which any strategy will have to be conducted and determines the political cost.

While it is feasible to design a theoretical model for limited nuclear war, the fact remains that fifteen years after the beginning of the nuclear age no such model has ever achieved general agreement. It would be next to impossible to obtain from our military establishment a coherent description of what is understood by "limited nuclear war." The Air Force thinks of it as control over a defined air space. The Army considers it vital to destroy tactical targets which can affect ground operations, including centers of communications. The Navy is primarily concerned with eliminating port installations. Even within a given service, a detailed, coherent doctrine is often lacking. The Strategic Air Command and the Tactical Air Force almost surely interpret the nature of limited nuclear war differently. Since disputes about targets are usually settled by addition—by permitting each service to destroy what it considers essential to its mission—a limited nuclear war fought in this manner may well become indistinguishable from all-out war. At least, it would diminish our assurance and subtlety in an operation in which everything would depend on the ability to remain in control of events.

The disagreements between our services are repeated in relations with our allies. Few of our allies possess nuclear weapons. Those that do have emphasized the retaliatory and not the tactical aspect of nuclear warfare. Public opinion in most allied countries has been mobilized against nuclear weapons by a variety of agents. And these attitudes are reinforced by current trends in arms-control negotiations. In these circumstances, it will become increasingly difficult to concert a strategic and tactical doctrine that is accepted by the alliance and maintained with conviction in the face of Soviet pressure. This raises doubt as to whether the West will possess either the knowledge or the daring to impose limitations. If it relies *entirely* on a nuclear strategy, its vulnerability to nuclear blackmail both before and during hostilities would be considerable.

To be sure, any limitation of war is to some extent arbitrary. There is probably some disagreement even as to the nature of limited conventional war. The problem of communicating intentions to an opponent during a conflict will be difficult regardless of the mode of warfare, but this makes it all the more important that the limitations which are attempted be reasonably familiar. Even with the best intentions on both sides, a nuclear war will be more difficult to limit than a conventional one. Since no country has had any experience with the tactical use of nuclear weapons, the possibility of miscalculation is considerable. The temptation to use the same target system as for conventional war and thereby produce vast casualties will be overwhelming. The pace of operations may outstrip the possibilities of negotiation. Both sides would be operating in the dark with no precedents to guide them and a necessarily inadequate understanding of the purposes of the opponent, if not their own. The dividing line between conventional and nuclear weapons is more familiar and therefore easier to maintain— assuming the will to do so—than any distinction within the spectrum of nuclear weapons. This uncertainty may increase deterrence. It will also magnify the risks of conflict should deterrence fail.

These considerations are reinforced by the strategic changes wrought by the advent of the age of nuclear plenty and the long-range missile. When nuclear material was relatively scarce, it was possible to believe that tactical nuclear weapons might give the West an advantage in limited war. Under conditions of nuclear scarcity, the Soviet Union would have had to make a choice: it could not simultaneously push the development of its retaliatory force and also equip its ground forces for nuclear war. Whatever alternative was chosen would produce a weakness in *some* category. Since the logical decision for the Soviets was to give priority to the retaliatory force, it was then held that tactical nuclear weapons could be used to offset Soviet conventional preponderance.

In the meantime, the Soviet nuclear stockpile has multiplied. A nuclear strategy will now have to be conducted against an equally well-equipped opponent. In these circumstances, numbers become again important. Because of the destructiveness of nuclear weapons, the casualty rate among combat units is likely to be high. The side which has the more replacements available therefore stands to gain the upper hand. The notion that nuclear weapons can substitute for numerical inferiority has lost a great deal of its validity.

The development of missiles has accentuated the strategic problems of limited nuclear war. As long as delivery systems were composed of airplanes, air domination over the battle area on the model of our experience in the Korean war was conceivable. And tactical skill in handling the weapons *within* the combat zone might lead to victory on the nuclear battlefield. However, as missile forces grow on both sides, as even airplanes are equipped with medium-range missiles, this possibility steadily diminishes. For one thing, it seems unnecessary to introduce major nuclear forces into the combat zone, since nuclear weapons can be delivered accurately at considerable distances. More importantly, the only way of achieving what used to be considered air superiority is to destroy most of the opponent's medium- and intermediate-range missiles. Such an operation is difficult to reconcile with an attempt to limit hostilities. If, however, the areas where these missiles are located become sanctuaries, it would appear that a stalemate is almost inevitably the outcome of a limited nuclear war.

Of course, such a result must not be minimized. An aggressor, certain that his attack would be checked, would presumably be deterred. The difficulty is the devastation of the combat zone, which would be the price of a stalemate. In some situations, it may be to the Communist advantage to settle for the *status quo ante* in a war that obliterates the disputed area. If a Soviet attack on Western Germany should lead to the desolation of the Federal Republic, the Soviet Union would score a major gain even if it offered at some point to withdraw to its starting point. The devastation of Germany might be a means of convincing all other threatened areas of the futility of resistance. An "unsuccessful" attack of this nature might insure the success of all future Soviet blackmail.

Finally, it would be idle to discount the impact on strategy of the pattern of arms-control negotiations. At each conference, nuclear weapons have been placed in a separate category and stigmatized as weapons of mass destruction without any distinction as to type or device. The goal of eventual nuclear disarmament has been avowed by all states. A moratorium of nuclear testing has been in existence for two years, and it is probable that a formal agreement will be signed. Future negotiations will almost inevitably reinforce this trend. The consequence will be that the inhibitions against using the weapons around which the West has built its whole military policy will multiply. Whatever the other consequences of a nuclear-test ban, it will reinforce the already strong reluctance to use nuclear weapons in limited war.

These factors will create an extremely precarious situation if the free world continues to rely primarily on a nuclear strategy. The more the pressures build up against *any* use of nuclear weapons, the greater will be the gap between our deterrent policy, our military capability and our psychological readiness—a gap which must tempt aggression. The years ahead must therefore see a substantial strengthening of the conventional forces of the free world. If strong enough to halt Soviet conventional attacks—as in many areas such as Europe they could be—conventional forces would shift the onus and risk of initiating nuclear war to the other side. Even where they cannot resist every scale of attack, they should force the aggressor into military operations which leave no doubt as to his ultimate aim. They would thereby make an ultimate recourse to nuclear weapons politically and psychologically simpler, while affording an opportunity for a settlement before this step is taken.

Many of the assumptions regarding the impossibility of conventional defense and of "hordes" of Communist manpower are either fallacious or exaggerated. Both in total available manpower and in its industrial potential, the free world still is superior. And conventional warfare favors the defense. It has been truly remarked that but for the development of nuclear weapons, the defense would long since have achieved ascendancy over the offense. Even in World War II, the attacker generally required a superiority of three to one.

To be sure, in other areas the problem is more complicated. In the so-called "gray areas" of the Middle East and Southeast Asia, the Communist bloc can concentrate its manpower and material against countries weaker and less closely allied than are those of the North Atlantic Community. On the other hand, these are also the areas where the political penalties for aggression would be the greatest. An attack on an emergent country would antagonize all the other uncommitted nations and would lead to an increased mobilization of Western resources. Moreover, difficulties of terrain and communications place a ceiling on the number of troops an aggressor could effectively utilize even there. The inability to protect every area locally is no excuse, nor is failing to secure those areas where protection is possible.

At a minimum, the conventional capability of the free world should be of such a size that a nuclear defense becomes the *last* and not the *only* recourse. The best situation is one in which the conventional forces of the free world can be overcome *only* by nuclear weapons. There is no technical reason why this should not be possible, in Western Europe, at least. Such forces would remove many opportunities for Soviet gains achieved merely by the use of threats. They would increase the flexibility of our diplomacy. They would enable us to negotiate the control of nuclear weapons with confidence.

SOME CONSEQUENCES

While a substantial build-up of conventional forces and a greater reliance on a conventional strategy is essential, it is equally vital not to press the conclusions too far. In their attempt to prove their case, many of the proponents of a conventional strategy have thought it necessary so to deride *any* reliance on nuclear weapons, or to paint so awful a picture of atomic war that they may defeat their own object. For, against an opponent known to consider nuclear war as the worst evil, nuclear blackmail is an almost fool-proof strategy. Conventional forces will be of no avail if an aggressor is convinced that he can probably force surrender by threatening to use nuclear weapons. A greater emphasis on conventional defense presupposes that the aggressor cannot promise himself an advantage either from the threat or the actuality of nuclear war. However much conventional war may be preferred to the use of nuclear weapons, limited nuclear war is preferable to all-out war.

Conventional forces should not be considered a substitute for a capability of waging a limited nuclear war, but a complement to it. It would be suicidal to rely entirely on conventional arms against an opponent equipped with nuclear weapons. Such a development would probably provide the precise incentive an aggressor needs to employ nuclear weapons and to sweep all before him. A conventional war can be kept within limits only if nuclear war seems more unattractive.

This becomes apparent when we analyze what options we have if, despite our best efforts in the conventional field, nuclear weapons are actually used against us. We would then seem to have three choices: to accept defeat; to resort to general war; or to seek to conduct limited nuclear war. If we are unwilling to accept defeat—and to do so under such circumstances would make us forever subject to nuclear blackmail—our choice resolves itself into all-out war or limited nuclear war. All-out war will become increasingly senseless as the missile age develops. Hence, conventional war can be kept conventional only if we maintain, together with our retaliatory force, an adequate capability for limited nuclear war. The aggressor must understand that we are in a position to match any increment of force, nuclear or conventional, that he may add. This realization would reduce the incentive to engage in aggression, and should deterrence fail, it will provide the best chance of limiting hostilities.

It may be argued that this line of reasoning demonstrates the absurdity of a greater reliance on conventional weapons. Nuclear weapons must favor one side or the other. If they favor us, we should use them. If they give an advantage to the Communists, they will use them. But this is not necessarily the case. Unless the superiority of one side grows overwhelmingly, the increased risks of an unfamiliar mode of warfare may outweigh the purely military benefits.

The relation between conventional and nuclear capabilities is subtle and complex. If we are serious about placing a greater reliance on conventional forces, we must reassess a notion which has become almost axiomatic in our military establishment: that our military forces can be equipped and trained as dual-purpose units capable of fighting both nuclear and conventional war. This concept has merit as regards the Navy and the Air Force—or any other unit not in constant contact with the opponent and therefore subject to more or less continuous control from higher levels. But it is fallacious with respect to ground operations. To be sure, troops can be trained to use both nuclear and conventional weapons. They should at least be aware of the elementary forms of protection against nuclear attack. But once committed to combat, the units actually engaged in military operations must opt for one mode of warfare or another. For one thing, it is probably impossible to shift from conventional to nuclear war at the opponent's initiative. The side using nuclear weapons first can disperse, while the side relying on conventional weapons must remain concentrated in order to have the necessary fire power. The front-line units of the side conceding the first nuclear blow will almost certainly suffer heavily should the war turn nuclear. Their protection is not so much nuclear weapons of their own as to have *available* within striking distance *other* units capable of conducting nuclear operations.

If nuclear weapons become an integral part of the equipment of *every* unit, it will be next to impossible to keep a war conventional, regardless of the intentions of both sides. Even if the intention is to employ nuclear weapons only as a last resort, this becomes empty when the interpretation of this step becomes more and more decentralized. A regimental or even a divisional commander should not be the judge. Lacking the over-all picture, he will always be tempted to utilize all his available weapons. When he is hard-pressed, it would require superhuman discipline not to use arms which he believes may solve his difficulties. And the further down a unit is in the chain of command, the less can its experience be taken as a guide to the general situation. Regiments or divisions have been destroyed even in the midst of an over-all victory.

While a great deal of attention has been given to the diffusion of nuclear weapons to new countries, the diffusion downward of nuclear weapons *within* our military establishment is also a cause for concern. The more foci of control, the greater the possibility that these weapons will be used—not so much by the action of the "mad" major of the horror stories of accidental war as by the best judgment of a hard-pressed officer in the confusion of combat. An action which would bespeak our increased emphasis on conventional weapons more convincingly than any declaration would be to create nuclear and conventional commands for purposes of combat. The units could be trained interchangeably. But once committed, the conventional forces would not have nuclear weapons at their direct disposal. Deterrence as well as the conduct of nuclear war would be in the hands of separate commands whose weapons would be made available to the conventional forces only on the basis of an explicit decision at the highest level.

The need for separate commands indicates that a conventional capability cannot possibly be accommodated within present force levels. In the absence of reliable arms control, larger military budgets will almost surely be required. This is a price worth paying. But we should not imagine that the shift to a greater reliance on conventional weapons requires only the decision to do so. It will involve substantial efforts, intellectual and material, and it will be neither cheap nor easy.

It is sometimes argued that a conventional strategy does not necessarily require an increase in conventional forces. Our national history reminds us of many wars where we prevailed, despite initial defeats, because of the might of our industrial potential. An aggressor, so the argument goes, would be more deterred by the possibility that we would build up our strength during a conflict than by the forces-in-being available to us at the beginning. The Korean war is only the latest demonstration of our ability to build up fairly quickly, provided only that we are able to hold the initial thrust of the aggressor for some time.

This view has great merit. Conventional weapons have a relatively low order of destructiveness and yet require a fairly substantial production effort. They therefore do place a premium on the West's industrial potential. At the same time, care must be taken not to draw extreme conclusions from this fact. In both World Wars our side not only had a superior industrial potential but also a vast preponderance of manpower. Nevertheless, victory required a build-up of nearly two years and protracted campaigns whose bloodiness must not be obscured by the horror of nuclear warfare.

Whatever the significance of prolonged mobilization in the era of what is now called conventional technology, it becomes an extremely risky course in the nuclear age. When both sides possess nuclear weapons, there is always the danger that they will be used, regardless of declarations and perhaps even intentions. The risk of "escalation" is a product of two factors: the nature of the limitations and the duration of the conflict. A limited nuclear war lasting one day may involve a smaller danger of "escalation" than a conventional war lasting a year. Aggression may be tempted by the prospect of dramatic victories and the possibility that the free world may not be willing to run the risks of nuclear war inherent in a prolonged mobilization. Forces-in-being are therefore more important than at any previous time in our history. This does not mean that they must be able to hold every square inch of every threatened area. It does indicate that enough of an area must be protected so that the governments concerned consider resistance not simply a quixotic gesture. And the prospect of restoring the situation must be sufficiently imminent so that the aggressor sees no prospect in creating a *fait accompli* and then "out-enduring" his opponents. In short, greater reliance on a conventional strategy implies that we are prepared to maintain conventional forces and mobilizable reserves in a higher state of readiness than ever before. It is as dangerous to think of a conventional strategy as if somehow nuclear weapons could be eliminated from our calculations as it is to continue to consider nuclear weapons from the perspective of our now-ended invulnerability.

These considerations bear importantly on the question of how the decision to place greater reliance on conventional weapons is to be made manifest. Many thoughtful persons have proposed that we should strive in arms-control negotiations to bring about a mutual renunciation of the first use of nuclear weapons. We should, it is urged, resist Communist aggression with conventional forces and resort to nuclear weapons only against nuclear attack. Nothing less, so the argument goes, will induce us to develop the necessary conventional forces and doctrine. It would end the possibility of nuclear blackmail. It would remove the immediate danger of a nuclear holocaust.

There is no doubt that such an agreement has many tempting aspects. It would be a stunning initiative if we proposed a formal agreement to renounce the use of nuclear weapons and perhaps a serious Soviet political setback if it were rejected. It would force us to come to grips with the problems of conventional strategy more urgently than seems otherwise possible. Indeed, *if* a mutual renunciation should be thought desirable, it may well be that a unilateral Western step would be the wisest course. A formal agreement has the advantage that the Soviet Union would have to violate a solemn treaty if it resorted to nuclear weapons or to nuclear blackmail. But this inhibition would hardly be greater than one produced by a unilateral renunciation by the United States. Nuclear blackmail would put an end to our renunciation, and *a fortiori,* so would the first Soviet use of nuclear weapons. In both cases the onus for returning to a reliance on nuclear weapons would be placed on the Soviet Union—within the limits of certainty produced by what will almost surely be a highly ambiguous situation. The slight additional advantage of a formal agreement would be more than made up for by the clarity and initiative achieved by a unilateral declaration.

However, the propagandistic gain does not outweigh the political and strategic disadvantages. A really effective renunciation would imply that either side—or at least the side renouncing nuclear weapons—would prefer to be defeated by conventional weapons rather than employ its nuclear arms. This in itself will be a hard decision to make. Would we be prepared to lose Europe to a conventional attack? If we are not—and we cannot be— a formal renunciation may be meaningless. On the other hand, if the aggressor accepts a renunciation of nuclear weapons at face value as indicating a decision to accept a defeat by conventional forces, aggression may actually be encouraged.

Assuming that it were possible to return to a *pure* conventional strategy —with either side preferring a defeat by conventional weapons to a nuclear war—what would be the consequences? It seems inevitable that deterrence would be weakened. The history of warfare in the conventional era indicates that it is not easy to convince an aggressor of the risks of embarking on war. Because of the relatively low destructiveness of individual weapons, the side which can suddenly mass its forces can usually achieve a breakthrough. The key to success is the ability to concentrate more forces *at any given point* than the opponent. In both World Wars, Germany began the war even though it was numerically inferior, relying on tactical skill and mobility. Victory was ultimately achieved only after prolonged and ruinous conflict, which indicated that the certainty of defeat required for deterrence is not easy to obtain with conventional weapons. Arms control can ameliorate this situation, but not eliminate it. Even if forces on both sides are stabilized, it will not be easy to stabilize tactical skill and mobility.

On the historical record, then, conventional weapons are not very effective for deterrence. This situation may even be magnified in the nuclear age. An aggressor may seek to achieve a victory by conventional means and then protect it by nuclear arms. We will then face the dilemma of either accepting the defeat or engaging in a kind of warfare which our renunciation of nuclear weapons was designed to avoid and which seems incapable of depriving the aggressor of his prize. If the Soviet Union should succeed in overrunning Europe or even Iran with conventional forces, it could then offer peace while threatening to resist the restoration of the *status quo ante* with nuclear weapons. It would appear extremely difficult to land on a hostile shoreline or to fight our way across the Continent, say, from Spain, against an opponent prepared to use nuclear weapons. In short, the combination of a conventional strategy for an overwhelming initial victory, coupled with a nuclear strategy to prevent a recapture of lost territories, may be the most effective form of Communist aggression.

All these risks, however, would be run for a gesture which may be meaningless. For, regardless of what we tell the aggressor or even ourselves, we could not guarantee that if pressed too hard we would not use nuclear weapons after all. This uncertainty about whether we "meant" our renunciation or knew our own mind would add to deterrence. It indicates, however, that at best a formal renunciation of the first use of nuclear weapons would not weaken deterrence; at worst it may open a new scope for blackmail.

In the nuclear age, therefore, actions speak louder than words. What we tell the Communist countries is less important in the first instance than what we tell ourselves. We should make immediate and energetic efforts to restore the conventional forces of the free world. We must adjust our doctrine accordingly. But it would be extremely risky to create the impression that we would acquiesce in a conventional defeat in vital areas. Once the conventional balance of forces is restored, we could then responsibly announce that we would employ nuclear weapons only as a last resort, and even then in a manner to minimize damage. To the extent that the Communists are unable to defeat the conventional forces of the free world without resorting to nuclear weapons, the practical effect will be to renounce the first use of nuclear weapons. Even where this is not the case, strengthened conventional forces would pose an increased risk for the aggressor and provide opportunities either for the mobilization of additional conventional forces or for negotiations before we make the decision to use nuclear weapons. The inability to defend every area with conventional forces should not be used as an excuse for failing to build up our strength. The free world must not become a victim of asserting that if it cannot do *everything*, it will not do *anything*.

The course we adopt with respect to the relation between conventional and nuclear strategy will determine the future direction of our strategy as well as our diplomacy. This is particularly evident with respect to arms-control negotiations. In this respect, the present state of our military establishment places us at a severe disadvantage. Given the disparity in Sino-Soviet and Western conventional forces, many measures such as a percentage reduction of forces or a troop freeze may be a means of perpetuating an inequality which will be an increasing source of danger as all-out war becomes more and more senseless. The same effect will be produced by our concentrating on nuclear disarmament without addressing ourselves to the gap in conventional forces. We can escape this vicious circle only if we realize that the price of flexibility is sacrifice and effort. If our military establishment continues to be built around nuclear weapons, and if we refuse to make the sacrifices involved in a greater reliance on conventional weapons, the current emphasis of arms-control negotiations must be shifted. In such circumstances, it will not be wise to lump all nuclear weapons into a separate category of special horror. Rather, we should then elaborate as many distinctions between various types of uses and explosive power as possible in order to mitigate the consequences of a nuclear war. On the other hand, if we really believe in the need for a greater emphasis on conventional weapons, we must be prepared to accept the paradox that the best road to nuclear-arms control may be conventional rearmament.

This is not to say that arms control should be reserved for the nuclear field. On the contrary, the balance in conventional forces should be based on a combination of an increase of our conventional strength and control schemes to stabilize an agreed level of forces. But we cannot rely on arms control as a *substitute* for an effort in the conventional field. For, if the disparity in local power becomes too great, the Soviet Union will lose any incentive for responsible negotiations. No scheme of arms control will then seem to enhance its security as much as its existing superiority. And the requirements of inspection become excessive when the strategic position of one or both sides is so precarious that it can be overthrown by even a minor violation.

This is the measure of the task ahead: simultaneously with building up our capability for limited war and our conventional forces, we will be embarked on arms-control negotiation of crucial import. Our leadership must convince public opinion that we have to increase our military expenditures even while making earnest efforts to negotiate on arms control. The danger of slighting one or the other effort is enormous.

Yet history will not excuse our failure because the task is complex. The divorce between diplomacy and strategy will produce paralysis. If we want limited war forces we will get them only by a major effort. If we are serious about disarmament, we must restore the balance of our military establishment. To continue to combine incompatible policies must lead to disaster.

8. Economic Implications
of Arms Control

KENNETH E. BOULDING

THE DISCUSSION OF THE ECONOMIC IMPLICATIONS OF ARMS CONTROL, FOR the United States or for other countries, depends greatly on the concept of arms control which is in the mind of the discussant. The very discussion of arms control is an indication that unilateral national defense is unsatisfactory and that some substitute is to be sought. The nature of the dissatisfaction, however, and the nature of the substitute, is subject to wide variation even among the authors of this book.[1] The concept of arms control as "military cooperation with potential enemies" seems to me the most fruitful, especially as extended to include the concept of organization for all kinds of cooperation with potential enemies designed to produce mutual security and to reduce enmity.

This concept is clearly shocking to those who are emotionally committed to the ethic of unilateral national defense, or those whose hatred of the potential enemy is so intense that they cannot bear the thought of cooperation. It is, however, a concept which is being forced upon us by the nature of modern war. So little serious intellectual attention has been given to the problem, in comparison with the enormous effort devoted to unilateral national defense, that we find ourselves on the threshold of doomsday unprepared to spell out even the larger framework of the changes which are now necessary in the world social system if man is to survive.

We do not even know, for instance, whether arms control will in fact lead to less government spending on defense, including the costs of inspection or of inter-armed-force or inter-nation organization. There are those who argue that arms control might lead to a larger military budget, especially if control were confined to the weapons of mass destruction. In the absence of adequate information on this point, any discussion of domestic implications must be highly speculative. It is important, however, not merely to speculate but also to build theoretical and statistical models of the domestic social system which can accommodate a number of different possibilities, even quite extreme cases. The economic system is that part of the social system in which such model building is most highly advanced, and where therefore the effects of various patterns of arms control can be most clearly followed. The economic system, however, is highly dependent on political decisions and on psychological attitudes, and we cannot be content with a mere economic analysis. Economic analysis, nevertheless, is a good place to begin, not only because in the present state of knowledge it offers the best chance of success, but also because in the minds of many people, and especially noneconomists, the economic consequences of arms control, and especially of disarmament, are a source of real anxiety.

The anxiety stems from the association of disarmament with depression and with extensive economic dislocation. The prosperity of the 1940's and 1950's, by contrast with the misery of the 1930's, is associated, whether the association is justified or not, in the minds of many people with the high level of war and defense expenditures in the former periods, and with the low level in the latter. The memories of the Great Depression are still strong in the minds of the middle-aged and the powerful, and the fear of another such experience, though by now driven down into the unconscious, is an active determinant of our value system. Nobody wants to suggest that the United States would deliberately sabotage an attempt at arms control because of this fear of depression; the frivolity and hypocrisy with which the subject of disarmament was treated in official circles in the pre-sputnik era was due almost entirely to an emotional and intellectual commitment to unilateral national defense, not to any fear of economic consequences.

Nevertheless, it is important to examine, and if possible to remove, this economic anxiety. Arms control is going to be a very difficult road to find, beset with legitimate anxieties and risky decisions. The advance clearing away of minor obstacles, illegitimate and unnecessary anxieties, and falsely imagined risks is an important part of the pathfinding process. It would be unspeakably tragic if the great moment in history arrived at which opportunity presented itself for a transition from the present system (the road to doomsday) to a system which offered at least a chance of human security and decency, and if we then found that illusions about economic systems caused us to stumble and take the wrong road.

There are, then, three major domestic economic problems which arms control may represent, summarized as *conversion, stabilization,* and *growth.* These are all general problems of the economy and are not peculiar to arms control. Conversion is the problem of how to adjust the structure of production in the economy—that is, the commodity mix of total output—to shifts in the structure of total demand, public and private. Stabilization is the problem of how to control the vicious dynamic processes of deflation, depression, and unemployment, on the one hand, or inflation on the other, which may be initiated by these shifts in the structure of total demand. Growth is the problem of achieving a structure of total demand which will give the society an optimum rate of economic growth; the latter might be defined as the maximum rate of growth which is subject to the constraints of its basic value system.

Conversion is a problem that is always with us. The movement of technology, trade opportunities, and public and private demand constantly imposes on any economy the necessity for altering its product mix and the occupational distribution of its labor force. In the course of the past two hundred years, for instance, the United States has shifted the proportion of its labor force engaged in agriculture from about 90 percent to 10 percent under the impact of a great technical revolution, which has resulted in a more than tenfold increase in output of food and fibers per man-hour. Agricultural policy testifies both to the magnitude of the conversion problem involved and also to the ability of governments to hamper it.

To come closer to the immediate topic, the United States has suffered enormous fluctuations in the proportion of the gross national product allotted to national security (defense) in the past twenty years; as of 1959 the latter was a little less than 10 percent of the gross national product, and the recent trend is illustrated in Table 1.

TABLE 1

United States Gross National Product (GNP) and National Security Expenditures (NSE) in real terms (billions of dollars) at 1959 prices, selected years.

YEAR	GNP	NSE *	NSE / GNP (%)	UNEMPLOYMENT AS % OF LABOR FORCE †
1939	211.5	3.2	1.5	17.2
1944	366.3	164.7	45.0	1.2
1945	359.4	139.8	39.1	1.9
1946	316.0	26.7	8.4	3.9
1947	315.7	15.3	4.8	3.6
				(3.9)
1953	417.1	60.1	14.4	2.5
				(2.9)
1954	408.8	49.5	12.2	5.0
				(5.6)
1959	478.8	45.5	9.5	(5.5)

SOURCE: *Economic Report of the President,* 1960.

* NSE figures are net of government sales, hence may be a little too small. There has been a substantial revision of these figures in recent years.
† The figures in parentheses are according to the new definition.

The rise in national security expenditures from the almost negligible levels of the 1930's to the heights of the mid-1940's (World War II) was, of course, accompanied by a sharp rise in GNP and a dramatic fall in the percentage of unemployment. Here we have the origin of the myth of defense-inspired prosperity. It is a myth which derives its power from the fact that it is not wholly untrue and is rooted in the personal experiences of millions of people. Nevertheless, it *is* basically only a half truth. The outstanding fact is the remarkable stability and success of the American economy under the impact of the massive armament and disarmament of the 1940's, when, for instance, in one year (1945–1946) we transferred an absolute amount of manpower and resources from war to civilian employments more than twice as much as would be involved (in real terms) in total and complete disarmament at present. The post-Korean disarmament was less well managed: unemployment rose to a disquieting 5 percent in 1954, but subsided again in later years in the face of a continued fall in the real defense burden.

Some of the problems of conversion do not show up in the aggregate data. Even within the defense program itself there are continual shifts involving conversion problems of the same order of magnitude as those which would be involved in substantial disarmament or even in conversion to "expensive" arms control. The shift which has taken place in the past few years from the wheel to the whoosh as the basis for military hardware, for instance, has created a substantial conversion problem within the defense industry of the same order of magnitude as that which might be expected in the shift-over from the present system to a plausibly expensive arms-control system. The current change-over temporarily created some mildly depressed areas, such as Michigan, but the economic impact of conversion has not presented itself as more than a minor national problem.

I am not arguing, of course, that conversion is costless, painless, and creates no problems, and least of all am I arguing that there should be no national policy about it and no organization to deal with it. I would argue indeed that this is a perennial problem, that even though the American economy is remarkably flexible and deals fairly well with this problem even in the absence of any governmental organization, there is a strong case for more positive social organization to deal with depressed areas and industries, whether these result from tariff changes, exhaustion of natural or human resources, shifts in technology or tastes, or changes in the defense industry. I argue also, however, that this is a manageable problem, and that it can be solved well within the limits of toleration which our value system imposes.

The ease with which the problem of conversion can be solved depends in no small measure on our ability to prevent depressions. It is dangerously easy for a free market economy with low levels of government expenditure to get into a vicious spiral of declining investment, resulting in declining incomes and profits, which lead to still another decline in investment, and so on. The remarkable resiliency of the American economy since 1945 by comparison with the 1930's can be attributed to the development of a number of "built-in stabilizers," as well as to a general expectation that government would intervene quickly to prevent a serious depression. Of these built-in stabilizers the sheer magnitude of the Federal budget is an important element. With a large over-all budget amounting to about one-fifth of the gross national product, with tax receipts amounting to an even larger proportion of disposable income, and with a tax system that is at least moderately progressive, general deflationary or inflationary forces in the private economy call forth an automatic counterforce in the public sector. Thus a deflationary movement in the private sector, due, say, to a decline in private investment expenditure or to a "buyers' strike" of consumers trying to increase their cash balances, is reflected in a decline in taxable income. With a system that is largely pay-as-you-go, this results in an immediate decline in tax receipts at both Federal and local levels.

There is also likely to be an increase in over-all governmental expenditure on unemployment insurance benefits, relief payments, agricultural price-support purchases, and so on. Government cash budgets rapidly become unbalanced: this results in an increase in the cash balances held by the public, and this is in itself an inflationary factor. It may not be enough to counteract the initial deflationary movement entirely, but it will slow down the deflation and hence tend to eliminate certain dynamic aggravations of the deflationary process. If in addition there are some deliberate policy measures, such as credit relaxation or tax reduction, a spontaneous deflationary force can easily be offset in principle, though in practice there are difficult problems involved in the timing of these changes. Similarly, if there is a spontaneous inflationary movement in the private sector, taxable incomes rise, government receipts rise and expenditures fall, and government runs a surplus which drains money out of private balances, thus reducing the inflationary pressure.

Thus, the critical question here is whether arms control will result in a sizable reduction in the over-all government budget. If we have what I have called "expensive" arms control, which seems most likely at the moment, with elaborate inspection systems and even an increase in conventional forces, the problem may not arise. The movement toward arms control, however, is more fundamental than a mere attempt to put back the clock of technology to the point where we can once more indulge ourselves in the luxury of war without the fear of annihilation. At some point in the development of a viable world social system, as we proceed from arms control to close organizational connections between opposing armed forces, or even as we proceed to a system of "absolute weapons" in which defense collapses altogether and unilateral disarmament begins to pay off, there may come a point where there is no payoff in the maintenance of expensive national armed forces and they will be dismantled. This may seem absurd to historians and political scientists who are not students of general social systems and who cannot usually imagine any social system beyond the present.

We know too little about social systems to predict their course, and there may be many possible dynamic paths to the world society—conquest, unions, agreements, tacit agreements, unilateral behavior, and so on. The possibility of "cheap" arms control must not, however, be left off the agenda, even though this is almost certainly not the next move. The problem of the reaction of the American economy to "cheap" arms control (for instance, total disarmament) is a question of more than academic interest, even though it is at the moment an "academic" question. It is important not only because it may someday happen and we should be prepared for it, but because the assertion that the American economy could not maintain its health without a large arms program is a widely held belief, not only by Communist propagandists (though this line seems at the moment to have been abandoned) but what is more important, by many Americans themselves, some of them in high places.

Suppose then, we look at a model of an American economy in, say, 1959, in which the national security budget has been virtually eliminated. The total government budget is still about 10 percent of the GNP. This is a situation surprisingly similar to that of 1929, as is shown in the following table:

TABLE 2

United States Nonmilitary Government Expenditure, in real terms ⋅(in billions of 1959 dollars).

| | TOTAL | | AS PERCENT OF GNP | |
	1929	1959	1929	1959
Federal nonmilitary expenditure	3.4*	8.1	1.8*	1.7
State and local government expenditure	17.4	44.3	8.9	9.2
Total nonmilitary government expenditure	20.8	52.4	10.7	10.9
GNP	203.6	478.8		

SOURCE: *Economic Report of the President,* 1960.

* This figure is for total Federal expenditure, as military expenditure is not available separately. The latter would be of the order of 1.0 billion.

It may come as a shock to many people to learn that apart from national defense, the proportion of real product actually absorbed by government in the late 1950's was almost exactly the same as in the late 1920's, in spite of a more than doubled real GNP. Creeping socialism does not seem to have crept very far, outside the Pentagon, which is in terms of GNP the world's third largest nonmarket economy, with only Russia and possibly China exceeding it. There may even be something in Galbraith's thesis that the public economy needs to expand, arms control or no arms control. The question needs to be raised, therefore, as to whether a nonmilitary American economy in 1961 would be any safer from depression than in 1929 without the introduction of organizational machinery which we do not now possess. No definite answer could be given to this question without a good deal more study.* There are many important differences between now and 1929. The national debt is larger. We have pay-as-you-go taxes, which are a great stabilizer (before this, income taxes were paid on the previous year's income and so went up as a percentage of income when incomes were falling). We have social security, and also agricultural price supports, which for all their vices are also built-in stabilizers. Nevertheless, it is a moot question whether these devices are quantitatively adequate to deal with a sharp deflation. We may not expect anything like 1929–1932, but something like 1937–1938 would not be beyond the bounds of possibility.

It must be emphasized, however, that the purely economic problems involved in an adequate stabilization policy have been solved at the level of first approximation. We know roughly what to do, and still more roughly how much to do and when to do it. It would be possible, for instance, to increase the sensitivity of the built-in stabilizers at a lower level of government expenditure by such devices as automatic tax-rate reduction when national income fell, and a similar increase when it rose. It would be possible also to pursue more vigorous monetary policies. I am personally against this step, but this is an internal row among the economists. The important thing is that there are many ways of stabilizing (within limits of tolerance) the gross national product. There is an important unsolved problem regarding the extent to which this can be done without long-run inflation, and how the answer to this question is related to noncompetitive labor, capital, and commodity markets, but this, in a sense, is a secondary problem. To put the matter in a rather crude form: If we take 40 billion dollars of defense production out of the gross national product, where can we find another 40 billion dollars' worth of goods and services which can be absorbed without causing deflation? The answer is partly in increased household purchases as a result of tax decreases, partly in increased investment by businesses, partly by increased government expenditure in civilian uses, and partly by an export surplus created by foreign investment or foreign aid.

It is easy to find four numbers that add up to 40 billion. The trouble may be that it is too easy: there are too many alternatives, and we may be paralyzed for want of ability to choose among them, for the choice will involve political decisions which we are not well set up to make. Furthermore, the choice involves a mixture of technical and political decisions which are hard to unscramble. Thus the decision to take steps to stabilize the GNP

* Such a study is in progress under the auspices of the Center for Conflict Resolution at the University of Michigan, directed by Professor Emile Benoit of Columbia University, and financed by a grant from the Carnegie Corporation and a Ford Foundation Faculty Research Fellowship.

and so expand other forms of product absorption by roughly the amount of decline in government military expenditure would be almost nonpolitical in the sense that there would be wide agreement and little conflict of interest about the objective. When it comes to allocating this increase among the various alternative methods of achieving it—tax reduction, debt decrease, shifts in the tax structure, additional government expenditure on various competing activities (health, education, social security, conservation, public works, roads, flood control, and so on), and finally foreign aid and public investment abroad—the battle of interests is on, and there is no machinery to insure that the sum total of these various decisions adds up to just the right amount. I have sometimes thought of a device like a "government dollar," in which taxes shall be collected and budgets reckoned, and a variable rate of exchange (set by an economic policy agency analogous to the Federal Reserve Board) betwen government money and private money: the interests could fight out the truly political problems of allocation in government dollars, and then the stabilization agency could from time to time determine the aggregate amounts by setting a rate of exchange with private money as stabiization policy demanded. The suggestion may be quite impracticable: it is offered only as an example of the kind of change in our existing economic institutions which a stabilization policy on a small government budget might require.

Perhaps the greatest immediate threat to a rational stabilization policy is the still common attitude toward the national debt which sees it as a great burden and wants to strain to reduce it. There is sometimes a case for monetizing part of the national debt (paying it off with newly created money). There is hardly ever any case for paying it off by running a budget surplus, except in periods of strong inflation of private origin. A sharp reduction in the total government expenditure will be seized on by the economic puritans as an opportunity to pay off the national debt by not reducing taxes and so producing a substantial budget surplus. Such a policy would almost certainly be ruinously deflationary, and would cause depression and prevent conversion.

The problem of designing an optimum rate of economic growth is even more difficult than that of stabilization, and arms control may well raise serious questions—questions, however, which again are capable of serious answers. Economic growth is maintained by devoting resources to the accumulation of things, skills, and knowledge, and of these knowledge is the greatest. National security expenditure generates, as an important byproduct, all three of these forms of accumulation. It results in the accumulation of buildings, roads, installations, and stocks of many commodities, many of which have potential civilian uses. It results also in the accumulation of skills in the population by dragging men out of their homes and teaching them crafts, trades, and professions, as well as the arts of dealing death and destruction. Finally, and this is becoming an increasingly important aspect of military expenditure, it organizes research on a scale of expense unknown to the civilian world. The Pentagon and Hollywood seem to be the only two places in our society where extravagance is cultivated as a virtue. Therefore, when research is hitched to the military rocket, it proceeds at a pace far beyond that of the civilian and merely peripatetic philosopher. I am quite willing to deplore this fact, but I am forced to acknowledge it. Perhaps the biggest social invention of the mid-twentieth century was the RAND Corporation, which perpetually makes obsolete the institution that fathered it.

Here again the economic problem is almost trivial. If we spent as much on research and training for human welfare as we spend for defense, it is hard to believe that the results would not be even more dramatic. If all science could be pursued without the smell of brimstone, and if all secrecy were abolished, how much more quickly, and joyfully, would knowledge grow. The problem is essentially one of the political consciousness: Can we organize, through both private and public organization, the same kind of effort, or an even greater effort, for pure knowledge, useful skill, and human betterment than we can for the road to doomsday? If we cannot, it can only be because of a failure of the imagination, of a lack of clear purpose, and a poverty of symbols. But if we lack these things, we do not deserve anything better than doomsday.

In spite of the fact that the main theme of this chapter is the domestic economic implications, we should take a brief glance abroad, for several reasons. One is that the internal economic implications of arms control for other countries may be different from what they are in the United States. In Russia, for instance, though exact information is not available, the proportion of the gross national product going into national security is considerably larger than in the United States—though in an economy that is substantially poorer. National security is correspondingly a much greater economic burden. In the United States the marginal significance of the arms dollar is in the realm of a little more or a little less luxury; in Russia it is much closer to basic comfort, and in India it is close to sheer necessity. The Russians correspondingly have a greater incentive than we do toward "cheap" arms control, and this may explain something of their (and our) attitudes. In really poor countries like India, Pakistan, and China, arms expenditure literally snatches life from the starving: there is an enormous economic interest in cheap security.

Indeed, economic development is such a tender plant in its early stages that a heavy arms budget may condemn a poor country to stagnation. The problem is complicated, however, by the fact that at least in its early stages arms control will probably not operate as a world system, and there will be sub-systems within it (such as the rivalries between India and Pakistan, Israel and the Arab world, Cuba and the Dominican Republic) which may escape the general system of arms control and yet may be very costly to the participants.

Another reason for looking at the world economic scene is that one of the domestic implications of arms control (at least, of "cheap" arms control) for the United States may be a release of resources for investment and development abroad. This has implications for the reduction, or increase, of world tensions which may be relevant to the success or failure of arms control itself. It is important, too, in the moral mythology of disarmament: the plea that disarmament would release large resources for economic development and for raising standards of life in the poor countries is a powerful part of the motivation which drives ordinary decent people toward it, even if it does not have much appeal for political realists and those who direct the destinies of states.

Like other myths, this also embodies an important half truth. It is true that disarmament (or cheap arms control) would release resources which could indeed be used for this purpose. They do not have to be used for this purpose, however, and there is no guarantee that they would be. If we assume that no method of domestic stabilization is acceptable, other than manipulating the export surplus, then of course the stabilization program which followed cheap arms control would involve extensive gifts and investments abroad. It is perfectly possible, however, to draw up a domestic stabilization plan which involves no increase in the export surplus and no contribution to the development of the rest of the world. The plain fact is that, beyond a certain point of profitable investment abroad, the increase in the American export surplus involves a real cost to Americans, in terms of consumption foregone, or what may be more serious, domestic growth impaired. Empire, whether political or economic, has frequently involved a high cost to the imperial power. In terms of per-capita income, for instance, the countries that stayed at home and minded their own business (like Sweden and Switzerland) have frequently done better than those who have spread their flag and their subsidies around the globe, like Portugal and Spain. The history of the technological revolution shows that man may squeeze a hundred dollars out of nature with the effort that he spends on squeezing one dollar out of conquest. The polite struggle to abandon empire, which is so characteristic and almost embarrassing a phenomenon of the modern world, may not be unconnected with a half-conscious realization that whatever may have been the case three hundred years ago, empire does not pay today. There may be exceptions to this rule: the Russians have probably got something out of East Germany, though it will be surprising if they get anything out of Cuba and Guinea. The whole subject needs much more careful study than has been given to it.

The impact of aid programs, both on the development of the recipients and on the level of world tensions, needs careful study. On the one hand, we must avoid the naïve expectation that progress and peace can be bought by the indiscriminate shoveling out of billions. On the other hand, we must equally avoid the niggardly naïveté of the xenophobes and economic isolationists. Without some acceptance of world responsibility on the part of the rich and powerful countries, it is difficult to visualize a successful system of world peace. Yet there is also a trick of being able to accept gifts, advice, and support without a collapse of internal morale and self-respect. It may be more blessed to give, but it is often a lot harder to receive. Nevertheless, this skill can be learned, as Japan has shown in regard to knowledge and Puerto Rico shows in regard to both things and knowledge. The problem of how to make the poor countries rich requires a degree of serious research and attention at least comparable to that put into the road to doomsday. If arms control can release this kind of resource, in the long run this may be its most important contribution.

The economic consequences of arms control are perhaps the easiest to trace of all the consequences for the social system. The impact of arms control on the other institutions and patterns of behavior in society may eventually be even more significant, but we have hardly begun to think about these deeper implications. Nevertheless, they exist—for religion, for family life, for ethics, for art, for culture in all its many dimensions, and for politics. This is true because arms control is the beginning of a great revolution in human affairs. It may look like an attempt to get national security cheap, or to safeguard the institution of limited war, or to prevent a nuclear holocaust— and it is all these things. However, arms control is only the beginning of a process of evolution of social institutions which leads to the abolition of war and the establishment of the institutions of permanent peace, even though we cannot now foretell in detail what these will be. A specter is haunting the chancelleries and the general staffs, more frightening perhaps than that which Karl Marx invoked in 1848; it is the specter of Peace—that drab girl with the olive-branch corsage whom no red-blooded American (or Russian) could conceivably warm up to. She haunts us because we cannot go back to Napoleon, or to Lee, or even to MacArthur: the military are caught in an implacable dynamic of technical change which makes them increasingly less capable of defending the countries which support them, except at an increasingly intolerable cost. The grotesque irony of national defense in the nuclear age is that, after having had the inestimable privilege of losing half (or is it three quarters, or all?) our population, we are supposed to set up again the whole system which gave rise to this holocaust!

We are, however, totally unprepared for peace. We have never had peace, and it may be forced upon us before we really want it. One can only, in the spirit of Newton's *Opticks,* raise some queries. What, for instance, can hold society together in the absence of an external threat? What are the institutions which can embody "conflict control"—that general social system of which arms control is only a special case? How do we catch the disintegrating dynamic processes in society—the epidemics of hatred, the infectious images of falsehood, the powerful symbols which lead to destruction—and stop them, by education, by quarantine, by counter-eloquence, before they spread too far? How do we give the individual an image of self-respect, of identification with some larger group, without permitting the development of images of hatred and intolerance? How do we preserve the richness and variety of cultural differences in a world of rapid communication and peace —how, in other words, do we preserve the very real virtues of nationalism in a warless world? How do we prevent the great latent social processes (population growth, emotional hysteria, charismatic leadership, mistaken images of social fact) from carrying societies to poverty, factionalism, and decay? More difficult perhaps, how do we prevent boredom, how do we preserve danger, excitement, and a sense of high purpose? How do we deal with sadism and masculinism, masochism and feminism, the strut and the swagger, the cringe and the death wish? How do we release people from the crippling "binds" of ambivalence, and release their creative potential? How do we raise children in a warless world? What kind of ethic do we inculcate, and what are our defenses against its corruption? What rituals shall we have, and what heroes? How can we prevent the corrupting influence of wealth, luxury, and the treacherous ability to satisfy the flesh? Peace, it is clear, insinuates her soft fingers into every nerve of life. We have dreamed of utopia, and secretly been thankful that it is only a dream. Now we are going to be compelled to think about it, and think hard and long, for we may be forced into it by the absence of any alternative but doomsday.

PART III

THE SUBSTANCE OF
ARMS CONTROL

9. Reciprocal Measures for Arms Stabilization

THOMAS C. SCHELLING

THERE HAS BEEN A WIDESPREAD CHANGE IN THE THINKING ON ARMS control in the last year or so. Much of it is due to the focus of attention on "measures to safeguard against surprise attack" (to use the official terminology). Although this subject is still listed anachronistically under "disarmament," it is differently oriented. It assumes deterrence as the keystone of our security policy, and tries to improve it. It accepts a retaliatory capability as something to be enhanced, not degraded—something to be made more secure, less accident-prone, less in need of striking quickly to avoid its own destruction, less capable of gaining advantage from a sudden attack of its own. An anomaly of this approach to arms control is that it does not necessarily involve "disarmament" in the literal sense.

Another anomaly, which rather shakes the disarmament tradition, is that weapons may be more stabilizing and less aggressive if they are capable of civilian reprisal rather than of military engagement. A standoff between two retaliatory forces is in some ways equivalent to an exchange of hostages; and "inhumane" weapons, capable of inflicting damage but not able to go after the enemy's strategic forces, acquire virtue because of their clearly deterrent function and the lack of temptation they give either side to strike first.

More important, though, is the fact that schemes to avert surprise attack are manifestly compatible with a national military policy, not a renunciation of it. They emphasize the possibility that one can simultaneously think seriously and sympathetically about our military posture and about collaborating with our enemies to improve it. To propose, as does the notion of "measures to safeguard against surprise attack," that military cooperation with potential enemies may offer opportunities to improve our military posture, opens a new field for imaginative scientific and military thinking, and may eventually enlist the support of the military services themselves.

Most of this progress is still ahead of us; the revolution in thinking about arms control is barely started. Officially we have taken only the most hesitant steps in defining arms control in a way that does not contradict our national security policies. We still talk officially as though "disarmament" can only save money, without noticing that under the new philosophy it could cost more. We still work officially with an image of disarmament that makes it solely a peacetime (cold-wartime) process of negotiating explicit detailed agreements in a multinational context for the reduction or elimination of weapons, without adequately recognizing that, as in limiting war, limiting the arms race can be a more tacit and less formal process than the "treaty" idea implies. More important, the prevalent image of disarmament is still one that gives the process a uniquely defined end point—the point of no arms at all, or virtually none except in the hands of some international authority or synthetic state that would have the power to police the world against international violence but against nothing else.

The cautious and the skeptical, the pessimists and the realists, have doubts about how rapidly that end point can be approached, whether it will be approached at all, and whether the process once started may not be reversed. But the goal itself is rarely challenged except by those who have no interest in arms control. And by far the most frequent argument raised in favor of particular limited measures of arms control, perhaps the most widely persuasive, is that these limited measures are at least "steps toward" the goal of ultimate disarmament. We have not faced up to the implications of the anomaly that "measures to safeguard against surprise attack" are designed to preserve a nuclear striking power, and are not easily construed as just another "step toward" ultimate disarmament.*

We still talk about "levels" of armament or disarmament, as though there were only two directions in which to go, up and down, the arms race going in one direction and arms control in the other. We have not yet admitted that, even in the framework of arms control, it could be an open question whether we ought to be negotiating with our enemies for more arms, less arms, different kinds of arms, or arrangements superimposed on

---

* It should be noted here that the term, "measures to safeguard against surprise attack," has become extremely ambiguous. Some use it to refer only to schemes to avert surprise by provision of last-minute tactical warning. Others enlarge the term to include reciprocal intelligence measures to provide strategic warning or to provide reassurance of the absence of intent or capability. Some use the term more broadly to include limitations on forces, their kinds, numbers, or deployment, to make the achievement of surprise more difficult. (In an extreme interpretation, any disarmament scheme that requires visible rearmament for the initiation of general war can be viewed as a "warning system.") Others use the term to include measures not aimed at surprise itself but at vulnerability to surprise, i.e., to weapon programs or limitations that make the initial attack less potent even when surprise is achieved. All these, and many other, interpretations and usages of the term have one thing in common, however; they are all concerned with the advantage that attaches to "going first" in a major war and are concerned to reduce it or to allay the false alarms and crises that it gives rise to. Additionally, there may be measures aimed at preventing surprise or reducing its consequences in local rather than general war; these have received comparatively little attention in the last few years, but some of the Europe-oriented surprise-attack proposals of 1955-1957 were of that character.[1]

existing armaments. We have given little thought even to the weapon system that would be required by that ultimate international authority that might police the world against armed violence, and to whether it, too, would be embarrassed by a "massive retaliation" doctrine that would lack credibility; whether it, too, might be subject to surprise attack; whether it, too, would lack resolution (as some think NATO might lack resolution) to reach an awful collective decision in response to nibbling aggression or bland violation.

The point of this chapter is that there is a vast new area to be explored once we break out of the traditional confinement of "disarmament"—the entire area of military collaboration with potential enemies to reduce the likelihood of war or to reduce its scope and violence. It is an area worth exploring because our present military policies and prospects, however we feel about the adequacy of current programs, cannot promise security from a major thermonuclear war; and even modest improvements achieved through cooperation with the Soviets should be welcome.

It is not true that in the modern world a gain for the Russians is necessarily a loss for us, and vice versa. We can both suffer losses, and this fact provides scope for cooperation. We both have—unless the Russians have already determined to launch an attack and are preparing for it—a common interest in reducing the advantage of striking first, simply because that very advantage, even if common to both sides, increases the likelihood of war. If at the expense of some capability for launching surprise attack one can deny that capability to the other, it may be a good bargain. We both have a common interest in avoiding the kind of false alarm, panic, misunderstanding, or loss of control, that may lead to an unpremeditated war, in a situation aggravated by the recognition on both sides that it is better to go first than to go second. We have a common interest in not getting drawn or provoked or panicked into war by the actions of a third party (whether that party intends the result or not). And we may have an interest in saving some money by not doing on both sides the things that, if we both do them, tend to cancel out.

This common interest does not depend on trust and good faith. In fact it seems likely that unless thoroughgoing distrust can be acknowledged on both sides, it may be hard to reach any real understanding on the subject. The intellectual clarity required to recognize the nature of the common interest may be incompatible with the pretense that we trust each other, or that there is any sequence of activities in the short run by which either side could demonstrate its good faith to the other.

Ancient despotisms may have understood better than we do how to tranquilize relations between them while hating and distrusting. They exchanged hostages, drank wine from the same glass, met in public to inhibit the massacre of one by the other, and even deliberately exchanged spies to facilitate transmittal of authentic information. And perhaps, having exchanged a son for a daughter in the cold-blooded interest of contract enforcement, they may have reduced tension sufficiently to permit a little affection to grow up in later generations.

ARMS CONTROL AND MILITARY TECHNOLOGY

The premise underlying my point of view is that a main determinant of the likelihood of war is the nature of present military technology. We and the Russians are trapped by our military technology. Weapon developments of the last fifteen years, especially of the last seven or eight, have themselves been responsible for the most alarming aspects of the present strategic situation. They have enhanced the advantage, in the event war should come, of being the one to start it. They have inhumanly compressed the time available to make the most terrible decisions. They have almost eliminated any belief that a really big war either could be or should be limited in scope or brought to a close by any process other than the sheer exhaustion of weapons. They have greatly reduced the confidence of either side that it can predict the weapons its enemy has or will have in the future. In these and other ways the evolution of military technology has exacerbated whatever propensities toward war are inherent in the political conflict between us and our enemies. It might be naïve to say that this is an unmixed evil for both us and the Soviets, since it powerfully affects the bilateral contest between us; nevertheless, it is hard to escape the judgment that nature might have been kinder in the way she let our military technology unfold itself over the last decade and a half.

It is interesting—more than that, it is useful—to ask what technological achievements (available both to us and to our enemies) we wish had never occurred, and what technological failures we wish had turned out otherwise. Do we wish the hydrogen bomb had never come along to make intercontinental missiles economical? Do we wish that nuclear-powered aircraft had made airborne alert so cheap that retaliatory aircraft could stay aloft rather than be vulnerable on the ground to a missile attack? Do we hope that no one ever discovers an economical means of nullifying ballistic-missile submarines, so that neither side can hope to preclude retaliation by sudden attack? Do we wish that warning systems were so nearly perfect that "false alarm" were virtually impossible, or so poor that we could never be tempted to rely on them? Do we wish that missiles had never become so accurate that they could be used to destroy an enemy's missiles in an effort to negate an enemy's retaliatory threat? Do we wish that radioactive fallout could not occur, or do we welcome it as a peculiarly retaliatory (and hence deterrent) weapon effect that is of little use in a pre-emptive attack? Do we wish that secrecy about weapons and weapon production were much more difficult to maintain than it is, or welcome certain kinds of secrecy as a form of mutually appreciated security against surprise attack?

The reason why it is productive to speculate on these questions, rather than merely fanciful, is that arms control can usefully be thought of as a way of changing some of the answers. In addition to what we can do unilaterally to improve our warning systems, to maintain close control over our forces, to make our forces more secure against attack, to avoid the need for precipitate decisions, and to avoid accidents or the mistaken decisions that they might cause, there may be opportunities to exchange facilities or understandings with our enemies, or to design and deploy our forces differently by agreement with our enemies who do likewise, in a way that enhances those aspects of technology we like and that helps to nullify those that we do not.

If we wish that radar were better and cheaper and less limited by the Earth's curvature, we might make it so by exchanging real estate with the Russians for the construction by each of us of observation posts on each other's soil. If we hope that no one can ever predict with confidence how his own missiles would do, in a surprise attack, against the hardened missile sites of his opponent, we might deny each other the necessary knowledge by banning tests of large weapons in the era in which anyone actually has a missile in a hard underground site that he could use a weapon-effects test. If instead we wish that each side might preserve the privacy of its railroad lines for mobile missiles, we might jointly eschew certain surveillance techniques; and if we thought that anti-missile defenses of missile sites might be more feasible, and retaliatory forces correspondingly less vulnerable, with the further testing of nuclear weapons and their effects, we might look with more favor on continued weapon testing. These considerations are by no means the whole story in arms control, but they do remind us that we and our enemies can both jointly welcome, or jointly deplore, certain technological developments (like the improved accuracy of long-range missiles) and may possibly find ways, jointly, to enhance them or to offset them, over and above the things that we can do unilaterally.

NEED FOR STRATEGIC ANALYSIS

These examples suggest some of the criteria that can be applied to limited arms-control schemes, and some of the difficulties in implementing them. As to criteria, the first thing to emphasize is that it takes a good deal of strategic analysis to decide whether a particular limitation or augmentation of weapons or facilities is a good one or a bad one. Viewing limited measures on their individual merits, and not as steps in a comprehensive program that can be justified only by a long sequence of steps to follow, one has to ask whether the technological and economic consequences of a particular scheme are or are not conducive to military stability; and the answer is very unlikely to be closely correlated with whether more weapons or fewer weapons are involved, bigger weapons or smaller ones, or even whether notions of "more" and "less," "bigger" and "smaller," can be applied. Whether we would like to see reconnaissance satellites banned or encouraged may depend, for example, on whether we think they will mainly provide targeting information to the initiator of war or mainly provide warning to a potential defender so that a potential attacker is the more deterred. Whether we like big missiles or not may depend on whether we believe, as so many believed a few years ago, that missiles would be simple and sturdy and hard to destroy in their underground sites or believe as so many fear now that increased accuracies and yields make the present generation of missiles better for a first strike than for a second strike. Whether we wish missile technology to be advanced or retarded may depend on whether or not we believe, as many do, that the next generation of missiles will be easier to protect, easier to hide, or easier to keep moving, and therefore less insecure. Whether one welcomes nuclear-powered ballistic-missile submarines on both sides or deplores them depends on whether they seem to be peculiarly good at surviving and retaliating, and hence "deterrent," or peculiarly good at getting up close for a no-warning strike on an enemy's retaliatory power. And if it were somehow possible to enforce a ban on "dirty" bombs, there would still be a genuine strategic question of whether or not we wish deterrent capabilities to be enhanced by the greater punitive power of dirty bombs, recognizing that comparatively slow-acting fallout may be of much less utility to a potential attacker, whose main interest is to minimize retaliation on himself.

IMPLICATIONS FOR ARMS AGREEMENT

The fact that developments such as these require strategic analysis before it can be decided whether they are good or bad is, aside from being true, discouraging. It means that even among the experts there will be disagreement about the consequences of any particular prohibition or exchange of military facilities; it may be next to impossible to get widespread understanding of the relevant arguments, even within governments. And if fairly detailed analysis is required, and careful distinctions have to be made, prohibitions might have to be specified in equally careful detail and with equally fine distinctions. This is certainly an obstacle to negotiation. Furthermore, any analysis—and any prohibition or agreement or exchange of facilities that is justified on the basis of such analysis—is subject to rapid obsolescence. The friendly warning satellite appears, a year later, as a vicious targeting aid to the surprise attacker; the network of warning systems originally designed for mutual reassurance proves in operation to have too high a false-alarm rate; the missile-guidance systems that we deplored because of their extreme accuracy and the advantage they would give the attacker may prove, after we outlaw them, to have been the main hope for mobile missile systems desired for their invulnerability and hence for their stability. By the time we reach agreement on precisely what to allow in our satellites, where to place our radar, or what missiles to ban, new evidence or new analysis comes along to suggest that the justification of the particular scheme we are about to subscribe to is all wrong.

Finally, by the time we look at individual schemes in sufficient detail to judge whether their strategic implications are "good" for both us and our enemies, we may have narrowed them down to the point where they are intolerably biased. It is probably a mathematically sound principle that the more measures we put in a package, the more their bilateral biases will cancel out, and hence the greater will be the joint gain relative to the competitive advantage. This may mean that once a potential arms-control system is dissected into sufficiently small pieces to apply the right kind of analysis, we shall have more individual bargaining counters too small and too biased for the negotiating process.

The recent negotiations on weapon tests may prove to be typical. First, there has been almost no public discussion of whether the further testing of weapons and weapon effects would really be conducive to the development of greater bilateral military stability or instability over the coming years.* Even if the public could be got interested in this crucial question, it would be unlikely to have the information it would need to judge the answer. (There has been a good deal of public discussion of the merits and possible demerits of preventing the further spread of nuclear weapons to small countries, but remarkably little discussion of just how a test ban would obstruct the spread.) Second, while it may seem a mischievous stroke of fortune that somebody discovered, between the two conferences, facts or ideas that made the policing of a test ban appear more difficult than it had appeared the year before, this may be exactly what we have to expect in every case. If today we had "completely solved" the new technical problems introduced by the "decoupling" technique, we should still have to be prepared for somebody's discovering next year a new possibility that had been overlooked, one that contemporary detection technology could not yet cope with.

The test-ban discussions also illustrate that, when an issue has been narrowed down, the bias in the advantages may seem to outweigh the joint advantages. There is more controversy, and understandably so, over whether a prohibition on small-weapon tests is in the American interest, than on whether a prohibition covering the whole spectrum is.

But of all the characteristics of the present test-ban negotiations, the most significant may be that we have had a moratorium for some time without a formal agreement. (We do not, of course, have rights of inspection; so we cannot be sure that the moratorium has been kept; but it

---

* That is, whether further testing would mainly facilitate the development of more secure retaliatory weapon systems with better communication and control, less subject to accident and false alarm, or instead would mainly enhance the potency of weapons for pre-emptive attack and aggravate the urge, when in doubt, to strike quickly and without restraint. The answer is by no means obvious for the period immediately ahead. It should be noted that tests involve not only new-weapon performance but weapon *effects* on previously untested targets, and the latter may be especially relevant to such things as anti-ICBM defense, civil defense, and the vulnerability of fixed or mobile weapons, warning systems, and communication and control systems.

likely has been, except possibly for the most easily disguised tests.) And this moratorium resulted from no detailed negotiations, no careful specifications, and no written documents to be initialed and ratified. I do not think this result can be wholly explained by the pressure of public opinion. Part of the motivation must be that, whatever one side is sacrificing in improved technology, the other side is also foregoing tests, and each would probably resume them if the other did. Thus the main sanction of an arms-control agreement—the expectation that each will abstain only if the other does—is probably present in this case. It is therefore a genuine instance of "arms control." If it suffers from being tentative, temporary, qualified, and conditional, so might any arms-control agreement, even if duly negotiated and signed; furthermore, who can say yet that the present "agreement," if such we may call it, will not be of some duration?

INFORMAL ARMS UNDERSTANDINGS

Here, I think we have an important clue to a process by which arms control may be reached, and the kinds of arms control that can be reached by that process. Maybe arms control is destined to be something more informal than is suggested by the great diplomatic deployments in Geneva. Maybe limited measures of arms control can be arrived at by quite indirect and incomplete communication; maybe they will take the form of a proposal embodied in unilateral action (or abstention from action) which continues if matched by corresponding action on the other side and only for so long as it is. Maybe instead of *arguing* about what we should do, we will simply do it and dare the other side to do likewise, or do it and quietly suggest that we would like to keep it up, but only if they find it in their interest to do something comparable.

But if arms control is to be arrived at by a more tacit and informal process, and if we are going to call "arms control" any of the military things that we and the Russians abstain from because of an awareness that as long as each abstains the other probably will too, we should look around and see whether we do not already have a good deal of arms control. If we have, we should look at it closely to see what lessons we can draw.

Offhand, it appears (but a more imaginative examination might prove otherwise) that the tacit understandings we have with the Russians concern what we do with our weapons more than what we possess.* We seem to have some understandings about traffic rules for patrolling bombers;

---

* A possible exception is civil defense. The extraordinary aversion to civil defense in the United States Government must be complex in its explanation; but an element is very likely a belief that a genuine civil defense program might open up a new dimension of the arms race, leading either to a "civil-defense race" with the USSR or just to an aggravation of the arms competition. The same may be true in the USSR. An interesting question is how much "clandestine" civil defense the Russians are undertaking, and their reasons for keeping it private. (In pointing this out, the author is not trying to justify the aversion to civil defense.)

there are apparently certain lines we stay on this side of, lines the Russians presumably can recognize, the crossing of which they can probably monitor to some extent. This is certainly a restraint that we unilaterally observe in the interest of reducing misunderstandings and alarms. As far as I know, the traffic rules are communicated, not explicitly, but simply by behaving in accordance with them (perhaps *conspicuously* in accordance with them) and possibly by having chosen the dividing lines in such a way that their significance is recognizable. We both abstain from harassing actions on each other's strategic forces; we do not jam each other's military communications, scare each other with fallout from weapons tests, or wage surreptitious peacetime undersea wars of attrition.* We may yet develop tacit understandings about zones and traffic rules for submarines, and may (or may not) develop a tradition for leaving each other's reconnaissance satellites alone. We both very obviously abstain from assassination. The Russians recently "negotiated" (by a process of nudging) a sharper understanding about sharing the Pacific for target practice. It remains to be seen whether the U-2 incident causes certain tacit or latent understandings to come unstuck.†

In all likelihood we may abstain from the use of nuclear weapons in some limited war, though both sides often seem to denounce officially the notion that a serious limited war should be, or could be, fought without nuclear weapons. Here is an interesting case of an arms limitation that may be tacitly recognized by both sides, and recognized only because each thinks the other may observe it too, yet one that is not only not formally agreed on but even denounced and denied by both sides. It seems doubtful whether this tacit understanding could be made much stronger by a written document.‡ A restraint on the use of nuclear weapons may be more persuasive if it seems to rest on the enemy's own self-interest—on his understanding that if he abstains we may too, but only if he does—than if it pretends to rest on the power of a written agreement or on a fiction of "good faith."

LIMITED WAR AS "ARMS CONTROL"

In fact, all of the tacitly agreed limits that do apply, or may apply, in limited war can be construed as a kind of informal arms control tacitly

---

* Not yet, that is, or not very much. Preserving some of the mutual restraints we now enjoy may be as important an "arms-control" objective as creating more.

† It seems a correct interpretation that there is still some element of implicit understanding about not transferring nuclear weapons to other countries. Its status is presently a great deal more ambiguous than the author expected a couple of years ago; nevertheless there must be a general awareness on both sides that the restraint of either will be weakened or dissolved by promiscuousness on the other's part.

‡ It could be made much stronger by various unilateral actions. One would be to increase our *capability* to get along without nuclears in limited war. Another would be to add symbolic support to the understanding; the test-ban negotiations—especially if a formal agreement is reached—almost certainly do this, whether they are intended to or not.

arrived at. My impression is that we and the Russians will go to some length to avoid having American and Russian troops directly engage each other in a limited war, simply because such an engagement might create extremely unstable expectations about whether the war could remain limited. We and the Russians both recognize many legalistic limitations in war, such as the distinction between North Koreans and Chinese, between volunteers and regulars, between the provision of materials to an ally and the provision of manpower, between doing an ally's reconnaissance for him and doing his bombing, perhaps even the distinction between local airfields that are fair game because they are on the ground within a disputed country and the decks of carriers offshore that might for some reason be construed as "sanctuary."

Most of these limits are arbitrary, conventional, and casuistic—purely matters of tradition and precedent. For that reason they are uncertain and insecure; nobody is even nominally committed to honor them. But they demonstrate that it is possible for potential enemies to arrive tacitly, or by indirect communication, at a meeting of minds about some rules, and about how to interpret intentions through the way one operates and deploys his resources. Most important, the limits that can be observed in limited war are a powerful demonstration that sheer self-interest—the recognition of a need to collaborate with an enemy in wartime, to reach understandings that transcend the formalities of explicit communications; the recognition of a mutual interest in avoiding accidents, incidents, misunderstandings, and unnecessary alarms, and in holding to any constraints that can be found—can provide potent sanctions that need not rest on explicit negotiation and formal agreements.

We may, then, increase our understanding of the nature of arms control, what it rests on and how it may come about, by recognizing limited war as a kind of arms control in itself. And perhaps it differs from peacetime (i.e., cold-war) arms control less than we customarily think. Perhaps the psychology and the sanctions and the mode of communication, the kinds of reasoning involved, the lack of formal agreement or even acknowledgment, that typify limited war, represent a more central and typical process of international negotiation than we usually give it credit for.

There is another aspect of limited war that deserves emphasis in this connection. The limits in limited war are arrived at not by verbal bargaining, but by maneuver, by actions, and by statements and declarations that are not direct communication to the enemy. Each side tends to act in some kind of recognizable pattern, so that any limits that it is actually observing can be appreciated by the enemy; and each tries to perceive what restraints the other is observing. For that reason the limits themselves must be clearcut, must be of an "obvious" character, must be based on qualitative distinctions rather than matters of degree. They must not be too selective, too gerrymandered in discriminating between what is inside and what is outside the limit. They must attach themselves to benchmarks, demarcation lines, and distinctions that come naturally. They must have simplicity. They must take advantage of conventions and traditions and precedents that exist, even if the precedents and traditions are biased between the two sides or a nuisance to both sides. Often they must involve all-or-none distinctions, or across-the-board distinctions like that between land and water, between material and manpower, between two sides of a border, or even some arbitrary but potent and highly suggestive feature like a parallel of latitude.[2]

This is certainly true in the case of the use of nuclear weapons in limited war. It is enormously more likely that a limit against any use of nuclear weapons could be recognized, sensed, and adhered to by both sides on condition that each other observe it, than that any particular quantitative limitation, target limitation, fission vs. fusion limitation, or limitation based on who is the "aggressor," could be jointly and tacitly converged on by the participants.

But the same is certainly true of a test suspension. A tacitly reached moratorium on testing nuclear weapons—mutual and reciprocal but essentially unilateral on both sides—is much more likely to be stable and durable, much less likely to be eroded by ambiguous behavior, than a selective moratorium. If we and the Russians are very selective in our unilateral restraints, each choosing the particular yields, altitudes, fission-fusion combinations, and localities for tests, it seems unlikely either that both sides will hit on the same limitations and maintain them with confidence, or that both will hit on "equivalent" though different restraints.

To some extent, then, the gains and losses of a particular agreement, i.e., the way any particular understanding that is reached may discriminate between the two parties (or among more than two parties), are likely to be dictated somewhat by the elements of the problem, and not altogether by the detailed preferences of the parties to the understanding or their bargaining skill. An absolute ban on weapon tests, for example, or any other across-the-board prohibition, is somewhat arbitrary in the way it distributes the advantages; but perhaps some of its appeal is precisely in the fact that it is somewhat arbitrary, somewhat determined by chance or by the very structure of the problem, dictated by circumstances rather than by either side to the other.

COMMUNICATION AND UNDERSTANDING

If an important part of our arms control—or let us call it "mutual arms accommodation"—with our enemies is going to be tacit and informal, a matter of reciprocated unilateral actions and abstentions, we need to take seriously the problem of communicating with our enemies about what we are doing, and of reaching understandings with them. In some respects informal communication is easier, in some ways harder; the process is different from that of formal, explicit, detailed negotiation, and imposes different requirements. Informal communication is usually ambiguous; a government speaks by hint as well as by overt statement and proposal, it speaks indirectly through the medium of press conferences, leaks of information, and remarks to third parties. It speaks with many voices, in the executive branch, in the congress, and even in private articles and news stories that are "inspired" or are inferred to be so. And it speaks through the actions it takes.*

The differences should not be exaggerated; even when large teams of professional diplomats and technical experts are assembled in Geneva, much of the communication takes these other forms. Nevertheless, the strategy of communication is different, particularly because of the greater need in informal negotiations to reach a real understanding. In formal and explicit negotiation, what eventually matters is to a large extent what gets written down and agreed to; even if there was not a meeting of minds, there may have been a meeting of words that provides a record of the expectations of both sides and the obligations perceived. In informal negotiation the ultimate sanction depends less on a piece of paper than on the clarity of the understanding reached. If one behaves in a particular way, in anticipation of the other's reciprocation, there is a need to make clear precisely how one is behaving, with what mutual purpose in mind, so that the other can read the proposal in it, infer what would constitute reciprocation, and design its own behavior accordingly.

There is furthermore a greater need to be persuasive. In explicit negotiation, it may be possible to reach an agreement whose terms are reasonably well understood without agreement on principles or any reciprocal understanding of each other's motives. If the letter of the agreement is clear, the spirit can remain somewhat in doubt. In informal negotiation, the spirit bears most of the burden; and if the *idea* behind what we think we are doing is not perceived by our partner (enemy), what we expect of him— or what we may reasonably be expected to expect of him—may be too dimly perceived to be the basis for genuine reciprocation.

Suppose we decide to put more emphasis on ballistic-missile submarines, for example, in the belief that they are peculiarly "stable" weapons because of their lesser susceptibility to destruction in case of a surprise attack and because they are not so much under obligation to strike quickly in the event of an ambiguous warning (or war itself), or else because their smaller warheads, with possibly a lesser degree of accuracy as compared with ground-based missiles, make them less of a threat to the enemy's retaliatory forces and more of a genuine deterrent. Suppose we decide that we could afford to do this only if the enemy himself oriented his own strategic program toward similarly "stable" weapon systems. It might not be at all clear to the Russians what our motives are, or what the conditions were for our going through with the program. Or suppose we have

* In a sense, the abortive summit conference of May 1960 did not involve less "negotiation" just because the meeting never took place.

a crash program for the development of a more secure ground-based missile force, this program to be financed by a sharp increase in the defense budget, with a good deal of expenditure on command, control, and communication arrangements so as to reduce both the vulnerability of our weapons and their sensitivity to accident or false alarm. In particular, suppose that our budget rises because of increased outlays associated with our desire for a *slow* reacting force, rather than one that must react rapidly. In such circumstances, our actions may be stabilizing or destabilizing, depending on whether the enemy can perceive that we are making the world safer for him rather than increasing his need (and ours) to jump the gun in a crisis. If we institute an airborne alert, it may be important to do so in a way that enhances the apparent as well as the real security and stability of our retaliatory weapon systems. This might mean that we would have to choose deliberately, say, flight patterns that manifestly enhance the security of our forces rather than the speed with which they could initiate a surprise attack of their own.

By far the most important prerequisite is that we understand our own motives well enough to take actions that are consistent with a deterrent philosophy, and well enough so that we can articulate it to ourselves. If we have such a philosophy, and if our actions are consistent with it, and if for our own purposes we articulate that philosophy in explaining our budget decisions here at home, we are probably well on the way to conveying that philosophy persuasively to our enemy, if he is at all receptive. A special problem here is that our overt position on disarmament must not be too inconsistent with the philosophy that we are trying to display and get across to our enemy. If, for example, we really believed in a policy of collaborating with the Russians to develop a stable situation of mutual deterrence, and if we determined to make important changes, to this end, in the configuration of our weapons but these changes were not in the direction of general disarmament, we would put a double burden on our communication if the front we presented on arms-control questions bore no relation to that philosophy. This does not necessarily mean that we have to speak in our formal disarmament diplomacy in a manner that is sincere and consistent with what we are fundamentally trying to get across to the Russians. It may just mean that our insincerity should be as manifest as the inconsistency, so that when we do contradict ourselves the Russians know that this is for show and that they should look for the real message elsewhere. Still, it would help if we could find the diplomatic courage to shift even the formal discussions of arms control more into accord with our basic military policy, at the same time as we try to adapt that military policy in directions that the Russians can appreciate and reciprocate, so that disarmament negotiations can help a little, or at least hinder as little as possible, the development of a genuine understanding.

Even so, it is still an unanswered question whether the Russians are at all disposed to participate in any "mutual arms accommodation" with us, beyond what we already do in a tacit way. And it is a difficult technical question whether, even if they are disposed to cooperate with us and appreciate the principle of stable retaliatory systems with minimum proclivity toward false alarm and minimum temptation toward surprise attack, there are any promising actions to be undertaken. Weapon systems can rarely be classified indisputably as first-strike or second-strike weapons, as "accident-prone" or "accident-proof"; a good deal of technical analysis has to lie behind a judgment, many of the technical judgments may not be made equally by us and our enemies, the judgment has to be made in the context of an evolving weapon system for which facts are really only forecasts, and what is known today may no longer be true tomorrow. It is, furthermore, too much to expect the massive bureaucracy of our defense establishment and our foreign service, and the partisan conflicts in Congress, to produce and maintain a coherent philosophy and transmit it with high fidelity to a suspicious enemy whose receptivity and reasoning processes we can only poorly evaluate. But it is worth trying.

RECIPROCATED DEVELOPMENT OF STABLE ARMAMENTS

One possibility, already adverted to, is to design our military forces conspicuously and deliberately in the direction of deterrence, stability, and slow reaction. That is, to articulate as a policy the design of a strategic force that is peculiarly good at waiting out crises, at surviving a surprise attack, and at punishing an attacker *ex post facto,* and not particularly good at initiating a preventive attack, not in need of responding rapidly to warning.

This may not be a bad policy to follow unilaterally; but the advantage of pursuing it is greater if the enemy pursues it too. The more each side perceives the other as designing his force for a sudden pre-emptive attack in a crisis, or for a premeditated surprise attack, the more one is tempted himself to develop a quick-reacting system, one that is peculiarly suited to catching the enemy's military forces before they have left the ground. Thus to some extent such a policy is a conditional policy; the motive is greater if the principle is reciprocated by the enemy.

It would be extraordinarily difficult, perhaps impossible, to negotiate a detailed understanding of precisely what kinds of weapons in what configurations, and how deployed, would meet the "stability" criterion. For that reason the idea may not be one that lends itself to explicit detailed negotiated agreements. But that does not rule out the possibility that both sides may perceive value in pursuing such policies in a general way, and may recognize that their own behavior not only helps the other side pursue a similar policy but helps to induce it by the tacit promise of reciprocation. As mentioned above, we already do this in such matters as the traffic rules we both unilaterally observe and reciprocate; there may be a good deal of room for gradually extending this kind of reciprocal unilateral action, even though the subject may never appear on the agenda of a diplomatic negotiation.

Compared with a *peaceful* world disarmed, schemes to stabilize mutual deterrence are a poor second best; judged against the prospect of war, measures to make it less likely may be attractive. This point of view will not appeal to any who believe that war results from the sheer existence of arms and the temptation to use them, or from the influence of militarists in modern society whose prestige increases in proportion to the arms budget, and who believe that distrust is only aggravated by people's acting as though distrust exists. History shows, it is said, that man cannot live in a world with arms without using them. History rarely shows anything quite that universal; but even granting it, the question is not whether it is asking much of man to learn to live in a world with arms and not to use them excessively. The question is whether it takes more skill and wisdom for man to learn to live in a world with arms and not to use them than it does for man to disarm himself so totally that he can't have war even if he wants it (or can't want it any longer). If modern social institutions are capable of achieving disarmament in the first place, and of avoiding arms races in perpetuity thereafter, perhaps they are capable of supporting a world with arms without war. Those who argue that peace with arms is impossible but act as though peace and disarmament are not, may be using a double standard.

And it must be remembered that total disarmament, even if achieved, does not by itself preclude subsequent arms races; nor does a good start toward total disarmament preclude a violent reversal. To the extent that an arms advantage is more easily obtained when the level of armaments on both sides is low—to the extent that the consequences of cheating are greater in a world with few arms—arms races might become more violent, the lower the level of armament from which they start. Particularly in a world in which the pace of scientific progress is rapid but jerky, uneven as between countries, and full of opportunities and uncertainties for weapons development, it is not at all clear that the world would be less uneasy about arms advantages if each side continually thought of itself as nearly naked. What can explain the complacency of the American response to the first Soviet sputnik except a feeling (superbly rationalized) that the existing level of arms provided so much security that no single new achievement, or even a revision of the comparative time schedules by a year or two, could quite upset the balance.

EXCHANGE OF STABILIZING INFORMATION

Another area of possible cooperation is in damping the arms race through the exchange of information. I am not much impressed with the budgetary fury of our participation in the arms race, but it is not hard to imagine that the budgetary arms race might get into much higher gear. If it does, part of the motivation (at least in this country) may be due to uncertainty about the level of armament on the other side. The "missile gap" that one estimates, or feels obliged to assume to exist in the absence of information, may exceed the actual missile gap, causing a more frantic increase in armaments than would be undertaken with better information. And it may induce reciprocal action on the other side, which also wishes to avoid an intolerably unfavorable imbalance.

To illustrate: suppose that either side felt reasonably secure against sudden attack as long as its enemy's numerical superiority in missiles never reached, say, 2:1. In this case, just knowing what the other possesses and is producing could make possible a stable equilibrium at a modest level of strategic armaments, while ignorance of the enemy's strength might seem to require an unlimited effort to avoid falling too far behind. With actual weapons such simple calculations are of course impossible; but the principle is valid.

An important difficulty of applying it, though, is that the ways by which one can get authentic information about the other's present and projected strength may provide more strategic information than the other side can tolerate.* A special difficulty is that the Soviets may already know most of what they need to know for this purpose; it is mainly we who do not.

But it is interesting that they might possibly prefer that we know the truth. If in fact we are on the verge of a crash program based on an exaggerated estimate of what they have already done, it could cost them money (and perhaps an increase in the risk of war) to keep up with us. It is also interesting that the truth is probably not something that they could readily reveal on their own. They have to find some way of giving us evidence for believing the truth (or a less exaggerated estimate of the truth) and give it in a way that does not yield targeting and other information that they would find intolerable. The fact that this intelligence gap is mainly on our side does not preclude Soviet interest in some means of conveying the information to us, and it does not obviate the need for cooperative techniques for receiving it.

MEASURES FOR REASSURANCE ON THE BRINK OF WAR

Measures to prevent "accidental war," war by misunderstanding, war by false alarm, are another possibility. One aspect of this has been mentioned: the reciprocal development of the kinds of forces and modes of behavior that minimize accidents or their consequences, minimize alarms and misunderstandings, minimize the need to react quickly in the face of ambiguous evidence. But there is another type of joint or reciprocal activity that could

---

* Also, one side yields a bluffing or bargaining advantage if it reveals that its weaponry is less impressive than may have been thought. It loses, too, the possibility of surreptitiously achieving a dominant superiority. But losses of this kind are the price of arms control in the first place.

help. It would be to arrange in advance, even if crudely and informally, communication procedures, exchange of information, and inspection facilities, for use in the event of an accident, alarm, or misunderstanding that created a crisis. Part of this is just procedural—making sure that we and the Russians have the same idea about who gets in touch with whom when communication or bargaining is suddenly required. Part of it is intellectual—thinking ahead of time about how one would go about reassuring the Russians in the event they had a false alarm, and what we could demand of them for our own reassurance if we ever got ambiguous evidence. Part of it is physical—making sure that, if we should need inspectors on a particular scene within a few hours to verify that something was an accident, or to verify that the Russians were calm, or to verify that the Russians were not taking actions we thought they were taking, the necessary inspectors and equipment would be available within a few hours' travel time from where we would need them. Just having some Russians available at strategic points around the United States, able to see things with their own eyes if we suddenly wanted them to and able to report home instantly through authentic channels, might be useful someday. And if we ever want them, we may want them in a hurry; there may not be time to identify them, brief them, ship them over there, and train them for their job, once the accident occurs or the crisis is on or the misinformation filters through the Russian warning system.[3]

"CRASH" ARMS CONTROL

There is a more ambitious possibility. Neither we nor the Russians at the present time take arms control terribly seriously; we do not view it as an alternative to a war that is imminent. But it is not difficult to imagine crises in which the likelihood of immediate war would become a grave preoccupation. Once the threat of imminent war rises above some threshold, the mere consciousness that each side is preoccupied with it—and with the importance of being the one to start it, if it should come—will aggravate the propensities that already exist. It is perfectly conceivable that in a real crisis there would be a sudden and drastic change in the attitudes of both sides toward arms control. "Preventive arms control" might begin to look like a risky but attractive alternative to a possibly inevitable preemptive war. Sudden and drastic "measures to safeguard against surprise attack" might have to be negotiated on an acutely demanding time schedule.

If so, success may depend on whether one or both sides is intellectually prepared for the contingency, whether some understandings have been reached in advance, and whether certain facilities can be improvised to monitor whatever arrangements might be forthcoming. One of the important "limited" arms-control measures that we might take in advance of such a crisis, either by ourselves or with our enemies, either informally or explicitly, is a development of understandings, procedures, personnel, and

equipment, of an imaginative and adaptable sort, capable of going into
action at such time as we and the Russians both decide that now is the
time for arms control and we can't wait.

ARMS CONTROL IN GENERAL WAR

A final possibility, a pessimistic but a serious one and one suggested
by the analogy between arms control and limited war, is the role of arms
control in general war if general war occurs. We usually think of arms control or deterrence as having failed if war breaks out; and so it has, but it
can fail worse if we give up at that point. It is not entirely clear that a
general war—a war between the USA and the USSR, involving their
strategic forces on a large scale—would necessarily be unlimited either in
the way it would be fought or in the way it would be concluded. Particularly
as we come to think about an inadvertent war—one that results by some
kind of accident or misunderstanding, or one that is reluctantly initiated
by the Russians or by us in the belief that it is urgent to pre-empt at once
—it is worthwhile to consider whether fury is the only guide we need in
conducting the war, and whether the exhaustion of weapons on both sides
is the only condition for terminating it.

It is commonly taken for granted that if the Russians initiate a general
war it would be in a vicious effort to exterminate us both as a nation and
as a people, and that they would be so impatient to do this as to spend
valuable weapons to create civil damage at the outset. But it is not obvious
that a coldly calculating enemy would afford himself the luxury of going
after cities and people when there are more urgent targets that he has to
destroy in order to reduce the scale of our retaliation. Nor is it obvious
that an impetuous attacker, one whose motivation is partly the fear that
if he does not strike first he will be second, would be immune to the
thought that he might want to surrender if the thing went badly, to accept
our surrender if it went well, or to negotiate a truce between those extremes.
If there is no immediate strategic need to kill our people, it may occur
to him that they are worth more alive than dead; the threat of killing them
gives him something to bargain with in the course of the war or at its
termination. Similarly for us: if the war was a mistake we might be more
interested in minimizing the consequences of the error, whosever error it
was, and in maintaining the possibility of a negotiated outcome that
limited damage on both sides. For this bargaining purpose, live Russians
and our unspent weapons are assets, and about the only ones we'd have.

The subject is a complicated one and cannot be decided here. It has to
be acknowledged that there are dangers in suggesting to the Russians that
we are even aware of the possibility that an attack on us might not be
cataclysmic for us both. But the possibility is so universally unmentioned
and so terribly important that it deserves to be brought into the open for
study. Its relation to arms control is that the mere possibility of limiting

a general war between us and our principal enemy may depend on some understanding, tacit and informal as it may be, that we share ahead of time. There may be little national advantage in abstaining from certain targets in the event of war, or in attempting to communicate, unless the enemy can be alert to what is going on.

TERMINATING WAR BY ARMS CONTROL

Terminating a war through anything other than the sheer exhaustion of weapons on both sides would require some form of arms control. It is a noteworthy characteristic of a possible World War III that even unconditional surrender may be physically impossible. How do the Russians persuade us that they have destroyed (or are prepared to destroy or deliver us) some or all of their significant weapons and are prepared to submit to our political demands? We cannot even trust them not to test weapons under a test-suspension agreement; in circumstances infinitely more desperate, when a one-hour pause in the war may be of strategic benefit to somebody, if they send us an urgent message acknowledging their guilt in the war and proposing that we preserve our world by letting them surrender to us, are we likely to be able to do anything? If they are fooling, and if we are fooled, the cost will be tremendous; if they are not fooling and we choose to ignore them, the cost will be tremendous. Can we think of what they might do to prove that they mean it? Have we got the facilities to monitor them and to police them? Have we incorporated in our strategic forces, and in the operating doctrine of those forces, recognition of their potential role in policing the disarmament by which the war might be brought to a close?

Actually "surrender" is a poor word here. Anywhere between the two extremes of unconditional surrender by one side or the other, the truce or understanding or scheme for bringing the war to a close might better be described as "disarmament" or "arms control." Historically one might have allowed an enemy, when he "conditionally" surrendered, to keep some purely defensive weapons as a hedge against the victor's violating his promise. This is a kind of asymmetrical disarmament scheme. In the future, at the close of a general war, one might have to allow the conditionally surrendering enemy to retain some retaliatory weapons, these being the only kind that two major powers can use to enforce promises from each other. In effect, "measures to safeguard against surprise attack," possibly one-sided, possibly bilateral, and certainly more drastic than any that have yet been considered, might be the minimum requirement of a conditionally surrendering enemy.

Thus anywhere between the two extremes of total surrender, the outcome should be viewed as a disarmament process, with the asymmetry presumably reflecting the degree of victory or defeat. But as remarked above, even the extremes of unconditional surrender require much the same kind of procedure for mutual relaxation, cessation of hostilities, inspection, enforcement, and so forth. Any general war that is terminated by a bilateral understanding, by anything other than the independent exhaustion of weapons on both sides, requires something in the nature of an enormous, complex, and dynamic scheme for arms control.

If this possibility is to be left open, we need to anticipate it in the design of our strategic forces and in our plans for their use. It may require special facilities and equipment to bring a war to a close, of a kind not necessarily provided for in a plan that considers only the contingency of an all-out war to the finish. But it also requires some mutual awareness ahead of time, on the part of both our enemy and ourselves, and perhaps some crude and tacit, if not careful and explicit, understanding about the modes and techniques of negotiation in the event of war.

10. The Case for Unilateral Disarmament

ERICH FROMM

THERE IS LITTLE DOUBT THAT THE PROPOSAL FOR A UNILATERAL DISARMA-
ment—in the broad sense of the unconditional dismantling of a country's
military establishment—will be acceptable neither to the United States nor
to the Soviet Union in the immediate future. Hence, inasmuch as this
chapter is concerned with *practical* suggestions for arms control, it pro-
poses another and very limited concept of unilateral disarmament, one
which has been called by Charles Osgood *"graduated unilateral action (or
disengagement)"* or which might be called *unilateral initiative in taking
practical steps toward disarmament.* The basic idea underlying this concept is that of a radical change of our method of negotiating multilateral
disarmament. This change implies that we give up the present method of
bargaining in which every concession we make is dependent on a corresponding and guaranteed concession on the part of the Russians; that, instead, we take, unilaterally, gradual steps toward disarmament in the
expectation that the Russians will reciprocate and that, thus, the present
deadlock in the negotiations for universal disarmament can be broken
through.

In order to describe the nature of this policy of unilateral steps, I cannot improve on the following description by Osgood, who, as far as I know,
was the first one to express this idea in two brilliant and profound articles.[1]
"To be maximally effective," he writes, "in inducing the enemy to reciprocate, a unilateral act (1) should, in terms of *military aggression,* be clearly
disadvantageous to the side making it, yet not cripplingly so; (2) should be
such as to be clearly perceived by the enemy as reducing his external
threat; (3) should not increase the enemy's threat to our heartland;[2] (4)
should be such that reciprocal action by the enemy is clearly available and
clearly indicated; (5) should be announced in advance and widely publicized to ally, neutral, and enemy countries—as regards the nature of the
act, its purpose as part of a consistent policy, and the expected reciprocation; but (6) should not demand prior commitment to reciprocation by
the enemy as a condition for its commission." [3]

As to the specific steps which should be taken in this fashion, it would
require a great deal of further thought, aided by competent specialists. But

in order to give at least an idea of the concrete steps this policy would envisage, I want to mention the following (some of them in agreement with Osgood): sharing of scientific information; stopping of atomic tests; troop reductions; evacuation of one or more military bases; discontinuation of German rearmament; etc. The expectation is that the Russians are as willing as we are to avoid war, hence that they will begin to reciprocate and that once the course of mutual suspicion has been reversed, bigger steps can be taken which may lead to complete bilateral disarmament. Furthermore, I believe that disarmament negotiations should be paralleled by *political* negotiations, which aim essentially at mutual noninterference on the basis of the recognition of the *status quo*. Here, too (and again in essential agreement with Osgood's position), unilateral steps such as the recognition of the Oder-Neisse line and admission of China to the United Nations would be taken in the expectation of reciprocation by the Russians (i.e., curbing of Chinese aggression, noninterference in the Middle and Far East).

What are the premises underlying the proposition for unilateral steps toward disarmament? (At this point I shall mention only some fundamental ones, while others will be discussed in the second part of this chapter which presents the argument for total unilateral disarmament.) They are briefly: (1) that, as indicated before, the present method of negotiations does not seem to lead to the goal of bilateral disarmament because of the deeply ingrained mutual suspicions and fears; (2) that without achieving *complete* disarmament, the armament race will continue and lead to the destruction of our civilization as well as that of the Russians or, even without the outbreak of a war, will slowly undermine and eventually destroy the values in defense of which we are risking our physical existence; (3) that while unilateral steps constitute a definite risk (and must do so by the very nature of the idea), the risk at every step is not a crippling one and is infinitely smaller than the danger we run by the continuation of the arms race.

Even though the broader concept of complete—rather than graduated —unilateral disarmament is, as stated before, not a practical possibility in the near future, as far as the United States and the USSR are concerned, I believe it worthwhile to present the arguments for this position, not primarily because the editor of this volume asked me to present this position nor even because I share it with a small minority of others who believe that the risks in the continuation of the armament race are far greater than the very serious risks of unilateral disarmament. While both reasons might not be sufficient to justify the following presentation, I do believe that it is not only justified but important for another reason: thinking through the arguments for a radical—even though practically unacceptable— position contributes to breaking through the thought barrier which prevents us now from getting out of the dangerous circle of seeking peace by means of threat and counterthreat. Taking seriously the reasoning which supports the unpopular position of complete unilateral disarmament can open up new approaches and viewpoints which are important even if our practical aim is that of graduated unilateral action or even only that of negotiated bilateral disarmament. I believe that the difficulty of arriving at complete disarmament lies to a large extent in the frozen stereotypes of feelings and thought habits on both sides and that any attempt at unfreezing these patterns and of rethinking the whole problem can be of importance in finding a way out of the present dangerous impasse.

The proposal for complete unilateral disarmament has been advocated from a religious, moral, or pacifist position by such men as Victor Gollancz, Lewis Mumford, and some Quakers. It has also been supported by men like Bertrand Russell, Stephen King-Hall, and C. W. Mills, who are not opposed to the use of force under all or any circumstances, yet who are uncompromisingly opposed both to thermonuclear war and to all and any preparation for it. This writer finds himself somewhat between the position of the strict pacifists and men like Bertrand Russell and Stephen King-Hall.[4]

The difference between these two groups, however, is not as fundamental as it may seem. They are united by their critical attitude toward the irrational aspects of international politics and by their deep reverence for life. They share the conviction of the oneness of the human race and faith in the spiritual and intellectual potentialities of man. They follow the dictates of their conscience in refusing to have any "part in making millions of women and children and noncombatants hostages for the behavior of their own governments."[5] Whether they think in theistic terms or in those of nontheistic humanism (in the sense of the philosophic continuum from Stoic to eighteenth-century Enlightenment philosophy), they all are rooted in the same spiritual tradition and are unwilling to compromise with its principles. They are united by their uncompromising opposition to any kind of idolatry, including the idolatry of the state. While their opposition to the Soviet system is rooted precisely in this attitude against idolatry, they are critical of idolatry whenever it appears in the Western world whether it is in the name of God or of democracy.

While there is no proponent of unilateral disarmament who does not believe that the individual must be willing to give his life for the sake of his supreme values, if such an ultimate necessity arises, they are all equally convinced that to risk the life of the human race, or even the results of its best efforts in the last five thousand years, is immoral and irresponsible. As warfare becomes at once more senseless and more devastating, the convergence between religious pacifist, humanist, and pragmatic opponents to nuclear armament grows.

From the standpoint of the proponents of unilateral disarmament, to continue the armament race is catastrophic, *whether the deterrent works or not*. In the first place, they have little faith that the deterrent will prevent the outbreak of a thermonuclear war.[6] They believe that the results of a thermonuclear war would be such that in the very "best" case they completely belie the idea that we ought to fight such a war in order to save our democratic way of life. There is no need to enter the guessing game as to whether one-third or two-thirds of the population of the two opponents and what proportion of the neutral world (depending on how the wind blows) will be destroyed. This is a guessing game that verges on madness; for to consider the possibility of the destruction of 30%, 60%, or 90% of one's own and the enemy's population as an acceptable (although, of course, most undesirable) result of one's policy is indeed approaching pathology. The increasing split between intellect and affect, which is so characteristic of our Western development in the last centuries, has reached its dangerous, schizoid peak in the calm and allegedly rational way in which we can discuss possible world destruction as a result of our own action. It does not take much imagination to visualize that sudden destruction and the threat of slow death to a large part of the American population, or the Russian population, or large parts of the world, will create such a panic, fury, and despair as could only be compared with the mass psychosis resulting from the Black Death in the Middle Ages. The traumatic effects of such a catastrophe would lead to a new form of primitive barbarism, to the resurgence of the most archaic elements, which are still potentialities in every man and of which we have had ample evidence in the terror systems of Hitler and Stalin. It would sound most unlikely to many students of human nature and psychopathology that human beings could cherish freedom, respect for life, or love after having witnessed and participated in the unlimited cruelty of man against man which thermonuclear war would mean. It is a psychological fact that acts of brutality have a brutalizing effect on the participants and lead to more brutality.[7]

BUT WHAT IF THE DETERRENT WORKS?

What is the likely future of the social character of man in a bilateral or multilateral armed world, where, no matter how complex the problems or how full the satisfactions of any particular society, the biggest and most pervasive reality in any man's life is the poised missile, the humming data processor connected to it, the waiting radiation counters and seismographs, the over-all technocratic perfection (overlying the nagging but impotent fear of its imperfection) of the mechanism of holocaust? To live for any length of time under the constant threat of destruction creates certain psychological effects in most human beings—fright, hostility, callousness, a hardening of the heart, and a resulting indifference to all the values we cherish. Such conditions will transform us into barbarians—though barbarians equipped with the most complicated machines. If we are serious in claiming that our aim is to preserve freedom (that is, to prevent the subordination of the individual under an all-powerful state), we must admit that this freedom will be lost, whether the deterrent works or does not work.

Aside from these psychological facts, the continuation of the arms race constitutes a particular threat to Western culture. In the process of conquering nature, producing and consuming have become Western man's main preoccupation—the goal of his life. We have transformed means into ends. We manufacture machines which are like men, and we produce men who are like machines. In his work, the individual is managed as a part of a production team. During his leisure time, he is manipulated as a consumer who likes what he is told to like and yet has the illusion that he follows his own taste. In centering his life around the production of things, man himself is in danger of becoming a thing, worshiping the idols of the production machine and the state while he is under the illusion of worshiping God. "Things are in the saddle and ride mankind," as Emerson has put it. Circumstances which we created have consolidated themselves into powers which rule over us. The technical and bureaucratic system we have built tells us what to do, it decides for us. We may not be in danger of becoming slaves, but we are in danger of becoming robots, and the human values of our tradition are threatened—integrity, individuality, responsibility, reason, and love. Talking about these values more and more becomes an empty ritual.

This trend toward a world of impotent men directed by virile machines (both in the United States and in the Soviet Union)—brought about by technological and demographic factors, and by the increasing centralization and bureaucracy in big corporations and government—will reach the point of no return if we continue the arms race. Dangerous as our present situation is, we still have a chance to put man back into the saddle, to effect a renaissance of the spiritual values of the great humanistic tradition. Unless such a renaissance occurs, unless we can achieve a radical revitalization of the spirit on which our culture is founded, we shall lose the vitality necessary for survival and we shall decay, just as many other great powers have decayed in history. The real threat to our existence is not Communist ideology, it is not even the Communist military power—it is the hollowness of our beliefs, the fact that freedom, individuality, and faith have become empty formulas, that God has become an idol, that our vitality is sapped because we have no vision except that of having more of the same. It seems that a great deal of the hatred of Communism is, in the last analysis, based on a deep disbelief in the spiritual values of democracy. Hence, instead of experiencing love of what we are *for,* we experience hate of what we are *against.* If we continue to live in fear of extinction and to plan mass destruction of others, the last chance for a revival of our humanist-spiritual tradition will be lost.

BENEFITS AND DANGERS OF UNILATERAL DISARMAMENT

If these are the dangers of the policy of the deterrent, what do the proponents of unilateral disarmament consider to be the benefits—and the dangers—of their policy?

The most likely result of unilateral disarmament—whether it be undertaken by the United States or by the Soviet Union—is that it would prevent war. The main reason which could impel either the Soviet Union or the United States to atomic war is the constant fear of being attacked and pulverized by the opponent. This position is succinctly expressed by Herman Kahn, who is in no way a proponent of unilateral disarmament. Kahn states that, "aside from the ideological differences and the problem of security itself, there does not seem to be any objective quarrel between the United States and Russia that justifies the risks and costs that we subject each other to. The big thing that the Soviet Union and the United States have to fear from each other is fear itself."[8] If, indeed, the main cause of war lies in mutual fear, then the disarmament of either the Soviet Union or the United States would most likely do away with this major cause and, thus, with the probability of war.

But are there motives other than fear which could prompt the Soviet Union to try for world conquest? One such motive could be economic interest in expansion, which was a basic motivation for the initiation of war in the nineteenth century and also for the first two World Wars. Exactly here we see the difference between the nature of the conflicts in 1914 or 1939 and the present situation. In World War I, Germany threatened British markets and the French sources of coal and iron; in 1939, Hitler needed territorial conquest for the economic expansion he wanted. Today, neither the Soviet Union nor the United States has overriding economic interests in the conquest of markets and supplies, since a 2 or 3 percent rise in the level of national productivity would bring a greater advantage than would any military conquest, and, moreover, each has the capital, raw material, supplies, and population for a constant increase in its general productivity.[9]

The more serious possible motive is found in the fear, widely held in the United States, that the Soviet Union is out to conquer the world for Communism and that, if the United States disarmed, Russia would be all the more eager to achieve her wish for world domination. This idea of Russian intentions is based on an erroneous appreciation of the nature of the present-day Soviet Union. It is true that under Lenin and Trotzky the Russian Revolution was aimed at conquering the capitalistic world (or at least, Europe) for Communism, partly because the Communist leaders were convinced that there was no possibility of success for Communist Russia unless the highly industrialized states of Europe (or at least Germany) joined their system, and partly because they were prompted by the belief that the victory of the Communist revolution in the world would bring about the fulfillment of their secular-messianic hopes.

The failure of these hopes and the ensuing victory of Stalin brought about a complete change in the nature of Soviet Communism. The annihilation of almost all the old Bolsheviks was only a symbolic act for the destruction of the old revolutionary idea. Stalin's slogan of "socialism in one country" covered one simple aim—the rapid industrialization of Russia, which the Czarist system had not accomplished. Russia repeated the same process of accumulating capital which Western capitalism had gone through in the eighteenth and nineteenth centuries. The essential difference is that, while in these centuries in the West the sanctions were purely economic, the Stalinist system now developed political sanctions of direct terror; in addition, it employed socialist ideology to sugar-coat the exploitation of the masses. The Stalinist system was neither a socialist nor a revolutionary system, but a state-capitalism based on ruthless methods of planning and economic centralization.

The period of Khrushchevism is characterized by the fact that capital accumulation has succeeded to a point where the population can enjoy a great deal more consumption and is less forced to make sacrifices; as a result, the political terror can be greatly reduced.

But Khrushchevism has by no means changed the basic character of Soviet society in one essential respect: it is not a revolutionary nor a socialist regime, but one of the most conservative, class-ridden regimes anywhere in the Western world, humanly coercive, economically effective. While the aim of democratic socialism was the emancipation of man, the overcoming of his alienation, and the eventual abolition of the state, the "socialist" slogans used in Soviet Russia reflect empty ideologies, and the social reality is the very opposite of true socialism. The ruling class of the Soviet Union is no more revolutionary than the Renaissance popes were followers of the teachings of Christ. To try to explain Khrushchev by quoting Marx, Lenin, or Trotzky shows an utter failure to understand the historical development which has taken place in the Soviet Union and an incapacity to appreciate the difference between facts and ideologies. It should be added that our attitude is the best propaganda service the Russians could wish for. Against the facts, they try to convince the workers of Western Europe and the peasants in Asia that they represent the ideas of socialism, of a classless society, etc. The Western attitude, of falling for this propaganda, does exactly what the Russians want: to confirm these claims. (Unfortunately very few people except democratic socialists have sufficient knowledge of the difference between socialism and its distorted and corrupt form which calls itself Soviet socialism.)

The role of Russia is still more emphasized by the fact that Russia feels threatened by a potentially expansionist China. Russia one day might be in the same position with regard to China as we believe we are in relation to Russia. If the threat to Russia from the United States were to disappear, Russia could devote her energy to coping with the threat from China, unless by universal disarmament this threat would cease to exist.

The above-mentioned considerations indicate that the dangers which might arise if the Soviet Union were not to give up its armaments are more remote than they seem to many. Would the Soviet Union use her military superiority to try to occupy the United States or Western Europe? Aside from the fact that it would be exceedingly difficult, to say the least, for the Soviet Union's agents to run the economic and political machines of the United States or Western Europe, and aside from the fact that there is no vital need for Russia to conquer these territories, it would be most inconvenient to try to do so—and for a reason which is generally not sufficiently appreciated. Even the pro-Communist workers in the West have no idea of the degree of coercion to which they would have to submit under a Soviet system. They, as well as non-Communist workers, would oppose the new authorities, who would be forced to use tanks and machine guns against the protesting workers. This would encourage revolutionary tendencies in the satellite states, or even within the Soviet Union, and be most undesirable to the Soviet rulers; it would especially endanger Khrushchev's policy of liberalization, and hence his whole political position.

Eventually the Soviet Union might try to exploit its military superiority for the penetration of Asia and Africa. This is possible, but, with our present policy of the deterrent, it is doubtful whether the United States would really be willing to start a thermonuclear war in order to prevent the Russians from gaining certain advantages in the world outside of Europe and the Americas.

All these assumptions may be wrong. The position of the proponents of unilateral disarmament is that the chance that they are wrong is much smaller than the chance that the continuation of the arms race will finish civilization as we cherish it.

SOME PSYCHOLOGICAL CONSIDERATIONS

One cannot discuss the question of what might happen as a result of unilateral disarmament—or, for that matter, of any mutual disarmament —without examining some psychological arguments. The most popular one is that "the Russians cannot be trusted." If "trust" is meant in a moral sense, it is unfortunately true that political leaders can rarely be trusted. The reason lies in the split between private and public morals: the state, having become an idol, justifies any immorality if committed in its interest, while the very same political leaders would not commit the same acts if they were acting in behalf of their own private interests. However, there is another meaning to "trust in people," a meaning which is much more relevant to the problem of politics: the trust that they are sane and rational beings, and that they will act accordingly. If I deal with an opponent in whose sanity I trust, I can appreciate his motivations and to some extent predict them, because there are certain rules and aims, like that of survival or that of commensurateness between aims and means, which are common to all sane people. Hitler could not be trusted because he was lacking in sanity, and this very lack destroyed both him and his regime. It seems quite clear that the Russian leaders of today are sane and rational people; therefore, it is important not only to know what they are capable of, but also to predict what they might be motivated to do.[10]

This question of the leaders' and the people's sanity leads to another consideration which affects us as much as it does the Russians. In the current discussion on armament control, many arguments are based on the question of what is *possible,* rather than on what is *probable.* The difference between these two modes of thinking is precisely the difference between *paranoid* and *sane* thinking. The paranoiac's unshakable conviction in the validity of his delusion rests upon the fact that it is logically possible, and, so, unassailable. It is logically possible that his wife, children, and colleagues hate him and are conspiring to kill him. The patient cannot be convinced that his delusion is *impossible;* he can only be told that it is exceedingly *unlikely.* While the latter position requires an examination and evaluation of the facts and also a certain amount of faith in life, the paranoid position can satisfy itself with the possibility alone. I submit that our political thinking suffers from such paranoid trends. We should be concerned, not with the possibilities, but rather with the probabilities. This is the only sane and realistic way of conducting the affairs of national as well as of individual life.

Again on the psychological plane, there are certain misunderstandings of the radical disarmament position which occur in many of the discussions. First of all, the position of unilateral disarmament has been understood as one of submission and resignation. On the contrary, the pacifists as well as the humanist pragmatists believe that unilateral disarmament is possible only as an expression of a deep spiritual and moral change within ourselves: it is an act of courage and resistance—not one of cowardice or surrender. Forms of resistance differ in accordance with the respective viewpoints. On the other hand, Gandhists and men like King-Hall advocate nonviolent resistance, which undoubtedly requires the maximum of courage and faith; they refer to the example of Indian resistance against Britain or Norwegian resistance against the Nazis. This point of view is succinctly expressed in *Speak Truth to Power* (see reference 4):

Thus, we dissociate ourselves from the basically selfish attitude that has been miscalled pacifism, but that might be more accurately described as a kind of irresponsible antimilitarism. We dissociate ourselves also from utopianism. Though the choice of nonviolence involves a radical change in men, it does not require perfection. . . . We have tried to make it clear that readiness to accept suffering—rather than inflict it on others—is the essence of the nonviolent life, and that we must be prepared if called upon to pay the ultimate price. Obviously, if men are willing to spend billions of treasure and countless lives in war, they cannot dismiss the case for nonviolence by saying that in a nonviolent struggle people might be killed! It is equally clear that where commitment and the readiness to sacrifice are lacking, nonviolent resistance cannot be effective. On the contrary, it demands greater discipline, more arduous training, and more courage than its violent counterpart.[11]

Some think of armed resistance, of men and women defending their lives and their freedom with rifles, pistols, or knives. It is not unrealistic to think that both forms of resistance, nonviolent or violent, might deter an aggressor from attacking. At least, it is more realistic than to think that the use of thermonuclear weapons could lead to a "victory for democracy."

The proponents of "security by armament" sometimes accuse us of having an unrealistic, flatly optimistic picture of the nature of man. They remind us that this "perverse human being has a dark, illogical, irrational side." [12] They even go so far as to say that "the paradox of nuclear deterrence is a variant of the fundamental Christian paradox. In order to *live,* we must express our willingness to kill and to die." [13] Apart from this crude falsification of Christian teaching, we are by no means oblivious of the potential evil within man and of the tragic aspect of life. Indeed, there are situations in which man must be willing to die in order to live. In the sacrifices necessary for violent or nonviolent resistance, I can see an expression of the acceptance of tragedy and sacrifice. But, there is no tragedy or sacrifice in irresponsibility and carelessness: there is no meaning or dignity in the idea of the destruction of mankind and of civilization. Man has in himself a potential for evil; his whole existence is beset by dichotomies rooted in the very conditions of his existence. But these truly tragic aspects must not be confused with the results of stupidity and lack of imagination, with the willingness to stake the future of mankind on a gamble.

Finally, to take up one last criticism, directed against the position of unilateral disarmament: that it is "soft" on Communism. Our position is precisely based on the negation of the Soviet principle of the omnipotence of the state. Just because the spokesmen for unilateral disarmament are drastically opposed to the supremacy of the state, they do not want to grant the state the ever-increasing power which is unavoidable in the arms race, and they deny the right of the state to make decisions which can lead to the destruction of a great part of humanity and can doom future generations. If the basic conflict between the Soviet system and the democratic world is the question of the defense of the individual against the encroachment of an omnipotent state, then, indeed, the position for unilateral disarmament is the one which is most radically opposed to the Soviet principle.

After having discussed the case for unilateral disarmament (in the broad sense), I want to return to the practical proposition of unilateral steps toward disarmament. I do not deny that there are risks involved in this limited form of unilateral action but considering the fact that the present method of negotiations has produced no results and that the chances that they will in the future are rather slim, considering furthermore the grave risk involved in the continuation of the arms race, I believe that it is practically and morally justified to take this risk. At present we are caught in a position with little chance for survival, unless we want to take refuge in hopes. *If* we have enough shelters, *if* there is enough time for a warning and strategic evacuation of cities, *if* the "United States' active offenses and active defenses can gain control of the military situation after only a few exchanges," [14] we might have only five, or twenty-five, or seventy million killed. However, if these conditions do not materialize, "an enemy could, by repeated strikes, reach almost any level of death and destruction he wished." [15] (And, I assume, the same threat exists for the Soviet Union.) In such a situation, "when nations are poised at the last moment when an agreement appears possible to end the risk of horrifying war, unleashed by fanatics, lunatics or men of ambition," [16] it is imperative to shake off the inertia of our accustomed thinking, to seek for new approaches to the problem, and above all, to see new alternatives to the present choices that confront us.

11. Comprehensive Arms-Limitation Systems

JEROME B. WIESNER

I. INTRODUCTION

MANKIND'S ALMOST UNIVERSAL DESIRE IS TO HALT THE FRIGHTENING ARMS race and to provide, by rule of law, the security now sought so futilely from nuclear armaments and ballistic missiles. While the goal is clearly visible, the course is not; until now it has not been possible for East and West to agree upon a mutually acceptable disarmament or arms-limitation scheme. This chapter will explore the variety of problems which must be solved if comprehensive arms-limitation systems are to be made acceptable.

The phrase "comprehensive arms-limitation systems" designates systems of arms regulation which seek to limit, under controlled conditions, all weapons of war regarded by the contracting parties as capable of being used for other than internal security purposes. The phrase "arms limitation," rather than "disarmament," is used for semantic reasons.

Though the writer believes in the importance of eliminating all military power from the arsenals of independent nations as rapidly as is feasible, he also believes that it will be extremely difficult to achieve this goal in one mighty agreement and that it may be necessary to reach it through a series of steps, in which the total available military force is successively reduced. "Arms limitation" describes this process better than the word "disarmament," which to many Americans implies an all-or-nothing situation.

During the past fourteen years international arms-control conferences have occurred more or less regularly. Starting with the meetings of the United Nations Atomic Energy Commission in 1946, which spent many months considering the Baruch version of the Acheson-Lilienthal proposal for the control of atomic energy, there have been a series of international meetings between the representatives of the Eastern and Western powers in an attempt to arrest the arms race. In 1952 the United Nations Disarmament Commission began a series of meetings in an attempt to get agreement on a plan for general disarmament. The Commission did not succeed in initiating serious discussions during its 1952 and 1953 meetings and was essentially moribund from 1953 until mid-1954. Then, and again in 1955, the Commission held a series of productive meetings in London, which were followed by the Summit Meeting of 1955, the London meetings of the United Nations Disarmament Commission in 1957, the Geneva Conference of "the experts to study the technical means of monitoring a nuclear test ban," the "Conference of Experts for the Study of Possible Measures Which Might be Helpful in Preventing Surprise Attack," the political conference to prepare a treaty prohibiting the testing of nuclear weapons, and, finally, the Ten Nation Disarmament Conference of March-June 1960. It is interesting to note that this series of international conferences oscillated between attempts to achieve very extensive arms-limitation agreements and efforts to find meaningful limited measures which could be implemented in spite of broad areas of disagreement. It has become evident by now that there is not an obvious, quick and easy path to military security through arms limitation. Nearly all significant limited arms-control measures, such as the nuclear test ban, the demilitarized zone in Europe, or the open-skies proposal, are judged to be unsafe—though it is not clear that they really are—and therefore undesirable by one or more of the many parties who would have to accept them. The limited proposals require either the Soviet Union and its allies to accept more inspection than they are prepared to have without extensive disarmament, or the West to accept arms limitations with what to it appears to be inadequate inspection. These asymmetrical views are the natural consequence of the security problems faced by each group.

II. WHAT MAKES ARMS-LIMITATION AGREEMENTS DIFFICULT?

Experience indicates that individual projects or proposals, no matter how promising, always will be evaluated in a negative state of mind born of fear. I have had considerable opportunity to observe this effect in the operation of the American government, and I assume from published statements made by Soviet leaders, and from discussions with many Soviet disarmament experts, that a similar protective mechanism operates there.

We are confronted by a serious communication block. In conflict situations between individuals, and in conflict situations in which individuals act for nations, statements of antagonists are evaluated not in terms of the intended meanings, but rather in terms of the most threatening alternatives. This is particularly true when survival is believed to be at stake. When this happens, there can be no meaningful communication. Every proposal by either side is scanned for the hidden purpose. The entire history of the atomic control negotiations is a demonstration of this effect. Starting with the Baruch-Lilienthal plan and coming up to the present negotiations with the Soviet government regarding a nuclear test ban, there has been a reluctance by all parties to consider that such proposals are put forward in good faith.

To succeed, arms-control measures must be of such a nature that their implementation gives participants a feeling of greater security, not less, and they should also be of such a character that they promote mutual understanding and trust. The problem confronting us is to design a comprehensive arms-control system which commences with low-risk measures that can be carried out in the atmosphere of suspicion and fear, but which clearly leads to the ultimate objectives. Thus, by having clear-cut and desirable goals, it may be possible to gain acceptance of the initial steps.

OBSTACLES TO ACHIEVING ARMS-CONTROL AGREEMENTS BY MEANS OF LIMITED MEASURES

The various limited arms-control measures discussed at the disarmament conferences have been unacceptable for many reasons. First of all, there is much evidence to support the allegation that until recently neither side was sincerely attempting to reach agreement on disarmament or arms limitations. Furthermore, none of the participants in the conferences have been sufficiently prepared to permit them to negotiate with confidence. The American delegations to the disarmament discussions, to the nuclear test ban conferences, and to the surprise attack conferences had very inadequate technical preparation to support them in the discussions. They were further handicapped by the lack of any definite national position on the subjects being discussed or even of any guidance regarding rational objectives. There is considerable evidence to support the view that the Soviet delegations were not much better prepared. In fact, it often appeared to Western observers that the Russian groups were even less well prepared technically than they.

OBSTACLES TO ACHIEVING ARMS-CONTROL AGREEMENTS BY MEANS OF COMPREHENSIVE SYSTEMS

The design of a satisfactory comprehensive arms-control system, i.e., one attempting to eliminate or control all major weapons of war, involves complex interrelationships between the various weapons systems affected and between each of them and whatever inspection system is required to monitor it, and even more complex interrelationships among the armament, inspection, and the policy objectives the security system is intended to support. The complexity of the inspection and control system will be determined by the exact nature of the weapons limitations to be imposed; some disarmament or arms-control systems which have been proposed appear to require elaborate inspection and control systems, others require much less.

Up to the present time, there has not been adequate examination of the technical details of any comprehensive system to make possible a really satisfactory evaluation of it. Unfortunately, in this circumstance, the West has always been suspicious of Soviet proposals, and furthermore has generally been ultra-conservative in the inspection requirements it places upon any system. Until there is an adequate understanding of the various components which go into the make-up of the comprehensive systems, it will be difficult, if not impossible, to arrive at a mutually acceptable system.

In this chapter I propose to discuss the inspection problems and the security problems associated with elimination or limitation of the major weapons systems now in existence, and I will also examine the problems of technological surprise created by the on-going research activities. Following this I will examine three possible forms of comprehensive arms-control systems.

In the design of a comprehensive arms-control system, not only are the ultimate objectives important, but the situation which will be created during the implementation phase must also be taken into account. It is extremely important that the timing, the build-up of inspection, the decrease in weapons, and the geographic distribution of the various activities must all be considered simultaneously—otherwise systems will be proposed which will appear too dangerous to one side or the other.

From the discussions in this chapter, it will be obvious that there are many gaps in my present understanding of the problem and that considerable further thinking and study is required before any one of these systems is likely to be accepted. The systems examined should not be considered as definitive proposals, but rather as being illustrative of the range of problems which need to be examined. In spite of the reservations expressed above, I am hopeful that a comprehensive arms-control system, acceptable to both the East and the West, can be developed, and that it will gain acceptance more easily than a series of individual limited measures.

There are many reasons why I suspect that a comprehensive system may be easier to negotiate than a series of independent limited measures worked through one at a time. If there exists an agreed upon long-term goal, a plan for reaching it by means of a sequence of arms-limitation measures and a timetable for doing so, there will be an enormous interest in the ultimate objective and individual steps will not have to be as finely balanced as if they were likely to persist for all time. Second, the inspection required to safeguard some limited measures absolutely may appear to be almost as great a breach of Soviet security as the inspection required for a comprehensive system. In fact, really adequate inspection for limited measures may be more difficult to achieve because the various components of an inspection system will reinforce one another. Finally, when extensive disarmament has taken place, there will be no need for military secrecy, so that the environment in which the inspection will have to function will be much more favorable for effective control. I do not mean to say that there are no useful limited measures; there are probably many; for example, an arms-free zone in central Europe might contribute to the reduction of tensions if it could be negotiated.

OBSTACLES TO REACHING ANY AGREEMENTS

Specific and overriding fears influence the point of view of each of the groups negotiating an arms-control agreement. They can cause different nations to react to a given proposal in very different ways. Some of the more important of these fears are:

On the side of the Soviet bloc:

1. Concern about American bomber bases and missile bases surrounding the territory of the USSR—not only about the possible deliberate use of these weapons, but also about the dangers of the so-called "accidental war" occurring as a result of tensions in areas where there are extensive military forces.

2. Fear of espionage; this factor is related to the previous one; much of the Soviet military security in the face of superior and close-by nuclear striking power has been obtained by carefully guarding knowledge of the location and size of important USSR military targets. It should not be surprising, therefore, if Western emphasis on inspection is viewed with considerable suspicion.

3. Concern about a rearmed, reunited Germany.

4. Widespread belief that capitalistic states may deem military adventure necessary to support their economies. This view, formerly widely held, seems to be a much less significant concern of Soviet leaders now than it was in the past.

5. A belief that the capitalistic states are dedicated to the extermination of Communist or socialist states.

6. The fact that the Soviet Union, its allies and satellites are outnumbered in the United Nations and cannot ever expect to get fair treatment.

On the Western side:

1. Fear that the large Soviet land armies could, and probably would, occupy Western Europe and many other areas of the world if not "deterred" by the threat of atomic retaliation or by adequate conventional forces.

2. Widespread acceptance of the view that the Soviet government is dedicated to the extermination of the Western way of life by any means available to it, including military force if its use is not too costly. This has its extreme form in the fear of a surprise attack. This fear increases continuously as the evolution of nuclear weapons and ballistic missiles makes such an attack appear to be easier to carry out and harder to defend against.

3. Fear of the unknown. Travel restrictions and other censorship devices imposed by the Soviet Union to provide it with military security make it appear possible for that country to carry out large-scale military deployment unbeknown to the rest of the world. Many Western experts believe that it would be possible for a decisive missile force to be built up behind

the Soviet security screen with little danger of detection. The fear of Soviet duplicity is so great among some Western experts who participate in disarmament planning that it is not possible to visualize a level of inspection which would actually alleviate this fear. Such individuals seem to prefer the unknown dangers of the arms race to arms reduction with any conceivable degree of inspection. Others would require a level of inspection so great that no nation, including ours, would be willing to pay for it.

4. A fear of military action by local Communist groups within countries such as France, Italy, Burma, and India, supported by aid from the Soviet Union.

CAN THE CONFLICTING SECURITY REQUIREMENTS BE RESOLVED?

Though many of the worries listed above are actually political, not military, in nature, they are affected by the military situation and will be affected by changes in the relative military positions of individual countries, whether due to unilateral actions or to arms-limitation agreements. Some of these problems will disappear as progress is made in limiting military force, others will have to be dealt with explicitly in negotiations.

One of the most serious stumbling blocks encountered in attempting to achieve agreement between the East and the West on arms-reduction plans is the seeming contradiction or conflict between steps required to reduce the fears and suspicions of both sides at the same time. The clearest example of this problem, and in fact the issue which has caused the most misunderstanding in all of the previous negotiations, is the apparent irreconcilability between the Soviet fear of espionage, which seems to dictate that there should be considerable disarmament before there is widespread inspection, and the Western fear that in the absence of an essentially perfect inspection system, the Soviet Union would be able to launch a successful surprise attack on the Western military forces.

These problems can be resolved, as will be shown in subsequent sections, provided there is adequate understanding and agreement on each side regarding the security considerations motivating the other, a considerable degree of objectivity in examining the consequences of various actions, and a sufficient understanding of the technical characteristics and actual performance of individual components of inspection systems to permit relatively objective assessments to be made.

It is unfortunately true, as was previously stated, that in the past there have been insufficient technical and military studies to permit adequate assessment of various alternative systems. Lacking sufficient understanding of basic matters, negotiating groups representing both sides have found being objective a serious liability and have therefore seldom attempted it. If progress is to be made in the future, the negotiating groups will have to be much better prepared and they will have to be determined to respect and consider fairly the actual, and possibly even the imagined, security needs of the other side. Furthermore, both groups must be realistic in their security objectives. That is, each must be prepared to accept some risks in implementing arms-control systems. The objective should be to find security systems less dangerous than the accelerating arms race rather than to achieve a system capable of providing absolute security, an obviously unobtainable goal. If this point of view were accepted by both sides, many different comprehensive arms-limitation systems capable of providing adequate security to all participants could be designed and in all likelihood one of these would be completely acceptable.

An even more serious difficulty encountered when attempts are made to judge disarmament proposals is the lack of explicit national goals or objectives beyond the statement of the national desire for a safeguarded disarmament. In particular, there is no clear-cut understanding of the kind of political environment we desire to live in. The acceptability or desirability of many proposed disarmament systems depends more upon political issues than upon military safety, though this is rarely realized or admitted. For example, the USSR proposal for "general and complete disarmament" would probably result in a world safe enough for the two countries, but one in which neither the United States nor the Soviet Union would have any control of conditions in other parts of the world. Is either of us really prepared to accept this situation?

There are many reasons for being optimistic at the present time. Since 1957 a number of developments have occurred—some technical, some military, some political—for whose achievement a comprehensive agreement appears to be more urgent and possibly even more feasible than was the case then. The most significant of these developments are:

1. The development of long-range ballistic missiles. This has had a number of important effects. Ballistic missiles and thermonuclear weapons taken together create a situation in which it is unlikely that any nation can achieve, in the foreseeable future, an overwhelming military position. There has been an increasing acceptance of the idea that the continued arms race will result in less, rather than more, security for everyone. Missile developments have also made possible, at least in principle, the creation of a highly secure deterrent force. This prospect provides a means for overcoming the "clandestine weapon" difficulty always present in designing an arms-limitation system. This point will be examined in considerable detail later on.

2. The apparent willingness of the Soviet Union to consider the creation of an inspection system in parallel with the reduction in forces and weapons levels. This is undoubtedly due in part to the improved military posture the Soviet Union has achieved by the development of ballistic missiles.

3. Nuclear weapons developments which now make available adequate warheads for any military need which can be visualized as arising during the implementation phase of an arms-control system, so that further developments are not vital for the maintenance of an adequate deterrent posture.

III. OBJECTIVES OF ARMS-LIMITATION AND CONTROL AGREEMENTS

The first and foremost United States objective in seeking arms-limitation agreements is to improve the national security—both short-term and long-term. Presumably it is the same motivation that compels other nations to join with the United States in seeking such agreements. Clearly many partial measures will improve the national security in the short run, but in the long run only a cessation of the arms race and a great reduction—or, hopefully, the elimination—of all major weapons, in the framework of an international security system capable of preventing the reappearance of large-scale national military forces anywhere, can guarantee military security. Total disarmament with a genuine international security system should be the goal toward which we strive. However, as will be shown, there are many comprehensive arms-control systems short of this ideal which could make a significant contribution to national security.

PRINCIPLES FOR A COMPLETE DISARMAMENT PROGRAM

The essential principles for a complete disarmament program were presented to the United Nations Disarmament Commission on April 24, 1952. These general principles, which can serve as a background to a discussion of today's problems, are repeated here:

1. The goal of disarmament is not to regulate but to prevent war . . . by making war inherently, as it is constitutionally under the Charter, impossible as a means of settling disputes between nations.

2. To achieve this goal, all States must co-operate to establish an open and substantially disarmed world (a) in which armed forces and armaments will be reduced to such a point and in such a thorough fashion that no State will be in a condition of armed preparedness to start a war, and (b) in which no State will be in a position to undertake preparations for war without other States having knowledge of such preparations long before an offending State could start a war.

3. To reach and keep this goal, international agreements must be entered into by which all States would reduce their armed forces to levels, and restrict their armaments to types and quantities, necessary for (a) the maintenance of internal security and (b) fulfillment of obligations of States to maintain peace and security in accordance with the United Nations Charter.

4. Such international agreements must ensure by a comprehensive and co-ordinated programme both: (a) the progressive reduction of armed forces and permitted armaments to fixed maximum levels, radically less than present levels and balanced throughout the process of reduction, thereby eliminating mass armies and preventing any disequilibrium of power dangerous to peace; and (b) the elimination of all instruments adaptable to mass destruction.

5. Such international agreements must provide effective safeguards to ensure that all phases of the disarmament programme are carried out. In particular,

the elimination of atomic weapons must be accomplished by an effective system of international control of atomic energy to ensure that atomic energy is used for peaceful purposes only.

6. Such international agreements must provide an effective system of progressive and continuing disclosure and verification of all armed forces and armaments, including atomic, to achieve the open world in which alone there can be effective disarmament.[1]

These essential principles apply as well today as when they were written, though to design security systems which fulfill all the requirements these statements imply is ever so much more difficult now than it was in 1952—and there are many indications that trends in research on and development of weapons will continue to make the task increasingly difficult.

At this stage in history it is extremely desirable to make a start on disarmament, no matter how modest a one. Consequently, we should be prepared to examine and, if reasonably safe, to implement limited systems which fall far short of satisfying all the requirements set forth here.

MINIMUM OBJECTIVES FOR A COMPREHENSIVE ARMS-LIMITATION SYSTEM

In planning comprehensive arms-limitation systems which fall short of total and complete disarmament, we must nonetheless have ambitious objectives. They should be:

1. to take away from each nation, or any probable coalition of nations, the power to defeat another major nation;

2. in the absence of international guarantees, to retain for each nation a fraction of its original military strength so that the threat of its use is available to deter those few actions by others which would threaten that nation's most vital interests;

3. to reduce the likelihood and danger of war by reducing the pressures toward an arms race, reducing the extent to which quick-reaction forces of great potency are needed, reducing the immediate destruction produceable by a war to the lowest level compatible with the other aims—and by

4. reducing, to whatever extent possible, the total economic and human cost of military power and arms control combined.

IV. POSSIBLE FORMS OF COMPREHENSIVE ARMS-CONTROL SYSTEMS

As previously stated, by comprehensive arms-control systems are meant those systems designed to eliminate or markedly limit the major instruments of war and to provide sufficient inspection and control of production, research, and development to prevent the creation of clandestine forces. Such systems may be designed so as to eliminate eventually all military weapons except those required for internal police action, or merely to reduce their numbers to a less dangerous level. During the past decade, several comprehensive arms-control systems have been outlined, some of them by official groups involving NATO and Warsaw bloc members and others by private individuals with an interest in the problem.

The comprehensive systems that have been proposed fall into two categories, those which involve essentially total disarmament and those which only reduce force levels and depend upon inspection systems and whatever inherent stability the system may have to deter the clandestine build-up of additional weapons or the use of the existing forces. Systems of the latter type are known as stable deterrent systems.

Total disarmament systems also may be divided into two categories, those which assume international military forces and associated legal apparatus, and those which do not.

ESSENTIAL FEATURES OF COMPREHENSIVE ARMS-CONTROL SYSTEMS

Proposals made in the past have many features in common. Many of them still appear to be essential even at this time. The most important of these are:

1. Agreement upon objectives of the system, i.e., the final weapons and manpower composition of the national military establishments and of any international military force that will be created.

2. Agreement to disclose information pertaining to armament stockpiles, armament production, weapons research and development, national budgets, etc., and to permit checking of the veracity of these disclosures.

3. Agreement upon a time schedule for reduction of the national forces' levels and weapons' levels, and of the build-up of the inspection organ and of the international security force if one is to be created.

4. Agreement upon details of the inspection apparatus to monitor critical components of point 2 above and upon the rights of the inspectorate.

5. Agreement on the legal aspects of the control authority.

6. Some description of the course to be followed in the event that violations of the agreement are discovered, or that activities of the inspection organ are impeded.

We will show the essential features of each of the types of comprehensive arms-control systems discussed above and make an effort to compare their relative desirability, considering such factors as ease of implementation, cost, and degree of assurance provided.

V. COMPONENTS OF ARMS-LIMITATION SYSTEMS— INSPECTION AND CONTROL

An essential part of any realistic comprehensive arms-reduction proposal will be the inspection and control system. The effectiveness of the inspection system in providing assurance thaat agreements are really being

respected will not only govern the security provided by the specific arrangement, but will obviously greatly influence the willingness of nations to
participate in it. It is also clear that the more extensive, complicated, and
costly a proposed inspection system is, the more difficult will be its acceptance and implementation. It is not necessarily true that the more elaborate
the inspection system, the greater the confidence it will engender, for this
is governed as much by the nature of the specific arms-limitation agreement
being monitored as by the actual inspection system. Two examples will
illustrate this point.

RELATIONSHIP BETWEEN SPECIFIC ARMS-LIMITATION MEASURES AND INSPECTION REQUIREMENTS

During the 1958 Geneva Conference on Means of Preventing Surprise
Attack, the Western delegates proposed a very elaborate and costly system
designed to detect and warn of the build-up or actual occurrence of a surprise attack. For a number of reasons the Western proposals did not include
any limitation on the number or deployment of the various weapons of
mass destruction the system was to control. Though in certain situations
this system would provide some additional security against surprise attack,
it was very costly for what it would accomplish. In addition, it was possible
to imagine situations where it could be exploited by an aggressor. The
difficulty with such a system is the necessity of providing continuous observation at many separate places as well as extremely rapid communication
and data-processing capability between each of the observation points and
national or international decision-making centers. The need for ultra-rapid,
extremely reliable communication and data processing is created by the
very short time of flight of ballistic missiles. In contrast to these severe
requirements, an inspection system designed to monitor complete disarmament, or even the stable deterrent system to be examined later, will have
no need for ultra-fast or perfectly reliable electrical communication since
nearly all required responses will be measured in days, weeks, or months.
In addition, to the best of my present ability to estimate, a total disarmament agreement would probably not require a larger inspection force to
monitor it than would be required by the proposed system to warn of a
surprise attack. These remarks are not meant to imply that there are no
useful limited measures which could be undertaken to reduce the dangers
of surprise attack, which there certainly are, but rather to indicate the
difficulty of going very far along this path.

The problems encountered in agreeing upon a system for detecting violations of a nuclear test ban are another illustration of the difficulty of implementing partial measures. At the time of this writing, the extensiveness of
an adequate system is the subject of disagreement not only between the
United States–United Kingdom delegation and the Soviet Union delegation
at Geneva, but between various scientific groups within the United States.

The system agreed upon clearly does not have a high probability of detecting small explosions. A considerable increase in the number of stations in the network would be required to improve this situation. The Soviet Union obviously fears such an increase in the number of seismic stations and the concomitant increase in the inspection force, while many people in the United States are equally fearful of clandestine testing within the Soviet Union. Two critical years have been spent attempting to negotiate this issue. Ironically, an inspection system for monitoring a truly comprehensive disarmament agreement would probably have no need at all for a system to detect underground nuclear tests.

With properly planned stable deterrent systems, the more extensive the inspection system is, the lower will be the levels to which forces can be reduced with safety. In an initial phase of disarmament, therefore, it may be easier to reconcile the two fears (the Soviet fear of widespread inspection while weapons remain, and the Western fear of clandestine USSR forces) by starting with a stable deterrent system than by attempting to implement one of the total disarmament plans.

Different weapons will pose different inspection requirements. Ships will be easier to control than aircraft, aircraft easier than missiles, etc., and the degree of assurance required in the information concerning different weapons will vary as well. For example, much more precise information will doubtless be needed regarding the number of ballistic missiles (if any) remaining in a country than will be needed concerning the number of fighter aircraft or short-range air defense missiles. All comprehensive arms-limitation systems that are to be examined require some inspection system, but the inspection requirements will differ greatly between the systems.

The *feasibility* of the systems to be studied will depend upon the feasibility of adequate inspection; the relative *desirability* of the different plans will be affected in part by the complexity of the inspection system. Though inspection techniques of arms control are examined in more detail in Bernard T. Feld's chapter in this book, a review of pertinent information regarding the inspection systems for use in controlling nuclear weapons and for controlling the principal means of delivering them will be presented here.

SPECIFIC TECHNIQUES OF CONTROL AND INSPECTION

The negotiability of any arms-limitation proposal will be determined, to a considerable degree, by the inspection and control measures it requires. The extent to which the production or deployment of any weapon can be restricted by agreement will be established by the ability of an inspection system to verify the agreement. Furthermore, the difficulty of implementation will be determined by the inspection techniques chosen to monitor the agreements. A highly technical system, requiring the development and production of specialized new equipment such as better seismic detectors for detecting underground explosions or special large radar instruments for detecting missile firings, will take longer to install and have operating than one that depends primarily upon the use of available devices, such as existing photo reconnaissance equipment, or just upon physical inspection by observers. Since a wide variety of inspection systems appears to be possible, it is likely that some of them will be more acceptable than others. Unfortunately, they have not been studied adequately, and are not well understood, so that meaningful comparisons cannot be made between them. The planning of comprehensive arms systems should only be undertaken after the control and inspection problems associated with the individual weapons are understood reasonably well.

Objectives of Inspection. An inspection system must serve two different functions. When the arms-limitation agreements are being implemented it will be necessary to verify military forces. Verification will consist of establishing the veracity of the actual disclosures by on-site inspection, and establishing that all existing military units and equipment were included in the initial disclosure. After the verification of the initial disclosures is completed, it will be necessary to continue search for possible clandestine activities, such as the secret production of nuclear material or the construction of missiles.

The degree of assurance required of the inspection system will depend very much on the nature of the arms-limitation agreement being monitored. For example, a stable deterrent agreement which permits relatively large missile forces to remain in national hands requires less assurance regarding the existence of a small clandestine missile force than an agreement completely outlawing missiles.

Inspection and Observation Techniques. In planning arms-limitation systems, it is desirable to limit the inspection and observation components to those of a strategic nature, i.e., to those depending on information regarding location, number, etc., and to avoid the use of tactical information requiring rapid transmission and quick reaction.

The techniques available fall into two basic categories: aerial (or satellite) inspection and observation; and ground inspection using resident or mobile inspectors.

Aerial Reconnaissance for Search and Verification. Photographic reconnaissance provides one of the most effective means of checking the accuracy of facility disclosures and searching for clandestine military or production installations. With modern photographic equipment, it is possible to identify small objects on the ground even though the camera is at high altitude. Because of its great effectiveness and relatively modest cost, photographic reconnaissance is often proposed as the basic means of verification and search in arms-control systems.

Two quite different capabilities are required for the most effective use of aerial photography for search and verification purposes in an arms-control system. There is need for general high-altitude coverage and for a modest amount of very-high-resolution low-altitude reconnaissance capability to be used for investigating suspicious objects which cannot be identified from the high-altitude films. Though the high-resolution capability is not absolutely required, its existence will greatly reduce the ground inspection effort.

A quite modest flying and photo-interpreter effort appears to be adequate to verify or repudiate the disclosures regarding present-day missile-launching sites; factory and camp locations, etc.

Ground Inspection Techniques. The ground inspection system will be used to fulfill a number of quite separate functions. Principal among these are:

1. to assist in the effort to detect or verify the existence and location of all significant military weapons, military test facilities, military research establishments, and manufacturing facilities with emphasis upon those not amenable to aerial and space techniques,

2. to investigate areas of suspected military activity uncovered by aerial inspection or by other means,

3. to maintain surveillance of known facilities capable of developing, testing, or producing military weapons to insure that no illegal activities exist. This could include extensive and continuing inspection of records, raw materials, output, surveillance of personnel, etc., and

4. to operate technical systems such as surveillance radars, seismic systems, and data processing centers, used in conjunction with the inspection operation.

While the functions listed are separate, the inspectorate would no doubt be an integrated system making use of common facilities and staff wherever possible and using the information gained by each of the operations to create as reliable a picture as possible of the military state of affairs. An inspection system adequate to monitor any degree of disarmament appears to be possible, though its acceptability is by no means certain. Detailed discussions of the individual inspection problems are given elsewhere in this volume.

Psychological Inspection. The preceding sections have dealt with the inspection of things. It is also possible to "inspect" people. A variety of means has been proposed for doing this, including newspaper campaigns to familiarize people with the nature of arms-control agreements, offers of rewards, interrogation of key personnel, and the use of lie detectors. Though psychological inspection has not been examined carefully, it does appear to be an important inspection technique. (See chapter 18 on this subject by Lewis Bohn.)

PHASING TO PROVIDE EQUITABLE IMPLEMENTATION WHILE RETAINING ADEQUATE SECURITY

One of the most difficult problems encountered in the planning of an arms-control system is that of balancing the level of disarmament and the completeness of the inspection system during the period of transition to the final conditions. One means of resolving this difficulty is by combining time-phased arms reductions with an inspection system based upon the concept of territorial disarmament proposed by Louis B. Sohn.[2] In this plan, thorough search for clandestine activities would be permitted in only a fraction of the territory of any one country at the beginning of the implementation period, and the search would progress to the point of complete coverage at the end of the period. The choice of the area to be searched at each stage is selected unpredictably by the inspecting authority and the information gained is combined with the information provided by the initial declarations and by the other inspection techniques. By the proper choice of conditions, it appears that the conflicting interests of the two sides may be made compatible.

INTERNATIONAL SECURITY FORCE

A serious point of difference between Western and Eastern proposals for comprehensive arms-control systems is the attitude taken toward the inclusion of some form of international "police force." In recent discussions the Western allies have insisted upon the creation of a modest military force for the international control authority before eliminating national forces, while the Soviet Union and its allies have, until recently, objected to it.

The Western view has been that, in the absence of an international force, a world disarmed down to the level required for internal security would not be stable because one of the participating nations could decide to violate the agreements and build up a dangerous nuclear force before the others could react and rebuild a nuclear deterrent. The Soviet view has been that it would not be possible to build up a very large clandestine force before the effort would be detected and counter-actions taken. It is also their view that arms-limitation agreements can only work if the large nations believe them to be preferable to an arms race, in which case they will observe the agreements. It is certainly hard to believe that a nation would deliberately eliminate a large share of the military force it has worked hard to create and then take an action that would start a new arms contest.

There are many way to create an international security force. An attractive way would be to have the smaller nations of the world take on this responsibility with financial and material support from the larger powers. It has even been suggested that France might be willing to join such a group and supply it with a nuclear capability, if it proved desirable to include a nuclear component.

SOME IMPORTANT INSPECTION PROBLEMS

The specific inspection techniques discussed in the preceding sections can be employed singly or in combination to monitor compliance of arms agreements. As already indicated, the intensity of the inspection activities will obviously be controlled by the risk involved if violations are undetected.

The most serious inspection problems are posed by the limitation of nuclear weapons and ballistic missiles, and by the need for surveillance of research and development.

The nuclear-weapon and missile-control problems are interrelated. If one could be absolutely certain of the size of any controlled nuclear stockpile, the need to carry out careful control of missiles would be reduced. Likewise, if very good control could be established over missiles, aircraft, and other carriers of nuclear weapons, less adequate control over the warheads could be accepted. In fact, it will probably be necessary to accept some uncertainty in each and take advantage of the reassurance provided by the overlapping control.

Inspection and Control of Ballistic Missiles. The control and inspection system visualized here is based upon the assumption that at appropriate times, specified in the Arms Control Agreements, complete and accurate information considered necessary for the monitoring of missile limitation agreements will be provided to the control authority by the participants in the agreements. The associated inspection system will have two distinct tasks: it must first verify, within tolerable error, the initial disclosures; and thereafter it must continue to ascertain that existing missile forces are not being augmented clandestinely. Furthermore, it must be so designed that the inspection system need expand only at a rate compatible with the progress being made toward the final armament levels.

The initial verification of missile force level and facilities disclosures can be achieved by direct examination of production facilities and records, and by interrogation of personnel involved in missile production, development, and operation. The initial verification would be reinforced by the phased disclosure and verification of missile locations. This step would be accomplished by physical search, using aerial reconnaissance and other techniques in the areas opened to complete inspection. The important property of a good search system for use in verifying missile force disclosures is that it have a high probability of detecting the existence of one, or at most a few, clandestine missiles if a substantial number exist and not that it be able to find all that may exist. This fact has two consequences; it makes possible the use of random sampling techniques and it makes the possession of a sizeable clandestine force very risky.

After the agreed-upon disclosures have been made, the control authority will have the task of authenticating the information disclosed and of insuring its completeness. A variety of complementary techniques are available to verify the completeness of the disclosed data and the continued compliance with the agreements. For these techniques to be effectively employed, the inspection authority must have the right to employ at will those inspection techniques previously agreed upon.

Detailed examination of this problem leads me to believe that it is feasible to create an inspection system in the near future to verify or repudiate good faith with regard to the production and deployment of missiles.

Nuclear Stockpile Control. At the present time the principal technical difficulty encountered in making safe disarmament arrangements stems from the existence of large stockpiles of nuclear materials and the impossibility of determining for sure how large they actually are. This uncertainty in the measurement has been estimated to fall in the range of from 50 to 500 large nuclear weapons if physical means only were employed to estimate past production. It is probable that an intensive study of the physical means of estimating past nuclear production could greatly reduce this uncertainty. There is also reason to hope that psychological inspection could reduce this number considerably, but it is premature to count on this.

A somewhat easier problem is the limitation of the production of new nuclear material. While it is probable that enough material to make a very few bombs per year could be produced clandestinely or diverted from peaceful uses, I do not believe that this problem is nearly as serious as that of establishing confidence in the location of previously produced material.

Because it is obviously possible for clandestine stockpiles to exist, I feel strongly the need to retain a small nuclear deterrent force at least until considerable confidence has been developed in the inspection system.

Technological Surprise. One of the most difficult military eventualities to prepare for is the technological surprise. In the kind of world we live in, the most effective safeguards from technological surprise are a very broad and intensive research program, as much exchange of scientific and technical information as the cold war permits, and an effective intelligence system.

In a disarmed world there will be no need for secret research and development and it should be strictly forbidden. If all legitimate scientific and technical work is open and observable, the danger of the sudden appearance of unexpected weapons resulting from secret research will be greatly reduced. The techniques of psychological inspection should be particularly useful in dealing with this problem.

It should be noted that after a weapon has been invented, it must not only be developed and tested, but it must also be produced, usually in substantial quantity, before it can be regarded as a serious threat. In an open world large-scale clandestine production and deployment will also be difficult.

One interesting characteristic of highly technical inventions is that such new ideas spring up in many places around the world at more or less the same time, being more dependent upon the sudden development of new scientific knowledge than any other single factor. Because this is so, the danger from technological surprise would be less in a world in which research was conducted openly and results published freely than in the present one.

VI. THE CONCEPT OF STABLE MUTUAL DETERRENCE

The arms-limitation systems examined in Section VIII below propose to achieve security against the disaster of nuclear war by getting rid of nuclear weapons. Stable deterrent systems, on the other hand, attempt to curb the arms race by creating a system in which a surprise attack by one side cannot prevent retaliation by the other and is thus deterred. This is an attempt to follow the course defined by Dr. Leo Szilard as "learning to live with the bomb." [3] While a system of mutual deterrence is less attractive in many ways then properly safeguarded total disarmament, it may be somewhat easier to achieve and could be regarded as a transient phase on the way toward the goal of total disarmament.

THE CONCEPT OF MUTUAL DETERRENCE

The concept of mutual deterrence, explored in considerable detail by a number of military writers, is basically quite simple. Fundamentally it stands upon the premise that it is now possible, or soon will be possible, to create offensive weapons systems sufficiently invulnerable to enemy attack to prevent their destruction by any practicably achievable force. In this circumstance there will be no need to fear an enemy surprise attack undertaken specifically to wipe out the force. If each side has a similarly protected and invulnerable force, there will be no opportunity and therefore no incentive for either to build up a so-called counter-force capability. In this situation, an attack is deterred by the certain knowledge that it will be followed by a devastating reply.

MUTUAL DETERRENCE USING BALLISTIC MISSILES

Obviously any of the existing delivery systems can be used as part of a stable deterrent system. Because bomber aircraft normally require large airfields for their operation and appear to be harder to protect than ballistic missiles, missiles are the favorite weapon for planning deterrent systems. Though it may be regarded as a gross oversimplification by the experts, this discussion will ignore the very great complications of the multiple weapon problem and consider the pure ballistic missile case.

In order to destroy missiles installed in protected underground bases and missile systems protected by mobility (Polaris missiles in submarines, or mobile Minuteman missiles, for example), an attacker would be forced to launch many missiles for each one being attacked. It is easy to conceive of situations in which the exchange rate could be ten or greater. If both sides in a military contest develop secure weapons, much of the incentive for an unlimited arms race disappears, even without controls. The ability to achieve relatively secure retaliatory systems makes it appear feasible to control the size of such forces by agreement. To do so requires only strategic inspection techniques, i.e., inspection methods which keep account of force levels rather than of the momentary readiness of forces. There is a minimum size to a deterrent force below which it may not provide security. This is determined by the number of missiles it may be possible to hide without serious danger of detection which obviously will be a function of the effectiveness of the missile inspection system. Herein lies the useful feature of the deterrence concept for the design of an arms-control system; there can be a mutual deterrence system to fit any desired level of inspection and the better the inspection the smaller the deterrent force required to insure stability. This provides a possible means of beginning arms limitations with only a modest inspection effort and a corresponding modest reduction in force, and allowing the system to evolve in the direction of fewer weapons and more inspection as confidence in it is built up.

It is important to note that a missile deterrent system would be unbalanced by the development of a highly effective anti-missile defense system and if it appears possible to develop one, the agreements should explicitly prohibit the development and deployment of such systems.

The possibility of a comprehensive arms-limitation and control system using stable deterrents will be determined to a significant degree by the feasibility of dealing successfully with the ballistic missile-control problem.

It is possible to conceive of a stable deterrent system using only a relatively small number of ballistic missiles and associate with it an inspection and control system adequate to provide a high degree of assurance that there can remain no clandestine force sufficiently strong to be a serious threat to the legal deterrent forces. This can be understood if we examine a simple example. Let us assume that the deterrent force consists of a number of Minuteman missiles installed in underground concrete emplacements. Depending upon the thickness of the concrete protection and other features in the design, the missile can be made secure against shock waves corresponding to overpressures up to about 1,000 pounds per square inch, though designs in the region between 100 and 300 psi are considered more practical. A 300 psi overpressure corresponds to the effect of a five-megaton bomb bursting on the ground approximately 0.7 mile from the point of measurement. The overpressure is a very sensitive function of the distance from the explosion, so that if guided missiles are used to deliver nuclear weapons in attacking hardened targets, their accuracy is very important. Missile accuracy is specified by quoting a median accuracy, which is the radius of a circle about the aiming point containing half of the impacts from a repeated series of trials.

If a nuclear weapon had to make impact within one-half mile of a target to destroy it, a missile having a median accuracy of half a mile would have a 0.5 probability of doing so, two missiles would have a 0.75 probability of doing so, three missiles a 0.875 probability and four missiles would have approximately a 0.94 probability of destroying the target. When the number of targets to be attacked is large and the number of survivors that can be tolerated is small, the certainty with which each individual target must be destroyed becomes extreme, and the number of attacking missiles required can become quite large.

This calculation is typical of many in which the methods are simple and obvious, but is one which should be held in considerable suspicion because of the unreliability of the assumptions. In particular, estimates of exchange ratios are very sensitive to estimates of missile accuracy, a bit of information that is very hard to get and dangerous to trust completely, and one that is subject to change as missiles develop. This does not imply that such calculations are not valuable, but rather that judgment and care should be applied when making and using them.

To demonstrate how difficult it is to destroy a hardened missile force, an example will be given. If it is agreed that each side is to have 200 missiles in its deterrent force and if the missiles were protected for 300 pounds/sq. inch overpressure, 1,000 missiles having a median accuracy of one mile would be required to have a 0.9 probability of reducing the attacked force to 10 missiles. It obviously would not require a very intensive inspection effort to detect an attempted build-up of this magnitude.

LIMITATION ON NUCLEAR WEAPON STOCKS

A more secure system can be made if limitations are placed upon the permissible nuclear weapon stockpile as well as upon the ballistic missile force. By limiting the size of the nuclear weapon stockpile, it is possible to place an additional constraint upon the maximum size of the surprise attack capability which could build up clandestinely. Though it might appear that adequate security could be obtained by effective controls on nuclear stockpiles alone, a system in which several independent controls are imposed upon each of the major weapon systems is obviously more secure.

In order to restrict the size of nuclear stockpiles in a meaningful way from the point of view of deterrent security, it will be necessary to limit the use of nuclear weapons to retaliatory purposes. This is so, for if they were to be permitted for limited war purposes or air defense, the number of weapons, and therefore the amount of fissionable material required, would be so great that large numbers could be diverted to the surprise attack force.

These restrictions do not appear serious. As missiles become the principal weapon for surprise attack, air defense becomes of limited value in actually protecting the country. Furthermore, limited nuclear war appears to be undesirable from a military point of view even in the absence of arms control. In that situation, however, one must be prepared for limited nuclear war, because the other side may introduce nuclear weapons, as pointed out by Henry A. Kissinger in this book. In the environment of a comprehensive arms-limitation system, on the other hand, it is possible to enforce reliable constraints against arming limited-war forces with nuclear weapons, which obviates this problem. We do not wish to preserve the institution of limited nuclear war.

What Constitutes an Adequate Deterrent? What does it take to deter the launching of a surprise attack? Obviously there is no specific answer to this question. From the Western point of view the question really is, "What does it take to deter the Soviet Union from launching a surprise attack?" This question cannot be answered very satisfactorily; it depends so very much on one's views of the objectives of the Soviet leaders. There are students of Kremlin policy who contend that the Soviet leaders are prepared to sacrifice a third of their inhabitants and most of their cities if by doing so they could achieve world domination. If one accepts this thesis, an extreme one, he must plan a deterrent system capable of inflicting such punishment after he has absorbed an attack; i.e., one large enough to permit one or two hundred missiles to survive after any possible Soviet attack. A more moderate view taken by others, myself included, is that the present Soviet leaders would be unlikely to risk the nuclear destruction of their major cities in the absence of a very serious threat, in which case the deterrent force could be small because in this situation belief that any missiles would survive an attack would provide adequate deterrence. There are valid arguments for making the deterrent force as small as possible in spite of the greater stability and ease of inspection of substantial deterrent forces. They relate to the dangers of accidental war and to the willingness of nonnuclear nations to allow the continued existence of large nuclear ballistic missile forces among other things.

It might be desirable to start with a substantial deterrent force (200-500 missiles) to reduce the danger discussed above, and as experience is gained with the system and confidence is achieved, the deterrent force could be reduced to a very small size or even eliminated completely.

THE USES OF MUTUAL DETERRENCE

The importance of a stable deterrent system used as a component of an arms-limitation arrangement is that it provides a means of reducing the danger from clandestine nuclear weapons and long-range delivery vehicles. It may be used in conjunction with any of the comprehensive disarmament systems described in Section VIII below. In this case, instead of completely eliminating nuclear weapons and delivery systems, a small number will be permitted to remain. While this situation is not as desirable as would be the actual elimination of all such weapons, it must certainly be preferred to the present unlimited arms race and actual elimination probably cannot be achieved. If a system of stable deterrents can be used to establish a condition of military security during which military forces and weapons stockpiles can be cut back, international tensions reduced, and a period of cooperation and mutual confidence achieved, total nuclear disarmament with or without an international security force may be much more easily agreed upon.

VII. A COMPREHENSIVE DISARMAMENT SYSTEM BASED UPON STABLE DETERRENCE

In Section V it was shown that a mutually agreed-upon stable deterrent system could provide the basis for comprehensive disarmament because it provided a means of reconciling the Soviet reluctance to permit inspection and the Western fear of clandestine weapons. The size of the deterrent force can be chosen large enough to provide adequate security with minimal inspection and subsequently reduced as the inspection effort grows and experience establishes confidence in it.

Nuclear deterrence, using aircraft and missile-delivery systems, provides the basis of military security for both the United States and the Soviet Union at the present time, so that one could contend that we are just proposing to endorse the present situation. However, the proposal for a stable deterrent system is an attempt first to end the nuclear race by imposing a limit upon the size of the legal deterrent, and then to carry out extensive disarmament under the security umbrella which it provides.

As has been stated many times, the ultimate objective of an arms-control system should be to achieve arms reductions to the levels required for internal police action, but, like most other Americans who have examined this problem, I believe that this condition can be achieved only if an adequate international security force exists, controlled by an adequate system of law, or alternatively, if the international tensions can be greatly reduced before disarmament to that level is undertaken. The attainment of either of these goals in a single step appears to be extremely ambitious and therefore it appears desirable to proceed toward this utopian goal in smaller steps. One method of doing this is described in the next section.

PHASES IN THE DEVELOPMENT OF THE STABLE DETERRENT DISARMAMENT SYSTEM

In selecting this particular system, I have consciously attempted to limit the amount of inspection needed during the early period of implementation in order to meet Soviet fears. I believe that the arrangement will provide adequate security for the West. The following four phases are included in this plan: preparatory phase, implementation phase, build-up of an international authority, and the final elimination of national forces.

Phase I: Preparatory Period. During this period the details of Phase II would be worked out and agreed upon. Among those things which would have to be settled would be:

1. The size of the deterrent force, its composition, etc.

2. The size and composition of nonnuclear forces for limited war to remain at the end of Phase II; this will involve agreements covering both land and sea forces.

3. Agreements to halt or limit development and production of new weapons.

4. A timetable for reaching the agreed upon levels of armament and troops.

5. Agreement upon an inspection agency to monitor the agreements and upon a timetable for its implementation. The implementation will involve geographic phasing as well as time-phasing so that the proportion of military facilities exposed to inspection can be made to correspond to the amount of disarmament that has taken place.

6. Agreements upon steps to be taken in the advent of violations.

7. Methods of adjusting forces and inspection within the framework of the treaty.

In this chapter I deliberately avoid making firm proposals for force levels because they should result from a detailed study. However, to provide some sense of what is visualized, a possible range will be indicated.

The initial deterrent force could consist of a force in the range of from 100 to 400 large nuclear weapons and accompanying delivery vehicles, either aircraft or missiles. Studies made independently by the United States Army and Navy have indicated that, even in the absence of agreements limiting force size and permitting inspection, 200 relatively secure missiles would provide an adequate deterrent. As the inspection system is put into operation and confidence is gained in it, the number of nuclear weapons can be reduced markedly below that required initially.

Conventional force levels can correspond to those in the USSR and Anglo-French proposals in which manpower was limited to the range of 1-1.5 million men for the United States, the Soviet Union, and China, somewhat lower limits for France and the United Kingdom, and can eventually be reduced to much lower levels. These numbers are not based upon adequate examination and may be altered considerably by further study. In addition to limiting total manpower, it is important to limit the amount of armaments allowed to remain in national arsenals. Careful consideration must also be given to the problem presented by the United States requirement for naval support and overseas transport as long as substantial conventional forces are permitted to exist.

Phase II: Implementation Period. During this period, which might be as short as three years, the agreements reached in the previous phase would be carried out. The steps would include the following:

1. The submission of previously agreed-upon information concerning military units, size of weapons stockpiles, information pertaining to production facilities, development establishments, test sites, etc. In some cases the information will be made available at the beginning of the implementation period, in other cases the disclosure of information may be made available according to a previously agreed upon schedule.

2. The elimination of surplus weapons. According to an agreed upon

schedule nuclear weapons, missiles, tanks, aircraft, and all other weapons included in the agreement will be placed in depots under international supervision or destroyed. In the early stages of the agreement it may appear prudent to leave the weapons in a supervised depot so that they may be turned back to their owners if subsequent agreements are not carried through. Later, when the good faith of all of the participants is fully accepted, these surplus weapons should be destroyed. In the beginning the transfers of weapons to international control will be checked against the declarations made by each nation. As inspection activities are established, the initial declarations will also be checked.

3. The build-up of inspection. In parallel with the reduction of arms, inspection activities should be started according to the agreed-upon schedule. The first inspection activity will be to verify arms declarations and to ascertain that arms production and development have stopped. A second responsibility of the inspection authority will be to establish that clandestine activities do not exist.

The precise nature of the inspection force is a matter to be worked out between parties to the agreement. As stated in Section V above, a large variety of inspection systems and modes of implementation appears to be feasible from the point of view of security; the deterrent force being used to compensate for any lingering uncertainty about the effectiveness of inspection during the build-up period.

Phase III: Consolidation of the Accomplishments of Phase II and Build-up of an International Authority. At the end of Phase II the military forces of the individual nations will have been reduced to the agreed-upon levels and the inspection system will have been sufficiently exercised to make possible a dependable estimate of its capabilities. At that time it will probably be possible to further reduce the deterrent force. The principal innovation to be made in this period will be the creation of a modest international security force and the legal authority to operate it. (See Arthur Larson's chapter in this volume.) As experience is gained, the international authority can be increased in size and authority until the point is reached where there is sufficient confidence in it to give it the task of maintaining the peace. At that time the last stage in the creation of a world security system can be undertaken—i.e., Phase IV, the complete elimination of all military capability not required for internal security.

In planning this system, I have attempted to take into account the conflicting security requirements and the fears, as I understand them, of the East and the West. I am almost certain that no matter how hard I try, I cannot really fully understand the concerns and logic of the Soviet arms-control experts. Furthermore, in my plans I have probably made more concessions to the American biases, which I know so well from personal contact, than I have to those of the Russians, at which I can only guess.

Nonetheless, I believe that a disarmament scheme not too unlike the one discussed above must be acceptable to all parties if they really desire to make significant strides in the elimination of the arms race and toward a secure and disarmed world.

It is useful to examine what will have been achieved if a system of the general character of that described here could be agreed upon and implemented. A nation's objective in attempting to achieve disarmament agreements should be to enhance the total national security, and the effect of agreements must be examined in a number of areas in addition to that of the military.

The achievement of the arms-control objectives outlined above would certainly improve the basic political conditions in the world. Many persons would challenge this assertion on the grounds that the arms race is a consequence of political conditions and not vice versa. While it is certainly true that the arms race began as a result of an unacceptable political situation, the arsenals of the East and the West are well past the point where they adequately deter each other, and each addition of a new weapon merely gives additional certainty to the expectation that a nuclear war will amount to mutual suicide. In spite of this fact, the arms race speeds on ever faster, spurred not by any rational estimate that a new weapon will greatly improve the military situation, but rather by the logic of the arms race: it is dangerous not to make any weapon the other side has—or may have. This situation is made worse by the determination of the leaders of both sides to bargain only from positions of strength, which in turn is made worse by the obviously sensible tendency to overestimate the opposition's weapons and underestimate one's own. These factors taken together create a situation which is ever accelerating, if we assume neither side collapses under the strain, and if both sides follow the course that their individual strategists regard as obvious self-interest. In fact, if an arms race of this sort is continued, any political adjustments will become impossible, for almost any political readjustment will involve changes which might, in someone's view, alter the military situation disadvantageously and thus be judged dangerous.

I am convinced that arms-control measures such as those outlined above would, if implemented in good faith, reduce tensions and provide an atmosphere in which it should be possible to make progress toward the solution of political problems. The more comprehensive disarmament measures are, the more likely it would be that both sides would recognize and respect their common interest in very extensive disarmament and consequently would become increasingly reluctant to initiate any actions, including military adventures, which might re-establish an arms race. Without the tensions of the present race and with the elimination of the possibility of achieving solutions by military means, it should be less difficult to reconcile the present differences.

Any comprehensive arms-control agreement will of necessity involve the participation of the government that controls the China mainland and will consequently force the United States to take a more constructive attitude on this problem than we have in the past. It is obvious that if we fail to gain their participation in arms-control agreements, we will have to accept a serious shortcoming in any security system we create.

If the arms race were halted, it would be possible for both the United States and Soviet Union to behave differently with regard to the problems posed by China, so that it may be necessary to begin by implementing disarmament agreements that do not require acceptance by China, and to include China in the agreements only after a substantial degree of mutual confidence is created.

I believe that an important aspect of the successful institution and implementation of comprehensive disarmament measures is that it will reduce the pressures which now compel other countries to consider creating an independent national nuclear capability. Much of the agitation within individual countries for doing this stems from prestige and political considerations rather than from real defense needs, though it is true that the motivation for an independent European nuclear capability stems from a desire to create a deterrent force not entirely dependent upon an American response. In any event, agreements which eliminate—or greatly reduce— the scale of Russian and American weapons should mitigate the pressures for the creation of additional nuclear forces.

The previous arguments are primarily political. Obviously, there will also be extensive, direct military gains from the implementation of these proposals. By suitably reducing the nuclear forces available to either side, the possibility and consequently the danger of a successful pre-emptive strike by either side will be greatly reduced, if not eliminated, provided it is done with reasonable care. In such an environment the need for instantaneous response to attack will disappear and with it much of the present tension and the danger of accidental war.

Many advocates of controlled mutual-deterrent systems derive considerable comfort from the fact that thus to limit the size of strategic nuclear forces will limit the damage that would occur if a war started in spite of our best efforts. While it is clearly true that a smaller force can do less damage, I am unable to get any real comfort from the fact that only one hundred bombs (instead of one thousand or ten thousand) could fall on our country and on Russia. In either case the possible scale of suffering and damage is beyond my comprehension. I regard a system of stable mutual deterrence only as a means of making the transition from the present situation to a state of comprehensive disarmament.

VIII. A SURVEY OF SOME PREVIOUS COMPREHENSIVE DISARMAMENT PROPOSALS

During the meetings of the United Nations Disarmament Sub-Committee in the years 1954 and 1955, both the East and the West made formal proposals for comprehensive disarmament systems. As might be expected, in their initial form each of them was one-sided and disregarded the known security worries of the other side. During the course of the Sub-Committee meetings, each side modified its proposal in an attempt to make it more attractive to the other. In spite of the fact that both sides modified their initial positions greatly, they were not able to reach agreement. Subsequently, the USSR has made additional proposals worthy of examination. It is informative to examine the past efforts to see whether or not they appear to be adequate from a security point of view, and if not, how they would have to be modified to make them satisfactory.

The following summary (taken from the book *The Arms Race* by Philip Noel-Baker [4]) shows how far the participants in the United Nations Sub-Committee discussions were able to progress before their work was halted.

ANGLO-FRENCH PROPOSAL, JUNE 11, 1954— MODIFIED APRIL 19, 1955

The Draft Disarmament Treaty . . . should include provisions covering the following:

(1) The total prohibition of the use and manufacture of nuclear weapons and weapons of mass destruction of every type, together with the conversion of existing stocks of nuclear weapons for peaceful purposes.

(2) Major reductions in all armed forces and conventional armaments.

(3) The establishment of a control organ with rights and powers and functions adequate to guarantee the effective observance of the agreed prohibitions and reductions.

The agreement to start with a reduction of conventional forces to a ceiling of 1-1.5 million men. A nuclear production cut-off to begin when 50 percent of the conventional force reduction has been made. After 75 percent of conventional force reduction has been made:

1. There should be "a complete ban on the use of atomic, hydrogen and other weapons of mass destruction."

2. Simultaneously, the elimination of these weapons and the final quarter of the agreed reduction in armed forces and conventional armaments shall begin and both processes shall be completed within the time limit laid down in the Disarmament Treaty. All atomic materials shall then be used only for peaceful purposes.

According to the British and French delegates, this proposal was dependent upon agreement upon: "1. Agreed-upon reduction in the levels of conventional forces [ceilings of 1-1.5 million men for United States, Russia and China and 650,000 each for Britain and France]. 2. The institution of an effective control system that would operate throughout the whole disarmament program."

Proposed Control Mechanism. The Anglo-French Memorandum made the following statement concerning the control problem:

I. In our view the control organ must have the right of full information and inspection of the following "objects of control" . . .

(1) numbers of armed forces and their equipment;

(2) conventional land, sea and air armaments, including certain categories of civilian aircraft and shipping;

(3) military installations, including barracks, ordinance depots, dockyards and airfields;

(4) factories capable of making armaments (including aircraft), explosives, and propellants;

(5) nuclear installations and reactors;

(6) plants capable of making chemical and biological weapons.

II. The control organ should be able to make use of the following methods of inspection and supervision: (1) aerial reconnaissance; (2) inspection on the ground; (3) budgetary controls; (4) observation at strategic points.

III. The control organ should also have the following rights:

(1) unrestricted rights of freedom of movement to, from and within all States party to the treaty;

(2) the right to make full use of the communication systems of the State which it is inspecting and to possess suitable transport and communications of its own;

(3) the right of access to all the objects which have just been mentioned; advance notice would be given of routine visits, but the right of inspection without warning would also be essential;

(4) the right to investigate alleged or suspected breaches of the treaty in any establishment or installation in the territory of any State party to the treaty; and, perhaps, in some respects, the most important of all,

(5) the right to use all necessary technical devices which may assist supervision and detection.

USSR PROPOSAL, MAY 10, 1955, AND AMPLIFIED IN 1957

1. the manpower ceilings of between 1 and 1.5 million, etc.;

2. "the 5 Powers shall undertake also to reduce their conventional armaments correspondingly";

3. the 50 percent arrangement for the "cut-off";

4. the 75 percent arrangement for the abolition of stocks of nuclear and other mass-destruction weapons;

5. "appropriations by States for armed forces and conventional armaments shall be reduced correspondingly";

6. there should be *one* "International Control Organ," with expanding powers;

7. the International Control Organ should:

(a) have "staff . . . selected on an international basis";

(b) enjoy the right "to require from States any necessary information on the execution of measures for the reduction of armaments and armed forces";

(c) "have *permanently in all States signatories . . . its own staff of inspectors having, within the bounds of the control functions they exercise, unimpeded access at all times to all objects of control"*;

(d) "have unimpeded access to records relating to the budgetary appropriation of States for military needs";

(e) have *"rights and powers to exercise control, including inspection on a continuing basis, to the extent necessary to ensure implementation of the above-mentioned Convention by all States. . . ."*

On the completion of all the measures enumerated above, it would be desirable that the Powers should further reduce their armaments and armed forces to the levels strictly necessary for the maintenance of internal security and the fulfillment of the UN Charter.

To this program was added in 1957 "the total abolition of all missiles, both intercontinental missiles and intermediate and short-range missiles as well."

CONTROL MECHANISMS FOR CONVENTIONAL ARMAMENTS AS PROPOSED BY THE USSR IN MARCH 1956

With a view to the establishment of effective international control over the fulfillment by States of the above-mentioned obligations with respect to the reduction of conventional armaments and armed forces, an international control organ shall be established having the following rights and powers:

1. [This deals with surprise attack and the establishment of ground control posts.]

2. The international control organ shall exercise control, including inspection on a permanent basis, to the extent necessary to ensure implementation of the agreement by all States.

3. The control organ shall have permanently in all States party to the agreement its own staff of inspectors, recruited on an international basis, having, within the bounds of the control functions which they exercise, unimpeded access at all times to all objects of control.

The objects of control are: military units; stores of military equipment and ammunition; land, naval and air bases; factories manufacturing conventional armaments and ammunition.

4. At a specified stage of the execution of the general disarmament program, when confidence among States has been strengthened, the countries convened shall consider the possibility of using aerial photography as one of the methods of control.

5. The control organ shall have unimpeded access to records relating to the budgetary appropriations of States for military needs, including all decisions of the legislative and executive organs on the subject.

6. The control organ shall establish in the capitals of States party to the agreement branches whose functions shall include maintaining liaison with the governmental organs of States, directing the work of the control posts and

inspectors operating in the territory of the State concerned, and analyzing the information furnished by States.

7. The international control organ shall be established within the two months following the entry into force of the agreement. It shall establish its local branches, set up the control posts and position its inspectors in good time to ensure that they are able to begin carrying out their functions at the moment when States begin the execution of the measures provided for in the agreement.

8. The international control organ shall make recommendations to the Security Council on measures of prevention and suppression with regard to violators of the agreement on the reduction of conventional armaments and armed forces.

9. The States party to the agreement shall submit to the international control organ within one month after its establishment complete official figures of their armed forces, conventional armaments and expenditures for military requirements.

COMPARISON OF THE RUSSIAN AND ANGLO-FRENCH PROPOSALS

Both proposals were so general that it is not possible to judge their adequacy. Whether or not either proposal would be acceptable to the nations who must participate in its implementation would be determined by the details of inspection and the details of scheduling or timing. The experience with the nuclear test ban negotiations would lead one to believe that getting agreement on the details on either of these two similar proposals would not have been easy. Note that there were many points of agreement in the two proposals and either could easily have served as a basis for the design of an adequate arms-control system if the desire to create one had been great enough to overcome the effects of fear, skepticism, and suspicion regarding each other's motives which seem to have governed United States and Russian actions at that time. Both proposals included measures to cope with the major problems of that period:

1. Both proposed the elimination of nuclear weapons production.

2. Both proposed the ultimate elimination of nuclear weapons and other weapons of mass destruction.

3. Both included a provision for the reduction of manpower in the military forces and limiting the conventional armament.

4. Both provided for an international inspection and control authority.

5. Both suggested a timetable for implementing of the systems, but both proposals were very vague.

It is also interesting to note that in 1955 neither side felt it necessary to eliminate nuclear delivery means—then the long-range bomber—though in 1957 the Soviet Union did hold out the prospect of eliminating missiles. Nor did either side propose the creation of an international security force to provide a means of enforcing compliance of the agreements.

These omissions probably indicate that in 1955 there was not yet sufficient appreciation of the fact that it was no longer possible to verify completely declarations concerning the size of nuclear stockpiles and that consequently small clandestine stockpiles might exist after completing the elimination of declared stockpiles.

The Western proposals were withdrawn in 1955, as Mr. Frye has already stated in this volume, because of a growing fear on the part of some American experts that the problem of the clandestine nuclear stockpile could not be solved. In some respects, it is a great tragedy that agreements were not reached and implemented in the period 1955–1957 before the development of the ballistic missile and lightweight thermonuclear weapons that have made the problem of inspection even more difficult than it was then.

Both proposals call for the ultimate elimination of nuclear weapons and other weapons of mass destruction, elimination of nuclear weapon production, and a major reduction in the size of conventional military forces and military armaments available in each country. If adequate controls on long-range aircraft and ballistic missiles were added to the preceding proposals, they would be applicable to the situation existing today.

We still face the question of clandestine armaments, especially clandestine nuclear weapons and clandestine ballistic missiles, but a solution of this problem appears to be possible if both sides really want it. Among the various means of minimizing the danger of clandestine weapons are the creation of an international security force sufficiently strong and dispersed to be an adequate counterthreat to any likely clandestine force, the creation of a sufficiently effective inspection system to make the retention or creation of a clandestine force extremely difficult, and the maintenance of nuclear weapons depots under international supervision to be available to their owners in the advent of the sudden appearance of such weapons in the hands of any other nation or group of nations.

PROPOSALS FOR GENERAL DISARMAMENT

During the past two years there have been several new proposals by the Soviet Union and various Western groups. The two most significant of these have been summarized in the following table, which is from a publication by the staff of the Subcommittee on Disarmament of the Committee of Foreign Relations of the United States Senate. The chart is reproduced with their kind permission.

The similarities between the two proposals are amazing, but also somewhat deceptive. Though the ultimate objectives of the two proposals are the same, despite the apparent agreement between them, a great deal of adjustment in both will be required if a single agreement is to be achieved.

A careful comparison of the two proposals will show that the differences in fears and security objectives which I have discussed earlier still dominate these proposals. In spite of this they are heartening documents—if they were actually proposed for serious negotiation, which many knowledgeable people doubt. Most important of all is the recognition in both papers of the need for a militia to preserve the peace.

The above proposal for a mutual deterrent system and for time-phased territorial disarmament and inspection was planned with the intention of resolving the conflicting security interests of the East and West, which show up so graphically in this table.

SOVIET PROPOSAL, JUNE 2, 1960	U.S. PROPOSAL, JUNE 27, 1960
First Stage	*First Stage*
Armed-forces reduction: (Removed to 2d stage and only U.S.S.R. and United States specifically mentioned.)	Armed-forces reduction: Initial force level ceilings to be: 2,500,000 for the United States and U.S.S.R. and agreed appropriate force levels for certain other states. After accession to the treaty of other militarily significant states and after these initial force levels have been verified, force levels of 2,100,000 shall be established for the United States and U.S.S.R. and agreed appropriate force levels shall be established for other militarily significant states.
Armaments reduction: Joint study to effect cessation of production of chemical and bacteriological weapons and on destruction of stockpiles of such types of weapons.	Armaments reduction: Agreed types and quantities of armaments in agreed relation to established force levels to be placed in storage depots by participating states within their own territories under IDCO (International Disarmament Control Organization) supervision pending destruction or conversion to peaceful uses.
Missiles and other delivery systems: All means of delivering nuclear weapons to be destroyed and their manufacture stopped, including: strategic and tactical missiles; pilotless planes of all types; all military aircraft capable of delivering nuclear weapons; surface warships capable of being used to carry nuclear weapons; submarines of all classes and types; all artillery	Missiles and other delivery systems: Prior notification to IDCO of all proposed launchings of space vehicles and missiles and their planned tracks, and the establishment of a zone of aerial and ground inspection in agreed areas including the United States and U.S.S.R. Declaration of and institution of onsite inspection at mutually agreed operational airbases, missile

SOVIET PROPOSAL,
JUNE 2, 1960
First Stage (*continued*)

systems and other means of carrying nuclear weapons. The penetration of warships beyond the limits of territorial waters and the flights beyond limits of their national territory of military aircraft capable of carrying weapons of mass destruction shall be prohibited.

Nuclear weapons: Joint study to effect cessation of production of nuclear weapons and on destruction of stockpiles of such weapons. States having nuclear weapons shall not transfer them or information necessary for their manufacture to states which do not possess such weapons. Nonnuclear powers shall refrain from manufacturing nuclear weapons.

Withdrawal of foreign troops, dismantling of bases: All foreign troops shall be withdrawn. Foreign bases and depots shall be abolished.

Outer space: Space vehicles shall be launched only for peaceful purposes in accordance with agreement on inspection of launching sites. Launching into orbit or placing in outer space of special devices shall be prohibited until after final destruction of all means of delivering nuclear weapons.*

Control measures: International on-the-spot control shall be established over the destruction of missiles, military aircraft, surface warships, submarines, and other devices which could be used to carry atomic and hydrogen weapons. International inspection

U.S. PROPOSAL,
JUNE 27, 1960
First Stage (*continued*)

launching pads, submarine and naval bases in order to establish a basis for controls over nuclear delivery systems in subsequent stages.

Nuclear weapons: The production of fissionable materials for use in weapons shall be stopped upon installation and effective operation of control system necessary for verification, and agreed quantities of fissionable materials from past production shall be transferred to nonweapons uses, including stockpiling for peaceful purposes, conditioned upon satisfactory progress in the field of conventional disarmament.

Withdrawal of foreign troops, dismantling of bases: (No mention.)

Outer space: The placing into orbit or stationing in outer space of vehicles carrying weapons capable of mass destruction shall be prohibited.

Control measures: An International Disarmament Control Organization (IDCO) shall be established within the framework of the United Nations and expanded as required by the progressive implementation of general and complete disarmament.

* The "special devices" would probably include the Midas and other United States reconnaissance satellites. This is the proposal criticized by Richard S. Leghorn near the end of his chapter.—ED.

SOVIET PROPOSAL, JUNE 2, 1960 *First Stage (continued)*	U.S. PROPOSAL, JUNE 27, 1960 *First Stage (continued)*

teams to be sent to military bases and troops on foreign territories to supervise elimination of these bases and withdrawal of troops to within national boundaries. Destruction of missile launching sites except for peaceful purposes. Control also established at airports and harbors. Right of inspection of all plants, factories, and shipyards involved in military production. By mutual agreement, permanent control groups may be set up at certain plants and installations. Right of inspection teams to examine rocket devices being launched for peaceful purposes and to be present at time of launching. Inspectors shall communicate with control council through existing channels of communication.

Keeping the peace: (No mention.)

Second Stage

Armed-forces reduction: Reduction of the armed forces of all states to agreed levels, United States and U.S.S.R. reduced to not more than 1,700,000.

Armaments reduction: Conventional weapons released by force reduction to be destroyed or used for peaceful purposes and destruction of all stockpiles. Prohibition of chemical and biological weapons production.

Missiles and other delivery systems: (No mention.)

Keeping the peace: (No mention.)

Second Stage

Armed-forces reduction: Force levels shall be further reduced to 1,700,000 for United States and U.S.S.R. and to agreed appropriate levels for other states.

Armaments reduction: Quantities of all kinds of armaments of each state including nuclear, chemical, biological, and other existing weapons of mass destruction and all means for their delivery shall be reduced to agreed levels and the resulting excesses shall be destroyed or converted to peaceful uses.

Missiles and other delivery systems: Agreed categories of missiles, aircraft, surface ships, submarines, and artillery designed to deliver nuclear and other weapons of mass destruction shall be destroyed or converted to peaceful uses.

SOVIET PROPOSAL, JUNE 2, 1960 *Second Stage (continued)*	U.S. PROPOSAL, JUNE 27, 1960 *Second Stage (continued)*

Nuclear weapons: Complete prohibition, cessation of production, and destruction of existing stockpiles of all nuclear weapons.

Nuclear weapons: Nuclear armaments to be further reduced.

Withdrawal of foreign troops, dismantling of bases: (No mention in 2d stage.)

Withdrawal of foreign troops, dismantling of bases: (No mention.)

Outer space: (No mention.)

Outer space: (No mention.)

Control measures: Inspectors shall verify destruction of existing stockpiles of nuclear, chemical, and bacteriological weapons. Rights to inspect all production of atomic materials or atomic energy. Inspection by military specialists of disbanding of troops. Control organization to have free access to all material on military budgets.

Control measures: (No mention.)

Keeping the peace: Joint study on measures to insure compliance with the treaty on general and complete disarmament after all measures provided for in treaty have been completed. Joint study on measures to maintain peace and security in accordance with the U.N. Charter. Control organization to report on progress toward disarmament to U.N. Security Council and General Assembly.

Keeping the peace: An international peace force, within the U.N., shall be progressively established and maintained with agreed personnel strength and armaments sufficient to preserve world peace when general and complete disarmament is achieved.

Third Stage

Third Stage

Armed-forces reduction: Completion of the disbandment of the armed forces of all states. States shall retain only agreed-upon police (militias) with small arms for internal law and order.

Armed-forces reduction: Forces and military establishments of all states shall be finally reduced to those levels required to maintain internal order and insuring the personal security of citizens and of providing agreed contingents of forces to the international peace force.

SOVIET PROPOSAL,
JUNE 2, 1960
Third Stage (*continued*)

U.S. PROPOSAL,
JUNE 27, 1960
Third Stage (*continued*)

Armaments reduction: All remaining conventional arms whether held by armed forces or in stockpiles shall be destroyed or used for peaceful purposes. Military production shall be wound up except for limited output of small arms to be retained by states after completion of program of general and complete disarmament.

Armaments reduction: The international peace force and remaining agreed contingents of national armed forces shall be armed only with agreed types and quantities of armaments. All other remaining armaments shall be destroyed or converted to peaceful uses. There shall be no manufacture of any armaments except for agreed types and quantities for use by the international peace force and agreed remaining national contingents.

Missiles and other delivery systems: (No mention.)

Missiles and other delivery systems: All remaining weapons of mass destruction and vehicles for their delivery shall be destroyed or converted to peaceful uses.

Nuclear weapons: (No mention.)

Nuclear weapons: (No mention.)

Withdrawal of foreign troops, dismantling of bases: (No mention.)

Withdrawal of foreign troops, dismantling of bases: (No mention.)

Outer space: (No mention.)

Outer space: (No mention.)

Control measures: Control organization can send inspectors to verify abolition of military establishments. As necessary, institute a system of aerial observation and aerial photography over the territory of states. Shall have right to send mobile inspection teams to any point and to any facility in the territories of states.

Control measures: (No mention.)

Keeping the peace: Measures to maintain peace and security in accordance with the Charter of the U.N. shall be carried out. States shall undertake to place at the disposal of the Security Council, when necessary, formations from the contingents of police (militia) retained by them.

Keeping the peace: The international peace force shall be armed only with agreed types and quantities of armaments.

12. Policy Considerations of a Nuclear-Test Ban

DONALD G. BRENNAN AND MORTON H. HALPERIN

INTRODUCTION

IN THIS CHAPTER WE SHALL DEAL WITH THE MAJOR POLICY CONSIDERATIONS of a ban on the further testing of nuclear weapons.* Many of the issues involved in such a ban have become extremely controversial. The primary objective of this chapter is to illuminate the relevant issues of policy as completely as space permits. There are some genuine potential costs of a test ban, and we have tried at least to indicate these, so far as we know them. However, sufficient technical information is now available to enable us to indicate just how serious these costs might be. In our opinion, these costs at worst do not outweigh the possible gains of a test ban, at least for the next five or ten years.

Another objective of this chapter is to provide an example of a fairly complete analysis of an arms-control measure. As such things go, it is a rather simple measure, and the analysis will indicate the potential magnitude of the problem of analyzing more complicated measures. Simply as an example of a fairly complete analysis, this chapter may be of value even if a test-ban treaty is signed and ratified by the time this book is published—which seems rather unlikely. And some of the issues involved are likely to remain live issues even if a treaty *is* signed and ratified. Since a rather detailed summary of the negotiations up through the fall of 1960 has been published,[1] we shall confine ourselves to the substantive issues, which for the most part have not been adequately discussed elsewhere.

Finally, we cannot emphasize too strongly that the present analysis is of *a test ban as a limited measure,* on the assumption that few or no other arms-control or inspection agreements will be implemented during the relevant period. This is not because we think this assumption is especially realistic, much less desirable, but because we think that as matters

---

* This chapter has benefited substantially from the comments and suggestions of many people. Since some of these prefer to remain anonymous, we shall not identify any of them, but the writers are much indebted to all of them.

now stand a test ban must be evaluated on its own merits, some of which include the possible effects on subsequent military cooperation.

THE CENTRAL STRATEGIC ISSUE *

Possible developments in nuclear weapons may be placed into two categories: the development of improved strategic weapons and development of improved tactical nuclear weapons for use on the battlefield. (Weapons for defensive purposes need not constitute a separate category.) The military evaluation of strategic-weapon developments and defensive developments will be treated in a later section of this chapter.

As with strategic weapons, the evaluation of possible developments in tactical nuclear weapons involves a consideration of what developments are possible and of the uses to which the tactical nuclear weapons can and should be put. The question, then, as to what role limited nuclear war should play in American military strategy is crucial in evaluating the desirability of a nuclear-test ban. In fact, much of the opposition to a test ban has been based on an erroneous evaluation of limited nuclear war. Most of the opponents of the test ban have argued that the United States must develop more efficient tactical nuclear weapons for use in limited war.

For example, Edward Teller[3] in a syndicated series of newspaper columns on the test ban has argued that the United States needs a capability of fighting a limited nuclear war. "It is to the interests of the Russians that we abstain from using [tactical] nuclear weapons. In the absence of such weapons . . . [Russian] tactics will work." He then goes on to deny that it is impossible to keep a limited nuclear war from exploding into an all-out war. This idea, that limited nuclear war is to the advantage of the United States, is echoed in a speech made in the Senate on May 12, 1960, by Senator Thomas J. Dodd[4] of Connecticut, entitled "The Eight Fallacies of the Nuclear Test Ban," in which he stresses the importance of developing clean nuclear weapons for tactical purposes and argues that this is the key to American supremacy in a limited war.

Few of the supporters of the nuclear-test ban have discussed this issue.† Most serious analyses of limited nuclear war, however, have concluded that it would not be to the advantage of the United States to use nuclear weapons in a limited war in which such weapons were used by both sides. Henry A. Kissinger, formerly a leading exponent of a limited nuclear war strategy, has substantially altered his views, as his chapter in the present volume indicates. For reasons given below, the writers of this chapter consider that limited nuclear war, as opposed to conventional war, might well be to the disadvantage of the United States, as well as being so

---

* For an extended analysis of the role of nuclear weapons in limited war and a discussion of the public debate on this issue, see reference 2.

† For an excellent exception see a Senate speech by Hubert Humphrey, in the *Congressional Record,* June 4, 1959.

mutually unattractive that the United States and Russia would prefer to fight with conventional weapons. Most professional students of national security policy agree, including the following (some of whom have changed their position in recent years): Hanson Baldwin, Bernard Brodie, Arthur Hadley, Herman Kahn, William W. Kaufman, James E. King, Robert Osgood, Henry Rowen, Thomas C. Schelling, and Albert Wohlstetter, as well as P. M. S. Blackett of Great Britain.[5]

There has been, as indicated in Kissinger's present chapter, a failure on the part of the government (or anyone else) to develop a coherent, plausible strategy for limited nuclear warfare, though of course this does not prove that one could never be devised. This lack of understanding of limited nuclear war makes it much more likely that such a war would be unstable and makes an American policy based on initiating the use of tactical nuclear weapons a highly questionable one.

As both sides begin to consider in detail the problems of limited nuclear war, it is not likely to look attactive to either the Soviet Union or the United States. The primary danger of limited nuclear war is the lack of knowledge as to whether such war could in fact be kept limited. Advocates of a limited nuclear war have argued that one cannot dogmatically assert that a limited nuclear war would be highly unstable. This is certainly correct. Our knowledge in this area is such that it is impossible to make any certain statements at all. However, what evidence there is suggests that the use of nuclear weapons in a limited war is likely to make that war highly unstable, and certainly less stable than a limited war in which only conventional weapons were employed.

We know from the experience in Indonesia, Korea, and elsewhere that conventional wars can be kept limited in the nuclear age. We have no similar experience with nuclear limited war. We have the evidence of army field exercises and war games. In such exercises the introduction of tactical nuclear weapons has had a very great tendency to lead to an unlimited expansion of the war, which strongly suggests the grave difficulties of keeping a nuclear limited war within reasonable bounds. We also have "pencil-and-paper analyses." Theoretical studies of this kind by private students of military policy, including both the present writers, have led to the conclusion that the use of tactical nuclear weapons would break one of the major barriers to the escalation of limited wars. The distinction between nuclear weapons and chemical high-explosive weapons is a clear one. It is readily observable on the battlefield and is understood by both sides. It probably would be relatively easy to preserve such a limitation during a limited war. No other natural differentiation in the use of nuclear weapons has been discovered. There is no sharp discontinuity either in the size of nuclear weapons or in the targets at which they could be aimed. Furthermore, while there is a joint understanding between both sides as to what abstaining from the use of nuclear weapons in a limited war means, there is no similar joint understanding of the possible tactical uses of nuclear weapons.

Aside from the problem of finding a stopping point in the spectrum of existing nuclear weapons, the use of nuclear weapons in a limited war is likely to increase the pressures for expanding the war in several other ways. Nuclear weapons can lead to rapid military reverses which are likely to be destabilizing and which make it more difficult to exercise civilian control over the war. Furthermore, the acceptance of "sanctuaries," which was so important in keeping the Korean war limited, is not likely to survive if planes taking off from these sanctuaries drop nuclear weapons of great explosive power on their targets.

Even if a limited nuclear war could be kept stable, the destruction such a war might cause is likely to make both sides hesitant about engaging in the use of nuclear weapons. The actual destructive power of nuclear weapons seems underestimated by at least some advocates of limited nuclear war. Nobody has been able to suggest a plausible strategy for limited nuclear war that would be unlikely to involve a mass destruction of the populace and the industry of the country being defended. The use of a few thousand tactical weapons in the kiloton range (certainly conceivable in such a war) would result in the devastation of several thousand square miles and possibly in many millions of civilian casualties. Very small selective nuclear weapons would not produce such a destruction, but it is unlikely that such weapons would continue to be used exclusively. An increasing lack of intelligence concerning opposing forces would probably force a commander to use weapons of increasingly larger yield in compensation. Degeneration of command and control would probably have the same effect.

The great destructive power of nuclear weapons highlights one of the major political costs of using them. Should either the United States or the Soviet Union employ nuclear weapons to defend a particular area against enemy attack, the devastation of that area would probably be immense. If this policy were declared in advance, or if it were once applied, it would quickly become clear to the allies of either the United States or the Soviet Union what the costs were of accepting help from a major power. The American system of alliances in particular is likely to be put to grave jeopardy should the United States destroy another country in attempting to defend it. In addition, most of the neutralist leaders of the world have come out strongly against the use of nuclear weapons, and there would be great diplomatic losses for either the Soviet Union or the United States in initiating the use of such weapons.

Besides these disadvantages to both the United States and the Soviet Union, there are several that would peculiarly affect the West if nuclear weapons were used in most areas in which such a war is likely. It has often been argued that to use nuclear weapons would be to the military advantage of the United States, so often that in some quarters this view has acquired the status of dogma. It has been asserted but never proved that the use of tactical nuclear weapons would compensate for the superiority of Communist manpower. The argument is based on the idea that numbers will not be a significant factor in a limited nuclear war, but this proposition does not stand the test of analysis. The great destructive power of tactical nuclear weapons and the consequently high rate of casualties show that the ability to send in troop replacements would be of great strategic importance. In addition, even if the troops are dispersed, as some suggest, their absolute numbers in battle would still be a crucial variable in determining the outcome.

The second major argument for saying that the United States would gain from the use of tactical nuclear weapons in limited war is that somehow the use of these weapons aids the side on the defensive. Here again, no one has made clear why this should be true. The unstated assumptions behind this argument seem to be that the West would be using nuclear weapons but that the enemy would not, or else would be using them inefficiently or only from fixed positions. Since none of these seems likely, there is no reason why they should be of more value to the defense than to the offense. In addition, it seems clear that the West will by no means be exclusively on the tactical defensive in a limited war. In Korea, for example, the United Nations forces were on the tactical offensive most of the time.

The third major argument for American supremacy in a tactical nuclear war is based on what might be called the "elitist" approach to international politics: that somehow American (and Western) troops are more intelligent, more dynamic, more resourceful, and that somehow these values will be of greater importance in limited nuclear war than they would be in conventional war. This argument seems based on a naïve logic; no one has presented evidence to support this *a priori* notion of the supremacy of democratic armies. The tactics of limited nuclear war resemble, if anything, guerrilla warfare, particularly after central control is lost. Both the Russians and the Chinese have amply demonstrated their competence in this kind of warfare, which depends on the initiative and ability of individual, local leadership. Guerrilla warfare and limited nuclear war also resemble each other in their methods of gathering and using target intelligence. This suggests a major Communist advantage in many areas.

Having rejected the argument that the United States would gain in the use of nuclear weapons in a limited war, we turn to the two major asymmetrical disadvantages from the use of nuclear weapons in limited war. The first is in the area of logistics. American supply lines in virtually all conceivable limited wars are likely to be long, vulnerable, and dependent on ports, airports, and other precise, easily destroyed targets. Communist supply lines, on the other hand, are likely to be short and not so vulnerable to the use of nuclear weapons. The port of Pusan in Korea, for example, could have been put out of commission for a long time with a single nuclear weapon. On the other hand, a supply line based on individual carriers could not have been destroyed short of a major nuclear attack which would have saturated North Korea. Similar situations are likely to evolve in future wars.

The second major disadvantage to the United States in the use of nuclear weapons in a limited war is that it destroys the advantage the United States would have in a conventional war because of its vastly larger gross national product (GNP) and industrial capability. The implements of war required to dominate a given target system completely will be significantly cheaper, both in monetary terms and in terms of industrial capacity, if nuclear weapons are used. This can be graphically illustrated in terms of the concept of saturation level. If we define saturation level as the force needed to destroy completely a given target, it is clear that the amount of productivity and the cost of destroying a particular area is much less if nuclear weapons are used. Thus, the Russians and the Chinese could easily match us in destructive capability in a limited nuclear war but either would have a great deal of difficulty in doing so in a large-scale conventional war.

For these two reasons, and because the United States is likely to be hurt more than the Soviet Union by the political costs in view of its far-flung voluntary alliance system, it seems clear that it has more to lose from the introduction of nuclear weapons in a limited war than the Soviet Union does. But it should be emphasized that both sides would be likely to lose, and that it is likely to be to the advantage of both to prevent the introduction of nuclear weapons in any limited war. On the other hand the United States must maintain a capability for limited nuclear war since the other side may introduce nuclear weapons, and the possibility that the United States might want to introduce nuclear weapons under some circumstances cannot be entirely ruled out.

We turn then to the relation of this analysis to the question of a test ban. First, we may reject the desirability of having both sides develop additional and improved tactical nuclear weapons. These improvements are not likely to eliminate the disadvantages discussed above, and they may make it more likely that these weapons will be used as they become more widely available or if both sides become more dependent on them. Furthermore, in so far as the advantage is slightly in favor of the United States in the fighting of conventional limited wars, we might in this regard gain from a test ban under which the Soviets refrained from developing a greater arsenal of tactical nuclear weapons. Even if the Soviets cheat, they are most unlikely to gain a major advantage. In any case, they would probably be inhibited from using nuclear weapons, and the present American arsenal is sufficient to fight a limited war up to (and beyond) any scale which one could expect would remain limited.*

The test ban is also likely to have positive effects which would inhibit the use of nuclear weapons in a limited war. For one thing, it would affect the expectations of both the United States and the Soviet Union. It would establish clearly that both consider nuclear weapons to be somehow differ-

---

* This point is elaborated below.

ent from high-explosive weapons. It would involve a joint implicit recognition that such weapons are not "conventional" and would reinforce the expectation that they would not be used in a limited war. This would increase the value of the nuclear-nonnuclear line as an important limit in a limited war. Furthermore, in so far as both sides want to keep the ban, they would likely refrain from the use of nuclear weapons, because even if a test ban could survive any limited war (which is not at all clear), it almost certainly cannot survive one which involved the use of tactical nuclear weapons.

A test-ban treaty would also be likely to have some desirable effect on American military planning. At the present time, with an ambiguous civilian policy, the military establishment has not been entirely clear as to whether or not it will be given permission to introduce the use of nuclear weapons in a limited war. The United States might find itself in a situation in which, because of its military planning, it must either intervene with nuclear weapons, or not intervene at all. In part, this stems from the fact that many in our military establishment simply do not believe that they would be denied nuclear weapons in a limited war if they believed them to be necessary. The signing of a test-ban treaty, thus establishing the psychological expectations discussed above, might have a significant effect on military planners enhancing the expectation that they might not be given permission to introduce nuclear weapons in any limited war. Probably this would be the case, even without a test ban, but a test-ban treaty would emphasize the point and perhaps stimulate the development of capabilities for conventional war.

Finally, the test ban might pave the way to additional arms-control agreements in the nuclear field that might further inhibit the use of nuclear weapons in limited war. For example, agreements not to introduce first use of nuclear weapons might be attainable. It may be that the signing of a test-ban treaty is almost a prerequisite for arms control in this area, since if it were honored it would make negotiations easier and more likely.

MAJOR POLITICAL CONSIDERATIONS

Although the suspension of nuclear testing seems on the surface to be primarily a military issue, political motives have in fact been important both for those supporting the ban and for those opposing it. In assessing any arms-control proposal, it is necessary to consider both the military-strategic implications and the international-political implications. It is dangerous to evaluate any proposal on the basis of either military considerations alone or political factors alone. Most discussions of the test ban have concentrated on either the first or the second. A review of the central strategic issue—that of the tactical uses of nuclear weapons—suggests that a test ban would be to the advantage of the United States as well as to that of the Soviet Union. We shall now consider the major political arguments for and against the proposal for a test ban.

While opponents of the test ban have talked primarily of the military-strategic implications, its proponents on the whole have concentrated on the political value of American acceptance of the ban. Several years ago much of the emphasis fell on the need to end the pollution of the atmosphere. Even without a formal test-ban agreement, it does not now seem likely that the United States by itself will resume tests in the atmosphere, and therefore this is no longer an immediate policy issue.*

Nth Country Considerations. The major political costs and gains of the test ban involve its effect on countries other than the United States and the Soviet Union and in particular the so-called "Nth" country problem. Many people have suggested that the spread of nuclear weapons to third, fourth, and Nth countries could lead to a great deterioration of the international scene; they therefore urge that every means be sought to halt the spread of nuclear weapons and have argued that the ban would help to do so. The test ban of itself could not solve the problem. Nevertheless, the effect it might have on the spread of nuclear weapons is also clear. For one thing, both the United States and the Soviet Union seem determined to use any test-ban agreement to enable them to withstand pressure from their allies for aid in testing nuclear weapons. The first clause of the draft treaty agreed to at Geneva in 1960 commits the parties to refrain from helping other countries to test weapons.

In addition, other states will be asked to join the treaty and to agree to abide by the clause barring the testing of nuclear weapons. Without testing, or without obtaining much information presently classified, no fifth or "Nth" country could independently construct nuclear weapons of high military efficiency and reliability. They could perhaps produce some relatively primitive weapons, but in the absence of testing (and therefore the absence of any possibility of conclusively demonstrating the existence of the weapons), the motive for producing them would undoubtedly be much reduced. Therefore, the ban as now envisaged, if generally subscribed to, might serve as an effective block to the spread of independent capabilities for producing and developing nuclear weapons.

Moreover, the test ban might reduce the desire of an Nth country for nuclear weapons in several ways. As suggested above, the test ban would tend to reinforce the expectation that the major powers might not use nuclear weapons. If the powers that had nuclear weapons were not planning to use them in limited wars, the arguments within an Nth country for obtaining such weapons would be greatly reduced. The idea that nuclear weapons are somehow different, immoral, and in many ways undesirable would be strengthened. The major powers would be in a much better position to withstand pressures from their allies for nuclear weapons, while neutralist powers might be sufficiently less willing to pay the price of obtaining them.

While in one sense the Nth country problem is the single problem of

* It is of course possible that resumption of underground testing by the United States would catalyze the resumption of atmospheric testing by the Soviet Union.

preventing the spread of nuclear weapons beyond the countries which now have them, in fact it is three separate problems: the problem of America's NATO allies' being given nuclear weapons or developing them themselves, the special problem of China, and the problem of neutralist nations acquiring nuclear weapons. In general, the points just made apply to a greater or lesser degree to the three Nth country problems, but it is necessary to distinguish the costs and gains in relation to the three groups.

A nuclear-test-ban treaty would have important short- and long-range effects on the North Atlantic alliance which are difficult to gauge or accurately predict. The French undoubtedly look upon the test ban as a device used to deny them nuclear weapons and are likely to be extremely unhappy about a ban, whether or not they are successfully pressured into signing a treaty. In so far as the nuclear-test ban reduced the likelihood of the use of nuclear weapons in a limited war, it would have an important effect on the present effectiveness of the NATO deterrent forces. While it is true that Europe could more effectively be defended without the use of nuclear weapons, the removal of the nuclear threat might tend to increase the likelihood of limited war in Europe, because such a war could be fought with a greatly reduced danger of escalation. While we would argue that this is to the advantage of the European members of NATO, as well as of the United States, it is not at all clear that the reaction of the NATO powers will in fact be in this direction. In any case until the European members of NATO adjust to a change to a conventional strategy for Europe, there are likely to be serious strains within the NATO alliance.

For the long run, America's NATO allies, particularly Britain, France, and Germany, are in effect asked by a test-ban treaty to accept a permanently inferior military position vis-à-vis the United States as well as the Soviet Union. While this may be of value to all members of NATO and in some sense is inevitable, it will have important repercussions and effects on the long-run cohesion and stability of the alliance which are difficult to assess.

The possible costs and great uncertainties in relation to the effect of the test ban on the NATO alliance are real and must be considered. Nevertheless, it is our belief that on the whole the test ban will be of value to NATO. Our allies will share with us, although perhaps not equally, the general gains from a test ban discussed in this chapter. In addition, it is our belief that if the test ban contributes even slightly to a shift toward the defense of Western Europe by conventional means, it will have made a substantial contribution to Western military policy.

The problem of China is a particularly difficult one to evaluate in terms of the test-ban treaty. It is, of course, by no means clear that the Chinese would accede to a treaty that committed them to abstain from testing nuclear weapons and to allow at least some inspection personnel into China. If the Chinese did join, it is virtually certain that they would demand at least some political concessions from the Western powers in return.

Whether the West should accept these demands depends very much on their nature and should not be judged in advance. It should be noted that most of the gains we see from a test-ban treaty would be enhanced by Chinese participation but they do not all depend on it. In addition, some people have seen a test ban as one means of opening the way toward Soviet-American cooperation in dealing with the Chinese problem. The test ban might well serve as a lever which the Russians could use to resist Chinese pressures to gain nuclear weapons, although we have no way of knowing whether they would use it in this way. We do not mean to overestimate the possibility of Soviet-American cooperation. The Soviets may well see the treaty as opening the way to Soviet-American cooperation in dealing with the problem of Western Germany.*

The gains from the West's accepting the test ban are clearest in relation to the neutralist Nth countries. The general pressures which the test ban would generate against the spread of nuclear weapons are most likely to be effective in these cases and, in addition, the neutral nations are strongly committed to support the test ban.

The General Assembly of the United Nations has on several occasions gone on record enthusiastically in favor of the suspension of all nuclear tests. To some people in the United States, the test ban is a gauge of American sensitivity to the opinions of the neutralist blocs. The cold war for the next decade will involve a struggle for the allegiance of the present neutral and uncommitted nations. These states, for reasons not clearly defined, have been enthusiastically in favor of a test ban; to some extent the United States was forced into the initial negotiations by this pressure, and by the willingness of the Soviet Union to champion the cause of nuclear disarmament. Should the test-ban negotiations break down, and should the West be blamed for this rupture, there might well be very serious effects on American standing in the underdeveloped areas. This is a reason advanced by many for accepting a test ban, even if the ban should be somewhat dubious on strategic grounds, and a reason why some (but not the present writers) have suggested that we should not even scrutinize very carefully the military implications. This pressure has also existed in some of the opposition parties in the allied countries, particularly in the Labour party in Great Britain.

Without denying the importance of neutralist opinion, the writers believe that the United States would be establishing a dangerous precedent if it yielded to this opinion on the test ban without a careful analysis of the other political and strategic considerations involved. If the strategic analysis suggested that there would be great military costs (and it does not), then, while the United States might gain some political propaganda from seeming to yield to neutralist opinion, it would also incur a cost, particularly within the American military establishment, if it seemed to be giving up an ap-

* The pessimism with which one must approach the problem of China in relation to arms control is detailed in the later chapter by Barnett.

preciable amount of American security in an attempt to win the propaganda battle with the Soviet Union. Despite the importance of international public opinion, the United States should not place itself in the position of seeming to allow this opinion to completely dictate its military policy.

We do not mean to overstate the possible effects of a test ban on the spread of nuclear weapons. Iklé [6] has made the following points: (1) The Nth countries may not accede to the treaty; (2) They may develop at least some weapons without testing; (3) Small tests are not detectable; and (4) No sanctions against violators are provided in the draft treaty. Iklé then adds: "In spite of all of these limitations, however, a test ban might have some inhibiting effect on Nth country capabilities by slowing down international competition so that even aggressive and irresponsible countries might move more slowly. We can hope for such an inhibiting effect, but we can't count on it." This is correct. However, we can be sure that the resumption of testing by the United States and the Soviet Union would increase the pressures on Nth countries to develop nuclear capabilities.

A good way to summarize the relation of the test ban to the Nth country problem is to observe that the test ban is likely to be a necessary but not a sufficient condition to inhibit the spread of independent nuclear-weapon capabilities. Critics of the ban often point to the fact that it may well not be sufficient. But it is equally important to stress that the ban *is* likely to be *necessary*.

An ambitious program aimed at discouraging the diffusion of nuclear-weapon capabilities might include the following political and arms-control objectives, in addition to the nuclear test ban: (1) the cessation of production of nuclear-weapon materials; (2) renunciation of all first use of nuclear weapons; (3) conducting all nuclear explosions for peaceful applications under international auspices, if at all; (4) destruction (or transfer to peaceful uses) of some stocks of nuclear materials; (5) prohibition of the deployment of tactical nuclear weapons outside the home territories of the major powers; (6) implementation of the controls and safeguards of the International Atomic Energy Agency on nuclear reactors; and (7) persuasion of Great Britain and France to leave the "nuclear club." Item (7) would probably be easy to accomplish if the preceding items were implemented (de Gaulle has said in the past that France would accede to the test ban if (1) is accomplished), and the first six items appear potentially feasible under sufficient safeguards. The implementation of this program would probably be quite effective on all Nth countries except China. Whether it would provide sufficient leverage (via the Soviets or otherwise) on the Chinese is doubtful. A detailed discussion of this program is not within the scope of this chapter.

Other Political Considerations. In addition to its effect on the Nth country problem, many have seen the test ban as a first step toward increased arms control and also toward increased political cooperation between the United States and the Soviet Union, with a consequent lessening of international tensions. This view has gained weight as the negotiations have proceeded in Geneva and as the number of issues have been reduced. It can now be argued that, should these negotiations fail, the possibility for any other formal and explicit arms control would be set back for a considerable time. On the other hand, should an agreement emerge, it would clearly establish the possibility of other important agreements between the United States and the Soviet Union, despite the hostile climate now existing. If the agreement proves satisfactory to both sides, it would possibly contribute to a slackening of tensions and would perhaps clear the way to cooperation in other areas.

Furthermore, the test-ban proposal, as envisaged, would serve at least partially to open up the Soviet Union. It would establish the principle of inspection, and for the first time there would be progress in getting the Soviet Union to permit Western inspectors within its territory. This would mean an advance toward the principle of "openness." Should this inspection work to the satisfaction of the Soviet government, it might reduce the latter's suspicion of Western proposals for inspection and make possible a far more substantial arms-control program with the necessary inspection. To many people this is the major benefit of the nuclear-test ban, although it should be clear that openness is not an unmixed blessing. Some claim that, whatever the risks involved, they are justifiable, because any agreement may open the way to a comprehensive arms-control agreement between the United States and the Soviet Union.

Not many people have viewed all the precedents that would be set by the test ban with satisfaction. The critical questions of the test ban, including the number of on-site inspections,* the composition of the inspectorate, and the composition and functioning of the control body, have yet to be determined. Should the United States agree to a treaty that provided only a very low probability of detecting nuclear tests, and should it agree indefinitely to a moratorium on certain tests without any inspection, then, in view of its past position on inspection, it might establish dangerous precedents for the future of arms control. It might then be more difficult for the United States to insist on adequate inspection safeguards when negotiating future arms-control agreements. In addition, it might provide the Soviet Union with the technique of pressuring the West into disadvantageous positions. The Soviet Union might force the United States to make dangerous compromises on really crucial issues, because it would not want to give up what would seem to be virtually a treaty in hand.

Finally, some of the first steps discussed above have a dangerous implication. Of itself, the test ban would not necessarily reduce the danger of Soviet strategic or tactical attack, but it might contribute to a feeling in the West that the danger of attack had been reduced and that consequently there was less need for military preparedness. The results might be disastrous if

* While the present writers do not view this particular problem as critical, the "official" view is otherwise at the time of writing.

a test-ban agreement caused the West to make less adequate military preparations.

Arms control and armament, therefore, are clearly two aspects of the same policy. It should not be assumed because some arms control seems to be working and an agreement has been signed that the value of armament has been lessened. If arms control is not to prove disastrous, it must be clear to our allies that a test ban signifies only that both sides have found it advantageous to sign the treaty—not that both had renounced all use of military force. Unless we are prepared to maintain adequate military forces—admitting at once that what is "adequate" may depend on other arms-control agreements—the test ban would loom as very dangerous rather than as at least marginally valuable.

It is by no means easy to balance the political gains and costs. Nevertheless, it would seem that not only is the test ban of strategic value to the United States but also that it would be of political value as well, *if* it does not lead to a great reduction in the American defense effort or prevent a possible increase in this effort.

POSSIBLE FURTHER WEAPON DEVELOPMENTS

Technical Preliminaries. In this section we shall discuss the nature of possible weapon developments that might be achieved with the aid of further testing, and the potential military significance of each development in three cases: first, both sides abstain from the development in question; second, the United States abstains but the Soviet Union does not (i.e., the case of Soviet cheating); third, neither side abstains from the development.* Although the belief is widely held that the United States nuclear technology is appreciably ahead of the Soviets, we do not have the relevant data to evaluate this contention. Therefore our discussion assumes essential parity and is not based on the argument that the United States would gain from a test ban because of its present lead over the Soviet Union.

There is at least a theoretical possibility of achieving some weapon developments, perhaps substantial ones, without further testing. These might be achieved on the basis of laboratory studies and experiments. For the most part, our discussion does not take this possibility into account; not because we think such developments unlikely—we have no basis for a judgment on this question—but because we believe that the United States' weapon systems should not in any event become wholly dependent on weapons that are quite far from tested designs, however much confidence the weapon designers may have in such developments. There is an obvious trade-off between improved weapon efficiency on the one hand, and con-

---

* Many potential arms-control measures also require evaluation for the possible case in which a violator openly breaks an agreement and suddenly resumes a prohibited activity. For reasons that should become apparent, the writers do not believe this case requires explicit attention for a test ban.

fidence in the reliability of the weapons on the other. It is not possible for us to evaluate this trade-off in detail, but our bias is distinctly a conservative one. On the other hand, we would argue strongly for such laboratory studies and experiments as may be feasible, perhaps extending to limited production of advanced but untested weapons.

In the last analysis, the whole argument of ceasing or resuming testing depends primarily on the military weapon problem. It is precisely this area that has not been fully illuminated in the national debate thus far. Many of those who advocate the resumption of nuclear testing promise revolutionary types of weapons, but the military-security value of these weapons is not usually evaluated. It is often implied that there is a third level or domain of weaponry, beyond the thermonuclear or "hydrogen" bomb, to which we can progress by further testing and where, presumably, we will rest more securely than at the present. While the technology of nuclear weapons is still somewhat obscure, and while we make no use of classified data, the basic elements of the nuclear weapon problem can be discussed freely without resorting to classified data.

We shall first review the basic facts of bomb technology.* The basic principle on which current nuclear weapons depend is that of *fission*, in which atoms of a suitable material split up into two or more smaller atoms, releasing energy in the process. The principal fissionable materials suitable for use in a bomb are plutonium (Pu-239) and a special isotope of uranium (U-235). In order for the fissionable material to detonate as a bomb, a certain minimum amount of the material, called the critical mass, is required. It is likely that the exact amount required depends on the material and the method of detonation, but it is generally thought [7] to be in the region of 5 kilograms (11 pounds). If all the fissionable material actually underwent fission in the reaction, the energy released would be equivalent to 9 kilotons of TNT per pound of material. Because the bomb starts blowing up before all of the material undergoes fission, however, this theoretical limit cannot be achieved. For example, if the Nagasaki bomb had 20 pounds of fissionable material, as is generally believed, the theoretical upper limit of energy yield would have been 180 kilotons, but it is known that the actual energy yield of the Nagasaki bomb was about 18 kilotons. Therefore, only about 10 per cent of the fissionable material actually was fissioned. (The bomb itself, which included a detonation mechanism, safety devices, and a casing, weighed 10,000 pounds, not 20 pounds.[8])

The reaction on which thermonuclear weapons are based is that of *fusion*, in which two atoms join together to form a new atom and release energy in the process. For example, fusing two atoms of heavy hydrogen yields energy at the rate of 26 kilotons per pound of material (KT/lb). Many other fusion reactions are possible. It is not generally known just what reactions are employed in actual thermonuclear weapons, but the various

* A more detailed discussion is given in a report by Davidon, Kalkstein, and Hohenemser,[7] on which the following is based.

theoretical possibilities (such as fusion involving tritium, lithium, and deuterium) are known to have theoretical upper-limit energy yields of about 25 to 30 KT/lb.*

Present-day thermonuclear bombs require a fission bomb to initiate the fusion reaction. Additional fission energy may be obtained by using the fusion reaction to induce the fission of natural uranium metal, which is much less expensive than U-235. The bulk of the radioactive fallout produced by a thermonuclear bomb is due to the fission yield, not to the fusion reaction. In current weapons, the fission yield may range from 5 per cent to 70 per cent or more of the total yield. Weapons having a low fission yield are sometimes termed "clean" bombs, since they produce relatively little radioactive fallout.

Ratios of Yield to Weight. The values given above for energy yield per unit weight relate only to the theoretical upper limit of energy yield and the weight of the material entering the nuclear reaction. In an actual military bomb, not all of the fissionable or fusionable material can react. In addition, a complete bomb or warhead includes a chemical high explosive, a detonation mechanism, safety devices, and a casing. Therefore, the actual yield per unit of weight of the complete bomb is considerably less than the values given above. Since the yield and weight of the total device are what count for military purposes, the yield/weight ratios of weapons are very important in describing their military effectiveness.

Such yield/weight ratios for several specific weapons have been estimated by Ralph Lapp [9] using Congressional testimony and other published sources of information. We are indebted to Lapp for the following estimates: the warhead weight for POLARIS and Minuteman (they use the same warhead) is about 600 pounds and has a yield of about 600 kilotons for a yield/weight ratio of 1 KT/lb. The Atlas ICBM has a warhead yield of about 4.5 or 5 megatons and has a yield/weight ratio of 1.5 KT/lb at present. Lapp estimates a current yield/weight ratio of 2 KT/lb for a more massive device of two-thirds fission yield, which would have more efficiency. (This would imply a total yield of 24 megatons for a 6-ton bomb. Since the B-52 has twice this bomb-carrying capacity,[10] the total B-52 bomb yield would be 48 megatons.)

These estimates agree generally with an independent estimate that can be deduced from a recent article by Hans Bethe: "If we want to increase the efficiency of our nuclear weapons by another factor of about 10 . . . from the presently achievable, we come to a point where the entire material in the weapon must undergo a nuclear reaction." [11] Since the theoretical fusion yields are in the region of 25 to 30 KT/lb, this indicates that present weapons must be about 3 KT/lb. Bethe further stated: "Since there must be assembly mechanism, triggers, bomb cases, and the like, this [increase

---

* Other reactions are, in some sense, possible in principle. As an extreme example, complete conversion of mass to energy according to the Einstein law $E = mc^2$ would yield 9 MT/lb. But such reactions are not thought to be feasible in weapons.

of efficiency by another factor of 10] is clearly impossible." In addition to the detonation mechanism and other nonreacting components, the fact that a bomb begins to explode before all the nuclear material has undergone reaction would further limit achievable yields. These data therefore indicate that current yield/weight ratios of large strategic weapons are in the region of 1 to 3 KT/lb, depending on weight, and that further testing and development might improve these ratios by a factor of 5.

It is important to understand that the possible improvement in efficiency is something like a factor of 5, not a factor of 500 or 5,000. For comparison, the efficiency of current bombs has been improved by about a factor of 1,000 over the Hiroshima and Nagasaki bombs, and by a factor of two or three million over chemical explosives. Quantitative considerations of this type are vital in evaluating the possible strategic significance of the further development of high-yield weapons.

If both we and the Soviet Union abstain from further improvements in efficiency, the situation will remain essentially as it is. If neither we nor the Soviets abstain from further testing, we both may increase the total deliverable yield by something like a factor of 5 (assuming that the delivery vehicles and systems remain fixed), or we may effect certain savings in the cost of delivery vehicles and systems (assuming that the total deliverable yield is held fixed), or there may be any combination of these two.* However, if we both pursue such developments, this will, broadly speaking, have no net effect on the relative military capabilities of the United States and the Soviet Union, though it might have some effect on the *stability* of the strategic balance. There are also some possible asymmetries. For example, if the Soviet Union wished to implement a counterforce doctrine and target their weapons against our hardened bases, while we wanted to implement a retaliatory doctrine with our weapons against Soviet population centers, then the symmetrical development of increased warhead yields could appear more valuable to the Soviets than to ourselves, since the increased yield would be of more significance for the counterforce posture. From the point of view of a United States analyst of strategy, the most important question is: How serious would it be if the Soviet Union achieved such improvements but we did not?

The writers believe that it would be serious enough to warrant some concern, but that this possibility is not an overriding consideration. The degree to which such potential clandestine developments could appear dangerous depends appreciably on the type of strategic posture the United States wishes to maintain. If we wish to maintain a clear-cut margin of strategic nuclear superiority, the potential costs of one-sided Soviet developments would be much greater than if we are willing to maintain a posture of approximate equality of strategic forces. As was indicated in chapter 1,

---

* The question of small mobile missiles (for invulnerability), or of defense missiles, which is often raised in this connection, is simply a special case of these two, and will be separately discussed below.

there has not been an explicit decision of national policy on this point at the time of writing, so far as we are aware. However, we believe—at least tentatively—that the posture of approximate equality is, on balance, to be preferred, and the tone of the discussion that follows is governed by this preference. A strong preference for a position of decisive superiority *could* make the possibility of one-sided Soviet improvements appear to be an over-riding consideration.

It is necessary to rely to some extent on the tone of the discussion to convey our sense of the magnitude of the risk, because a more complete (and possibly more objective) analysis would require detailed consideration of several specific hypothetical weapon systems, and space does not permit this. A more thorough discussion would also disclose cases in which "yes or no" decisions about entire systems might hinge on the possibility of achieving developments of the type under consideration.*

Let us first assume that the Soviet Union used this increase in efficiency to increase their total deliverable yield by a factor of 5, assuming that the number and type of delivery vehicles remain fixed. Now, the area of blast damage of a warhead is proportional to the two-thirds power of the yield, and $5^{2/3}$ is approximately 3. Therefore, this development would be roughly equivalent to multiplying their missile and bomber forces by about a factor of 3.† As pointed out in the chapter above by Jerome B. Wiesner, we can (and probably will) build strategic-force systems that are effectively invulnerable (in the sense discussed by Wiesner) against forces that might be larger by a factor of 10 or more. Therefore, while we should not willingly give the Soviets a factor of 3 in strategic forces unless we achieved something of comparable advantage ourselves, it is at least possible to contemplate such clandestine Soviet developments with some equanimity, and it is also possible to think that there may be gains that would more than offset this possible risk. (As noted above, this possibility depends to some extent on strategic doctrine, and depends even more on the general levels of hostile forces and capabilities.)

The same conclusion follows in the event that the clandestine improvements in weapon efficiency were applied to reducing the cost of delivery vehicles and systems, while maintaining the total deliverable yield fixed. If other factors such as range and guidance are constant, the cost of a missile is roughly proportional to its payload. This would not mean, however, that the Soviets could reduce the cost of their total strategic system by a factor of 5, since the system involves much more than the missiles themselves. Other components include command, control, and communication systems; test facilities; launching-pad facilities (including submarines);

* Experts are likely to find the ensuing discussion too abstract; the writers apologize for this, but we see no short way of solving this problem.

† This assumes that the target system was not already saturated by the old forces. Against a target that can be destroyed with certainty by a 2 MT weapon of available accuracy, there is no point in going to 10 MT. Allowing an equivalent factor of 3 in total forces is therefore *very* generous.

and ground crews. All things considered, it does not seem likely that reducing warhead weight by a factor of 5 would reduce the cost of the system by more than a factor of 2.* The same considerations suggest that, if the Soviets wished to triple the effectiveness of their strategic forces, they could do it just as well by doubling their investment in the system as by improving warhead efficiency by a factor of 5, and this might possibly be cheaper than an extended program of clandestine tests conducted in outer space.

In this general problem one particular case is of sufficient importance to warrant discussing it as a specific example. It is often held that we need to develop small, mobile missiles as part of an invulnerable deterrent force, and it is sometimes held that a test ban would inhibit the development of lightweight warheads needed for such missiles and would therefore be destabilizing. Now, if it is argued that the POLARIS-Minuteman warhead (600 pounds) is too heavy for this purpose, and if a warhead of 200 pounds is desired, an extrapolation of the estimates given above suggests that current technology (without further testing) would enable the fabrication of 200-pound warheads with a yield of roughly 50 to 100 kilotons. The total deliverable yield could then be raised to virtually any value desired simply by multiplying the number of missiles. This is just a special case of the general principle discussed above.

In contradistinction to the argument that a test ban would be destabilizing because it would prevent the development of mobile missiles, it is sometimes held that the increased yield achievable by further testing would contribute to the counterforce capability of strategic weapons, which would be *destabilizing*. It is difficult, if not impossible, to see whether a test ban would, on balance, enhance or degrade the stability (in the usual narrow military sense) of strategic nuclear deterrence.

The foregoing discussion represents, we believe, a reasonable outlook on the situation to be expected. It is not meant to suggest that there are not special cases in which, for example, the advantage in cost might be more or less than a factor of 2—there are. But a special case that could reasonably be of decisive significance does not seem possible. We might be wrong about this. Other considerations discussed below should be understood as qualified in this same sense.

Pure Fusion Weapons. One development that might be obtained with the aid of further experimentation would be pure fusion weapons, that is, thermonuclear weapons that did not require a conventional fission bomb as a trigger and would require little or no fissionable material. The energy yield from such weapons would result entirely (or almost entirely) from nuclear-fusion reactions. These reactions are generally thought to require

---

* Of course, this depends on what one counts as part of the "system." If the "system" is taken to be the entire military establishment, a factor of 2 is far too large. A representative "system" might include a fleet of POLARIS submarines with their missiles, bases, and tenders, but would not include basic training centers, research and development centers, etc., in which case the factor of 2 would be vaguely right.

ignition temperatures achievable only with fission reactions, but some other means of ignition (detonation) might be found. The question of whether or not this development is likely to be achieved with further research and testing is quite controversial among weapon scientists, and the present writers have no basis for an independent judgment. However, it is possible to discuss a number of consequences that would follow if this development were achieved.

One of the original motives for pursuing the development of pure-fusion weapons was that such weapons would produce little or no radioactive fallout. In general, of course, this would make such weapons less hazardous to neutrals, allies, and ourselves. A less immediate consideration, on the other hand, is that the development of clean weapons might itself reduce the barriers to their use and thereby make it more likely. But the major issues hinge on more specific cases.

One motive for the development of "clean" weapons may be their use as defensive weapons, especially in the realm of air defense. It is obviously to our interest to minimize the fallout on our own territory or on that of our allies. Although it is rather difficult to assess the urgency of this motive, it does not appear to be overwhelming, since the damage produced by fallout from purely defensive weapons seems likely to be relatively small in absolute terms, and certain to be small in comparison to the damage produced by weapons used by the other side.*

The preceding paragraph should be considered in the light of the fact that thermonuclear devices now exist in which the fission yield is only 5 per cent of the total yield. However, such low-fallout weapons are probably not the most efficient as measured by yield/weight ratios.

Another reason sometimes advanced for the development of pure-fusion weapons is that they might be much cheaper than present nuclear weapons, for the fissionable material used in the latter is extremely expensive. For example, the cost of a pure-fission weapon of a few kilotons yield is in the region of a half million dollars, while a multimegaton thermonuclear weapon does not cost very much more. This indicates that the bulk of the cost of present thermonuclear weapons is probably associated with the fission trigger.

If we could produce pure-fusion weapons that required only relatively common materials such as lithium and did not require enormous production facilities, the cost of the large-scale production of nuclear weapons might be greatly reduced. It might then be possible to produce high-yield or low-yield weapons for, say, a few thousand dollars each (apart from the costs of development).

In the present state of the world, such a development would be inimical to the security of the United States, because it would permit any nation with even a modest industrial base to go a long way toward equalizing the

---

* This is especially true of weapons exploded at high altitudes (as for defense against aircraft or missiles), which produce negligible local fallout.

military power of the United States. The same consideration must appear just as forcefully to the Soviet Union. From the point of view of international security, we are already disturbed at the prospect of additional nations acquiring a few primitive fission bombs; we should be much more disturbed at the prospect of many nations acquiring a virtually unlimited stockpile of weapons of arbitrary yield. Since the development of simple and cheap fusion weapons has been pursued for several years without any visible sign of success, there is at least some reason to hope that, even if testing is resumed, such weapons will never be developed. If they ever are developed, it is virtually certain to prove impossible to keep the technology involved sufficiently secret.

From the point of view of the United States, the notion that the most wealthy nation on earth should encourage the development of weapon systems that provide "more bang for the buck" is the height of absurdity. Only a certain amount of "bang" is required to dominate or destroy any given military objective. Therefore, the development of systems providing "more bang for the buck" means that nations with many fewer "bucks" can equalize our military power with respect to the target systems of the type involved. We have already seen this phenomenon with respect to present-day nuclear weapons; the Soviet Union, which has a comparable population and a considerably inferior industrial base, has virtually equalized the military power of the United States with respect to certain types of nuclear conflicts. The development of cheap and simple fusion weapons would enable many nations to move in this direction.

It may not be entirely up to us to decide whether or not such weapons shall be developed. Although the Soviet interest in abstaining from this development would appear to be at least as large as our own, it is important to ask: How seriously (if at all) would the military position of the United States relative to the Soviet Union be degraded, if the Soviets achieved this development (by clandestine testing or otherwise) but if we did not? The answer, while complicated, appears to be that the threat would be manageable.

The first problem is whether our present stockpile of weapons is sufficient for any possible conflict, or whether we ourselves should need a greatly increased supply of weapons to offset the possibility of a large-scale Soviet production of cheap fusion weapons *per se*. A recently reported estimate [12] placed the current United States production of U-235 at about 70,000 kilograms (150,000 pounds) per year. It was not stated how long production rates have been at this level, but the current rate suggests that estimates of 600,000 to 1,000,000 pounds for the total production through the end of 1960 of U-235 would be a reasonable range. If we use the million-pound figure, and assume that this can be detonated with current techniques at 20 per cent efficiency (mass fissioned to mass fissionable), or about 2 KT/lb, this stockpile would imply a total available *fission* yield from U-235 of 2,000,000 kilotons, or 2,000 megatons. We do not know how this is fabricated into stockpiled weapons, but we can look at some possibilities. To begin with, if this were all fabricated into large thermonuclear weapons of 5 per cent fission yield, this would imply a total yield capability of 40,000 megatons. If we assume that 5 per cent represents the yield of the fission trigger and that additional yield can be obtained by using the fusion reaction to fission natural uranium metal (i.e., U-238, as opposed to U-235), this could imply a total weapon stockpile of about 80,000 megatons with a 50 per cent fission yield; for example, 10,000 bombs of 8 megatons each. These would be sufficient, if delivered, to obliterate the Soviet Union and China together. If all of the U-235 stockpile were fabricated into tactical fission weapons, each using 20 pounds, it would provide 50,000 tactical weapons of 40 kilotons (or less) each. What is more likely than any one of these possibilities is some mixture of them, for example, a total of 25,000 tactical weapons and a collection of large strategic weapons having a total yield of perhaps 30,000 to 40,000 megatons.

It is easy to show that a total of 2,000 tactical weapons of a few kilotons' yield is certainly sufficient to destroy completely a very large field army of 25 line divisions, even if we assume any practical degree of dispersion of the forces. In practice, a much smaller number of bombs would probably suffice. Therefore, even if we allow several thousand weapons for air defense or antisubmarine purposes, and a stockpile of strategic weapons of obliterating proportions, it is quite clear that we shall not have an urgent need of multiplying our possible weapon stockpiles by anything like a factor of 5 or 10. This fact is virtually independent of Soviet weapon stockpiles *per se*. In other words, even if the Soviets did develop cheap fusion weapons while we did not, they would not gain an overwhelming military advantage from this fact alone.

The problem becomes more complicated if it is assumed that the Soviets also might develop new delivery systems and tactics to accompany the cheap fusion weapons, and then deployed the resulting weapon systems in a large-scale manner. Possibilities of this kind include, for example, novel types of air defense systems, capabilities for antisubmarine warfare, and a new spectrum of infantry weapons and tactics. Large-scale Soviet achievements of this type, if unmatched by corresponding developments in the United States, could be genuinely hazardous. So long as the Soviet developments remained clandestine, they would not of themselves provide the Soviets with additional political influence or bargaining power. However, they might well tempt the Soviets to aggressive or even reckless courses of action. And if deterrence failed, in consequence of Soviet aggressiveness, the United States might then be at a considerable disadvantage in the conduct of the resulting war.

This problem should not be minimized. On the other hand, it should be emphasized that Soviet achievements on the scale necessary for a decisive effect are most unlikely to remain completely invisible. In order to utilize cheap fusion weapons in a significant way, the production and deployment of tens or hundreds of thousands of weapons and weapon systems would be required, as would the training of tens or hundreds of thousands of troops. Out of many thousands of possibilities, a single informed defector is not at all unlikely. Even without an overt defection, activity on the required scale should be readily detectable by the Central Intelligence Agency, especially if the Agency is actively "looking" for such activity. In view of this fact, plus certain other considerations to be summarized in the next paragraph, the possibility of clandestine development by the Soviets of cheap fusion weapons does not presently seem to be an unacceptable risk.

In outline, the major considerations bearing on this problem appear to us as follows: (1) The possible development of cheap fusion weapons is an uncertain matter; (2) If achieved, the mere multiplication of weapon stocks would not itself be particularly hazardous; (3) The development could be hazardous if accompanied by the development and large-scale deployment of new weapon systems and tactics; (4) However, the accomplishment of (3) would constitute a major activity extending over several years and involving many thousands of people; (5) It is probable that such activity would be detected in sufficient time to take whatever remedial measures would have been possible in the absence of a test ban. In connection with this last point, we believe it important for the United States to maintain a strong laboratory research and development program on cheap fusion weapons, together with paper studies and "war games" on the possible utilization of such weapons, as a means of keeping abreast of the possibilities. This program might even extend to the prototype production of such (untested) weapons if laboratory studies and designs should eventually appear workable (or if such "success" has happened already).

Refined Tactical Weapons. So far as acceptance by the United States is concerned, it appears to us that the most delicate issues involved in the test-ban controversy are likely to be those surrounding the further development of tactical nuclear weapons. This is partly because the detection of clandestine tests of low-yield tactical weapons is most uncertain, and partly because of the widespread misunderstanding, and some degree of genuine uncertainty, as to what limited nuclear war is. There is a nearly complete coincidence between people who favor a limited nuclear war strategy for the United States and people who are opposed to a complete test ban without "adequate" inspection.

The extent to which further improvements in tactical weapons are possible is a matter of some controversy among weapon scientists. Some hold that we already have almost everything that might be desired for tactical weapons, as to size, weights, yield, etc. Others hold that this is not the case and that further developments are likely to prove very important. This apparent division of opinion actually rests on the issue of a limited nuclear war, for the purely technical facts involved seem less in dispute. It seems likely that further improvements in yield/weight ratios of tactical weapons are possible, perhaps something like the factor of 5 discussed above. Additional flexibility in the physical shape of tactical weapons would also be a likely development, as would the development of weapons of very low yield (e.g., 1 ton). The possible development of pure fusion weapons for tactical purposes, while controversial, is at least conceivable. Finally, a special type of tactical weapon, called a neutron bomb, might be developed. According to Senator Dodd, in a Senate speech of May 12, 1960, a neutron bomb "can theoretically be produced by tailoring the energy of a fusion explosion so that, instead of heat and blast, its primary product is a burst of neutrons. Such a burst would do negligible physical damage, but it would immediately destroy all life in the target area." [4] Evidently such a bomb would be purely an antipersonnel weapon. There has been little public discussion of neutron bombs, and it is not known whether the likelihood of their development is controversial, but we are willing to assume for the time being that the weapon can be developed with further testing.

The question then arises as to what the strategic significance of this development would be. If we are to use nuclear weapons at all, we should prefer to use weapons that produced the least in undesirable side effects, such as unwanted damage to property. However, it is equally clear that the avoidance of unnecessary damage is of negligible importance from a purely *military* point of view, and in particular is unlikely to affect the purely military outcome. The same statement appears to be true of other possible developments in tactical weapons, such as reduced weight or improved weapon shapes. As noted above, a very large field army can be completely saturated with a few thousand weapons. We have the weapons and the delivery systems to do this, and, if we were engaged in a limited nuclear war with the Soviets, whether we could do it or not is likely to depend much more on whether we have sufficient target intelligence as to the disposition of their forces than on whether their weapons are one-fifth as heavy or twice as heavy as ours. This fact, it should be emphasized, is no less true in reverse; the Soviets are perhaps equally indifferent to factors of 2 or 5 in the relative weights (or yields) of our respective tactical weapons.

The sharpest way of stating this argument is to observe that a *military* counter to the possibility of clandestine Soviet development of small tactical weapons is a willingness to "escalate" the level of conflict in the event that unexpected weapons are introduced by the other side. Although the present writers are not in most cases sympathetic to the nuclear escalation of limited wars, the relatively low likelihood that it would be required for this purpose combines with the relatively modest degree of escalation necessary if it were required to make the risks of this strategy seem acceptable in comparison to the alternative (of resuming testing at the present time). Where other considerations (such as this one) are not dominant, we should argue that it is important to maintain approximately the same spectrum of capabilities as that that might reasonably be possessed by prospective opponents.

It is worth stressing that our argument assumes that a limited nuclear war would be quite different in character from a conventional war. We should otherwise feel obliged to conclude that the military outcome of a limited nuclear war might very well be sensitive to a factor of 5 in comparative yield/weight ratios of weapons. (The military outcome of a nonnuclear war would probably be very sensitive to a factor of 5 in fire power.) In this respect, we differ from some of our friends who argue that the test-ban issue can be fought out on the basis of the "sufficiency" or "insufficiency" of our present weapons without any reference to the character of a limited nuclear war. But both the present writers have devoted considerable study, separately and jointly, to the problems of limited nuclear war, and we do not believe that it would resemble the conduct of a conventional war. In view of the probable character of a limited nuclear war, we do not believe that a further factor of 5 (or more) would be militarily significant, whether achieved by both sides, neither side, or one side only.*

Whether this conclusion is accepted or not, we believe that the debate would in any event be greatly improved if the participants would argue the specific issues of their images of the probable conduct of a limited nuclear war. In view of the fact that we have lived for fifteen years in the nuclear age and that no sensible doctrine for the tactical employment of nuclear weapons has yet been devised, a considerable burden would thereby fall on the advocates of a limited nuclear strategy; but we believe this same fact shows that the burden of proof should fall on them.

Testing for Weapon Effects. Some military tests involving the detonation of nuclear weapons are intended to yield information about weapon effects, not developmental information about the weapons themselves. Such information includes blast, heat, and radiation effects on various types of structures and mechanisms; patterns of fallout distributions; certain upper-atmosphere phenomena; and effects on the propagation of electromagnetic waves from radar and communication systems. In contrast to certain weapon development tests that might be conducted underground or in outer space without detection, most significant tests for weapon effects would take place in or near the atmosphere and would be easily detectable. Therefore, the principal cases to be considered are those in which both sides abstain or neither side abstains; clandestine cheating to determine weapon effects is not generally feasible. (There may be one or two significant exceptions.)

One of the major areas for testing of this type is in testing the vulnerability of "hardened" weapon systems. Some of our missiles (and related components of strategic weapon systems) will be protected against blast and radiation damage by concrete silos and bunkers and by being placed partly or wholly underground. These structures are designed to withstand a certain blast overpressure, such as 100 pounds per square inch, and a certain level of radioactive contamination. In other words, it is thought that an enemy

---

* This applies also to possible types of limited nuclear war of a more sophisticated variety than that discussed above.

warhead of a given yield would have to be closer than a certain distance (depending on the yield) in order to render the system inoperative. For the most part, such systems have not been tested by actual nuclear explosions. It is not known, therefore, whether they are slightly or considerably better than the (conservative) theoretical design values, or whether they might have hidden defects that would only be disclosed by an actual attack. But this uncertainty cuts both ways; the Soviet planner of an attack would be concerned that the structures might be very much better than the nominal design values, while we would be concerned about the possibility of unforeseen defects. This uncertainty may well be more deterring to a would-be attacker than would precise knowledge of the vulnerability of the targets he wishes to attack. Therefore, it appears to be about as much to our interest that both we and the Soviets should abstain from such testing as that we should both pursue experiments of this type. (This depends to some extent on which types of strategic problems seem most worrisome.) This same fact appears true of most other types of testing for weapon effects, for example, testing the vulnerability of underwater objects such as submarines.

However, one area of testing weapon effects that may not have this character involves the vulnerability of communication systems. It is obviously in our interest to retain control over our strategic forces in the event of a war; it may be less obvious but probably no less true that it is equally in our interest that the Soviets should also retain control over their forces, at least until their weapons were either exhausted or destroyed. This is because if there were a general nuclear war, they might be persuaded at some point to stop firing at us or they might decide to fire only in limited ways, and it would be important that they should be able to implement such decisions. For similar reasons, it might be important to the Soviets that we should remain in control of our forces. In both cases, this question hinges on operational doctrine and war plans. If the enemy plans call for the independent firing of all weapons if the central communication system is disrupted, we do *not* wish to destroy their control system. But there are potential hazards to existing communication systems from uncertain weapon effects.

To begin with, there is a problem of the vulnerability to blast of facilities such as transmitter installations and underground cables. However, problems of this type are better understood and fairly predictable. What are less predictable, and potentially more important, are certain weapon effects that influence the propagation of radio waves. Two weapons in the megaton range were detonated at high altitudes in the Pacific in the summer of 1958, and were observed to disturb some communication transmissions throughout an area of at least 1,500 miles in radius.[13] The phenomena involved are probably not entirely understood, and the development of adequate communication systems might possibly be facilitated by further experiments of this type. (However, such experimental information might be destabilizing.) This is therefore one area in which it might be to the interest of both the Soviets and ourselves to pursue further testing, if it were not for other considerations. It seems likely that the communication problem can be adequately solved by other means, but it is worth pointing out that a reduced vulnerability of communication and control systems might mitigate the consequences of a war.

Antimissile Weapons. The problem of warheads for antimissile missiles is mentioned so often by opponents of a test ban that the subject deserves some comment, though it has often been much overrated. The major problem of an antimissile missile has nothing to do with warheads, and if this major problem can be solved, the further development of warheads is not critical, although budgets may be affected.

The major problem in question is that of discriminating by radar (or other) techniques between an actual incoming warhead and target decoys sent along with the warhead. This problem is so formidable that many experts feel that the terminal-phase interception of enemy missile warheads at sufficiently high altitudes to protect cities will never be practicable, although low-attitude interception to protect "hardened" retaliatory forces may be more so. If this problem of discrimination and others relating to the guidance of the interception vehicle can be solved, the problem of a suitable warhead can also be solved, with or without further testing. The principal effect of further testing might be the projected improvement in yield/weight ratios discussed above. Again, a reduction in warhead weight by a factor of 5 might result in a reduction in system cost by something like a factor of 2, or perhaps even less in this case because of the necessary large investment in radar systems. The practicability of a system of this type, for either the United States or the Soviet Union or both, is not likely to stand or fall on a factor of 2 in the system cost. The present Nike-Zeus program in the United States is presumably proceeding on the basis of current warhead technology.*

Two other problems relating to this warhead development deserve brief mention. First, it seems unlikely that a specific warhead design for the Nike-Zeus missile has been tested. Any warhead eventually employed should, in our view, therefore be based on existing designs. This would not mean, however, that the weapon would be unreliable without an actual test; we would infer this fact if for no other reason than that leading weapon scientists who are opposed to a test ban never mention this problem. In addition, the total number of weapon tests conducted to date (100-odd), when coupled with Bethe's statement [11] that we have "an enormous arsenal of . . . weapons" and Teller's statement in his chapter of this book that "each nuclear explosion is . . . an experiment whose outcome is very much in doubt," clearly indicates that we have many operational weapons that have

---

* As noted above in an earlier footnote, there is little motivation to develop low-fallout weapons for this application because they would be exploded at high altitudes, and would therefore produce negligible local fallout.

never actually been proof-tested, although their reliability does not thereby seem to be in doubt.* Most of the basic designs (as contrasted with operational weapons) have probably been tested. Second, some testing of the weapon effects of the Nike-Zeus warhead might be desirable to establish the distance at which it could destroy an incoming enemy warhead. However, this can probably be estimated reasonably well on the basis of theoretical calculations and past weapon experiments.

THE INSPECTION PROBLEM

In this section the general character of the inspection problem is indicated, without any detailed analysis. Additional material on inspection can be found in the article by Bethe and in the earlier chapter in this book by Teller. An extremely detailed discussion of inspection problems (as of April 1960) can be found in the hearings of the Joint Committee on Atomic Energy.[14]

The basic facts can be summarized as follows. Tests in or near the atmosphere, even of fairly small bombs, are easily detectable. If no system of inspecting rocket vehicles before launching is instituted, then clandestine tests (of an arbitrary yield) can in principle be conducted in outer space. Any projected satellite system for detecting tests in outer space would have a finite range of detection, and the use of sufficiently large rockets would always make it possible to conduct tests beyond the range of the detection system. This would undoubtedly be very expensive and very troublesome, but it is possible at least in principle. With respect to any projected seismic network for detecting underground tests, clandestine underground tests of high-yield weapons would probably not be feasible, but the testing of sufficiently small weapons would always escape detection by the network. The efficacy of both concealment and detection techniques is changing rapidly at the time of writing.

One of the difficulties associated with seismic detection of underground tests is that it is possible to detonate the weapon in a large underground cavity; this would reduce the seismic signal, a process called "decoupling." In order to reduce the seismic signal by a factor of 120 for a fixed medium, the required hole must have a volume of 70,000 cubic meters per kiloton of yield. (A smaller hole would give a lesser reduction, not necessarily proportional, in the seismic signal.) An additional decoupling factor of $2\frac{1}{2}$ can be obtained by constructing the cavity in a hard medium such as salt, and the total decoupling thus obtained is often quoted as a factor of 300 relative to our underground tests in volcanic material in Nevada. Whether or not it is possible to make such cavities sufficiently large to decouple completely an explosion of several tens of kilotons, say, 50 kilotons or

---

* The context of Bethe's statement makes it apparent that "enormous arsenal" was meant in the sense of "enormous variety."

more, especially without a large risk of detection of the hole-building process, is a highly controversial matter.[14] However, it would probably be feasible to construct such holes to decouple explosions of 2 or 3 kilotons or less; indeed, it appears that several holes adequate for this purpose already exist. These holes might also be sufficient to decouple 20- or 30-kiloton explosions by a factor of 30 or more. In addition, several other methods of improving the concealment of underground explosions are under investigation and may well prove feasible.

On the other hand, it may also be possible to improve the performance of detection systems. At the time of writing, no specific detection system has been adopted by the Test Ban Conference at Geneva, and several detection systems have either been proposed or are under investigation. One of the more attractive systems has been discussed by Bethe,[11] who suggested the use of twenty large manned stations in the Soviet Union (as originally envisaged by the 1958 Geneva Conference of Experts), supplemented by 200 additional unmanned ("robot") stations suitably distributed throughout the Soviet Union. This system would detect *and* identify (as underground explosions, in contrast to earthquakes) fully decoupled * tests down to 20 kilotons in the seismic regions of the Soviet Union.[11] It would similarly identify explosions without decoupling down to 70 tons yield. Further improvement in the performance of detection and identification systems may well prove possible.

One troublesome problem is that of on-site inspection. A seismic network would identify as earthquakes or explosions only a certain fraction of all seismic events; it would detect many more events that could not be so identified. At the Test Ban Conference, the Western position, which has been accepted in principle by the Soviets, is that at least some unidentified events should be subject to veto-free, on-site inspection at the location of the event.† As of October 1960, the Conference was considering a treaty to prohibit underground tests resulting in a signal of seismic magnitude (a specified numerical measure of such events) 4.75 or larger, which would correspond to 20 kilotons (or more) without decoupling, and a moratorium of limited duration on smaller tests. There would be roughly 100 natural seismic events per year of magnitude 4.75 or more in the Soviet Union, of which about 50 to 70 would be unidentified by the original network proposed at Geneva.‡ The United States has proposed that 20 per year of these be subject to on-site inspection; the Soviet Union has proposed 3 per year. We shall return to this point in the following section.

Technology for both concealment and detection is in a state of flux at the time of writing. (United States research efforts in this field are budgeted at 66 million dollars for the fiscal year 1961.) Much of the discussion of the

---

* I.e., a decoupling factor of 300. Larger decoupling factors may be achieved.

† Problems in locating such events are mentioned in the chapter by Teller.

‡ There are large uncertainties in these numbers; "100 events" should be understood as "between 50 and 200 events." See pp. 89–102 of the JCAE hearings.[14]

inspection problem has concentrated on the detection and identification of 20-kiloton tests, but there is nothing especially magical about 20 kilotons; the emphasis on this yield probably stems from the historical accident that the Hiroshima and Nagasaki bombs were approximately of this size, as was one of the five seismic tests in the Hardtack II series. The detection probabilities for tests of small weapons will always be lower, and the detection probabilities for large tests will always be higher. *No conceivable change* in the state of detection technology can alter the *qualitative* fact that underground tests of sufficiently small weapons will not be detected by the system. (They may, of course, be detected by means of intelligence or through the defection of someone to whom the test was known.) At the time of writing, this fact has scarcely been recognized, much less widely discussed; however, we believe it important to an understanding of the role of inspection in connection with a weapon-test ban, especially as weapon scientists (at least in the United States) are particularly interested in weapons of much less than a kiloton.

It is useful to distinguish several orientations to inspection, of which we shall mention three: inspection to insure detection of noncompliance; inspection to deter evasion; and inspection to guarantee security. In compliance-oriented inspection, the objective is to guarantee that the other party is in fact complying with the letter of the agreed constraints; in deterrence-oriented inspection, the objective is to create a system of risks such that the expected utility of successful evasion is less than the expected disadvantages of getting caught; and in security-oriented inspection, the objective is so to arrange the total posture of armament and inspection that the security of the participants cannot be seriously impaired. It is obvious that these distinctions are by no means completely sharp, but they are useful and serve to indicate differing inspection requirements.

Early discussions of the inspection problems of a weapon-test ban, and many public discussions up to the present time, have been based on a compliance-oriented view of inspection. This view is emphasized by critics of a test ban. However, so far as national security is concerned, we have little interest in compliance *per se*. Fairly recently, the more sophisticated students of these matters have emphasized deterrence-oriented inspection for a test ban. From this position, advocates of a ban usually argue that even the rather imperfect detection system discussed at the Geneva Conference of Experts (one which would certainly not *guarantee* compliance with a total ban) is sufficient to deter the Soviets from evading the ban. Although this position is not usually accompanied by a detailed analysis of what the Soviets might accomplish by further testing, we believe, on the basis of the analysis in the preceding section, that this position is in fact correct. It does not appear that the Soviets would have a considerable motive for pursuing the further development of nuclear weapons. In this case even rather slight risks of detection and minor potential costs should be sufficient to deter evasion.

It appears to us, however, that the most relevant criterion for inspection in a weapon-test ban is that of insuring adequate national security. According to the analysis of the previous section, the military security of the United States would probably not be disastrously impaired by even completely unrestricted * Soviet testing, while we abstained from all testing. The question then arises: Are the potential net gains—political, psychological, and military—of a test ban sufficient to compensate for the potential military costs of *unrestricted* clandestine Soviet testing? If this question can be answered in the affirmative, the inspection problem becomes nearly vacuous. And we believe that it can.

CONCLUSIONS

It is useful to divide our conclusions into two aspects, those relating to what might be called the "objective merits" of the case and those relating to internal political problems and problems of negotiation.

So far as the objective merits of the case are concerned, we believe that the potential gains of a weapon-test ban are substantial. There would be military advantages stemming from reduced expectations of conducting a limited war with nuclear weapons, and a consequent tendency to strengthen Western conventional forces; political advantages relating to opinion in neutralist countries and reduced pressures on Nth countries to develop independent weapon capabilities (which, ultimately, is also a military advantage); and psychological advantages relating to retarding the technological development race and to creating a more favorable climate in which to negotiate further measures of East-West cooperation.

Some of these gains are more nebulous than others. As suggested, the effect on the Nth countries is uncertain and there will be political costs in relation to those Nth countries which are allied to the United States. But, it must be added, we *can be certain* that the resumption of weapon testing by the United States and the Soviet Union will enormously increase the political and military pressures on Nth countries to develop their own weapon capabilities. We believe that we can and should keep this pressure turned off, at least until such time as it is unequivocally clear that the problem has become hopeless or that other risks have become too great. In this last connection, it cannot be argued that the widespread diffusion of independent weapon capabilities would be invisible; for example, France has made no attempt to conceal the existence of her weapon program or her weapon tests.

It should be noted that most of the potential gains would *not* be realized to the same degree by a partial test ban, say, on atmospheric tests alone. A complete test ban has a clarity of meaning and intention that is simply

---

* Or unrestricted except for weapon-effects testing. We believe we could show in some detail that it is probably not necessary to admit this exception, but since most such testing is readily detectable, we have not done so above.

not achievable with an atmospheric ban or a ban on underground tests above the seismic magnitude 4.75.*

It is also important to note that most (not all) of these objectives are virtually unaffected by whether the Soviets are or are not conducting clandestine tests. All the political and psychological pressures on the Nth countries depend only on what seems to be the case, not on what it actually may be. This points to the peculiar fact that even if we were to obtain intelligence evidence that the Soviets were conducting clandestine tests, we might decide it was in our interest to bring the matter to their attention privately rather than denounce them publicly. In any event, it is clearly desirable to retain flexibility and an open mind with respect to the treatment of discovered violation.

The potential military costs of the ban to the United States definitely depend on whether or not the Soviets conduct extensive clandestine testing, but the dependence is not likely to be an extreme one. If the Soviets comply with the ban, the military costs are virtually negligible, consisting primarily of some surmountable uncertainties concerning weapon effects on communication systems. There is also an increased dollar cost associated with certain weapon systems; however, for reasons discussed above, this is not a *relative* cost, and may well be a relative gain. If the Soviets were to conduct *unrestricted* clandestine testing, then the costs would not be negligible, but neither would they be likely to be overwhelming. The major cost would consist in giving the Soviets something like a factor of 3 in their strategic systems or a factor of 2 in the cost of these systems, or some possible combination in between. (Even to give them a factor of 2 in system cost is to discount completely the cost of a clandestine test program, which might possibly exceed the possible saving in their strategic system.) This advantage in the cost factor is comparable to the ratio of the United States GNP to the Soviet GNP, and we can well afford to put at least this much margin into our own strategic forces as a hedge against this problem, among others. (We are here assuming that no other arms-control or inspection measures are brought into being; this problem is simplified considerably if certain additional inspection measures are provided.) We can regard the total potential cost to the United States of the test ban, assuming the possibility of unrestricted clandestine Soviet testing, as the price of achieving the potential objectives of the ban. When so regarded, it seems to us to be at least a reasonable bargain, if not an overwhelming one. It is an overwhelmingly good bargain, if the Soviets comply with the ban or conduct only limited clandestine testing.

Although we believe that we can and perhaps should spend twice as much as the Soviets on our strategic nuclear forces, as we probably have in the past, we should also point out that to assume unrestricted clandestine testing by the Soviets is probably unrealistic. Apart from the engineering

---

* There is, however, much merit in prohibiting only clearly detectable tests by *treaty*, while all others are "prohibited" by a simple moratorium. This is discussed below.

difficulties of undertaking a substantial clandestine-test program, the same reasons why the United States can afford to feel relaxed about the possibility of clandestine Soviet development illustrate why the Soviet Union is not likely to be strongly motivated to pursue such developments. In other words, even the slightest risk of detection, which might lead to some political embarrassment at the least, should be sufficient to deter the Soviets from undertaking such a program. For example, the possibility of the defection of someone connected with the program should be enough for this purpose. We do not rest our case on this fact; rather, we rest on the feasibility of constructing our own strategic forces with a sufficient margin to hedge against the possibility of clandestine development. But we do believe that this would be a "hedge" against a most unlikely possibility.

This brings us to the troublesome question of on-site inspections. The situation may well have changed by the time this book is published, but at present, there appears to be a large difference between United States (20 inspections) and Soviet (3 inspections) positions on this subject. Both friends and foes of the test ban in the United States have widely criticized the Soviet position as absurd. However, we are unable to evaluate the significance of this factor of 6⅔ in the relative detection probabilities.* Moreover, we suspect that no one else can either.† From the point of view of deterrence-oriented inspection, it is clear that an additional factor of 7 in detection probability increases deterrence. However, even if deterrence-oriented inspection were the proper framework in which to view this problem, it is impossible for us to see why the deterrence might (or might not) be sufficient with this added factor of 7 or why it might be insufficient without it. The factor may well be important, but we do not know how to evaluate it.

This brings us to our conclusions concerning internal political problems and related matters, all of which have the property that we have the capability of dealing adequately with them if only we have sufficient collective wisdom to do so. First among such problems is the question of whether or not the achievement of a test ban, by itself, might not relax national efforts below a safe level. We tend to think it would not, partly because a test ban alone is unlikely to moderate the cold war very much.

A more difficult problem concerns the negotiation of the number of on-site inspections. Several United States Senators, our negotiators in Geneva, and many others have taken a rather firm position as to the point of 20 inspections. This probably derives from a lack of disciplined efforts to understand the test-ban problem in its entirety; to our knowledge, no correspondingly complete discussion of the subject has ever been set forth

* If we (rashly) assume the perfect efficacy of on-site inspection, this is, for example, the difference between a 28 per cent and 4 per cent probability of detection of a single underground 20-kiloton shot without decoupling in a particular environment. (The Geneva network is assumed.) The uncertainty of the efficacy of on-site inspection is likely to be greater than a factor of 6. Different yields might imply a much greater factor.

† Both the number 20 and the number 3 were probably plucked out of thin air.

elsewhere. Whatever the merits of the case may be, it will be very difficult for these people to withdraw from such firmly held positions. A somewhat related problem is suggested by the fact that it might be undesirable to establish a precedent with the Soviet Union in the direction of accepting "low-grade" inspection. The fact that a test ban would appear to be reasonably safe for national security even with no inspection whatever is not one likely to carry over into all possible arms-control measures. It is important that both we and the Soviets should clearly understand this fact if we relax our requirements for inspection of the test ban. It appears to us that the primary motivation for on-site inspection in the Soviet Union is to contribute to the "openness" of Soviet society. For this purpose 20 inspections per year are obviously better than 3, but the difference does not strike us as justification for throwing away all the possible gains of a ban. One hopes that the difference will prove negotiable.

Similar questions obscure the problem of how much pressure to apply to the Soviets in the bargaining process, such as whether and under what conditions testing should be resumed (or threatened to be resumed) unilaterally if an agreement is not obtained. If the test ban were a completely isolated issue (which it is not) we would tend to believe that United States testing should be unilaterally resumed only in two cases: First, if it is *overtly* clear that many other nations in the world are already conducting test programs; in this case few of the objectives of the ban would be achieved by our further abstention. Second, in the event that the risks of continued abstention begin to appear much more dangerous than they do at present.

But the test ban is not a completely isolated issue, and it probably would be necessary at some point to resume testing if the Soviets remain in an unacceptable negotiating position or if for some other reason a treaty cannot be obtained. Both the domestic political effects and the consequences for future arms-control negotiations would be much too adverse to permit indefinite abstention from testing without any form of agreement.

The problem of accommodating the possibility of a considerable increase in the apparent risk indicates the advantage of prohibiting only clearly detectable tests by treaty, and leaving open the possibility of resuming small underground tests. This could be accomplished by various mechanisms, such as a moratorium that would expire after a prescribed period but might be renewed. However, in contrast to recent United States negotiating positions, continuation of a moratorium should *not* be made to appear dependent on the outcome of a research program on detection. It is perfectly clear that detection technology will never advance to the point where all tests of potential significance can be detected with even modest reliability. The continuation of a moratorium should rather be made dependent on a decision by the President that, all things considered, the risks of continuing the moratorium appear smaller than the risks of resuming testing.

PART IV

THE OTHER
PARTICIPANTS

13. Negotiating with the Soviet Union

BERNHARD G. BECHHOEFER

THE WESTERN POWERS HAVE BEEN NEGOTIATING WITH THE SOVIET UNION on the subject of arms control almost continuously since the end of the Second World War. Yet on the surface, any agreement seems even farther away than when the negotiations commenced in 1946.

A large number of the observers of the arms-control negotiations have concluded that the Soviet Union has no genuine interest in disarmament and that in its approach it is motivated solely by considerations of propaganda. A smaller but probably better informed segment of the public views the negotiations solely from the technical standpoint of military strategy. Another segment of the public takes at face value all Khrushchev's orations about his desire for world peace, and denounces the West for failure to accept the Soviet terms. All of these viewpoints oversimplify the issues and the negotiations to resolve them.

The purpose of this chapter is to point out certain broad characteristics of the negotiations that have persisted year after year. The study has no precise conclusion except that there is no simple nostrum that will cure all the world's ailments. The terms of reference of the negotiations are extremely complex, and progress in the negotiations depends upon a high degree of expertise, both political and technical.

THE IMPORTANCE OF NEGOTIATIONS

Since the Second World War, the Soviet Union has consistently differentiated the subject of arms control from all other political issues and in its public positions has stressed the top priority it attaches to agreement in this field. The greatest propaganda campaign conducted by the Soviet Union in the last years of Stalin's rule was the so-called Stockholm Appeal, which may be summarized by the phrase, "Ban the bomb." When Khrushchev addressed the United Nations in the fall of 1959, at a time when Soviet smiles had replaced the more usual scowls, his plea was for total disarmament. As recently as August 1960, when East-West tensions were acute, a comparatively sophisticated Soviet journal, in an exchange of articles with the *London Economist,* stated, "Disarmament is the categorical imperative of our time."

We need not consider here the motivation behind this Soviet attitude. It may well be that the Soviet leaders, after studying the disarmament by the West after World War I that led to the temporary successes of Hitler, came to the conclusion that the process could be repeated after World War II, with the Soviet Union reaping the benefits. Certainly, not only the Soviet positions in the arms-control negotiations from 1946 to 1954, but also the accompanying propaganda campaigns were admirably suited to such a policy. While the preferred Soviet position was probably to secure the unilateral disarmament of the West, it became increasingly evident after 1954 that the Soviet leaders not only realized that a nuclear holocaust would destroy both East and West, but also that they had brought this idea home to the Russian people. Therefore, the Soviet Union may genuinely wish some arms control. Whatever the motivation, the continued Soviet public emphasis on disarmament and arms control as the main problem of the age has profoundly influenced the substance of the negotiations and also the negotiating atmosphere.

THE AUDIENCES

Apparently the prime requisite of all Soviet disarmament proposals is that on the surface they must be politically appealing. Whenever the negotiations probe beneath, some Soviet proposals have considerable content, while others are pure froth. On the surface, however, they are all glib and attractive.

This appearance has placed the Western powers on the defensive. The Soviet representative will exclaim: "Ban the bomb." The West will reply, "*Yes, but* we insist on safeguards to ensure that both sides are observing their agreements." From the standpoint of broad propagandistic assaults, a position beginning with "Yes, but . . ." is unattractive.

Arms-control proposals are directed to two separate audiences: the delegations of the United Nations and world public opinion. Until 1955, the Soviet Union consistently put forward positions which outraged the United Nations delegates. In consequence, during the entire period from 1949 to 1955, the Western powers received a virtually unanimous endorsement within the United Nations for their positions. Only on rare occasions was the Soviet Union able to muster even a single vote outside the Soviet bloc for its proposals. After the United Nations actions to resist the Communist aggression in Korea and, to an even greater degree, after the death of Stalin, the Soviet leaders began to realize the importance of securing United Nations support for their positions. It gradually dawned on them that among the majority of the members of the United Nations there is probably no coherent public opinion apart from the intellectual and social elite which dominates both government and industry. In general, this elite furnished the United Nations delegates from these states, and therefore, the United Nations votes truly reflected and molded the views of the states themselves.

In the fall of 1954, the Soviet Union began to take positions which on the surface were more plausible and less outrageous. Almost concurrently, Governor Stassen, who was then the United States negotiator, reversed all the previous United States positions which had had such a favorable reception in the United Nations. While technically his action may have been justified because of weapons developments requiring a reappraisal on all positions, it was a great mistake from the standpoint of world public opinion. Ultimately in this year the United States returned to advocating the broad objectives of disarmament which the then United States delegate —Benjamin Cohen—had first submitted in the United Nations in 1952. In the meantime, however, Khrushchev had appropriated much of the position in his address to the United Nations in September 1959, which quoted literally (but without attribution) both Cohen and the leading exponent of disarmament in France, Jules Moch. In 1957, the Western powers took two steps which again might have been technically justifiable but which had no universal appeal: they combined all the Western proposals into one package and insisted that the General Assembly vote its endorsement of the package over Soviet opposition.

Since then, the Western powers have had great difficulty in securing widespread support within the United Nations. Today many of the so-called "neutral" States frequently support the Soviet positions, and some of the best friends of the Western powers at times abstain from voting. This change in the situation arises from two circumstances. The Soviet proposals are less blatantly propagandistic than formerly, and they are directed to the United Nations delegations rather than to the media of mass propaganda. At the same time, the Western proposals are phrased more timidly and in technical terms, with little appeal either to the United Nations delegations or to the larger audience of the world.

GENERAL VS. DETAILED PROPOSALS

Over the years, one test of the seriousness of Soviet negotiations has been the length and degree of detail of their proposals. In June 1946, the Soviet suggestions for an organ of international control were somewhat detailed. Thereafter, the Soviet proposals became shorter and less detailed, and finally degenerated into mere slogans of propaganda. Not until 1955 did the Soviet Union reverse itself sufficiently to submit proposals approximately as detailed as in 1946. The Soviet positions in 1959 and 1960 on the cessation of tests are sufficiently detailed to permit a precise treaty, if agreement can be reached. This is an unprecedented development in the negotiations. On several occasions John Foster Dulles pointed out that an agreement in principle on arms control with the Soviet Union might have little significance. The true test of Soviet intentions would arise with the negotiating of the detailed annexes intended to implement the agreement in principle. The only negotiation of this nature since World War II is the present (1961) conference on the cessation of nuclear testing. The system of safeguards evolving in these negotiations is totally different from any of the more general proposals for safeguards made over the years by either the Soviet Union or the West. The difficulty in securing agreement, even on the limited machinery necessary to monitor the cessation of nuclear tests, is a strong indication of the obstacles to agreeing on a broader disarmament program that would require far more complicated systems of safeguards.

NEGOTIATORS

The Soviet Union has always assigned its top foreign office representatives to the arms-control negotiations. These have included Vyshinsky and Gromyko, Soviet foreign ministers, and Malik and Zorin, deputy foreign ministers. Furthermore, all the negotiators and most of the top advisors have had many years of experience in the field. As early as 1946, Gromyko, Malik, Tsarapkin, and Skobeltzyn participated in the negotiations over the Baruch plan for the international control of atomic energy. Zorin first appeared in the negotiations about 1950. All, except Malik (who had a heart attack) and Vyshinsky (who died), are still active in this field. This continuity in the Soviet representation has greatly benefited the Soviet Union. The Soviet leaders are thoroughly versed in their subject and are sufficiently high in the official hierarchy to assure speedy high-level decisions on important issues. In contrast, the United States, on at least two occasions, has appointed representatives with no previous diplomatic experience, who were thrust into the fray with scanty preparation—in one instance, on two weeks' notice. Furthermore, the United States representatives have usually not had an easy access to the President or even to the Secretary of State. This has not been lost on the Soviet Union. The appointment of Stassen at the cabinet level raised high hopes that the United States was at last giving an appropriate emphasis to arms control. However, in the summer of 1957, it became only too apparent that Stassen also had an exceedingly limited authority. One logical consequence of this situation may have been the repeated suggestions of the Soviet leaders to raise the negotiations from the commissions of the United Nations to the summit. An additional motive for doing so is the fact that agreements at the summit must of necessity be broad and general, with few of the details. As pointed out, the Soviet Union has invariably preferred the broad general approaches suitable for a summit meeting to detailed programs.

THE PROBLEM OF SAFEGUARDS

The basic issue differentiating the Soviet position from that of the West might be stated in Western terms as follows: Will the Soviet Union permit a sufficient penetration of its iron curtain to assure the observance of its commitments? While this is the main question, only rarely have the lines of battle been drawn up squarely on this front. On one occasion in

1954, a speech of Vyshinsky raised the issue directly, and the United States representative made a brilliant reply.

[Vyshinsky]: During the last World War, even button factories—at least in my country—began to make weapons to fight Germans, and they did so successfully. Do you suggest that with a view to the reduction of armed forces and armaments we have to supervise every factory making buttons for ladies' suits and men's trousers?

[Wadsworth]: Mr. Vyshinsky pointed out yesterday that during the war certain button factories in the Soviet Union manufactured munitions. This, I can assure him, is quite parallel to the history of United States industry during the war—and indeed that of most of the countries in the war. The international control commission must, therefore, in our view, have the right to inspect button factories in order to determine whether or not they are manufacturing munitions. That is precisely what the Soviet Union representative denied to us during the London talks. . . . If . . . we correctly interpret Mr. Vyshinsky's statement yesterday, any country can frustrate the international inspection simply by posting on a munitions factory a sign reading: "Keep out. This factory is making buttons."

Generally speaking, the Soviet representatives have shown great skill in avoiding the issue. The Baruch plan for the international control of atomic energy probably could have been framed in terms which would have compelled a Soviet rejection solely on the ground of Russian unwillingness to permit the establishment of an adequate safeguards system within the Soviet Union. However, the plan as presented raised certain extraneous issues, such as the veto in the United Nations Security Council, and the international ownership of nuclear facilities, issues in which the United States position was inherently much weaker. This permitted the Soviet Union to reject the Baruch plan, but for the wrong reasons.

From 1947 to 1955, the Soviet Union avoided the issue through a number of devices, the most important of which was the refusal to discuss a control system before a prior decision on what was to be controlled. For example, the Soviet Union insisted on a decision to prohibit atomic weapons prior to a discussion of the control system so as to ensure the observance of the prohibition. This shifted the issue from the extent to which the iron curtain was to be penetrated to the much more obscure issue of the phasing of the program.

On May 10, 1955, the Soviet Union suddenly conceded the general principle advocated by the West that safeguards should be continuously adequate to insure the observance of commitments. This shifted the emphasis for the next two years from safeguards to arms limitations. Only in 1958 with the setting up of technical groups to study the cessation of nuclear tests and defense against surprise attack did the issue of the extent of penetration of the iron curtain once more become central. Without going into the complicated substantive issues of stopping nuclear tests, it is suggested that, if the conference broke up today, the state of the record would not permit the conclusion that the sole cause of the breakdown was the Soviet unwillingness to permit a sufficient breach of its iron curtain, even though this may be the fact.

The Soviet Union generally describes the Western proposals for a safeguard system operating behind the iron curtain in terms of Western espionage, yet at the same time it concedes the necessity for such a system. This equivocal attitude seems to be a façade for a realistic Soviet appraisal of the world situation. The Soviet Union recognizes that because of its iron curtain, any international safeguard system operating behind the curtain will benefit the West more than an equivalent system operating in the West, where the Soviet Union probably has already most of the information the system would develop. It is only realistic to anticipate that the Soviet Union will demand a price from the West for breaching its iron curtain. The Soviet proposals, then, call for an excessive price; but many of the Western proposals are equally unrealistic in reducing this price to zero.

PERIODS OF HOT AND COLD

On numerous occasions over the years the Soviet Union has shown no desire to discuss arms-control problems. It is interesting to study both the circumstances under which the Soviet Union has wished to avoid such discussions and the techniques which the Soviet Union has followed to secure this objective.

In the winter of 1952, when the United Nations Disarmament Commission began its discussions, it was obvious that the Soviet Union had no desire or intention to make any serious proposals. At that time it had embarked upon two tremendous propaganda campaigns, more or less directly related to disarmament: the "Ban the bomb" campaign and the charges that the United States soldiers were carrying on bacteriological warfare in Korea. These campaigns would have provided a sufficient motive to account for the Soviets' efforts to block the discussions in the Disarmament Commission, since the United Nations negotiations might well have softened the impact of the Soviet propaganda. Another possible motive which may well have influenced the Soviet Union at this time was that the Western positions were becoming politically much more attractive. In the last years of Stalin's rule, Soviet policy had become so rigid that any successful Soviet initiative to meet the Western positions was highly unlikely.

The obvious method of avoiding a discussion (a walk-out from the conference room) was unavailable. Two years earlier, the Soviet Union had walked out from all of the organs of the United Nations because of the United Nations' refusal to seat the Chinese Communists. This tactic had failed, and the Soviet Union had gradually returned to the United Nations, commencing in August 1950.

The opening speech of the Soviet delegate in the meetings of the Disarmament Commission in 1952 was a propaganda blast accusing the United States of using bacteriological warfare in Korea and calling for a

United Nations investigation. This, of course, had nothing to do with the work of the Disarmament Commission. In order to prevent the Commission from coming to grips with the problems with which it was supposed to deal, the Soviet Union submitted a plan of work, the adoption of which would have decided all the substantive issues as the Soviet Union wished and would have prevented the Commission from considering any proposals except those advanced by the Soviet Union. For example, the item on the reduction of conventional armaments in the agenda read as follows:

Preparation of agreed recommendations on the reduction by the Five Powers —the Union of Soviet Socialist Republics, the United States of America, the Peoples Republic of China, the United Kingdom and France—of the armaments and armed forces in their possession by one-third within a year.

The Soviet substantive proposals had been for the reduction of armaments and armed forces by one-third within a year. The Western governments in the previous General Assembly had indicated their intention of submitting a proposal for the establishment of numerical ceilings on armed forces, which would not have been admissible under the item on the Soviet agenda. The item would also have gone a long distance toward recognizing Communist China. The discussion of the program of work lasted for more than two weeks, and it was not until the eighth meeting of the Commission that the Western powers succeeded in bringing these preliminary issues to a vote which rejected the Soviet plan and accepted a French plan over Soviet opposition.

The Soviet representative immediately announced that he had no intention of adhering to the plan which had been adopted, and his speeches in fact ranged far and wide, not only over the field of disarmament but virtually all other political issues dividing the East and the West.

In March 1955, the Soviet Union adopted similar tactics at the opening of the second session of the Subcommittee of Five of the Disarmament Commission. Apparently, the reason for the Soviet Union's wishing to delay the negotiations at this time was a pending reappraisal of policy in the Kremlin, which emerged suddenly three months later in the famous Soviet proposals of May 10, 1955, which have been the foundation of all Soviet proposals since that time.

From May 10, 1955, until the latter part of August 1957, the Soviet Union was consistently willing to discuss the subject of disarmament. However, in the latter part of the summer of 1957, Chancellor Adenauer was campaigning for re-election. In his campaign, he placed considerable stress on improved relations between Western Germany and the Soviet Union. He even cited the relative harmony of the disarmament negotiations as evidence of such improvement.

During the entire negotiations from March until the end of August, the Soviet representative had consistently spoken with moderation. Suddenly, on August 27th he read a prepared speech which changed the entire tone of the negotiations. It was a violent attack on the West, in particular on the United States and on Adenauer, containing all the Soviet clichés about the cold war which heretofore had been conspicuous by their absence from the negotiations. Zorin carefully explained that he had been instructed to make this speech. Within a week the subcommittee meetings had adjourned with no plans for reconvening. Thereafter, the Soviet Union declined to participate in further disarmament discussions until the entire framework for the discussions had been changed in accordance with its wishes.

While the forthcoming German elections were probably not the only factor to cause the Soviet shift in tactics, there seems little doubt of the relation between the two events. Another factor may have been the fact that the Western positions in August became more rigid and moved farther away from the Soviet position than the positions advanced by Stassen in May and June. Thus the Soviet leaders may have felt that there was very little chance of progress in the near future in the field of arms control, and were willing to break up the negotiations in order to help defeat Adenauer. Actually, if this was the Soviet appraisal, it was totally erroneous. The Soviet attacks on Adenauer apparently increased his support and resulted in his re-election by a majority far larger than had been anticipated.

CLIMATE OF NEGOTIATIONS

In the main, the atmosphere of the arms-control negotiations has reflected the general temperature of international relations. When on the surface the relations have been relatively cordial, the arms-control negotiations have progressed smoothly. Usually, when general international relations became worse, the arms-control negotiations have likewise deteriorated. However, there have been variations in this pattern which may be far more significant than the pattern itself.

The Hungarian and Suez incidents in the fall of 1956 vastly increased East-West tensions. However, within three months, the Disarmament Commission and its Subcommittee of Five embarked on a negotiation which until the end was virtually free of the invective and name-calling so usual in negotiations with the Soviet Union. The moderation of the discussions in the 1957 Subcommittee was in sharp contrast to the violence of Khrushchev's pronouncements outside these negotiations.

After the U-2 episode and the break-up of the scheduled summit meetings in Paris in April 1960, arms-control negotiations were resumed, both in the conference on the cessation of nuclear tests and in the Committee of Ten States dealing with the broader problems of disarmament. The discussions of stopping nuclear tests still continue with a distinctly perceptible stiffening of position on the part of the Soviet Union. In the Committee of Ten States, immediately after the U-2 episode, the Soviet Union came up with a revised position, which in appearance (though probably not in fact) met some important Western objections to previous

Soviet positions. Regardless of the substantive importance of the new Soviet proposal, its tone was moderate, in sharp contrast to the simultaneous Soviet threats of missile warfare outside the negotiations, and the intensified propaganda campaign launched against the United States.

To be sure, the Soviet Union broke up the meetings of the Ten Nations shortly afterward, so as to prevent the West from introducing its own revised program. This Soviet action may not have been too significant. The Khrushchev policy of increasing contacts with the West has always had its opponents within the Soviet Union. Khrushchev himself made it clear that, pending the American elections, there was no possibility of progress toward any agreed disarmament program. Therefore, the break-up of the meeting of the Ten Nations may well have been a concession to Khrushchev's opposition: a concession which in the long run would not materially dim or delay the prospects for future agreements.

In short, the years of negotiation seem to indicate that the Soviet Union is somewhat more moderate in arms-control negotiations than in other equally controversial political negotiations. This may suggest a greater desire on the part of the Soviet Union to reach some agreement in this field which would diminish the possibility of a nuclear holocaust.

RELATION TO MILITARY CAPABILITIES

Fortunately, there seems to be little relation between the relative military postures of the Soviet Union and the West, and Soviet attitudes in the arms-control negotiations. In 1952, when the Soviet Union was most intransigent, the West was probably in a stronger military position vis-à-vis the Soviet Union than it was earlier or later. The recent development of the so-called missile gap does not appear to have had any perceptible influence on the Soviet position on arms control. In all probability, part of the Soviet opposition to the Baruch plan for the international control of atomic energy rested on the belief that the Soviet Union would be in a better position to negotiate after it developed its own nuclear weapons. Except for this one instance, any possible connection between Soviet disarmament proposals and Soviet military capabilities is too subtle for ready comprehension. This may mean that the Soviet disarmament proposals are not serious and therefore need not be coordinated with Soviet military strategy. A more plausible reason may be the Soviet faith in the inevitable ultimate triumph of Communism, coupled with a genuine belief that a stabilization of weapon programs at a relatively low level, rather than at a high one, will speed that triumph. The Soviet leaders seem convinced that the Western economy would collapse without the stimulus of its huge weapon program.*

---

* For whatever reasons, Soviet views on this matter appear to be changing. Khrushchev and others now (1961) argue that the Western economy would not collapse.— ED.

PERSONAL RELATIONS

From 1946 until 1954, informal contacts between the Soviet and the Western representatives were almost entirely confined to the ambassadorial level. In 1954, these contacts began to broaden. In the Spring of 1954, the United States delegation took the initiative by inviting all the Soviet advisors to a cocktail party. The Soviet delegation returned the invitation, and ever since then social contacts at the advisor level have continued. This has greatly facilitated the negotiations. On nonsubstantive matters, such as the scheduling of meetings and the working out of the formal reports of the Disarmament Commission or its subcommittees, relations have generally been satisfactory and often cordial. The Western delegates and advisors have great respect for the ability and knowledge of their Soviet counterparts, and in some, though not in all, instances this attitude is apparently reciprocated. In a figurative sense, the legal doctrine of *caveat emptor* applies to nearly all international negotiations. While the Western negotiators must be more careful in dealing with the Russians than with some other states, the main reason for such respect is the greater skill and expertise of the Soviet negotiators.

DELEGATIONS

Since the fall of 1951, the United States, the United Kingdom, and France have invariably consulted in advance before presenting their positions in the arms-control negotiations and have reached agreed positions. With the establishment of the Subcommittee of Five of the Disarmament Commission in 1954, Canada, a member of the Subcommittee, entered the consultations. The advantages of joint Western proposals have far outweighed the disadvantages. One advantage, involving negotiating tactics rather than substance, is that the capabilities of the various negotiators have frequently supplemented one another. The fact that ever since 1951 Jules Moch has been the leading spokesman for disarmament has frequently placed him in a better position to reply to the equally experienced Soviet delegates than that of the usually less experienced American delegate. Thus Moch has overcome some of the handicaps of the American delegation as a result of the frequent changes in its negotiating and advisor personnel. At the same time, the number of United States personnel engaged in the arms-control negotiations is greater than the combined numbers of French, British, and Canadian personnel, though it is sometimes less than the Russian personnel. Therefore, the American delegation is in a position to furnish much of the background data required by the other Western delegations. The American delegation, as a result of its greater number of members, is likewise in a much better position to maintain liaison with the numerous other states not actively participating in the negotiations.

THE SMALLER POWERS

States other than the great powers have usually taken the position that arms-control negotiations, particularly in the field of atomic energy, are the sole responsibility of the great powers. These other states intervene only when a complete impasse seems to have developed among the great powers, and even then their intervention is confined to efforts to break the impasse.

The first of these interventions on the part of the smaller powers took place in 1948, after the Soviet Union had completely rejected the Baruch plan for the control of atomic energy. At that time, the Western powers recommended discontinuing the negotiations but could not secure a majority in the General Assembly for their position, despite the General Assembly's support for all other phases of the Western position.

In 1951, when the General Assembly was laying the groundwork for the new Disarmament Commission, the Political Committee of the General Assembly suggested private meetings of the representatives of the Soviet Union, the United States, the United Kingdom, and France, under the chairmanship of the President of the General Assembly, Padilla Nervo of Mexico. These private meetings successfully ironed out some (though not most) of the differences between the Soviet Union and the West. The resolution of the General Assembly that resulted from this initiative furnished the framework for arms-control negotiations from 1952 through 1957.

After the collapse of negotiations in 1957, a number of states sought to develop formulae which would permit the resumption of negotiations. The disarmament discussions in the General Assemblies, both in 1957 and in 1958, were extremely extended, and many states developed proposals which, whether substantive or procedural, were all directed toward breaking the impasse among the great powers. Among the states making constructive suggestions were Mexico, India, Japan, Yugoslavia, Ireland, and even Poland. The Polish suggestions, though slightly more moderate than the Russian, were probably dictated by the latter.

These states (except Poland) were proceeding independently of the Western powers or of the Soviet Union, and in many instances, both the Soviet Union and the West opposed their suggestions. The result has been, however, that a number of states have gained the reputation of complete impartiality as to East and West. All of this is helpful, since it has some effect in limiting the irresponsibility of Soviet positions and assures greater efforts on the part of the West to develop the best possible positions consistent with its broader political and strategic policies.

COMMENT ON THE SURPRISE ATTACK CONFERENCE

An excellent example of the West's failure to appreciate the fundamentals of arms-control negotiations with the Soviet Union can be found in connection with the conference on surprise attack, which took place in Geneva in November and December 1958. The background of this conference is most significant. In November 1957, the Soviet Union had announced its refusal to participate in the reconstituted Disarmament Commission, thus bringing to an end the United Nations negotiations, which had gone on almost without interruption since World War II. Strong pressures throughout the world for a resumption of negotiations had apparently influenced the Soviet Union to accept United States proposals for two conferences of experts— one dealing with the cessation of nuclear testing, and the other, with a "study of possible measures which might be helpful in preventing surprise attack."

This conference took place at the same time as the meeting of the United Nations General Assembly, which spent almost two months trying to devise a means of resuming the general discussions of disarmament and to lessen the differences between the Soviet Union and the West. This was certainly an occasion when political wisdom dictated the necessity of a moderate Western position which might open the door to further negotiations and some measure of agreement. The United States apparently recognized the importance of the conference and produced a delegation of fifty experts and advisors. (The Soviet delegation numbered seventeen.) The United States delegation included outstanding scientists (George B. Kistiakowsky, Jerome B. Wiesner, Albert G. Hill) and high-ranking military leaders (led by General Otto P. Weyland) as members, and a prominent businessman with no experience in negotiating with the Russians (William C. Foster) as head. This delegation produced a series of splendid studies identifying the instruments of surprise attack and the techniques which would be required to prevent such an attack, with an evaluation of the results of applying these techniques. All this would have required a massive breach of the Soviet iron curtain, with vast strategic advantages to the West. The United States position never mentioned the price the West might be willing to pay to secure these advantages.

It is difficult to conceive of a position which would have been more distasteful to the Soviet Union. This was clear even before the meeting, when a Soviet note stated: "The Soviet Government . . . considers that the work of the forthcoming conference of experts should be directed to working out practical recommendations on measures for prevention of surprise attack *in conjunction with steps in the field of disarmament.*"

In 1952 the United States had taken an analogous position, when it submitted to the Disarmament Commission its paper on the "Disclosure and Verification" of armaments before producing any plan to reduce armaments. The explosive Soviet response—despite the United States assurance that a plan for reducing armaments would soon appear—should have urged caution in repeating this approach. The United States delegation of fifty to the surprise attack conference, however, included only one State Department officer, with far less rank than ability, who had observed the 1952 episode. Apparently, the United States had learned nothing from the earlier experience. Fortunately, instead of the Soviet explosion of 1952, this conference ended merely in "the suspension of meetings in view of the Christmas and New Year holidays," with an expression of "the hope that discussions . . . will be resumed as early as possible." They never have been resumed.

CONCLUSIONS

These observations about the atmosphere and the techniques of negotiating lead to a few broad comments. First, the Western positions in arms-control negotiations must be both sound and politically attractive. If they are unsound, the Soviet negotiators have the skill and experience to demonstrate that unsoundness, with great political damage to the West. If the Western positions are politically unpalatable, the Soviet Union will invariably interrupt the most serious of negotiations to secure a propaganda victory. Therefore, in the interests of successful negotiations, the positions should be both sound and politically attractive. Second, no matter how hopeless the prognosis, the Western powers must continue to seek to negotiate. The menace of all-out nuclear warfare is so great that the rest of the world will simply not allow negotiation to die. Third, a United Nations decision approving a Western proposal is completely futile in the absence of Soviet agreement. Western insistence on securing such United Nations approval without Soviet agreement has done great harm to Western prestige. Fourth, the subject is so complicated that years of experience are needed to develop a negotiator who knows the answers. Both the Soviet Union and France have learned this lesson, but apparently the United States has not. Fifth, up to this point, the disarmament negotiations have barely scratched the surface; they have merely dealt with general principles, and (except in one field, the cessation of nuclear tests) have scarcely begun to delve into the problems which must be solved precisely and in detail before a significant program of arms control and reduction can come into being. Sixth, disarmament is only one of the many areas in which the Soviet Union challenges the West, with the objective of speeding the ultimate triumph of Communism. The West must be in a position to meet all the challenges—the attempts to extend the area of Communist domination as well as the challenge to disarm. There is no conflict between a strong, well-armed West, able to meet all challenges, and progress toward the equilibrium of armaments between East and West at a relatively low level.

14. The Inclusion of Communist China in an Arms-Control Program

A. DOAK BARNETT

COMMUNIST CHINA POSES SOME EXTREMELY COMPLEX AND PERPLEXING problems for the other major powers concerned with worldwide arms control. To date, these problems have remained largely in the background, partly because of Peking's exclusion from the international councils debating the issues, and partly because the other major powers have failed to reach conclusive agreements even without the involvement of Communist China. If and when the other powers can make significant progress toward international agreements, however, the dilemmas posed by Communist China will come rapidly to the forefront, and even before that day arrives they deserve much more careful analysis and public consideration than they have so far received.

In view of the urgent need for control of nuclear weapons, and the widespread concern that a diffusion of nuclear capabilities will present a serious threat to world stability, special attention should be devoted to nuclear developments in Communist China and their implications both for Peking's present and future military position and for the international problem of nuclear arms control.

When the Chinese Communists came to power, just over a decade ago, they knew little about modern weapons of mass destruction, and apparently Chinese leaders greatly underestimated their significance. At that time, of course, even the Russians had not yet fully grasped the revolutionary implications of nuclear weapons for modern military doctrine and strategy, and it is not surprising, therefore, that the Chinese Communists, emerging from over two decades of guerrilla struggle in isolated rural areas, gave almost no sign of recognizing the tremendous importance of these new weapons for large-scale warfare.

At the start of the Korean War, in 1950, Peking went to great lengths to depreciate the significance of nuclear weapons, asserting that Communist China's huge territory and population made it relatively invulnerable to nuclear attack.* In an article published in one of Peking's principal

---

* They may well have been correct, considering 1950 fission bombs and the stockpile thereof. The same judgment of 1960 thermonuclear capabilities would be quite

282

propaganda journals soon after the Chinese Communists' intervention in Korea, it was argued, for example, that "the atomic bomb itself cannot be the decisive factor in a war," since "the more extensive the opponent's territory is and the more scattered the opponent's population is, the less effective will the atom bomb be." [1] To some extent this may simply have been a propaganda line, and the Chinese Communists may, in fact, have been relying upon the deterrent effect of the atomic capabilities of their ally, the Soviet Union, to prevent atomic attack against China—even though Moscow carefully avoided any explicit commitment of nuclear backing. "The atomic bomb . . . is now no longer monopolized by the U.S.," the same article quoted above also said; "the Soviet Union has it too." Yet, there are some indications that Peking's leaders may actually have considered the possibility of atomic attack against China, and, basing their calculations on the presumed defensive assets of their geographic, demographic, and economic position, decided they could risk it. On the eve of Communist China's entry into the war, a top Chinese Communist general said to Indian Ambassador K. M. Panikkar, in private conversation: "The Americans can bomb us, they can destroy our industries, but they cannot defeat us on land . . . We have calculated all that. They may even drop atom bombs on us. What then? They may kill a few million people. Without a sacrifice a nation's independence cannot be upheld . . . After all, China lives on the farms. What can atom bombs do there?" [2]

Three years of war in Korea—the Chinese Communists' first real exposure to effectively used airpower and other modern "conventional" weapons—clearly had a profound impact on the military-strategic thinking of Peking's leaders and greatly spurred the modernization, with Soviet assistance, of Peking's entire military establishment. Perhaps the Russians' gradual assimilation of the implications of nuclear weapons into their military doctrine—which was then in progress—also began to affect the Chinese Communists' views on the scientific, technological, and military prerequisites for great-power status. In any case, it was not long after the end of the war that Peking started to show signs that it was paying increased attention to the urgent need to develop modern science and technology, and while the economic motivation for this new emphasis was obvious, from the start it was also clear that military and strategic considerations played a very significant role in the calculations of Peking's leaders.

In the period 1954–1956 several significant developments marked the first steps toward what was to become a major drive by Communist China to foster modern science and technology and, more specifically, to prepare itself—with Russian assistance—for the atomic age.

One of the first signs of Peking's increased interest in these fields was the strengthening of the Chinese Communist Academy of Sciences in 1954;

---

wrong; complete obliteration of China would be quite feasible. It is not clear that the Chinese realize this.—ED.

following the Soviet pattern, Peking decided to convert the Academy into a semi-independent body under the State Council (Cabinet).[3] In the same year, the Chinese Communists and the Russians signed their first important agreement for cooperation in science and technology; it called for the establishment of a new Sino-Soviet Scientific and Technical Cooperation Commission.[4]

Then, in January 1955, Moscow launched a major new program of "scientific and technical assistance" to other Communist-bloc nations— including Communist China—for the development of "atomic energy for peaceful purposes," and promised to supply them with research reactors and "the necessary amounts of fissionable materials for the reactors and for research purposes." [5] This marked an important change from Moscow's earlier policy of keeping most nuclear matters secret even from its Chinese ally and East European satellites. Soon thereafter, the Chinese Communists and the Russians signed an implementing agreement for cooperation in the atomic energy field.[6] In response to these developments, and in line with Peking's growing recognition of the necessity of accelerating Communist China's general progress in science, the Chinese Academy of Sciences, together with the State Planning Commission in Peking, began in 1955 to formulate a long-term scientific development plan. In mid-1955, the head of the Academy, Kuo Mo-jo, in listing the "keypoint tasks and the needs of scientific development in the future," ranked "physics (particularly nuclear physics)" first.[7]

Finally, in January 1956, Premier Chou En-lai, at a special conference on "the question of intellectuals" convened by the Chinese Communist Party Central Committee, publicly revealed that a long-range plan for scientific development was being mapped out, "taking into account the needs and possibilities to introduce the world's most advanced scientific achievements into our country and fill in our most urgent gaps in science as quickly as possible." [8] At the same time, he called for a new policy toward China's non-Communist intellectuals, designed to stimulate their creative initiative and to obtain increased cooperation from them. In describing and explaining this increased emphasis on science, the Chinese Communists stressed, significantly, that "science is a decisive factor in our national defense," as well as in "economic and cultural enterprises." [9]

Later in the same year, the Chinese Communists officially unveiled the new long-term scientific development plan, covering a twelve-year period, 1956–1967. They also set up within China a Planning Commission for the Development of Science, which included over six hundred scientists and technicians,[10] and began sending Chinese scientists to the Joint Institute of Nuclear Research, organized by the Russians in 1956 at Dubna in the Soviet Union, in cooperation with scientists from throughout the Communist bloc.[11]

In this 1955–1956 period, although the Chinese Communists still had little to say publicly about their intentions regarding atomic bombs, and while they supported the worldwide Communist line calling for the banning of all nuclear weapons, it is significant that they showed signs of adopting for the first time what was, in effect, a sort of nuclear posture, emphasizing, in their propaganda aimed at the Japanese, the vulnerability of Japan to atomic warfare.

The period immediately following these developments, from 1956 to 1958, was in many respects an extremely difficult one in China. It was a period marked by numerous signs of increased domestic strains and tensions. The Chinese Communists' new policy of encouraging increased freedom of expression on the part of the intellectuals—which reached its peak in early 1957—proved to be worse than a failure, and after it had backfired against the regime, Peking initiated a tough crackdown, in the form of an intense "anti-Rightist campaign" followed by a strenuous drive to reindoctrinate the intellectuals and institute greater control over them. All of this doubtless slowed down the implementation of Communist China's new scientific development plan, and it probably helps to explain why the Chinese Communists later referred to the period just before 1958 as one characterized by a "dreary situation [in science] in which research was carried on by only a few people." [12] Even during this period, however, Peking clearly pushed forward as rapidly as it could in the development of science, with particular stress on the nuclear field. Communist China's educational system, already greatly expanded and reorganized to place primary emphasis on science and technology, continued to grow rapidly. The Russians sent an exhibition on the peaceful uses of atomic energy which toured China; Soviet and Chinese scientists jointly lectured in China on nuclear science; teaching and research in nuclear physics spread; and some industrial use of isotopes began.[13] Most important, construction proceeded steadily on the research reactor provided by the Russians to China.

Then, in early 1958, Communist China decided to launch a "great leap forward," in science as in most other fields, and during the months that followed, its scientific training programs—along with its entire educational system—were significantly expanded. Many new research organizations were set up under the Academy of Sciences, including an Institute of Atomic Energy Research which split off from the older Physics Research Institute. Numerous universities and institutes started training courses on atomic energy, and even some local government bodies were reported to have established organizations to conduct "research" in the nuclear field. And in June 1958 Communist China's first nuclear reactor went into operation near Peking.[14]

During this period, as Peking's reactor neared completion, and only a few months before the Chinese Communists initiated the second Quemoy crisis, the first hints appeared of Communist China's intention ultimately to obtain nuclear weapons. The initial statement of this intention was made by Peking's Foreign Minister, Ch'en Yi, in May 1958, during an interview with some German correspondents. Exactly what he said is not wholly clear since the reports on the interview vary. One correspondent quoted him as saying that, "At the moment China does not own atomic weapons, but we shall have them in the future." [15] Another correspondent implied, however, that Ch'en's statement had been somewhat more ambiguous and conditional; he reported that Ch'en said: "No Asian country possesses long range atomic weapons, not even China. If the U.S. should station such weapons in Asia, Peking would examine if China, too, must have nuclear weapons, because such American weapons would be chiefly directed against China." [16] The implied warning that Communist China might well obtain nuclear weapons was clear, in any case. At about the same time, Communist China also announced its intention ultimately to enter the space age; Kuo, head of the Chinese Academy of Sciences, declared that China was planning to launch an earth satellite.[17]

Even more important, during the same month, May 1958, a top Chinese Communist military leader also declared that it was Peking's intention to obtain nuclear weapons; his statement was more specific and unambiguous than Ch'en's. In an article in a Chinese Communist military journal, *Chieh Fang Chün Pao,* Peking's Air Force Commander Liu Ya-lou said: "China's working class and scientists will certainly be able to make the most up-to-date aircraft and atomic bombs in the not distant future." [18] Then, in early 1959, the Italian Communist Party paper *Unita* quoted the Vietnamese Communist leader Ho Chi-Minh as saying, "In the not distant future, the Chinese as well will have atomic bombs." [19]

During the period marked by these various statements, there were a number of indications that the Chinese Communists might be applying increased pressure on the Soviet Union to provide China with stronger military backing in the nuclear field (as well as in other military fields); there were some indications, in fact, that Peking in this period might actually have started preparing in various ways for the time when it ultimately would have access to nuclear weapons—perhaps counting on having access to the Soviet stockpile of atomic bombs even before achieving any independent capacity to produce such weapons.

A careful reconstruction of the events before, during, and after the 1958 offshore-islands crisis suggests either that Peking, during the crisis, consciously and successfully exerted pressure on Moscow to extract promises of significantly increased nuclear support or, alternatively, that even prior to the crisis the Russians agreed to play a supporting role that implied a willingness to make such commitments. Little is known, even today, about what took place at the Mao-Khrushchev meeting in Peking in July-August 1958—a meeting which followed close on the heels of an important national conference of Chinese military leaders and immediately preceded Peking's renewed pressure on Quemoy—but it is conceivable that some agreement may have been reached at that time on the nature, and perhaps the limits, of the nuclear backing which Moscow was prepared to give

China in the forthcoming offshore-islands crisis. It is also conceivable, however, that as the crisis actually unfolded, Peking may have exerted increasingly strong leverage on the Russians to obtain greater commitments of Soviet support than Moscow had ever made before, or perhaps initially intended to make in this instance.

Almost immediately after the 1958 Mao-Khrushchev meeting, rumors began circulating in Eastern Europe that the Soviet Union had agreed both to supply Communist China with atomic weapons and ballistic missiles and to assist the Chinese in launching an earth satellite.[20] The Russians remained silent, and avoided all comment on the subject, but perhaps it is significant that Moscow's censors passed at least one story on the reports. Whether these rumors had some basis in fact at that time, or were merely planted for political purposes by either the Chinese or Russians or both, is still unclear.

Once the Chinese Communists had started their intense bombardment of Quemoy in late August, however, Moscow began to back up Peking with various kinds of threats and commitments which became increasingly broad as the crisis progressed. On August 31, a little over a week after the bombardment had begun, *Pravda* declared that the Chinese Communists would be given the "necessary moral and material aid." [21] Less than a week later, on September 5, it began to accuse the United States of "resorting to brazen, provocational blackmail by threatening China with atomic war," and it warned that aggressors should "not calculate that a retaliatory blow will be confined to the region of the Taiwan Strait and offshore islands." [22]

Then, on September 7, Khrushchev sent a letter to President Eisenhower which not only stated that "An attack on the Chinese People's Republic . . . is an attack on the Soviet Union," but also used very strong nuclear threats to back up Communist China against the United States. "Military leaders in the United States," Khrushchev asserted, "are trying also, with the tacit agreement of the American government, to resort to atomic blackmail against China,* acting, evidently, under the residual impression of the moods that reigned in Washington during the period of the United States short-lived monopoly of atomic weapons . . . It is needless to say that the attempt to frighten other states by atomic weapons are utterly hopeless in the present circumstances as the United States has long lost the monopoly of atomic arms . . . It can be said with full confidence that no threats and blackmail can scare the Chinese people . . . The Chinese people will strike back at the aggressor in a fitting manner." [23]

Finally, on September 19, Khrushchev sent another letter to Eisenhower, one considered to be so threatening and offensive that it was not even answered by the United States. "I must tell you outright, Mr. Presi-

---

* During the crisis, 8-inch howitzers (which can fire atomic shells) were conspicuously deployed on the Nationalist-held islands. This fact was widely publicized, as were statements by the Navy indicating an atomic capability that might be used.—ED.

dent," he said in this letter, "that atomic blackmail with regard to the People's Republic of China will intimidate neither us nor the People's Republic of China. Those who harbor plans of an atomic attack on the People's Republic of China should not forget that the other side too has atomic and hydrogen weapons and the appropriate means to deliver them and, if the People's Republic of China falls victim to such an attack, the aggressor will at once get rebuff by the same means." [24] On September 21 the Peking *People's Daily* echoed Khrushchev's line: " 'Eye for eye, and tooth for tooth' the Chinese people will deal redoubled blows at the aggressors," it said, warning, "the U.S. is not the only country in the world which has atomic and hydrogen weapons." [25]

In evaluating the significance of these statements, it should be noted that Khrushchev's two letters to Eisenhower were both sent after, rather than before, Premier Chou En-lai had already announced Communist China's willingness to resume ambassadorial-level talks with the United States; Peking may, in short, have already assured Moscow, before Khrushchev made his threats, that it would not push the crisis to the point of risking major war with the Americans. Moreover, one month later, in October, Khrushchev qualified his promises to Communist China somewhat, explaining that the Soviet Union did not intend to "interfere" in the Chinese Communist struggle to gain control of Taiwan and indicating that the pledges of aid he had recently given would apply only "if the Chinese People's Republic is attacked from without or, more concretely, if the U.S.A. attacks the Chinese People's Republic." [26]

Despite these qualifications, however, it seems evident that the promises made by Khrushchev in 1958 went far beyond the pledges inherent in the 1950 Sino-Soviet alliance and that Khrushchev has now, in effect, committed the Soviet Union either to use nuclear weapons itself to support Peking, or to turn over nuclear weapons to the Chinese Communists, in the event of a nuclear attack against the China mainland. The September 7 statement that the "Chinese people will strike back" seems to imply the latter possibility, but the September 19 statement merely warning that the "other side" has atomic weapons which could be used for such a "rebuff" is more ambiguous. In either case, it has been much clearer since 1958 than it was before that Peking is now able to use direct or indirect threats of nuclear retaliation against possible threats of nuclear attack.

During the offshore-islands crisis, and since, there have been a variety of other new developments and reports—none of them conclusive, by any means, but all of them suggestive—pointing toward the possibility that Peking may already have begun preparing for the possibility of nuclear war. It is worth noting, for example, that the Quemoy crisis itself coincided with a massive drive within China to communize the rural population and to organize local militia on an unprecedented scale. While numerous economic and political motives underlay these drastic steps, resulting in the increased militarization and tighter organization of China's peasantry in units which have an improved capacity to achieve local self-sufficiency, it is clear that Peking's leaders believed these steps to be of significant value for defense in the event of nuclear war. In the fall of 1958, for example, Mao Tse-tung called for the organization of a "tremendous number of militiamen" to be ready for "criminal acts and atomic threats to world peace." [27] Some months later, Defense Minister Lin Piao, while analyzing the value of the communes to Communist China's military position, declared that "the people's communes in which industry, agriculture, trade, education, and military affairs are combined and government administration and commune management are merged are a powerful reserve to realize in a most effective way the plan of making everybody a soldier, to support the front line, protect the motherland, and to lead the enemy to fatal disaster when once the imperialists launch a war of aggression against our country." [28]

There have also been many other kinds of reports since late 1958—of varying credibility—which suggest that Peking has been moving steadily toward the goal of acquiring a capability of its own to wage nuclear war. In the summer of 1959, for example, Governor Averell Harriman reported that Khrushchev had told him, in an interview in the USSR, that Russia had shipped numerous rockets to China.[29] In June 1959, a *Christian Science Monitor* report from Singapore, citing "military intelligence experts" there, declared that it was "known" that a Soviet military mission with four high-ranking generals was currently in Communist China advising on the modernization and reorganization of Peking's army; the report further stated that China was believed to be forming some pentomic divisions capable of using "nuclear tactical equipment," and that military intelligence experts in Singapore "inferred" that "Moscow may be preparing to supply its Chinese ally with nuclear weapons." [30] In the early autumn a similar report regarding Soviet assistance for the organization of pentomic divisions in Communist China was dispatched from Hong Kong to the *New York Times*,[31] and in February 1960 a Chinese Nationalist Defense Ministry spokesman declared that the Chinese Communists had already constructed a string of rocket bases along the China coast.[32] In January 1960, another *New York Times* story from Washington, D.C., cited a "government intelligence report" predicting that Communist China would be able to launch an earth satellite in two years, possibly with Russian rockets if not its own, and asserted that the Chinese Communists had started a rocket program of their own, utilizing the expertise of a prominent Chinese rocket expert who returned from the United States to Communist China in 1955.[33]

The most extensive of all claims to date concerning Peking's recent progress toward membership in the "nuclear club" appeared in January 1960, in a Hong Kong–datelined story in *U.S. News and World Report*, written by a correspondent who cited "intelligence experts in Hong Kong" as his source.[34] This article claimed that in addition to the one Chinese research reactor known to be located near Peking, Communist China has already built one other reactor, in northern Manchuria, and is in the process of constructing two more, one at Sian in northwest China and another at Chungking in the southwest. It also stated that the Chinese and Russians have established a jointly operated factory in Urumchi, in Sinkiang, to refine Chinese uranium ores, and that China sends the refined uranium produced by this factory to the Soviet Union for processing and enrichment and receives some of it back in an enriched form. The article also claimed that Communist China has started a rocket-research program, and that 950 Chinese students have already been enrolled in or graduated from the Joint Institute of Nuclear Research in the USSR. On the basis of all of this, the author asserted, "Experts here [in Hong Kong] now believe Communist China will be able to fire its first atomic device late in 1961 or early in 1962."

There have even been a few isolated claims in recent years that atomic bombs have already been stored in Communist China [35]—presumably still under Soviet control—although the majority of informed observers appear to believe, and the bulk of the available evidence seems to indicate, that this is not the case.

It is extremely difficult to evaluate these fragmentary reports and bits of data. Some may be based, at least in part, upon speculation. Possibly others might be based on deliberately spread misinformation; conceivably, for example, either the Russians or the Chinese or both may believe that it is to their advantage, politically and militarily, for the Western powers to overestimate the rate of progress which Peking has already achieved, or can achieve, in the nuclear field. Yet, one cannot dismiss such reports or ignore completely the estimate made by some observers and "experts" that Communist China might be able to enter the "nuclear club" by exploding an atomic device as early as late 1961 or 1962.

Moreover, even if one discounts all reports and estimates which could be based partly on speculation or misinformation, and examines only the most reliable data available on nuclear developments in Communist China, the known facts—derived largely from official Chinese Communist and Soviet sources—point to conclusions about Peking's potential for developing an independent capacity to produce nuclear weapons which provide no basis for complacency.[36]

It seems clear that Communist China is currently developing the basic resources, technical skills, and equipment necessary to produce and explode a nuclear device in the relatively near future. It is believed to be mining uranium in Sinkiang (when the Soviet Union announced in January 1955 that it would help Peking build a research reactor, and would provide it with fissionable materials, Moscow stated that the Chinese were "supplying appropriate raw materials to the Soviet Union" [37]), and they are, in any case, receiving some enriched uranium from the Russians. While it may be a long time before Communist China can develop the complex and expensive facilities required to enrich uranium on its own, in due time Peking can be expected to construct new nuclear facilities capable of using natural uranium without enrichment. Communist China's pool of technically qualified personnel is clearly growing quite rapidly, and Peking may already have enough scientists competent in nuclear matters to produce and explode an atomic device. While admitting that just prior to 1949 there were only about ten scientists in China actively engaged in atomic energy research, Peking now claims that in the past ten years "a strong scientific and technological force has grown up in the field of atomic energy." [38] The practical effects of the Chinese Communists' remarkable expansion of education, focusing primarily on scientific and technological training, will probably not, it is true, be fully felt for some years—perhaps not until the 1970's. But in the interim Peking's supply of highly trained scientists and technicians has been, and is being, built up very significantly, as a result of the return of qualified Chinese scientists from abroad, the training of others in the Joint Institute of Nuclear Research in the USSR, and the development of a group of men who have acquired experience working with the aid of Soviet advisors on the construction of China's first reactor and other installations. Peking has doubtless established the necessary priorities and organizational framework, and has allocated the required resources, to spur the development of nuclear science and supporting scientific activities. The Institute of Atomic Energy Research, established in 1958, is under the leadership of a former collaborator of Joliot-Curie,[39] who has asserted that the Chinese Communist Party Central Committee has attached "great weight to scientific research in and the applications of atomic energy" and has given "continuous support" in personnel and "financial and material resources." [40]

Most important of all, the Chinese Communists now have in operation the basic facilities necessary both to conduct the required research, and to produce the needed plutonium, in order to construct an atomic device. These facilities include a 6½–10-megawatt research reactor, a 25-mev cyclotron, and an accelerator provided by the Soviet Union, as well as a high-voltage multiplier and several accelerators built by the Chinese themselves.[41]

The reactor, which has been operating since mid-1958, is a heavy-water research model, originally rated at 6½ megawatts by the Russians but capable of operating at a higher level and now classed as a 7–10-megawatt reactor by the head of the Chinese Institute of Atomic Energy Research. Its fuel consists of enriched uranium (enriched to 2 per cent in isotope content of U-235) supplied by the Soviet Union. According to one careful estimate,[42] if one assumes new fuel loadings every six months (each of which would result in irradiated rods having an accumulation of 675 grams of plutonium usable for weapons), and allows for minimum stoppages both for refueling and repairs and for experimental research purposes, this reactor could produce enough plutonium in approximately four and a half years for the manufacture of a nuclear bomb or device with an explosive power of roughly 20 kilotons—approximately the size of the Nagasaki blast in 1945—even though the technology of the first bomb might be primitive. If one further assumes that the Chinese Communists have, in fact, been using the reactor for this purpose since mid-1958, that they have also in this period been constructing the necessary plutonium separation and fabricating facilities, and that they would need a minimum period of six months for the extraction of the final plutonium and the fabrication of a device, this means that with the output of this one reactor the Chinese Communists conceivably could build and explode an atomic device by mid-1963.

This estimate indicates when the Chinese Communists might be able to produce an atomic explosion "on their own," but it definitely assumes a minimum degree of continued Soviet cooperation. It assumes, first of all, that the Russians are willing to provide the Chinese with roughly nine batches of fuel loadings over a four-and-a-half-year period, starting from mid-1958, and secondly, that Peking is not, and will not be, restricted in how it can use the plutonium produced by its reactor. If and when the Chinese Communists wished to embark on a bomb-producing program that would not be dependent upon access to the Russians' supplies of enriched uranium, and therefore upon tacit Soviet approval or acquiescence, they would doubtless build power reactors which use natural uranium as fuel and produce larger quantities of plutonium.

In the light of the available evidence, it seems prudent to assume that the Chinese Communists are proceeding with plans to produce an atomic explosion, using their existing nuclear facilities to work toward that end, and that Moscow is giving tacit approval, since the Russians are providing the necessary fuel. This does not mean, however, that one must assume that the Russians are necessarily enthusiastic about the prospect of Communist China developing an independent nuclear capacity. It seems likely, in fact, that while the Soviet Union has probably felt—perhaps under continuous pressure and prodding from Peking—that in order to maintain the solidarity of the Sino-Soviet alliance it must provide the Chinese Communists with at least minimum assistance in the nuclear field, it has probably also felt quite ambivalent about the prospect of Communist China joining the "nuclear club." A number of facts suggest such an ambivalence on the Soviet part and point to the possibility that even though the Russians have provided the Chinese Communists with some aid they have held back from giving the kind of full-scale support that they have been capable of providing in the nuclear field.

It is worth noting that the research reactors given to Communist China and Yugoslavia by the Russians are different from those given to the European satellite states; although technically they are better reactors, with a higher operating level, it may be significant that they use as fuel uranium which is enriched with only 2 per cent U-235, while the reactors in the satellites, where the Russians exercise firm political control, are more standard Soviet models using fuel which is enriched with 10 per cent U-235 (a grade of U-235 which, if diverted, could be reprocessed far more easily to weapons grade than can 2 per cent material).[43] It may also be significant that despite an obvious desire on the part of the Chinese Communists to obtain power reactors (apart from their economic value, such reactors can use natural uranium for fuel, and can produce large quantities of plutonium usable for weapons purposes), the Russians have still not made a power reactor available to Peking, even though they have promised them to such satellite nations as Czechoslovakia, East Germany, Poland, and Hungary.[44] As early as 1956, the Chinese Minister of Power declared that "atomic power stations would be built" in China, and a Chinese Communist magazine asserted that "atomic power stations will . . . be constructed with the aid of the Soviet Union." [45] But in late 1959, the Chinese were still vague on how and when they would acquire such power stations; all that the head of the Chinese Institute of Atomic Energy Research could say was that "the construction of atomic power stations in the Soviet Union and the continuous progress made in study pertaining to the control of thermo-nuclear reaction have opened up for us a new source of energy supply with unlimited capabilities." [46] There is other supporting evidence that Peking has been unable to obtain a power reactor from the USSR; according to private reports from European atomic energy specialists, in the spring of 1958 Chinese Communist purchasing agents, who were then attempting to buy a power reactor in Western Europe, asserted that they had been told in Moscow that prior Soviet commitments precluded the Russians from accepting a new order for power reactors at that time.

In addition, there are certain other aspects of Soviet policies, particularly in the period since 1957, which may provide additional clues to Soviet attitudes toward Communist China and the nuclear weapons problem—although the meaning of such clues is subject to varying interpretations. Since late 1957, for example, it has been the Russians, interestingly enough, rather than the Chinese, who have taken the initiative in promoting the idea of a "nuclear-free zone" in Asia, and Peking, while it eventually endorsed the idea in a dutiful fashion, at no time has seemed to show great enthusiasm for it.

The zone idea was one of many promoted at the Cairo Afro-Asian Conference in late 1957. After that conference's Political Committee had passed a resolution on nuclear weapons and disarmament which stated that there should be a peace zone, free from nuclear and rocket weapons, in Asia and Africa, *Pravda* echoed this demand almost exactly, but the Peking press virtually ignored it. This pattern, indicating Soviet initiative in pressing for such a zone, and a relative lack of enthusiasm on the Chinese part, was subsequently repeated several times. For example, Khrushchev, speaking at the Soviet Twenty-first Party Congress in January 1959, once again endorsed the idea of an atom-free zone, to cover the Far East and Pacific basin, but Chou En-lai, who spoke after him, had nothing to say about this idea.[47] Later, Peking did declare thaat it "fully" supported Khrushchev's proposal, but there is room for doubt that this was in fact the case.

It is also noteworthy that while the Soviet Union, since 1957, has shown increasing signs of a desire at least to negotiate seriously with the Western powers about arms controls, and since 1958 has promoted its "peaceful coexistence" line in a most energetic fashion, Communist China in this period has shown little interest in the arms-control problem, has on several occasions adopted a militant posture on issues directly affecting its interests, and has made a number of official declarations which seemed out of step with current Soviet tactics. In 1959 when Peking exerted strong pressures on India, in regard to the Tibetan border question, and on Indonesia, because of a dispute concerning the overseas Chinese, the Russians appeared to disassociate themselves from Peking's actions.

Then, when Khrushchev visited Peking on the occasion of Communist China's tenth anniversary celebration, he seemed particularly determined to impress upon his Chinese hosts the importance of pursuing "peaceful coexistence" tactics, which Peking had itself earlier stressed but now seemed to be compromising. "Marxists have recognized and still do recognize," he said, "only wars of liberation, wars that are just, and have condemned and still do condemn wars that are predatory and imperialistic . . . No. We have no need for war in general. Even a system as noble and progressive as socialism should not be imposed if the people do not want it." [48]

By contrast, a number of statements made by Chinese Communist leaders in this period have had a very different tone. In early 1960, for example, *Hung Ch'i,* organ of the Chinese Communist Party Central Committee, printed an article on Lenin's birthday warning that the present relaxation of East-West tensions is more apparent than real and stressing the continuing possibility of war between the Communist and capitalist nations. "While juggling with peace, Eisenhower and his like are making active preparations for war," the article declared.[49] "It is absolutely impermissible for us to mistake certain tactical changes on the part of imperialism for changes in the nature of imperialism." "If the imperialists insist on unleashing another war, we should not be afraid of it," it went on to say, adding that if there is "a third world war," "it is certain several hundred millions more will turn to socialism. Then there will not be much room left in the world for imperialists, while it is quite likely that the whole structure of imperialism will utterly collapse."

One of the most specific hints of a possible divergence between the Russians, with their energetic advocacy of nuclear arms controls (including a test ban), and the Chinese Communists, with their presumed desire to join the "nuclear club," was made by Mikoyan in February 1960. After delivering a speech in Oslo to the Norwegian Students' Association, Mikoyan was asked what effects the recent French atomic explosion would have on "peaceful coexistence," and whether it would lead Communist China also to desire possession of atomic bombs. "We wish to forbid all atomic tests," he is reported to have replied.[50] "If there will be no agreement on this, China may have atomic weapons. The sooner we get an agreement the greater are the chances that there will be no more explosions."

However, while it might be reassuring to draw extreme inferences from statements of this sort, it would be unwise to do so; as former Secretary of State Christian Herter has pointed out, things may be more complicated than they seem. "The Chinese at the present time are taking a very different line from the point of view of relaxation of tensions, if you want to call it that, than are the Russians," Herter said at a press conference in early 1960, but "whether this is a deliberate play between the two of them or whether they are actually taking different lines, it's very difficult to tell."[51]

In the light of all the above, plus what is known in more general terms about the character of the Chinese Communist regime and its present leadership, it seems reasonable, prudent, and necessary to assume not only that Peking will attempt to join the "nuclear club" as soon as possible, but also that it may be able to do so within a relatively short period of time—perhaps within the next three years.

In attempting to estimate the possible consequences of this eventuality, it is necessary to keep a number of important factors in mind. First of all, Communist China's leaders are clearly determined to achieve major-power status, and as their power grows their demands for international acceptance, and for a greater voice in world affairs, might well become increasingly strident and insistent. These leaders, it should be remembered, place great stress upon the intimate relationship between military power and political influence—it was Mao Tse-tung who coined the phrase "political power grows out of the barrel of a gun"[52]—and they can be expected to use, in every way possible, the increased influence in international affairs which they would doubtless achieve first, from the psychological impact of their exploding any kind of nuclear device, and second, from the real improvement in their power position which would eventually result if in time they produce or acquire a usable stockpile of nuclear weapons.

Even more important, perhaps, it would be a mistake to ignore the fact that Communist China is at present a frustrated nation, and the combination of great ambition, growing power, and deep frustration can be a dangerous mixture. Of all the major powers, Communist China is the only one with significant unsatisfied claims to territories that it promises ultimately to "liberate," by military force if necessary. (The offshore islands and Taiwan are by far the most important of these.) It is also the only major power that is excluded from the most important international councils.

Moreover, if one compares Peking's leaders with those of the other major powers, even including the Soviet Union, they still appear to be motivated by a particularly strong revolutionary zeal, which greatly affects their view of the world. Moved by a combination of this ideological fervor and intense Chinese nationalism, these leaders have shown little evidence to date that they consider international stability—even military stability in a precarious nuclear age, which does appear to concern Soviet leaders— to be an important goal.

Contrary to widespread opinion, the Chinese Communists are by no means wholly rigid or reckless; they are, in fact, capable of calculated self-control and restraint, as well as considerable flexibility and agility, at least in a tactical sense. But there is little to indicate that they regard tensions and crises as being necessarily undesirable; on the contrary they seem to regard them as an important part of the essential stuff of which the dialectic of history is made.

Furthermore, even if Peking's leaders could be expected under most circumstances to calculate with care the possible consequences of the use of their power, nevertheless at the present time they are clearly prepared to be militant in pursuing some of their basic goals, and in the pursuit of these goals, they seem prepared to take considerable risks in a calculated fashion.

One might add that it is difficult to know how fully they understand, even now, the nature of the risks of modern nuclear warfare, or to what extent they may still believe, as seemed to be the case in earlier years, that they are relatively favorably situated to risk atomic war, because of the presumption that mainland China's huge population and territory make for relative invulnerability.

Given the nature of the Chinese Communists' motivations, goals, and patterns of behavior, the prospect of Peking acquiring an independent nuclear capacity is an extremely disquieting one. It poses the "nth power problem" to the nth degree.

While it would be hazardous to attempt to predict precisely what new lines of policy the Chinese Communists might adopt on achieving membership in the "nuclear club," in general terms a number of developments would seem possible.

The first real impact of an initial atomic explosion, whether of a bomb or of some other sort of nuclear device, would probably be more psychological than military, but undoubtedly Peking would exploit this impact to the maximum to build up China's prestige and give added weight to all of its claims and policies.

Then, if Peking began slowly to accumulate even a few bombs (it would take several years to build a stockpile of any real size) it might well be tempted to exert increased military pressures on neighboring countries, or to adopt a nuclear posture in support of friendly insurrectionary forces in these countries, or to try outright nuclear blackmail in certain situations. Even if it refrained from crude, overt pressures and threats, while switching back to tactics placing increased stress upon "peaceful coexistence" —which is possible—its possession of nuclear weapons might nevertheless add greatly to Communist China's influence. Doubtless it would attempt to deter the United States from intervening in Asian crises and would do its utmost to neutralize American nuclear power in the region (perhaps especially in the area of the offshore islands and Taiwan Strait); it might attempt to do this through a form of atomic blackmail—by threatening, in effect, to trigger a nuclear conflict which could soon involve the Soviet Union and thereby expand to global war. Even if Peking possessed only a few bombs, because of its alliance with the USSR it would have a theoretical ability to convert a limited conventional conflict into a general nuclear war, and consequently either an open or implied threat that it might do this would carry a good deal of force. It is very possible, in short, that the situation in East Asia, which is already sufficiently unstable, as the history of the past decade amply demonstrates, could become considerably more dangerous and volatile if and when Peking joins the "nuclear club."

The desirability of forestalling these consequences is hardly arguable, but in realistic terms the possibilities of doing so seem relatively unfavorable.

Perhaps the first requirements for a successful effort to prevent the consequences suggested above would be: the conclusion of an effective atomic test ban; Peking's adherence to it; and adequate inspection within Communist China to enforce Peking's verbal commitments. However, even this would not necessarily prevent the Chinese Communists from accumulating fissionable material and constructing "primitive" bombs, without testing them. The fact that all four of the present members of the "nuclear club" successfully exploded their first bombs would probably lend credibility to any claims, or suspicions, that Peking had accumulated a supply of fissionable material and had built up a stockpile of usable "primitive" bombs, even without testing. The existence of a test ban might well deter Peking, it is true, from publicly revealing any such bomb-building program, but it would not preclude the possibility that the Chinese Communists might decide, at some later date, to renounce the ban and reveal their possession of a stockpile of bombs.

The only really dependable means of ensuring that the Chinese Communists could not carry out a clandestine program to produce nuclear weapons would be to conclude an international agreement, with Peking's participation, for the control of all fissionable materials, a program that would require on-the-spot inspection at every nuclear reactor, in China as elsewhere.

Granting that a test ban would not, in and of itself, provide foolproof safeguards against Communist China developing a program to produce atomic bombs, there are many who argue, nevertheless, that it is an important first step toward worldwide nuclear arms control, and it is amply clear that even this "first step" cannot be made effective and enforceable unless the Chinese Communists are ultimately included. Technical studies of the detection problem leave no room for doubt on this score. Unless and until detection techniques improve, any worldwide monitoring and inspection network would probably require at least 37 manned posts on the Asian mainland, about twelve of them on Chinese Communist territory, in order to ensure that a reasonable proportion of all underground explosions of over 19 kilotons could be detected and identified.[53] There are some who maintain, in fact, that because of the possibilities of muffling underground explosions, an even larger number of posts would be desirable. Whatever the exact number of posts that might be required, unless there were adequate coverage of the China mainland, either Peking itself could in due time conduct small underground explosions, or it could, at any time, permit its Soviet ally to do so.[54]

Since even the "first step" toward international controls of nuclear weapons cannot be effectively implemented without Peking's participation, it seems clear that the key question—assuming international agreements on nuclear controls are practicable at all—is not "if" Communist China should be included, but rather "how and when."

The evolution of United States policy on this question, and the assumptions which seem to underline official policy, deserve careful examination.

Four years ago, in February 1956, Secretary of State John Foster Dulles, discussing the problem of inspection to enforce any agreed-upon arms-control program, stated that any "ultimate comprehensive system certainly must" involve the Peking regime "sooner or later," but he asserted that the inclusion of Communist China did not have to be "necessarily at the inception." [55] Somewhat over a year later, in July 1957, he declared, "I think one can have a disarmament agreement without including Red China," but then he went on to say, "Of course, if it were not possible to have it without including Red China, then it might be possible to have undertakings from Red China." [56] "It is quite possible," he explained, "to have an agreement which stands on certain presuppositions. Some of these presuppositions might relate to Communist China without it being a party to the agreement. Then if those presuppositions proved unfounded the agreement would be called off." Elaborating further, he said, "I think we believe that a system can be devised, without necessarily the Chinese Communist regime being a contractual party to it, which would state certain terms and conditions, and certain presuppositions, certain assumptions as regards countries which were not parties." He "doubted very much" whether Communist China would attempt to produce atomic weapons on its own.

In June of the following year, 1958, Dulles again expressed his views on this problem, but by this time they had changed considerably—apparently as a result of a more careful technical examination of the problems of enforcing a test ban. To have an effective ban, he now said, "I would suppose that we would want to have—that the experts would feel we needed to have—inspection posts with some mobility not only in the Soviet Union but also on the mainland of China and other areas of that sort." [57] He added that, "I don't think I ever said that I excluded the possibility that the Soviets might themselves conduct tests on Chinese Communist territory." Then he went on to remark: "I don't know what the attitude of Communist China will be to having control posts on its territory. It doesn't seem to want to have outsiders in its territory." When asked whether "at some point there would have to be negotiations involving Red China," he seemed deliberately to sidestep this important question.

Assistant Secretary of State for Far Eastern Affairs Walter S. Robertson, discussing this problem in February 1959, agreed with the proposition that Peking should be included in any sound arms-control program, but he stressed—with justification—the difficulties of implementing arms controls. He seemed to imply, in fact, that the problems of implementation would be so great as to make the task of arms control virtually hopeless.[58] "If it were possible to establish a sound, workable system for controlling armaments or nuclear tests or surprise attacks—a system that truly protected our national security—then, of course, I believe Red China should be included," he said. "But I would lay great stress on the words 'sound, workable system,' because of the experience which we have had in the Far East in the last decade not only in dealing with Red China's repeatedly broken promises but, more pertinently, with the Communists' methods of undermining the work of control commissions established in Korea and in Indo-China."

More recently, the official view has appeared to change in one basic respect, since Christian A. Herter succeeded Mr. Dulles as Secretary of State. While Dulles sidestepped the question of whether it would ultimately be necessary to negotiate with Peking on arms control, Herter has frankly acknowledged that at some point it will be necessary to do this and to bring Communist China directly into the arms-control picture—although when, or under what circumstances, is still unclear. In September 1959, when asked "if there were a possibility that at some stage Communist China could take part in the discussions of the present Disarmament Commission which is outside the UN on the matter of controls?" Herter replied that it "is, of course, wholly possible." [59] He added, however, that he did not "see the necessity of bringing Red China in until the nations that are going to be sitting at that table come nearer to agreement." (Two days earlier State Department spokesman Lincoln White had said: if "substantial progress" could be made in current discussions, "then it would be logical to consider participation in such a disarmament program by other countries—including, of course, Red China." [60] In February 1960, Herter elaborated on this, saying that if the nations currently discussing a nuclear test ban reached agreement, "At that time the question of the adherence of Communist China would become an important factor and would, I assume, be asked for." [61] In regard to general disarmament, he asserted that if the negotiating powers reached agreements, the United Nations would probably "carry on from there" with the task of obtaining "general adherence." In this case, he said, the United Nations "might well seek Communist China's adherence to the agreement. But," he added, "I don't think it would necessarily require Communist Chinese membership in the United Nations any more than it would require recognition by any power of China."

Briefly summarized, the present United States government position on this problem seems to be that, if and when the nations currently negotiating on arms control can reach agreements, then the need to make these agreements fully effective will require consideration of how to obtain Peking's adherence, but that in the interim there is no necessity either to bring Communist China into the negotiations, or to take preparatory steps to lay the groundwork for dealing with Peking at some later stage.*

This position seems to rest on some optimistic, and perhaps dubious, assumptions. First of all, it seems to assume that if and when Peking is brought directly into the arms-control picture, even if it tries to exploit the situation by bargaining for recognition, United Nations membership, or other political gains, there will not be any necessity to make concessions or even to deal with broad political questions that would immensely complicate the problem from the American viewpoint. This hope seems to be based, in part at least, upon the assumption either that the Soviet Union would exert sufficient pressure on Peking to induce it to adhere to any agreements previously endorsed by the Russians, or that there would be other imperatives that would impel the Chinese Communists to cooperate even if they could not achieve any of their major current political aims or claims.

In realistic terms, the prospects may be much less optimistic than assumptions such as these would seem to imply. While there is no doubt that theoretically Peking could adhere to, and participate in, any arms-control agreement previously concluded by the other major powers without its being accorded diplomatic recognition or a seat in any existing international organization (the Soviet Union adhered to the Kellogg Treaty for outlawing war in 1928 when Moscow was still not a member of the League of Nations or recognized by the United States), the prospect that Communist China would actually do so, and would forego raising broad political questions, seems very dubious.

Peking has not shed very much light on its intentions in this regard, but it has made it clear that it cannot be expected automatically to adhere to any arms agreements concluded by the other powers. "Any international

---

* However, articles under consideration at the Test Ban Conference provide for withdrawal from the treaty in case important states do not accede to it, or in case the required control system is not installed.—ED.

disarmament agreement which is arrived at without formal participation of the Chinese People's Republic or signature of its delegates," Foreign Minister Ch'en Yi said in January 1960, "cannot, of course, have any binding force on China." [62] Probably the key words in this statement are "formal participation"—they doubtless mean participation in basic negotiations—and one fundamental question which they raise is what Peking might demand as the price of its participation and agreement.

It is difficult to believe that if and when the Chinese Communists were to be invited to adhere to an arms-control agreement they would cooperate automatically. Judging by their international behavior throughout most of the past decade, it seems highly probable that in such a situation they would engage in some very hard bargaining. They might, in fact, bargain for sizable political gains as the price of even agreeing to negotiate. Conceivably, they might raise not only issues such as United Nations membership and recognition, but also their territorial claims to the offshore islands and Taiwan. Moreover, whatever price they might try to exact as the precondition of negotiating, it is very possible that even after agreeing to talk, they might insist on going over the ground already covered by the other powers, raising again many of the technical issues concerning inspection and control—as they would affect China specifically—which have, from the start, required long and excruciating negotiations between the Western powers and the Soviet Union. Their bargaining position in such a situation would be a relatively strong one, since really they could bargain by merely doing nothing—by being obstructionist—in the hope that the pressures of world opinion might ultimately impel the Western powers to make concessions.

What are the prospects that the Soviet Union might be induced to bring effective pressure on Communist China to cooperate on arms controls? As noted already, there are reasons to believe not only that Moscow is more concerned about the need for arms control than Peking, but also that it may have definite reservations about the possibility of Peking becoming a nuclear power. Yet, the character and evolution of Sino-Soviet relations over the past decade provide little basis for hope that Moscow could or would force the Chinese Communists to cooperate on arms control if Peking were to decide firmly to be obstructionist. The record of recent years indicates that the Russians do not dictate to the Chinese Communists; they negotiate with them. It also indicates that in the interplay between Moscow and Peking, the Chinese Communists' influence and stature have steadily grown. And, perhaps most important, it indicates that preservation of the Sino-Soviet alliance is still of primary importance to both Moscow and Peking and takes precedence over lesser aims and considerations. None of this should be taken to mean that every effort should not be made to induce Moscow to exert pressures on Peking to cooperate regarding arms control. It does mean, however, that the Russians may not be willing to exert very strong pressures—which could threaten the basic solidarity of the Sino-Soviet alliance—and that, consequently, it seems unlikely that the Western powers can rely on the Russians to solve their problem of how to deal with the Chinese.

All of this leads to a question which may be at the heart of the matter: To what extent is it realistic even to consider the possibility of arms-control agreements with Communist China as long as the present over-all political situation in East Asia remains unchanged?

In hearings on disarmament and foreign policy held by the Disarmament Subcommittee of the Senate Committee on Foreign Relations in 1959, one distinguished observer, concerned primarily with European rather than Asian problems, declared: "It is the political issues which are basic . . . armaments are more apt to be a function of political disagreement than vice versa, and . . . efforts to reduce tensions by seeking agreement on the reduction and control of armaments, while leaving the political issues unresolved, are not hopeful." [63] If this statement has relevance to the situation in Europe,* it doubtless has even more relevance to East Asia.

At present the existing tensions and conflicts of interest in East Asia are so fundamental that one can question whether there is any immediate prospect of discovering successful approaches to the basic problem of arms control in that area. And if, as seems to be the case, even a "first step" on the international arms-control problem, such as a nuclear test ban, must be dealt with on a worldwide basis to be effective, this fact poses some far-reaching dilemmas.

Does this suggest that if the current arms-control negotiations do achieve some success, the United States must consider making major political concessions in order to obtain Peking's cooperation? There is no easy answer to this question. But there are cogent arguments against the idea of making major concessions to Communist China under duress; the political effects of such concessions—on the United States' allies in Asia, and even, for that matter, on the neutralist nations—might be extremely adverse. Perhaps, therefore, if arms control is important, and if the implementation of worldwide arms control will require Peking's participation, and if this seems unachievable or impractical unless there is some lessening of existing tensions in East Asia, the most reasonable course of action might be for the United States government to take the initiative in pressing much more actively to stabilize the existing situation throughout the East Asian region and to reduce existing tensions, modifying its present policies toward China in whatever ways seem desirable and possible toward this end.

Such a course of action would require a careful re-examination of United States policy toward China and a realistic determination of what is essential, and what is adaptable or negotiable, in that policy. This is an area of great controversy in the United States. However, it is the view of the author [64] that while there is no room for negotiation or change in the

* The statement, while correct in a sense, requires elaboration. See the earlier chapter by Bowie.—ED.

United States' basic commitment to defend Taiwan and the other non-Communist states bordering Communist China against aggression, the United States can legitimately explore the possibilities for a constructive change of posture with respect to the offshore islands, Peking's representation in the United Nations, and the possibility of *de facto,* or ultimately even *de jure,* American recognition of the Communist regime's jurisdiction on the China mainland. A more flexible American policy would not necessarily elicit immediate concessions from Peking, but if it tended over time to reduce the intensity of existing conflicts of interest in East Asia, the possibility of considering arms-control negotiations relating to that area would certainly be improved.

Throughout this discussion, it has been assumed that the issues of nuclear arms control—starting with the problem of enforcing a test ban—will come to the forefront in relation to China before issues of general disarmament. Perhaps at least a footnote should be added on the relationship of the Peking regime to the problem of general disarmament.

While Peking's relationship to the problem of nuclear controls is based on the fact that it has the potentiality of becoming a nuclear power, and is already allied with one, it would be a dangerous error to forget that Communist China is already a major power in terms of military manpower and conventional weapons. Over most of the past decade, it has posed a serious threat to the stability of East Asia despite its lack of nuclear weapons. It possesses a regular army of about 2,500,000 men; at present this is the second largest army in the world, and if the Soviet Union carries out its promised manpower cuts, it may become the first. Peking also maintains sizable public security forces, a large organized reserve, and huge militia forces. In addition, its air force of at least 2,500 planes—1,800 or more of which are jets—is the largest in Asia and cannot be ignored.[65] Peking's total forces are greater, in fact, than those of all the other nations of non-Communist East Asia combined. The principal basis for maintaining any sort of military balance in that region over the past decade has been the fact that the United States has backed up the weaker forces of the non-Communist nations in the area, and, since the Korean war, the Communists have had to weigh the possibilities of American intervention in any important conflict in that region.

Considering the size of Peking's conventional forces, it seems clear that no general disarmament program involving a worldwide reduction of forces would be practicable without Communist China's participation.[66] Moreover, since progress toward the achievement of effective agreements on comprehensive disarmament would, under the best possible circumstances, take considerable time, in the short run the United States, while working toward nuclear arms control, must devote increased attention to the improvement of its capacities to meet a variety of possible Chinese Communist threats with conventional military forces. It is true that this further complicates an already extremely perplexing problem, but there is little merit in ignoring complexities that are real and inescapable.

15. The Role of the Smaller Powers

PAUL M. DOTY

AS FRANCE GREETED THE FIFTEENTH YEAR OF THE NUCLEAR AGE WITH the explosion of her first atomic bomb, the nuclear club expanded for the first time in nearly eight years. Without international agreements or a display of national self-control uncommon to these times, admissions will come with much greater frequency. Today the smaller powers, the twenty-odd nations that by their own efforts could gain admittance to the club within another eight years, await their inevitable rendezvous with Mephistopheles. The magical power can be theirs, but they are haunted by the uncertainties of the exchange. It is with the question of the desirability of the smaller powers' possessing nuclear arms, and the alternatives they have if the temptation is denied, that this article will be chiefly concerned. The issues are viewed both from the standpoint of the smaller powers and the strategic position of the Western alliance.

The identification of the smaller powers cannot be exact but a useful approximation is available as a result of a study undertaken in 1958 by a small group of scientists working under the auspices of the American Academy of Arts and Sciences to determine the capabilities of nonnuclear nations for producing nuclear weapons. This group concluded in their report [1] that twelve nations (including France) were technically able to embark on independent, successful nuclear-weapons programs in the near future and that eight others could follow shortly. Of these twenty, six were members of NATO (Belgium, Canada, Denmark, France, Italy, The Netherlands, and West Germany), four were members of the Warsaw Pact (Czechoslovakia, East Germany, Hungary, and Poland), five were other European nations (Austria, Finland, Sweden, Switzerland, and Yugoslavia), three were major Asiatic powers (Communist China, which is dealt with in the previous chapter, India, and Japan), while standing alone in the Southern Hemisphere was Australia. At least six others should be ready to join this list a decade hence. These then are the Nth countries, those nations for whom nuclear-weapon capabilities can be secured by their own efforts. What will their choices be?

THE EXPERIENCE OF BRITAIN AND FRANCE IN
THE NUCLEAR CLUB

Thus far, the nations that have joined the nuclear club have done so in the order of their technological and economic capability. For the Soviet Union, admission was an overwhelming strategic necessity: for Britain and France, the decision turned not only on strategic but also on political and economic considerations, prestige, influence in Washington, commercial interests, and scientific ambitions, as well as other reasons only remotely related to the Russian threat. An assessment of what membership has brought Britain and France is clearly relevant to whether or not capability alone should continue to be the condition on which the decision to qualify is decided.

Unlike France, Britain's decision to become a nuclear power was made at the dawn of the nuclear age, when the consequences of success were unclear but full of military promise. From her experience, however, nuclear weapons are seen to have played a dominant but unpredictable role in her changing military posture and accommodation. On the point of expectation, however, it is clear that early membership has brought them a specially favored relation with the United States in the determination of policy and has made possible a unique acquisition of American nuclear techniques. Yet from the day of her admission to the club in 1952, Britain has had to contend with a series of unforeseen difficulties. The first was Russia's unexpectedly early qualification for membership, so that by the time Britain began stockpiling atomic bombs, it was vulnerable both because of its newly independent position and because of its previous acceptance of American bombers on its airfields. Then began under joint Anglo-American responsibility the vast military blunder of our neglecting conventional war capabilities, in the mistaken view that nuclear weapons would do instead. This generated the greatest stresses on NATO, quickened the insistence on rearming Germany, and introduced tactical nuclear weapons, with no doctrine to cover their use.

With the arrival of nuclear parity in the mid-fifties and the imminence of longe-range missiles shortly thereafter, the doctrine of massive retaliation needed a successor. In 1957 the British Minister of Defence stated, "We have decided not to defend the whole country, but to defend only our bomber bases," and in 1958 it was affirmed that any major acts of aggression by the Russians, even with conventional weapons, would be countered by British nuclear weapons. But since it had been made clear that the consequences would likely be the total destruction of the country and its people, the credibility of this policy was questioned abroad, while at home, the citizenry began to take exception to the self-sacrificial role for which they had been cast. It was this realization that sparked the campaign for nuclear disarmament, "the most powerful non-party political movement since the War," and initiated an intense debate, which has not yet reached its zenith, over the wisdom of denouncing membership in the nuclear club and setting up a nonnuclear club. This dramatic shift recently received the sanction of one of Britain's best known writers on military affairs, P. M. S. Blackett, who concluded his analysis:

In fact, I can see no plausible way in which the European defense community can survive either with its own nuclear forces or with individual national nuclear forces. I feel that the present situation, with an American safety catch on all its nuclear weapons, wherever situated, is much more stable than either of those alternatives. However, to keep it stable, it is essential that Britain renounce her own nuclear forces, otherwise their spread to other countries will never be checked.[2]

In the ethical field as well, new voices, independent of the campaign, called for the redress to the erosion of morals that was required to justify the deliberate plan (in certain military circumstances) to annihilate tens of millions of men, women, and children, as against which the victims of Hitler's gas chambers would hardly be remembered. It remained for Lt.-General Sir John Cowley to sum it up:

The professional fighting man chooses death (instead of dishonor) so that his country may survive, or, on a grander scale, so that the principles for which he is fighting may survive. Now we are facing a somewhat different situation, when the reply is not to be given by individuals but by countries as a whole. Is it right for the government of a country to choose complete destruction of the population rather than some alternative, however unpleasant? Should we in any circumstances be morally right to choose not only the termination of our own existence as a nation, but also the existence of future generations of our own countrymen? [2]

Nor is this the end of Britain's difficulties. Nuclear bombs are essentially useless without delivery systems. In attempting to keep up with the transition from bomber to missile, Britain has spent more than £100,000,000 on developing the Blue Streak Rocket. Early in 1960 it became clear that this rocket would be obsolete before it could be tested. It was consigned to the scrap heap, and Britain opted out of the missile race. This raised the fundamental question: Could Britain by itself muster the resources to stay in the nuclear race over the long pull and maintain its posture of an independent nuclear deterrent?

Thus the price Britain has paid for membership in the nuclear club has been very high and is rising. Yet Britain survives and as a nation prospers. Many think that this would probably be the case if it had not been a member; but some find grounds for doubt, taking unassailable refuge in the indisposition of history to allow experiments to be repeated.

If we turn to France, matters simplify, since we have to deal only with motives and expectations, which de Gaulle and Moch have articulated rather clearly. The French decision began with the proposition that no alliance or commitment would be strong enough to compel any nation to risk nuclear destruction to aid another. Thus, it is argued, the only nuclear power that will deter an attack on France is one that rests entirely in French hands. Some Frenchmen go on to make three further points: the only nuclear deterrent that will protect other European countries is one that lies completely in the hands of each country; therefore, each European country should have an independent nuclear capability; and since the interests of France are closely enmeshed in those of Europe, France will be safer if every major European country has its own nuclear weapons. De Gaulle's speeches suggest that the mission of French nuclear arms is to build a spearhead of a third force with the rest of the "Europe of Six" constituting the shaft of the spear. In November 1959 he stated, "We must have this atomic force, whether we build it or buy it." But in the real world of 1961, France does not have this choice. Alone, within the next few years, she can only load obsolete and highly vulnerable bombers with bomb loads that are so indecisive as to make the pretension to a third force a mockery. Of course, a major motive in their developing atomic bombs has been their hope that the initiation fee for the nuclear club would bring with it the privilege of sharing in atomic plenty and the means of delivery thereof. This has not been forthcoming, nor can it realistically be expected that either major nuclear power would yield to France the essential components of a third force capable of being pointed at any future date in whatever direction France's particular idea of "balance" required. Thus, by self-deception, France postpones until some future date the reappraisal that tortures Britain today. Already many prominent Frenchmen are questioning the wisdom of the present course, and such men as François Mauriac, Georges Duhamel, and others have denounced the French tests and petitioned for the renouncing of nuclear weapons, "thereby bringing to other peoples the example of a confident and generous will to cooperate and to reinforce the hope of a humane peace which alone will permit world disarmament."

THE SMALLER POWERS AND THE NUCLEAR CLUB

Despite the sketchiness and unbalance in our summary of the British and French experience with membership in the nuclear club, it provides invaluable guidelines to other smaller powers pondering the decision to join, and it confronts the two major nuclear powers with the problems that will be multiplied if membership in the club increases.

If a potential nuclear power judges that its prestige and influence outweigh the cost, and that the threat in Britain of the first split of its bipartisan defense policy in modern times and the helplessness in France to turn a few bombs into a third force are special to those countries, there still remains the question of how much security, if any, is being bought.

For NATO members (and in so far as they are free to choose, the Warsaw Pact countries), the strategic arguments vis-à-vis a major power threat cannot be dominant, because they cannot hope to challenge the massive concentration of explosive power and the variety of advanced delivery systems being built up in the Soviet Union and the United States. Nor is it reasonable to expect that an independent nuclear capability of modest proportions could be used to insure the involvement of the American striking force in a crisis, although the risk of doing so would be a destabilizing factor. In short, only a rather low-class, apprentice type of membership seems to be open in the nuclear club, at least in the 1960's.

This conclusion needs perhaps the qualification that those nonnuclear powers with large land masses should be excepted. The reason is that during the coming decade the two major powers will have the capability of devastating a physically small country without diverting their guard against the other major powers. Communist China, India, and Australia obviously fit these conditions. For all the others a modest nuclear capability carries no real threat in a potential conflict with either of the major powers. It could only be punitive when used in a first strike, but that would bring a devastating retaliation. In a second strike, the result would be the same, but the damage to the major power would be greatly reduced. Even France must recognize this inescapable asymmetry.

For the other European powers, the situation is little different in effect. Switzerland, Sweden, Austria, and others enjoy an independence that rests upon a strong tradition which is protected by virtue of the fact that a threat to their independence would produce tensions and the risk of a thermonuclear war quite out of proportion to any gain that would come to the instigator. Indeed, it is this condition, together with the weight of quickly reacting world opinion, that extends to all neutrals a protection against military aggression that was almost unknown before the nuclear age.

For the nations somewhat removed from the East-West balance of power, considerations of security are focused on other potential sources of aggression. If China becomes a nuclear power, India, Japan, and even Australia may consider themselves threatened and become actively interested in reacting in kind. The common denominator is the same in all these cases: if a country can gain a nuclear capability that is significant in terms of the potential threats it faces, it can be strategically justified in doing so.

This last point suggests that even in Europe, in the shadow of the Soviet and American atomic umbrellas, a smaller power may develop a small nuclear arsenal, and, by inciting suspicion among neighboring states, induce them to proceed likewise to protect themselves against a day when the mutual concern of the United States and the USSR may be diverted from them. For example, if Spain and not France had become the fourth member of the nuclear club, the reaction in France could have been accurately predicted. So it is that, while most of the smaller powers do not have strategically valid reasons to justify nuclear arming, the decision to do so by any of a number of individual nations could trigger others into following suit, since the threat presented by a nation with a few newly acquired nuclear arms is a challenge they could dare to meet.

Yet strategic considerations, as viewed by the smaller nations, are not likely to be the point upon which the decision to acquire nuclear arms will turn. A diffusion of nuclear arms is more likely to arise in two ways. Other nations experiencing the same heady drive of nationalism as is France will find the acquisition of nuclear arms irresistible as a source of prestige and a symbol of status. Alternatively, if either the Soviet Union or the United States and Britain come to believe that a wider dissemination of nuclear weapons is inevitable, or if the stresses of the cold war intensify and require the ultimate demonstration of faith in "trusted allies," the *carte-blanche* transfer of nuclear weapons and delivery systems might be expected. It is well known that the United States came close to making this decision in February 1960, and it can be easily imagined that the Soviet Union continues to be hard pressed, particularly at times like the Quemoy crises, to share her atomic plenty with Communist China. It may be well to examine briefly the restraints that both the nuclear powers and the smaller powers will face in contemplating these possible actions.

THE INCENTIVES OF THE NONNUCLEAR CLUB

The case for the major nuclear powers' keeping the nuclear club limited to its present membership is fairly obvious and this is the major motive behind the negotiations for the cessation of nuclear tests. First, there is the natural incentive of the nuclear powers to keep for themselves the vast military power of nuclear weapons. Moreover, the present nuclear powers, having the most to lose if nuclear weapons are used, consider themselves the safest keepers. And then there is the statistical argument: the fewer fingers on the nuclear triggers, the fewer chances of their being pulled. And finally, the dissemination of nuclear weapons, once begun, will have no limit, so that in the end, nations, or rather national leaders, unhampered by the responsibility of the present nuclear powers, will be tempted to use them under trivial provocation. This dissociation of action from responsibility points the way to atomic chaos, where the attacked might not even know the attacker.

Of course, a number of possibilities exist between the present position with Anglo-American and Russian safety catches on all nuclear weapons (except those few in French hands) and the extensive diffusion of such weapons without responsible control. But even to proceed from the present position to one in which NATO members had independent control of weapons provided to them would represent substantial risk to any common defense policy for NATO. Given its present centrifugal tensions, it seems unlikely that a breakup of NATO into a number of nuclear-armed and mutually suspicious states could be avoided. The idea of having a jointly operated nuclear deterrent in Europe likewise does not bear inspection, since it would be too ponderous to be effective and would risk the involvement of all the partners by the careless action of any one.

Nor is the transfer of nuclear weapons to allies any more attractive when tactical weapons are considered. This raises the whole unsettled question of tactical nuclear weapons in the NATO context and can be summarized thus. With no experience in their actual use, it remains uncertain how they would be deployed to be effective, whether more or fewer troops would be required, how supply would be maintained with ports highly vulnerable, how escalation could be avoided, how the people one wishes to protect could be saved from obliteration and even whether such weapons favor the offense or the defense. Obviously, confusion would only be compounded by allowing these questions to be judged by a number of independent authorities.

The uncertainties in the use of tactical nuclear weapons remain, even when they are under Anglo-American and Russian control. The disadvantages to either side that would follow from its initiating tactical nuclear war loom so great that it seems safe to predict that this possibility would be delayed until all other less dangerous means were exhausted. In short, more prolonged exposures to the rigors of nuclear strategy have led to increasing disenchantment with proposals for limiting nuclear war. The consequence is a reassessment of the role of conventional land armies in dealing with the explosive clashes of national wills, so as to maintain a risk that is commensurate with the provocation. The basic military mission of NATO is to provide just such a series of graduated responses. In the end the argument leads unavoidably to the conclusion that the only sensible military policy for the West would be to counter the Soviet conventional offensive forces in Europe by conventional counterforces. This conclusion immediately suggests that the European democracies should again take up the old-fashioned and unpopular job of raising armies by conscription—probably no more popular now than when suggested in a somewhat different context in 1958 by George Kennan.[3] In short, the harsh fact is that it is in conventional arms, together with their continued development, that the West has been lulled into a dangerous neglect, and it is in the redress of this unbalance that the smaller powers could make their strongest contribution to the defensive strength of NATO. This would mean the abandoning of any pretense that the use of nuclear weapons in Europe would be likely to do other than lead to widespread nuclear war. But, in exchange, it does provide a reliable means of dealing with a range of more likely problems, a means that is known to favor defense by a factor of at least three, and a means in which independent national control can be exercised to a large extent.

Parenthetically, it should be noted that by offering an alternative to tactical nuclear weapons this development would indeed contribute to disarmament. Moreover, it would appear likely that any disarmament process will at some stage put considerable reliance on conventional forces.

These views are, of course, quite contrary to those now officially held by the French, which by the extension of their logic would lead to the development of an independent nuclear capability for every nation. By thus littering the world with nuclear booby traps, a fatal Soviet-American thermonuclear exchange would almost certainly be triggered.

If we put aside the French view, it would appear that the present precarious balance of world power has, nevertheless, a certain stability which is vulnerable to an extension of independent nuclear capabilities. By abstaining from nuclear weapons, the smaller powers can contribute to this stability; by taking certain military measures, they can actually strengthen it. But we have not dealt with the several positive steps they can take to improve their own security and contribute to a less militarized and more peaceful world.

THE SECURITY AND DEFENSE OF THE SMALLER POWERS

The military revolution of the postwar period has for all time taken from "security" and "defense" much of their meaning. It was recently revealed [4] that the estimated explosive power of the United States's nuclear weapons exceeds the equivalent of ten tons of TNT for every inhabitant of the world. If all the other nuclear powers together have a similar amount, the total would be an amount of TNT sufficient to cover the entire land area of the world with a blanket an eighth of an inch thick. For a small country, at least, defense against this level of explosive power magnified by its radiological consequences is, in any direct sense, impossible, and security can only really describe the relative effectiveness with which such a power is restrained.

This way of describing by analogy the potential destructiveness in which we are immersed is particularly dismal, precisely because it pictures a situation in which the destructiveness has spread to its limit and is uncontrolled. The source of such security and defensive possibilities as the smaller powers may possess derives largely from the concentration and control of nuclear power in a few nations. Hence, as we have concluded earlier, the security interests of the smaller powers lie in keeping nuclear weaponry stored up in a few countries, in which the variables affecting its release remain manageable.

In the area of defense the outlook is not so limited. While the smaller powers would be impotent to deter the major nuclear powers if they became bent on mutual destruction, the much more realistic concern is the prevention of small wars, or their containment, if they do start. Here the smaller powers play a crucial part, beginning with the insuring of their own defense and their abstaining from any provocative action.

The defensive posture of a smaller power, directed as it must be to a relatively small locale, will be strong only as it incorporates purely defensive components. These include reliance on conventional forces which have in so many cases proven their value in defense over offense. In many instances, the Swiss example of a citizen soldiery may be superior to military units on the pattern of World War II. As such, they could provide the core of a civil-resistance movement on any territory overrun by the invader. The neglect of this role, like the neglect of civil defense by the nuclear powers, greatly weakens the military posture. However, this is not the place to repeat Mr. Kennan's arguments for this course.

It may be well, however, to introduce one other facet of this situation, by calling attention to the unique role which chemical (and perhaps biological and radiation) weapons can fill in the defense of smaller countries.

The emotional reactions so often directed against these weapons are inconsistent with a realistic appraisal of modern weapons. Indeed, with the practical development of nonlethal but incapacitative modes of action, these weapons stand alone in allowing an improvement that is not coupled to increased destructiveness. And it is in a defensive role for smaller countries that their advantages are most obvious. For example, by their use a border can be made impassable without destruction and at low cost. The citizenry can be provided with inexpensive and effective protection in advance. In short, chemical agents are increasingly adaptable to the graduated needs of the defense of small countries, and their development and use deserve careful reconsideration in the over-all effort to diminish the risk of nuclear war by reducing the likelihood of aggressive acts by the smaller nations that may by chain reaction lead to an involvement of the major powers.[5]

DISARMAMENT AND THE SMALLER POWERS

Beyond the counsel of abstention in regard to nuclear weapons and beyond the military preparations for effective defense lie a number of positive actions by which the smaller powers could guide the world through its present perils and on to the ultimate reconciliation of the human race. Several possibilities can be envisaged in which the smaller powers could play a leading role.

The first area in which the smaller powers can demonstrate their interest in arms control and disarmament is, of course, by contributing ideas and criticism to discussions and negotiations already underway or soon to begin in this area. It is widely admitted that the thought and planning devoted to problems of arms limitations by the major powers is quite inadequate when the magnitude of the problem is viewed in perspective. That is, for twenty years there has been a ceaseless application of the world's best scientific and technological talent, supported by the resources and national will of the great powers, to the improvement of competing military forces. The forces which this has put in motion easily constitute the most extensive and organized effort of modern man. To find a means of controlling and reversing this prodigious effort will require much more than the modest attempts now underway. With the major powers preoccupied with negotiating positions and detailed evaluations, a special need could be filled by the smaller powers by initiating new ideas, suggesting means of resolving conflicts and offering their judgment of the value of each successive development. Indeed, the complexity of the problems that must be solved if disarmament is to be approached is such that the active, informed, and sustained interest of the smaller powers may well be an absolutely essential ingredient for maintaining the interest of world opinion as successive attempts and failures tend to breed a fatalistic apathy.

This coin has an opposite side as well: the need for constructive cooperation in each stage of arms control that the great powers can agree upon. The Nuclear Test Cessation negotiations provide a clear and cogent test to the smaller powers on this point. In the negotiations themselves the smaller powers do not have a direct voice. But by informal approaches and better liaison with the participants the informed concern of the smaller powers could have a useful impact. If a treaty in this area is achieved, the smaller powers will have a new and greater opportunity to contribute. This obviously arises because the success of such a Test Cessation Treaty will depend upon the agreement to restraints among the smaller powers just as much as among the nuclear powers. In this, or whatever may be the first disarmament measure agreed to by the major powers, the critical phase will be that in which the adherence of all the smaller powers (and China) will be sought. It is difficult to foresee a more searching test of the concern, the vision, and the diplomatic skill of the smaller powers. Their role would be vital in reaching the nearly unanimous agreement essential to such measures. Failure at this stage would bring to an end the disarmament effort that had gone furthest toward fulfillment.

Another example of a situation in which the cooperation of the smaller powers would be vital is in the often discussed proposal for disengagement, particularly in Europe. The details of the several specific proposals need not be discussed here. What is important is the growing acceptance of such proposals in the West as well as in the East. As the Anglo-American nuclear deterrent becomes less and less credible in the eyes of West Europeans, the land defense of their homeland receives a higher priority. This is compatible with, and could be aided by, the creation of a zone of disengagement in Central Europe. With different reasoning, the East European countries are led to similar conclusions. As time passes, the Soviets have less need on several counts to insist on the political and ideological conformity of the members of the Warsaw Pact. Thus, if this is not a misreading of the many indications of increasing flexibility, the time is near when an initiative by smaller powers may elicit an acceptance of an area disengagement by the major powers. Of course, an experiment in disengagement, by itself, will not assure progress on the road to peace, but it will present new opportunities for the relaxation of tension, for the return of more nearly normal contacts in Central Europe, and for the trial of a new kind of accommodation between East and West. Beyond this, it offers a test case for disarmament, since denuclearization and later disarmament itself could find their initial trials in this arena.

In addition to the general area of responsible involvement in the planning and early stages of disarmament measures, other roles[6] of the smaller powers can be mentioned briefly. For example, there is the unique role that the smaller powers could play in the evolution of a permanent and effective United Nations Emergency Force or its equivalent. That this is an urgent need at present and an essential device in maintaining a balance of power as disarmament might proceed has been widely documented. While such a force has often been opposed by the Soviet Union and some other nations such as India, the establishment of at least a stand-by force has been sanctioned by the Uniting for Peace Resolution passed by the United Nations Assembly in 1950. Moreover, it is widely agreed that if such a force were established on a permanent basis, it should not include permanent Council members. Hence, there is here a vital opening for wise initiative and concerted action by the smaller powers.

Third, there will be a large and demanding role for the smaller powers to play if and when disarmament gets under way. Whether the route of partial measures or of comprehensive disarmament is followed or not, the need for technical and military personnel trained in modern weaponry and communications, skilled in languages, competent in administration, and perceptive and understanding in human relations will be very great indeed.

Finally, the smaller powers cannot remain oblivious to the opportunities for moral leadership that their abstinence from nuclear weapons affords. The unselfish aid of many such nations in the area of refugee relief testifies to their responsiveness to human need. The power of example remains a valid means of influencing the conduct of nations as it does the conduct of individuals. The nations that share the benefits of industrial civilization are divided by ideological prejudices and human passions that many smaller powers can help to put into a perspective based on civilized values rather than the arbitrament of unreasoned and unlimited power.

PART V

TECHNIQUES OF
ARMS CONTROL

16. Inspection Techniques of Arms Control

BERNARD T. FELD

INTRODUCTION

THIS AUTHOR REGARDS IT AS AXIOMATIC THAT MOST SIGNIFICANT ARMS-control arrangements require for their successful achievement the solution of some technical problems. The scope of the technical problems includes more than just the working out of mechanical inspection devices and the definition of the role of control and verification agencies. Satisfactory technical solutions require as well explicit attention to problems of devising measures for justifying and enhancing confidence in the arrangement, for minimizing tensions and conflicts growing out of it, and for encouraging the development and extension of accommodations into other aspects of international life so as to insure a continual increase of the mutual security of nations.

It is not intended to imply that arms control is entirely or even predominantly a technical problem. Clearly, the achievement of any significant form of arms control involves agreement on issues which are at the same time political, economic, strategic, military, social, historical, and legal as well as technical. Nevertheless, the solution of the technical problems is certainly a prerequisite to the achievement of an acceptable agreement, and the form of the available solutions is crucial for determining the possible types of accommodations.*

Nor can we automatically equate arms control with disarmament. Indeed, as will be detailed in the next section, "arms control" may be defined as comprising the entire spectrum of possible arrangements—from armed "deterrence" schemes, which may require the building up

---

* The solutions may be simple for some agreements, such as the recent treaty to insure only the peaceful use of the Antarctic regions. Unfortunately, this simplicity in this case applies to an arrangement which yields little in the way of arms control. On the other hand, the degree of technical complexity is not necessarily a measure of the degree of significant disarmament involved in an agreement. Thus, while there are many arguments to justify the continued pursuit of a nuclear-weapons test-ban agreement, despite the great (and growing) complexity of the system being devised to monitor it, it can hardly be said that the cessation of testing will reduce the arsenals of the great powers to any appreciable degree.

of certain types of armaments, all the way to universal disarmament—with the common feature, however, that these arrangements are adopted as part of a conscious effort to decrease and eventually minimize the likelihood of uninhibited armed conflict.

But it would be less than candid of me not to admit to the conviction that the possible solutions that have the greatest interest, now and in the foreseeable future, lie more in the direction of disarmament than in deterrence through mutual terror. This conviction is based mainly on two considerations: first, I feel that any system, no matter how ingeniously contrived or how meticulously constructed and balanced, is inherently too dangerous if it contains within it the possibility that a single nation, through unilateral action, can touch off a rapid chain of worldwide destruction. The instability might be triggered by a madman bent on international murder and suicide, or by a military or strategic miscalculation, or by a fortuitous series of accidents of inherently low probability; but the consequence could in any case be a catastrophic and irreversible holocaust.*

Systems involving appreciable controlled disarmament, such as those discussed in the chapter by Jerome B. Wiesner,[2] if they are attainable, have the important feature that there is of necessity an appreciable time lag between the inception of an armed conflict and the accumulation by the antagonists of stocks of nuclear weapons sufficient to cause the type of unacceptable damage referred to above. This time is available for the consultation, negotiation, and external intervention which might stop the conflict short of a catastrophic conclusion.

Universal disarmament without controls, however, may be excessively unstable in so far as it would encourage evasions and military adventuring. It would appear that the appropriate arms-control arrangements may lie somewhere between the extremes, possibly closer to the stabilized deterrence systems at the beginning, but evolving, as rapidly as feasible, in the direction of disarmament under the control of effective international organizations.

The second consideration pointing toward the importance of disarmament measures is essentially a political one. The great powers and their leaders are all publicly and firmly committed to the aim of comprehensive disarmament.† Talks are now going on, and, regardless of any mental

---

* This problem is discussed in detail in the chapter by Herman Kahn.[1]

† "I want to . . . emphasize that the United States is prepared to explore every possible avenue to find a way toward general disarmament" (Dwight D. Eisenhower[3]).

"The Soviet Government . . . has come to the firm conviction that the way out . . . should be sought along the road of general and complete disarmament" (Nikita S. Khrushchev[4]).

"Our aim is to move forward by balanced stages towards the abolition of all nuclear weapons and . . . the reduction of all other weapons . . . to levels which will rule out the possibilities of aggressive war" (Selwyn Lloyd[5]).

"France believes that . . . peace . . . involves the limitations and control of armaments by both camps" (Charles de Gaulle[6]).

reservations either side may harbor, there is a firm moral commitment to continue to seek measures leading to the elimination of armaments, together with some kind of control.

If eventual comprehensive disarmament is the stated policy of the major powers, the specific steps and even the avenues of approach have remained exceedingly vague. Beyond the general outlines of the Russian and American approaches,[4, 7] practically nothing has been published on the details of proposed disarmament measures.* More information is available on the history of disarmament negotiations,[8] and a number of general studies have been carried out in recent years by the United States Senate Subcommittee on Disarmament.[9] But the most comprehensive published study of techniques in this field remains that of Melman,[10] carried on outside the government.

In one field, the monitoring of a possible ban on the testing of nuclear weapons, a great deal of information is available.[11] Although such measures can hardly be said to constitute serious disarmament,† the difficulties are in many respects characteristic of the types of technical problems which will be encountered in future arms-limitation negotiations. Thus, it is possible to make a comprehensive list of the problems which need to be solved and to outline the research program required, as has been done in the report of the Berkner Committee.[12] As a result, it is clear that the technical problems raised in the test-ban negotiations, and their suggested solutions, appear formidable indeed (see reference 1), so much so that it is worth noting what has been pointed out in some detail by Szilard,[13] that it might be possible to settle for a greatly simplified inspection system by placing a greater reliance on human, in contrast to purely physical, devices for inspection.

The author of this chapter has participated in an effort to summarize the status of research, as of March 1960, relating to the technical problems of arms control and to identify areas in which further research is most needed. This study was undertaken by the Committee on the Technical Problems of Arms Limitation of the American Academy of Arts and Sciences, as part of a broad program of the Institute for International Order aimed at stimulating research on Peace Problems. The discussion which follows draws liberally on the results of this study.[14]

---

* Enough has emerged, however, to make clear the serious difference in emphasis on the role of control and inspection. Thus, Khrushchev says: "If disarmament is comprehensive and complete, then *upon its attainment* control shall likewise be general and complete"[4] (italics ours). Compare this statement with the official Western proposal at Geneva: "The task of the . . . conference shall be to work out measures of general disarmament, which can only be attained by balanced, phased and safeguarded agreements."[7]

† This fact may diminish their significance, but not their importance.

CHARACTERISTICS OF ARMS-CONTROL AGREEMENTS

As previously indicated, our definition of arms control is intended to encompass all possible arrangements designed to decrease the probability of international armed conflicts, from unilateral "deterrence" measures to universal disarmament requiring stringent international controls.

There are many factors which are important in relating what is desirable to what is feasible. Thus, the technical solutions which are relevant to a given arms-control negotiation are determined to a large extent by the type or level of international agreement which is politically negotiable at the time. But what is negotiable is of course strongly influenced by what is regarded as desirable, and this, in turn, is influenced by other considerations, including the strategic advantages which might be gained or lost by the control scheme, the costs and other economic implications of the proposed system, and the relationships of the contemplated measures to the ideological positions and self-images of the nations involved.

Still, provided the political and other such constraints can be reasonably well defined, the problem of the arms-control "technician" is to choose from among the possible solutions, or to devise new ones, in such a way that the *system as a whole* is the best which can be achieved—due account being taken of the whole set of pertinent criteria, including capabilities and effectiveness, limitations, cost, acceptability, and a number of other criteria relating to the impact of the contemplated agreement on the further development of arms-control measures and the growth of international law and of enforcement agencies.

Since the end of World War II, a number of proposals for arms-control systems have been explored on the international level. These include the Acheson-Lilienthal-Baruch plan [15, 16] for the international control of all nuclear-energy activities, the Rapacki plan [17] for "the establishment of a denuclearized zone in Central Europe," proposals for eliminating the possibilities of surprise attack [18] (including the "open skies" proposals), and the latest Russian proposal [4] for general and complete disarmament in four years. On the whole, none of these plans has achieved the required balance between the technical and the other considerations; the Western plans have tended to overelaborate the former at the expense of the latter, while the Eastern plans have generally exhibited an almost total disregard of the technical problems.*

Among the criteria for acceptability of arms-control arrangements, those which relate to stability and to the elimination of sources of tension are perhaps the most difficult to satisfy. Although the technical requirements often appear to demand extensive controls, it is important to recognize

---

* Thus the West accuses the USSR of desiring disarmament without control, and the Russians counter that they "are in favor of genuine disarmament under control but . . . against control without disarmament." [4] Neutral observers of a cynical bent have contended that in fact practically all proposals so far have taken into consideration only strategic and ideological problems, and were in effect designed to increase the military and propaganda position of whichever side advanced them.

that the more elaborate the system, the more numerous are the potential sources of friction, and the greater is the likelihood of increasing tensions, rather than decreasing them.

This problem represents just one of the reasons why considerable attention is being devoted to arms-control measures which rely as little as possible on explicit agreements among the powers. It appears that a great deal of effective arms control (in contrast to arms limitation or reduction) might be achieved through unilateral actions on the part of the great powers. However, for such actions to be effective, it is necessary that the motivations behind them should be so obvious as to render them acceptable without explicit agreement.

This category of arms control includes most of the deterrence schemes which emphasize the development of invulnerable retaliatory weapons at the expense of first-strike capabilities. As pointed out by Schelling,[19] there are many simple unilateral actions which can contribute to the stability and effectiveness of such systems. A more elaborate scheme, aimed at the achievement of stability in an armed world, has been explored by Szilard.[20] This approach to arms control emphasizes techniques of self-inspection. A self-inspecting arrangement is one in which the burden of proof of compliance rests with each of the parties to the arrangement; it is possible only in so far as the incentives for compliance and for convincing the potential antagonists of this compliance exceed the gains which could possibly accrue from a violation.

Whether it will also be possible to develop and utilize techniques of self-inspection in agreements involving an appreciable degree of arms reduction is a question whose answer will require much more study.

GENERAL TECHNIQUES FOR INSPECTION

The methods available for the inspection of various possible agreements for arms control have many common features, so that a relatively small number of techniques can be utilized, by varying some of the details, in the control and limitation of many types of weapons and delivery systems. These general inspection techniques can be separated into physical, records, and nonphysical inspection.

A. *Physical inspection* comprises those techniques of direct surveillance and verification of specific weaponeering activities which depend on physical contact with the activity in question, or with a direct by-product of this activity. These techniques, which are those usually associated with control systems, include:

1. *General (ground) surveillance* of factories, military installations, forbidden production activities or unusual movements or deployments harbors,* transportation centers, airports, etc., aimed at detecting either

---

* In this category we include the sea as part of the "ground." This relates in particular to agreements that contemplate control of the numbers and distribution of nuclear-powered submarines.

indicating preparation for unusual military activities. Studies of such controls have been reported by Melman,[10] and in connection with the Geneva Conference on Preventing Surprise Attack.[18]

2. *Inspection of known facilities* for the verification of compliance with agreements. These techniques apply in an operating system for arms control, and are designed to ascertain that known and normally permissible laboratories and factories are not clandestinely engaged in military development or production activities. Inspection problems in this category have been studied extensively in relation to the control of plants producing fissionable materials,[21] but there has also been some study relating to the control of other arms systems.[10]

3. *Aerial and outer-space reconnaissance and surveillance* for illegal activities. There are three permutations of this application as it affects the observer and the observed:

(a) Surveillance of objects on the ground by air-borne or space-based systems, including aerial reconnaissance [10] and, looming on the horizon, reconnaissance satellites. Such surveillance aims at detecting significant changes in the normal pattern of activity, such as might accompany preparations for a surprise attack. The U-2 incident has resulted in considerable open discussion of the uses and capabilities of these techniques.

(b) Surveillance of objects in the air by ground-based systems, comprising radar systems for the observation of missile launchings and, possibly, air traffic control.[22] This category of techniques is of interest mainly for possible arrangements involving restraints on the development of long-range missiles and satellites, with surveillance of launchings included as part of the agreement.

(c) Surveillance of objects in the air or in space by air-borne or space-based systems relates to the same functions as discussed in paragraph (b). However, additional detection possibilities are available above the atmosphere, such as infrared detection, and these systems may have special applicability with respect to the detection of missile launchings and the detection of outer-space testing of nuclear weapons.

4. *Special techniques for the detection of radioactivity* from the ground, in the air, or in the seas are specifically applicable to problems of nuclear weapons production and test detection. Almost all nuclear materials activity—production or use—gives rise to some residue of radioactivity; since the detection of the products of radioactive disintegrations provides an extraordinarily sensitive inspection device (by the use of appropriate techniques, literally a single nuclear disintegration can be distinguished), many methods can be conceived for the detection of those hidden activities which require the disposal of some radioactive substance at some stage.

5. *Problems of maintenance of weapon stockpiles* are worthy of special attention since the difficulty of discovering nuclear weapons (and missiles) hidden before the institution of an inspection system is

generally regarded as the major technical obstacle to the adoption of agreements contemplating drastic reduction of armaments. In particular, this requires investigation of whether there are aspects of the maintenance of secret stockpiles which require activities susceptible of detection. Such studies appear to call for highly classified information.

B. *Records inspection* involves the detailed analysis of industrial and governmental activities by methods with which there is considerable experience,[10] although most of it is applicable to the governments and societies of the West. There are two approaches to the examination of plant and agency records:

1. *Budget and expenditure inspection* may provide a means of verifying the nature and extent of declared activities, and possibly of detecting the existence of undeclared activities of large scope, although a number of examples exist where the expenditure of large sums for military purposes was kept relatively secret (e.g., the Manhattan project during World War II).

2. *Production and inventory records* are subject to verification by strict accounting procedures. There are probably not many difficulties associated with the verification of operations and production after the adoption of a control agreement. But the accurate estimation or verification of past production presents a major problem, involving the consistency, authenticity, and completeness of past records, which may be crucial for determining what kind of arms-control agreements are possible. The solution of this problem could be one of the keys to the future prospect for disarmament.

C. *Nonphysical inspection* covers those techniques of control, surveillance, and verification primarily involving the use of human agencies. In view of the inadequacy of physical and records inspection techniques with respect to at least two crucial problems—namely, the possibility of appreciable stockpile accumulation before the initiation of the agreement and the difficulty of detecting research and development activities which could result in major breakthroughs—it is important to seek other means of verification of compliance with agreements and of control over clandestine activities. The first systematic appraisal of nonphysical techniques, as far as we know, is due to Bohn;[23] specific applications have since been suggested in a number of instances.* Nonphysical inspection techniques have received very little study to date. Subjects of obvious interest for future study include:

1. *Utilization of the general population for information* on compliance and for detection of clandestine activities. This approach raises questions of the extent of supranational loyalties and the possibilities for their enlargement, the availability of secure channels for the transmission of information to an outside agency from inside a closely con-

* Such as Melman's "inspection by the people"[10] and Szilard's plans for test-ban control.[13]

trolled nation, and the evaluation of the validity and reliability of information received. Beyond some very preliminary studies,[10] practically no information is available.

2. *Utilization of key people* for the location of key activities. For this approach to be usable, it is necesary first of all to determine who are the key people with respect to any activity of possible interest to the control agency. If we assume this information, it is then necessary to determine which individuals are likely to know of or to be involved in clandestine activities and to devise techniques of interrogation and surveillance which are most likely to elicit information concerning such activities. As a possible means of obtaining information, such special psychological testing devices as depth interviews, polygraphs (lie-detectors), drugs, hypnosis, etc., invite study, if only because so little is known. At the same time, it is necessary to pay close attention to the necessary restraints imposed on the use of such devices by constitutional requirements and by the general rules of conduct which should be practiced in civilized nations.

3. *A census of the activities of specialists* could provide a means of detecting when a significant sector of the scientific community disappears from peacetime activities. The difficulty with such a census is that it requires full information, including knowledge of those who have gone directly from school into secret laboratories and who are accordingly not known to the scientific and technical community through their professional work. Hence, the effectiveness of this approach may depend on the availability of complete records of student interests and activities in institutions which provide advanced training, as well as the provision of means of tracing individuals of possible interest to the inspectorate.

4. *Establishment of an international intelligence network* would probably be necessary for the institution of any comprehensive control system. Although considerable experience exists with national agencies, there is neither experience nor precedent relating to the use of such agencies for the detection of violations of international agreements.

A more detailed discussion of some of these techniques appears in the chapter by Lewis Bohn.

COMMON PROBLEMS OF INSPECTION SYSTEMS

The specific form of inspection system required to implement a given agreement will depend on the constraints imposed by the terms of the agreement as well as on what is to be inspected. However, common to all inspection systems will be certain problems, such as the use of sampling techniques to accumulate and evaluate relevant data, the development of methods of organization and staffing of inspectorates to insure maximum effectiveness, and the devising of means for insuring the continued maintenance of this maximum effectiveness.

A. *Statistical sampling techniques* are required for any of the inspection methods discussed in the preceding section, since it is manifestly impossible to observe every act, record, and person involved in a widespread industrial complex. There are two sides to the sampling problem, however, and the methods they require may be quite different. On the one hand, if the problem is to verify permitted activities in disclosed facilities, the methods of sampling are relatively standard, having been worked out in connection with such well-studied industrial problems as quality control and inventory maintenance.[10] On the other hand, the design of techniques to search for undisclosed facilities and weapons or for clandestine activities in a sovereign nation, part or all of whose officials and nationals may be bent on evading the agreement, presents a relatively virgin field. The evolution of appropriate sampling patterns and procedures is in large measure an operations-research problem, but it also involves many aspects of "game theory," since the appropriate techniques may depend on decisions concerning the strategic aims of the inspectorate.*

We need information directly relating to specific control systems, but there is also need for a more theoretical approach through mathematical models which treat in a general way statistical sampling in an evading population under various assumptions concerning its behavior patterns.

B. *The organization and staffing of the inspectorate* presents problems which are critical for the success of any control agreement. It is necessary to provide for supplementary functions of a positive, constructive nature if the inspectorate is to attract and retain personnel of a sufficiently high calibre to enable it to perform its supervisory tasks with the requisite ability and efficiency. Such additional responsibilities, if appropriately designed, can also help to minimize frictions between the inspectorate and the host countries, especially if they develop vested interests in the successful operation of the control system for the countries involved.

C. *Maintenance of the effectiveness* of the inspectorate requires more than just the provision of interesting and useful supplementary functions. Research on inspection problems, especially on possible means of evasion, will be required to perfect the inspection system. Besides, an inspectorate will be in a much better position to fulfill its functions and to anticipate new developments if, as a result of its own research, its knowledge of a given weapons technique is at least as advanced as that of any of the nations involved.

Research on inspection techniques and on the detection of possible evasions might well be instituted by the various powers involved, on a unilateral basis, before the achievement of an agreement. Such research,

* Is it better to let the evaders know (publicly or privately?) that their evasion has been detected, or to keep this secret, etc.? A start has been made on the study of some of these problems, in and out of the government, but these studies have not been made public and this author does not know whether they are being continued.

if properly balanced between studies of evasion possibilities and detection methods, might help delineate the possible fields of agreement and might enable the negotiators to enter into the discussions with reliable prior information relating to detection and inspection capabilities. Such a situation never has prevailed in international negotiations on arms controls.

SOME EXAMPLES AND APPLICATIONS

The possible use of the available control techniques, singly or in combination, is best illustrated by a consideration of the specific control schemes which at one time or other have been considered seriously enough to receive more than a superficial study. Only suggestions made after 1945 are included, since only these could take into account nuclear weapons and modern delivery systems, but it is by no means certain that some of the studies carried out by the League of Nations may not have relevance.

A. *The Acheson-Lilienthal plan* [15] was devised as a means for controlling nuclear weapons through the prevention of their production and development beyond the 1946 level. Since at that time no nation other than the United States had facilities for the production of weapons materials, it was possible to adopt a simple and unsubtle technical solution for achieving complete control. The plan was to vest in an international agency the sole right to engage in any activity relating to nuclear energy. All nuclear plants and related activities (the mining of uranium, chemical processing, etc.) were to be constructed, operated, and controlled by the international agency.

The plan, especially as elaborated by Baruch,[16] involved such unprecedented infringements on national sovereignties and contained possibilities for such all-pervasive outside controls over important aspects of national economies that it was almost inevitable that it should be rejected by the USSR.* In fact, the plan may be taken as a classic example of the perfect "technical" solution which is, however, rendered useless by the failure to take sufficient account of the political, economic, and psychological realities. Of course, at the opposite extreme is an oft-repeated (pre-1955) Russian proposal of a treaty banning nuclear weapons.†

The more recent discussions of nuclear-weapons limitation have, on the one hand, reflected a growing realization on the part of the USSR that limitations without effective controls are unacceptable to the West

---

* This conclusion is perhaps one of hindsight. On the other hand, there is a serious question, in view of what is now known about the internal politics of the USSR in the late 1940's, that any control plan at all would have received serious consideration.

† This remark does not apply to proposals for an agreement to renounce the *first use* of nuclear weapons. Such proposals represent, in fact, a good example of possible self-inspecting arms-control arrangements.

and, on the other hand, a growing scepticism in the United States relating to the possibility of finding adequate technical measures for detecting treaty violations. This scepticism has lately been heightened owing to the difficulties of devising an evasion-proof agreement for banning bomb tests, but for many years it has pervaded every discussion of a reduction of nuclear-weapons stockpiles. But if for some people these uncertainties have tended to discourage the exploration of possible control arrangements, the reaction of others has been to seek alternative verification techniques and to study more intensively some nonphysical inspection measures.

B. *Production controls and the Nth-country problem*. The search for techniques for the control of nuclear weapons has been intensified as a result of the growing realization on both sides of the importance of impeding the further uncontrolled spread of nuclear-weapons capabilities.[24, 25] One result has been an enhanced interest in the utilization of international organizations, in particular the International Atomic Energy Agency (IAEA), in place of the heretofore prevailing systems of bilateral agreements, as an effective means of aiding in the development of nuclear-power capabilities while at the same time maintaining a reasonable international control to prevent the diversion of fissionable material into weapons production.

Although the charter of the IAEA, established in 1957 as an Agency of the United Nations with headquarters in Vienna, contains provisions for a number of controls aimed at preventing the diversion of fissionable materials, there has been a considerable reluctance on the part of some of the signatory nations to sanction the setting up of an effective control system. Nevertheless the IAEA organization has shown an increasing interest in such controls, and the Agency's Governing Board has adopted a safeguards program.

The powers of the IAEA which could be applied to controls include [24]: the right of approval of facility designs, the responsibility for establishing health and safety measures, the ability to require adequate production records and reports, the responsibility to prevent diversion of fissionable material during and following processing, and the right to terminate assistance in the event of noncompliance with IAEA regulations. The techniques available and the measures which could be taken by control agencies have been studied in considerable detail in this country (and by the other nuclear powers); further study under the sponsorship and support of the IAEA is in progress in many countries. A detailed discussion of control measures was given in testimony in connection with ratification by the United States Senate of the Statute of the IAEA.[26]

C. *The Melman study*[10] of "Inspection for Disarmament" represents the most comprehensive published investigation of problems and techniques applicable to the enforcement of agreements for the partial or complete prohibition of nuclear weapons and the means of their delivery. Most of the eighteen papers comprising the study assume the existence of an agreement, including a provision for the unhindered access by an international inspectorate to facilities inside the signatory nations. However, the United States has been taken as the prototype nation to which the inspection techniques are specifically applied.

These papers, which cover the whole range of inspection problems, include: direct physical surveillance by aerial inspection methods, the detection of underground nuclear explosions, the detection of high-altitude missile tests, inspection for the production of agents of biological warfare, the direct inspection of factory operations, the use of fiscal and records inspection, as well as problems of psychological inspection, especially those relevant to the utilization of national populations for uncovering clandestine activities. Also included are interesting studies of past evasions of arms-control arrangements, in Palestine under the British mandate and in the Weimar Republic, as well as studies of possible techniques for evading the agreement under consideration made by "evasion teams" constituted for this specific purpose.

In his analysis of the results of the studies, Melman, while taking cognizance of the possibilities for systematic evasion inherent in many of the proposed inspection techniques, adopts the position that a combination of many techniques can serve to reduce to an essentially negligible level the net probability of significant evasions of the agreement by any single nation. However, this conclusion is also based on the assumption of a successful utilization of the technique of "inspection by the people," some possibilities of which are explored in the study.

It is of course possible to quarrel with this conclusion, to question the relevance in the present state of international relations of some of the controls envisaged, to point to differences between the American and Russian societies, especially as regards inspection problems, to urge greater attention to the interactions between different control measures, etc. But, such criticisms notwithstanding, this is a bold and imaginative first attempt, which, by bringing into the realm of public discussion the serious problems whose solutions are required for comprehensive disarmament and especially by calling attention to the importance of nonphysical inspection techniques, has made a major contribution to the study of arms control.

D. *The prevention of surprise attack* [18] is an aspect of arms control, of greatest significance in the absence of controlled arms limitation or in an interim period during which armaments are being reduced. As examples, the Rapacki plan and the "open skies" proposals are aimed at the reduction of surprise-attack capabilities and at the provision of mutual assurance concerning the peaceful intentions (or the contrary) of both sides.

Such assurances are especially important in a situation such as the present one, in which both sides rely for the maintenance of the peace on a mutual recognition of the effectiveness and readiness of deterrent forces. These assurances will remain important as deterrence systems become more powerful and more invulnerable, even in the absence of any but the most tacit of international arrangements.[19] On the other hand, their existence can contribute materially to the easing of tensions and to the establishment of an atmosphere of relative trust in which more inclusive agreements may become possible.

At the "surprise attack conference" of experts from the East and the West,[18] held in Geneva toward the end of 1958, no discernible progress was made toward agreement on prevention of surprise attack, owing to the participants' inability to agree on terms of reference. Nevertheless, the conference served at least to focus attention on a number of serious and difficult technical problems, of which we single out just one in the following brief discussion.

It is clear that the development of submarines of unlimited range and of submarine missile-launching systems (i.e., POLARIS) capable of firing nuclear weapons from under the sea, introduces new dimensions into the surprise attack problem. The control of such weapon-delivery systems depends on the ability to control the submarines. Two aspects of the problem need to be considered. On the one hand, submarines, like bombs and missiles, can be stockpiled, and the detection of their storage (for example, in remote locations on ocean bottoms) and knowledge of the numbers stored raise serious questions; however, these do not appear to be as difficult as those associated with the problem of a nuclear-weapons stockpile. On the other hand, the problem of locating submarines in operation, or even of forming a reasonably accurate estimate of their numbers, is also a formidable one, although it appears possible to conceive of systems of surveillance of major ports and straits, by using appropriate underwater location techniques, which might serve to enforce an agreed limitation on the number of active submarines without necessarily requiring a detailed knowledge of their location.

E. *Control of biological, chemical, and radiological weapons* is a field whose importance remains rather difficult to assess, despite some recent studies by competent authorities.[27, 28] Although there is little doubt that many nations are carrying on serious efforts in this field, the impression still prevails that such weapons represent more of a potential for nuisance than for decisive influence in possible major conflicts.* Still, the usefulness of such weapons may be much greater when viewed with the eyes of a small nation, because of their relative cheapness and the

---

* "As means of immediate and certain destruction, these weapons cannot compare with hydrogen bombs. The dependence of biological weapons on uncontrollable factors, such as meteorological conditions, and the difficulty of confining the effects to the attacked territory, make them especially unpredictable in scope and effect. . . . But, however difficult the international control of atomic weapons may be, the international control of biological and chemical weapons by any system of inspection seems incomparably more difficult" (from the Statement of the Pugwash International Conference of Scientists on Biological and Chemical Warfare[28]).

universality of their availability, and they might be capable of playing a decisive role in a relatively localized conflict.

A number of aspects of those weapons suggest possible special control methods. Thus, while the research and development stage would require minimal facilities normally available as a result of legitimate biological, chemical, and nuclear-power activities, their field testing and deployment for use might require special preparations and concurrent activities—such as the large-scale immunization of populations in the case of biological agents affecting man—which could be readily detectible by an inspection system.

CONCLUSIONS

Any survey of the techniques available for the implementation of possible arms-control systems is bound to conclude with remarks concerning the woeful inadequacy of past and present research in this field. The painfully obvious need for an organized governmental effort, also capable of developing a governmental group with a "vested interest" in arms control comparable with that normally devoted to the enhancement of military capabilities, has been forcefully pointed out on many occasions. With such remarks I concur. Beyond this, I would like to call attention to two specific problems in which it appears that further research is most urgently needed. Their solutions, if such are possible, lie at the very heart of the questions of the feasibility and possible extent of comprehensive arms-limitations measures. These are:

A. *The stockpile problem,* or the question of the degree of certainty with which it may be possible to ascertain (by a study of past records, inventories, plant characteristics, etc.) the amount of weapons material which may have been sequestered by a nation, or by an influential group within the nation, before the institution of a control agreement. There is a considerable overlap between the methods of attacking this problem and those developed for the prevention of clandestine diversion of new weapons materials; but almost all discussions found in the open literature refer to the latter.

Of course, the stockpile problem applies to all weapons on which there might be some agreed limitation; however, this discussion will be limited to nuclear weapons and long-range missiles. Given free access to all plants capable of producing appreciable fissionable material, and to all of their records, the problem of ascertaining past production has many approaches which taken together can help to narrow the uncertainty of the estimate. Thus, the records of past power production (or heat removal), together with a knowledge of plant design characteristics, provide an estimate of production of plutonium or uranium 233. Records of mining operations and of uranium ore-processing activities yield information on the raw materials which have gone through the plants, including plants for the separation of uranium 235. Waste products, through their chemical and radiochemical analysis, yield information on past production.

The uncertainty in the estimate of past production increases with the total amount of material processed and with the length of time over which there has been uninspected production. As of this writing, the stockpile problem applies only to the three or four nuclear powers. With the exception of the Melman study,[10] the existing information is mainly classified. The numbers which one occasionally hears quoted by apparently reliable sources for the amount of fissionable material which could be sequestered from present stockpiles in the USSR, if an agreement were to take effect now, with little chance for subsequent detection that a diversion had been effected, range from enough to produce about fifty large thermonuclear bombs up to enough for about five hundred. Clearly, it is important to develop techniques for reducing the actual upper limit of uncertainty. It would be important for the purpose of public discussion and planning for the presently accepted upper limit to be made public.

The stockpile problem with respect to ICBM's has been discussed in considerable detail in the Melman report.[10] On the one hand, the problem is less difficult because of the relatively short time during which it has been possible to accumulate hidden stockpiles and because of the size of the objects. On the other hand, missiles require many components, some of a rather specialized nature, whose production is widespread throughout the normal industrial activities of an industrialized country; this aspect tends to increase the difficulty of detecting any one clandestine activity, but it provides for a large number of possible points of detection.

After the production of fissionable materials and the manufacture of missile components, these must be assembled into weapons, deployed and maintained in readiness if they are to be used by a potential aggressor. While such activities might also be rooted out by physical inspection techniques, it may be precisely in this field that nonphysical techniques (psychological inspection, inspection by the people, etc.) will have their most fruitful application.

In any event, the possible size of clandestine stockpiles is likely to be among the crucial factors which will set the level of possible disarmament agreements at any time.

B. *Research and development constraints* are implicitly assumed in most control systems envisaged, since practically all such systems are unstable with respect to a technical breakthrough capable of providing a decisive military advantage to one member of the agreement. This instability applies in schemes of armed deterrence perhaps even more than in situations of relatively comprehensive disarmament. Although the inspection techniques discussed above may all be relevant to some forms of research and development activities, this inspection problem is one which by definition defies general solution; for how does one predict the unknown? Nevertheless, some techniques have greater relevance than others, e.g., methods of records inspection. In particular, the nonphysical techniques would appear to offer the greatest promise, especially in those aspects which provide for a continuing census of the activities of key specialists.

Any serious attempt at inspecting research and development activities implies the complete elimination of secrecy from research. This openness would have to apply not only to basic research, but to governmental and industrial research activities as well. In the final analysis, however, stability with respect to technological progress could probably only be achieved through the adoption and exercise of stringent self-restraints on the part of sovereign nations; the solution of this problem may, in fact, demand the greatest self-restraint of all—the eventual relinquishment of absolute national sovereignty in favor of an international order with the enforcement capabilities necessary to establish and preserve the peace.

17. Public Opinion and the Control of Armaments

ITHIEL DE SOLA POOL

THE THESIS OF THIS CHAPTER IS THAT AN EFFECTIVE SYSTEM OF ARMS limitation should embody the conscious use of propaganda as an instrument of control. The thesis rests on two premises which not everyone accepts: that the state of public opinion in the major powers can greatly affect how an arms-control system will function; and that the state of public opinion both at home and abroad is capable of being influenced by a well-planned strategy of action.

THE SHAPING OF PUBLIC OPINION

The primitive science of public opinion has many hallmarks of mythology and folklore, including the simultaneous acceptance of contradictory propositions. For example, proverbs say, "Look before you leap," but also, "He who hesitates is lost." Similarly, proverbs abound in the lore of public opinion. We are told that there is no real public opinion on foreign policy—Congressmen often say that no one ever lost an election on the score of foreign policy—yet we are also told that "wars are made in the minds of men." Both statements partake of truth. We talk about the magic weapons of the "hidden persuaders," and, on other occasions, deplore the apparent inability of persuasion to overcome public apathy about such important causes as arms control.

Truth is more complicated than such proverbs, though not antithetical to them. The serious student of public opinion must start by making distinctions. There is a difference between public opinion in situations in which people feel effectual and situations in which, dealing with issues they cannot understand or with a regime they cannot effect, they feel impotent. There is a difference between public opinion on matters which affect the believer at first hand, e.g., unemployment or juvenile delinquency, and public opinion on matters known only through mediated experience.[1]

Foreign policy is generally a matter where knowledge is of the mediated kind. War, it is true, is part of the immediate experience of most of us but armament policy is not. The technical problems of arms control are an extreme example of an important public issue in which people are asked to judge things far outside their range of experience. Since our topic here is public opinion on arms control, what we need now to review is how public opinion is formed in circumstances in which the information the public receives consists of messages about things seen only in the mind's eye.

We have some knowledge of how people handle information when first-hand experience does not provide a guide. In part, they use homely analogs. People judge international disputes by reference to familiar principles about private quarrels, just as they reach conclusions about public finance by reference to familiar principles of household management.

Besides analogs, they use authority. Of the various types of authority, one is of transcendent importance. That is the behavioral model provided by an authority figure such as a head of state. (This point is discussed by Freud in *Group Psychology and the Analysis of the Ego*.)

The essential function of an authority figure in the shaping of public opinion is not the dissemination of information. Eight out of ten, or even ninety-nine out of a hundred of their countrymen would not normally know what Eisenhower or Khrushchev or de Gaulle or Nehru had said in his last major policy speech. More people, indeed, would know than if the same information had been disseminated by any other statesman, but for the sheer diffusion of information, speeches seldom compare with the headlines about the day's top news events. A satellite shot into space, a congressional filibuster, a lunch counter sit-down, or a U-2 shot down will outscore a Presidential speech on a public information test. True, there are exceptions. There were Roosevelt's fireside chats or Churchill's "blood, sweat and tears." But these were exhortations more than expositions. They were speeches which moved men's souls. There is power in the truly great orator, but his power as a leader of public opinion is even more important in other directions than it is in imparting information. His power is that he demonstrates how a man should act in the presence of the facts at hand.

Facts are only raw ingredients of public opinion, for facts do not talk for themselves. The learner needs guidance on how to interpret information and how to conduct himself in the face of it. It is for that reason that a behavioral model is crucial. Let us think back to when Soviet missiles were first reported to be making successful flights of intercontinental range. That was a fact disseminated in the press. Suppose the President of the United States had immediately called for emergency spending, had placed one-third of the Strategic Air Command in the air, and had himself started sleeping in a bomb shelter. The "fact" would have assumed quite different proportions than if the President found it barely worthy of comment, played golf, and left the budget untouched.

There are few limits to what a respected national leader can call on his people to do if by his own conduct he gives a model of appropriate response to the facts of a situation. In 1940 Winston Churchill, in magnificent prose, exhorted a people, whose armies were in full retreat, to act with heroic courage, promising neither hope nor reward. But no rhetoric could have turned the trick if Churchill had spoken with wavering voice or from a hiding place overseas. It was the character of the man and his personal conduct which carried the exhortation and provided the model of how to handle the facts he disseminated.[2] The miracle of British courage—a manifestation of public opinion—was inextricably linked to an extraordinary feat of leadership.

In much the same way the miracle of present American unconcern in the face of the danger of obliteration has been linked to another feat of leadership. In the decade of the fifties, the United States passed from being the foremost military power on earth with a monopoly of atomic power, consonant with its traditional self-image as fiercely competitive in striving to be the biggest, the strongest, and the best, to a nation for the first time under the constant cloud of destructibility. The might of America's nuclear arsenal was thus rendered useless as an instrument of policy except for deterrence of nuclear attack, for we lie open at all times to obliteration. Yet this dire decline of America in the world was accepted by the American people with utmost equanimity. There were no riots, no war party formed, no calls for impeachment. The stock market continued at reasonably high levels and a mood of confidence persisted. It is indeed a bit of a miracle, the explanation of which lies in the extraordinary behavioral model of serene self-confidence provided by the President who was in office. His peaceful mien, his insistence on normal behavior, effectively prevented any fact from becoming a signal for military alarm. This conduct enhanced America's reputation for peacefulness among the nations of the world. It probably lessened national security. But whether one approves or disapproves, it remains a feat of leadership.

The moral is that public opinion and leadership are joint products, not mathematical complements in which the more of one means the less of the other.

Public opinion, it appears, is something more than facts the public knows and values to which it adheres. There is a third ingredient, which may be described as the implication for personal action seen in the facts and values: how much attention should one pay them, what personal consequences are they felt to have, and what mode of behavior is seen as fitting in the light of them. For matters outside the spheres of men's private experience, the implications for personal action are largely derived by reference to the behavioral models provided by leaders. Among these reference persons the head of government is pre-eminent.

Such are some principles about public opinion when it operates in realms where the public has no first-hand experience. What are their applications to opinion on arms control?

There exists in the stock of information available to the American and

Russian people full evidence of the destructive potential of modern weapons. Surveys on civil defense in the United States have shown that public estimates of technical facts on the destructive power of thermonuclear weapons are, relatively speaking, not inaccurate. Apathy about nuclear warfare and failure to draw appropriate political conclusions are not the result of mere ignorance of weapons technology.

Furthermore, at least one value conducive to arms control exists in the public, the desire for peace. But, the presence in the public of such facts and such values does not determine what operational implications the public will draw. A further ingredient needed before public opinion will emerge as a significant force for arms control is leadership. On operational conclusions from the existing information, public opinion is amorphous, inchoate, ready to be led.

But ready as it is to respond to leadership, public attitudes toward arms control cannot be led by words alone. The public is not to be had for the asking or the ordering. It will draw its own conclusions consonant with the behavioral models offered it by those whom it respects.

INFLUENCING OPINION FROM ABROAD

One implication of the above discussion is that neither leader nor led is free in relation to the other. They are coupled parts of an interacting system. The leader who would shape opinion is constrained to behave in appropriate ways. And when he has succeeded in creating opinions he limits his further freedom to change his stand. What he has led the public to believe in, the public will demand. A Churchill-like stand destroys support for seeking compromise or an Eisenhower-like stand makes it hard to ask sacrifices. He who would shape public opinion must give hostages to it.

And so it follows, if we look at opinion and leadership as a coupled system, that the goal of foreign propaganda addressed to a country is to act on the system in that country, not on either of its halves alone. Propaganda efforts for arms control can, indeed, help to bend the course of nations and to make control more feasible. The main purpose of such a propaganda effort if it is to succeed should, however, not be to sell disarmament to the public as such but rather to commit the propagandizing governments themselves to the scheme for control and to make it more difficult for them to cheat.

Let us illustrate by reference to the effects of propaganda in quite a different recent situation: the American exhibition in Moscow.[3] The exhibit portrayed the consumer goods available to the American people. The Soviet propagandists felt constrained to reply. Soviet citizens, they said, have the same things, and to underscore the point they opened their own exhibition of Soviet cars, television sets, housing, etc., at the entrance gate to the American exhibit. To compete in the propaganda field, the regime itself became a perhaps unwilling agent of liberalization. Its propaganda sanctioned the demand of the Soviet public for more and better consumer goods and added to whatever pressures are put on Soviet military production by the people's urge for better living.

The planned purpose of the American exhibit, to convey an image of the American way of life, was of secondary importance in and of itself. What difference does it make how Russians visualize the daily life of an alien tribe dwelling 6000 miles away? But the portrayal became by indirection a powerful political instrument, for it forced Soviet domestic propaganda, at least temporarily, into that branch of the Soviet line more advantageous to American interests.

This example is not an odd, special case of propaganda trickery. It illustrates a mode in which international efforts to influence public opinion typically function. It is seldom that foreign propaganda operates to any great extent directly upon a people. There are circumstances in which it may, as when a revolutionary underground awaits word from outside. But the usual mode of impact of foreign propaganda is that a small volume of external communications serves as a catalyst to a specific and large flow of domestic messages. Commonly the catalyst works in the manner just illustrated; fear of losing a propaganda battle compels a regime to commit itself in ways or to degrees which it would not otherwise consider.

DO PUBLIC OPINION AND PROPAGANDA
AFFECT ARMS CONTROL?

But, it may fairly be asked, does it matter what a regime tells the public about arms control? Do public statements affect what diplomats may eventually achieve by way of agreement? And in particular does it matter in action what a totalitarian regime tells its people in propaganda?

The relevance of propaganda and attitudes to arms control has been underlined recently by the discussion of what is called, in Lewis Bohn's phrase, psychological inspection. A valid point in this discussion is that no inspection scheme is likely to succeed in the face of a unitedly hostile populace, set to deceive the inspectors and to protect their own government, whether it is cheating or not. Guerrilla warfare teaches a parallel lesson. Even a small conspiratorial minority cannot be suppressed when the populace favors them and will hide them in its midst. But guerrillas cannot survive if they cannot rely on at least passive support of the populace.

The analogy between antiguerrilla action and arms inspection holds. A cabal of cheaters (officially sanctioned or not) preparing a massive enough scheme for nuclear triumph would necessarily engage large numbers of persons in untoward activities which would come to the attention of even larger numbers of persons. This kind of cheating may work among a supportive population, antipathetic toward inspecting agencies. But every step which increases the probability that some individual or individuals will identify with the inspectors instead of with their government and will expose illicit activity makes such cheating harder and riskier.

Propaganda in support of the inspectors is such a step to jeopardize cheating. The propaganda which will make cheating hardest is propaganda in which a nation's own top officials repeatedly tell their people that it is their duty to cooperate with an arms-control and inspection system. If Mr. Khrushchev or his successor, in accordance with an international agreement, periodically lectured the Soviet people on their duty to open their portals to inspection for peace, if the Soviet law and the Party congress resolutions formally enunciated this obligation, it would become substantially harder to organize safe contrary activities even through the abundant covert channels of the secret police, army, and party. Not every *apparatchik* and technician would understand that the sacred words were to be taken as mere window dressing.

Of course, that image of future developments is fantastic. Like many arms-control ideas, there is no immediate prospect of agreement to a plan as far-reaching as that just mentioned. We have described admittedly extreme measures, but they are of interest because they are not all-or-none proposals.

Partial steps, either by competitive propaganda or by international agreement, leading to repeated and public proclamation of the legitimacy of inspection and encouraging full and fair cooperation with the inspectors, makes the successful hiding of violations less manageable. Conversely, a regime which protects its power to cheat by using propaganda to isolate or alienate its people from the agents of inspection casts doubts upon its true acceptance of controls and may cause others to back away from agreements and concessions. Thus, the Soviets, to gain the advantages which disarmament has for them, are under pressure to use their instruments of public persuasion in ways which lend support to systems of control. It is not easy for them to conduct an effective worldwide campaign for disarmament without thereby popularizing the idea in the Soviet Union too. And it is hard for them to go far in the direction of creating public support for disarmament without accepting the risks of popular support for effective controls. To some extent they may become prisoners of their own propaganda. Arms-control schemes can be designed to maximize that possibility.

CASES OF ENTRAPMENT BY PROPAGANDA

What we are proposing is not an innovation without precedent. On the contrary, national policies are constantly being entrapped by the demands of competitive propaganda. American policy has been forced by the demands of competitive propaganda to accept, at least tacitly, two themes of dubious value from our point of view, namely, peaceful coexistence and disarmament as distinct from arms control.

"Peaceful coexistence" as distinct from, say, "peaceful nonintervention" implies acceptance of Soviet domination in their Bloc. The duality of the coexistence image says in effect that not 50 or 80 nations may each peacefully choose its course, but that each of two systems may. That is a subtle redefinition of what constitutes the preservation of peace and what constitutes aggression, which, because of its propagandistic skillfulness, our side has not been able to reject.

Similarly, we have become bemused by the notion of disarmament as an economy measure. The prevention of nuclear warfare is far too important an objective to be entangled in matters of economy. The preservation of mankind is worthwhile even if it costs more than the present arms race —and it possibly will. The manning of an effective arms-control scheme may require a professional "unarmed service" comparable in size to a small armed service and expensively equipped. Such a service may require persons of high professional competence who will live under unpleasant circumstances in remote parts of the world, and who will have to be compensated accordingly. Add to that the cost of maintaining a secure second-strike capability, preferably in the hands of an international agency, to deter sneak attacks. Add to those items the further cost of whatever policing (international or other) against limited war is necessary, for the danger of small wars would probably grow if the deterring fear of starting a nuclear holocaust out of a small fracas were eliminated. Clearly, effective arms control may cost a great deal.

From the Soviet point of view such a costly arms-control effort would be partly self-defeating, for among their major objectives is to relieve themselves of the strain of armament spending. We, however, are rich enough wholly to subordinate the goal of economy to the goal of security for mankind. An expensive though effective system of arms control would be desirable for us.

But public opinion has not been brought to an awareness of the expense of effective arms control and our national policy suffers because of that. Appeals for arms reduction with the implication that they would mean economy have produced a public response in this country which imposes limitations upon our diplomacy. We have tended to accept a definition of arms limitations (proffered by the Russians, among others) in which it is assumed that banning of weapons is part of a complex including mutual trust, reduced tensions, reduced military expenses, and reduced military activity. And, conversely, it is believed that if hostility and tensions grow then arms tend to become unlimited and military budgets and activities to increase.

This analysis of the security problem is, however, simple minded. If tensions and differences were sufficiently relieved, perhaps instead of banning the bomb we could survive without abolishing nuclear weapons.

But if the bipolar conflict remains sharp, and wars remain probable events, then national survival will require the elimination of the large-scale use of the most dangerous weapons so as to permit the battling out of national differences without incurring the risks of total war. Or to put the same point differently: if by some miracle we and the Soviets were to mutually abolish our nuclear weapons, far from necessarily entering an era of good feeling, we might find ourselves having to increase our military effort to a fantastic degree so as to be able to deter Soviet invasion of, for example, Iran or Berlin with conventional weapons. In the absence of a nuclear danger, some checks to localized military action would be gone, and we might have to prepare for increased warfare even if we had regained the marvelous security, that in our time there would be no nuclear war.

While it is thus clear that abolition of certain weapons is not in any logical sense necessarily a part of reduction of tensions or of arms spending, these things are associated as one in the mind of the public. In public opinion the urge for disarmament arises from attitudes essentially antithetic to the burdens and processes of international politics. Disarmament is seen as an alternative to a responsible foreign policy. It is seen as an escape from the burdens of a national security effort. To those who find distasteful the nasty, tough, expensive processes of using national power for national objectives, disarmament presents itself as a pleasant alternative. It offers itself as a way in which we can with apparent impunity start behaving as liberal godly gentlemen, not only within the in-group of an organized society, but to all humanity. And at the same time it promises a release of resources for more civilized purposes than arms.

But the effort to achieve disarmament on such an irresponsible business-as-usual or moralistic basis is self-defeating, for in the end a nation will not thus risk its survival. Disarmament, if it is to be achieved at all, requires that at each step of the way each side have adequate assurances of military security. Abolition of particular weapons needs to be but part of a coherent security policy of which other parts include defense spending, military alliances, diplomacy, inspection, etc. Disarmament is a proper part of such a military security policy, for no nation can be secure in a world in which modern weapons are uncontrolled.

As long as the public is not made aware of this view of arms control, as long as disarmament is the slogan of those who would shuffle off the burdens of national security policy, and is correspondingly opposed by those who make our defense plans, it is hard for a democratic government to deal with disarmament realistically. The government is caught in the middle. On the one hand, the military become a pressure group against arms-control measures when the military should as part of their job be seeking those controls which maximize national security. On the other hand, to the extent that the government accepts disarmament defined as relaxation of defense, it undermines its ability to demand effort and sacrifice from the public for it is signaling to the public a condition of normalcy.

None of these things need be. Arms control could have been defined by the President as an arduous and expensive, but necessary security measure, and the public would have responded accordingly. But in the propaganda battle we were seduced into accepting a Soviet definition of the issue. We reject the Soviet proposals, but we discuss them in the same terms as they were offered: reducing tensions and reducing the arms burden.

PUBLIC OPINION IN THE SOVIET UNION

The reader may appreciate that a democratic government can be hamstrung by public opinion, but may doubt that this limitation also applies to the Kremlin. The usual view, that in Russia public opinion is nothing, has a superficial plausibility based on the fact—of course true—that the Kremlin elite does not share our ideology that the government should follow the desires of its public. They do, however, view public opinion as a force, and a dangerous force, to be taken carefully into account and manipulated. That is neither a democratic view, nor one of indifference or disregard. The dangerous force may be taken into account by brutal suppression, which is how public opinion against rural collectivization was handled. It may be taken into account by creating diversions or by camouflage. But to assume that such devices attest to an absence of interaction between public opinion and policy decision is to underrate seriously the role of public opinion in a totalitarian society.

Soviet leaders have always received detailed police reports on the state of opinion. More recently public opinion polls of a sort have been started in Russia. Evidence of sharp sensitivity even to minor waves of feeling is abundant. For brevity we note here but two points of evidence: (1) the attention paid by totalitarian regimes to molding public opinion; (2) the impact of Western cultural movements within Russia. The iron curtain is a porous one.

There is in Russia a vast press and radio network every word of which is carefully weighed, for Soviet *public* propaganda is a form of esoteric communication. *Pravda* articles are directives. They are not just noise irrelevant to a more important confidential communication system. On the contrary, what the public is told is treated as of vital importance. The struggles within the Soviet elite are largely carried out in terms of controversy about what criticism or praise of whom is to be allowed into the public press. When Lenin died the struggle was on his so-called testament: whether it would be acknowledged and published, and if so in which bowdlerized version. Khrushchev's struggle for power centered at one stage on how his title as first secretary of the Party should be printed— capitalized or not. The great purge trials of the 1930's were but an extreme form of the Soviet pattern of political struggle by public allocation of praise and blame. Clearly any action which can influence what statements the Soviet regime makes in public places has, in such a communication system, very great importance indeed.

The fact that public opinion is important in Russia, at least in that the regime behaves as if it is, is not enough to show that it can be manipulated by foreigners. But in fact totalitarian controls do not suffice to isolate Soviet thought from major concepts circulating in the world or from major news events.[4] Word-of-mouth channels are so effective that, for example, when Soviet defectors became disillusioned with their treatment at Western hands and returned in moderate numbers, the Soviet mass media did not publicize their complaints. The Soviet authorities realized that conversational reports would get around and would be accepted as more reliable than claims in the Soviet press. Also the elite are themselves a significant chink in the Soviet wall against foreign concepts. Those Soviet officials who travel, those who read foreign publications or monitor reports are deeply imbued with the notion of emulating and surpassing the West, but that implies following a path which has been defined by the West. The regime fails in its attempts to keep out interest in jazz, lipstick, TV, or French Impressionism. Political ideas of freedom continue to penetrate the Soviet wall and create sporadic ferment and dissent. The existence of such ideas becomes a fact of public opinion to which the Soviet regime does respond in some form even if only that of attack.

A PROPAGANDA PROGRAM FOR ARMS CONTROL

Among the propaganda options open to us, there are some which may make a difference to arms control. Specifically, propaganda devices may be among those used:

1. to open up Soviet society;
2. to add to the technical difficulties of surprise attack or arms-control violations;
3. to influence the internal political balance in the Soviet Union against elements with more strongly expansionist or dogmatic programs;
4. to reduce the chances of crises arising from miscalculation and ignorance of the facts;
5. to increase awareness of the disastrous consequences of nuclear warfare;
6. to increase awareness of the risks attendant on limited military actions; and,
7. to increase awareness of attractive opportunities for growth and success with arms limited and war prevented.

Of all these objectives, perhaps most important is the opening of Soviet society. True, there are dilemmas even about that goal, for the exposure of *defensive* weapons by penetrating their secrecy may make them less secure and thus be destabilizing. But what we fear from Soviet secrecy is an *offensive* capability which an open society would not have. As long as a great power retains such secrecy, long-term successful arms control is not conceivable. So, for arms control to succeed, secrecy among nations must become disreputable. A public opinion must arise, and be disseminated to the Soviet Union, one which accepts the equation, secrecy equals war, openness equals peace.

There is an inherent logic in our demand for inspection. By strongly posing the issue of inspection to provide security against surprise attack and by keeping discussion of that issue going in the world over a period of years, we would be able to make it a recognized consideration in internal Soviet opinion. The Soviet regime may not share our conclusions, but they will have to respond not only to our demands at the bargaining table, but also to an awareness of the force of these demands among themselves. They will in short have to find a debater's "answer" and incorporate it into their line. To that extent their strategic freedom is constrained.

Western strategy can be designed to compel the Soviet propagandists to deny to their people that the Soviet Union is a closed society enveloped in secrecy. Every pontifical statement by Soviet propagandists that there is no iron curtain, that they welcome visitors to see whatever they wish to see, that they do not prevent contact between their people and the West, and that the blame for closed areas and restricted travel is America's, is a triumph for liberalization and for those seeking effective arms control. Every statement, such as those following the U-2 incident, reaffirming the right to secrecy, condemning access as espionage, and hardening the defense of a closed society is a setback. To the extent that the Soviets deny that they are a closed society, they accept grounds for debate and magnify issues not of their choosing, which are favorable to realistic arms-control negotiations.

Likewise, it would be helpful if the Soviet leadership were repeatedly to assert publicly that nuclear warfare is suicide and that they would never launch a nuclear strike first. Clearly, such public statements could coexist (as they do) with a relatively covert military doctrine justifying a pre-emptive strike. Public promises are not assurance against deception. In nuclear warfare indeed the advantages are so loaded on the side of prevarication that an aggressor would hardly be inhibited by the consideration that world opinion (whatever was left of it) would realize that he had lied. This, in short, is about as hard a case as there is in which to demonstrate that public propaganda commitments make a difference. Yet, even in this instance, repeated public statements denying warlike intentions and condemning nuclear weapons have a constraining effect.

Such statements do several things. They make it more difficult to use nuclear blackmail in limited conflict situations because of the domestic anxiety which the threat to drop even one bomb on an enemy base might engender in a public thus indoctrinated. They strengthen the hand of

those factions in the Soviet internal debate on nuclear policy who have
concluded that nuclear strategy is a futile and dangerous game. (Such a
debate has taken place in Russia.) And finally, such statements may even
raise the complexity and expense of the communication and control
system needed by the Soviets to assure themselves of success in a first strike,
i.e., success of such certainty as to relieve them from anxiety about retaliation by residual forces. A simple attack system relies upon large numbers
of human beings understanding and obeying orders in the myriad operations involved in getting a massive firing off the ground. If any substantial
number of these persons have been affected by solemn public propaganda
as to how inconceivable it would be for their side to launch a war, there
may well be critical failures to understand or carry out orders at a number
of key places. (Studies have shown that a high proportion of soldiers
either do not fire or do not aim to kill when ordered to fire in battle.)
One way to reduce such failures of understanding or morale is to
whip up war fever in advance, but to do so is to surrender the advantage
of being able to launch an attack that is a complete surprise. A launching
system that could be counted upon to work at any moment despite widespread opposition to the launching of a first strike would have to use
extremely centralized electronic controls and would therefore need a high
degree of mechanical reliability. Setting up such a system would be both
difficult and expensive.

So there are good reasons for desiring the Soviet leadership to tell their
own people (as our leaders tell us) that their purposes are peaceful and
that they would not use their nuclear weapons in a first strike. The desire
for peace by the Soviet people is unquestionably a genuine grass-roots
feeling. The Soviet rulers have tried to capitalize on it by repeatedly
presenting themselves as peace-loving and as far as we can tell this element
of their domestic propaganda has been a success. The peaceful intentions
of the regime are apparently believed in. But even if a success, this propaganda is a constraint on the Soviet rulers. They are reinforcing the somewhat unsophisticated pacifism of their populace and thereby slightly limiting
their own alternatives.

There are still other ways in which propaganda addressed to the public
may facilitate the functioning of an arms-control scheme. One way is to
humanize the enemy and to inculcate a more differentiated image of him.
Let us consider how the character of the images of foreign nations may
affect strategic reasoning.

Any sane strategist views nuclear warfare as a last resort, if it is a
resort at all. As long as there seem to be possibilities for influencing the
course of enemy action, nuclear warfare will not seem attractive. Note, for
example, the debate in the United States a decade ago about preventive
war. The case *for* preventive war was that the military balance of power
would turn increasingly against us, and it has. The case *against* rested
upon the belief that Stalinist oppression instead of getting worse and worse

until an intolerable 1984 would give way either to revolution, or, as has begun to happen, to the creation of new bourgeoisie attitudes and strata and to the decay of the spirit of the revolution. Prospects of change from within made war an unattractive alternative. Only the view of Russia as an unmitigated blackness becoming blacker made war seem reasonable at all.

A second illustration of how the image of the enemy affects strategic thinking is offered by the problem of nuclear weapons in half-friendly theatres. If we think of the satellites as Communist countries we might use nuclear weapons in fighting over their territory, but if we think of them as allies to be liberated, we hardly could. Few of them would survive such liberation.

In short, the more pinpointed the enemy, the more restricted the targets, the more sense arms limitations may make even to military planners. This applies to Soviet planners too. A Europe containing strong Communist movements serving as fifth columns would be a target for which weapons of highly limited destructive potential would make more sense for the Soviets than would a solidly anti-Communist Europe. For Americans this sobering thought may be no reason for wanting Communists strong in Europe, though it might be a good reason to keep the Soviets adequately aware of the opportunities conceivably available there for the Left.

In Europe, in fact, the Communist prospects do not seem good enough for the Communists to take them very seriously. In Asia and Africa, however, they do, and it is clear that Soviet manners and the course of Soviet conduct are modified by a desire to bolster potential supporters who are recognized as significant forces in the population.

As a general matter, the more complex the image of the target, and the more aware the planner is of the possibilities of maneuver within the enemy sphere of influence, the less useful will unselective weapons of mass destruction seem. This is significant, for complexity of image is one aspect of public opinion which we do know how to influence. The evidence is strong that intercultural contact leads to increased differentiation of images. It does not always lead to friendship or liking. It may do the opposite. But it almost invariably leads to increased awareness of the complexity of individual and group characteristics. For this reason, East-West cultural exchanges are probably a powerful force favoring the prospect of ultimate arms-control agreements. Without necessarily increasing friendship, they may increase consciousness on both sides of the possibilities of subtle manipulations to influence the potential enemy's course of action as alternatives to such blunt concepts as massive retaliation.

One of the outcomes that may be most hoped for from the presence of arms inspectors in potential enemy territory is that they will provide more intimate and complicated interactions with the populace of the observed society than do present exchange missions. We should be concerned to avoid the isolation of the inspectors. For the long run progress of effective arms control, it is desirable that they be in as intimate contact as possible with the society in which they are stationed. It is often maintained that the Soviet regime could easily isolate inspectors. It could indeed isolate them, but not easily. It could do so only by a kind of terror which would prove once more to the Soviet people that their government does not trust them.

In the absence of vigorous terror the probability of Soviet citizen cooperation with foreign inspectors is at least as great if not greater than it would be in a free country. Alienation of the people from the regime has ever been a price of totalitarian control. The unrelieved din of propaganda for loyalty not only fails to stem alienation but is one of its sources. Alienation, it must be understood, is not lack of patriotism. It is distrust of the authorities and failure to identify with them; it is quite compatible with love of country. Those Russians who stuff unsigned notes into the hands of visitors, who criticize freely or are silent, depending on whether a third person is around, who talk of the government as "they," not "we," are not unpatriotic. They love their country and they also love peace with an emotional fervor at least as great as that of any other people. The evidence is that they also believe in "socialism."[5] But neither socialism, fatherland, nor peace is seen by alienated Russians, of whom there are many, as the same as that gang in the Party and government to whom they must adjust if they are to get along. True, a totalitarian regime has many weapons for intimidating the alienated and for creating façades of unity in public affairs. But any inspection device which opened up the possibilities of confidential contact between foreigners and alienated Russians would tap a great and vigorous stream of rumors, gripes, and disaffection which flows close beneath the surface of a totalitarian regime.

For that reason the Kremlin may be expected initially to reject free contact even though they have already admitted the principle of inspection. For the immediate future they will continue to label the free search for knowledge as espionage and for friendship as subversion. But we have the chance, by way of Soviet opinion, to make this an uncomfortable position to maintain. We can create an appealing ideology of the inalienable rights of friendship, of free movement, of an open world with open skies. If we conduct ourselves in ways which make the message meaningful, we may in time influence the coupled system of the Kremlin and Russian public opinion; we may move the Russian regime to counterpropaganda claims which may by halting and partial steps in turn lead toward practices which will enable us to know better whether arms controls are being observed. And this state of affairs will make it more probable that they be observed.

18. Non-Physical Inspection Techniques

LEWIS C. BOHN

PROGRESS IN ARMS CONTROL, AS IN OTHER MATTERS, REQUIRES THAT past thinking and past action should not determine future thinking or action. This chapter discusses some rather different approaches to arms-control inspection as compared with those considered in international negotiations hitherto or in most writings on arms control.* Many measures considered here may strike the reader as novel, drastic, and at first incredible; but the dangers of the nuclear age with which such techniques would be designed to cope are also novel, drastic, and at first incredible. The real question is, not that they are novel, but whether these techniques can indeed cope with these dangers.

"KNOWLEDGE DETECTION"

In the conventional image, a system for disarmament inspection consists of highly instrumented detection stations, perhaps equipped with radar, infrared, acoustic, seismic, and other detection devices, supplemented by mobile inspection teams in the air and on the ground, to seek forbidden installations or activities and to investigate suspicious events "on the spot." The inspectors are equipped with appropriate communication facilities to report their findings. The exact nature of the system will

* Many of the ideas in this chapter were first developed in the writer's internal memorandum at the RAND Corporation, January 12, 1956. They were presented verbally at a conference at Dobbs Ferry, New York, in June 1956. Some of the concepts were developed independently in the study edited by Seymour Melman, *Inspection for Disarmament* (New York, Columbia University Press, 1958), especially in the section by Melman, pp. 38–44. Similar concepts are also present in Grenville Clark and Louis B. Sohn, *World Peace through World Law* (Cambridge, Harvard University Press, 1958), especially pp. 261–262; and in Tom Slick, *Permanent Peace: A Check and Balance Plan* (New York, Prentice-Hall, 1958), especially pp. 79–80. A more recent version of the 1956 memorandum is the writer's paper, "Psychological Inspection," RAND P-1917, February 19, 1960. The present chapter has benefited from the work of Miriam Salpeter and others on "psychological inspection" (I now prefer the term "knowledge detection") at the Summer Study on Arms Control at the American Academy of Arts and Sciences, June–September 1960. Preparation of this chapter was supported by the Systems Research Center of the Lockheed Electronics Company, Bedminster, N. J.

vary rather widely with the nature of the violation it is designed to detect. Teams of accountants and experts on detecting forgery may be appropriate for monitoring the records of nuclear plants, while highly trained and equipped military and technical specialists may be required to detect a secret testing of a new missile, the launching of forbidden payloads into orbit around the earth, or a sudden surprise attack. But in every case, the focus is on discovering the violation itself: physical objects, installations, or activities which under the terms of the international arms-control agreement are prohibited. This conventional approach is sometimes called "physical inspection."

A very different approach to arms-control inspection is the following. Instead of focusing on the violation itself as a secret physical phenomenon, one can focus on *knowledge* concerning it, as a mental phenomenon in the heads of individual human beings. Instead of searching with various instruments and inspectors through whole countries or even in interplanetary space for devices or activities which have been prohibited, one can attempt to motivate those individuals who in one way or another learn of violations to bring their knowledge to the international inspection organization. Such individuals might include guards, scientists, clerks, accountants, explorers, aviators, police, technicians, and others. Also, for those few people "in the know" who may themselves have decided on a violation and therefore are unlikely to report it, one can attempt by various means and with full legal safeguards, to get at their knowledge of the violation even against their will, through judicial and other measures similar to those accepted in the United States for the detection of ordinary crime. Such a non-physical or "knowledge-detection" approach to arms-control inspection is by no means a panacea. But by giving a different coverage from the conventional approaches of physical inspection, with some chance of revealing violations that the latter are apparently unable to detect, it may be a very important part of an effective over-all system of inspection.

VOLUNTEERED KNOWLEDGE

We shall consider first the possibilities for motivating voluntary reports of violation to the international inspection organization. In democratic societies an appreciable number of citizens might report a violation of an international arms-control agreement, provided only that there was some way for them to do so. If the press is not under the control of the government, some journalists would probably gain and publish knowledge of violations, for a variety of motives. But the assurance that adequate information would reach the control organization would be small, even in "open" societies, especially if in the country concerned there was considerable popular feeling that violation of the agreement was for some reason appropriate and justified. And in police-state conditions, citizen reports of violation would be anything but automatic.

Conditions that might help motivate reports by individuals appear to be mainly the following. First, the successful operation of the control agreement, including its provisions for inspection, must be beneficial to the countries and peoples participating, and preferable to a collapse of the agreement or an evasion of the inspection system. For, unless it is an obvious fact that the success of the agreement is beneficial, there is too much danger that substantial fractions of the population will support a violation and not report what they may learn of it to the international authorities. Real patriotism, in other words, must clearly consist in reporting violations. While at first sight this may seem a somewhat difficult condition to meet, since the interests of the various countries involved in the agreement may well conflict at many points, it is in any case ("knowledge detection" quite aside) probably a requirement for the continued success of the agreement.

Second, all measures must be taken to explain why the agreement is beneficial and to give it official support. The purpose is to promote the necessary degree of popular support, and to avoid the possibility that a government wishing to violate its provisions secretly might give its people to understand that such secret violations were in the national interest, were approved by the government, and therefore should not be reported by those who might learn of them. The specific need is for a provision in the original arms-control agreement requiring all participating governments to pass laws making it a crime, punishable by domestic law, to violate the provisions of the arms-control agreement or to keep secret from the agency for international control any information of such a violation. Moreover, these provisions of the law of the land should be publicized by each government, and failure to support them by such publicity (or by other ways) should be declared to be a major violation of the control treaty.

Third, the legal penalties for keeping secret any knowledge of a violation of the control agreement might well be supplemented by rewards for reporting. If the information proved on investigation to be not only valid but of major importance, appropriate rewards might include large sums of money, lifetime pensions, possibly political office, medals, and even visas to live abroad for the informant and his designated relatives and friends. The solidarity of small groups conspiring to evade an arms-control agreement might be disrupted by a proper system of rewards far better than by threats of punishment or appeals to patriotism.

Fourth, there should be channels for the safe communication to the control agency of information on violations. One such channel would involve anonymous communications, mainly by telephone or by mail. Just as the police receive many tips on past crimes or on those being planned from individuals preferring to conceal their identity, so the international control agency might arrange to maintain mailing addresses and telephone offices in major cities and elsewhere. The freedom of these contact points from official or other interference could be tested by planted communications introduced by the control agency itself; if these failed to get through, investigation would be called for and action required of the country concerned to correct such interference. Most anonymous messages could of course be monitored by the host government, by wire-tapping or other techniques; but those reporting violations would have a reasonable chance of avoiding identification if they took sensible precautions, the nature of which might legitimately be publicized by the control agency.

Finally, it would be very useful to check the operation of the entire reporting system by having the international control agency introduce dummy violations. The over-all efficiency of the system could thereby be tested periodically and adjustments made as appropriate (perhaps even in the terms of the control agreement). More important still, an individual gaining knowledge of an apparent violation would have to allow for the possibility that it was a decoy object, installation, or activity deliberately planted by the control agency, and if he failed to report it, he would be subject to prosecution and legal penalty, provided it could be shown that he should have recognized it as a violation of the control agreement. A checking procedure of this sort, explicitly provided for in the control agreement, could in this way substantially improve the efficacy of the system it was checking.

In summary, the principal conditions tending to motivate reports of violations (or apparent violations) include: provisions in the control agreement making the agreement advantageous to the nations participating; the assuring of public support of the agreement by national governments; the establishment of legal penalties and rewards; the guarantee of the personal safety of informants; and permitting dummy violations to be introduced by the international control organ.

I would maintain that a system embodying these conditions could give a substantial, but by no means a guaranteed, probability that information of violations would be "volunteered" to the control agency. At a cost probably far less than that of the conventional highly instrumented "physical-inspection" measures which it would supplement, this component of a "knowledge-detection" scheme could give important leads on many types of violation. If large numbers of individuals were involved in a violation, the probability of receiving the relevant reports might approach certainty. An important case might be the concealment of prohibited missile sites. Burying the missiles and their associated installations so that they were undetectable by aerial or ground surveys or other "physical-inspection" systems might well be an entirely feasible operation. But it would also have to involve dozens, hundreds, or even thousands of individuals—and probably their families. "Knowledge detection" of such concealment would appear certain enough to deter the attempt. Or take another case: a nuclear test might be conducted on the far side of the sun, with results telemetered (by relay) to the testing country. Direct physical evidence of the test would be very difficult for the international inspection system to acquire. To conduct such a test in secret, however, would involve the launching of a major rocket vehicle (or vehicles) with secret payloads, the preparation of the nuclear device, the operation of the telemetering equipment, the interpretation of data, the application of the results, and decisions to undertake the whole operation, probably involving scientists, military men, and politicians. Again, the number of people with knowledge of an attempted violation must apparently run into tens or hundreds; and the success of an appropriate "knowledge-detection" system appears quite likely. Much the same situation appears to hold, incidentally, for a nuclear test conducted underground with proper "decoupling": in terms of knowledge detection, this is a sort of combination of the two cases just discussed.

In addition to its giving some prospect of uncovering violations which might otherwise escape an inspection system, knowledge detection gives unique coverage in the dimension of time. Let us suppose that the present moratorium on nuclear tests is formalized in an agreement: as of some initial date, neither the United States, the USSR, nor Britain will conduct any nuclear tests. Let us suppose further that it is only at some later date that an agreed world-wide test-monitoring system is installed, giving a physical-inspection capability for at least those tests above a certain yield conducted in the vicinity of our planet (including underground). At that same later date a knowledge-detection system of the sort we have described is also installed in these countries, as a supplement to the physical-inspection system and perhaps serving other (and more important) arms-control functions than the monitoring of nuclear tests. Not only might this system detect nuclear tests attempted at the later date *regardless of their yield or proximity to the earth:* it could also give information on violations of the agreement attempted *between* the initial date and the later date. It might do still more: it might yield information on a *contemplated* violation of an agreement, for which preparations were either under way or perhaps had only reached the discussion stage among a substantial number of people. For the knowledge of violation may be the knowledge of preparation, or even of mere intent. The conditions sketched earlier could motivate reports of violation well before "signals" could possibly be present in conventional inspection devices.

The contrast with conventional physical inspection is rather dramatic. In the latter, the violation may transmit a "signal" to the control organ that is brief in duration and appreciable only in the immediate vicinity. (Consider as typical "violations": nuclear explosions, missile tests, concealed nuclear stockpiles, concealed missile sites, biological or chemical gas weapon research or stockpiles, military training, surprise attack, etc.) The nature of the signal is entirely dependent on the nature of the violation, and the devices and techniques used to detect it. The signal can be hidden, muffled, jammed, decoyed, or otherwise interfered with at the choice of the violator. What it is, where it occurs, and when it occurs is largely controllable. But the "signal" from volunteered knowledge may be quite different. Because it is in the minds of human beings, it has a nature of its own, a location of its own, and a peculiar durability. It exists in various different places simultaneously and continuously. If the proper motivating conditions have been created, any of these embodiments may take an active initiative and bring itself to the attention of the international control agency. The signal that does reach the control agency is only partly dependent on the nature of the violation and only partly controllable by the violator (he can influence who knows how much), and his assurance of adequate secrecy may be small, since partial knowledge—or even mere suspicion—may do the job. Instead of an infinity of places and methods for the concealment of his violation, a violator may confront tens or hundreds of possible active "carriers" by which a signal may reach the control agency.

But of course there are problems.

The information collected by any inspection system must be processed, evaluated, and interpreted before it is of value. For knowledge detection, this is especially important, since the "signals" are not direct physical evidence of violation but only "leads." They must be followed through, to see if they are leads to actual violation or merely false alarms. (Follow-throughs are also necessary for some physical-inspection data. For example, seismographic signals may be from an earthquake; only on-the-spot investigation can establish, in some cases, whether they were caused by a nuclear detonation.) This is a major reason for using knowledge detection as a supplement to physical-inspection procedures, rather than by itself: unless there are means for on-the-scene investigation or some other appropriate follow-through, it will be impossible to establish the validity of reports of violation, and they will be all but worthless. The approaches to arms-control inspection discussed in this chapter should therefore not be imagined to circumvent the need for free access to places, installations, or people, which is a basic requirement—and a politically difficult one—in more conventional inspection systems as well.

Furthermore, just as a seismic (or other) signal from a nuclear test may be masked by a background of signals from other sources, so too there may be a high level of false reports in a system relying for its "signals" entirely on the impressions, reactions, and motivations of human beings. Indeed, since (one hopes!) there would be very few or no real violations of the control agreement, all or nearly all the reports received would turn out to be false alarms. One serious problem this raises (inherent also for many physical-inspection techniques) is to keep the inspection system and its personnel thoroughly alert and sensitive to the chance that the *latest* signal is of a real violation, when in the past most or all have been false. Another problem is that a violator may deliberately introduce false signals, both to lull the inspectors and perhaps to jam the system with a serious overload. The combination of incentives and punishments described earlier might well encourage anyone with even a faint suspicion to report it; a high data-handling capacity would therefore be a requirement of the system in any case. Deliberate false alarms could in general be tracked down and penalized. But the arrangements for anonymous tips would be very vulnerable to abuse by violators, pranksters, cranks, and others, and present a real problem, because penalties for deliberate false alarms cannot be imposed, their source being unknown. But perhaps a rise in the frequency of anonymous tips beyond the normal level (which the system must be able to handle) would itself at least be useful evidence of "foul play."

In order for information on violations to be likely to reach the control agency, those individuals having the information must be (1) fairly numerous, (2) effectively motivated to report their knowledge, and (3) able to report it. We have suggested how motivation and ability to report may be furthered by appropriate provisions in the agreement and other arrangements, and we have mentioned several inspection problems which (though almost inaccessible to conventional physical approaches) appear to involve substantial numbers of people. There remains the fact that some important violations (for example, the concealment of nuclear materials) might involve very few individuals; some or all of those involved might themselves have initiated the violation, and be determined not to report it; and the ability of any waverers to report might be drastically curtailed by the simple expedient of their enforced confinement or their murder. However, certain factors tend to counter this problem, at least partially.

WITHHELD KNOWLEDGE

The "knowledge-detection" approach may have relevance even in the more difficult arms-control inspection problems, through the development and application of techniques able to get at information even though the person involved may wish to withhold it.

A major point here is that there is a relatively small and identifiable group of individuals in each country, among whom there is very likely to be—and possibly must be—one or more individuals with knowledge of any major and deliberate violation of an arms-control agreement.

Prominent among this group are top-level political decision-makers: president, dictator, cabinet, or presidium members, behind-the-scenes "strong men," etc. In general, these are the individuals most directly responsible for the military and national security posture and decisions of their state. Having this responsibility, whether it is democratically entrusted to them by the people or assumed autocratically, they will have a direct interest in the fullest possible understanding of their country's strategic position and of the military capabilities that are or are not available for their use. A dictator, especially, is unlikely to permit the retention or development of important military capabilities that are beyond his control or knowledge.

Despite their strong concern, these national decision-makers might conceivably still be ignorant of the existence of a violation. But the point is that, if the national decision-makers do not know about it, they cannot make use of it. For a violation to have political or military significance in the international arena, it *must* first be known to a national ruler (or rulers). Of course, he may know few if any details. But he would have to know the general nature and dimensions of the violation if it is to be of any potential use to him and if he is to be able to prevent its use as an internal threat to his political power.

Other identifiable individuals of interest belonging to this group include lesser but still important members of the governing elite: political figures, top military men, and perhaps industrialists, bankers, and others, who in the Communist image (at least) have political influence in "capitalist" society. These "second-rank" personalities would probably include a substantial number who in greater or lesser measure would have knowledge of a significant violation of an arms-control agreement. However, if it became necessary to keep such information from them in order to maintain secrecy from techniques of knowledge-detection inspection, this might in many cases be arranged. The role of this group is therefore not so critical as that of the first.

Finally, certain types of violations would require the participation of one or more top-level scientists. If the identity of a country's able scientists is known to the outside world (in China, for example, this may soon not be the case), then those whose specialty might be required for the particular type of arms-control violation to be detected should be included in the key group to be surveyed by knowledge-detection techniques.

The result is that it would be possible to draw up for each major power an agreed list of possibly one thousand * individuals in that country who would be candidates for this type of inspection. My assertion is that a violation of an arms-control agreement that could be of sufficient significance to threaten world security or otherwise be of international political or military importance would be known to at least one member of this group, and in all probability to more than one. (If the number "in the know" is tens or hundreds, then there is a reasonable chance for the operation of the techniques of volunteered knowledge discussed earlier.)

The significance of this fact is that in contrast to the typical physical-inspection situation, where a violation may be in any one of millions of places, we have knowledge, in an important sense, of "where to look." We have a relatively well-defined and identifiable group of people, not

---

* This number might easily be ten times larger or smaller; it could be less for smaller or economically less developed countries than for the major powers.

too many in number, who have knowledge of a violation. If we can develop good methods of surveying and detecting the knowledge of these key groups in each country, we have a whole new approach to arms-control inspection.

And it does appear as if a moderate research effort might be able to achieve this end. The main hope appears to lie in the application of advanced scientific techniques in measuring the physiological reactions of an individual as he is questioned (under elaborate safeguards discussed below) about his participation in, or knowledge of, a violation of an arms-control agreement.

We already know that there are many aspects of the human system that react to emotional strain, and that many of these reactions are not subject to conscious control. It was observed many centuries ago, for example, that some individuals who are deliberately lying may experience a sudden blush or pallor; that is, the pattern of their blood circulation suddenly changes. The eyes of the deliberate deceiver may shift; his Adam's apple may jiggle; his hand may shake; his pulse may rise; his breathing may change its normal rhythm; his speech may falter. Such phenomena have long been known because they can readily be noticed, at least by a trained observer familiar with the subject: the perceptive parent may become something of an expert in the deception behavior of his child. But today these same phenomena can be observed and recorded objectively through the use of "electric eyes," optical devices of various sorts, a variety of instruments highly sensitive to motion, standard devices for measuring blood pressure, microphones to monitor heart or other muscle action, etc. And new devices, some of them only recently invented, now enable the continuous monitoring of activity in the human body, formerly undetectable and in some cases unimagined. Moreover, the use of sophisticated techniques (e.g., highly miniaturized radio receivers or transmitters) permits the measurement of most or all of these without major discomfort to the subject. In this category of newly observable body reactions we have "brain waves," skin resistance (a function of sweat-gland action), skin potential, the oxygen content of the blood stream, the physical and chemical action of the stomach, salivary action, muscle tension, radio-wave emission from the muscles (only recently discovered), and probably others.

Very little scientific investigation has been undertaken as to the relation of these physiological responses to the truthfulness of a subject's response under questioning. The efforts that have been made in this general area have mostly been crude and unscientific, and directed toward immediate application in the so-called "lie detector." Early in this century, simple measurements of pulse rate, respiration, or blood pressure were found to have some correlation with whether a subject was attempting to conceal information from an interviewer. More recently, the measurement of skin resistance (also known as the galvanic skin response or GSR, and psychogalvanic response or PGR) has also been used. The results achieved by these crude techniques indicate that there is indeed a correlation between physiological responses and attempted concealment. The claims of some of the practitioners of "lie detection" are frequently impressive: often a reliability of 80 or 90 per cent is alleged, and sometimes a much higher per cent.

But such claims are very suspect. Field data, where the emotional involvement of the subject is real, have rarely been gathered under controlled conditions. Laboratory efforts fail to simulate the real situation. The interpretation of the recorded data has involved a large measure of subjective judgment. Users of "lie detectors" in police work, private investigation, industry, and elsewhere frequently have a vested interest in the results. Manufacturers of the equipment naturally want to sell it. The operators and interpreters of the results are often poorly trained, unsophisticated, and inexperienced. Frequently, the real objective has been to impress a criminal suspect with the infallibility of the "machine," and thereby encourage his confession. Wide-ranging questioning may violate the personal rights of the subject, or create the fear of such violation. Frequently the only apparent safeguard has been for the subject to refuse the "lie detector" (or "polygraph") test altogether.

The unfortunate but inevitable result is that the physiological measurement of veracity has earned itself a very bad name. "Lie detectors" have come to be associated with "police-state" methods, the "third degree," violations of constitutional rights, and assaults on personal dignity. Evidence obtained in this way is frequently not admissible in legal proceedings. Public denunciation of such methods has extended even to the Soviet Union. L. N. Smirnov, deputy chairman of the Soviet Supreme Court, was quoted in connection with the trial of U-2 pilot Francis Gary Powers as asserting that "such methods as using lie detectors and brain washing techniques are loathesome to our legal ideals." (One hopes they are also loathesome to MVD practice.)

A vicious circle has developed. There is little incentive to do the necessary scientific research when the entire subject is so distasteful. And in practical application, there is little incentive for properly qualified and well-trained individuals to become involved, when the subject is so grossly deficient in scientific basis and so generally lacking in prestige.

My suggestion is that if a carefully designed, well-financed, full-scale research effort is undertaken, it *may* be possible in the course of a very few years to improve vastly the reliability of the whole process, and to reduce or eliminate the need for subjective judgment in interpreting the results. I would contend further that it appears possible to devise appropriate safeguards that can fully protect the legitimate rights of those few individuals who might be "surveyed" with these techniques for the purpose of arms-control inspection. All in all, there is a reasonable chance of lifting an unsavory business to scientific and social respectability, and of putting it to very valuable use.

An appropriate research effort would include the following. Methods for an accurate and painless measurement of physiological responses should be further developed, with the full application of newly available techniques for chemical, mechanical, electrical, radio, and optical measurement. Efforts should be made to discover still further kinds of physiological reactions than the already impressive list known at present, and to monitor these. More and more of these variables should be measured simultaneously, extending far beyond past "polygraph" techniques of measuring two and sometimes three variables. Intensive efforts should be made to process and interpret the total data resulting from these simultaneous measurements, rapidly and automatically, with little or no requirement for human judgment in the interpretative process. Intensive efforts should be made to understand what it is that we are measuring, why the measured variations occur, and the relation to the personality, the social and cultural environment, and the physiological makeup of the particular individual, and in general to improve our whole comprehension of relevant theory. On the "input" side, various techniques of presenting questions should be studied, drawing heavily on the techniques developed over the centuries by lawyers, and even by parents, and experts at "twenty questions." A questioning technique that should be further explored is the so-called "peak of tension." In the arms-control situation this might take the form of presenting a subject with lists of items, to one or more of which a noticeable "signal" should be detected if the subject had information on a violation. Such lists might include the names of people who might conceivably be involved, of research institutes, of dates, of types of violation or sections of the control agreement, of different types of weapons, of different geographical areas, and so forth. Possibly the modern developments in theoretical logic could be applied to the questioning process, to reduce the ambiguity of questions and increase their susceptibility to a "yes" or "no" answer. In this and perhaps in other ways, it may be possible to develop almost as much specific, detailed information on a violation as a subject may possess, even though these techniques at best cannot achieve "mind reading," but only an indication of whether a "yes" or "no" response is given honestly or otherwise. It might even be desirable to investigate other types of material than questions: fictional accounts of violations of the control agreement, for example.

As part of the over-all research effort, a thorough study should be made of countermeasures—and counter-countermeasures. Even though many physiological responses are not under the subject's conscious control, they can be conditioned to take various forms, or even to become controllable. A subject with knowledge of a violation might be made to "forget" his knowledge by hypnosis. Other countermeasures are conceivable and must also be prepared against, since they would be exploited to the fullest by a group attempting to conceal its evasion from this form of knowledge detection. In some cases counter-countermeasures can be devised. It is frequently possible to detect whether an effort has been made to affect the responses, and this in itself could be a serious violation. Perhaps the principal hope would lie in maintaining a most active research program under the control of an international agency, whose competence could be expected greatly to exceed that of individuals in a particular country who were attempting to conceal an evasion. One may with reason hope that it will turn out to be a very formidable task to condition or otherwise interfere with as wide a range of physiological responses as could be measured simultaneously with the full application of the new techniques. If the extensive research that must be done on this problem should show that the countermeasure problem cannot be coped with adequately, then clearly this whole "polygraph" approach would be less valuable for arms-control inspection.

As for the equally important question of safeguards: the first point is that unless the technical capability of these approaches is very high (including the ability to cope with countermeasures), they would not be used at all. Therefore, there would be very much less danger that the data obtained was false than is the case with present "lie detectors." Assuming there still was some margin of error, its existence would be fully appreciated and due allowance made before any application of the results. If the technique is known to have a reliability of (say) approximately 95 per cent, then the appearance of five "deceivers" in every hundred individuals surveyed will by no means lead to the assumption that they are involved in a genuine violation; before action can be taken against these individuals or against their country, further investigation must have developed corroborative evidence. The range of questions or other subject matter to be presented to each individual would be carefully defined beforehand, in the treaty or by appropriate vote of the control commission. Perhaps a list of questions to be asked would be presented beforehand to each subject, as has been found quite feasible in "lie detector" investigations. The quality and training of the questioners and of all others involved in the operation should be above reproach. The very highest quality in technique and personnel could be reserved for studying those individuals for whom a preliminary survey indicated some questionableness. The individual and his government could be given every right to cross-examine any of those examining him or interpreting the technical data, and to challenge the procedure, the data obtained, or the means of interpreting the results. As in the case of more conventional inspection systems, when disputes arose, they would have to be settled by commissions, boards, tribunals, or other groups formally established for this purpose under the control agreement. In these and other ways, safeguards comparable to those developed over many hundreds of years to protect individual rights in more conventional legal proceedings would be developed for this novel context and new technology.

I suggest that a procedure based on this kind of thorough scientific-research program, occurring only if that research leads to positive results (including a satisfactory solution to the problem of countermeasures), and surrounded by carefully elaborated safeguards, would be a very far cry from "lie detector" techniques. And the negative connotations surrounding the latter might well give way in this "knowledge-detection" operation to highly positive ones. The subjects of the process would themselves be a very distinguished group, including in their number all the most influential and important political and military figures, and perhaps some very distinguished scientists. The examiners should also be a distinguished group, including perhaps international figures in the law, diplomacy, the physical sciences, psychology, anthropology, and perhaps other fields. If technically appropriate and consistent with proper safeguards for the subjects, the proceedings might be held in the presence of other government officials, distinguished citizens, and visitors and witnesses from many countries. The investigations would be held at intervals appropriate to the types of violation which it is desired to detect, but in any case each round would be a major event.

No doubt some of the subjects would nevertheless regard the procedure more as a nuisance and an inconvenience than as a tribute to their personal positions in their countries. But what there was of such inconvenience might more properly be considered the legitimate price to be paid by these select individuals for the positions they have attained or accepted in the political, military, scientific, or business life of their country. In the event of an elaborate physical-inspection system, some of these same individuals, and many more of their compatriots at lower prestige levels, would be called upon to make much greater personal sacrifices in manning remote inspection posts for long periods of time. In any case, the price is very much less than the price they would be called upon to pay, along with millions of their fellow citizens, in the event of major war. I suggest that it is a wholly reasonable price for them to pay for the opportunity to make a real contribution in preventing war by sustaining the arms-control agreement.

ACCEPTABILITY AND APPLICATION

The knowledge-detection approach to arms-control inspection is a distinct departure from the more conventional physical inspection that has generally been considered in the past. It may therefore seem too novel and extraordinary to be realistic or acceptable. But care must be taken not to exaggerate this novelty, or to be too hasty in concluding that these techniques would be less acceptable than physical inspection.

We now have tips on income-tax evasion, smuggling, and other crimes, at the same time as we have a generally effective secrecy as to military affairs, industrial secrets, personal scandals, and social lies. In general, wherever the tip deals with an illegal act—especially one of obvious gravity, such as kidnapping or murder—it is fully sanctioned, both legally and socially. An arms-control treaty, once ratified by the Senate (or by the corresponding procedure in other countries), becomes the law of the land, quite equal to laws against treason, kidnapping, murder, etc. To report a violation of an arms-control agreement that might threaten millions of lives should be as legally and socially acceptable as to report a violation of the laws against kidnapping and murder. Nor does the high station of the violators give them special privilige: we do not accept corruption, tax evasion, or worse crimes among political leaders, prominent military men, or scientists; no more need we grant them immunity for secret violations of the terms of an arms-control agreement. Just as there are legal channels for the revision of domestic laws if they are unjust and improper, so also there could be legitimate channels for the modification of an arms agreement, or withdrawal from it altogether. Violation of the one law is no more justified than the violation of the other; and encouraging tips on violation is equally feasible and appropriate.

The novel element is, of course, that the reporting is done, not to the domestic authorities, since these may be under the control of those planning the violation, but to the international authority. To report the corruption of the municipal police chief to one of his policemen is less likely to bring satisfactory results than to report it to a state or federal authority. Nor are the "withheld knowledge" aspects of knowledge detection without their parallels in common usage. Again, because the physical-inspection task is very difficult or simply impossible for many crimes, such as smuggling, tax evasion, or kidnapping, all countries accept as part of their legitimate legal procedures the intensive questioning of suspects and witnesses, conducted usually in open court under elaborate safeguards. The judge or jury observes as closely as possible the reactions of those questioned, in full recognition of the fact that clues as to the truthfulness of the testimony may be revealed by the unconscious and sometimes uncontrollable behavior of those on the stand. And, outside the legal framework, we do have the press conferences of top political officials, including the President, in which questions are asked freely and physical reactions observed closely. On the Soviet side, Mr. Khrushchev, too, has exposed himself to wide-ranging questioning, often with a television audience of none-too-friendly millions.

Although the shortcomings of the lie detector have rightly prevented its general acceptance in legal proceedings, it has been both useful and unobjectionable as an accepted means to check petty larceny by employees in banks and other commercial enterprises. If the time comes when the measurement of physiological reactions becomes a valid and reliable indicator of truthfulness—perhaps as a result of intensive research directed toward knowledge detection in arms inspection—it may take on a role of honor and real importance in criminal proceedings. Like all inventions, this one can be used either to jeopardize human rights and aspirations, or to defend and strengthen them.

Even if they do have counterparts in the domestic context that are useful and at least partially accepted, do knowledge-detection techniques really have any chance of acceptance in the context of international agreements for arms control? Would any national government take them seriously as part of a genuine arms-limitation proposal?

First, it must be pointed out that the position of a particular government on a particular proposal is obviously a function of many other things than the methods proposed for inspection. Who made the proposal? What arms limitation does it envisage? How would these affect national security if they are strictly observed by all? How, if they are not? What are the probable political, economic, and social consequences of the agreement? And so forth. Only if the balance *on the whole* seems favorable will a given scheme be acceptable.

Part of this assessment involves the inspection system. Here, some of the questions to be weighed are: What is its ability to detect violations? Can it adapt successfully to new scientific developments? What will it cost? How long will it take to install? How many people and installations will it bring into the country? What other ways might accomplish the job of inspection more satisfactorily?

The introduction of arms-control inspection systems into any country raises many problems and difficulties. In a conventional, physical-inspection system there is the presence of many "foreigners," with privileged status, and perhaps with rights of free travel and access to normally secret or private military, transportation, industrial, or scientific installations. There are special communication systems, perhaps elaborately instrumented inspection posts, interpreters, supply systems, and headquarters buildings. There may be provisions for the families of the inspectors. The over-all bulk of the inspection operation depends, of course, on the specific tasks it must perform. A variety of disputes can be expected, from arguments over the abuse of no-parking zones and allegations of discrimination in housing to top-level disagreements on whether there has been a deliberate interference with the legitimate functioning of the inspectorate, whether the latter has interfered in domestic affairs, whether an apparent violation is one in fact, etc., etc. And there is an unending task of developing and modifying the inspection operations to keep up with new weapon systems, new possibilities for evasion, and new possibilities for more effective or more economical inspection.

The increment of physical difficulties added by knowledge-detection systems does not seem unduly large. The installations needed for gathering volunteered information would be relatively modest, even if privileged locations for diplomatic sanctuary were established quite widely. The follow-through investigation of tips, if it depended mainly on the physical-inspection system, would provide an additional burden which is difficult to estimate at present, but that might be large. Possibly some of it could be done with polygraph techniques. Checking the special groups in each country for withheld information (assuming this turns out to be technically feasible) would occur only periodically and might be done in borrowed facilities in each country's capital, or at one or more permanent international centers established for the purpose. The permanent personnel needed even in a large country might run into the hundreds, and they would be able to handle a very comprehensive arms-limitation agreement for which the physical-inspection operations would require many thousands.

The distinctive new problem presented by knowledge-detection techniques is political. To give individuals an officially encouraged channel for direct communication with an international agency is obviously an important addition to normal political structure and "chain of command." And certainly it would be a political innovation to monitor the physiological responses of eminent persons while they were being questioned about possible violations of an international agreement. One may indeed ask whether national governments will accept such changes voluntarily. But we may hope that if they are called for, at least they will be accepted by those governments more responsive to the popular will and to the needs of the times.

One may well wonder whether more autocratic governments will be even as favorably inclined toward knowledge detection as they have been toward more conventional physical arms-inspection techniques, which themselves may appear to offer unacceptable threats to the present regime's political power. Certainly safeguards must be used to see to it that knowledge detection invades the legitimate rights and prerogatives of states no more than those of individuals. For example, only volunteered information that bears directly on possible violations of a control agreement should be accepted and processed by the control agency; and the questions asked officials and others must be similarly limited. It is interesting that Premier Khrushchev has apparently accepted at least the principle of volunteered knowledge.* As for the measurement of physiological reactions as an indicator of truthfulness under questioning, it is at present (in the absence of the necessary research) such an uncertain and suspect technique that it should not now be accepted for arms inspection by any government, democratic or autocratic—any more than it is at present acceptable in domestic legal proceedings. If future research develops this technique into one that is scientifically valid and reliable, its acceptance may extend in all countries to arms-control inspection—or it may not. Perhaps it would improve both

* According to a report by Harrison E. Salisbury in the *New York Times* (September 27, 1960), "During a question-and-answer period, Mr. Khrushchev was asked by a scientist [David Hill] whether he would be willing to agree on turning the whole population into an inspection force, reporting any violation of disarmament to an international control agency. The idea would be that populations of all countries would be educated to detect and report violations. 'I solemnly assure you on behalf of the Soviet government,' Mr. Khrushchev said, 'that I accept all that was set forth by the distinguished scientist here, and I am ready to undersign such a proposal at any time.' " [Khrushchev subsequently reaffirmed both this position and his understanding of the measures envisaged in private conversations with Leo Szilard.—ED.]

its scientific and political prospects if there were international participation in the necessary research from the start.

If the balance of gains and drawbacks of a specific arms-control proposal appears on the whole favorable, it is probably unlikely to be rejected simply because it uses knowledge-detection techniques in its inspection system. If the Soviet government, for example, could accept a full panoply of physical inspection as a necessary accompaniment of a complete and general disarmament scheme, would it draw the line at all non-physical measures? This is perhaps made less likely by the peculiar features of knowledge detection discussed earlier: broad coverage, flexibility and adaptability, economy, and relatively small requirements in personnel. Unless Communist governments are prepared to trust fully the adherence of the "capitalist" governments—and of their own major allies—to the terms of an arms agreement, these features may be not without appeal to them as well as to others.

At the same time, for several reasons it does seem likely that knowledge-detection methods will be applied to the more advanced measures of arms control rather than to more modest preliminary measures. Soviet acceptance of thoroughgoing inspection of any sort has for some years been declared conditional on Western acceptance of thoroughgoing arms limitations. Since knowledge-detection measures so readily cover a wide range of limitations, it somehow seems wasteful to apply them only to a single one. The installations and personnel they require, while modest relative to elaborate physical-inspection requirements, may be physically and (especially) politically conspicious if used only (for example) to monitor nuclear tests.*

But if it is to the arms-limitation measures of the more distant future that these inspection approaches are chiefly relevant, this may also be to their credit. For without such approaches it is increasingly difficult to envisage the effective inspection and enforcement of the more throughgoing disarmament arrangements, and it is partly for this reason that progress toward them has been so slight. In terms of physical inspection, the world has already passed the point of no return relative to nuclear weapons, since no physical instruments are capable of locating hidden stockpiles of nuclear materials; it appears about to pass this same point relative to long-range ballistic missiles, which soon may be buried beyond the scope of known detection systems; and biological and chemical weapons present at least as much of an inspection problem.

These technical difficulties have been cited by both East † and West as reasons for turning to the more limited measures of arms control. Knowledge-detection techniques find no particular difficulty with the inspection

---

* If polygraph research gives positive results, I confess I would see much value in applying these techniques to top political, military, and scientific figures for the single purpose of nuclear test inspection. Especially interesting would be its ability (if this were desired) to "detect" past tests, as well as those planned weeks or months in the future, regardless of yield or location of burst.

† Notably in the Soviet proposal of May 10, 1955.

problems cited, nor with any others: whatever can be specifically pro-
scribed by a control treaty can become the subject of tips from the populace or the polygraph questioning of elites. If these techniques can be made
to work for any violations, they will work for all. This is of course a main
reason for advocating their thorough investigation and development. It
may also be a reason for resuming serious attention, in study and eventually in negotiation, to more complete disarmament measures, with all their
unmatchable advantages—and with the problems they present, even if
they can be effectively inspected.

19. Adjudication and Enforcement in Arms Control

LOUIS B. SOHN

THE PURPOSE OF THIS CHAPTER IS TO EXAMINE THE PROBLEMS OF AD-judication and enforcement in the context of a limited agreement on arms control. Its premise is, therefore, that one or more agreements will be concluded, providing for various measures of disarmament and for their effective supervision and control, but not for a complete system of world law.

Among friends, a pledged word is sufficient and there is no need for the establishment of a complicated machinery for the adjudication of disputes or the enforcement of decisions. But, in a situation where mutual trust does not exist, where suspicions are rife, and many disagreements are likely to arise, adequate methods must be provided in advance for the settlement of disputes and for ensuring compliance with both the basic rules and the decisions rendered to implement them.

The record of past relations between the nations of the Atlantic community and the Soviet bloc shows the importance of inserting in an agreement as many precise provisions as possible, leaving little to future determination. It is evident that even the relatively simple problem of the suspension of nuclear tests will require a long and detailed treaty. A comprehensive agreement on arms control is likely to be at least as detailed as recent agreements in the economic area, such as the treaty establishing the European Economic Community, which is some 150 pages long.[1] It is not possible, however, to foresee all the probable difficulties, and means must be found to deal with them in an adequate manner.

It would destroy the effectiveness of a treaty on arms control if any party to it were permitted to decide on the scope of its obligations. While each party to the treaty would like to limit its obligations to a minimum, it desires at the same time to impose as strong obligations as possible on the other parties. Treaty provisions are usually reciprocal, and impose equal obligations on all parties. In order to achieve the desired measure of control over other parties, each party must accept some limitations on its own freedom of decision. The ordinary way of achieving such control is to entrust to a third party the power to interpret the treaty in case of a disagreement between the parties.

ALTERNATIVE METHODS FOR SETTLING DISPUTES

There are many methods of settling such disagreements. Sometimes the parties can agree only to submit the dispute to a commission of investigation for a clarification of facts by means of an impartial inquiry. Quite often they also empower a commission to engage in conciliation and to present to the parties not only its conclusions about the facts but also its recommendations for a friendly settlement of the controversy. To ensure themselves further against the danger of an unwelcome decision, some countries have insisted that such commissions be composed of an equal number of persons from the two countries involved in the dispute. Such a joint commission is able to impose a decision, or even to make a recommendation, adverse to one of the parties only if at least one of that party's representatives agrees to it. Surprisingly, that method has proved quite successful in the settlement of disputes between the United States and Canada, where, through patient exploration, in many cases equitable solutions have been developed which both parties found it possible to accept.[2]

Nevertheless, this method is not a reliable one, especially if the relations between the parties are full of suspicions. In most instances, a more adequate method of settlement is needed, one which would lead to a binding decision. Three institutions are available for that purpose: an arbitral tribunal, the International Court of Justice, or a specialized court.

The oldest method is to create an arbitral tribunal for each dispute (or group of disputes) after the dispute has arisen. In such a case, a tribunal can be specially tailored to the requirements of a particular dispute; its members may be experts on the subject in dispute, and their nationalities may reflect the wishes of the parties with respect to an appropriate balance between representatives of the parties and neutral members.[3] It is possible, of course, to sabotage an arbitration by refusing to nominate the arbitrators, but methods can be devised to take care of this difficulty. Model rules on arbitral procedure were prepared in 1958 by the International Law Commission, and when properly followed they can ensure effective arbitration.[4] While an arbitral tribunal can solve satisfactorily a particular controversy, its period of existence is relatively short and it cannot develop a system of constant jurisprudence which could serve as a guide for the future conduct of the parties. A more permanent tribunal is necessary for that purpose.

The International Court of Justice at The Hague is the principal judicial organ of the United Nations. It is composed of fifteen judges, no two of whom may be nationals of the same state. Five of them are nationals of the permanent members of the Security Council, though this is not guaranteed in the statute of the Court; four judges come from Latin America, two from Western Europe, one from Eastern Europe, two from Commonwealth countries, and one from the Arab group of nations. Only two members of the Court come from Communist countries, and only one from a neutralist nation (the United Arab Republic).[5]

It can easily be seen that the Soviet Union would be reluctant to submit to the jurisdiction of the International Court of Justice in view of its predominantly Western composition. On the other hand, the Western nations might be reluctant to change the composition of the Court for all cases in order to obtain the agreement of the Soviet Union to submit to the jurisdiction of the Court in cases arising out of the arms-control agreement. If it should prove possible, however, to increase the number of judges from the neutral countries to at least three, the parties to the arms-control treaty might ask the Court to establish a special chamber for disputes relating to arms control. Such a chamber might be composed of two judges coming from the Atlantic community, two Communist judges, and three neutral judges. Such a special chamber of the Court could develop a consistent system of interpretation of the arms-control agreement, and would have behind it the prestige of the Court. A procedure might even be developed by means of which the arms-control chamber could obtain the advice of the full Court on questions of general international law which might be involved in a particular case, thus ensuring that the chamber would not depart too far from the general trend of the decisions of the Court.

It might be argued, however, that the problems of arms control require special technical knowledge and that many questions which would arise might require a method of approach more characteristic of constitutional and administrative law than of international law. Consequently, it might be preferable to establish a separate tribunal, composed of persons especially qualified to deal with matters of this type. It might also be easier to reach an agreement on the composition of such a tribunal than to make the choice of the judges of a chamber from the limited membership of the International Court of Justice. While the United Nations or the proposed International Disarmament Organization (IDO) cannot be a party to contentious proceedings before the International Court of Justice, and can only take part in proceedings relating to advisory opinions, an agreement creating a separate court may open such a court to these international organizations on a basis of equality with states. Finally, it might be possible to open the special tribunal to private parties (individuals and corporations) which claim to have suffered an injury because of the activities of the International Disarmament Organization. The International Court of Justice cannot be opened to them except through an amendment to the statute of the Court which might be difficult to push through in view of the tradition that this Court should be reserved for interstate disputes.

Such a special court might be modeled on the Court of Justice of the

European Coal and Steel Community, the jurisdiction of which was extended in 1958 to the other European communities, the European Economic Community and the European Atomic Energy Community (Euratom).[6] It may be noted that the Euratom Treaty contains both provisions concerning safety control against diversion of fissionable materials and provisions empowering the Court of Justice to deal with violations of the Treaty.[7] Similarly, the Convention on the Establishment of a Security Control in the Field of Nuclear Energy, signed in Paris on December 20, 1957, established a special tribunal to supervise the activities of the European Nuclear Energy Agency of the Organization for European Economic Cooperation.[8]

Additional difficulties might be created by the fact that certain inspection activities might require approval by an international court; in other cases, judicial action on the spot might be needed, rather than a decision at the seat of the court which might be quite distant from the place where emergency action is required. It might be suggested, therefore, that one court would not be sufficient and that a system of international courts needs to be created. The alternative would be to delegate these local functions to national courts, and to provide only for a right of appeal to an international court. Unfortunately, there is little inclination on either side to trust the judicial system of the other, and only a true international solution would be acceptable to all concerned.

If the idea of a system of special courts is accepted, it will not be necessary to create a large number of these courts. There might be one court for North America, one for Western Europe, one for the Soviet Union and Eastern Europe, one for China, one for Southeast Asia and the Far East, one for the Arab countries and North Africa, one for the rest of Africa, and one for Latin America—altogether, eight lower courts, each composed of three judges none of whom would be a native of the region. In addition, an appellate tribunal would be established which would also have primary jurisdiction over more important disputes between the states that are parties to the arms-control agreement and over disputes between states and the International Disarmament Organization. The appellate tribunal might be composed of nine judges (three Western, three Communist, and three neutral).

The advantages of the prestige and judicial impartiality of the International Court of Justice and of the easier accessibility and specialized knowledge of the special disarmament courts might be combined in a system which would combine lower tribunals with a right of appeal to the International Court of Justice. Such a system might be preferable to one equipped with a separate appellate tribunal, which would require a long time before it developed a reputation for impartiality and freedom from political influences equal to that of the International Court of Justice. It might be noted that such a system of appeals was developed after World War I, when disputes arose about the validity of the decisions of various mixed arbitral tribunals established to deal with disputes between Hungary and her neighbors. Several appeals were actually brought to the Permanent Court of International Justice in accordance with an agreeemnt of April 28, 1930,[9] and the Court developed an effective procedure for dealing with them. In particular, no difficulties were caused by the fact that the judgments of the tribunals were rendered in disputes between individuals and a state, while the appeals were brought by one state against another; the Court found it quite proper that two states might submit to it a dispute about the correctness of a judgment of another tribunal rendered in a case involving directly only one of these states.[10]

An appellate procedure established for disputes under an arms-control treaty need not be available in every case; it might be limited to cases in which at least two judges of the International Court of Justice have made a preliminary finding that the lower tribunal, from which an appeal is being made, appears (1) to have decided wrongly a question of the interpretation of the arms-control treaty; (2) to have exceeded its jurisdiction; (3) to have departed from the previous jurisprudence of the International Court of Justice; or (4) to have committed a serious procedural error resulting in a denial of justice.

SUBJECTS OF ADJUDICATION

Whatever the tribunal selected to deal with disarmament disputes, it might be necessary to state in more precise terms what its jurisdiction should be, i.e., what the range of matters which could be submitted to it should be. There would seem to be five main categories of cases: (1) disputes between two or more states with respect to the interpretation or application of the arms-control agreement; (2) disputes between the International Disarmament Organization and a state about the state's nonperformance of its obligations under the arms-control agreement; (3) requests by the International Disarmament Organization for judicial authorization to take certain inspection or enforcement steps against states; (4) appeals by a state against decisions of the International Disarmament Organization, asking for annulment on the grounds of lack of competence, major violations of procedure, violation of the arms-control treaty, or abuse of power; (5) appeals by private persons against decisions of the International Disarmament Organization enforcing the arms-control treaty against them, and complaints against acts of officials of the Organization who allegedly caused an injury to a private person. The cases in the fifth category and some of the cases in the third would be within the jurisdiction of the lower courts, subject to appeal to the appellate court; other cases would be within the original jurisdiction of the appellate court. In many respects, the jurisdiction of these courts would be similar to that of the Court of Justice of the European communities.[11] As in those communities, the purpose of the proposed arrangements will be to ensure the rule of law in the interpretation and application of the disarmament treaty.

It may be expected that direct disputes between states about the interpretation of the disarmament treaty are not going to be frequent. It is more likely that such disputes will ordinarily arise between the International Disarmament Organization and a state, though it is possible that the action of the Organization against a particular state might in some cases be the result, not of a report by its own inspectors, but of information supplied by another state. The first steps will be taken usually through the administrative process. For instance, if the management of a nuclear power plant should obstruct an inspection of the plant, the International Disarmament Organization would first ask the state in which the plant is situated to arrange for the admission of the inspectors. If the state should refuse to make such an arrangement, it might base its refusal on legal grounds; it might contend, for instance, that the plant in question is not subject to inspection under the treaty, or that the permitted annual number of inspections has been exhausted, or that the inspectors did not proceed through proper channels in seeking an admission to the plant. In another case, the International Disarmament Organization might request that a para-military unit be disbanded, while the state concerned might contend that the unit in question was not military but a training camp for athletes. Should the International Disarmament Organization consider these contentions unjustified, and should it prove impossible to settle the matter by negotiations, the Organization might bring the matter to the competent disarmament tribunal for a final decision.

SAFEGUARDS AGAINST ABUSES BY INSPECTORS

The provisions of the disarmament treaty relating to inspection might also include various guarantees against a possible abuse of power by the International Disarmament Organization. For instance, it might be provided that inspections outside a specified quota would be permitted only if the Organization had obtained a special authorization from the disarmament tribunal. Such an authorization would be issued by the tribunal only upon the showing of reasonable cause to believe or suspect that a prohibited or unlicensed activity was being conducted in a certain area. If there should be provisions empowering the International Disarmament Organization to grant, suspend, and revoke licenses to produce small arms, to engage in certain kinds of research, or to utilize nuclear materials, appeals to international tribunals might be granted against a refusal to grant a license or an allegedly unjustified suspension or revocation of a license.

It might be expected that the disarmament treaty would require that international inspectors should have due regard for all rights of personal privacy and private property, and should take into consideration the laws and customs of the respective nations to the fullest extent consistent with the effective discharge of their duties. In particular, safeguards would be necessary to prevent the disclosure of industrial secrets discovered during an inspection, except, of course, in a case in which such disclosure was necessary in order to accomplish the purposes of the arms-control treaty. In all these situations, recourse to an international tribunal might be necessary if an inspector violated his obligations under the treaty; in proper cases, just compensation would be granted to the injured state or person.

If the International Disarmament Organization should abuse its power to classify certain materials as "war materials" or as "nuclear materials," and should order their destruction or subject them to international controls, the state concerned, or even a private person owning such materials, might appeal to the disarmament tribunal against the decision of the Organization. There might also be cases in which a state would consider that the International Disarmament Organization should take certain action required by the treaty; e.g., if the Organization has neglected to inspect the territory of some states for a long period of time, another state might ask the tribunal to order the Organization to conduct such an inspection. Complaints might also be brought against the Organization if it should discriminate against some states and submit them to stricter controls without any special justification.

Finally, a state or a private person might have recourse to an international tribunal even before action has been taken by the International Disarmament Organization or one of its inspectors, if the contemplated action is considered as exceeding the powers of the Organization. In such a case the tribunal might issue an injunction prohibiting the taking of such action until the matter is decided by the tribunal.

Injunctions might also be issued by an international tribunal in the reverse situation, when an activity of a state or of a private person is alleged by the International Disarmament Organization or by another state to be contrary to an international obligation. Under its statute, the International Court of Justice is entitled to indicate provisional measures, and it has developed the necessary arrangements to treat requests for the indication of interim measures of protection as a matter of urgency.

REVISION OF TREATY PROVISIONS

As stated above, it may be anticipated that the disarmament treaty would contain not only some general principles but also a large number of detailed provisions. While the institution of an impartial tribunal would provide a method for removing at least some of the difficulties caused in the past by divergent interpretations of agreements between the West and the Soviet Union, it would still seem wise to try to solve most of the ambiguities in the treaty itself.

This method, however, has its own limitations. Circumstances change, unforeseen scientific or technical developments make certain provisions of the disarmament treaty obsolete, and there might be sudden shifts in the careful system of checks and balances established by the treaty. The negotiations on the suspension of nuclear tests have shown the impact of new discoveries which invalidate the premises of the first agreement on the subject. Similar problems may arise in the future, and methods must be found for dealing with them in an effective manner; otherwise the whole system might fall apart.

It might be noted that the treaty establishing the European Coal and Steel Community provides a procedure for dealing with special situations in which an amendment would be required in the rules for the exercise by the High Authority, the administrative organ of the Community, of the powers conferred upon it by the treaty. In particular, such amendments might be needed because of unforeseen difficulties experienced in executing the treaty or because of a profound change in the economic or technical conditions directly affecting the common market for coal and steel. The necessary amendments may be proposed jointly by the High Authority and the Council of Ministers of the Community, acting by a five-sixths majority. They are then submitted to the Court of Justice of the Community for an opinion on the question of whether or not the conditions prescribed in the treaty have been in fact fulfilled, and whether the proposed amendments are compatible with the articles of the treaty stating the basic purposes of the Community and whether those amendments do not change the relation between the various institutions of the Community. If the Court finds that the amendments conform to these requirements, they are submitted to the Common Assembly of the Community for approval. Should the Assembly approve them by a majority of three-quarters of the votes cast, representing a two-thirds majority of the total membership, the amendments come into force without need for further action by member states.[12]

A similar procedure might be devised for the arms-control treaty. It has been proposed by L. C. Bohn and others that amendments for taking into account changes in the technology of weapons and in detection devices should be adopted by a simplified procedure. Thus, the disarmament treaty might provide for the submission of amendments proposed by the executive organ of the International Disarmament Organization, and approved by its supervisory organ, to the international tribunal empowered to interpret the treaty. The tribunal would render an opinion about the compatibility of the amendments with the basic objects of the treaty and with the division of powers among the various institutions of the Organization. In case of a favorable opinion on the part of the tribunal, the amendments would be submitted to the Assembly of the Organization (or the General Assembly of the United Nations). If approved by that body by a two-thirds majority, including a majority of the principal powers, the amendments would come into force without further reference to member states for ratification. However, should the amendments introduce major changes in the disarmament treaty, the ordinary procedure of amendment would have to be followed, i.e., ratification in accordance with their respective constitutional processes by a prescribed large number of members, including almost all the principal powers.

One might have to deal also with a situation in which an amendment, found to be necessary by the executive organ of the International Disarmament Organization and to be compatible with the disarmament treaty by the international tribunal, has nevertheless failed to obtain the required majority in the Assembly or the necessary number of ratifications. In such a case, those states which consider that the nonadoption of the amendment would prejudice the further execution of some of the provisions of the disarmament treaty might request the tribunal to make a finding releasing them from those treaty obligations which can no longer be inspected in a satisfactory manner. The tribunal may make such a release conditional on a second submission of the amendment to the Assembly and its final rejection.

ENFORCEMENT

The enforcement of the arms-control treaty must be based on the principle that sanctions should be proportioned to the violations. There should be a number of sanctions available to the international authorities, and, to the extent that circumstances permit, there should be a slow progression from minor to major sanctions.

It might be important to avoid as far as possible the implication that each violation is one for which the government of a country must be directly responsible. In many cases it might be possible to take action against an individual or company engaged in a prohibited activity. In such cases, the main burden of enforcement should be put on the state in the territory of which such a prohibited activity has taken place. The International Disarmament Organization might request that state to stop the activity and to punish the persons concerned. Only if no steps are taken by the state, or if the steps taken are inadequate, would further action by the International Disarmament Organization be required. If a question of interpretation of the arms-control treaty should be involved in the case, and a state court should find the person not guilty of any violation or should order insufficient punishment, an appeal from the state court to the international tribunal could be taken by the International Disarmament Organization. Final judgments of the international tribunal in such cases of appeal should be entitled to forced execution in the territory of the state concerned to the same extent as local decisions. If the international tribunal has imposed a fine, such a fine may also be collected from any property which the person fined owns in some other country.

In another group of cases, the International Disarmament Organization might consider that a particular violation of the disarmament treaty
is due only to negligence, error, or an improper action of subordinate
officials, and that it does not constitute a deliberate act of the government
of the state concerned. In such a case, it might again be sufficient to call
on that government to take such action as is necessary to remedy the violation. If, however, the violation is not remedied within a specified period,
further action would be necessary.

The most difficult problem of enforcement arises in situations in which
a state itself has committed a major violation, or in which there is a
dangerous pattern of minor violations or of unremedied violations by private persons. If there should be a dispute as to facts, or if the state
concerned should contend that the facts in question do not constitute a
violation of the arms-control treaty as interpreted by that state, the matter
would be submitted by the International Disarmament Organization to the
disarmament tribunal for decision. Should the tribunal find that a violation
has occurred and should the state refuse to take any remedial action ordered by the tribunal, two types of sanctions would be available.

In the first place, economic sanctions might be taken against the state
concerned: economic assistance might be canceled, payments on international loans might be stopped, international trade relations might be
severed, and the foreign assets of the state and of its citizens might be
frozen. If the state is relatively small and is not supported by a large bloc
of other states, strict economic sanctions should be sufficient to ensure
compliance. In view of the economic interdependence of most states, even
relatively large states would have to comply, especially if the two super-
powers should support these sanctions, or at least do not interfere with
them. The "cold war," however, has shown the limited efficacy of economic sanctions against a superpower, and, in case of a violation by a
superpower or by a nation strongly supported by such a power, economic
sanctions might prove of no avail.

In such a case, it might be necessary to resort to the other alternative—
the cancellation of the disarmament treaty, or at least a threat of such
cancellation. It may be expected that a treaty on arms limitation would
come into effect only if it is so well balanced that all the parties to it will
have a vested interest in its enforcement and permanency. Should a state
be faced with the possibility that the disarmament treaty would cease to
be binding on all other states if it should continue to violate the treaty,
it would certainly have to weigh carefully the danger of a new arms race
and the fact that it alone would be held to blame. In most cases, these
considerations should be sufficient for it to accept the decisions of the
International Disarmament Organization and the disarmament tribunal.
If the violator should refuse to mend his ways, it would be necessary for
other states to follow up the threat and to start rearming, at least to the

extent necessary to even up the balance disturbed by the first state's violations.

It would be dangerous to leave this important decision about the withdrawal of the other states from all or some provisions of the arms-control treaty to the sole judgment of those states. The circumstances in which such a withdrawal would be permitted should be defined in the arms-control treaty itself, and the states relying on the relevant provision of the treaty would have to prove before the international tribunal that these circumstances have actually occurred. Only if the tribunal should agree with the contentions of these states, would they be entitled to withdraw and the disarmament treaty canceled in whole or in part. In an emergency situation, the tribunal would, of course, allow the states concerned to take such preliminary steps as might be needed to keep up with the state which has committed the violations forming the basis for the cancellation proceedings. Thus, the security of states would not be endangered by the delay caused by judicial proceedings.

This brief survey shows the role which might be played by international tribunals in the enforcement of an agreement on arms control. Such tribunals can solve disputes between the parties to that agreement and ensure that the rule of law is observed in the day-to-day interpretation and application of the agreement. Even in case of a serious disruption of the disarmament process, the tribunals can help to make certain that the treaty will not be terminated on a flimsy pretext. The different procedures outlined above would have to be worked out in finer detail, and many theoretical and practical difficulties would probably be encountered. But the task is not impossible, and with diligence and perseverance the required solutions can be discovered.

PART VI

FORMATION OF AMERICAN POLICY

20. Recent Policy Making in the United States Government

SAVILLE R. DAVIS

THERE IS LITTLE USE IN REVIEWING THE EXPERIENCE OF ARMS-CONTROL efforts before the nuclear age, except to contrast it with the present. Apart from the simple longing of mankind for release from war, which is an honorable attitude in any age, the chief carry-over from the pre-nuclear period has been a negative one. In the 1920's there was a hopeful but ill-fated experiment in partial disarmament which was based on a premise that later proved fallacious and a technique that proved irresponsible.

It was thought at the time that war was caused in good part by efforts of the arms merchants to improve their market. Limit the market, it was argued, and reduce the incentive to war. The resulting attempt to disarm was undermined by cheating in the 1920's because there was no system of policing through inspection. Disarmament was then modified in principle during the 1930's, when the Axis powers showed that there were other causes of war than the greed of the Zaharoffs. It became obsolete after World War II, when the rebuilding of armed force became the order of the day, and the West braced itself for the task of denying to Stalin the easy aggressions which it permitted to Hitler. It is possible that the concept was graded down further than it deserved, considering the size of the arms lobby in the United States today.

In any event, as the naïve type of unsafeguarded arms control of the 1920's became clearly inappropriate to the problems of the next three decades, there developed a relatively harmless tradition in politics of paying it lip service, so as not to offend the gentler elements of public opinion, and of ignoring it in practice. This tradition of the white lie carried over into the nuclear age, when the need for arms control revived and caused great havoc before it was exposed. For in the mid-fifties the nuclear arms race began in earnest, and the need to check it began to

---

All quotations in this chapter are from newspaper clipping files of the *New York Times*, the Washington *Post*, and the *Christian Science Monitor*, except the comment by a "supporter of the Killian group," which is from a private source.

override the incessant struggle to build a better deterrent. For several critical years the habit of pretending to work for disarmament served to mask the fact that the political leadership of the United States did not want disarmament. More specifically, those in Washington who considered arms control undesirable or impractical clearly had the upper hand in the process of making and administering policy, with the help of others who thought the Russians would never sign anyway, or would sign and cheat.

President Eisenhower's first term and the opening year of his second must be understood in terms of this gulf between official speech and action. This was the period when the military high command and the officials in charge of making nuclear weapons were confident that they possessed, and could sustain, a decisive advantage over the Soviet Union in nuclear arms.

History may say that the time for serious negotiation with the Soviet Union had not yet come. As long as the United States was clearly stronger, the Kremlin would come off second best in any negotiation. Moscow was not likely to make an unfavorable agreement at a time when it was confident of catching up and conceivably surpassing the United States within a short time.

The central figures in the drama which then unfolded were the President himself and Secretary Dulles. The close relation between the two is well understood, but the arms-control story shows a particular aspect of it. The President had certain basic concepts which he himself developed and supported as if they were tenets of his administration. One of these tenets advocated arms control, if it could be worked out with safeguards against cheating. His strong sense of direction in this respect came partly from his personal determination to rise above the narrowly military background which he brought to the White House and his desire to be a civilian president, responsive to the highest political, rather than military, values and aspirations. He also was convinced that safeguarded arms control made military sense. From the period of his first Colorado vacation, when he thought deeply about nuclear weapons off by himself in the mountains by the trout streams, he was convinced that "there is no longer any alternative to peace," as he told a State Department audience on his return. When Mr. Eisenhower developed a fundamental conviction like this, he gave it regular support on the highest policy level. He was to rule repeatedly in favor of the State Department and against the Pentagon and Atomic Energy Commission when key disputes on arms-control negotiation were referred to him for decision.

Why, then, did his strong general support for this cause result in policies which looked like the reverse, when they were put into action?

This was the role of Secretary Dulles. Mr. Dulles, unlike the President, was an intensely complex individual. Although the President tended to reduce an issue to some fundamental line of reasoning or to a few basic facts from which he could draw a decision, Mr. Dulles enjoyed the stimulus of an intricate situation. As a passionate student of the many contradictions which are built into a nation's foreign policy and into its domestic formulation, his mind was entirely at home in situations in which he had to say one thing one day and another the next, or to talk oppositely to groups with opposing interests. He kept his counsel for the most part as to whether his particular object at a given time was to confuse or disarm his critics, deal with pressing day-to-day situations with realism, or fit his apparent contradictions into some larger plan.

It was not out of character, then, for him to respect the President's deep desire to keep nuclear arms under control, and at the same time to see the many obstacles more clearly than the President, and to think in his own mind that arms control was probably a hopeless exercise for the present. Since the President let himself be guided by Mr. Dulles in day-to-day actions, it was natural that, while the President proposed optimistically, Mr. Dulles disposed skeptically, and with the President's own agreement.

There are subtle degrees of difference here which need to be defined with some care. It is not enough to say, as Walter Lippmann, Marquis Childs, Chalmers Roberts, and others have said, that the President's wishes were sabotaged on lower echelons. Mr. Dulles was in charge. The "lower echelons" did his bidding. Many lesser officials in the State Department itself believed in the possibility of arms control more than he did. While the final effect of the Dulles realism on the President's wish and faith was to frustrate them, the relation between the two men was honorable and close, and there was more to it than what looks like a simple betrayal of his chief on Mr. Dulles' part. Had it been merely that, the Dulles stratagem would not have worked.

The Russians gave Mr. Dulles continual and abundant opportunities to persuade the President that they did not mean business at almost any stage of a disarmament negotiation. Dulles could count on this kind of negative cooperation from Moscow to buttress his own stern and disciplinary concept of how to face down the Communist threat.

Mr. Dulles was in his element during this period. This writer knew him well when covering the earlier postwar conferences with the Russians, and watched him become the acknowledged master of cold-war maneuver. His legal mind took keen and relentless delight in the business of checkmating his opponent. Furthermore, if anyone else knew how to moderate or shortcut this quarrelsome bargaining procedure, he did not come forward. Democrats and Republicans, liberals and conservatives, genial negotiators and those born tough—all tried, and the results were approximately the same.

It was not argued seriously in Washington that the cold war could be brought to an end. Or even that the beginning of the end was in sight. It is a false dilemma to say that the cold war must be abandoned or continued. The advocates of arms control wanted to introduce one element of stability into the content, at a point where the high pressures inherent in a policy of deterrence might explode. It was assumed that we would seek to manage a two-level policy, with calculated disagreement over most of the range of our relation with the Communist governments, and a few areas where a common interest in survival demanded mutual concessions.

It is now possible to explain what happened in Washington when the course of international strategy reached a turning point. The mutual belligerence of policy between the United States and the USSR, which had served a national aim on both sides, found itself surrounded by new conditions in which it was causing a drift toward severe instability and the danger of nuclear war. What could be done?

A good time to pick up the story is the spring of 1957, when a United Nations conference on disarmament was scheduled at London, when nuclear testing was in full swing, intercontinental missiles seemed uncomfortably close, and the President had chosen Harold Stassen as his Special Assistant on Disarmament. The President wanted to make a fresh effort to negotiate. Mr. Dulles considered that this was the thing to do, but offered the President no hope that it would be successful. The chief opponents of any agreement— Admiral Arthur W. Radford, chairman of the Joint Chiefs of Staff, and Rear Admiral Lewis L. Strauss, chairman of the Atomic Energy Commission—were not greatly perturbed, because Mr. Dulles seemed mainly on their side. Then the unexpected happened.

Stassen became keenly interested in arms control.

His motive is of less importance than its result. He doubtless wanted his mission to succeed. It might have given his political career a fresh start. And, the more he studied arms control, the more he was impressed with its merit. In any event, he violated the tacit gentleman's agreement not to try too hard.

The Stassen episode should go down as a classic in the politics of arms limitation. It got under way in April and May, with Dulles saying, "We consider that control and reduction of arms are possible, desirable, and in the last reckoning indispensable." The President said he felt the Russians were "taking a different tone," because they were "feeling the pinch of building, supporting and maintaining those tremendous military organizations."

At the end of May, Stuart Alsop described a "bitter internal struggle" which took place when Stassen returned from London for consultation. Admiral Radford was the most vocal opponent. "It is not generally known," said Alsop, "how fierce and uncompromising Radford's opposition was, nor how powerfully he was supported. Radford used every conceivable argument against agreeing to mutual inspection in any form." Dulles "adopted a position of cautiously benevolent neutrality."

Radford said publicly to newsmen, "We cannot trust the Russians on a disarmament agreement or anything. They have broken their word too many times."

The President let it be known that he was nettled by the Radford statement, ruled in general terms for Stassen after a series of meetings on lower levels, and told his press conference, "The United States must be ready to meet the USSR halfway on a first-step disarmament agreement." This country is not "recalcitrant or picayunish" and should have an "open mind," the President said. Americans must "keep exploring every facet of this whole great field, to see if something can't be done. It just has to be done in the interest of the United States." Stassen went back to London.

Lippmann wrote, "For the first time in the long history of talking about disarmament, we are in sight of negotiation." The Russians, he said, were "behaving seriously," and the President "decided the costs of not negotiating are greater."

It was almost immediately clear that the result of the policy battle in Washington had been to put Stassen in an even tighter harness of day-to-day instructions from Washington and to embolden him to the point of an indiscretion which enabled Dulles to pull sharply on the checkrein. This was a reckless action on Stassen's part, one that went beyond his instructions: on May 31st an uncleared memorandum was delivered to Soviet chief delegate Valerian Zorin. The risk to Stassen from this action was wholly disproportionate to any possible gain for his cause. An unnamed Washington official told the press that Stassen had been "naïve," which was true, and Dulles announced that Stassen had been rebuked with the President's approval.

To repeat: "with the President's approval."

Lippmann said Stassen's mandate was still "thin, weak and tentative." Chalmers Roberts of the Washington *Post* said this was "a story of how Stassen has been undercut at home . . . by others in the administration, once it appeared the Kremlin might really be serious in an arms agreement." Marquis Childs wrote that the President, "while helping to create a climate of American opinion in which negotiation is possible, has yet to give Stassen the kind of backing necessary in the crucial weeks ahead. The President can do that only by making it clear to Messrs. Radford, Strauss and Co. that they cannot cut the guts from American proposals while pledging fealty to the principle of agreement itself."

"More serious," said Roberts, "the United States is in the position of having reneged on disarmament proposals. . . ." Another Roberts dispatch said that the effect of the Administration debate "is to cast in doubt the nation's good faith in the London disarmament talks." Soviet Foreign Minister Andrei Gromyko in Moscow took advantage of the situation to tell a press conference that the United States was using the London talks as a "screen to continue and intensify the arms race." It is probable that he was making the usual propaganda point. It is not inconceivable, however, that his colleagues had begun to be seriously interested in attempting to negotiate and now concluded that the United States did not mean business.

Late in June, Admiral Strauss took physicists Edward Teller and Ernest O. Lawrence to the White House to argue for continued nuclear testing in order to perfect "clean" weapons. The President was impressed. "But for the moment," he said publicly in noticeably less vigorous terms than before, "it would appear that the psychological factors and the fears of the world are such that we should go ahead with the plan" to offer a conditional suspension of tests.

During the summer Dulles tied the American test-ban offer to an entire package of proposals—a maneuver not unlike the frequent tactic of the Russians of linking a reasonable offer to more radical steps the other side would surely not accept. Stuart Alsop wrote, "The President has hobbled Stassen. Radford and Strauss have won a signal and probably final victory. The President placed conditions on suspension of tests which hardly anyone expects the Soviets will accept."

Mr. Dulles ignored the charge. "This can be said with assurance," he said, like an ardent advocate of arms control, "the risks of seeking to move forward are far less than the risks of being frightened into immobility." Having won his point, he was taking steps as he so often did to conceal his victory by talking as if he leaned generously the other way. "We must assume that since an agreement is necessary, it is possible and that we must make it possible," he declared.

In September the chapter was closed. The AEC announced new tests in Eniwetok. Henry Cabot Lodge told a private group at the United Nations that the test-ban proposal should be unhooked from the rest of the package offer if negotiations were to get anywhere. Stassen told two officials in Washington, according to Childs:

If you deliberately want to prevent achieving any disarmament, then you do the following:

1. You make your proposals so complicated and far-reaching that the other side is almost certain to reject them.

2. You impose on the negotiator the necessity to check and recheck and check again with officials back home before he can advance another step in the negotiations. In other words, you make it as difficult as possible to carry on a frank face-to-face discussion on the terms of a disarmament agreement.

3. You tolerate—if you do not actively encourage—officials who say publicly that there is no possibility of getting a disarmament agreement and that an agreement would, in any event, be unworkable if not undesirable.

Lippmann had said a little earlier: "The great underlying issue which in the end must be decided by public debate, has been debated in secret within the administration and has been decided but not settled." This issue was: "Whether, if an enforceable agreement to limit armaments could be reached, it would be wise to make the agreement."

On October 4, 1957, Sputnik went up. Four weeks later the President brought President James R. Killian, Jr., of the Massachusetts Institute of

Technology, to the White House with authority to bring the best available talent into the President's scientific advisory committee. A new weight was added to the balance. By May 1958, six months later, the balance had tilted to the opposite side. It is an oversimplification, but a useful one, to say that the President now listened primarily to men whose information and judgment of fact indicated that a safeguarded arms-control agreement would be to the advantage of the national interest and security of the United States, whereas before that time he had listened chiefly to men who said such an agreement would gravely damage national security.

It is an even riskier oversimplification, but still a useful one, to say that the net policy of the United States toward arms control was reversed in this short period of months. Like most shifts of policy, this one will not be found in documents. Policy is determined by political momentums operating on the existing balance of forces in Washington. The arrival of the new group of presidential advisers set up such a fresh momentum.

How did this change come about? To begin with, this is an era in which considerations of power are determined by weapons (those existing and those in prospect) which are beyond the experience and reckoning of typical military professionals. Second, and granting exceptions, the quality of scientists and weapons experts within the government, and particularly within the Atomic Energy Commission, had deteriorated. Liberal-minded scientists who were high enough in the ranks to influence policy had in general left the government, partly to return to their creative work and partly to escape the conservative and security-minded restraints imposed by the McCarthy era, by the formalism of the Pentagon, and especially by Mr. Strauss in his administration of the AEC and in his role as special presidential adviser. Those scientists who were sympathetic to this environment and remained in government service were inclined to be conservative to the degree that they concerned themselves with policy. Few of the first team were left. The quality of scientific advice available to the President was both partisan, after being channeled through Mr. Strauss, and in many cases second-rate.

Meanwhile, scientists outside the government were inhibited from open discussion by their former or continuing access to classified information. Those who did not have such information could make general comments on national policy, but could not keep authoritatively abreast of the detailed questions at issue, such as the feasibility of inspection, the relative trends of United States and Soviet weapons, and so on, and therefore were not in a position to speak out.

Evidence is available to the writer which clearly indicates that the President and Mr. Dulles were unwitting prisoners, in their lonely isolation at the top of the government pyramid, of the special selection of knowledge and attitudes which came to them through official channels and especially through Mr. Strauss. They had no alternative against which to measure the partisan quality of this advice or its scientific inadequacies.

The Killian group brought such an alternative to the White House. It was one more effort to solve the prickly question of how to adjust science, technology, weaponry, strategy, and political policy making. The President needs the special pleading of his weapons makers and users, but he is helpless if their arguments are not tested by men of equal knowledge and standing who are not committed; otherwise there is no horse race. The President and Mr. Dulles now had a two-sided debate to help them make up their minds.

The scientists sought to provide a good quality of scientific information and judgment and to let the chips fall where they might. They recognized that policy making was the task of the President and that negotiation must rest in the hands of the State Department. Their function was to be disinterested. But however carefully they hewed to this line, the effect of their information and judgment on a situation and on men who had not been confronted with this order of scientific thinking and knowledge was to dislodge a good deal of fallacious information and inference. The facts provided by the scientists clearly pointed in a different direction of policy from those previously available. They called for a re-examination of what constitutes security for both sides. They persuasively introduced the concept of inspection as a deterrent, replacing the notion that it must be an absolute to be useful.

Mr. Dulles and his client, the President, listened with profound interest. For Mr. Eisenhower, here was authoritative technical support for the concept he had been clinging to, despite all obstacles, as an article of faith. For the Secretary of State, here was a new element of unpredictable but obviously formidable strength in the balance of forces at home and abroad over which he had been shrewdly presiding. He was so impressed with the newcomers' depth of scientific knowledge and authority, which obviously outclassed almost all of their opponents', that he admitted he had been given poor scientific advice before the new group arrived. Yet the evidence all goes to show that he did not change his own inner conviction that a new effort would be futile because the Communists would not sign. He had a deep suspicion of the Communists, abundantly justified by events. He believed that a nation operating by principles was at a disadvantage when dealing with an unprincipled nation, and feared that if we were drawn into agreements with the Kremlin on particular issues the effect on public opinion might be to undermine our ability to keep up our guard. He was determined that we should not be taken in.

As always, he bent with the breeze when the Killian committee showed its mettle. He even gave the impression that he had shifted his position and was going forward enthusiastically with the new tide of affairs. But he did not yield more than a few inches of his hour-to-hour grip on all negotiations with the Soviet Union. Dulles was still in ultimate control.

What had changed was the flow of scientific information and judgments to the President and Mr. Dulles. When the Defense Department or the

AEC made statements which were inaccurate or shortsighted or slanted to a partisan purpose, the Killian group put them straight. The very fact that such statements would be scrutinized by the scientific advisers who had no vested interest acted as a brake on the self-confidence of less informed special pleaders. More and more responsibility was placed on the Killian group as the disinterested quality of its judgment became evident.

It is clear that the key to the decision-making process on arms control in Washington during this period is to be found in the thought processes, the methods of working, the policy concepts of Foster Dulles. It is a rash reporter who will give a snap judgment on this intricate individual, who kept most of the world, including his own closest associates, guessing much of the time with respect to the full dimensions of the strategy he was conducting and the specific meaning of his maneuvers at any given moment.

During the several years under discussion, he managed to persuade the President that he was doing as much as was practicable for arms control, considering the limits set by the Communists; to keep the Pentagon sullenly subservient to his primacy in foreign affairs but not greatly troubled about the likelihood of disarmament; to keep Strauss at arm's length but to confirm the Strauss pessimism with respect to any agreement with the Kremlin; to make enough positive statements about disarmament so that the American people, who were apt to be sentimental on this point, could not detect any hostility on his part to the idea; to keep the Communists aware of the fact that he would not deal with them on this issue and intended to keep more propaganda pressure on them than they could apply in return. The only hard fact in this carefully contrived mixture was that arms control did not move forward.

Dulles, as the world knows, tirelessly administered policy as well as made it. On arms-control matters he wrote many of his notes or instructions to negotiating delegations, or worked carefully over drafts written by his associates. His deep distrust of Stassen caused him to spend an inordinate amount of time on day-to-day instructions during the Stassen episode. He kept this function in his own hands. Often he would work and make decisions at his house on a quiet week-end, with one or two subordinates present.

When he took over the State Department, there was a formal structure and process for arms control which he promptly modified. President Truman had set up an interdepartmental Regulation of Armaments Committee, including Secretary of State Acheson as chairman, the secretary of defense, and the chairman of the Atomic Energy Commission. The principals met infrequently. Most of the work was done at the staff level. It was sincere. General Omar Bradley encouraged it, and Mr. Acheson did not interfere. But the goal was far off. Mr. Acheson took disarmament, even as a public-opinion problem, less seriously than Mr. Dulles. Indeed, the subject was an anachronism at that period, given the onset of the cold war.

When the Eisenhower administration took over in 1952, a new pattern developed. Since Dulles took charge and worked with his peers, members of the Cabinet took a more active part in setting policy. The meetings of the formal interdepartmental committee and its staff lapsed, and when Mr. Dulles wanted help he chose it from his own staff, from the Disarmament Division of the State Department. Dulles never let this subject become implicated in the processes of the National Security Council, whose descent into formalism, frustrated infighting, and stalemated positions was recently described to a committee of Congress by Robert Lovett. When the time came for an action, Dulles worked it out, did such clearing with other departments as was necessary, obtained the President's approval, and acted. The other departments knew that he was irresistibly persuasive with the President, and treated him with proportionate respect. He in turn often disregarded or overrode them. He was capable of saying in effect, "Nonsense, Lewis, I couldn't go along with that," to Admiral Strauss and then going his own way. He was, however, more or less at the mercy of scientific verdicts from Mr. Strauss and the Pentagon, and until the Killian group arrived he had to quote them as authority on what science had in store for weapons and strategy.

An example of his working habits was the President's letter to Soviet Premier Bulganin in April 1958. The Killian group was pressing for direct talks between the scientists of both sides. The letter suggesting technical consultations was drafted by Dulles and an associate or two on a Sunday afternoon at his house, with Dulles doing most of the writing. He never cleared it with other departments. He simply telephoned the President and got his approval. Usually he would have no more than two or three members of the staff present on such an occasion, and when he telephoned or directly consulted the President, the latter almost never made a change in the Dulles text.

The Bulganin letter opened the way to the conference of scientists of both sides at Geneva in the summer of 1958 which reached a speedy and spectacular agreement on the preliminary technical aspects of suspension of nuclear tests. This was regarded by optimists at the time as a major break-out from the earlier pattern of sterile negotiation. This was probably the case, but it set in motion counterforces in Washington which plunged the whole subject into confusion again. Opponents in the Atomic Energy Commission, with its almost unlimited resources from the public purse, went full steam ahead with research designed to prove that test inspection was much more difficult than the scientists of the Killian group, with no research at their disposal, had initially estimated. And it was not long before Mr. Killian had to announce that the first estimates of what was necessary to distinguish underground nuclear explosions from earth tremors had been overoptimistic in terms of the detection equipment then available. Moscow immediately took this announcement for what it was —a victory for the opposing forces in Washington as well as a legitimate increase of knowledge about the problem. Since the Geneva agreement by the scientists had been based on these initially oversanguine estimates, the Russians began a long stone-walling operation of their own in which they refused to accept the new calculations or to review the Geneva agreement. It took time for the Killian group to gain headway in Washington with the argument that its fundamental position was not altered by the new findings; that detection with existing instruments and procedures would be more difficult than expected, but that these instruments were antiquated and built for other purposes. New and appropriate instruments could doubtless be developed. There were methods, such as supplementing the work of inspectors with automatic nets of underground recording instruments, and there were procedures such as random inspection, greatly increasing the deterrent effect of a given quota of trips by inspectors, which could overcome the handicap raised by the new AEC findings.

It was the position of those scientists arguing for arms control that a constructive approach to the problem called for a quite different motive than that of the leaders of the AEC. Instead of spending resources and talent to prove that a task could not be accomplished with existing methods and equipment, the situation called for spending resources and the best available talent in an effort to develop new methods and equipment to do the job. An inspection system should be started at once, it was argued, on the best terms obtainable from the Russians and without yielding the right to resume testing if the effort failed. Its purpose would be to acquaint both sides with the actual problems of detection and to assist the task of developing more adequate detection systems.

Once again, the line that divided the two factions was that between an *a priori* conviction that arms control was neither feasible nor desirable, and the conviction that every effort should be made to develop adequate solutions and to see if the Kremlin would accept them. As one supporter of the Killian group put it, "We surely don't know whether the Russians would or would not sign, if a reasonable inspection system were achieved and if we made our best effort in good faith to negotiate it. But one thing is sure. Considering the certain results of nuclear war and the dangers of this new kind of arms race, we could not look history in the eye if we did not try to find out. And if we do not try, we will never know whether they would be prepared to agree or not."

While pro and con arguments over these points continued, and while the Killian committee tried to arrange for research facilities in friendly hands, Mr. Dulles reasserted control. He himself made the decision and issued the instructions which transferred talks with the Russians back from the summer's technical phase to the political level, where they languished during the fall and winter. He scarcely needed to resume his familiar methods of tough and protracted bargaining because the Russians had already done it for him. But he did not lag behind. American delegations, both to a second Geneva conference on the suspension of testing and to a new Geneva conference on the control of surprise attack, were rigidly forbidden to go beyond their specific instructions at any given moment. The instructions were not to make our most favorable offers at the start, but to demand an initially high price which the Russians could be counted upon to reject and to counter with a similarly impossible price of their own—and so the usual process of haggling began again.

The scientists had hoped that the new conference on surprise attack could pass quickly into a technical stage, like the successful meeting on nuclear testing during the summer. The Soviets never permitted it to leave the political stage. Both conferences developed into the type of slug-fest for which Mr. Dulles had so great a talent. There was ample data with which to persuade the President from week to week that the Russians were not cooperative.

The weight of evidence available suggests to this writer, at least, that Mr. Dulles had been impressed by the technical knowledge of Mr. Killian and his colleagues, and by their humane understanding of the implications of the nuclear age for civilization as a whole, but that he had not altered his own estimate of the Communists and of the way to deal with them to any significant degree. There are those who were close to him and who think they detected signs that he at least came to question this attitude shortly before his death. But if this was more than a questioning, he kept his own counsel to the last.

This is the point where the present review must cut off. It is still too early to appraise the change of riders in the middle of the arms race from Foster Dulles to Christian Herter, and much too early to comment on the change from Dwight D. Eisenhower to John F. Kennedy.

21. Government Organization
for Arms Control

HUBERT H. HUMPHREY

THIS CHAPTER IS A DISCUSSION OF ORGANIZATION PROBLEMS AFFECTING government formulation and implementation of arms-control policies.* It does not discuss what the policies should be, but rather ways in which individuals should work together in order to reach and implement decisions regarding policy.

Before there can be intelligent discussion of the possible forms of governmental organization, the government and the people must know how much importance to attach to arms control. Is the control and reduction of armaments a realistic goal to seek in today's world? What priority should arms control be given? Answers to these questions are required in order to place arms-control organization in the framework of our system of values and goals and so that efforts to make progress proceed from commonly accepted assumptions.

The control and reduction of armaments, in my opinion, should be at the heart of United States foreign policy. Of necessity, we have been indulging in the first arms race in our history. Now there is evidence that our major adversaries would prefer to reduce the tensions resulting from a build-up in armaments and take steps to minimize the danger of war. No one can predict with certainty that progress on arms control is possible, or that success in controlling and limiting one category of weapons will lead to success in other categories. But we shall never know what accomplishments are possible unless we make the effort. Arms control may be the key to the future security of this nation, and, indeed, of the peoples of the entire world. It should be given the highest priority by the government.

Given these assumptions there are basic tasks the government should be prepared to carry out. Effective organization for arms control requires: (1) joining together the relevant political, military, and scientific factors;

* In the preparation of this chapter, I wish to acknowledge the helpful assistance of Miss Betty Goetz, member of the staff of the Foreign Relations Committee and the Staff Assistant to its Subcommittee on Disarmament.

and (2) utilizing these political, military, and scientific factors, to form decisions regarding arms-control policy and to execute expeditiously the decisions reached. Whatever government machinery is involved should be geared to facilitate the accomplishment of these basic tasks.

No amount of organization, however, can be expected to act as a substitute for Presidential leadership. At the top there must be a person who believes in the importance of arms control and who is willing to give the subject adequate and sustained attention. The President must also be willing to involve himself in the inevitable controversies that will surround policy questions in the arms-control field; he must be willing to take the time to listen to the arguments and then make firm decisions. Certain organizational structures may be superior to others, but none can be a replacement for Presidential leadership and prompt and firm Executive decision-making.

The Secretary of State also has an important role in arms-control policy. Although several agencies of the federal government are concerned with arms-control policies, the Department of State has a key function in formulating and executing them. The attitude of the Secretary of State, therefore, is vital. If he believes there is an opportunity to halt the race in armaments and to divert the two major power blocs from military competition to competition in more peaceful pursuits, he will make certain that arms control receives the time and study it deserves. If he thinks that arms control is not a feasible alternative to an arms race or that other nations are not prepared to treat it seriously, then it will likely receive but limited attention.

These considerations point to the conclusion that juggling, reshaping, and drawing new lines on an organization chart cannot determine conclusively that the United States will earnestly and persistently seek progress on arms control. Always more important than organizational structures are people—their views, their convictions, their dedication to tackling a problem and solving it.

Governmental organization, nevertheless, deserves serious thought and scrutiny. In the next section I shall first describe briefly the organizational structures and methods of carrying on arms-control activities within the Executive branch, and then evaluate their effectiveness and workability.

ANALYSIS OF PAST FORMS OF ORGANIZATION

From 1946 until mid-1955 the Department of State had the major responsibility for problems of disarmament. The Atomic Energy Commission, however, played an important role in the development of the Baruch Plan for the control of atomic energy. The Commission also furnished the Department of State with technical data to be presented before the United Nations Atomic Energy Commission. But disarmament negotiations in the United Nations and with individual countries were handled through the State Department's Bureau of International Organization Affairs. Benjamin Cohen, Morehead Patterson, and James Wadsworth, and all the other United States negotiators reported directly to the Secretary of State.

In March 1955 the President appointed Harold Stassen, then head of the Mutual Security Program, to be his Special Assistant for Disarmament. Mr. Stassen was directly responsible to the President and was given a seat in the Cabinet and on the National Security Council. He was also considered to be under the general supervision of the Secretary of State.

Mr. Stassen gathered together a group of persons from various departments and agencies in the government: the Department of State, the Central Intelligence Agency, the Atomic Energy Commission, the Department of Defense, the Department of Justice, and the United States Information Agency. In addition, he appointed the chairmen of several task forces to study appropriate disarmament inspection systems, i.e., nuclear materials, aerial inspection, army and ground units, navy and naval weapons, national budgets, steel, power and industry, and the use of communication in inspection. These task forces were charged with the responsibility of devising workable inspection measures. The Special Disarmament Assistant said of the task forces:

As a result of their studies . . . I believe we shall have something we have never had before—a detailed operating manual of what to inspect, how and where it would be inspected, and a knowledge of what can and cannot be profitably inspected if we seek to provide a safeguard against surprise attack and to supervise an international arms limitation agreement.[1]

All negotiations on disarmament during Mr. Stassen's tenure of office were handled by him on the basis of negotiating papers approved by the National Security Council, except discussion of arms control in the United Nations, which was the chief responsibility of the United States Ambassador to the United Nations, Henry Cabot Lodge. Even in the United Nations debates, however, Mr. Stassen played an active part.

With Mr. Stassen's resignation at the beginning of 1958, the main responsibility for arms-control policy was returned to the Department of State. Jurisdiction over disarmament, however, was removed from the Bureau of International Organization Affairs and transferred to the newly established Office of the Special Assistant to the Secretary of State for Disarmament and Atomic Energy. In the fall of 1960 a new United States Disarmament Administration was created by Executive order. As of the writing of this chapter (February 1961) the Kennedy Administration has not yet determined whether this Disarmament Administration, a part of the Department of State but somewhat semi-autonomous in its operations, should be retained.

Until recently the Department of State has had no funds or staff to conduct any studies of the various political, military, and scientific problems involved in arms control. Some studies, particularly those on the technical aspects of detection and identification of nuclear weapons tests, were made under the general direction of the Office of the Special Assistant to the President for Science and Technology. Other technical studies on this subject were carried out by the Air Force Technical Applications Center in the Department of Defense, by the Division of Military Application of the Atomic Energy Commission, by the Central Intelligence Agency, or by private research groups under contract to these government agencies. In most cases these studies were made on an *ad hoc* basis, with little coordination by a central authority. Few studies were made on the relation of arms-control plans and proposals to national security interests, military strategies, and United States political objectives throughout the world.

Under this organizational structure, policy on arms control was formulated by a Committee of Principals consisting of the Secretary of State, the Secretary of Defense, the Chairman of the Atomic Energy Commission, the Special Assistant to the President for Science and Technology, and the Director of the Central Intelligence Agency. Before meetings of the Committee of Principals, discussions of policy questions were usually held by an interdepartmental committee of officers from these five agencies. The drafting of proposals was done by the Department of State, and the technical details to buttress such proposals were supplied by way of the President's Science Adviser.

PROBLEMS IN IMPROVING THE PRESENT ORGANIZATION

Each of these various forms of organization has its advantages and disadvantages. As one who has closely observed the workings of government in this field over the past five years, I have reached certain conclusions about the problems which developed and which should be avoided. I have also noted those methods of organization that, in my opinion, should be retained and expanded.

Let us first consider the case of a Special Assistant to the President for Disarmament. The greatest advantage of such a Special Assistant is that he has the ear of the President. He can go directly to the President and confer with him on policy, proposals, and even problems with government agencies. He need not be restricted by the budgets of the regular departments, and by being a member of the Cabinet and the National Security Council he is on a par with the heads of other departments.

There are three main disadvantages to the status of a Special Assistant for Disarmament. First, by being outside of the Department of State, the agency with primary responsibility for dealing with foreign policy and carrying on relations with other countries, there is always the danger that the Special Assistant will act counter to other foreign-policy considerations. During the period of the Special Assistant this did occur, with the consequence of antagonizing officials within the State Department and causing confusion and uncertainty in the capitals of other nations as to what United States policy was.

Second, the Special Assistant acted as the chief United States negotiator at disarmament conferences and, therefore, was often away from the seat of government. When questions of policy then had to be resolved back in Washington, the Special Assistant had no one of sufficient stature to represent him before the President and to argue policy matters with other agencies having an interest in the position being taken by the United States. During 1957, when Mr. Stassen was out of the country, he evidently acted quite contrary to the wishes of Mr. Dulles, then Secretary of State. In the absence of Mr. Stassen, Mr. Dulles was in a position to prevail upon the President to curtail Mr. Stassen's authority. This experience has made the Department of State reluctant to transfer any of its jurisdiction and authority over arms-control matters to anyone outside the Department.

A third problem connected with the role of a Special Assistant involves the availability of information to be released outside the Executive branch. The Disarmament Subcommittee of the Senate Committee on Foreign Relations has experienced the not uncommon difficulty of obtaining information from the Executive branch of the government. This difficulty is compounded under the status of Special Assistant in that he is able to plead executive privilege and thus deny to any committee of the Congress, public group, private citizen, or member of the press information on any aspect of the problem which it is to his interest to deny. The Special Assistant to the President for Science and Technology and the Special Assistant to the President for Disarmament have used executive privilege to deny information to the Senate Disarmament Subcommittee, as well as to the public at large. Earlier I mentioned the creation of eight task forces by the Special Assistant for Disarmament. When committees of Congress requested information pertaining to these studies, executive privilege was used as a reason for the refusal to share information. If the claim of executive privilege is to be used by any officer or individual connected with the White House on such important matters as disarmament, even when they are not highly classified, then this is an important drawback to a similar organizational pattern for the future.

Just as there are advantages and disadvantages in having a Special Assistant for Disarmament in the White House there are advantages and disadvantages in having disarmament matters be primarily the responsibility of the Department of State.

The main reason for giving the Department a primary role in arms-control matters is that little can be accomplished except through negotiation with other countries. This is clearly the responsibility of the Department of State. It must coordinate policy with friendly governments; it must select and instruct the negotiators to arms-control conferences; and it must determine that arms-control proposals do not conflict with other aspects of United States foreign policy.

During the decade after World War II, when disarmament was viewed almost solely as a political problem of foreign policy, other agencies of the government were apparently content to give the Department of State a free rein over the formulation and execution of policy. Furthermore, the cold war, as well as a hot war in Korea, were at their height, and any progress toward arms reduction was considered remote.

Beginning about 1955, arms control as an instrument of national policy began to grow in importance. Thus when the State Department in 1958 reclaimed its authority over policy, the interests of other agencies had been aroused, and the gaps in our machinery and the disadvantages of relying on the Department of State for policy formulation became apparent. During this period almost every decision had to be thrashed out in endless argument among at least five principal agencies: the State Department, the Atomic Energy Commission, the Defense Department, the Office of the Special Assistant to the President for Science and Technology, and the Central Intelligence Agency. On the four occasions from 1958 until mid-1960 when arms-control discussions took place, the United States entered these conferences in various degrees of unpreparedness.[2] Decisions were taken only after prolonged debate and delay. For months during the conference on the discontinuance of nuclear-weapon tests, the United States negotiators in Geneva lacked direction on key proposals because of the inability of the government back in Washington to reach any workable compromise. I am told that if it had not been for the President's Science Adviser, who had access to the President, it is questionable that any progress could have been made during this period. The State Department was unable by itself to exert leadership in this field.

An added complication to the formulation of arms-control policy was the existence within the Department of State of serious differences of opinion. What appeared feasible and acceptable to the Office of Disarmament and Atomic Energy was objected to by other bureaus in the Department. For example, the Disarmament Office has been known to be interested in developing possible proposals for anti-surprise-attack zones in Europe and possibly in other areas. This suggestion has met with the firm opposition of the Bureau of European Affairs, where there is a strong view that the development of zones in Europe might jeopardize the reunification of Germany. There has been discussion of possible zones of arms control in Asia, but the attitude of the Far Eastern desk toward any participation of Communist China in these agreements has precluded effective and intelligent discussion of such possibilities.

Conceivably, the Department of State should have been able to resolve these political controversies by utilizing its own Policy Planning Staff. At least there was machinery in existence that could be given the assignment of studying such problems. However, other problems arose, particularly in the technical field, for which no government machinery existed. The result was to set up *ad hoc* groups which were expected to produce solutions within short periods of time.

The Stassen task forces mentioned earlier are an example of the use of *ad hoc* groups. Although it was claimed that the studies to be undertaken by these groups would contribute significantly to our understanding of arms-control problems,[3] it is unlikely that most of these groups fulfilled their assignment. No reports have ever been made public, and there is little indication that American disarmament policy reflected any accomplishment on the part of these groups.

Three years later, in the fall of 1959, another *ad hoc* appointment was made and with about the same degree of success. The Secretary of State appointed Charles Coolidge, a Boston lawyer, to assemble an *ad hoc* staff to conduct a review of disarmament policy. Evidently this study was thought to be totally inadequate. It has been kept highly classified, even though the appointment of Mr. Coolidge was hailed as an important development.[4] Unfortunately, the State Department placed its full confidence in this group, and when its report in January 1960 was found to be useless, the Department had to begin to formulate a policy from scratch, only a few days away from high-level meetings with other nations which had been called for the purpose of coordinating the policies reached by each nation individually.

These examples illustrate an important point, namely, that *ad hoc* groups cannot be expected to review in the space of a few weeks or months so important a subject as arms-control policy and produce sound and substantial results.

A further example of the lack of machinery can be seen in the experience of the government in attempting to acquire additional information on the detection and identification of nuclear explosions. In this case regular agencies of the government were called upon to carry out the assignment, with the following results.

Reference has been previously made to special studies being undertaken on the detection and identification of nuclear explosions by the Department of Defense and the Atomic Energy Commission. That additional studies should be conducted was decided at a meeting on April 23, 1959, attended by the Deputy Secretary of Defense, the Chairman of the Atomic Energy Commission, and the Special Assistant to the President for Science and Technology. Among the projects to be carried out by the Atomic Energy Commission was one (Project Cowboy) on ways to conceal nuclear tests. The Department of Defense was assigned the study of ways to improve the detection and identification of underground nuclear explosions (Project Vela). Before the end of the year the AEC had completed a series of experiments on concealment. The Defense Department, however, did not start its research on Project Vela until the following year. There was a delay of several months while two divisions of defense (the Air Force

Technical Applications Center and the Advanced Research Projects Agency) argued which should be responsible for the project.

The enthusiasm with which the AEC entered into the study of possibilities of concealment, compared to the haphazard way in which the Department of Defense approached the study of improving possibilities for detection, illustrates an important lesson aptly described by Dr. James B. Fisk, former President of the Bell Telephone Laboratories, Vice-Chairman of the President's Science Advisory Committee, and former chief United States delegate to two international technical conferences concerned with the discontinuance of nuclear weapons tests. Dr. Fisk said:

> While the Department of Defense and the Atomic Energy Commission will always have a great interest and responsibility and will make contributions in this field [of arms limitation], they should not be expected to carry the burden both of maximizing and, simultaneously, minimizing arms.[5]

Disarmament raises difficult political as well as technical problems. Whatever type of organization is established, it must be able to meet these problems effectively and in a way that permits the United States to present its case before the world in the most positive form.

NEED FOR A SPECIAL EFFORT

The principal functions of special organizational machinery dealing with arms-control problems should be: to conduct research, to coordinate policy, and to formulate arms-control plans and proposals. This recommendation follows from the analysis in the preceding section which points up an important conclusion, namely, that arms control involves foreign-policy considerations and aspects of scientific and technological developments.

The research and experimentation to be undertaken can be grouped in three major categories. The first deals with military and political considerations in arms control, and how these would be affected under certain kinds of proposals. Some needed studies in this category are as follows:

1. The military significance of various types of agreements and their effect on specific military strategies and weapons systems.

2. The political and military advantages and disadvantages of linking together various arms-control proposals.

3. The political and military significance of inspection techniques and their possible impact on the Soviet Union and other states.

4. The importance and efficacy of intelligence as a supplement to functions of control systems to verify compliance with agreements.

5. The effect of technological development on various types of arms-control agreements.

6. Studies of demilitarized zones and the possible stationing of an international police force in areas of potential armed conflict.

7. Political problems connected with the inclusion of Communist China in an arms-control agreement.

8. Studies of control measures to halt or slow down the arms traffic to disturbed areas, such as Latin America, the Middle East, and Africa.

A second category concerns research on the technical and scientific requirements of verification, inspection, and the monitoring aspects of agreements on the control and reduction of armaments. Many of the elements in these studies must be integrated with the studies in the above category concerning military and political problems. Studies in the technical and scientific group include:

1. The detection and identification of nuclear-weapons tests.

2. The detection of missile tests and the launching of vehicles into outer space.

3. Measures to guard against surprise attack by long-range weapons, missiles, bombers, naval craft, conventional armaments, and armed forces.

4. Control systems to verify the cut-off of production of nuclear weapons.

5. Verification measures for a reduction in conventional armaments and armed forces.

6. Verification measures for the reduction and/or elimination of the production of chemical, biological, and radiological weapons.

A third category of studies concerns the economic aspects of arms control. Although the national economy would ultimately benefit from a reallocation of resources from weapons development to peacetime goods, certain industries and specific geographical areas would have adjustment problems. These should be looked into in advance of any arms-control agreement. Some of the questions to be studied in this connection are:

1. How would specific arms-control proposals affect certain segments of the economy?

2. What adjustments might be considered?

3. What policies and action should be formulated and carried out by the Federal Government to assure the least disruptive transition of the economy under conditions of substantial disarmament?

It would not be necessary for an arms-control agency itself to undertake each research project. Many could be contracted out to private institutions and industry. Some could be carried out by other government agencies. In the economic field, for example, the Business and Defense Services Administration of the Department of Commerce would be equipped to conduct certain studies. In the field of military strategy the Department of Defense would obviously have a key role, and on political questions an agency should be able to call on the Policy Planning Staff of the Department of State for assistance.

What is important is that an agency have the authority to engage in the studies that should be made if our arms-control policies and negotiations are to be grounded in solid support. Furthermore, it is vital that the results of studies in one area be related to the conclusions reached in other areas. The requirements for measures for inspection and measures for control of individual disarmament might be different if two or more were combined. In other words, some of the features of one control system probably can be utilized in another control system, with the advantage of reducing the complexity of control measures in general.

Any arms-control agency should have responsibilities other than those in the area of research. One of these should be in coordinating policy. Ways should be found to join together diplomatic and political policies on the one hand, with defense policy on the other.

On many occasions during the past few years the Defense and State Departments have followed contradictory policies affecting arms control. These are some examples. Beginning in 1954, the Defense Department devised a military-defense strategy of massive retaliation which involved giving first priority to nuclear weapons with vast destructive power, the equivalent of hundreds of thousands and even millions of tons of TNT. To deliver these weapons, the Defense Department concentrated on building a long-range strategic bomber force. To provide facilities for such a force required the construction of special air bases in key countries around the world.

At the same time the Defense Department ordered a cutback in conventional military strength, in part because the need for military manpower and conventional arms under a defense policy of massive retaliation was minimized, and in part to reduce the defense budget.

In the meantime one important development was becoming apparent to the State Department. The major military threat to the United States and the free world was not solely one of a knockout blow resulting from surprise attack. Most of the threats of war were on the periphery of the Soviet Union and were of a type which was more likely to require the availability of conventional arms and armed forces than heavy nuclear armaments. Furthermore, it was becoming apparent that many of the countries along the Soviet periphery did not want to be part of the battlefield for a nuclear war. They wanted to be free, not only free from the tyranny of Soviet and Chinese Communism, but also free from the evils of radioactive fallout.

The Department of State, therefore, began talking about nuclear disarmament at the very time when the Defense Department and the Atomic Energy Commission were at the peak of their interest in the development of nuclear weapons and in reliance on nuclear weapons for defense. Every move for the control of nuclear weapons made by the State Department was opposed by the Department of Defense and the Atomic Energy Commission.

Another example. Occasionally the State Department would suggest to the Soviet Union that armed forces be reduced. No sooner was such a proposal made on our part than an announcement would be made from the Pentagon that armed forces would be cut back unilaterally. Thus, any bargaining power the United States negotiators might have had was dissipated. The unilateral cutback might have had some use at least if it had been publicized as evidence of the sincere desire of the United States to work toward peace. No such message was carried to the people of other countries.

Other illustrations could be given to show that what political officers were proposing in the area of disarmament was contrary to, or was undercut by, the military. They point up the need for a centralized authority to coordinate national security policy so as to blend defense, disarmament, and political objectives so that United States policy-makers will make sound decisions and so that United States negotiators and information specialists can sell and publicize our proposals to full advantage.

THE ROLE OF CONGRESS

Although it is not responsible for the formulation and execution of policy, Congress, and particularly the Senate, has important functions in arms control. They can be grouped in five categories: (1) to appropriate funds to cover the cost of arms-control activities; (2) to give advice and consent to the making of treaties (Senate consent to treaties requires a two-thirds vote); (3) to provide general advice to the President and his chief advisers in foreign policy and national security affairs; (4) to enact laws that can affect both policy and organization; and (5) to approve all officials appointed by the President under legislative authority.

Since some discussion of the substance of possible legislation has already been given above, and since the approval by Congress of the appointment of officials is not very germane here, I shall limit my remarks on the role of Congress in arms control to the first three functions.

Until very recently appropriations for arms-control research and related activities have not been asked for, granted, or even considered necessary. The idea that millions of dollars should be spent on developing a control system for prohibiting the production of nuclear weapons, for example, is new and strange. Actually it is just as important to know what types of control are necessary for disarmament as it is to know what types of armaments are necessary for defense. Both intimately affect our national security.

On four occasions during the First Session of the 86th Congress, I tried to obtain funds for special arms-control studies: State Department appropriations, Defense Department appropriations, the Supplemental Appropriations bill, and appropriations for Mutual Security. Each time I was unsuccessful, in part because Congress did not realize the need was urgent and in part because the Executive branch gave practically no support to this effort.

That defense and disarmament are twin features of national security is only beginning to be comprehended. The committees of the Congress that have jurisdiction over foreign relations, armed services, and atomic energy have the special responsibility to make known to other members of Congress and to the public the importance of arms control today, and also the need to prepare for negotiations by conducting the appropriate studies and research, lest the proposals offered at the conference table are found too late to be either not feasible or else inimical to interests of national security.

The role of the Senate in the ratification of treaties is a vital one. The requirement of a two-thirds vote means that very large support and an understanding of the position of the Executive branch on any treaty that is negotiated must be forthcoming from the Senate. A two-thirds vote also means that the subject of any treaty must transcend partisan politics. Seldom does the political party in control of the Executive branch have the strength in the Senate to command or expect the support of 67 Senators. The Executive branch should not wait until a treaty has been negotiated before it consults the Senate. If it does, the Senate has the awkward choice of either a routine approval of the treaties submitted to it or of refusing consent to the product of months and perhaps years of labor and negotiation.[6]

To what extent the Executive branch should consult the Legislative branch in the formulation of arms-control policy and the negotiation of treaties must be worked out through experience. In the recent past little actual consideration took place, and much of that was initiated by members of Congress.

It is important to distinguish the act of consulting from the act of giving information. Although the submission to Congress of information pertaining to arms control is by no means thorough, it is far greater than the amount of consultation that has taken place. The Disarmament Subcommittee frequently has received information from the Executive branch about policies that have already been decided. Seldom has it been invited to participate in a discussion before policy decisions have been reached.

The third major function of Congress (especially the Senate) in the area of arms control comes under the broad category of advising the President. This is, of course, closely related to the procedure of Executive consultation of the Senate regarding the negotiation of treaties.

Because I myself believe that the Senate must be kept informed of the policy of the Executive branch during the course of negotiating any treaty dealing with arms control, as chairman of the Senate Foreign Relations Subcommittee on Disarmament, I have held hearings on numerous occasions during the entire period of the negotiations for the discontinuance of nuclear-weapons tests. The Joint Committee on Atomic Energy also held hearings during this period. These hearings, plus discussion and debate on the Senate floor, give every member of the Senate the opportunity to become informed. Moreover, by being apprised of developments in negotiations, Senators can if they wish register their views before the President and the Secretary of State, either collectively through the passage of resolutions, or individually through private discussion and communications. Through such procedures the Executive branch is in a much better position to judge the receptivity of the Senate to a treaty than if the Senate remained silent during the course of negotiations with other countries.

The Senate, however, should not wait until a treaty is being negotiated before advising the President and his appointed officers about arms-control matters. If it did, the Senate would have little voice in influencing policy, and it would not be properly performing its constitutional role of advising the President. Most of the work of the Senate Disarmament Subcommittee has been directed to informing the members so that they could perform their advisory role intelligently. The studies, hearings, reports, speeches, inquiries, and correspondence of the Subcommittee and its members have had an effect on the formulation of arms-control policy—to what extent, it is difficult to measure.

CONCLUSIONS

In concluding my discussion of government organization for arms control, I think one point must be stressed. The United States cannot proceed with arms-control negotiations at its own pace. Negotiations cannot be postponed for years while our organizational structure evolves. Nor can we expect other countries to bide their time while we decide how to put our own affairs in order. Science itself cannot be held back. In the absence of control and elimination, the nuclear and other weapons resulting from advances in technology will spread to many countries. The weapons being produced and developed today are becoming increasingly automatic. Once they are sent on their mission, they cannot be recalled, and they are weapons against which there is little or no defense. Thus the danger of a runaway war is becoming greater all the time. Outer space may become a battle field for military competition if progress is not made through international agreements in reserving it for peaceful exploration and pursuits. This is a new dimension in arms control that necessitates immediate attention. These are the realities with which governmental organization for arms control must cope with all dispatch.

PART VII

TOWARD A PEACEFUL WORLD

22. The Pursuit of Rational World-Security Arrangements

RICHARD S. LEGHORN

THE CRUX OF THE SO-CALLED "DISARMAMENT" OR NATIONAL-SECURITY problem for the United States today is the resolution of a dichotomy which exists between deterrence and disarmament policies in the nation's approach to security, and the definition of our national-security objective as the construction of rational world-security arrangements.*

It is the purpose of this chapter to suggest that certain factors in the current military-technological situation make progress in arms control newly feasible; that mutual deterrence through national armed strength can be the basis upon which more stable and rational world-security arrangements can initially be founded, provided certain arms regulations are instituted; and that such a system of stabilized national deterrents—while inherently too insecure and potentially too devastating to constitute world security in the long run—can preserve the peace while the world develops United Nations machinery for enforcing the peace, and nonviolent methods for resolving international conflicts, both of which are necessary conditions for achieving ultimately the goal of universal, complete disarmament of nations.

RESOLVING THE PRESENT DICHOTOMY IN UNITED STATES SECURITY

The internal dispute within the United States between the "armers"—the advocates of security through armed strength, or *deterrence*—and the "disarmers"—those advocating security through arms reductions, or *disarmament*—has led this country to pursue inconsistent and frequently conflicting courses. Both deterrence and disarmament are legitimate, indeed vital, approaches to security planning. They are only two sides of the question. But today neither pursued independently of the other is acceptable or adequate.

* I am indebted to T. C. O'Sullivan and Miss Faith Wright for considerable assistance in the preparation of this chapter.

These two aspects of the security problem are mutually compatible and complementary means to a single objective, enhanced national and world security. They should be harmonized within one coherent, over-all security concept. Until they are, the dichotomy in the United States' handling of its security affairs will continue to engender confusion at home and abroad, both as to ultimate goals and short-term tactics; it will forestall this country's exercise of world leadership and impede progress toward a rational system for national and world security.

Identifying a New United States Security Objective. The key objective of building rational world-security arrangements has not yet been politically identified and is a gap in our foreign-policy objectives. The preoccupation of the United States with the means of achieving arms control has obscured the definition of its ultimate goal in this area, which has too often been equated, erroneously, with disarmament *per se.*

To set an early goal of "general and complete disarmament," as advocated by Khrushchev, is a delusion and invites disaster. Unless one postulates a millennium in which there will be no conflicts of interest or violently aggressive tendencies among nations, or in which governments will have withered away, as in Communist theory, peace cannot be an absence of arms. We should have learned this lesson from the experiences of the Rhineland, South Korea, World Wars I and II, and the history of families, tribes, states, and nations.

At present the maintenance of national deterrent forces is the only factor serving to secure such stability as does exist. These deterrent forces must not be eliminated until new machinery for enforcing peace has been created to insure order, under law and justice. Complete disarmament without such arrangements for security would merely lead to rearmament in the face of international conflicts; peaceful rocket and nuclear technologies would quickly be converted to military uses.

It is irresponsible to encourage the hopes of mankind for the sake of an unrealistic and unfeasible goal. Alone, the term *disarmament* is an inadequate and misleading description of the fundamental United States objective, and is more descriptive of Communist than of Western goals. It should be viewed not as the direct goal but as a result feasible only after the world has built reliable international means for enforcing the peace.

Neither can we be satisfied with the establishment of controlled mutual deterrence as a satisfactory long-range goal. The political and technological factors affecting deterrence are dynamic and would always threaten to upset the stability, again making it possible to revert to the old patterns of the arms race. Controlled mutual deterrence is, however, a valid interim step which would act as an umbrella under which we could develop effective United Nations machinery for dealing with the peace. The United States must take immediate steps to enhance stability through a combination of deterrent arms and arms control.

Nor is the elimination of conflicts of interest our goal. There is a high level of ideological conflict between the Communist and non-Communist worlds. What is more important is to create security systems which will prevent the resort to violent means for resolving such conflicts and permit the build-up of alternative, nonviolent techniques for settlement. Our proper concern is to make the world safe for differences in ideology.

Nor is reduction in national expenditures through reduction in armaments a primary or immediate goal. Elaborate systems will be required to implement the new security structures, and these will be expensive. We must not continue, either, to talk mostly of national security, forgetting that the military-technological situation is such that the United States alone can no longer increase its own security without agreements which also increase the security of other nations. We should harmonize these policies into one pursuit with an international scope—the building of stable world-security arrangements.

The real goal is security—security for our own and other nations, within a framework of world order under law and justice, in which peaceful change is facilitated and conflicts are resolved nonviolently. Our task is to build rational world-security arrangements based initially on stabilized and controlled national deterrent arms, and as soon as feasible, on reliable United Nations machinery to enforce the peace.

This aim must be achieved in the face of the Communist threat and "total conflict" strategy. Our policies must facilitate construction of an acceptable system of world order, while simultaneously countering the Communist threat.

The Relation to Other National Objectives. It is useful to note the relation of this security objective to four other national objectives that we may expect to dominate our foreign policy during the immediate future.

Maintain world leadership so that it may be exercised to achieve our goal of a system of world law, order, and justice under which freedom can flourish.

While the United States still enjoys the advantages of relative over-all superiority in power, it must develop and use its advantages in power to move the world away from security systems based on unrestrained national power to more stable and durable arrangements consistent with the principles of constitutional democracy. During this period, a partial Pax Americana can help insure world peace. But considered estimates of the duration of the over-all superiority of United States power vis-à-vis that of any other nation or probable combination of nations are in terms of decades, not centuries, and America's advantage in military power is already fast disappearing.

Our national power must be purposefully directed during this period to achieve a world social order in which human activity is not predominantly directed by central purposes. This goal is more positive and constructive than the declared World War II objective of "saving the world for democracy," or the cold-war objective of containing Communism. The United States must:

1. strive to maintain power advantages where we now unquestionably have them, such as economic superiority;

2. firmly establish advantages in those areas in which we have been seriously challenged, as in science, technology, and education; and

3. attempt to establish at least an equality if not a superiority in these areas in which Communist advantage is too often presumed to be inherent, as in informational (ideological) functions.

The sole exception to this competition for power advantages lies in the military area, where a stable stand-off should be our pursuit, as discussed later in this chapter.

United States leadership cannot be exercised to achieve our basic national political aim until deterrent and arms-control policies are adjusted within a consistent security program. A nation which quite evidently is divided and does not know what it wants in the "disarmament" area cannot possibly lead the world in any direction.

Reduce the Communist threat through measures which tend to promote the evolution of Communist countries toward societies compatible with our basic national political goal.

Until recently, the declared position of the United States, if not always its action position, has been to reduce the Communist threat by attempting to reduce its capabilities. To develop enervating fissures within and even to bring down the system was an avowed purpose of liberation policies and of extreme containment pressures to deny Communist countries access to other resources.

The lack of realism and the bankruptcy of this negative approach, so evident in many areas, has brought a shift, if not a firm decision in national policy, in favor of measures designed: (1) to improve our capabilities relative to those of the Soviets, and (2) in the long range, to alter the intentions of Soviet society and to cultivate the evolution of these intentions in a manner consistent with our own basic political goals. Military containment (deterrence) is still valid, but not ambition to bring down the system or turn the clock back.

Rather than anti-Communism, our overriding purpose must be the pursuit of an enforced, competitive peace under law and justice. We must be more "for" than "against." This is not the place to discuss cultural-exchange, trade, or other policies in relation to this evolutionary objective. However, it is useful to note two circumstances that bear directly on arms-control policy.

First is the contribution which the adoption of the evolutionary objective can make to further arms controls. Realistic liberation policies would have required decisive military superiority. Containment policies in their extreme forms also tend to require United States and allied military superiority; there are still voices advocating major United States arms-budget increases as a measure to strain the Soviet economy in an unproductive arms race.

The goal of decisive military superiority blocks the consideration of arms-control measures, except those whose effect is to freeze the Soviets in a position of military inferiority, a situation they steadfastly refuse to accept, and one which in pursuit of their basic political goal they must continue to refuse to accept. It has also tended to result in defining our arms-control objectives as agreed measures whose effect is to reduce the relative Soviet military position. This is an unrealistic and unproductive ambition.

Second are the ways in which arms controls support our evolutionary objective. Dictatorships tend to lean on alleged outside threats; the establishment of rational world-security arrangements for arms controls will tend to remove these fears and this prop of dictatorship. Arms controls will require exchanges of personnel and information, thus tending to move Communist countries toward more open societies. Freedom can hardly flourish in a climate of fear, and well-constructed arms controls will tend to diminish tensions. When eventual comprehensive controls are able to reduce security costs appreciably, the released economic and technological resources will tend to enhance the Soviet status as a "have" nation, with more conservative and less revolutionary inclinations.

In short, arms-control measures and measures to facilitate the evolution of Communist societies support one another in an important way.

Reduce causes of international conflicts and tensions, both short and long term.

It is frequently stated that substantial progress in the elimination of political, economic, ideological, propaganda, and other causes of conflict must be made before there can be substantial progress in disarmament and that arms are the result and not the cause of tension. While this view might have been acceptable when wars and arms were limited to degrees of destruction that did not threaten the very existence of civilization and humanity, this syllogism is no longer an acceptable basis of policy.

While it is an important national objective to work to eliminate the various causes of war, we must take the view that there will always be conflicts of interest among nations, and violently aggressive tendencies among some. Many international political problems are rooted in the security issue, and, as we build stable world-security arrangements, political settlements will be facilitated. Thus, while recognizing that political settlements and reduction in the causes of conflict will tend to facilitate arms-control negotiations, we cannot regard a substantial elimination of conflict as the condition to progress in arms controls.

Develop international methods for the nonviolent resolution of conflict and peaceful change.

To progress from the present and no longer adequate institutions of international diplomacy to those of world law and justice, vast efforts are required to develop techniques for the nonviolent resolution of conflicts and techniques for peaceful change. It is not within the scope of this chapter to detail these techniques or how they might best be developed. But the path almost certainly lies through the repeal of the Connolly amendment, a substantial revision of the United Nations Charter, and the steady development of a body of world law. It is necessary to identify this key national objective and to examine its relation to disarmament and arms-control policies.

A PROPOSED APPROACH TO RATIONAL WORLD-SECURITY ARRANGEMENTS

The United States should approach its objective of building rational world-security arrangements in three ways.

First is the enforcement of international order through stabilized and controlled national deterrent arms, in which levels of national arms would be stabilized and controlled downward to the lowest level sufficient to deter resort to war.

Second is the development of international law and United Nations authority to enforce the peace: the build-up of the reliable machinery which will make feasible the transfer of enforcement power from individual nations and power blocs to the United Nations.

Third is a comprehensive national arms reduction down to the levels required for internal police duties, with the decisive transfer of responsibility for enforcing international peace to the United Nations; this situation is what should be intended by the phrase "universal and complete disarmament."

These three elements in our national approach must be pursued simultaneously. They are closely interrelated, and progress in each will contribute to, and depend largely upon, progress in the others. Yet we should expect them to be fully accomplished only in sequence. It is important to understand this sequential relation, and to recognize in particular that real progress in the third area, universal and complete disarmament, depends upon success in the first two.

There is a tendency to think of carrying out this last phase according to a master plan, with an agreed-upon timetable beginning immediately. I view this tendency as a dangerous one. Until reliable United Nations machinery exists for enforcing the peace, it would be most unwise to embark upon the scheduled creation of an absence of arms.

First Element: the enforcement of international order by a system of national deterrent arms, stabilized and controlled down to the lowest level sufficient to deter resort to war.

The term *stabilization* as used in this chapter refers to the maintaining of a world situation in which the evaluation of a proposed military action by any nation indicates that the probable loss will be far greater than the possible gain, with the result that the action will be discarded as unprofitable. In speaking of stabilization, of course, I refer to the degree of stability, and not to perfect stability. Our goal should be to move from levels of lesser stability to levels of greater stability, at lower world-armament levels. Rather than seeking an illusory static equilibrium, we should manage the dynamic factors involved and constantly make adjustments, both unilaterally and through agreements, which build greater stability at lower force levels.

I am convinced that national deterrent arms, on which we now rely, can be organized into a rational "collective security" system for preserving the peace without the madness of the current spiraling arms race, and with substantial arms reductions. But the national deterrent forces of the major powers must first be stabilized. Caught in a headlong arms race, the world cannot turn around until it first stops racing.

In all probability we shall have to live under the umbrella of mutual deterrent forces for a considerable length of time. We should face the difficult fact that there is in the world today a high degree of ideological conflict, a type of conflict extremely difficult to deal with. At the same time, there is a very low degree of ability to resolve such conflicts in a nonviolent manner. As long as this condition prevails, the deterrent force levels on both sides of the iron curtain will have to remain rather high in order to make any resort to violent means clearly unprofitable.

We should not regard a temporary system of stabilized national arms as an unmitigated evil, however. The more certainly these forces deter war, the more they will require the resort to nonviolent techniques, such as diplomacy, arbitration, world law, and judicial decision. This period should be considered as a helpful condition to the development of a functioning system of world law and enforcement machinery, which, in turn, is a necessary condition to the eventual reduction of national arms to the level of internal police forces. Indeed, it is likely that the reduction of force levels will be paced by the evolution of effective nonviolent techniques, rather than by any arbitrary timetable.

There should be a substantial reduction of certain arms as we achieve rational world-security arrangements based on controlled mutual deterrents. However, a reduction to too low a level will tend to lessen rather than increase stability, if carried out too soon in relation to the development of United Nations enforcement machinery and methods of nonviolent resolution of conflict.

Second Element: the development of international law and of United Nations authority to enforce the peace.

Major progress in this area can hardly be made quickly. The problem is not the relatively straightforward matter of organizing a United Nations security force, but rather the monumental job of achieving a legal, judicial, and political context in which it can operate. These elements are treated more fully in the following chapter by Arthur Larson; our present concern is directed to the development of United Nations authority and experience in peace-enforcement action, and the build-up of a United Nations force for this purpose. While we should pursue this approach vigorously and concurrently with the programs to stabilize national deterrent forces, we should not expect too rapid progress.

We have seen in the past ten years a few early examples of direct action by the United Nations in situations of military conflict. In Korea, major national contingents entered the country at the invitation of the South Korean government and in the name of the United Nations. Later in the Middle East, a force recruited by the United Nations and stationed on the border provided inspection functions as well as deterrence to border incidents. In the Congo, a force recruited in a similar manner acted in a quite different capacity.

These precedents suggest that there is sufficient reason to consider establishing a permanent United Nations security force of moderate size, capable of performing a broad spectrum of functions. These would include observation and inspection, deployment for purposes of deterrence, and military action in support of self-defense measures in repelling invasions. This force should be of a highly mobile nature and could be supplemented as is appropriate by national contingents recruited by the United Nations. It should be used only when authorized by the United Nations, when invited by the nation in which it would be physically located, and only in the defense of that nation's territory. The key to the successful development of United Nations security forces may well be the acceptance of the concept that they will be used only to support actions of pure self-defense— that is, only on the defender's side of the pre-aggression, de facto, political boundary.

As United Nations enforcement authority develops, new nations and nations not protected by alliances can be expected to rely more and more on the United Nations for security against external aggression, rather than on national forces. As the United Nations expands its ability to provide such security, under the umbrella of stabilized mutual deterrent forces maintained by the two blocs, more and more nations would accept its protection, cutting back national forces to levels required for internal police duties.

It is possible that the build-up of United Nations enforcement authority during this period may be assisted by the creation of regional groupings, organized to provide defensive security to nonbloc nations. Such regional arrangements might for example be established by Africa or Latin America. Or, alternatively, an initial United Nations security force might be recruited from and used by the so-called "neutral" group for strengthening their measures for security.

Third Element: comprehensive national arms reduction under United

Nations controls to levels required for internal security, with an effective transfer of the enforcement authority to the United Nations.

Significant progress here must await the development of the United Nations as a reliable keeper of the peace. As of today, the West remains reluctant to accept the Khrushchev formula for complete disarmament in four years, principally because of its concern about effective arms controls and a substitute system to enforce the peace. This reluctance is well founded. It is national armaments that are maintaining whatever stability there is in the world today. We should not plan to get rid of these arms until the necessary international legal and judicial institutions are established and until United Nations enforcement authority under proper political direction has proved its adequacy. When we arrive at this stage, it would be safe to complete the transfer of forces for the maintenance of peace from national and alliance control to United Nations control. We may expect this evolution to take place in two phases.

First, when all but the nuclear-power blocs have come to rely on the United Nations' ability to enforce peace, we can anticipate the reduction, under adequate controls, of *conventional* forces throughout the world, down to the levels required for internal security. After that would come the controlled elimination of *nuclear* weapons of mass destruction from national armaments. I find it hard to believe that we shall reach this latter stage until the institutions for the peaceful resolution of international conflicts are well developed and until world armament laws are enforceable on individuals. In the sequence of steps I am suggesting, the elimination of retaliatory rocket weapons would come last, not first.

STABILIZATION MEASURES

Success in building rational world-security arrangements depends heavily on the early control and stabilization of national deterrent arms at the lowest levels still adequate to deter resort to violence. This is an urgent problem. The military situation will never be self-stabilizing or self-regulating, and world nuclear stockpiles are approaching, or have achieved, a size sufficient to destroy twentieth-century civilization. Listed below are proposals to implement a controlled stabilization of national arms. They are grouped into two sections, as they relate to nuclear or conventional forces.

The measures proposed in the first section, which deals with nuclear weapons, have as a common aim the stabilization of retaliatory deterrents and involve reducing the need for quick reactions. It is believed that a war fought with nuclear weapons would be a general war, or would deteriorate into general war. This section, then, can be thought of as relating to stabilization against general war.

The recommendations in the second section are directed toward the stabilization—under the umbrella of mutual nuclear deterrence—of conventional weapons, by strengthening the defense relative to the offense, and by giving it a quickened reaction capability to remove the prospect of profit from any conventional offensive. It is believed that a very widespread war would be fought with nuclear weapons, and that strategies limited to conventional weapons relate only to local wars.* Therefore, this section can be thought of as relating to the controlled stabilization of deterrents to local wars.

We have already defined controlled stabilization as a continuing and dynamic process in pursuit of lower force levels and a military situation in which the expected loss through an aggressive action, as estimated by either side, is substantially greater than the expected gain.

There are several ways to institute specific measures. In recent years, we have focused on formal negotiation and the achievement of tacit understanding. Writings in the arms-control field are now increasingly stressing the importance of conditional unilateral acts in achieving stability. These unilateral acts may either add to stability or help establish the conditions necessary to tacit or explicit agreements.

Pending the development of substantial United Nations forces, every effort must be made to maintain the bipolarity of the military world. It should be apparent that both nuclear retaliatory stability and conventional defensive stability will decrease appreciably as the number of major independent power centers increase beyond two. Many believe that the world situation, if not brought under control first, will be virtually uncontrollable if the number of truly independent centers of nuclear power rises beyond three or four. It is important, therefore, to achieve reasonable control while bipolarity exists and to adjust the controls to allow the maintenance of maximum stability if power shifts from bipolar to multicentered arrangements.

Earlier, we discussed arrangements to provide, outside of the bipolar power-bloc structure, defensive security for newly emerging nations and some bloc members. These arrangements can play an important role in preserving the bipolar power structure while controlled mutual deterrence is being pursued.

Nuclear Weapon Problems. In the late 1940's, after World War II, we placed our primary reliance on retaliation against cities. We had a few bombers and atomic bombs; the Russians had none. We had little conventional power, so the threat of atomic bombing was our primary security reliant.

During the early part of the 1950's, we shifted our aim from Russian cities to Russian military installations. That is, we put our primary reliance on a *counterforce* strategy, instead of a *countereconomy* strategy. This was the correct strategy for the 1950's, when we had overwhelming superiority in both bombs and bombers. With the Soviet development of atomic

---

* However, some strategists believe that a conventional war on something like the scale of World War II is not impossible.—ED.

weapons, the best strategy in the event of war was to destroy Russia's few long-range bombers and the atomic weapons which could really hurt us.

Now, in the 1960's, a different situation faces the United States. The Russians, no matter what we can practically do, will be able to inflict unacceptable damage on the United States in the event of war. A basic counterforce strategy can no longer provide the security it did in the 1950's. Furthermore, a counterforce posture by a nation, such as the United States, which expects to receive the first blow requires major arms superiority. And the pursuit of superiority means an indefinite arms race.

Counterforce strategy must now give way to the pursuit of controlled mutual deterrence. Stability of deterrence in the 1960's will be based on approximate strategic parity between the West and the Soviet Union. Parity in nuclear rocket weapons would, initially, be at a relatively high level, but this level should be substantially lower than that which would allow mutual annihilation.

Once both sides have the capabilities and understand that a first-strike initiative cannot sufficiently eliminate second-strike capability, the stage will be set for a serious discussion of ways to bring about controlled mutual deterrence.

Invulnerable weapons will permit abandoning our declared policy of *instant, massive* retaliation in favor of *certain, sufficient* retaliation. We can introduce enough delay in retaliation to reduce substantially the risks of accidents and miscalculations. These characteristics will also facilitate agreements with our allies for sharing control of these weapons, as it will be easier to define the conditions under which they may be used.

Certain kinds of advances in technology tend to increase stability and should therefore be encouraged. As already mentioned, the availability of solid and possibly storable liquid rocket propellants will provide retaliatory weapons highly invulnerable to counteroffensive blows and to aerospace defenses. Because it will take very many weapons either in offense or in defense to destroy one retaliatory weapon, the achievement of decisive supremacy by either side will be impractical. This situation can eliminate the decisive advantage of a first-strike initiative, which currently exists with vulnerable aircraft and first-generation missiles. Furthermore, the current advantage of surprise nuclear attack tempts pre-emptive action and, because it compels instant reaction to warnings, risks war through accident and miscalculation. Thus, the technology of relatively invulnerable solid-fueled rockets will provide major opportunities to stabilize the world's military environment during the 1960's.

The United States and the Soviet Union—or NATO and the Warsaw Pact group—might have 1,000 highly invulnerable, long-range rocket weapons. I slightly prefer 500 to 1,000, while some experts prefer 300 to 500, but the exact number is not too important in this discussion. One hundred is too few because too unstable, and ten thousand is both unnecessary and too risky of the annihilation of twentieth-century civilization.* The danger of technological surprise would be minimized by mixing qualitatively different methods of launching—mobile land-launch, submarine and sea-surface launch, and perhaps airborne launch—with dispersal and hardening of sites.

Stability of mutual deterrence with these invulnerable retaliatory weapons does not depend on precise equality in numbers, provided we do not stabilize at excessively low levels. Thus, tacit agreements backed by intelligence information may prove a useful interim to formal agreements on force levels. And formal agreements will be facilitated because inspection does not need to maintain precise equality, as a few violations cannot upset the strategic balance.

In the early stages of pursuing stability, arms information, however secured, must be adequate to warn of any impending counterforce superiority, whether from technological breakthrough or through the building of additional armed forces. We shall soon have reconnaissance satellite systems which, with other open sources, intelligence techniques, and a limited amount of inspection, should provide enough information for the stabilizing process. This information need not be exhaustive, since exact equality in weapons, item for item, is not required for this stability of deterrence.

Once second-generation rocket weapons, which can be hidden completely and fired instantaneously, become available in quantity, systems to warn of impending surprise attack will be of minimum value. In fact, agreed inspection to warn of impending surprise attack with second-generation rocket weapons is not desirable for the pursuit of deterrent stability of nuclear weapons. Such acquisition of target-deployment data might tend toward instability. The key to nuclear stability is information adequate to preserve the qualitative and quantitative parity of retaliatory systems.

In the initial stages, to keep nuclear-armed aircraft from upsetting the retaliatory stand-off, surprise warning systems will remain useful, as will controls on bomber deployment and continued emphasis on nuclear air defense. Regulation of bomber-force levels will help to consolidate stability and help to prepare for comprehensive arms control, but they are not a first essential to the achievement of nuclear stability.

The controlled limitation of the production of large rocket weapons can be an excellent means of consolidating mutual nuclear deterrence. Also, experimental and practice launchings might be controlled through a mutually agreed system of reporting and observation. In addition, the agreed suspension of nuclear tests or limitations on large tests will help nuclear stability through impeding the development of rocket counterforce capabilities. The cessation of production of nuclear materials for weapons purposes and the transfer of substantial amounts of nuclear material from military to peaceful stockpiles are not essential to the pursuit of deterrent stability

---

* The question of warhead yield is important in this connection. Ten thousand 20-kiloton weapons would be less destructive than one thousand 20-megaton weapons.— ED.

of nuclear weapons. They are, however, important in bringing stockpiles down to levels well below those required for mutual annihilation and for impeding the spread of nuclear weapons to other countries.

What seems immediately feasible, both technically and politically, is the establishment of a control system to keep weapons of mass destruction out of orbit. The West should press the initiative it took in March 1960, while there is still some question as to the military usefulness of outer space weapons.

Conventional Weapon Problems. Military technology and certain political factors are such today that the conventional local defense could be made strong enough decisively to repel, and therefore deter, any local conventional offense. There are at least eight types of action we should pursue to achieve the deterrent stability of conventional arms:

1. We should strive for an approximate equality of Communist and Western conventional strengths at progressively lower levels. To overcome a conventionally equipped defense, a conventionally equipped offense will require in men, tactics, and equipment a superiority of something like two or three to one. Thus, equality favors the defense, in the sense that an offense only equally strong is faced with a high probability of failure. It is well to underline the fact that today the Communist bloc, including China, has only about 15 per cent more in active military personnel than the Western bloc. If Khrushchev carries out his announced reduction to 2,400,-000 men, the total men under arms on each side will be roughly equal.

2. The strategic mobility of Western conventional forces is essential to balance the current Communist advantage of internal lines of military communication throughout the Eurasian land mass, and to reduce the advantage of initiative. Air and sea lift, supplemented by a few selected overseas bases for conventional forces, can provide strategic mobility to strengthen Western conventional deterrent power and thus enhance conventional military stability.

3. Information to warn of surprise attack should be our third pursuit. Surprise is an advantage for the offense. Eliminating surprise strengthens conventional defense and thus also enhances military stability. Aerial inspection—while of limited value in warning of rocket surprise attack—can very adequately warn of mass conventional attacks.

4. Disengagement of conventional forces will promote deterrent stability by reducing tension and accidents and by insuring more time to ready the defense.

5. Technology can greatly strengthen the conventional defense. The machine gun has long been effective against men, but recent developments will greatly improve antitank and antiaircraft weapons. Additionally, technology can provide a greatly improved air lift, and greatly improved reconnaissance and warning systems. Also, if arrangements are possible which permit a nation in pure self-defense against massed conventional attack to use certain unconventional weapons, such as chemical weapons or special

types of nuclear devices (for instance the "neutron bomb" discussed in Chapter 12 of this book), on its own territory only, deterrence to mass conventional attack would be vastly increased. This latter measure could be employed only if the use of unconventional weapons were limited to the defending force; however, the advantages for stabilization are sufficient to warrant study of ways of establishing conventions for the one-sided defensive use of unconventional weapons.*

6. Control over conventional arms can help insure parity of numbers. Reductions should be aimed first at arms that tend to be employed offensively, such as tanks and bombers.

7. An important element of deterrence is the intent to resist, and the clear demonstration of this will to a potential aggressor. Mutual security pacts and the presence of allied soldiers on the territory of weak nations will strengthen conventional deterrence.

8. Lastly, United Nations deterrent power can greatly improve conventional deterrent stability. While we must not expect that it will be adequate in any Western-Communist confrontation, it could exert a stabilizing conventional deterrence in other areas. It would be especially effective initially in dampening intra-Free World conflicts, which will continue to develop in the Middle East and Latin America and among the new and emerging nations of Africa. United Nations forces, by providing reliable security for these nations, will reduce or eliminate their need for nuclear weapons and thus can curb the diffusion of nuclear weapons from the present bipolar power structure to a multi-centered power structure.

Some people have questioned the wisdom of deliberately strengthening defensive technology relative to the offense, considering that in the past the United States has repeatedly found itself on the tactical offensive, fighting to win back territory lost in an initially strong enemy offensive. However, it should be noted that, had the initial defense been strong enough to be successful, this concern would be unwarranted.

Other possible objections to this policy relate to potential problems which might develop in certain special situations, such as reopening a road to Berlin. Situations like Berlin, in which the policy would be disadvantageous, do not imply that it is invalid. Rather, they underscore the need, if we adopt this policy, to avoid the creation of situations in which it does not work.

THE ROLE OF ARMS INFORMATION

In concluding, I should like to emphasize the importance of arms-information systems in the pursuit of stability. Information facilitates tacit agreements and counteractions to destabilizing perturbations. Information is stabilizing because it warns of impending attack, force-level build-ups, or technological surprise, identifies accidents, and helps avoid miscalcula-

* Many students of these matters are intensely skeptical of this proposal.—Ed.

tions. In the psychological sense, the broad availability of arms information is important; fear of the unknown is behind much of the arms race and behind international tensions and distrust. The basis of confidence is not only experience but also information. In the absence of knowledge of the actual threat, countermeasures tend to be built against all imaginable threats, thus further spiraling the arms race.

To achieve military stability, both sides must have all the information that can be gained from agreed inspection sources, from open sources, and from intelligence sources, with the single exception of nuclear counterforce targeting intelligence. The West is faced with a vastly greater paucity of information than are the Communists. Now that Russia is reaching a nuclear retaliatory parity with the West, we in turn must achieve a parity of conventional forces and parity in information in order to maintain a military stand-off. In allocating priorities, we must put arms information on an equal footing with armed deterrence.

It should by now be obvious that the overflight of Russia is vital to our security. For a number of years we have been able to overfly the Soviet Union at very slight military risk. The military vulnerability of our overflight systems has been small. The political vulnerability, however, has been extremely high. The reader may recall the Russian protests in 1955 and again in 1958 because certain United States balloons flew over the USSR, allegedly carrying reconnaissance equipment. More recently, the Soviet outcry over the U-2 made this overflight program politically impossible.

The last technological opportunity that we have to gain vital information from overflights is the reconnaissance satellite. From a political standpoint, this satellite is inherently less vulnerable than either aircraft or balloons. It does, however, have some degree of political vulnerability, and the Soviet Union has launched a political attack against it. Their first major move came in their disarmament proposal of June 2, 1960, which demands that Midas and similar satellites be declared illegal in the very first phase of disarmament. This, I think, is the beginning of a major political offensive to shoot down these satellite systems politically. A close examination of the systems involved will suggest that they are not very effective for gathering the types of information the Russians most fear will be obtained, and it is important that the Soviet Union be reassured on this point.

Some understanding must be reached with the Russians about the essentiality of arms information for military stability. Uncertainty about military facts tends to increase tensions, fears, and the risk of miscalculation and accidents. Uncertainty impedes progress with arms regulation.

CONCLUSION

In this chapter I have tried to suggest that the key to true national security lies first in harmonizing our deterrence and arms-control policies in one over-all concept of world security. We should first urgently pursue a secure world peace based on the controlled stabilization of national arms, with reduction to the lowest level needed to deter resort to violence by any nation. As United Nations machinery is developed, both to enforce the peace and to resolve international conflicts in a nonviolent manner, we can foresee a further reduction of national force levels, as more and more nations become willing to rely on the United Nations for protection against external aggression. Only the successful development of such United Nations authority to preserve the peace will permit universal and complete disarmament—the comprehensive reduction of all national force levels to those required for internal security.

23. Arms Control through World Law

ARTHUR LARSON

THERE ARE TWO MAIN ELEMENTS IN WORLD LAW RELEVANT TO ARMS control: settling disputes, and ensuring compliance. This dual nature of the world law task needs stressing at the outset because the first of the two jobs, dispute-settling, is usually slighted in discussions of this kind. Too often it seems to be assumed that if somehow we could only create a decisively powerful international police force under central control in a relatively disarmed world, the problem of achieving world law would be largely solved. This assumption contains a pair of fatal flaws.

The first flaw is this: before a police force is sent into action to deal with an international quarrel, except in the case of overt violence directly witnessed or verified by the force, there must first be a decision on who is right and who is wrong in the quarrel. Since most quarrels nowadays are the result, not of clean-cut lawless invasions, but of complex and subtle clashes of alleged rights, this settling of the rights and wrongs of the situation requires a body of principles to guide the decision and an impartial mechanism to apply the principles—both acceptable to the states affected.

The second flaw is this: a relatively disarmed world with a powerful international force is not going to come into existence except as a satisfactory dispute-settling system is developed simultaneously. Armaments have not been built up entirely out of sheer "cussedness." They have been built up, in part at least, to perform a legitimate function: that of trying to protect the state against wrongful infringements of its rights, including its right to security. It follows that we cannot merely get rid of armaments and leave a vacuum. Something has to be put in their place. In the human story that "something" has always been law.

The general approach of this chapter will differ from some earlier treatments of the subject. Here the attempt will be to describe, not just an end result, but a process. That is, the primary effort will be, not to draw a blueprint of an idealized system of world law and arms control, but to inquire whether it is possible now to begin a series of gradual and phased steps that ultimately could lead to something approximating such an idealized system.

This approach is suggested by the thought that our plan for building up world law must match our plan for disarming. We reject sweeping Russian proposals for total disarmament in a few years as unrealistic. We propose gradual and phased disarmament, with the strength of the central international police force rising as the strength of national armaments falls, until the international force in effect outweighs the national. A program for achieving world law to match this arms-reduction program, then, would not be one of a sweeping revision of the United Nations Charter within a few years to create a limited World Government. Such a program, rather, must gradually strengthen the body, the machinery, and the acceptance of law for settling international differences—not before, not after, but contemporaneous with and in phase with the reduction of armaments. Consequently, just as we may envisage a world in which an international armed force will decisively outrank the national, so we may envision a world in which an international rule of law will eventually outrank national license and self-judging.

SETTLING DISPUTES

Before we can discuss how disputes should be settled in a world of law and reduced arms, we should look round and ask what kind of disputes we have to deal with in today's world. In so doing, we must distinguish actual active disputes from generalized tensions and unpleasantness between states. Strain and struggle, suspicion and exasperation, must for our purposes be taken as given quantities on the international scene. Our concern here is how to keep them from breaking the peace.

In discussions of the problem of arms control and war prevention, one often gets the impression that the actual onset of hostilities is treated as a kind of mathematical abstraction. The concept that "A attacks B" or "B attacks A" is taken as a given quantity, and various deductions and equations are then based upon this concept. (This is like a classical opening in a murder mystery: the corpse is found in the library; the murder is a given quantity; and the story proceeds from there.) Much of the elaborate analysis of deterrence and arms-control policy will be found on close examination to assume that a major attack will come about either as the result of a "preventive strike" by a power which has no better reason for striking than a conviction that it has a certain ratio of military superiority, or as the result of an "accident" based on a mistaken notion that another power had launched a major attack.

Both these ways of setting off a war are within the realm of possibility and must be reckoned with, but to treat them as almost the only ways in which war starts is to give an air of unreality to discussion and planning. Most wars nowadays are set off by a specific dispute, not by a vague state of tension or rivalry. Until you identify what the nature of the dispute is, and where it is, and what countries and issues it involves, and how big it is, you cannot very well discuss either how to prevent its breaking into war or how to anticipate the form that any such war would take.

As this chapter is being written, four active disputes are prominent on the front pages and in the editorial columns. The first is the Berlin crisis, which stems mainly from the right claimed by the USSR to relieve itself of its obligations by full recognition of the German Democratic Republic, and thus allegedly to destroy all Western right of access to West Berlin. The second is the Sino-Indian boundary dispute, with both sides claiming a number of frontier territories as of legal right. The third is the continued stoppage by Egypt of Israel-connected shipping desiring to transit the Suez Canal, under claim of alleged belligerent rights. The fourth is the real or threatened interference with foreign rights in Cuba. Perhaps one should add, in view of World Refugee Year, the continuing dispute about the rights of Arab refugees from Palestine. Other controversies around the world include assorted disputes over national boundaries and a number of clashes over the relative rights of co-riparians to the use of waters of international rivers.

All of these quarrels have several common features of prime significance for our purposes: they involve claims of legal rights by both sides; questions of international law are imbedded in them all—sometimes as many as a dozen; and thus in no single case could an international enforcement agency be automatically or administratively set in motion against one of the parties.

These examples should serve as a useful corrective to the commonly heard assumption that today's major disputes are all political, not legal. In one loose sense, these disputes are "political" because the parties insist on trying to solve them by political rather than legal means. That misses the point. The point is that, in their inherent nature and quality, these controversies have legal questions at their core. Of course, there are other controversies involving changes in existing legal relations that are diplomatic and political in their very nature, such as the future of Germany, the recognition of the People's Republic of China, and the evolution of a government for the Congo. But as to the essentially legal disputes, they are being handled by nonlegal means, not because their intrinsic nature compels this course, but because the parties do not choose to settle them by legal means. The problem is not "can't"—it is "won't." Thus, the nationalization of the Universal Suez Company gave rise to what was basically a legal dispute. It became political because of the way it was handled.

Since Hungary and Suez there has not been a case of overt and violent invasion of another's territory by force of arms. Even in these two instances the invaders made emphatic claims of legal justification: in the case of Hungary, "invitation"; in the case of Suez, "protection" of the Canal under treaty right.

Simple Invasions. The lesson seems to be that, while the problem of protection from old-fashioned open attack or overrunning of boundaries will continue to exist, it is not the largest and certainly not the hardest part of the world law task. But it is definitely a part, and we should therefore quickly take note of the specific question of how to deal with it. Let us assume that mobile units of the international force are gradually built up at key points in the world, with their strength and number increasing as arms reduction progresses. The force will have an administrative body exercising immediate control over its actions. In the case of a simple, gross invasion, reported by an inspector who witnesses it or verifies it by observation, there would be neither time nor occasion for anything other than a direct administrative decision by the force's controlling body to order the invaders to halt and retire, and to back the order by immediately moving international units to the scene.

Similarly, if an imminent offensive aerial or missile attack were detected, the right of an international force to take direct action would be clear.

Ample analogy can be found in domestic law for the distinction between this kind of peremptory administrative action in emergencies and the normal procedures of law enforcement. Thus, a police officer who sees a burglar climbing through the window of a church can on his own authority make the decision to arrest him on the spot and may use such force as is necessary. By contrast, recall the case of the two ministers who both claimed the legal right to the pulpit of a church in Brooklyn. If the policeman on the beat had been called in, could he have made a legal decision between the two and then have arrested and detained the loser? Certainly not. The normal domestic law enforcement procedure always involves the judicial function, in the issuance of warrants, informations, indictments, and, of course, convictions and sentences.

Since the function of the police includes not only defending right against wrong, but also preventing breaches of the peace as such, an international force should also have the power, wherever violence has occurred or is imminent, to step into contested territories and prevent further clashes. Thus, just as such a force might have been able to act to stop the invasion of South Korea by North Korea, so also it might even occupy disputed areas between China and India for the sole purpose of preventing violence —recognizing that the ultimate question of legal rights in particular territories must later be settled by other means.

It would be highly desirable to work out more detailed understandings on the conditions under which virtually automatic action by an international force could take place. Secretary of State Herter stressed "the need to create certain universally accepted rules of law which, if followed, would prevent all nations from attacking other nations."

Clashes of Alleged Legal Rights. Let us now see what can be done about the commoner type of quarrel involving more complex questions of legal rights. It must be stressed again that the function of a legal order here is not merely to restrain any violence that might grow out of these disagreements, but also to assure all nations that they can safely disarm because all their rights—not just their right to be free from deliberate unexcused physical aggression—will be systematically and fairly protected.

The Body of Law. The first requisite of a system of world law competent to dispose of disputes and protect rights is a body of law that is both accessible and acceptable. The present body of international law is capable of substantial improvement on both these scores. Moreover, in line with our main approach of stressing actions that can be taken now to move us gradually toward our idealized objective, we should particularly note that this improvement can be undertaken, and is being undertaken, on an increasing scale by the techniques of both research and diplomacy.

As to the accessibility of existing law: much of the principal material, such as current treaties, is reasonably available. But there is nothing in international law to compare with either the completeness or the convenience of an ordinary domestic law library, with its up-to-date digests, key-number system, elaborate cross-reference and finding aids, definitive reporting and annotation systems, loose-leaf services, and the like. The multifarious sources of customary international law in particular are scattered and unorganized. The same is largely true of international law decisions to be found in opinions of national courts throughout the world. The prosaic task of simply finding and publishing and adequately indexing the law we already have may seem a far cry from visions of a world living under law. But how can you live under law if you cannot find out what it is?

Even if all the existing law were accessible, this would be only a start. The larger part of the task is to develop a body of law acceptable to more than ninety nations. International law as we know it is largely the handiwork of Western Christendom. Many states do not think of it as *their* law, but rather as a legacy from the days of imperialism. Is there anything we can do—and do now—about this?

A solution sometimes proposed is to create an international legislative body comparable to Congress, to pass binding international laws. People favoring this course sometimes ask, "How can you have world law if you have no world legislature?" Such people are surprised to learn that by far the greatest part of Anglo-American law was not the product of legislation at all, but of judicial decision. In any event, since our approach calls for actions that can be initiated now in phase with gradual disarmament, we must face the fact that states are not going to agree to a general world legislature in the foreseeable future. The distinctive feature of legislation, as distinguished from making new law by multilateral treaty, is that the treaty binds only those who agree to it, while legislation can bind a minority over its protest. Does anyone seriously suppose that today's nations, including our own, would entrust the changing of their basic legal rights to legislative action by any coalition of other states that might be able to assemble the necessary voting majority?

There are three major sources of law specified in the Statute of the International Court of Justice. These are customary law, treaties, and the "general principles of law recognized by civilized nations." It is the last

two that hold the greatest promise for our purposes, because their acceptability is built into them.

The reference to "general principles" seems to mean this: if you can
delve into the basic legal principles developed within the major legal systems—such as Common Law, Civil Law, Islamic, Hindu, Jewish, Chinese,
Japanese, African, and Soviet—and find a common element, that common
element becomes elevated to the status of international law. The tentative
conclusion reached by Wilfred Jenks in his book, *The Common Law of
Mankind,* is that there is a surprising degree of consensus among these
systems on the great principles relevant to international peace, such as the
principles that the sovereign is under the law, that disputes must be decided
through independent third-party adjudication, that the right of self-defense
is subject to certain defined limitations, that agreements must be kept and
are released only in a small number of named situations, that acquired
rights (with some exceptions) are to be protected, that there is a duty to
consult before acting to affect the rights of others adversely, and that harm
to others without justification is a legal wrong. Beyond these broad principles, there are many others that are more specific. For example, the Duke
University project on illegal propaganda is investigating the possibility of
applying such general principles as the wrongfulness of using words to
harm, and the culpability of incitement to harm, to the problem of international propaganda.

The acceptability of this source of law lies in the fact that, when you
cite it, you are not shoving alien concepts down the throats of countries
who had nothing to say about forming those concepts; rather, you are
merely reminding them of their own deepest legal traditions. The difficulty
with this source—and it is not an insuperable one—is that an immense
amount of far-flung research is obviously necessary if these general principles are first to be distilled from the many different systems, then analyzed
and compared to find a true consensus. Semantic difficulties abound, and
one must constantly ask whether apparently similar words really mean the
same thing. This is a rich opportunity for present research, and at least
two law schools, Cornell and Duke, have launched several projects in this
area.

Treaties as a source of law also enjoy the advantage of inherent acceptability for the obvious reason that they are the product of the voluntary
act of the party bound. This point is of particular interest when the question is raised of acceptability of world law to Communist countries. Andrei
Vyshinsky has written: "The Soviet theory of international law considers
treaties . . . to be the main source of international law. Their legal significance and validity must be unconditionally observed."

The more we can, through energetic diplomacy, blanket troublesome
new areas of international relations with law-making treaties, the more we
shall increase the chances of creating a body of law that is both made to
order for current needs and endowed with maximum prospects of accepta-

bility. We already cover large segments of activity in this way—civil aviation, postal service, narcotics and white-slave traffic, patents and copyrights, and so on. Recently, a good start was made on an agreed regime in Antarctica. In the same way, without waiting for an international legislature, we should be getting on with possible codes on Atomic Energy, International Propaganda, Space Law, the Law of International Rivers, protection of private international investment, and a number of other current fast-moving subjects.

Indeed, the British have suggested that what we need most now is a "code of co-existence" which would define in precise form those activities of states which would no longer be permitted, such as hostile propaganda, economic warfare, and subversion.

The creation of new law through treaties should be accompanied by the clarifying of existing law through codification and restatement. This is primarily the responsibility of the International Law Commission of the United Nations. This Commission has had some successes and many frustrations. Its work could be facilitated in a number of practical ways not involving any Charter amendments, including such obvious and down-to-earth changes as putting the members on a full-time basis with adequate funds at their disposal to hire staff and handle efficiently the volume of complex work expected of them.

What is most directly relevant to the present analysis, of course, is a disarmament treaty. Indeed, if we could only postulate a highly intelligent self-interest in each of the parties, such a treaty, in addition to its enormous intrinsic value, might have the added value of being the vehicle by which an unusual advance is accomplished in dispute-settling under law. The hypothetical process could run as follows: hypothesis 1, all parties sincerely want a disarmament treaty that works; hypothesis 2, all parties are wise enough to realize that, as Louis B. Sohn points out in the opening passages of his chapter, "Adjudication and Enforcement in Arms Control," a disarmament treaty will work best if it has an impartial dispute-settling mechanism built into it to handle controversies on interpretation.

If this kind of clause were tried in a disarmament treaty and if it worked well, it could be extended to more and more treaties until a considerable part of international relations had been effectively brought within an orbit of impartial adjudication under law.

The Machinery of Law. So far we have considered the body of world law, and have examined ways in which it could be gradually strengthened, diversified, modernized, and made more universally acceptable, without waiting for any dramatic change in world organization. But how about the machinery of world law? Can this too be strengthened, diversified, modernized, and made more universally acceptable by a gradual process that is within the realm of reasonable possibility? The answer is that it can.

There is now only one court of general international jurisdiction, the International Court of Justice at The Hague, which is the judicial arm of the United Nations. As matters now stand, it is as if, in domestic law, you had to run to the Supreme Court every time you had a dented fender or a back alimony claim. Of course, with the present scarcity of business in the Court—about one and one-half contentious cases are decided per year —the awkwardness of having only one such court does not make itself seriously felt. But we are assuming that, as disarmament progresses, and as the body of world law is built up, resort to judicial settlement will increase—if convenient judicial tribunals are available.

As a blueprint for an ultimate optimum system, to be accomplished by an intelligent revision of the United Nations Charter, the judicial, arbitral, and conciliation structure set forth in Clark and Sohn's *World Peace through World Law* would be difficult to improve upon. Since the present essay attempts to begin with steps that can be taken at once, and since the assumption of an extensive revision of the United Nations Charter in the near future does not seem a realistic one, the effort will be to show first that considerable diversity and flexibility could be gradually achieved within the present Charter and Court Statute if certain statutory sections were exploited to the full.

Article 26 of the Statute provides:

The Court may from time to time form one or more chambers, composed of three or more judges as the Court may determine, for dealing with particular categories of cases.

Thus, a panel of three or five could be set up to handle all interpretation disputes under a disarmament treaty. Again, since the Court can sit anywhere in the world, presumably it could assign particular panels to sit from time to time in different regions of the world, and thus approximate the regional court system that many people have urged. This same freedom to travel would even permit the Court or its panels to ride circuit and thus increase its accessibility even more.

Article 50 of the Court's Statute states:

The Court may, at any time, entrust any individual, body, bureau, commission, or other organization that it may select, with the task of carrying out an enquiry or giving an expert opinion.

This opens vast possibilities for dealing with a large volume of detailed business. It is a familiar experience in administrative law to find that the bulk of the business is disposed of at various stages of fact-finding and opinion-rendering by referees, hearing examiners, masters, and assessors. By a skillful use of this Article, the Court could, if the amount of business required, in effect set up the equivalent of a hierarchy of lower courts, the only difference being that the lower bodies could only render opinions and not judgments. But for a large proportion of litigants, an adverse fact-finding or expert opinion is a sufficient signal to induce retiring from the field.

Under a disarmament treaty, such a system could be used to handle detailed controversies of interpretation in the first instance, right in the region.

Article 41 of the Statute provides:

The Court shall have the power to indicate, if it considers that circumstances so require, any provisional measures which ought to be taken to preserve the respective rights of either party.

Thus, the Court can issue the equivalent of a temporary injunction to stop an alleged disarmament violation, for example, pending a more complete hearing on the merits.

This, then, is a sampling of the possibilities for finding variety and flexibility within the present constitutional framework of the Court. These and similar moves, supplemented when appropriate by special tribunals outside the United Nations, such as the Court of the European Economic Community, should make it possible to achieve a large part of the desirable improvement in world judicial machinery, even prior to the time when a more perfect structure can be achieved through a revision of the United Nations Charter.

If these various expedients were reasonably successful, the "habit of law" would gradually increase to the point which would make constructive United Nations Charter revision more realistically possible than it now is. As states become accustomed to the advantages of a convenient and impartial settlement of disputes, they will more readily favor building into the structure of the United Nations Charter those advantages which under the gradual process were worked out by comparatively makeshift means.

This is not unlike the evolutionary process of change by which the United Nations has been transformed in other respects: the growth of the function of the Secretary-General; the creation of the small police force; and the enhanced role of the General Assembly, including the device of the investigatory commission, employed in the Laotian case. Just as any future United Nations Charter revision might well ratify and incorporate these *de facto* changes, so it might also incorporate and improve upon the changes in the scope and variety of dispute-settling mechanisms worked out within the present Charter and Statute.

It is to be hoped that the confidence in international tribunals created during the first stage of growth here described would permit the members of the United Nations to accept the more complete and regular kind of judicial, arbitral, and conciliatory system described by Clark and Sohn. This system (which should be studied in its full form in *World Peace through World Law,* if justice is to be done it) includes: a revised and strengthened International Court of Justice; a World Equity Tribunal to hear cases that cannot be settled on essentially legal principles; a World Conciliation Board to help the parties to arrive at voluntary settlements, whether legal or nonlegal, by the techniques of mediation and conciliation; Regional Courts of the United Nations, whose jurisdiction would extend, among other items, to certain international offenses of private parties and to questions of inspection under arms control, and from which appeals would lie to the International Court of Justice; a United Nations police force; and an Attorney-General of the United Nations, who would have the responsibility for the prosecution of offenses and for the general direction of the police force.

Up to this point, the conclusion is that, if we first make the most of the opportunities now realistically available to us, we can steadily build up both the body and the machinery of world law in such a way as to set the stage for the eventual acceptance of an optimum system of world law, and at every step of the way we can gradually transfer to law the function of protecting legitimate national rights, and so permit nations, with growing confidence, to reduce their national armaments.

ENSURING COMPLIANCE

Now that we have examined the problem of settling who is right and who is wrong—which nation shall feel the lash of international enforcement, and which nation shall sit by, wearing the smile of vindicated righteousness—we are entitled to consider the process of enforcement itself. One or two observations should be made to place this element in proper perspective. The first is that the part to be played by physical force in the attainment of compliance with world law is probably not as great as is usually supposed. There is only one recorded case of disobedience to a final judgment of the International Court of Justice; and among the hundreds of arbitral decisions and thousands of other decisions of international tribunals, there is only a handful of cases in which any question of noncompliance can be found. The lesson seems to be that, if we can obtain acceptance of the body of law and of the machinery of law by the nations affected, compliance will generally follow. In other words, once a country has so far accepted the body of law and the tribunal as to entrust a case to it, it is "in so deep" that noncompliance with the decision finally rendered becomes unthinkable.

The second observation is that physical force is only one item in the armory of sanctions for compliance with law. The enforcement measures now available include diplomatic pressures, economic measures, attachment of property belonging to the debtor state, enforcement through national courts, various kinds of enforcement through international organizations, and enforcement measures under international arrangements apart from the United Nations. A good example of a device of obvious potency for inducing compliance without the use of force is that of the International Civil Aviation Organization. If its Council finds that a member nation has refused to comply with a final decision of the International Court of Justice or of an arbitral body, the contracting states undertake not to allow the airlines of the offending state to operate in their territory. A more crushing sanction could hardly be imagined. This sanction is the equivalent of a death sentence for the international air commerce of the recalcitrant state. The availability of such measures as this should serve as a reminder that the strengthening of enforcement of world law should proceed, not just through the strengthening of methods employing force, but equally through the strengthening of every other kind of diplomatic, economic, and collective pressure that can be devised. The Collective Measures Committee of the United Nations has indicated in its reports some of the ways this strengthening could be accomplished.

The nature of a possible international security force remains to be considered. Any attempt at picturing such a force at this point in time must necessarily be viewed as merely illustrative of what could conceivably be done, since details about the size, composition, and disposition of such a force will in fact depend upon a host of variables which cannot now be settled.

The idea of an international military force is not entirely new. As long ago as 1910, the United States Congress, in 36 U.S. Statutes at Large 885, suggested creating a commission which would study "constituting the combined navies of the world [into] an international force for the preservation of universal peace" in connection with arms limitations. In 1919, a joint military force under an international general staff was proposed by the French government, and the suggestion was renewed in more detailed form by the same government in 1932, in both instances in connection with disarmament proposals.

At the Dumbarton Oaks Conference in 1944, both the Soviet Union and the Chinese delegation called for an international air force. The result was a provision in Article 45 of the Charter, which obliges member states to "hold immediately available national air force contingents for combined international enforcement action." The Charter provides for national contingents for international enforcement action, but this obligation was to arise only upon the conclusion of special agreements, and these agreements have never been made. As a result, the United Nations forces assembled for action in Korea in 1950, in the Middle East in 1956, and in the Congo in 1960 were not the result of a regular advance creation of available contingents. The Korean force became largely the responsibility of the United States to assemble from among nations willing to contribute. The Middle East force and the Congo force were largely made up of contingents furnished by nations with relatively small military forces.

An international armed force for a world of disarmament and world law would have to be quite differently constituted from either of these. As to the size of such an ultimate force, the common-sense formula now being advocated by the United States is this: the size of national armaments should be gradually reduced, and the size of the international armed force should be gradually increased, until the point is reached at which the strength of the international force is superior to that of any nation or combination of nations with which it might reasonably be expected to have to deal. This formulation indicates that the size of the international security force cannot be stated in absolute terms, but will depend on the relative size of national armaments at any given point. Theoretically, an absolute limit beneath which national armaments cannot be expected to fall might be stated, since a certain minimum would always be considered appropriate for the maintenance of internal order. As for adding up the combined strength of the combinations of nations that might have to be dealt with, this does not mean that the central force would have to be greater than the forces of all of the countries in the world combined. A common-sense judgment would have to be made on realistic possible aggregations, and the size of the international force calculated accordingly. It has been estimated that, on the assumption of a reasonably successful disarmament process, the size of the international force might ultimately be around 500,000.

Because of the potential idealistic appeal of this kind of force, coupled with the provision of good salaries and incidental benefits, it should be possible to staff such a force with young people of high quality, without the necessity for any kind of international selective service. The distribution by nationalities should be such that no single nation would have more than a very small percentage of the force represented. The nationalities should not be clustered into separate units, but should be commingled throughout the force, for obvious reasons. Similarly, the command structure should be subject to regular rotation among nationalities. The force should be stationed at its own bases at strategic points around the world. It should be liberally equipped with air-transport facilities, paratroop equipment, and other aids to mobility, because of the unusual importance of its ability to reach trouble spots promptly.

The planning for the size and composition of the international force must constantly look in two directions. It must aspire to sufficient size and effectiveness to do the job assigned to it. On the other hand, it should be so adjusted, both as to size and as to detailed constitution, that it will not give rise to fears of a Frankenstein monster that will take over the world. Although superficially the postulated mathematical preponderance of strength in the central force might seem to lend some support to such fears, a closer look at the realities of such a situation will serve to dispel them. The force would be made up of people drawn from dozens of nationalities, all of whom expect to serve for a limited time and then resume their normal lives and friendships in their home countries. Such people are going to have small appetite for becoming the hated tools of some power-mad potential world dictator. Moreover, the force will be widely scattered geographically, and will have a rotating command; thus, having no single national industrial base to support it, it will be incapable of any sustained autonomous activity.

A force of this size and character could presumably be built up gradually without a revision of the United Nations Charter, since we have the precedent of the Middle East force to build on. As indicated earlier, under the Clark and Sohn proposal such a force would be subject to the direction of an Attorney-General. Until such an office is created by amendment to the Charter, it might be desirable to have the staff of the force responsible to the Secretary-General, who is in the logical position to take executive action. The United Nations Charter now contains in Article 94(2) a permissive provision under which a party seeking enforcement of a decision by the International Court "may" apply to the Security Council, which then "may" make recommendations or decide upon measures—which might include using the security force. Although the point may be debatable, this vague permissive procedure ought not by implication exclude other enforcement procedures for which general authority may be found in the Charter.

So far, we have contemplated the use of an international force only when there has been (1) an administrative decision to stop an overt invasion actually observed, and (2) an authoritative determination of rights by the impartial dispute-settling structure.

For this reason, it seems possible to entrust its direction to an officer such as an Attorney-General or Secretary-General. The range of policy decision or discretion will have been reduced to the minimum by the precise rules governing automatic action by the force and by the assumption of responsibility by the dispute-settling mechanism in less precise situations. Conceivably, a political body, such as the Security Council or General Assembly, should have the power to overrule the officer and stop action by the force. But should there be, in addition, the possibility of initiating action by the international security force through a decision of a political body? The only important type of case in which this might seem appropriate would be the necessity of dealing with some outlaw nation or group not a party to the system of disarmament and law which this discussion assumes. In relation to such a troublesome outsider, the disarmament collectivity would be somewhat in the position of a sovereign nation which must necessarily decide the question of a declaration of war by political means. But in relation to the members of the collectivity, the situation is entirely different. To apply central force to them as a result of political decision would be comparable to the bill of attainder and other ancient attempts by nonjudicial domestic bodies to arrogate to themselves the right to apply punishments directly by vote of a deliberative assembly. The hazards of entrusting this power to a political body are somewhat the same as the hazards which made the bill of attainder and similar procedures anathema to our sense of fair play. No matter how the present imperfect voting system might be revised, is there any great likelihood that assurances satisfactory to United Nations members can be devised against the fear that some kind of political coalition of nations might "gang up" on a minority and enforce its will through the use of the international security force?

CONCLUSION

It is a good thing, even at this early stage of arms-control discussion, to hold up a picture of the system of world law and arms control toward which we would like to strive. This is useful to give direction to our efforts, and it is useful to enlist the support of people everywhere who are eager for a plan that is full of hope and daring. But it must not be a plan that reminds us of that oldest of all jokes, the story of the farmer who, after several futile attempts to give directions to a motorist, concludes, "Mister, you can't get there from here."

This chapter, then, has tried to depict a world of law and how to get there from here, in such a way as to satisfy the aspirations of the strife-weary without offending the common sense of the tough-minded. At this point, someone may once more cite Lloyd George's dictum that the most dangerous thing in the world is to try to leap a chasm in two jumps. That depends. If the longest distance you can leap is fifteen feet, and if the chasm is a hundred feet across, one leap can be rather dangerous too, and it might be better if you walked down and climbed up a step at a time.

PART VIII

FOREIGN COMMENT

In order to provide some international perspective on the foregoing material by American authors, comments on selected chapters by well-qualified foreign observers were solicited. These were secured by Stephen R. Graubard, Historian at Harvard, and Victor F. Weisskopf, Professor of Physics at Massachusetts Institute of Technology. The comments that follow first appeared in the Winter 1961 issue of Dædalus in substantially their present form. Remarks by three Soviet observers were solicited but were never received.

RAYMOND ARON

Born in Paris in 1905, Raymond Aron, scholar and political commentator, is professor in the Faculty of Letters at the University of Paris, and at the Institut d'Études Politiques, and a contributor to *Le Figaro*. His writings, which have often appeared in English, include: *The Century of Total War; The Opium of the Intellectuals; On War;* and *France, Steadfast and Changing: The Fourth to the Fifth Republic.*

I SHOULD LIKE TO MAKE SOME OBSERVATIONS ON THE CHAPTER BY PAUL Doty, "The Role of the Smaller Powers." The thesis he presents seems to me can be summarized in these terms: It is preferable for the Atlantic Alliance, as well as for the smaller powers, that the latter abandon the idea of having a retaliatory atomic capability and that they protect themselves by improving their other means of defense.

The futility of a retaliatory capability for the smaller powers is demonstrated as follows. France or Great Britain within the next ten years, at least, will have at their disposal only a small capability in comparison with that of the great powers. In particular, they will have only strategic bombers and intermediate missiles that will be vulnerable to attack on the part of a great power. Now, a small power will never take the initiative in atomic warfare, since such a step would bring down on it a total catastrophe. Therefore, an atomic capability can help only if it survives attack by a great power. This capability must be serviceable as a *second strike*. As technology has so far developed, the French or even the English capability would in all likelihood be almost completely eliminated by a Soviet attack. The conclusion is that neither France nor probably Great Britain will have their security increased by the atomic power they themselves can produce.

This reasoning seems convincing to me (I myself have argued thus in discussing the French atomic program), but it is important first of all to define under what technical conditions it is applicable. How does a small atomic capability differ from a big one? How does a capability that Great Britain or France can acquire differ from that of the United States or the Soviet Union? As for bombs, it does not seem that the cost of producing thermonuclear bombs is beyond the means of France. (Great Britain produces thermonuclear bombs, although the strategic bomb and bomber ensemble represents no more than 20 per cent of the defense budget.) In the next ten years, by devoting from one to two hundred billion old francs (from two to four hundred million dollars) to its atomic program, France can acquire a certain number of thermonuclear bombs. The problem is one of reducing the size of these bombs to such a dimension that they can be transported by British or French carriers.

This brings us to the second argument: In the present state of technology, as it is known, strategic bombers will be vulnerable, and so will ballistic intermediate missiles. The English have just discarded the Blue Streak precisely because it would be too vulnerable. Such in fact is the present idea, but it would be dangerous to draw any conclusions from it. If we suppose that between now and 1970 the smaller powers cannot reduce the vulnerability of their striking power, they can do so perhaps by 1970 or 1980. They have no chance of succeeding in this, however, unless they work on this from now on, since, according to American legislation, the communication of secrets to an ally depends on the progress the latter achieves. (A second argument has been presented by a well-known French technologist, Camille Rougeron, who declares that a smaller power from now on can acquire retaliatory power that is relatively cheap and only slightly vulnerable by adopting certain solutions—dirty bombs, above-ground explosions, etc.[1])

I am not competent to decide whether this "atomic force for the use of poor countries" can be acquired, or, if so, within what period. But it seems to me essential to remind American readers of two ideas: first, so long as American scientific cooperation depends on the knowledge that is accumulated among allied countries, the latter will be compelled to carry on their own research, if only to profit someday from this cooperation. In the second place, American opinion would be wrong in excluding, on principle, the hypothesis of a "cheap solution" of a problem whose solution in the United States has been costly. As the Greeks long since recognized, poverty is the mother of invention.

Let us turn from this point to the next. Suppose Dr. Doty is right, and that Great Britain and France between now and 1970 can deploy only an atomic capability that is small and relatively vulnerable. Would this be an entirely useless capability? Dr. Doty's theory is that it would be both useless and dangerous. It would guarantee no supplementary security to any secondary power, but would increase the risk of conflict through misunderstanding, accident, or irrationality. In order to reconcile these two propositions—the English or French striking power would contribute nothing to either country but would increase the danger of an undesired war—we must suppose that the secondary powers could take no recourse to atomic arms, or the threat of such arms, unless by behaving in an irrational manner. If this is true, however, the French government might argue that it would be diplomatically stronger the day the American government fears being drawn into conflict by some unconsidered initiative.

The two arguments Dr. Doty attributes to French spokesmen are: the difficulty a country has in protecting another country by deterrence; and the law of proportion between the risk and the stake. Up to what point would the Soviet Union be convinced that the United States would accept unlimited destruction solely to protect an ally? Up to what point is a small country, which represents a small stake, unprotected by the capability of striking one or two cities of the enemy with A or H bombs?

The best proof that this first question is a real one is that the American government has envisaged putting thermonuclear arms at the disposal of its allies. Finally, a contrary decision has been taken, but the actual solution, provisionally the best one, can be discussed by the allies from two points of view: by installing launching sites on its territory, a country allied to the United States makes an attack on itself inevitable in case of a general war; therefore, it accepts them only if it considers that, in spite of all, these launching sites confer more security than they do risk, and therefore that it does not have to dread an adventurous or irrational attack on the part of the American government. In other words, if a secondary power accepts protection from a great power, this implies that the first has confidence in the second. It is the lack of such confidence that in part explains the decision of the French government to try to create a striking force that will obey its commands only.

As for the second argument (the proportion between the risk and the stake), this in itself does not seem to me absurd but only untimely. In fact, the small powers who are now neutral and who would eventually acquire atomic arms, according to this reasoning will not do so before such armament is almost invulnerable. As for France, she is too involved in East-West relations to admit any probability to the hypothesis of having to resist alone a pressure or threat of aggression. It is necessary, therefore, to consider a last point: How can the French determination to acquire a striking force that is wholly national be explained? Dr. Doty considers this only an anachronistic expression of nationalism. It is always dangerous not to try to put oneself in another's position. To justify his policy, General de Gaulle has invoked none of the preceding arguments (no country can protect another, the proportion of risk and stake). He feels impelled to advance again the classic theory that a state must be capable of assuring its own defense. If it lacks military autonomy, it is no longer a state. In private conversation, he is said to employ the following arguments. Today the United States protects us, but will it do so tomorrow? France will not be listened to so long as she herself lacks decisive arms. At the present moment, thanks to its atomic monopoly, the United States unilaterally makes decisions that involve her allies. The interests of France will be better preserved when supported by a national striking force.

What is the central problem, therefore? Under present circumstances, the United States argues that the best thing for everybody is to accept its monopoly of atomic arms; but, then, because of this monopoly, it claims the right to make decisions alone in major circumstances. Perhaps France is wrong in believing that a small atomic capability would allow her to exercise greater influence; but to call "nationalism" the desire not to depend entirely on a protector that is indifferent to the specific concerns of its allies would be an unwarranted enlargement of the meaning of the word. At the time of the Suez expedition (no matter what one thinks of it), the French and the English did indeed realize that the American capability did not protect them *in all circumstances* from Soviet pressure or threat. Perhaps the autonomy to which they aspire is not to be had, but their aspiration is neither unintelligible nor irrational. The fact that the American writer does not find any sense in the French decision is explained by the formula attributed to Charles Wilson, "What is good for General Motors is good for the United States." We have only to replace it with this formula, "Whatever is in the interest of the United States is in the interest of Europeans." Unfortunately, the latter remain unconvinced.

As a result, there arises a final problem. Let us suppose that the French are fundamentally wrong, that their atomic capability reinforces neither their security nor their influence within the alliance. What attitude is the United States going to adopt? The present policy of France is contrary to the good functioning of the alliance and will be even more so tomorrow. Conventional armaments will be wanting. World security will be impaired by the lack of agreement as to a common military policy between the United States and its allies. Smaller powers, assuming that they cannot deter the great powers, retain a "nuisance capacity" within their alliances. Although Doty's conception may be a reasonable one (that the United States keep a monopoly of atomic arms in the free world), and although it may become reality, American leaders must convince the governments of the European countries, not only that they would use their power wisely, but also that they will take account of the interests of their allies in using that power.

This is not the place to ask who is responsible for this unhappy situation, but the fact is that the European leaders until now have not been convinced. In the absence of mutual confidence, it is probable that the attempts of the Europeans to acquire atomic arms will go on.

ALASTAIR BUCHAN

Born in London in 1918, third son of the late Lord Tweedsmuir (John Buchan), Alastair Buchan is Director of the Institute for Strategic Studies (London) and the editor of its publication, *Survival*. He was previously on the staff of *The Economist* and also *The Observer*, first as its Washington correspondent, then as its diplomatic and defense correspondent. His publications include *The Spare Chancellor: The Life of Walter Bagehot* and *NATO in the 1960's*.

THE AMOUNT OF INTELLECTUAL ENERGY NOW BEING DEVOTED TO THE study of the problems of arms control and disarmament in the United States cannot fail to impress the non-American. It is clear that a far more intensive and also dispassionate effort is being made to think through the problems involved than is the case either in Europe or the Soviet Union. The question a European has a right to ask, is whether such thinking is along the right lines, that is, whether it is realistic in terms of what can be negotiated, both with the allies of the United States and with the Soviet Union, and whether it will produce a more stable world if such negotiations are successful.

Superficially, there is something of a conflict between the growing consensus of opinion in the United States that limited arms control offers a more fruitful prospect than do schemes of comprehensive disarmament, and the European belief in the latter. It would be surprising if there were not such a conflict; for one thing, European strategists, especially the British, are for some reason—perhaps it is temperamental, perhaps it is just parochialism—less concerned with the dangers of surprise attack and war, and more concerned with the burden of the arms race as a whole than the Americans. For this reason, and also because they fear that Western concentration on arms control will enable the Soviet Union to maintain a psychological and diplomatic advantage in terms of world opinion as the only major power clearly committed—however cynically— to the abolition of all armaments, the instinctive European preference is for the kind of comprehensive scheme so clearly laid out here by Wiesner.

However, I myself belong to what is, I think, a growing minority in Europe which finds more validity in the kind of approach outlined by Schelling and others, namely, the stabilizing of mutual deterrence by taking both unilateral and multilateral action and at the same time attempting to identify and control the most dangerous features of the arms race, rather than continuing to beat our heads against the stone wall of comprehensive multilateral disarmament.

In a limited space I can touch only briefly on the reasons why I find the arguments for giving first priority to limited measures of arms control compelling, but they may be worth stating, for they seem somewhat different from those which are generally advanced in the United States.

The first is concerned with the progression of the arms race in time as well as space. As Bowie points out, "Military instruments, while still related to political conflict, have taken on a life of their own and have become a separate source of tension and danger." While there are certain technological developments which are working in favor of stability, there are others which are not, and Kahn's analysis graphically illustrates how complex and delicate the weapons systems of 1969 will be if military technology is allowed to pursue its present rampant course. Now, it should be easier for both sides to agree mutually to deny themselves weapons systems which are still on the drawing board or in the laboratories than to dismantle those which have become embedded in national defense or defensive systems. In the last ten years we have missed several priceless opportunities to get future weapons under control, and since the developments of the 1960's may be even more potentially destructive of stability than those of the 1950's, this is an approach we can no longer ignore. While I do not imagine for a moment that the major part of controlled mutual deterrence can be based on a static technology, I am sure that the presidents and prime ministers and peoples of the 1970's will have legitimate grounds for upbraiding their predecessors if they find themselves saddled with the problem of maintaining a pattern of international order in a world in which, say, nuclear weapons have spread all round the globe and into outer space. Time, in other words, is against us.

The second reason for according a higher priority to limited agreements on arms control and inspection than disarmament lies, as several writers point out, in the importance in their own right of such agreements. By this I do not mean to endorse the rather naïve view sometimes put forward about "confidence building" between East and West. We live in a revolutionary age and must accommodate ourselves to the continuance of a high degree of distrust and animosity between men and states. My own belief in the importance of limited agreements derives from a sense that we are on the edge of a fundamental change in the world balance of power as it has existed in the last fifteen years, and that the axis of world tension is about to shift from "East-West" to "South-East—North-West," or even to "North-South." If so, there is no time to be lost, given the inevitable time lag in the adjustment of governments and policies to reality, in seeking to identify the areas of common interest with the Soviet Union. It would be one of the major tragedies of world history if two powers the size of Russia and the United States were to remain locked in a position of implacable hostility because of their inability to overcome the barriers raised by competing military technologies after the political basis of that hostility had been transmuted into something approaching a common cause against new dangers.

Superficially, the third reason for a belief in the necessity of giving first priority to limited measures of arms control, based on the principle of mutual defense, may seem a contradiction of the second. The reason is that the only forms of inspection that will be acceptable to the Soviet Union—for the foreseeable future at least—are those that make the minimum demands on national sovereignty. The Soviet repugnance to inspection has, I think, been given insufficient weight by many writers in this book. It is a national blind spot, but it is also a deeply rooted national prejudice that has little to do with Communism and would persist even in the face of *diktat* to the contrary from the Kremlin. The merit of the concepts being employed by Schelling and others, namely, of a system of mutual deterrence in which the object of inspection is to detect evasions of the agreed *size* of the deterrent force, rather than its state of readiness or physical location, is that it suggests a sufficiently light degree of interference with national sovereignty as to enable a Soviet government to insist that the Russian people respect it. (The Soviet repugnance to inspection is, of course, only one illustration of the problem created by rising nationalism in the world and would apply *a fortiori* among the even newer states of Asia and Africa.)

Clearly, there has been a great deal of homework done. I fully agree with Brennan that the only way in which we can educate the Russians (who have as yet applied nothing like the same degree of intellectual energy and talent to the problem, to help us identify the areas of common interest) is first to educate ourselves. In this respect, the work of American analysts and thinkers is both timely and encouraging.

JULES MOCH

Born in Paris in 1893, Jules Moch, naval architect, is chairman of the French delegation to the United Nations Disarmament Commission, on which he has represented France since 1951. He was Minister of Public Works before the war and in 1945–1947, Minister of the Interior from 1947 to 1950 and again in 1958. He was also Prime Minister and Deputy Prime Minister in 1949–1950. As Minister of National Defense (1950–1951) he promoted the rebuilding of the French armed forces and their integration into NATO. His writings treat contemporary political problems, ranging over a wide field. His best known works are: *Alerte: Le Problème Crucial de la Communauté Européenne de Défense; L'U.R.S.S.: Les Yeux Ouverts; The Human Folly* (with a foreword by Einstein); and *En Retard d'une Paix.*

THREE OBSERVATIONS COME TO A EUROPEAN'S MIND IF HE READS WITH care some of the foregoing chapters on arms control. On the one hand, the sufferings war inflicts have affected our two hemispheres differently. Though we are allies, and what is more, friends, our reactions at times are divergent, as Kissinger notes regarding nuclear strategy. On the other hand, too many disarmament strategists indulge in talk of war, and thus swim off, so to speak, into unreality. Third, their statements force a conclusion that is not given: all the compromise solutions that mingle partial disarmament with a limited "deterrent" are worthless. Security cannot be attained except by controlled disarmament, achieved as fast as is reasonably possible.

Such are the issues that emerge from a reading of these papers, and I should like to develop them.

First: *reactions differ between one hemisphere and the other.* Twice in a quarter century America has saved Europe: when the latter was at the end of her rope in 1917, after three years of frightful bloodshed; and again when she was groaning from four years of the most ferocious oppression. Our ineradicable gratitude, however, does not veil the facts from us: these two liberations have cost the United States losses that were certainly cruel

This article was translated by Katharine Strelsky. Several passages indicate that Moch did not always understand the points being made in the chapters (in English) under discussion. For example, the quoted view ascribed to Kissinger is completely contrary to Kissinger's actual position, which is: "Forces-in-being are . . . more important than at any previous time in our history." And Moch's interpretation of some of my own views is rather wide of the mark. But the comment, by one of the world's leading students of disarmament, illustrates vividly an outlook toward war and disarmament that is common in Europe.—ED.

but that hardly exceeded the cost in manpower in a colonial campaign. The French dead, if reckoned on the American scale, would number thirteen millions, while the USSR estimates seventeen million actual victims of World War II. There is hardly a single family in the Old World that does not mourn a lost member.

In America there was no destruction whatever. Since 1945 France has rebuilt almost ten thousand highway or railroad bridges more than 120 feet in length, at the rate of three completed installations a day—a technological record without precedent, requiring ten years of uninterrupted effort. The same thing is true of harbors, railways, air or maritime fleets, factories, and housing, which are not entirely rebuilt even now after fifteen years. The area devastated in the USSR exceeded the total land surface of the United States. Whole cities in Britain and Germany were wiped out by bombs. Above all, the United States and Britain were spared the horror of wartime occupation—but not France or Russia. These are the facts that account for the European reaction to the rearming of Germany and to the arms race.

When Donald G. Brennan analyzes the policy of strategic "deterrence," which he describes as being as old as man, and revives the old Latin formula, *Si vis pacem, para bellum* (If you desire peace, make ready for war), he must understand our preference for this transposition, *Si vis pacem, para pacem.* By the very process of preparing for war one finally provokes it. Moreover, when it comes to massive nuclear retaliation, it is the survival of all humanity that is risked.

Further, how can a European accept Brennan's classification, which distinguishes the "deterrence of a direct nuclear attack" (that is, on the United States) from an "extreme nuclear provocation" (on the European allies of the United States) or from a "nonnuclear but extreme provocation," including the occupation of Europe by attacking armies with conventional arms?

The distinction between the first two kinds of provocation is immediately suspect; this explains the refusal of certain states to allow American bases on their soil. As for the distinction between the first two and the third—Europe is left with no other hope than years of occupation that will convert her into a vast cemetery, to be succeeded by a liberation from tombs after the formation and equipment of an army of several million men. The same view is discernible in the paper by Kissinger, where he considers the mobilization (after the beginning of hostilities) of factories as "more significant than the achievement of a local tactical superiority . . ." and this is undoubtedly how the defense of Europe is envisaged.

Furthermore, let us not conceive of disarmament as a system of "arms control," but rather as a massive reduction in arms, including the elimination of the most fearsome. *Our object is to render purposeless Brennan's and Kissinger's various hypotheses and to control, not armaments, but disarmament.* Otherwise, salvation does not exist, at least for Europe.

Second: *the futility of war planning dear to the major powers.* Since I have had to sacrifice ten years of my life to actual warfare first in the land army, then in the navy and the resistance, and then having served as Minister of National Defense at the allied war councils, I declare that there is an absence of any common principle between these meetings and modern war: they take no account of the morale of the soldier, who, according as he blows up a vehicle with his bazooka or hides to save his life, changes the course of battle—nor of the morale of the civilians, who sooner or later influence their governments' course of action.

To conduct this kind of discussion of war—Kissinger gives some examples—is to imagine that it would be possible to measure out retaliation after an attack that can destroy dozens of millions of men, and to take no heed of panic and disorganization. In America the posters that closed certain parkways to civilians in case of an aerial bombardment, so as to keep the roads open for officials, symbolized obliviousness to a mass frenzy that is certain to rage without limit.

It is mere dreaming to imagine isolated troops, fatally trapped, yet forebearing to use tactical nuclear arms because they have been commanded to retaliate only with conventional weapons. It is pure utopianism to assert that cities will go on existing more or less normally under nuclear threat.

In the same sense, it is living outside reality to believe in tacit or explicit agreements limiting the power of nuclear arms in combat. Who is to be the judge? What is tactical for one side will be strategical for the other. Gas, which was not used between 1939 and 1945, is no example: masks were recognized as conferring only a tactical advantage, not a decisive effectiveness. And what sort of mask can protect against radiation?

There cannot be any rules of war, for war itself is a violation of all humane laws. Each side will decide its own action, in every situation, according to its own interest, as it conceives it, regardless of whether this involves breaking agreements. All peacetime talk of limiting war can be nothing but an intellectual game. Disaster cannot be dammed back if a hole in the dike is allowed. A people at war will understand no law but one: to try to destroy the enemy for the sake of their own safety.

Hence my third point: *war must be made impossible.*

Bowie gives a precise analysis of the reasons for distrust between the two blocs. He emphasizes that the Soviets have not always kept bad faith, that we are able to evolve solutions that are in the interest of both parties, which, according to my old formula, "increase at each stage the security of either bloc, not just the security of one at the other's expense," and last that the corresponding control must verify not only the truthfulness of the declarations of either side, but also their sincerity, and hence the nonexistence of munitions other than those at designated locations. Though the

Soviets were but recently opposed to any effective controls, today they accept the concept of verifying the truthfulness of such declarations, though not as yet their sincerity. Disarmament is indeed a school for patience.

Wiesner believes that no delegation truly desires agreement. I have headed the French delegation for ten years—a continuity unparalleled by any other delegation—and so I can say that his statement is inaccurate as regards my own country. France believes in disarmament because she considers it indispensable. Therefore, she does desire it and has multiplied her efforts toward conciliation—by the French proposals of 1952 and 1953, the Franco-British proposals of 1954 and 1955, as well as the attempt to make recent Western proposals more acceptable to the East, etc. Without ever disengaging herself from her allies, she will try to unite them in the essential compromises.

In order to appease the world's anguish, in our view we must begin disarmament with nuclear disarmament. But this must be undertaken in a realistic manner. Today it has become impossible to detect *a posteriori* and with sufficient precision the fissionable materials that have already been accumulated. "The point of no return," as I have said again and again since 1952, has long since been passed.

On the other hand, we can still control the bases from which such missiles are launched, as well as their vehicles—planes, ships, submarines, ramps, satellites, and rockets. We must forbid these vehicles' carrying nuclear loads and prevent them from being diverted to such purposes. We do not need to destroy all such missiles at once—they have peaceful uses too—but we have to establish permanent inspection on either fixed or floating bases, on ramps, or wherever else they may be situated, on national as well as foreign soil. These are concrete measures that are applicable at once, and they must be set quickly in motion if the evolution of technology is not to sweep us once more to the point at which all control will be illusory. Thus by excluding vehicles, we will render the stores of fissionable materials pointless. The powers would then agree to convert them to peaceful purposes (for this would be in each one's interest) and would doubtless proceed to such conversion faster than the treaty envisaged. In addition, they would agree to produce no more—under control—except for peaceful purposes.

Simultaneously, the manpower would be reduced step by step, and, above all, so would conventional armaments, which would have to be strictly proportioned according to declared strengths, with the controlled destruction of those in excess. In this sense, weapons matter much more than men, for they cannot be reconstituted as quickly as trained reservists can be remobilized and sent to their posts.

The entire operation, of course, would be carried out under a permanent, international, and total control, to which the Russians continue to object, but which we see as the sole means of progressively assuring confidence, by giving every nation the certainty that all the others are fulfilling their obligations in every respect.

I share some of Bowie's views. The two blocs alike want to disarm. The Soviets are still convinced of the final victory of their "faith." They count on what their industrial progress has already exhibited (even now it is rapid and, at rather long range, threatening to the West), and on their consequent ability to raise their standard of living—not on rockets—to conquer the world. They are not going to risk their entire future by hazarding a devastating war. But, to achieve their goals, their need for civilian manpower is enormous, forcing them to disarm and to take various other steps I will not stop to examine here.

In spite of recent failures, the moment is propitious for serious negotiations. There must be two conditions: that the East agree to a satisfactory system of inspection, without which all disarmament would be merely a snare; and that in the West all governments decide on disarmament and take the initial risks which this requires and which can be measured and defined.

Convinced as I am of the necessity for putting an end to man's insanity, I remain an optimist, and I set myself toward the building of a genuine peace.

PHILIP NOEL-BAKER

Born in 1889, Philip Noel-Baker has been a leading figure in the British Labour Party for over three decades, being a former chairman, and in 1959 was awarded the Nobel Peace Prize. From 1945 to 1951 he held many posts in the Labour Governments, including that of Secretary of State for Commonwealth Relations and Secretary of State for Air. His writings on arms control are extensive. *The Arms Race: A Programme for World Disarmament*, published in 1958, is the most recent of his six major books on disarmament.

IT IS DIFFICULT TO MAKE USEFUL COMMENTS ON THESE CHAPTERS IN A short article; if what I say seems to their authors to be didactic and superficial, I can only express my regret, and plead that the limitations of space have prevented me from offering more adequate and more respectful observations. The chapters seem to me individually and collectively to make most valuable new contributions to current thinking about our armaments.

A. Doak Barnett brings important new evidence for the view that China will soon have nuclear weapons of her own, and that within ten or fifteen years she will have a modern armory, perhaps as powerful as that of any nation in the world. When the repercussions of this development in Japan, India, and elsewhere are considered, together with the present attitude of the German General Staff, his paper shows the fallacy of trying to deal with the arms race as a "two-giant" affair.

Louis B. Sohn's discussion of adjudication and enforcement opens up new lines of thought. Of his suggestions for tribunals to deal with disputes about alleged violations of a disarmament treaty, his plan for a special Arms Chamber of the International Court of Justice seems the best; it will be desirable to have disputes dealt with as urgently as possible by judges of the highest standing; regional tribunals might involve delay, and it may be hoped that there would not be enough disputes to justify so elaborate a system of lower courts. Dr. Sohn puts the difficulties about sanctions against a government which violates a disarmament treaty into proper perspective, and shows that in a disarmed world they would not be nearly so formidable a problem as many people have believed. He states powerfully the case against allowing each signatory state an individual right of withdrawal from a disarmament treaty; the history of the League of Nations is evidence that, in spite of Mr. Bowie's arguments to the contrary, Dr. Sohn is right.

Donald G. Brennan renders a service by reminding us that the yardstick by which nuclear weapons must be measured is that of the Hiroshima and

Nagasaki bombs. It is necessary to learn by heart the grim statistics of the death and devastation wrought upon these two cities, if one is to understand the real meaning of the General Staffs' euphemistic phrases about "tactical atomic bombs" and "low-yield thermonuclear devices."

If, as is so often said, inspection is the crux of the disarmament problem, then Bernard T. Feld has done an important piece of work; he has carried further our understanding of the difficulties of international control and of the solutions that can be found. He powerfully reinforces the conclusion reached by Seymour Melman and his colleagues in their 1958 study, that if the governments seriously desire to disarm, there is no technical difficulty in effective inspection, even in respect of bacteriological, chemical, and radiological weapons and of military research, that should prevent agreement.

Jerome B. Wiesner makes a most cogent case for thinking that a comprehensive system of disarmament "may be easier to negotiate than a series of independent limited measures worked through one at a time"; and that "adequate inspection for limited measures may be more difficult to achieve." He explodes a lot of false arguments based on the Tests Conference in Geneva when he points out that an inspection system for monitoring a truly comprehensive disarmament agreement "would probably have no need at all for a system to detect underground nuclear tests." I hope that Dr. Wiesner's paper, like the others, may be widely studied in Europe and Russia, as it will be in the United States.

Inevitably, there are points in these chapters with which I find it less easy to agree.

Some writers speak of "status quo powers," as though the old distinction between "haves" and "have nots," so often used to justify Hitler in the 1930's, had some validity today. As President Eisenhower frequently observed, no nation can now promote any true national interest by resort to war.

Thomas C. Schelling says that "nature might have been kinder in the way she let our military technology unfold itself over the last decade and a half." There is a hint of historical determinism in this sentence that I find disturbing; nature can hardly be blamed for the development of the "modern" weapons.

Dr. Schelling also appears to assume, as do several other authors, that it will be possible to have a general nuclear war, and that mankind will survive. Dr. Schelling even says that "in the future, at a close of a general war, one might have to allow the conditionally surrendering enemy to retain some retaliatory weapons." Such rosy optimism strikes strangely on European ears; we remember Oppenheimer's recent speech in Berlin, in which he said that in our present weapons system we are "adding chance to anger" as a cause of cataclysm, and that, if war occurred, none of us would have enough living to bury our dead.

There is a similar assumption by several authors that an increase of conventional armaments would be a step toward disarmament. This paradox is gaining ground with some sections of the European general staffs, as they come to realize that the use of "tactical" nuclear weapons would reduce our continent to a radioactive desert. But can it be the right way to deal with present dangers, when Khrushchev is offering to reduce conventional armaments to any level we desire, and when, as we know, there is, for conventional armaments, no danger of undetected violation of the disarmament treaty, provided we have the comprehensive inspection which Khrushchev has proposed?

Is it really possible to hope that these present dangers would be less, if the smaller powers were not only to increase their conventional forces but also to develop biological, chemical, and radiation weapons, as Paul M. Doty has proposed? True, "biologicals" and poison gases are, as he argues, no more immoral than nuclear bombs; but should we not be more faithful to our Western principles if we reversed that proposition and said that nuclear bombs are as immoral as "biologicals" and poison gas? But morality apart, all of them have now become weapons of mass destruction; to spread their distribution to all the nations must surely accentuate the dangers we know today.

But the real crux of the armament problem lies in military research. "The dynamic character of military technology," says Robert R. Bowie, "forces each side to strain constantly to produce new or improved weapons systems in order to better its position or at least maintain the balance." This is the harsh truth; Mr. Bowie states the remorseless logic of the arms race. But "the dynamic character of military technology" results from the fact that the leading governments have vastly increased, and are still increasing, the sums which they devote to military research and development. In 1940, the United States government spent $25 million on employing scientists and other experts to improve their weapons; in 1953, it spent $1,570 million; in 1960, $8,400 million. *Thus United States expenditure on military research has been multiplied by 5 in the last seven years. No doubt Russia has spent even more, since missiles are the costliest weapons of all. Britain, France, Sweden, and other countries have made a corresponding effort.* The fact is that the competition in military research *is* the arms race of today; and, as the figures of expenditure reveal, this race is still gathering momentum every year. While it continues, it is academic to hope for any stable balance of military power, or for any worthwhile disarmament or arms control. Research is the root evil; the dynamo that is driving the war machine forward to mounting peril, and, it may be, to ultimate disaster.

To some readers, these may seem brash assertions. But I believe they are fully supported by Herman Kahn's brilliant analysis of the changes that have occurred in weapons systems since 1945. He tells us that, since Hitler was defeated, there has been a "complete technological revolution in the art of war" once every five years; and that for the next and succeeding revolutions, the period will certainly be less. To those who know the real nature of the weapons to which Mr. Kahn refers by their service names, the picture which he paints, both of the past decade and a half and of the future, must be terrifying in the extreme. Let me remind the reader of some of his predictions.

He tells us that by 1965, four years from now, we shall have bacteriological and chemical warfare; he means, no doubt, that by then they will be fully perfected for instant and large-scale use. He tells us that we shall have astronauts, and *"experimental climate control."* He says that almost certainly he has made "large underestimates of the total change" which we shall see in weapons systems by the 1970's, "since one can almost guarantee that many startling and unexpected developments will occur." No less terrifying is Mr. Kahn's account of the various ways in which war might come, his assessment of the cumulative risks, and his categorical assertion that *"one must eventually introduce a major change in the situation, or expect to get into a war anyway."*

But there are two sentences in Mr. Kahn's paper which stood out, when I read them, in letters of fire.

He asks the question: How many lives would we be willing to risk to protect ourselves from surprise attack? He says in answer: "It is clear that both the United States and NATO would reluctantly envisage the possibility of one or two hundred million fatalities (i.e., about five times more than those in World War II) from the immediate effects, even if one does not include long-term effects due to radiation, if an all-out thermonuclear war results from a failure of Type I Deterrence. Under somewhat more controversy, similar numbers would apply to Type II Deterrence."

Two hundred million dead, plus those myriads who would perish from the long-term effects of radiation—"it is clear" that the United States and NATO have agreed to that? Who has agreed? The Cabinets of the United States and of the NATO countries? Their Congress and Parliaments? Their electorates? Mr. Kahn does not tell us. But I venture the confident belief that no cabinet of any democratic country has decided to risk a war in which the losses would be as great as that. Certainly no government of any NATO country has asked its parliament to approve any such decision, and no people has yet "envisaged" such a holocaust.

Perhaps Mr. Kahn is telling us that, since governments have shirked the decisions which the possession of modern weapons must involve, the general staffs have simply made decisions of their own and have prepared their plans on the hideous hypothesis which he reveals? No one could blame the general staffs if this were so; the governments have told them to make the weapons; the parliaments have voted the money; the staffs must make plans for how they shall be used; plans are impossible without decisions. But it is surely vital that the truth about Mr. Kahn's statement should be known. Edward Teller has recently said: "The dangers of the nuclear age require split-second decisions. These decisions can be submitted to the voter only after the fact. This is unavoidable." [2] But the voter can and should be told the scale of the catastrophe in which, by these split-second decisions, he may be engulfed. Otherwise, the whole basis of democracy is destroyed.

The second of Mr. Kahn's statements which appalled me was this: if the United States, expecting an attack from Russia, were to evacuate 60 million people from its fifty largest cities, this would effect, he says, a great "psychological stiffening of the backbone" of the American people, and "an enormous decrease of the risks this country would be running, if it went to war."

I was a member of a Cabinet committee which dealt with evacuation in Britain in Sir Winston Churchill's war coalition. On the basis of that experience, I believe it would be utterly impossible for the United States to evacuate 60 million people from fifty cities; if it did, many millions more would evacuate themselves in panic from the smaller cities; the whole social and economic system of the country would collapse; the morale of the people would be most grievously undermined; and the damage which resulted from a nuclear attack would be no less, since the homes and factories of the 60 million would be destroyed, and they themselves would die from fall-out.

Indeed, I find it impossible to believe that any measure of civil defense, however elaborate and expensive, could produce any significant result. Dr. Schelling speaks of "the extraordinary aversion to civil defense in the United States Government." In Britain there is no aversion to civil defense; we developed it on a large scale in Hitler's war, and we found it useful; but our present government have made no serious preparations for shelter programs or for evacuation, because they know that in nuclear war they would be of no avail.

Dr. Brennan is right to take us back to the Hiroshima and Nagasaki bombs. When I was Secretary of State for Air in 1947, the Air Staff advised me that Britain's military resistance could be broken by a small number of those primitive atomic weapons—perhaps as few as 30, at the most 120. They said that Britain, which had resisted Hitler and Mussolini virtually alone for two years, would "cease to work." * That may recall to those who too easily forget it the real scale of the devastation which present stockpiles would produce. Let me repeat it: the new military vocabulary now in current use does not clarify, it obscures, the facts about the modern weapons. Dr. Brennan says: "Even among professionals, I have observed an occasional tendency to think of 'kilotons' as 'tons.' " This is a very frightening observation; and the tendency is very common among politicians and other nonprofessionals. Mr. Kahn says that the weapons systems have developed so fast that there are "doctrinal lags" in strategic thinking. This is a polite way of saying that, under the relentless

* Experts now estimate that ten modern high-yield thermonuclear weapons could virtually depopulate Britain, not merely break its military resistance.—ED.

pressure of the arms race, the weapons have been invented first, and that the general staffs have only then considered whether and how they could be used. A rereading of the writings of military theorists since 1950, and of the speeches made by ministers of defense, shows that "strategic thinking" has been in chaos during these fateful years.

It is high time to concentrate on the simple facts. War is an absurd monstrosity; it must be abolished. Historically, this reform is long overdue. The last forty years have proved, not only that international institutions are needed, but that they work, if they are used. But no doubt, as Mr. Kahn has argued, "a major change in the situation" is required, if the United Nations is to save us from a general war.

I believe this major change would come about, if Mr. Kahn's warnings were generally known and understood. If the peoples were plainly told that the general staffs had prepared plans which "envisaged" the death of two hundred million people, plus a vast number of fall-out victims, there would be from all nations a popular demand for a comprehensive, drastic, controlled disarmament—a demand so universal and so powerful that, in President Eisenhower's phrase, the governments would have to "get out of the way and let them have it." If war is now an absurd monstrosity, so are the armaments by which it would be fought, if it should come. If "arms control" is regarded as an alternative to disarmament, may the phrase not be a dangerous semantic aberration? What controls will really mitigate the dangers of the present situation, while military research creates the kind of arms race which Mr. Kahn describes? What controls will reduce the risk of surprise attack, while governments continue to spend thousands of millions of dollars a year to improve the power of surprise attack? How can confidence and trust be created—surely the U-2 and RB-47 episodes must prompt the question—while the nations continue to make immense efforts to increase their power of mutual, instantaneous destruction? A great English thinker, John Stuart Mill, said long ago: "Against a great evil, a small remedy does not produce a small result; it produces no result at all."

References

Editor's Preface

1. Louis Henkin, *Arms Control and Inspection in American Law* (New York: Columbia University Press, 1958).

1. Setting and Goals of Arms Control
DONALD G. BRENNAN

1. Arnold Wolfers and others, *Developments in Military Technology and Their Impact on United States Strategy and Foreign Policy*. Study No. 8 prepared at the request of the Committee on Foreign Relations of the United States Senate (Washington, D.C.: United States Government Printing Office, 1959).
2. William W. Kaufmann (ed.), *Military Policy and National Security* (Princeton: Princeton University Press, 1956).
3. Henry A. Kissinger, *Nuclear Weapons and Foreign Policy* (New York: Harper, 1957).
4. Bernard Brodie, *Strategy in the Missile Age* (Princeton: Princeton University Press, 1959).
5. Klaus Knorr (ed.), *NATO and American Security* (Princeton: Princeton University Press, 1959).
6. Oskar Morgenstern, *The Question of National Defense* (New York: Random House, 1959).
7. Thomas C. Schelling, *The Strategy of Conflict* (Cambridge: Harvard University Press, 1960).
8. Henry Rowen, *National Security and the American Economy in the 1960's*. Study paper No. 18 prepared for the Joint Economic Committee, Congress of the United States (Washington, D.C.: United States Government Printing Office, 1960).
9. Herman Kahn, *On Thermonuclear War* (Princeton: Princeton University Press, 1960).
10. Henry A. Kissinger, *The Necessity for Choice: Prospects for American Foreign Policy* (New York: Harper, 1960).
11. Raymond L. Garthoff, *Soviet Strategy in the Nuclear Age* (New York: Frederick A. Praeger, 1958).
12. H. S. Dinerstein, *War and the Soviet Union* (New York: Frederick A. Praeger, 1959).
13. Thomas C. Schelling, "The Retarded Science of International Strategy," *Bulletin of the Atomic Scientists* (March 1960), *16*: 103–106.
14. ———, "Bargaining, Communication, and Limited War," *Conflict Resolution* (1957), *1*: 19–36.
15. ———, *Nuclear Weapons and Limited War* (RAND Corporation Report P-1620), February 20, 1959.
16. Herman Kahn, *The Nature and Feasibility of War and Deterrence* (RAND Corporation Report P-1888-RC), January, 20, 1960.

17. Albert Wohlstetter, "The Delicate Balance of Terror," *Foreign Affairs* (January 1959), 211–234.

18. John B. Phelps, Raymond Foye, and Daniel Howland, *Some Calculations on Counterforce Strategies in a General Nuclear War* (The Mershon National Security Program, Ohio State University, Columbus [referred to below as *Mershon*], Report RP-1), August 27, 1959.

19. Raymond Foye and John B. Phelps, *Counterforce Calculations: Attack and Retaliation with Mixed Weapons Systems* (Mershon Report RP-2), November 24, 1959.

20. S. M. Rosow and John B. Phelps, *Measures of Destruction: Some Observations on Damage Levels in a General Nuclear War* (Mershon Report RP-3), December 14, 1959.

21. John B. Phelps and Raymond Foye, *A Technique for Fallout Casualty Calculations* (Mershon Report RP-5), January 22, 1960.

22. Samuel Glasstone (ed.), *The Effects of Nuclear Weapons* (Washington, D.C.: United States Government Printing Office, 1957), p. 505.

23. Joint Committee on Atomic Energy, Congress of the United States, *Summary Analysis of Hearings on Biological and Environmental Effects of Nuclear War* (Washington, D.C.: United States Government Printing Office, 1959).

24. Herman Kahn and others, *Report of a Study of Non-Military Defense* (RAND Corporation Report R-322-RC), July 1, 1958.

25. T. C. Schelling, *Surprise Attack and Disarmament* (RAND Corporation Report P-1574), December 10, 1958. (Published in Knorr,[5] also in abridged form in *Bulletin of the Atomic Scientists* (December 1959), *15*:413.)

26. ——, "Proposal for a Special Surveillance Force," *World Politics* (October 1960), *13*: 1–18.

27. United Nations General Assembly, *Report of the Conference of Experts for the Study of Possible Measures Which Might be Helpful in Preventing Surprise Attack and for the Preparation of a Report Thereon to Governments* (United Nations Document A/4078-S/4145, 5 January 1959).

5. The Arms Race and Some of Its Hazards
HERMAN KAHN

1. The *New York Times*, April 22, 1958.

2. Peter Bryant, *Red Alert* (New York: Ace Books, 1958).

3. Bertrand Russell, *Common Sense and Nuclear Warfare* (New York: Simon and Schuster, 1959).

4. T. C. Schelling, *The Strategy of Conflict* (Cambridge: Harvard University Press, 1960).

5. The term seems to be due to Amrom Katz.

6. While I would not care to guess the exact form an efficient Doomsday Machine would take, I would be willing to conjecture that if the project were started today and were sufficiently supported, one could have such a machine (or close approximation to such a device) by 1970. I would also guess that the cost would be between ten and a hundred billion dollars. Even then it might not be possible to destroy groups of especially well-prepared people. The mechanism one would use would most likely involve, not the breaking up of the

earth, but the creation of really large amounts of radioactivity, or the causing of major climatic changes.

7. I should make the point, though, that contrary to many common statements, current (1961) weapon systems are not Doomsday Machines or even close to being such devices.

8. This is actually an extreme view of the German situation. During most of the period 1933–1944 Hitler was restrained by "responsible" elements, and many of his gambles were actually hedged. On many occasions on which he seemed too reckless, military groups prepared a *coup d'état* should he go too far.

9. It is more feasible to survive and recuperate from a war than is generally thought. RAND Report R-322-RC, *Report on a Study of Non-Military Defense,* June 1958, has a description of the possibilities.

10. Testimony of General LeMay before the 1956 Subcommittee on the Air Force, Senate Armed Services Committee, p. 135.

11. See Fred C. Iklé, *Nth Countries and Disarmament* (RAND Corporation Report P-1956), April 1960, for further discussion of this important problem.

12. An international agency with a near-monopoly for force might come from any of the following possibilities, listed in order of apparent probability rather than desirability: (1) a Soviet- or United States-dominated world arising most likely out of war; (2) some other results of a war; (3) a Soviet Union–United States combination which is in effect a world government, though it may not be openly called so; (4) some of the NATO nations and China added to the above combination as influential, if not equal partners; (5) the haves against the have-nots, probably without exploitation, and, perhaps, with aid to underdeveloped nations, but with stringent arms control in which authority and responsibility are roughly proportioned to military and economic development; (6) a sort of world federal state in which power is proportioned to sovereignty and population, as in the United States Congress.

While many of the above possibilities may strike most readers as unpleasant or undesirable, it is quite possible that even a "bad" world government is preferable to an accelerated and uncontrolled arms race. It is to be hoped this last will not be the only choice available.

7. Limited War: Conventional or Nuclear? A Reappraisal
HENRY A. KISSINGER

1. For a fuller discussion of limited nuclear war, see the author's *Nuclear Weapons and Foreign Policy* (New York: Harper, 1957), chap. VI, "Problems of Limited Nuclear War," pp. 191 ff.

2. *Ibid.,* pp. 174 ff.

8. Economic Implications of Arms Control
KENNETH E. BOULDING

1. The recent literature on this subject is almost entirely confined to pamphlets and journals; there is a startling absence of formal or academic studies.

Many of the peace groups have published pamphlets relating to the economics of disarmament: see, for instance, *If the Arms Race Ends* (two papers by Albert L. Gray, Jr., and Byron L. Johnson, Board of World Peace of the Methodist Church, 740 Rush Street, Chicago 11, Illinois); *Fact Sheet: Economic Consequences of Disarmament* (Committee for World Development and Disarmament, United Nations Plaza, New York, October 1959); see also publications by the Friends Committee on National Legislation, 245 Second Street N.E., Washington 2, D.C., and by the Women's International League for Peace and Freedom, 2006 Walnut Street, Philadelphia 3, Pennsylvania.

Some of the more "neutral" policy research groups have also published pamphlets: the National Planning Association (1606 New Hampshire Avenue N.W., Washington, D.C.), Joint Statement, *Can the American Economy Adjust to Arms Reduction* (January 4, 1960); and the Committee for Economic Development (711 Fifth Avenue, New York 22, New York), *The Defense We Can Afford*, by James F. Brownlee. The Senate Subcommittee on Disarmament of the United States Senate Committee on Foreign Relations published *Hearings* (1957), of which Parts 8, 9, and 13 are particularly relevant.

Periodical and newspaper articles include: Emile Benoit, "Will Defense Cuts Hurt Business," *Michigan Business Review*, March 1957; Seymour Harris, "The Economics of Disarmament," *Current History*, October 1957; "Can We Prosper Without Arms," *New York Times Magazine*, November 8, 1959; and Senator Hubert H. Humphrey, "After Disarmament—What?" *Think,* January 1960. *The Nation* had a special issue, "Economic Hazards of Arms Reduction," March 28, 1959.

9. Reciprocal Measures for Arms Stabilization
THOMAS C. SCHELLING

1. See T. C. Schelling, "Surprise Attack and Disarmament," in Klaus Knorr (ed.), *NATO and American Security* (Princeton: Princeton University Press, 1959), or the shorter version in T. C. Schelling, *The Strategy of Conflict* (Cambridge: Harvard University Press, 1960), chap. 10.

2. For an extensive study of tacit bargaining, with special reference to limited war, see T. C. Schelling, *The Strategy of Conflict* (Cambridge: Harvard University Press, 1960), chaps. 3 and 4 and Appendix A.

3. A more extensive discussion of this point appears in T. C. Schelling, "Arms Control: Proposal for a Special Surveillance Force," *World Politics,* October 1960.

10. The Case for Unilateral Disarmament
ERICH FROMM

1. Charles E. Osgood, "Suggestions for Winning the Real War with Communism," *Conflict Resolution* (December 1959) *3*: 131, and also "A Case for Graduated Unilateral Disarmament," *Bulletin of Atomic Scientists* (1960), *16*: 127 ff.

2. This condition is in my opinion to be taken only as an optimal *desidera-*

tum, since any weakening of one power's aggressive potential means strategically some increase in the opponent's aggressive potential.

3. Charles E. Osgood, *op. cit.,* p. 316.

4. Bertrand Russell, *Common Sense and Nuclear Warfare* (London: G. Allen & Unwin, 1959). Stephen King-Hall, *Defense in the Nuclear Age* (Nyack, N.Y.: Fellowship Publications, 1959). Jerome Davis and General H. B. Hester, *On the Brink* (New York: Lyle Stuart, 1959). Lewis Mumford, *The Human Way Out* (Pendell Hill Pamphlet No. 97, 1958). C. W. Mills, *The Causes of World War Three* (New York: Simon & Schuster, 1959). George F. Kennan, "Foreign Policy and Christian Conscience," *Atlantic Monthly,* May 1959. Richard B. Gregg, *The Power of Nonviolence* (Nyack, N.Y.: Fellowship Publications, 1959). American Friends Service Committee, *Speak Truth to Power, Quaker Search for an Alternative to Balance* (1955).

5. George F. Kennan, *op. cit.,* pp. 44 ff.

6. This premise is shared by the report of the National Planning Association of America: *1970 without Arms Control; Implications of Modern Weapons Technology* (by NPA Special Project Committee on Security through Arms Control, Planning Pamphlet No. 104, May 1958, Washington, D.C.), which states: "Not only does the danger of war remain a possibility, but the probability totalled over time increases, becoming a certainty if sufficient time elapses without succeeding in finding alternatives." Or, E. Finley Carter, President of the Stanford Research Institute, writes: "In the search for security through the application of technology to weapons for destruction, the Soviet bloc and the Western allies have created a mortal common enemy—the threat of accidental nuclear war" (*SRI Journal,* Stanford Research Institute, Fourth Quarter 1959, *3*: 198). Herman Kahn also concludes, "It is most unlikely that the world can live with an uncontrolled arms race lasting for several decades" (*ibid.,* p. 139). He emphasizes that it is unrealistic to believe that war has become impossible because of its extremely destructive character.

The advisor on Science and Technology of the Democratic Advisory Council of December 27, 1959 declared: "All-out nuclear war seems not only possible but probable as long as we pursue our present military policies and fail to achieve international agreements of broad scope designed to alleviate this unstable situation. The triggering of a nuclear war by mistake, by misadventure or by miscalculation is a constant danger." It must be stressed that the danger lies not only in technical errors, but equally in the blundering decision-making by political and military leaders. If one remembers the political and military blunders committed by many of the leaders in the conduct of wars of 1914 and 1939, it is not difficult to visualize that, given present-day weapons, the same type of leaders will blow the world to pieces, in spite of good intentions.

7. For a detailed analysis of modern society cf. my *The Sane Society* (New York: Rinehart and Co., 1955).

8. *SRI Journal* (1959), *3*: 140.

9. For the very same reasons, there is a real chance for the future abolition of war, a chance which never existed in the past. In most of man's history, the improvement of his material situation required an increase in human energy (slaves), additional land for cattle raising or agriculture, or new sources of raw materials. The techniques of the present and of the future will permit an

increase in material wealth by an increased industrial and—indirectly—agricultural productivity, without the need of enslaving or robbing others. At present and in the future, war would have as its only "rationale" the irrationality of human desire for power and conquest.

10. Whether or not political leaders are sane is not a matter of historical accident. Any government which has set out to do the impossible—for instance, to achieve equality and justice when the requisite material conditions are lacking—will produce fanatical and irrational leaders. This was the case with Robespierre, as it was with Stalin. Or, a government which tries to reconcile the interests of the most backward social class (the lower middle class) with those of the economically progressive classes (workers and businessmen) as the Nazi government did, again will produce fanatical and irrational leaders. The Soviet Union today is on the road toward solving its economic problems successfully; hence it is not surprising that her leaders are realistic men of common sense.

11. *Op. cit.*, pp. 52, 65.

12. Peter B. Young, "The Renunciationists," *Airpower,* the Air Force Historical Foundation, 7, 1: 33.

13. *Ibid.*

14. Herman Kahn, *Report on a Study of Non-Military Defense* (RAND Corporation Report R-322-RC, July 1, 1958), p. 13.

15. *Ibid.*

16. General de Gaulle, in a speech in April 1960.

11. Comprehensive Arms-Limitation Systems
JEROME B. WIESNER

1. Submission to the United Nations Disarmament Commission, April 24, 1952.

2. Louis B. Sohn, "Territorial Disarmament," a private memorandum, November 2, 1959.

3. Leo Szilard, "How to Live with the Bomb and Survive," *Bulletin of the Atomic Scientists* (1960), *16*: 58.

4. Philip Noel-Baker, *The Arms Race* (London: Stephens and Sons, 1958).

12. Policy Considerations of a Nuclear-Test Ban
DONALD G. BRENNAN AND MORTON H. HALPERIN

1. United States Senate Subcommittee on Disarmament, *Conference on the Discontinuance of Nuclear Weapons Testing. Analysis of Progress and Positions of the Participating Parties* (October 1958-August 1960; October 1960).

2. Morton H. Halperin, "Nuclear Weapons and Limited War," mimeographed, Harvard Center for International Affairs, 1960 (forthcoming in *The Journal of Conflict Resolution*).

3. The series appeared in The Washington *Post and Times Herald,* August 1960, as well as in a number of other papers.

4. Thomas J. Dodd, "The Eight Fallacies of the Nuclear Test Ban," *Congressional Record,* May 12, 1960.

5. Hanson Baldwin, "Limited War," *The Atlantic* (May 1959), pp. 35–43. Bernard Brodie, *Strategy in the Missile Age* (Princeton: Princeton University Press, 1960), pp. 319–335. William W. Kaufmann, "The Crisis in Military Affairs," *World Politics* (1958), *10*: 507–603. James King, "Nuclear Plenty and Limited War," *Foreign Affairs* (1957), *35*: 238–256. Robert Osgood, "Stabilizing the Military Environment," *American Political Science Review* (March 1961), *55*:24–39 (footnote, p. 28). Henry Rowen, "National Security and the American Economy in the 1960's" (Joint Economic Committee, Study Paper No. 18), January 30, 1960, pp. 45–48. Thomas C. Schelling, *Nuclear Weapons and Limited War* (RAND Corporation Report P-1620), February 20, 1959. Albert Wohlstetter, *The Delicate Balance of Terror* (RAND Corporation Report P-1472), December 1958, pp. 33–36. P. M. S. Blackett, "Thoughts on British Defence Policy," *The New Statesman* (1959), *58*:783. Also, private communications from Herman Kahn and Arthur Hadley, 1960.

6. Fred C. Iklé, "Nth Countries and Disarmament," *Bulletin of the Atomic Scientists* (December 1960), *16*:391–394.

7. National Planning Association, *The Nth Country Problem and Arms Control* (Planning Pamphlet No. 108), January 1960.

8. *Aviation Week* (October 17, 1960), p. 25.

9. Private communication, October 1960.

10. Jane's, *All the World's Aircraft 1957–1958* (New York: McGraw-Hill, 1958).

11. Hans A. Bethe, "The Case for Ending Nuclear Tests," *The Atlantic* (August 1960), pp. 43–51. Reprinted in *Survival 2* (September-October 1960), pp. 179–188.

12. *Nucleonics* (September 1960), p. 18.

13. "Results of the Teak and Orange Shots in the 1958 Hardtack Series" (reprinted in reference 14 below, pp. 865–932).

14. Joint Committee on Atomic Energy, *Hearings*, "Technical Aspects of Detection and Inspection Controls of the Nuclear Weapons Test Ban" (2 parts), April 1960.

14. The Inclusion of Communist China in an Arms-Control Program
A. DOAK BARNETT

1. *Current Affairs Handbook* (Peking, Vol. 1, No. 2), November 5, 1950; *Current Background* (American Consulate-General, Hong Kong, No. 32), November 29, 1950, p. 10.

2. K. M. Panikkar, *In Two Chinas* (London: G. Allen and Unwin, 1955), p. 108.

3. George A. Modelski, *Atomic Energy in the Communist Bloc* (Melbourne: Melbourne University Press, 1959), p. 186.

4. See *NCNA* (*New China News Agency*), October 12, 1954; *SCMP* (*Survey of the China Mainland Press*, American Consulate-General, Hong Kong) 906, October 12, 1954, p. 6.

5. Communique of the U.S.S.R. Council of Ministers, *Tass*, January 17, 1955, in Modelski, *op. cit.*, p. 125.

6. See *NCNA*, April 30, 1955; *SCMP* 1038, April 30-May 2, 1955, p. 16.

7. *People's Daily* (Peking), June 12, 1955, in Modelski, *op. cit.*, p. 187.

8. *NCNA*, January 29, 1956, in Modelski, *op. cit.*, p. 187.

9. *Ibid.*, p. 186.

10. Nieh Jung-chen, "China's Progress in Science and Technology in Ten Years," *People's Daily*, September 27, 1959; *Current Background* (No. 608), January 8, 1960, p. 4.

11. Ch'ien San-ch'iang, "China Marches Forward in Big Strides in Regard to the Peaceful Use of Atomic Energy," *People's Daily*, October 11, 1959; *Current Background* (No. 608), January 8, 1960, p. 13.

12. Nieh, *op. cit.*, p. 8.

13. Ch'ien, *op. cit.*, p. 13.

14. *Ibid.*, p. 14.

15. *Die Welt* (Hamburg), May 12, 1958.

16. *Stuttgarter Zeitung*, May 12, 1958.

17. *NCNA*, May 16, 1958; *SCMP* 1777, May 22, 1958, p. 28.

18. *Chieh Fang Chün Pao*, May 23, 1958; *SCMP* 1900, November 24, 1958, p. 9. See also Washington *Post and Times Herald*, July 19, 1959.

19. *Unita* (Rome), July 1, 1959. See also Washington *Post and Times Herald*, July 19, 1959.

20. See, for example, the *New York Times*, August 18, 1958.

21. *Pravda*, August 31, 1958; *Current Digest of the Soviet Press* (Vol. 10, No. 35), October 8, 1958, p. 17.

22. *Pravda*, September 5, 1958; *Current Digest of the Soviet Press* (Vol. 10, No. 36), October 15, 1958, p. 9.

23. *New York Times*, September 9, 1958.

24. *New York Times*, September 20, 1958.

25. *People's Daily*, September 21, 1958; *SCMP* 1860, September 24, 1958, p. 48.

26. *Pravda*, October 6, 1958; *Current Digest of the Soviet Press* (Vol. 10, No. 40), November 12, 1958, p. 18.

27. *New York Times*, October 1, 1958, and *The Times* (London), October 1, 1958.

28. Lin Piao, "Hold High the Red Banner of the Party's General Line and Chairman Mao Tse-tung's Military Thought and Advance in Big Strides," *NCNA*, September 29, 1959; *Current Background* (No. 596), October 7, 1959, p. 7.

29. John L. Steele, *Life*, July 13, 1959, p. 36. Such rockets are probably short-range ones rather than long-range missiles but even short-range rockets could probably reach most targets in East Asia. Peking also has IL-28 bombers capable of carrying atomic bombs.

30. *Christian Science Monitor*, June 25, 1959.

31. *New York Times*, September 18, 1959.

32. *New York Times*, February 20, 1960.

33. *New York Times*, January 11, 1960. The expert mentioned was Dr. Chien Hsüeh-shen, formerly professor of jet propulsion at California Institute of Technology.

34. *U.S. News and World Report*, January 11, 1960, pp. 47–48.

35. Fred Greene, "Military Bases and Programs of Communist China," p. 4

(typescript, unpublished, prepared for the Senate Disarmament Subcommittee by the Legislative Reference Service, Library of Congress, March 22, 1957), cited in *Disarmament and Security in Eastern and Southern Asia* (see note 66), p. 9.

36. W. Davidon, M. Kalkstein, and C. Hohenemser, *The Nth Country Problem and Arms Control* (Washington, D.C.: National Planning Association, Planning Pamphlet No. 108, January 1960), pp. 27–28, lists Communist China as one of twelve countries, including France, "able to embark on a successful nuclear weapons program in the near future." This study estimates that "a typical weapons program for the manufacture of a few bombs per year" would require about five years to get into operation; see p. 21.

37. Modelski, *op. cit.,* p. 125.

38. Ch'ien, *op. cit.,* p. 12.

39. Modelski, *op. cit.,* p. 192.

40. Ch'ien, *op. cit.,* p. 12. In April 1960, Chou En-lai was reported to have told a Burmese official that Communist China expects to build atomic submarines within five years (*New York Times,* April 17, 1960).

41. Ch'ien, *op. cit.,* p. 14.

42. The data and analysis here are based on a personal communication from Arnold Kramish (RAND Corporation).

43. *Ibid.*

44. Modelski, *op. cit.,* p. 47, and information provided by Arnold Kramish.

45. *NCNA,* April 21, 1956, and *Wang Po,* September 10, 1956, in Modelski, *op. cit.,* p. 193.

46. Ch'ien, *op. cit.,* p. 18.

47. *NCNA,* January 28, 1959; *SCMP* 1948, February 4, 1959, pp. 2–7.

48. *Current Digest of the Soviet Press* (Vol. 11, No. 39), October 28, 1959, p. 22.

49. *New York Times,* April 3, 1960.

50. *Arbeiderbladet* (Oslo), February 15, 1960.

51. *New York Times,* April 9, 1960.

52. Mao Tse-tung, *Selected Works* (New York: International Publishers, 1954), I, 75.

53. See *Disarmament and Foreign Policy,* Hearings, Subcommittee on Disarmament, Committee on Foreign Relations, U.S. Senate, 86th Congress, 1st Session (Washington, D.C.: United States Government Printing Office, 1959), Part 1, pp. 4, 196.

54. Curiously enough, by far the largest detonations of conventional explosives anywhere in the world have been in Communist China. In 1956 several "immense explosions" took place in northwest China; they were reported to have been nonnuclear blasts detonated by a Soviet technical group. Their magnitude was as follows: July 19, 1.6 kilotons; November 15, 4.0 kilotons; December 31, 9.2 kilotons. Up to 1958, the largest nonatomic explosion ever detonated in the West was 1.3 kilotons. See Arnold Kramish, *Atomic Energy in the Soviet Union* (Stanford: Stanford University Press, 1959), p. 137. Speculating, it is conceivable that during this period, the Sino-Soviet partners were able to test the problems of detecting, and perhaps concealing, large blasts in that remote area of China.

55. *Control and Reduction of Armaments,* Hearings, Subcommittee on Disarmament, Committee on Foreign Relations, U.S. Senate, 84th Congress, 2nd Session (Washington, D.C.: United States Government Printing Office, 1956), Part 2, pp. 75–77.

56. *Secretary Dulles' News Conference of July 2, 1957,* Department of State Press Release No. 405, July 2, 1957, pp. 5–6.

57. *Secretary Dulles' News Conference of June 10, 1958,* Department of State Press Release No. 319, June 10, 1958, pp. 2, 9.

58. *Disarmament and Foreign Policy, op. cit.,* Part 2, p. 379.

59. *Text of Remarks by the Honorable Christian A. Herter,* Department of State Press Release No. 667, September 23, 1959, p. 7.

60. *Statement Issued by Lincoln White,* Department of State, January 21, 1960.

61. *Secretary Herter's News Conference of February 8, 1960,* Department of State Press Release No. 53, February 8, 1960, pp. 3–4, 7.

62. *New York Times,* January 20, 1960. Later, in April, Chou En-lai said: "An international agreement made without the participation and signature of China's representatives will have no binding force whatsoever on China" (*New York Times,* April 11, 1960).

63. George Kennan, *Disarmament and Foreign Policy, op. cit.,* Part 2, p. 204.

64. For further elaboration, see A. D. Barnett, *Communist China and Asia, Challenge to American Policy* (New York: Harper and Brothers, 1960), esp. chaps. 13–15.

65. *Ibid.,* chap. 6.

66. See *Disarmament and Security in Eastern and Southern Asia,* Staff Study No. 9, Subcommittee on Disarmament, Committee on Foreign Relations, 85th Congress, 1st Session (Washington, D.C.: United States Government Printing Office, July 1957), pp. 15–23, and *Disarmament and Foreign Policy, op. cit.,* Part 2, pp. 364–368.

15. The Role of the Smaller Powers
PAUL M. DOTY

1. The National Planning Association, *Pamphlet No. 108* (Washington, D.C.: NPA, 1959); also, Howard Simons, "World-wide Capabilities for Production and Control of Nuclear Weapons," *Dædalus, 88*: 385–409.

2. P. M. S. Blackett, "Thoughts on British Defence Policy," *The New Statesman* (1959), *58*:783.

3. George R. Kennan, *Russia, the Atom and the West* (New York: Oxford University Press, 1958).

4. Major-General John B. Medaris, in the *New York Times,* April 21, 1960.

5. The consequences of research and development in weapons systems are difficult to predict, hence such recommendations require some caution. In the case of agents of chemical warfare, their further development and deployment by the smaller powers could stimulate the major powers to a greatly expanded effort in this area, resulting perhaps in a breakthrough to a different lead in efficiency. This would have unpredictable effects. However, the possibility of a

substantial breakthrough in chemicals seems unlikely, since effectiveness as based on weight appears to be approaching a limit. To increase the yield, therefore, one can depend only on increasing the efficiency of dispersal at the target.

6. A discussion of many specific roles that the smaller powers could play cannot be included here since they depend on particular disarmament plans which are beyond the scope of this article.

16. Inspection Techniques of Arms Control
BERNARD T. FELD

1. Herman Kahn, "The Arms Race and Some of Its Hazards," in this volume.

2. Jerome B. Wiesner, "Comprehensive Arms-Limitation Systems," in this volume.

3. Letter of instruction to Fredrick M. Eaton, United States Representative at the Ten-Nations Geneva Disarmament Conference, the *New York Times,* March 13, 1960.

4. Speech before the United Nations General Assembly, the *New York Times,* September 19, 1959.

5. Speech before the United Nations General Assembly, the *New York Times,* September 18, 1959.

6. Speech before the British Parliament, the *New York Times,* April 8, 1960.

7. Western Five-Nation Proposal for General Disarmament, the *New York Times,* March 15, 1960.

8. United States Department of State, *Disarmament: The Intensified Effort* (Publication 6676), July 1958.

9. United States Senate Subcommittee on Disarmament, *Hearings and Reports on the Control and Reduction of Armaments* (Washington, D.C.: 1956–1959).

10. Seymour Melman (ed.), *Inspection for Disarmament* (New York: Columbia University Press, 1958).

11. *Report of the Conference of Experts to Study the Possibility of Detecting Violations of a Possible Agreement on the Suspension of Nuclear (Weapon) Tests* (United Nations Document A/3897, New York, 28 August 1958).

12. Lloyd V. Berkner *et al., The Need for Fundamental Research in Seismology:* Report of the Panel on Seismic Improvement (Washington, D.C.: Department of State, July 1959).

13. Leo Szilard, "To Stop or Not to Stop," *Bulletin of the Atomic Scientists* (March 1960), *16*: 82.

14. B. T. Feld, D. G. Brennan, D. H. Frisch, G. L. Quinn, and R. S. Rochlin, *The Technical Problems of Arms Control,* Program of Research No. 1 (New York: Institute for International Order, May 1960).

15. United States Department of State, *A Report on the International Control of Atomic Energy* (the Acheson-Lilienthal Report), Publication 2398 (Washington, D.C.: March 14, 1946).

16. United States Department of State, *United States Atomic Energy Proposals* (as presented by B. M. Baruch to the United Nations Atomic Energy Commission, June 14, 1946), Publication 2460 (Washington, D.C.).

17. The Polish proposal, submitted to the United Nations General Assembly on October 2, 1957, the *New York Times,* February 18, 1958.

18. *Report of the Conference of Experts* (Held from November 10, to December 18, 1958, in Geneva) *for the Study of Possible Measures Which Might Be Helpful in Preventing Surprise Attack* (United Nations Document A/4078, New York, 5 January 1959).

19. Thomas C. Schelling, "Reciprocal Measures for Arms Stabilization," in this volume.

20. Leo Szilard, "How to Live with the Bomb and Survive," *Bulletin of the Atomic Scientists* (February 1960), *16*:58.

21. United States Department of State, *International Control and Prohibition of Atomic Weapons,* Recommendations of the United Nations Atomic Energy Commission, Publication 3646 (Washington, D.C.: October 1949).

22. Donald G. Brennan, "Why Outer Space Control," *Bulletin of the Atomic Scientists* (May 1959), *15*: 198.

23. Lewis C. Bohn, unpublished memorandum, January 12, 1956; Bohn called this "psychological inspection."

24. William C. Davidson, Marvin I. Kalkstein, and Christoph Hohenemser, *The Nth Country Problem: A World Wide Survey of Nuclear Weapons Capability,* National Planning Association, Planning Pamphlet No. 108 (Washington, D.C.: January 1960).

25. Paul M. Doty, "The Role of the Smaller Powers," in this volume.

26. Richard L. Kirk, Testimony on May 14, 1957, in the *Hearings on the Statute of the IAEA,* United States Senate, Committee on Foreign Relations (Washington, D.C.: United States Government Printing Office, 1957).

27. United States House of Representatives, *Research in Chemical, Biological and Radiological Warfare,* Report No. 815, August 10, 1959.

28. *Proceedings of International Pugwash Conference of Scientists on Biological and Chemical Warfare,* The Terminal Tower, Cleveland, Ohio, August 24, 1959.

17. Public Opinion and the Control of Armaments
ITHIEL DE SOLA POOL

1. For a discussion of the character and consequences of mediated experience, see Daniel Lerner, *The Passing of Traditional Society* (Glencoe, Ill.: The Free Press, 1958).

2. E. Kris and N. C. Leites, "Trends in 20th-Century Propaganda," in Geza Roheim (ed.), *Psychoanalysis and the Social Sciences* (New York: International Universities Press, 1947), vol. I.

3. See John R. Thomas, *Report on Service with the American Exhibition in Moscow* (RAND Corporation Report P-1859), March 15, 1960.

4. Alex Inkeles and Raymond A. Bauer, *The Soviet Citizen* (Cambridge: Harvard University Press, 1959), chap. 7.

5. Inkeles and Bauer, *op. cit.*

19. Adjudication and Enforcement in Arms Control
LOUIS B. SOHN

1. *United Nations Treaty Series, 298*: 11–165.
2. See, e.g., Louis M. Bloomfield, *Boundary Waters Problems of Canada and the United States: The International Joint Commission, 1912–1958* (Toronto: Carswell, 1958).
3. Manley O. Hudson, *International Tribunals: Past and Future* (Washington, D.C.: Carnegie Endowment for International Peace, 1944), pp. 32–47.
4. "Report of the International Law Commission Covering the Work of Its Tenth Session, 28 April–4 July 1958," United Nations General Assembly, *Official Records,* 13th Session, Supplement No. 9, pp. 5–8.
5. International Court of Justice, *Yearbook, 1958–1959* (The Hague: 1959), p. 13.
6. *United Nations Treaty Series, 261*: 165–173, 247–267; *298*: 271–272.
7. *Ibid., 298:* 197–200, 212–217.
8. International Atomic Energy Agency, *Multilateral Agreements.* Legal Series, No. 1, pp. 192–193, 197–200 (Vienna: 1959).
9. Manley O. Hudson, *International Legislation* (Washington, D.C.: Carnegie Endowment for International Peace, 1936), V (1929–1931), 436–444.
10. Manley O. Hudson, *World Court Reports* (Washington, D.C.: Carnegie Endowment for International Peace, 1938), III, 326–327.
11. See references 6 and 7.
12. *United Nations Treaty Series, 261*: 225–227.

21. Government Organization for Arms Control
HUBERT H. HUMPHREY

1. United States Senate. Senate Foreign Relations Subcommittee on Disarmament, Hearings on the Control and Reduction of Armaments, Part 1, January 25, 1956, p. 12.
2. The four conferences referred to are: (1) the Conference of Experts to Study the Methods of Detecting Violations of a Possible Agreement on the Suspension of Nuclear Tests, held from July 1, 1958, to August 20, 1958; (2) the Conference of Experts for the Study of Possible Measures Which Might Be Helpful in Preventing Surprise Attack, held from November 10, 1958, to December 18, 1958; (3) Conference on the Discontinuance of Nuclear Weapons Tests, convened October 31, 1958, and still in session; and (4) Conference of the Ten-Nation Committee on Disarmament, held from March 15, 1960, to June 27, 1960.
3. See the testimony of President's Disarmament Assistant quoted on p. 393.
4. In a major speech on disarmament on October 13, 1959, before the United Nations General Assembly, United States Ambassador Henry Cabot Lodge said of the Coolidge appointment: "As for the United States, President Eisenhower has recently set in motion a new and thorough review of disarmament in the light of present-day technology. This review will prepare us to participate fully and constructively in the deliberations scheduled for next year."

5. United States Senate. Senate Government Operations Subcommittee on National Policy Machinery, Hearings, April 26, 1960.

6. The Senate does not have the option of substantially altering the language of a treaty without running the risk of subjecting it to complete renegotiation.

Foreign Comment

1. Camille Rougeron, *Science et Vie* (July 1960).
2. *The Reporter,* September 5, 1960.

Notes on Contributors

A. DOAK BARNETT, born in Shanghai in 1921, is a program associate of The Ford Foundation. His extensive diplomatic and journalistic experience in the Far East as well as in Washington has led to his publishing these studies: *Communist Economic Strategy: The Rise of Mainland China; Communist China in Asia;* and (as coauthor) *The United States and the Far East.*

BERNHARD G. BECHHOEFER, born in St. Paul, Minnesota, in 1904, is an attorney in Washington, D.C. He served with the Department of State from 1942 to 1958, participating in international arms-control negotiations. He is the author of a number of studies dealing with political aspects of arms-control problems.

LEWIS C. BOHN, born in Boston in 1924, was a junior scientist at Los Alamos in World War II. After graduate study in physics, international relations, and Soviet affairs in Geneva and at Harvard, he joined the Social Science Division of the RAND Corporation in 1955 as a specialist in arms limitation. Since 1960 he has been associated with the Systems Research Center in Bedminster, New Jersey. Among his papers are "Psychological Inspection" and "On Motives for Disarmament Research."

KENNETH EWART BOULDING, born in Liverpool in 1910, and a graduate of Oxford University, is professor of economics at the University of Michigan, to which he has returned after a year on leave at the University College of the West Indies. His most recent publications are: *The Organizational Revolution; The Skills of the Economist;* and *Principles of Economic Policy.* He is preparing a book on the pure theory of conflict and defense.

ROBERT RICHARDSON BOWIE, born in Baltimore in 1909, is director of the Center for International Affairs and Dillon Professor of International Relations at Harvard University. He is a frequent contributor of articles on legal and other aspects of foreign affairs. He was editor and coauthor of *Studies on Federalism.* From 1953 to 1957 he was Assistant Secretary of State for Policy Planning.

DONALD G. BRENNAN, born in Waterbury, Connecticut, in 1926, is a research mathematician and communication theorist at the Lincoln Laboratory of the Massachusetts Institute of Technology. In addition to several research studies, he is coauthor of *Inspection for Disarmament; Statistical Methods in Radio Wave Propagation;* and *Lectures on Communication System Theory.* He is a consultant in the Executive Office of the President on arms-control problems, and was codirector of the 1960 Summer Study on Arms Control of the American Academy of Arts and Sciences and a participant in the 1960 Pugwash conference.

SAVILLE R. DAVIS, born in Watertown, Massachusetts, in 1909, is managing editor of the *Christian Science Monitor.* As a specialist on American foreign policy, he frequently lectures and appears on leading radio and television programs.

PAUL M. DOTY, born in Charleston, West Virginia, in 1920, is professor of chemistry at Harvard University and a member of the President's Science Advisory Committee. He has served as a United States delegate to the first and sixth Pugwash conferences and as chairman of the Federation of American Scientists (1956–1957). He is editor of the *Journal of Polymer Science* and a Fellow of the National Academy of Sciences.

BERNARD T. FELD, born in Brooklyn, New York, in 1919, is professor of physics at the Massachusetts Institute of Technology, and was chairman of the Operating Committee on the Technical Problems of Arms Limitation and vice-chairman of the Committee on Public Responsibilities of Scientists—both sponsored by the American Academy of Arts and Sciences. Twice the recipient of a Guggenheim fellowship, he participated in the 1958, 1959, and 1960 Pugwash conferences. His publications include: *The Neutron* (Vol. II of *Experimental Nuclear Physics*); and (with others) *A Program of Research on the Technical Problems of Arms Control.* He was director of the 1960 Summer Study on Arms Control of the American Academy.

ROGER FISHER, born in Winnetka, Illinois, in 1922, is Professor of Law at Harvard Law School. He has served with the Economic Cooperation Administration in Paris and with the Department of Justice. He practiced law for a number of years in Washington, specializing in international legal problems. His current work centers on the process of bringing law to bear on governments.

ERICH FROMM, born in Frankfurt-am-Main in 1900, is professor of psychology at Michigan State University, and professor of psychoanalysis at the National Autonomous University of Mexico. His publications include: *Escape from Freedom; The Sane Society;* and *Man for Himself.* He is active in peace groups interested in unilateral disarmament.

WILLIAM R. FRYE, born in Detroit, Michigan, in 1918, is chief of the News Bureau of the *Christian Science Monitor* at the United Nations, which he has covered since 1950. Recently he attended the Ten-Nation Disarmament Conference in Geneva. His books include: *Disarmament: Atoms into Ploughshares?* and *A United Nations Peace Force.*

MORTON H. HALPERIN, born in Brooklyn, New York, in 1938, is a research fellow of the Harvard Center for International Affairs and a consultant to the RAND Corporation. He is coauthor with Thomas C. Schelling of *Strategy and Arms Control* (New York, 1961), and is currently working on a study of the theory of limited war.

HUBERT H. HUMPHREY, born in Wallace, South Dakota, in 1911, has been United States Senator from Minnesota since 1948, where he has sponsored legislation on farm and labor problems, civil rights, and disarmament. Since 1953 he has served on the Foreign Relations Committee of the Senate, where he is chairman of the Subcommittee on Disarmament. He was made Majority Whip of the Senate in 1961.

HERMAN KAHN, born in Bayonne, New Jersey, in 1922, is a strategic analyst and military planner with the RAND Corporation, from which he was on leave in 1959 to serve as research associate at the Center of International Studies at Princeton University. His publications include: *Report on a Study of Non-Military Defense; The Nature and Feasibility of War and Deterrence;* and *On Thermonuclear War.*

HENRY A. KISSINGER, born in Fürth, Germany, in 1923, is associate professor of government at Harvard University, director of the Defense Studies Program, and executive director of the Harvard International Seminar. Besides his many articles on foreign affairs, he is the author of *Nuclear Weapons and Foreign Policy* and *The Necessity for Choice: Prospects for American Foreign Policy.* He has been consultant to the Weapons Systems Evaluation Group of the Joint Chiefs of Staff since 1956, and is currently a consultant to the President.

ARTHUR LARSON, born in Sioux Falls, South Dakota, in 1910, is director of the World Rule of Law Center at Duke University and a former special consultant to the President. He has served in many governmental agencies and was successively counsel for the Industrial Materials Division of the OPA, dean of the University of Pittsburgh Law School, Undersecretary of Labor, and director of the United States Information

Agency. Among his publications are: *Cases and Materials on the Law of Corporations* (with R. S. Stevens); *The Law of Workmen's Compensation* (awarded the Henderson Memorial Prize); and *Know Your Social Security*.

RICHARD S. LEGHORN, born in Brookline, Massachusetts, in 1919, is President of Itek Corporation, Waltham, Massachusetts. He has served as a consultant to the National Aeronautics and Space Administration and USAF Scientific Advisory Boards; the National Advisory Committee for Aeronautics; the Special Assistant to the President for Science and Technology; the President's Special Assistant for Disarmament Affairs; and the Surprise Attack Disarmament Conference, 1958. He served in 1959 as Technical Deputy to the President's Joint Disarmament Study Commission, prior to the Ten-Nation Geneva Conference in 1960. He is Chairman of the National Planning Association Committee on Security through Arms Control, and a regular participant in the international Pugwash meetings. He is author of articles in the *Bulletin of Atomic Scientists, U.S. News and World Report, The Reporter,* and others.

ITHIEL DE SOLA POOL, born in New York City in 1917, is professor of political science and member of the Center for International Studies at the Massachusetts Institute of Technology. His main field of research has been public opinion and communications, with special reference to political movements. Among his publications are: *The Prestige Papers; Symbols of Democracy; Satellite Generals;* and *Trends in Content Analysis*.

THOMAS C. SCHELLING, born in Oakland, California, in 1921, is professor of economics and associate of the Center for International Affairs at Harvard University. After serving in Washington on foreign-aid programs (1948–1953), he was associated with the RAND Corporation (1958–1959). His publications include *International Economics* and *The Strategy of Conflict,* and (with M. H. Halperin) *Strategy and Arms Control*.

LOUIS B. SOHN, born in Lwow, Poland, in 1914, graduated from the faculty of law and diplomacy of the John Casimir University of Lwow, and is now Bemis Professor of International Law at the Harvard University Law School. He participated in the San Francisco Conference that established the United Nations and for two years served as legal officer of the UN Secretariat. Among his publications are *World Peace through World Law* (with Grenville Clark) and *International Legislation* (with M. O. Hudson).

EDWARD TELLER, born in Budapest in 1908, is professor of physics and former director of the Lawrence Radiation Laboratory of the University of California at Livermore. His recent research has been directed to the practical application of thermonuclear principles in the development of thermonuclear weapons. He is a member of the General Advisory Committee of the Atomic Energy Commission, of the Scientific Advisory Board of the Air Force, and a Fellow of the National Academy of Sciences. His publications include *The Structure of Matter* and *Our Nuclear Future* (with Francis Owen Rice).

JEROME B. WIESNER, born in Detroit, Michigan, in 1915, is director of the Research Laboratory of Electronics of the Massachusetts Institute of Technology. He was staff director of the United States delegation to the Surprise Attack Conference (1958). He is the Chairman of the President's Science Advisory Committee, and a Fellow of the National Academy of Sciences. Besides his studies on radio-wave propagation and on communication techniques and systems, he is coauthor of: *Modern Physics for the Engineer; Fortschritte der Hochfrequenztechnik;* and *Lectures on Communication System Theory.* In January 1961, he was appointed Special Assistant to the President for Science and Technology.